INTERNATIONAL
Vital Records
Handbook

INTERNATIONAL
Vital Records
Handbook

Thomas Jay Kemp

4th Edition

GENEALOGICAL PUBLISHING Co., Inc.

Published by Genealogical Publishing Co., Inc.
1001 N. Calvert St., Baltimore, MD 21202
Library of Congress Catalogue Card Number 00-134946
International Standard Book Number 0-8063-1655-1
Made in the United States of America

Dedication

To my wife, Vi, and children, Andrew and Sarah

A family without a genealogy
is like a country without a history

A traditional Chinese saying

CONTENTS

About the Author

Thomas Jay Kemp, a well-known librarian and archivist, is the Chair of the Genealogy Committee of the American Library Association and a past Chair of the ALA History Section. He is a member of the Board of Directors of the Federation of Genealogical Societies and has served as the Chair of the Council of National Library and Information Associations and as President of the American Society of Indexers. He is also a life member of the Association for the Bibliography of History; The New York Genealogical and Biographical Society; the New England Archivists; and the New Hampshire Library Association.

He is the author of numerous books and articles, including *The Genealogist's Virtual Library: Full-text Books on the World Wide Web* (2000); *The American Census Handbook* (2000); *Virtual Roots: A Guide to Genealogy and Local History on the World Wide Web* (1997); and the *Connecticut Researcher's Handbook* (1981). His articles have appeared in *Library Journal*, *The New York Genealogical and Biographical Society Newsletter*, *NAGARA Clearinghouse*, *School Library Journal*, *Archival Outlook*, *Illinois Library Reporter*, *Connecticut Libraries*, and many other publications.

INTRODUCTION

At one time or another all of us need copies of birth, marriage, or death certificates for driver's licenses, passports, jobs, social security, family history research, or for simple proof of identity. But the fact is that the requirements and fees needed to obtain copies of vital records vary from country to country, often requiring a tedious and time-wasting exchange of correspondence before the appropriate forms can be obtained and the correct procedures followed. The *International Vital Records Handbook* is designed to put an end to all that, as it offers complete, up-to-date instructions on how and where to request vital records. It also includes copies of the application forms, thus simplifying and speeding up the process by which vital records are obtained, regardless of the number or type of application forms required.

This new 4th edition of the *International Vital Records Handbook* contains the latest forms and information for each of the fifty states and also furnishes details about records that were created prior to statewide vital records registration; then, in alphabetical sequence, it covers all the other countries of the world, giving, where available, their current forms and instructions. Where neither a centralized vital records registration system nor vital records application forms are available, this book provides key addresses of repositories or institutions that might help you obtain copies of vital records. It also provides names of publications that might help you in your search.

Application forms issued by the various civil registration offices and the current procedures for obtaining a birth, marriage, death, divorce, or adoption certificate are given, where available, for each state, province, territory, or country. Simply photocopy the form you need, follow the instructions, and send the fee and the completed form to the appropriate record office.

A new development since the previous edition of this book is the availability of information, and in some cases forms, on the Internet; in fact, it is now possible to order certificates online for some states and countries. Whenever possible, this book lists web sites for civil registration offices and other useful repositories. The URLs given were accurate at the time of publication but—like postal addresses, phone and fax numbers, and e-mail addresses—they are subject to change.

In obtaining copies of vital records, it should be kept in mind that copies of the original certificate might be on file in several different jurisdictions, depending on the state or country. For example, if a vital record is not available from the national office of vital records you should check with the appropriate provincial or city office to see if they have a copy.

The Family History Library of The Church of Jesus Christ of Latter-day Saints in Salt Lake City, Utah has microfilmed millions of vital records from church registers and government record offices all over the world. This ongoing and extraordinary program has made the Family History Library the world's largest repository of vital records. For further information please write to The Family History Library, 35 North West Temple Street, Salt Lake City, UT 84150. Their web site is **http://familysearch.org**.

ACKNOWLEDGMENTS

In preparing and keeping current the 4th edition of the *International Vital Records Handbook*, I am grateful for the guidance and assistance of registrars, archivists, keepers of public records, librarians, and scholars from around the world. We owe the modern-day custodians of the world's vital records our gratitude for preserving the records of the past four centuries and providing the records and documentation of the individual lives of the majority of the 6 billion people alive on the earth today. In particular, I would like to thank the following:

Bettina Kann, Österreichische Nationalbibliothek; Mrs. Suzanne M. Ducille, Deputy Registrar General, Bahamas; M. Thompson, Regisration Office, Barbados; Miss. L.A. Danies, Assistant Registrar and Raymond A. Usher, Deputy Registrar, Registrar General's Office, Belize; Anita Lisbey, Belize Archives Department; M. Nestor Houeto, Director General, Institut National de la Statistique et de l'Analyse Economique, Contonou, Benin; Esterley M. Patterson, Administrative Assistant to the Registry General, Bermuda; S.G. Otladisa, Registrar, Civil Registration and Vital Events, Botswana; Codru Rasvan Vrabie, Blagoevgrad, Bulgaria; Berta Belmar Ruiz, Director General, Servicio de Registro Civil e Identificacion, Chile; Roné Béyom Ncakoutou, Director of Statistics, Economic & Demographic Studies, Chad; Mrs. M.Y. Li, Office of the Director of Immigration, Hong Kong; Leonardo Luis de Matos, Director, Direcão de Serviçços de Justiça, China/Macau; Lic. María Isabel Acebedo Isasi, Directora de Registros y Notaria, Ministerio de Justicia, Cuba; Jindriska Pospisilova and Zdenek Matusik, Czech National Library; Henrik Stissing Jensen, Statens Arkiver Rigsarkivet, Denmark; Hanne Willumsen, Indenrigs Ministeriet, Denmark; Jan Tuxen, Kerteminde, Denmark; Ruth Hedegaard, Vendsyssel Historiske Museum, Aalborg, Denmark; Margit Tammur, National Library of Estonia; Eeva K. Murtomaa, Helsinki, Finland; Anna Mantakou, Hellenic Institute of International & Foreign Law, Athens, Greece; Carolyn R. Garrido, Registrar, Guam.

Dr. Márta Dóczi, Budapest, Hungary; R.G. Mitra, Deputy Registrar General of India; Anup K. Pujari, Office of the Minister for Law and Justice, India; G.B. Hanumantharayappa, Deputy Registrar, High Court of Karnataka, India; Mr. M. Halder, Special Officer, Office of the Registrar General West Bengal, India; G. Prakasam, Joint Chief Registrar of Births & Deaths, Bangalore, Karnataka, India. Raj Gautam Mitra, Deputy Registrar General, India, New Delhi, India; Andrea Capaccioni, Biblioteca dell'Universitá per Stranieri, Perugia, Italy; Shotaro Hamura, Okayama University of Science, Okayama, Japan; Yoshiaki Omura, Japan; Judy Rao, University of the West Indies, Jamaica; J.G. Kinyua, Department of the Registrar General, Kenya; Mr. Uriam Reiti, Registrar General of Kiribati; Jichang Ryo, Seoul, Korea; Dr. Abdus Sattar, Secretariat of Planning, Libya; A Šoliūnas, Director, Lietuvos Archyv Departamentas, Lithuania; T. Gustiene, Director of Information Centre, Lithuanian National Library; Flossie Matenje, Malawi Library Association; Mrs. Yatimah Rimun, Malaysia National Archives.

Lic. Susana E. Natali Abella, Coordinadora de Estudios Poblacionales, Dirección General del Registro Nacional de Población e Identificación Personal, Mexico City, Mexico; Snyder H. Simon, Clerk of Courts, Pohnpei Supreme Court, Federated States of Micronesia; Prof. Paul Vlaardingerbroek, Tilburg University, Tilburg, Netherlands; Thomas van Ek, Wageningen, Netherlands; E.J. Rowland, Deputy Registrar General, New Zealand; J.G. Moore, Commonwealth Recorder, Commonwealth of the Northern Mariana Islands; Orana S. Castro, Vital Statistics Division, Northern Mariana Islands; Gunnar Thorvaldsen, Registreringssentral for Historiske Data, Tromsø, Norway; Torbjørn Låg, Riksarkivet, Oslo, Norway; Felix Murillo Alfaro, Jefe Instituto Nacional De

Estadística e Informatica (INEI); Carlito B. Lalicon, Chief, Civil Registry Division, National Statistics Office, Philippines.

Munvazese Paustin, Minister de l'intérieur et du Developpement Communal, Kigali, Rwanda; Georgina Strickland, Deputy Registrar General of Births, Deaths & Marriages, Apia, Western Samoa; Alymana, Panos Institut, Dakar, Senegal; V. Labiche, Director General, Ministry of Administration and Manpower, Victoria, Seychelles; Joeanne Lee, NHB, Singapore; Chua Ser Ching, Assistant Registrar, Supreme Court, Singapore; Mrs. Tan Yeow Liang, Office of Registrar of Marriages, Singapore; Lee Fook Wah, Registrar of Births & Deaths, Singapore; PhDr. Peter Kartous, CSc., DirectorMinisterstvo Vnútra Slovenskej Republiky, Bratislava, Slovenia; L. Coetzee, Head National Archives Repository, Pretoria, South Africa; Elisabeth Thorsell, Järfälla, Sweden; D.M. Mwita, Registrar General, Tanzania; Mrs. Fatai L. Vaihu and Frederick E. L. Tuita, Office of the Registrar, Supreme Court, Tonga; K.S. Harripersad, Registrar General, Trinidad and Tobago; Barney Tyrwhitt-Drake, United Kingdom; Dale Westerterp, Petaluma, CA; Richard C. Fipphen, Stamford, CT; S. Mususa, Acting Registrar, Department of National Registration, Passport and Citizenship, Zambia.

1. United States

UNITED STATES—Citizens Abroad

Send your requests to:

Passport Services   Tel. (202) 955-0307
Passport Correspondence Branch
1111 19th Street, NW, Suite 510
Washington, DC 20524

Cost for a Certification of Birth Report, or Consular Report of Birth	$40.00
Cost for a Certificate of Witness to Marriage or Consular Report of Death	$20.00
Cost for a Report of Death of an American citizen, or Consular Report	$20.00

The vital statistics of a person born to United States citizens abroad is documented by a U.S. embassy or consular office with a "Certification of Birth Report (DS-1350)," a "Certificate of Witness to Marriage," and a "Report of the Death of an American Citizen." Prior to November 1, 1990 these documents were called a "Consular Report of Birth, Marriage, or Death."

Vital records are kept by state and local registrars in the United States. If the birth, marriage, divorce, or death occurred inside the United States, you need to consult the listing in this book for the state where the event occurred. If the event occurred in another country and the person was a United States citizen or his dependent, contact Passport Services.

If the person was a member of the Armed Forces, write to the Secretary of Defense; Washington, DC 20301. If the person was a member of the Coast Guard, contact the Commandant, P.S., U.S. Coast Guard, Washington, DC 20226.

If the birth or death occurred on the high seas while the vessel or aircraft was outbound from the U.S. or at a foreign port, write to the U.S. Department of State, Washington, DC 20520. If the vessel was inbound and first docked in the U.S. after the event occurred, write to the Bureau of Vital Records for the state where it arrived.

It is possible to obtain a copy of an original application for Social Security services. Please see the instruction form given.

CONSULAR VITAL RECORD SEARCH REQUEST FORM

DATE:_____ PURPOSE OF REQUEST:_____

NAME AT (CIRCLE ONE)
BIRTH/DEATH/MARRIAGE:_____

NAME AFTER ADOPTION (IF APPLICABLE):_____

DATE OF (CIRCLE ONE)   COUNTRY OF (CIRCLE ONE)
BIRTH/DEATH/MARRIAGE:_____   BIRTH/DEATH/MARRIAGE:_____

FATHER'S NAME:_____
DATE & PLACE (STATE/COUNTRY) OF BIRTH:_____

MOTHER'S NAME:_____
DATE & PLACE (STATE/COUNTRY) OF BIRTH:_____

**IF YOU POSSESS A REPORT OF BIRTH/DEATH OR CERTIFICATE OF WITNESS
TO MARRIAGE, PLEASE ENCLOSE A COPY TO AID IN OUR FILE SEARCH.**

PASSPORT - FIRST ENTRY INTO THE UNITED STATES
NAME OF BEARER:_____
DATE OF ISSUANCE:_____ PASSPORT NUMBER:_____
DATE OF INCLUSION (IF PASSPORT WAS NOT ISSUED TO THE SUBJECT):_____

CURRENT PASSPORT INFORMATION
NAME OF BEARER:_____
DATE OF ISSUANCE:_____ PASSPORT NUMBER:_____

SIGNATURE:_____
         (SUBJECT, PARENT, OR GUARDIAN)

ADDRESS:_____ TELEPHONE (DAYTIME):_____
        _____

NOTICE: If you are requesting an amendment or correction to a Consular Report of
Birth Abroad, please include certified copies of all documents appropriate for effecting t
change (i.e., foreign birth certificate, marriage certificate, court ordered adoption or n
change, birth certificates of adopting or legitimating parents, etc.). The original or
replacement FS-240, or a notarized affidavit concerning its whereabouts also must be
included.

PLEASE INDICATE THE NUMBER OF DOCUMENTS DESIRED

REPORT OF BIRTH (FS-240) ($40.00 ONLY ONE COPY AVAILABLE)   _____
(***NOTE:*** Request for an FS-240 MUST include the original FS-240 or a notarized affidavit attesting to
        its disposition.)

For the following documents $20.00 for first copy; $10.00 for each additional copy:
CERTIFICATION OF BIRTH (DS-1350)   _____ (MULTIPLE COPIES AVAILABLE)
REPORT OF DEATH   _____ (MULTIPLE COPIES AVAILABLE)
CERTIFICATE OF WITNESS TO MARRIAGE   _____ (MULTIPLE COPIES AVAILABLE)
CERTIFICATION OF NO RECORD   _____ (MULTIPLE COPIES AVAILABLE)

Check or Money Order must be signed, dated, and made payable to **Department of State**.
Remittance must be payable in U.S. dollars through a U.S. bank.
PLEASE DO NOT SEND CASH.

RETURN THE RECORD SEARCH REQUEST FORM TO:

Passport Correspondence Branch
1111 Nineteenth Street NW, Suite 510
Washington, D.C. 20524

Social Security Number Record
Third Party Request for Extract or Photocopy

Mail to: Office of Central Records Operations
Baltimore, Maryland 21201

Refer to: **SPPE-1**

<u>INSTRUCTIONS</u> – <u>Print or type all data. Sign in ink. Allow 4 to 6 weeks for a reply.</u>

AS A REPRESENTATIVE OF THE PERSON WHOSE FULL IDENTIFYING INFORMATION IS SHOWN BELOW, I HEREBY REQUEST AN EXTRACT OR PHOTOCOPY OF THAT PERSON'S APPLICATION(S) FOR A SOCIAL SECURITY NUMBER.

SOCIAL SECURITY NUMBER (if known)	FULL NAME NOW USED
NAME SHOWN ON LAST SOCIAL SECURITY CARD (if different from full name now used)	
FULL NAME AT BIRTH	
DATE OF BIRTH (month, day, year)	

PLACE OF BIRTH (city, county, and state or foreign country)	SEX ☐ MALE ☐ FEMALE

FULL MAIDEN NAME OF MOTHER (whether living or dead)
FULL NAME OF FATHER (whether living or dead)

☐ The person I represent has completed and signed the authorization shown below which is required to release this confidential information to me since I am not a court-appointed legal representative.

☐ I am attaching a certified copy of my current court-appointment as this person's legal representative to obtain the release of this confidential information to me. Please return this copy with my reply.

PENALTY STATEMENT (read before signing)
Deliberately furnishing or causing to be furnished false information on this form is punishable by fine, or imprisonment, or both under federal law.

SIGNATURE OF REPRESENTATIVE	DATE
STREET ADDRESS	CITY, STATE, AND ZIP CODE

AUTHORIZATION TO RELEASE CONFIDENTIAL INFORMATION TO A THIRD PARTY – I am the person to whom this request pertains; and I hereby authorize the Social Security Administration to release an extract or photocopy of my Social Security number application(s) to my representative whose signature and address appear above.

SIGNATURE (do not print unless this is your usual signature)	DATE
STREET ADDRESS	CITY, STATE, AND ZIP CODE

NOTE: A printed signature or a signature by mark (X) must be witnessed below by two adults.

(1) SIGNATURE	(2) SIGNATURE
STREET ADDRESS	STREET ADDRESS
CITY, STATE, AND ZIP CODE	CITY, STATE, AND ZIP CODE

Department of Health and Human Services
Social Security Administration

Form **SSA-L997** (2-83)

ALABAMA

Send your requests to:

Alabama Department of Public Health   Tel. (334) 206-5418
Center for Health Statistics   Tel. (334) 206-5426
Office of Vital Records   http://www.alapubhealth.org
P.O. Box 5625
Montgomery, Alabama 36103-5625

Birth and death records are on file at the Office of Vital Records from January 1, 1908. Births are filed under the father's name by the date and place the event occurred. Birth records are confidential with restricted access for 125 years; death records are restricted for 25 years. Marriage records are on file from August 1, 1936, and divorce records from January 1, 1950. Marriage and divorce certificates are not confidential and may be obtained by anyone.

The Center for Health Statistics sells microfilm copies of the following vital records indexes for $40.00 a roll: Marriages (1936–1969), Divorces (1950–1959), and Deaths (1908–1959). Expedited service is available (with payment by credit card) for an additional fee of $10.00, plus shipping.

Cost for a certified Birth Certificate	$12.00
Cost for a certified Marriage or Divorce Certificate	$12.00
Cost for a certified Death Certificate	$12.00
Cost for a duplicate copy, when ordered at the same time	$4.00

For Marriage Records before August 1936 write to:

Probate Judge
County Court House
(County Seat), Alabama

For Divorce Records before 1950 write to:

Circuit Court
(County Seat), Alabama

For Adoption Record information write to:

Office of Adoption
State Department of Human Resources
50 North Ripley Street
Montgomery, Alabama 36130

Fairfield, Alabama, birth records from 1921 to 1933 are in the Tutwiler Collection, Birmingham Public Library (2100 Park Place; Birmingham, AL 35203). Alabama Department of Archives and History (624 Washington Avenue, Montgomery, AL 36130-0100; 334-242-4363; fax 334-240-3433) has copies of early county vital records.

The Family History Library of The Church of Jesus Christ of Latter-day Saints in Salt Lake City, Utah has microfilmed many of the original and published vital records and church registers of Alabama. For details on the holdings please consult your nearest Family History Center.

For further information see:

Manual for Clerks and Registers. Montgomery, AL: Administrative Office of Courts, 1979. Looseleaf.

Manual for Clerks and Registers of the Circuit Courts of the State of Alabama. University, AL: University of Alabama School of Law, Department of Court Management, 1974. Looseleaf.

USE ONLY FOR A VITAL EVENT WHICH OCCURRED IN ALABAMA

The fee for a birth, death, marriage or divorce is $12.00, which includes the cost of one certified copy OR Certificate of Failure to Find. For each additional copy of the same record ordered at the same time, the fee is $4.00. For information on how to expedite a document, call 334-206-5418. Make check or money order payable to "State Board of Health" or to the County Health Department. **Fees are non-refundable.** • Do not request two different types of certificates on the same form • **PRINT ALL INFORMATION** • You must **complete & sign the applicant section** or your request cannot be processed.

TAKE THIS FORM TO YOUR LOCAL COUNTY HEALTH DEPARTMENT OR MAIL IT TO:
Alabama Department of Public Health, Center for Health Statistics, P.O. Box 5625, Montgomery, Alabama 36103-5625

APPLICANT SECTION (THIS SECTION MUST BE COMPLETED) Birth certificates less than 125 years old and death certificates less than 25 years old are restricted records. You must be an immediate family member OR demonstrate a legal right to the record in order to obtain a copy of the record (§ 22-9A-21). Anyone falsely applying for a record is subject to a penalty upon conviction of up to three months in the county jail or a fine of up to $500. Code of Ala. 1975, § 13A-10-109. By signing, you are certifying you have a legal right to the record requested.

Your Signature _____ Date_____

Print Your Name _____ Address _____

City _____ State _____ Zip _____ Daytime Phone (   ) _____

Your Relationship to Person Whose Record is Being Requested _____

Reason for Request (if not immediate family) _____

I allow the following individual to pick up the certificate (s) _____

BIRTH:
NUMBER OF COPIES _____ AMOUNT PAID $ _____

FULL NAME AT BIRTH_____
FIRST / MIDDLE / LAST

DATE OF BIRTH _____ SEX _____

COUNTY OF BIRTH _____ HOSPITAL _____

FULL MAIDEN NAME OF MOTHER_____
FIRST / MIDDLE / LAST

FULL NAME OF FATHER _____
FIRST / MIDDLE / LAST

DEATH:
NUMBER OF COPIES _____ AMOUNT PAID $ _____

LEGAL NAME OF DECEASED_____
FIRST / MIDDLE / LAST

DATE OF DEATH _____ COUNTY OF DEATH _____ SEX_____

SSN _____ DATE OF BIRTH OR AGE _____ RACE _____

NAME OF SPOUSE _____
FIRST / MIDDLE / LAST

NAME OF PARENTS_____

STARTING WITH 1991 DEATHS, CERTIFICATES MAY BE ISSUED WITHOUT A CAUSE OF DEATH. Indicate the number of copies of each type of certificate you want:_____WITH CAUSE OF DEATH _____WITHOUT CAUSE OF DEATH

☐ MARRIAGE OR ☐ DIVORCE:
NUMBER OF COPIES _____ AMOUNT PAID $ _____

FULL NAME OF HUSBAND_____
FIRST / MIDDLE / LAST

FULL MAIDEN NAME OF WIFE _____
FIRST / MIDDLE / LAST

DATE OF MARRIAGE_____ (OR) DATE OF DIVORCE_____

IF MARRIAGE, COUNTY WHERE LICENSE WAS ISSUED _____

IF DIVORCE, COUNTY OF DIVORCE _____

COUNTY REGISTRAR USE: This application has been reviewed for the individual's right to receive the requested document(s).

_____ _____ _____
County Registrar's Signature   Date   County Health Department Receipt Number

Informational materials in alternative formats will be made available upon request.   ADPH-HS 14/Rev. 3-97

ALASKA

Send your requests to:

Bureau of Vital Statistics
Alaska Department of Health & Social Services
350 Main Street, Room 114
P.O. Box 110675
Juneau, AK 99811-0675

Tel. (907) 465-3392
Fax (907) 465-3618
E-mail: BVSOFFICE@health.state.ak.us
http://hss.state.ak.us/dph/bvs/bvs_home.htm

The Bureau of Vital Statistics has birth, marriage, and death records from January 1, 1913, and divorce records from January 1, 1950. These can also be obtained from the Clerk of the Superior Court where the divorce decree was issued. Write to: Superior Court, (County Seat), Alaska. Expedited service is available (with payment by credit card) for an additional fee of $10.00, plus shipping.

Cost for a certified Birth Certificate	$10.00
Cost for a plastic, wallet-size Birth Certificate	$10.00
Cost for an heirloom Birth Certificate	$35.00
Cost for a certified Marriage Certificate	$10.00
Cost for a certified Divorce Record	$10.00
Cost for a certified Death Certificate	$10.00

For Adoption Record information write to:

Adoption Coordinator
Alaska Division of Family & Youth Services
P.O. Box 110630
Juneau, Alaska 99811-0630
(907) 465-3631

Adoptees may receive copies of their original birth certificate at age 18.

The Family History Library of Salt Lake City, Utah has microfilmed many of the original and published vital records and church registers of Alaska. For details on their holdings please consult your nearest Family History Center.

For further information see:

Alaska Vital Signs. (Serial). Juneau, AK: Alaska Bureau of Vital Statistics, Vol. 1, No. 1, 1991– .

ALASKA BIRTH CERTIFICATE REQUEST FORM

Mail this form with a check or money order	or you may pay by Credit Card (Additional $10)
Payable to: Bureau of Vital Statistics Alaska Department of Health and Social Services P.O. Box 110675 Juneau, AK 99811-0675 **Phone** (907) 465-3392 **Fax** (907) 465-3618 **Email:** janet_brown@health.state.ak.us	Name on credit card Number Expiration Date: Visa Mastercard Discover AmEx *(Write in expiration date and circle type of card)* Signature

Full Name of Child:

Certificate Number (if known):

Date of Birth or
Period Covered by Search:

Place of Birth:

Mother's First, Middle, and Maiden
Names:

Father's Full Name:

Signature of Applicant:

Individual named on certificate, legal guardian, or parent

Applicant's Full Name (printed):

Address:

City, State, Zip:

Daytime Phone:

Relationship to Child: **(REQUIRED)**

(i.e. self, parent, legal guardian)

_____ Standard Size Certificates @ $10/each =

_____ Wallet Size Certificates @ $10/each =

_____ Ship by Regular Mail (No extra Charge)

1/7/99

The Alaska Children's Trust and the **Alaska Bureau of Vital Statistics** present the Heirloom Birth Certificate. *The Embrace,* by Rie Muñoz, poignantly depicts a parent's love. Each 9x12 inch certificate also includes the child's name, date, and place of birth, and the name(s) of the parent (s).

Click to view enlargement

A collaborative effort between the Alaska Children's Trust and the Alaska Bureau of Vital Statistics, the Heirloom Birth Certificate contributes to the well-being of all Alaska children. The Trust earns $25 from the sale of each certificate, and provides grants to Alaska communities for the prevention of child abuse and neglect. Available for purchase by parents, family or friends, an Heirloom Birth Certificate makes a unique baby gift. Birth certificates aren't just for newborns. Commemorate birthdays, anniversaries, retirements and other special occasions with the purchase of an Heirloom Birth Certificate.

To order your own or your child's birth certificate, print this page and complete the following information. Friends or relatives can purchase a gift certificate to be redeemed by the individual or immediate family member. Provide as much information as possible.

Name of Child:	
Date of Birth:	
Place of Birth:	
Mother's Maiden Name:	
Father's Name:	
Signature:	
	Individual named on certificate, legal guardian, or parent
Purchaser's Name:	
Address:	
City, State, Zip:	
Daytime Phone:	
Relationship to Child:	**(REQUIRED)**
	(i.e. friend, relative, legal guardian, parent)

1/7/99

ALASKA MARRIAGE CERTIFICATE REQUEST FORM

Mail this form with a check or money order **Payable to:** Bureau of Vital Statistics Alaska Department of Health and Social Services P.O. Box 110675 Juneau, AK 99811-0675 **Phone** (907) 465-3392 **Fax** (907) 465-3618 **Email: janet_brown@health.state.ak.us**	or you may pay by Credit Card (Additional $10) Name on credit card _____ Number _____ Exp Date: _____ ○ Visa ○ Mastercard ○ Discover ○ AmEx *(Type in expiration date and indicate type of card)* Signature

Name of Husband:	
Maiden Name of Wife:	
Date of Marriage (month/day/year):	
Place of Marriage:	*(IN ALASKA ONLY)*
Signature of Applicant:	
Applicant's Printed Name:	
Address:	
City, State, Zip:	
Daytime Phone:	
Relationship to Person Whose Record is Requested:	**(REQUIRED)**
	(i.e. bride, groom, legal representative)

_____ Certificates @ **$10/each** =

Ship by ○ Regular Mail **(No extra charge)**   ○ Express Mail **(Add $11.75)**
○ DHL **(CANNOT SHIP TO P.O. BOX) (Add $15.50)**

Payment by Credit Card **(Add $10.00)**

TOTAL CHARGE

ALASKA DIVORCE CERTIFICATE REQUEST FORM

Mail this form with a check or money order **Payable to:** Bureau of Vital Statistics Alaska Department of Health and Social Services P.O. Box 110675 Juneau, AK 99811-0675 **Phone (907) 465-3392** **Fax (907) 465-3618** **Email: janet_brown@health.state.ak.us**	or you may pay by Credit Card (Additional $10) Name on credit card _____ Number _____ Exp Date: _____ O Visa O Mastercard O Discover O AmEx *(Type in expiration date and indicate type of card)* Signature

Name of Husband:	
Name of Wife:	
Date of Marriage (month/day/year):	
Place Divorce or Dissolution was Granted:	*(IN ALASKA ONLY)*
Date of Final Decree or Period to be Searched:	
Purpose for Which Record is Required:	
Signature of Applicant:	
Applicant's Printed Name:	
Address:	
City, State, Zip:	
Daytime Phone:	
Relationship to Person Whose Record is Requested:	**(REQUIRED)**
	(i.e. husband, wife, legal representative)

_____ Certificates @ **$10/each** =

Ship by O Regular Mail **(No extra charge)**   O Express Mail **(Add $11.75)**
O DHL **(CANNOT SHIP TO P.O. BOX) (Add $15.50)**

Payment by Credit Card **(Add $10.00)**

ALASKA DEATH CERTIFICATE REQUEST FORM

Mail this form with a check or money order **Payable to:** Bureau of Vital Statistics Alaska Department of Health and Social Services P.O. Box 110675 Juneau, AK 99811-0675 **Phone (907) 465-3392** **Fax (907) 465-3618** **Email: janet_brown@health.state.ak.us**	or you may pay by Credit Card (Additional $10) Name on credit card _____ Number _____ Exp Date: _____ ○ Visa ○ Mastercard ○ Discover ○ AmEx *(Type in expiration date and indicate type of card)* Signature

Name of Deceased:	
Date of Death or Period to be Searched:	
Social Security Number of Deceased:	
Date of Birth and/or age of Deceased:	
Place of Death:	*(IN ALASKA ONLY)*
Signature of Applicant:	
Applicant's Printed Name:	
Address:	
City, State, Zip:	
Daytime Phone:	
Purpose for which Record is Required:	
Relationship to Deceased:	**(REQUIRED)**
	(i.e. spouse, child, sibling, legal representative)

_____ Certificates @ **$10/each** =

Ship by ○ Regular Mail **(No extra charge)** ○ Express Mail **(Add $11.75)**
○ DHL **(CANNOT SHIP TO P.O. BOX) (Add $15.50)**

Payment by Credit Card **(Add $10.00)**

ARIZONA

Send your requests to:

Office of Vital Records
Arizona Department of Health Services
2727 West Glendale
P.O. Box 3887
Phoenix, Arizona 85030-3887

Tel. (602) 255-3260
Tel. (602) 255-1072
Fax (602) 249-3040
http://www.hs.state.az.us/vitalrcd/vitalrcd.htm

The Office of Vital Records has birth and death records from July 1903. Expedited service is available (with payment by credit card) for an additional fee of $5.00, plus shipping.

Cost for a certified Birth Certificate (1950 to present)	$6.00
Cost for a certified Birth Certificate (prior to 1950)	$9.00
Cost for a certified Death Certificate (1950 to present)	$6.00
Cost for a certified Death Certificate (prior to 1950)	$9.00

For earlier records contact:

County Clerk
(County Seat), Arizona

Send your requests for Marriage or Divorce Certificates to:

Clerk
Superior Court
(County Seat), Arizona

For Adoption Record information write to:

Arizona Confidential Intermediary Program
Arizona Supreme Court
1501 West Washington
Phoenix, Arizona 85007

Tel. (602) 364-0387
Tel. (602) 542-9580
In area code 520: (800) 732-8193
TT (602) 542-9545
E-mail: cip@supreme.sp.state.az.us
http://www.supreme.state.az.us/cip/default.htm

The cost for the Adoption Intermediary Program is $20 per hour, with an average cost of $225 per case.

The Arizona State Library (Archives Division, State Capitol, 3rd Floor; 1700 West Washington, Phoenix, AZ 85007; 602-542-4159) has early Arizona marriage records from the counties.

The Family History Library of Salt Lake City, Utah has microfilmed many of the original and published vital records and church registers of Arizona. For details on their holdings please consult your nearest Family History Center.

ARIZONA DEPARTMENT OF HEALTH SERVICES
VITAL RECORDS SECTION

REQUEST FOR COPY OF BIRTH CERTIFICATE

DATE _____

ENCLOSED $ _____ IN _____ FOR _____

AMOUNT

(PRIOR TO 1950 ONLY) CERTIFIED PHOTO COPY $9	(1950 TO PRESENT ONLY) CERTIFIED COMPUTERIZED COPY $6

I. BIRTH CERTIFICATE OF:

			FOR OFFICE USE ONLY
FULL NAME AT BIRTH	DATE OF BIRTH	SEX	DATE ISSUED
PLACE OF BIRTH (City, County, State)	MOTHER'S MAIDEN NAME (First, Middle, Last)	MOTHER'S BIRTHPLACE	STATE FILE NUMBER
HOSPITAL OR FACILITY	FATHER'S FULL NAME	FATHER'S BIRTHPLACE	

II. PERSON MAKING REQUEST

PRINT PLAINLY - RETURN ADDRESS

WARNING: False application for a birth certificate is a punishable offense.

For the protection of the individual, certificates of vital events are NOT open to public inspection. Signature of applicant MUST BE NOTARIZED (MAIL ONLY) OR this form must be accompanied by a copy of a valid Government issue picture I.D. which contains the applicant's signature.

Your Signature ☞ _____

YOUR NAME _____

YOUR ADDRESS (Number and Street) _____

(TOWN, STATE, ZIP CODE) _____

RELATIONSHIP TO PERSON NAMED IN CERTIFICATE (e.g. parent, attorney, etc.)	FOR WHAT PURPOSE DO YOU NEED THIS COPY?	TELEPHONE NO (Optional)

Send completed application and correct fee to:
OFFICE OF VITAL RECORDS
Arizona Department of Health Services
P.O. Box 3887
Phoenix, Arizona 85030

SUBSCRIBED AND SWORN TO OR AFFIRMED BEFORE ME THIS _____ DAY OF _____

NOTARY'S SIGNATURE _____

MY COMMISSION EXPIRES _____

ADHS/ADM Vital Records
VS-15A (Rev. 3/94)

ARIZONA DEPARTMENT OF HEALTH SERVICES
OFFICE OF VITAL RECORDS

APPLICATION FOR COPY OF DEATH CERTIFICATE

DATE _____

ENCLOSED $ _____ IN _____ FOR _____

AMOUNT

COPIES OF THE FOLLOWING DEATH CERTIFICATE	FOR OFFICE USE ONLY
	STATE FILE NUMBER

1. NAME OF DECEASED - First, Middle, Last	IF ANOTHER LAST NAME (except by marriage) WAS EVER USED ENTER HERE	

2. DATE OF DEATH - Month, Day, Year	SEX	SOCIAL SECURITY NUMBER (necessary for positive identification)	DATE ISSUED

3. PLACE OF DEATH - Hospital or Residence	Town or City	County	ARIZONA

THE FEE IS $6 FOR EACH CERTIFIED COPY

4. IF MARRIED, IS WIFE/HUSBAND OF DECEASED NOW LIVING? ☐ YES ☐ NO	IF YES, LIST NAME - First, Middle, Last

5. HOW WILL COPIES BE USED?	ARE COPIES TO BE USED FOR U.S. GOV'T CLAIMS? ☐ YES ☐ NO	IF YES, LIST EACH TYPE OF CLAIM

WARNING: False application for a death certificate is a punishable offense.

For the protection of the individual, certificates of vital events are NOT open to public inspection. Signature of applicant MUST BE NOTARIZED (Mail ONLY) OR this form must be accompanied by a copy of a valid Government issue picture I.D. which contains the applicant's signature.

7. SIGNATURE OF APPLICANT (The regulations require a signed application)	RELATIONSHIP TO THE DECEASED?

7. TYPE OR PRINT NAME AND CORRECT MAIL ADDRESS BELOW

NAME	
STREET ADDRESS OR P.O. BOX NUMBER	
CITY AND STATE	ZIP CODE

SEND COMPLETED APPLICATION AND CORRECT FEE TO:
OFFICE OF VITAL RECORDS
Arizona Dept. of Health Services
P.O. Box 3887
Phoenix, Arizona 85030-3887

SUBSCRIBED AND SWORN TO OR AFFIRMED BEFORE ME THIS _____ DAY OF _____

NOTARY'S SIGNATURE _____

MY COMMISSION EXPIRES _____

ADHS/ADM/Vital Records
VS-158 (Rev. 3/94)

ARKANSAS

Arkansas Department of Health
Division of Vital Records
4815 West Markham Street, Slot 44
Little Rock, Arkansas 72205-3867

Tel. (501) 661-2174
Toll free (800) 637-9314
Fax (501) 663-2832
http://health.state.ar.us/certificates/certificates.html#

The Division of Vital Records has birth and death records on file from February 1, 1914. Marriage records have been kept since January 1, 1917, and divorce records since January 1, 1923. Also on file are Little Rock and Fort Smith births and deaths from 1881 (incomplete). For a copy of the original record, write "PHOTOCOPY ONLY" in red across the top of the form. Expedited service is available (payment by credit card) for an additional fee of $5.00, plus shipping.

Cost for a certified Birth Certificate	$5.00
Cost for a plastic, wallet-size Birth Card	$5.00
Cost for a certified Marriage or Divorce Certificate	$5.00
Cost for a certified Death Certificate	$4.00
Cost for a duplicate copy, when ordered at the same time	$1.00

For earlier records contact:

County Clerk
County Court House
(County Seat), Arkansas

For Adoption Record information write to:

Arkansas Division of Human Services
Arkansas Mutual Consent Voluntary
  Adoption Registry
P.O. Box 1437 Slot 808
Little Rock, Arkansas 77203-1437

Tel. (501) 682-8462

TDD (501) 682-1442
http://www.state.ar.us/dhs/adoption/adoption.html

The cost to register with the Adoption Registry is $5.00.

Arkansas History Commission (One Capitol Mall, 2nd Floor, Little Rock, Arkansas 72201; 501-682-6900) has microfilm copies of marriage records from selected counties from 1814.

For further information see:

Arkansas Records Survey (Serial). Little Rock, AR: Arkansas Records Association, 1972—. Quarterly.

Shaw, Mary Nell. *Arkansas Records Management Manual*. Little Rock, AR: Arkansas Historical Commission, 1981. 43p.

Date _____

ARKANSAS DEPARTMENT OF HEALTH
Division of Vital Records
4815 West Markham Street, Slot 44
Little Rock, AR 72205-3867

BIRTH CERTIFICATE APPLICATION

Only Arkansas births are recorded in this office. There are no original birth records for events which occurred before February 1, 1914. The fee is $5.00 per certificate copy or birth registration card. This fee must accompany the application. Send check or money order payable to the Arkansas Department of Health. DO NOT SEND CASH. Of the total fee you send, $5.00 will be kept in this office to cover search charges if no record of the birth is found. Only the names and dates listed will be searched for the $5.00 fee. Names and/or dates submitted later will require an additional $5.00 non-refundable fee.

List Below All Possible Birthdates and Names Under Which the Certificate May Be Registered   (Type or Print)

1. Full Name at Birth	First Name	Middle Name		Last Name		

2. Date of Birth	Month	Day	Year	Sex	Race	Age Last Birthday

3. Place of Birth	City or Town	County	State	Order Of This Birth (1st, 2nd, 3rd, etc.)
	Name of Hospital or Street Address		Name of Attendant at Birth	

4. Full Name of Father	First Name	Middle Name	Last Name

5. Full Maiden Name of Mother (Name Before Marriage)	First Name	Middle Name	Last Name

If this child has been adopted, please give original name if known.

_____

If you have received a copy before, please give certificate number. _____

If this is a delayed certificate, when was it filed? _____

What is your relationship to the person whose certificate is being requested?

_____

What is your reason for requesting this certificate?

_____

Is the person whose certificate is being requested still living? ☐ Yes ☐ No

Signature and telephone number of person requesting this certificate.

DO NOT WRITE IN THIS SPACE	
Name of Searcher	
Index	
Delayed	Prior
Volume Number	
Page Number	Year

Arkansas Department of Health
Division of Vital Records
BIRTH REGISTRATION CARD

CERTIFICATE NUMBER

NAME

BIRTHDATE   SEX

TOWN   DATE FILED

COUNTY   DATE ISSUED

THIS CERTIFIES THAT THE ABOVE IS A TRUE ABSTRACT OF THIS PERSON'S 98TH RECORD WHICH IS FILED WITH THE STATE REGISTRAR.

SHARON M. LEINBACH
STATE REGISTRAR

BIRTH REGISTRATION CARD
(Actual size 3 3/8" x 2 1/8")

Please PRINT below the name and address of the person who is to receive the copy(s) or card(s).

_____

_____

_____

STATE OF ARKANSAS

ARKANSAS DEPARTMENT OF HEALTH
DIVISION OF VITAL RECORDS
CERTIFICATION OF BIRTH

DATE FILED: DATE ISSUED:
CERTIFICATE NUMBER:
NAME: SAMPLE
BIRTHDATE: SEX:
TOWN: COUNTY:
MOTHER'S MAIDEN NAME: AGE:
MOTHER'S BIRTH PLACE:
FATHER'S NAME: AGE:
FATHER'S BIRTH PLACE:

SEAL

Sharon M. Leinbach
State Registrar

360506

CERTIFICATION OF BIRTH
(Actual size 7 1/2" x 6 1/2")

For Charge Card Calls Only -
Call (501)661-2726 to charge copies to a VISA, DISCOVER, or MASTERCARD

DISCOVER   VISA   MasterCard

Charge Card Fee is $5.00. This is in addition to fee for each certified copy requested.

ALL TYPES OF COPIES ARE LEGAL PROOF OF BIRTH

	HOW MANY
COPY OF ORIGINAL RECORD ($5.00 Each)	
CERTIFICATION OF BIRTH** ($5.00 Each)	
BIRTH CARD ($5.00 Each)	
AMOUNT OF MONEY ENCLOSED $_____	

** If Certification of Birth cannot be issued, copy of original record will be substituted.

Any person who willfully and knowingly makes any false statement in an application for a certified copy of a vital record filed in this state is subject to a fine of not more than ten thousand dollars ($10,000) or imprisoned not more than five (5) years, or both (Arkansas Statutes 20-18-105).

VR-7 (Rev. 3/99)

DATE _____

ARKANSAS DEPARTMENT OF HEALTH
DIVISION OF VITAL RECORDS
4815 WEST MARKHAM STREET, SLOT 44
LITTLE ROCK, ARKANSAS 72205-3867

MARRIAGE RECORD APPLICATION

Only Arkansas events of marriage are filed in this office. Marriage records start with 1917. The fee is $5.00 per certified copy. This fee must accompany the application. Send check or money order payable to the Arkansas Department of Health. DO NOT SEND CASH. Of the total fee sent, $5.00 will be kept to cover the search charge when the record is not located in our files.

FILL IN FOR A MARRIAGE RECORD

NAME OF GROOM _____

MAIDEN NAME OF BRIDE _____

DATE OF MARRIAGE _____
　　　　　　　　　　　　　　　Month　　　　　　　　　　　Day　　　　　　　　　Year

COUNTY IN WHICH LICENSE WAS ISSUED _____

_____

PLEASE ANSWER ALL QUESTIONS

What is your relationship to the parties named on the requested record?

_____

What is your reason for requesting a copy of this record? _____

_____

Signature and telephone number of person requesting this record:

_____

DO NOT WRITE IN THIS SPACE
Searcher _____
Index _____
_____
Volume No. _____
Page No. _____ Yr.

FOR CHARGE CARD CALLS ONLY-
　Call (501)661-2726 to charge copies to a VISA,
　DISCOVER or MASTERCARD.

VISA　**MasterCard**　**DISCOVER**

CHARGE CARD FEE IS $5.00. IN ADDITION TO FEE FOR EACH
CERTIFIED COPY REQUESTED.

- -

DO NOT DETACH

THIS IS A MAILING INSERT. PRINT NAME AND ADDRESS OF
PERSON TO WHOM THE CERTIFIED COPY IS TO BE MAILED.

THIS IS NOT AN INVOICE. ➤

NO. OF COPIES REQUESTED
_____
(Fee is $5.00 per copy)
Marriage _____
Amount of Money Enclosed _____

NAME _____

ADDRESS _____

CITY _____ STATE _____ ZIP _____

VR-9

　　　　　　　　　　-3689

Any person who willfully and knowingly makes any false statement in
an application for a certified copy of a vital record filed in this state is
subject to a fine of not more than ten thousand dollars ($10,000) or
imprisoned not more than five (5) years, or both. (Ark. Statutes
20-18-105).

ARKANSAS DEPARTMENT OF HEALTH
DIVISION OF VITAL RECORDS
4815 WEST MARKHAM STREET, SLOT 44
LITTLE ROCK, ARKANSAS 72205-3867

DIVORCE RECORD APPLICATION

Only Arkansas events of divorce are filed in this office. Divorce records start with 1923. The fee is $5.00 per certified copy. This fee must accompany the application. Send check or money order payable to the Arkansas Department of Health. DO NOT SEND CASH. Of the total fee sent, $5.00 will be kept to cover the search charge when the record is not located in our files.

FILL IN FOR A DIVORCE RECORD

NAME OF HUSBAND _____

NAME OF WIFE _____

DATE OF DIVORCE OR DISMISSAL _____
                                  Month   Day   Year

COUNTY IN WHICH DIVORCE WAS GRANTED/DISMISSED _____

_____

PLEASE ANSWER ALL QUESTIONS

What is your relationship to the parties named on the requested record?

_____

What is your reason for requesting a copy of this record? _____

_____

Signature and telephone number of person requesting this record:

_____

DO NOT WRITE IN THIS SPACE	
Searcher _____	
Index _____	
_____	
Volume No.	
Page No. _____	Yr.

FOR CHARGE CARD CALLS ONLY-
  Call (501)661-2726 to charge copies to a VISA,
  DISCOVER or MASTERCARD.

VISA   **MasterCard**   **DISCOVER**

CHARGE CARD FEE IS $5.00. IN ADDITION TO FEE FOR EACH CERTIFIED COPY REQUESTED.

- -

DO NOT DETACH

THIS IS A MAILING INSERT. PRINT NAME AND ADDRESS OF PERSON TO WHOM THE CERTIFIED COPY IS TO BE MAILED.

THIS IS NOT AN INVOICE.

NO. OF COPIES REQUESTED
_____
(Fee is $5.00 per copy)
Divorce _____
Amount of
Money Enclosed _____

NAME _____

ADDRESS _____

CITY _____ STATE ____ ZIP _____

VR-10

-3689

Any person who willfully and knowingly makes any false statement in an application for a certified copy of a vital record filed in this state is subject to a fine of not more than ten thousand dollars ($10,000) or imprisoned not more than five (5) years, or both. (Ark. Statutes 20-18-105).

Date _____

ARKANSAS DEPARTMENT OF HEALTH
Division of Vital Records
4815 West Markham Street, Slot 44
Little Rock, AR 72205-3867

DEATH CERTIFICATE APPLICATION

Only Arkansas deaths are recorded in this office. There are no original death records for events which occured before February 1, 1914.
The fee is $4.00 for the first copy and $1.00 for each additional copy of the same record ordered at the same time. The fee must accompany
the application. Send check or money order payable to the Arkansas Department of Health. DO NOT SEND CASH. Of the total fee you send,
$4.00 will be kept in this office to cover search charges if no record of the death is found. Only the names and dates listed will be searched
for the $4.00 fee. Names and/or dates submitted later will require an additional $4.00 non-refundable fee.

List Below All Possible Dates of Death and Names Under Which the Certificate May Be Registered   (Type or Print)

1. Full Name of Deceased	First Name		Middle Name	Last Name		
2. Date of Death	Month	Day	Year	Age of Deceased	Sex	Race
3. Place Where Death Occurred	City or Town	County	State			
If Unknown, Give Last Place of Residence	City or Town	County	State			
4. Name of Funeral Home						
5. Address of Funeral Home						
6. Name and Address of Attending Physician						

If deceased was an infant, was it stillborn? ☐ Yes ☐ No

What is your relationship to the person whose certificate is being requested?

_____

What is your reason for requesting a copy of this certificate?_____

_____

Signature and telephone number of person requesting this certificate:

_____

DO NOT WRITE IN THIS SPACE	
Name of Searcher	
Index	
Delayed	Prior
Volume Number	
Page Number	Year

- -

DO NOT DETACH

For Charge Card Calls Only
   Call (501)661-2726 to charge copies to a VISA,
   DISCOVER, or MASTERCARD

Charge Card Fee is $5.00. This is in addition to fee for each
certified copy requested.

THIS IS A MAILING INSERT. PRINT NAME AND ADDRESS OF
PESON WHO IS TO RECEIVE THE COPY OR COPIES.
THIS IS NOT AN INVOICE

_____

_____

Copies Requested	
ONE COPY $4.00 ADDITIONAL COPIES $1.00 EACH	HOW MANY
AMOUNT OF MONEY ENCLOSED $_____	

Any person who willfully and knowingly makes any false statement in an
application for a certified copy of a vital record filed in this state is subject
to a fine of not more than ten thousand dollars ($10,000) or imprisoned
not more than five (5) years, or both (Arkansas Statutes 20-18-105.)

VR-8 (Rev. 9/94)

Send your requests to:

Office of Vital Records
Department of Health Services
304 S Street
P.O. Box 730241
Sacramento, California 94244-0241

Tel. (916) 445-1719
Recording (916) 445-2684
Fax (800) 858-5553
Fax (916) 442-6766
http://www.dhs.ca.gov/hisp/chs/OVR/Ovrindex.htm

The Office of Vital Records has births, marriages, and deaths on file from July 1, 1905. The State makes available a microfiche index to deaths from 1905–1995. There is a $7.00 processing fee for credit card orders.

Cost for a certified Birth Certificate	$12.00
Cost for a certified Marriage Certificate	$12.00
Cost for a certified Divorce Record	$12.00
Cost for a certified Death Certificate	$8.00

For earlier records contact:

County Clerk
County Court House
(County Seat), California

For Adoption Record information write to:

California Department of Social Services
Adoption Branch
774 P Street, MS 19-31
Sacramento, California 95814-6401

Tel. (916) 322-3778
E-mail: wbeers@dss.ca.gov
http://www.childsworld.org/adoption/index.htm

California State Archives (1020 O Street, Room 130, Sacramento, CA 95814; 916-773-3000) has vital records from some counties. The Family History Library of Salt Lake City, Utah has microfiche copies of the statewide marriage indexes from 1960 to 1981 and the statewide death indexes from 1940 to 1995.

For further information see:

County Recorders' Legal Manual, a Reference Book of Laws, Legal Opinions and Rules Governing Recording Procedures in the State of California. Los Angeles, CA: County Recorder's Association of California, 1992. 2 vols.

Handbook for Local Registrars of Births and Deaths. Sacramento, CA: Office of the State Registrar of Vital Statistics, 1973. 113p.

State of California – Health and Human Services Agency   Department of Health Services

APPLICATION FOR CERTIFIED COPY OF BIRTH RECORD

INFORMATION: Birth records have been maintained in the Office of the State Registrar of Vital Statistics since July 1, 1905. The only records of earlier events are delayed birth certificates and court ordered delayed birth certificates registered as provided by law.

INSTRUCTIONS

1. Use a separate application blank for each different record of birth for which you are requesting a certified copy. Send **$12** for **each** certified copy requested. If no record of the birth is found, the $12 fee will be retained for searching as required by statute and a Certification of No Record will be sent.

2. Give all the information you have available for the identification of the record of the registrant in the spaces under **Certificate Information**. If the information you furnish is incomplete or inaccurate, it may be impossible to locate the record. If this person has been adopted, please make the request in the adopted name.

3. Complete the **Applicant Information** section.

4. Indicate the number of certified copies you wish and include with this application sufficient money, in the form of a personal check, postal or bank money order (International Money Order only for out-of-country requests), made payable to the **Office of Vital Records**. The fee is **$12** for each certified copy. Mail this application with the fee to the Office of Vital Records, 304 S Street, P.O. Box 730241, Sacramento, CA 94244-0241. You may also FAX your request and charge it to a credit card to: 1-800-858-5553 or (916) 442-6766 (out of country). There is an additional fee of $7 for using the charge card service. If requested, express courier fee will be applied to credit card.

CERTIFICATE INFORMATION – PLEASE PRINT OR TYPE

Name on Certificate – First Name	Middle Name	Last Name or Birth Name if Married
City or Town of Birth		Place of Birth – County
Date of Birth – Month, Day, Year (If unknown, enter approximate date of birth)		Sex ☐ Female ☐ Male
Name of Father – First Name	Middle Name	Last Name
Name of Mother – First Name	Middle Name	Last Name (Maiden Name)

APPLICANT INFORMATION – PLEASE PRINT OR TYPE

Purpose for Which Certified Copy is to Be Used	Today's Date	Telephone Number – Area Code First ( )
Name of Person Completing Application (Please Print)	Signature (Person Requesting Record(s) or Cardholder, if Different)	
Address – Number, Street	City	State	ZIP Code
Name of Person Receiving Copies, if Different From Above	Number of Copies	Amount Enclosed	E-mail Address
Mailing Address for Copies, If Different From Above	City	State	ZIP Code
Credit Card # for FAX Orders	Expiration Date	Shipping Method: ☐ Express Courier ☐ Regular Mail

DO NOT WRITE IN SPACE BELOW – FOR REGISTRAR ONLY

BIRTH

VS 111 (11/99)

APPLICATION FOR CERTIFIED COPY OF MARRIAGE RECORD

INFORMATION: Marriage records have been maintained in the Office of the State Registrar of Vital Statistics since July 1, 1905. We are unable to search records from 1987 to 1995.

INSTRUCTIONS

1. Use a separate application blank for each different record of marriage for which you are requesting a certified copy. Send **$12** for **each** certified copy requested. If no record of the marriage is found, the $12 fee will be retained for searching as required by statute and a Certification of No Record will be sent.

2. Give all the information you have available for the identification of the record of marriage in the spaces under **Bride and Groom Information**. If the information you furnish is incomplete or inaccurate, it may be impossible to locate the record.

3. Complete the **Applicant Information** section.

4. Indicate the number of certified copies you wish and include with this application sufficient money, in the form of a personal check, postal or bank money order (International Money Order only for out-of-country requests), made payable to the **Office of Vital Records**. The fee is **$12** for each certified copy. Mail this application with the fee to the Office of Vital Records, 304 S Street, P.O. Box 730241, Sacramento, CA 94244-0241. You may also FAX your request and charge it to a credit card to: 1-800-858-5553 or (916) 442-6766 (out of country). There is an additional fee of $7 for using the charge card service. If requested, express courier fee will be applied to credit card.

BRIDE AND GROOM INFORMATION – PLEASE PRINT OR TYPE

Name of Groom – First Name	Middle Name	Last Name	
Date of Birth	Place of Birth	Name of Father of Groom	
Maiden Name of Bride – First Name	Middle Name	Last Name	
Date of Birth	Place of Birth	Name of Father of Bride	
Date of Marriage – Month, Day, Year	If Date Unknown, Enter Year(s) to be Searched	County of Issue of License	County of Marriage

APPLICANT INFORMATION – PLEASE PRINT OR TYPE

Purpose for Which Certified Copy is to Be Used	Today's Date	Telephone Number – Area Code First ( )	
Name of Person Completing Application (Please Print)	Signature (Person Requesting Record(s) or Cardholder, if Different)		
Address – Number, Street	City	State	ZIP Code
Name of Person Receiving Copies, if Different From Above	Number of Copies	Amount Enclosed	E-mail Address
Mailing Address for Copies, if Different From Above	City	State	ZIP Code
Credit Card # for FAX Orders	Expiration Date	Shipping Method: ☐ Express Courier ☐ Regular Mail	

DO NOT WRITE IN SPACE BELOW – FOR REGISTRAR ONLY

MARRIAGE

State of California – Health and Human Services Agency

Department of Health Services

APPLICATION FOR CERTIFICATION OF DISSOLUTION OF MARRIAGE

INFORMATION: The Office of the State Registrar of Vital Statistics maintains records of divorces from 1962 through June 30, 1984. We issue a Certification of Record, not the Decree. A Certification of Record gives the names, filing date, county, and case number of the divorce only.

INSTRUCTIONS

1. Use a separate application blank for each different record of marriage for which you are requesting a certification. Send **$12** for **each** certification requested. If no record of the marriage is found, the $12 fee will be retained for searching as required by statute and a Certification of No Record will be sent.

2. Give all the information you have available for the identification of the record of the divorce in the spaces under **Husband and Wife Information**. If the information you furnish is incomplete or inaccurate, it may be impossible to locate the record.

3. Complete the **Applicant Information** section.

4. Indicate the number of certified copies you wish and include with this application sufficient money, in the form of a personal check, postal or bank money order (International Money Order only for out-of-country requests), made payable to the **Office of Vital Records**. The fee is **$12** for each certification. Mail this application with the fee to the Office of Vital Records, 304 S Street, P.O. Box 730241, Sacramento, CA 94244-0241. You may also FAX your request and charge it to a credit card to: 1-800-858-5553 or (916) 442-6766 (out of country). There is an additional fee of $7 for using the charge card service. If requested, express courier fee will be applied to credit card.

HUSBAND AND WIFE INFORMATION – PLEASE PRINT OR TYPE

Name of Husband – First	Middle	Last
Name of Wife – First	Middle	Last
Date of Divorce – Month, Day, Year	If Date Unknown, Enter Year(s) to be Searched	County of Divorce

APPLICANT INFORMATION – PLEASE PRINT OR TYPE

Purpose for Which Certified Copy is to Be Used	Today's Date	Telephone Number – Area Code first ( )		
Name of Person Completing Application (Please Print)	Signature (Person Requesting Record(s) or Cardholder, if Different			
Address – Number, Street	City		State	ZIP Code
Name of Person Receiving Copies, if Different From Above	Number of Copies	Amount Enclosed	E-mail Address	
Mailing Address for Copies, if Different From Above	City		State	ZIP Code
Credit Card # for FAX Orders	Expiration Date	Shipping Method: ☐ Express Courier ☐ Regular Mail		

DO NOT WRITE IN SPACE BELOW – FOR REGISTRAR ONLY

DISSOLUTION

VS 120 (11/99)

State of California – Health and Human Services Agency

Department of Health Services

APPLICATION FOR CERTIFIED COPY OF DEATH RECORD

INFORMATION: Death records have been maintained in the Office of the State Registrar of Vital Statistics since July 1, 1905

INSTRUCTIONS

1. Use a separate application blank for each different record of death for which you are requesting a certified copy. Send **$8** for **each** certified copy requested. If no record of the death is found, the $8 fee will be retained for searching as required by statute and a Certification of No Record will be sent.

2. Give all the information you have available for the identification of the record of the decedent in the spaces under **Decedent Information**. If the information you furnish is incomplete or inaccurate, it may be impossible to locate the record.

3. Complete the **Applicant Information** section.

4. Indicate the number of certified copies you wish and include with this application sufficient money, in the form of a personal check, postal or bank money order (International Money Order only for out-of-country requests), made payable to the **Office of Vital Records**. The fee is **$8** for each certified copy. Mail this application with the fee to the Office of Vital Records, 304 S Street, P.O. Box 730241, Sacramento, CA 94244-0241. You may also FAX your request and charge it to a credit card to: 1-800-858-5553 or (916) 442-6766 (out of country). There is an additional fee of $7 for using the charge card service. If requested, express courier fee will be applied to credit card.

DECEDENT INFORMATION – PLEASE PRINT OR TYPE

Name of Decedent – First (Given)	Middle	Last (Family)	Sex
Place of Death – City or Town	Place of Death – County	Place of Birth	Date of Birth
Date of Death – Month, Day, Year (Or Period of Years to be Searched)		Social Security Number	
Mother's Maiden Name		Name of Spouse (Husband or Wife of Decedent)	

APPLICANT INFORMATION – PLEASE PRINT OR TYPE

Purpose for Which Certified Copy is to Be Used	Today's Date	Telephone Number – Area Code First ( )
Name of Person Completing Application (Please Print)	Signature (Person Requesting Record(s) or Cardholder, if Different)	
Address – Number, Street	City	State	ZIP Code
Name of Person Receiving Copies, if Different From Above	Number of Copies	Amount Enclosed	E-mail Address
Mailing Address for Copies, if Different From Above	City	State	ZIP Code
Credit Card # for FAX Orders	Expiration Date	Shipping Method: ☐ Express Courier ☐ Regular Mail

DO NOT WRITE IN SPACE BELOW – FOR REGISTRAR ONLY

DEATH

VS 112 (11/99)

COLORADO

Send your requests to:

Vital Records Section
Health Statistics and Vital Records Division
Colorado Department of Health
4300 Cherry Creek Drive South
Denver, Colorado 80246-1530

Tel. (303) 692-2234
Recording (303) 692-2200
Fax (800) 423-1108
E-mail: comments.hsvrd@state.co.us
http://www.cdphe.state.co.us/hs/certs.asp

The Vital Records Sections has birth records from 1910 and death records from 1900. For marriage and divorce records, if you know the county where the license was issued, contact the county clerk's office in that county. Vital Records does, however, have an index that covers the years 1900–1939 and 1975 to the present for marriage records, and from 1968 to the present for divorce records. Also available is an online index to marriages (1975–Dec. 1999) and divorces (1975–April 2000): **http://www.quickinfo.net/madi/comadi.html**.

Certified copies of vital records can be ordered online, as well as by mail, phone, or fax. There is a $5.00 processing fee for credit card orders, plus an additional fee for express shipping.

Cost for a certified Birth Certificate	$15.00
Cost for verification of a Marriage Record, date known	$15.00
If the exact date is not known	$20.00
Cost for verification of a Divorce Record, date known	$15.00
If the exact date is not known	$20.00
Cost for a certified Death Certificate	$15.00
Cost for a duplicate copy, when ordered at the same time	$6.00

For earlier records write to:

County Clerk
County Court House
(County Seat), Colorado

For Adoption Record information write to:

Colorado Voluntary Adoption Registry
Colorado State Department of Health
4300 Cherry Creek Drive South
Denver, Colorado 80222-1530

Tel. (303) 692-2188
http://www.cdphe.state.co.us/hs/adoption.html

Cost for copy of Adoption Decree (Send Copy of Court Order with Request)	$35.00
Cost for registration with the Adoption Registry	$15.00

For further information see:

Oldemeyer, Shirley. *Colorado Historical Records Assessment and Reporting Project, Final Report for the National Historical Publications and Records Commission, 1982.* Denver, CO: Colorado State Historical Records Advisory Board, 1982. 71p.

Colorado Department of Public Health and Environment
Vital Records Section/HSVR-VR-A1
4300 Cherry Creek Drive South
Denver, Colorado 80246-1530
303-692-2200

Application for Certified Copy of Birth Certificate

Colorado has birth records for the entire state since 1910. Certified copies of certificates are also available from county offices (see reverse side).

Information about person whose birth certificate is requested — *please type or print.* If adopted, use adopted name.

Full name at birth	First		Middle			Last		
Date of birth	Month	Day	Year	Is this person deceased? Yes ☐ No ☐ If yes, date: ___/___/___ State where death occurred:				
Place of birth	City		County				State Colorado	
Full name of father	First		Middle			Last		
<u>Maiden</u> name of mother	First		Middle			<u>Maiden</u>		
Reason for request								

Signature of person making request	Relationship to registrant*	Date

Address	City	State	Zip	Daytime Phone ( )

*See other side

Ways to order:
- Order certificates online** at www.cdphe.state.co.us/hs/certs.asp. Certificate(s) mailed on next work day.
- Fax your application with credit card information**: within continental USA fax 1-800-423-1108; outside continental USA fax: 1-303-691-9307. Certificate(s) mailed on next work day.
- Apply in person for same day service. Office hours are from 8:30 a.m. to 5 p.m.
- Mail in application with credit card information**, check or money order. Certificate(s) mailed within two weeks.

**Convenience charge to be added. See fees below.

Charges:
- $15 for first copy (or search of files when no record is found)
- $6 for each additional copy of the same record ordered at the same time
- $5 convenience charge on credit card orders
- $11.25 for FedEx; $11.75 for Express Mail

<u>Make check or money order payable to to Vital Records Section. Please do not send cash.</u>

Number full size copies _____

Number pocket size*** _____

Total copies ordered _____

***Pocket size is 4" x 2 3/4"; contains name, sex, date, place of birth, state file number, date filed, and date issued; available for birth years 1935 to present.

Credit card orders:

Card Type: VISA ☐   MasterCard ☐   Discover ☐   American Express ☐

Cardholder name:_____

Card Number: |__|__|__|__|__|__|__|__|__|__|__|__|__|__|__|__| Exp. Date: _____/_____

PLEASE COMPLETE THIS AREA

PRINT name and address of person to whom the certified copy is to be mailed to or issued to over the counter:

_____
Name

_____
Address

_____
City/State/Zip

Cost of certificates ($15 for 1st copy; $6 for each additional copy of same record ordered at same time)	$_____
Convenience charge (credit card orders only, $5)	$_____
*Express Mail ($11.75) or *FedEx ($11.25) (circle one)	$_____
Total Charges	$_____

*Within continental U.S.

bircert.p65 (Rev. 8/00)

COLORADO DEPARTMENT OF PUBLIC HEALTH AND ENVIRONMENT
VITAL RECORDS SECTION/HSVRD-VR-A1
4300 Cherry Creek Drive South
Denver, Colorado 80246-1530
303-692-2200
World Wide Web Home Page: http://www.cdphe.state.co.us/hs/cshom.html

Application for Certified Verification of a Marriage Record

INFORMATION ABOUT PERSONS WHOSE MARRIAGE RECORD IS REQUESTED -- *please type or print*
This office has indices for 1900 to 1939 and 1975 to present.

Name of Groom (required for 1900-1939)	First	Middle	Last
Name of Bride	First	Middle	Last
County Where License Was Obtained			Date of Marriage
Signature of Person Making Request			Today's Date
Street Address	City	State / Zip	Daytime Phone ( )

This office will not have a record of the marriage if the county did not forward the information for the State Index. Verifications for the years 1940-1974 are <u>not</u> available from this office and must be obtained from the county where the license was obtained. You may need to contact each of the counties if you do not know where the license was obtained. County clerk offices are located in the county seat. A list of counties, county seats, and ZIP codes is provided for your convenience on the reverse side of this form.

Fees: $15 per verification or per search whether found or not. $5 per each additional index searched. (Indices for the following years are available from this office: 1900 to 1939 and 1975 to present.)
*Additional $5 per order convenience charge for use of VISA, MasterCard, Discover, or American Express.

Include appropriate additional fees if you wish your verification returned by certified mail, Express Mail, or Federal Express. Make check or money order payable to Vital Records Section. Please do not send cash.

Types of Service: ◆ Apply in person--same day (office hours are Monday-Friday from 8:30 a.m. to 5 p.m.).
◆ Mail in your application with check or money order--mailed within 2 weeks.
◆ For expedited or emergency service, fax a copy of your order with VISA, MasterCard, Discover, or American Express number--**MAILED** next business day.* Fax: 1-800-423-1108 within continental USA. Fax: 1-303-691-9307 outside continental USA.

For Credit Card Use:*   VISA No. _____   Exp. Date _____
MasterCard No. _____   Exp. Date _____
Discover No._____   Exp. Date _____
American Express No._____   Exp. Date _____

*Convenience charge to be added

Please complete this area also
DO NOT DETACH

PRINT name and address of person to whom the certified marriage verification is to be issued over the counter, or mailed:

Certified copies of marriage records are available from the county clerk where the license was obtained (see reverse side).

_____
Name

_____
Adddress

_____
City/State/Zip

ADRS 3 (12/97)

COUNTY	COUNTY SEAT	ZIP
Adams	Brighton	80601
Alamosa	Alamosa	81101
Arapahoe	Littleton	80120
Archuleta	Pagosa Springs	81147
Baca	Springfield	81073
Bent	Las Animas	81054
Boulder	Boulder	80301
Chaffee	Salida	81201
Cheyenne	Cheyenne Wells	80810
Clear Creek	Georgetown	80444
Conejos	Conejos	81129
Costilla	San Luis	81152
Crowley	Ordway	81063
Custer	Westcliffe	81252
Delta	Delta	81416
Denver	Denver	80202
Dolores	Dove Creek	81324
Douglas	Castle Rock	80104
Eagle	Eagle	81631
El Paso	Colorado Springs	80900
Elbert	Kiowa	80117
Fremont	Canon City	81212
Garfield	Glenwood Springs	81601
Gilpin	Central City	80427
Grand	Hot Sulphur Springs	80451
Gunnison	Gunnison	81230
Hinsdale	Lake City	81235
Huerfano	Walsenburg	81089
Jackson	Walden	80480
Jefferson	Golden	80401
Kiowa	Eads	81036
Kit Carson	Burlington	80807
La Plata	Durango	81300
Lake	Leadville	80461
Larimer	Fort Collins	80521
Las Animas	Trinidad	81082
Lincoln	Hugo	80821
Logan	Sterling	80751
Mesa	Grand Junction	81501
Mineral	Creede	81130
Moffat	Craig	81625
Montezuma	Cortez	81321
Montrose	Montrose	81401
Morgan	Fort Morgan	80701
Otero	La Junta	81050
Ouray	Ouray	81427
Park	Fairplay	80440
Phillips	Holyoke	80734
Pitkin	Aspen	81611
Prowers	Lamar	81052
Pueblo	Pueblo	81000
Rio Blanco	Meeker	81641
Rio Grande	Del Norte	81132
Routt	Steamboat Springs	80477
Saguache	Saguache	81149
San Juan	Silverton	81433
San Miguel	Telluride	80737
Sedgwick	Julesburg	81435
Summit	Breckenridge	80424
Teller	Cripple Creek	80813
Washington	Akron	80720
Weld	Greeley	80631
Yuma	Wray	80758

COLORADO DEPARTMENT OF PUBLIC HEALTH AND ENVIRONMENT
VITAL RECORDS SECTION/HSVRD-VR-A1
4300 Cherry Creek Drive South
Denver, Colorado 80246-1530
303-692-2200
World Wide Web Home Page: http://www.cdphe.state.co.us/hs/cshom.html

Application for Certified Verification of a Dissolution of Marriage

INFORMATION ABOUT PERSONS WHOSE MARRIAGE DISSOLUTION IS REQUESTED -- *please type or print*
This office has indices for 1900 to 1939 and 1968 to 1994.

	First	Middle	Last
Name of Husband			
Name of Wife	First	Middle	Last
County Where Decree Was Issued			Date of Decree
Signature of Person Making Request			Today's Date
Street Address	City	State / Zip	Daytime Phone ( )

This office will not have a record of the divorce, separation, or annulment if the county did not forward the information for the State Index. Verifications for the years 1940-1967 and 1995 to present are not available from this office and must be obtained from the county where the divorce was decreed. You may need to contact each of the counties if you do not know where the decree was granted. District courts are located in the county seat. A list of counties, county seats, and ZIP codes is provided for your convenience on the reverse side of this form.

Fees: $15 per verification or per search whether found or not. $5 per each additional index searched. (Indices for the following years are available from this office: 1900 to 1939 and 1968 to 1994.)
*Additional $5 per order convenience charge for use of VISA, MasterCard, Discover, or American Express.

Include appropriate additional fees if you wish your verification returned by certified mail, Express Mail, or Federal Express. Make check or money order payable to Vital Records Section. Please do not send cash.

Types of Service: ◆ Apply in person--same day (office hours are Monday-Friday from 8:30 a.m. to 5 p.m.).
◆ Mail in your application with check or money order--mailed within 2 weeks.
◆ For expedited or emergency service, fax a copy of your order with VISA, MasterCard, Discover, or American Express number--**MAILED** next business day.* Fax: 1-800-423-1108 within continental USA. Fax: 1-303-691-9307 outside continental USA.

For Credit Card Use:* VISA No. _____ Exp. Date _____
MasterCard No. _____ Exp. Date _____
Discover No. _____ Exp. Date _____
American Express No. _____ Exp. Date _____

*Convenience charge to be added

Please complete this area also
DO NOT DETACH

PRINT name and address of person to whom the certified verification is to be issued over the counter, or mailed:

_____
Name

_____
Adddress

_____
City/State/Zip

Certified copies of decrees are available from the clerk of the district court in the county where the decree was granted (see reverse side).

ADRS 4 (12/97)

COUNTY	COUNTY SEAT	ZIP
Adams	Brighton	80601
Alamosa	Alamosa	81101
Arapahoe	Littleton	80120
Archuleta	Pagosa Springs	81147
Baca	Springfield	81073
Bent	Las Animas	81054
Boulder	Boulder	80301
Chaffee	Salida	81201
Cheyenne	Cheyenne Wells	80810
Clear Creek	Georgetown	80444
Conejos	Conejos	81129
Costilla	San Luis	81152
Crowley	Ordway	81063
Custer	Westcliffe	81252
Delta	Delta	81416
Denver	Denver	80202
Dolores	Dove Creek	81324
Douglas	Castle Rock	80104
Eagle	Eagle	81631
El Paso	Colorado Springs	80900
Elbert	Kiowa	80117
Fremont	Canon City	81212
Garfield	Glenwood Springs	81601
Gilpin	Central City	80427
Grand	Hot Sulphur Springs	80451
Gunnison	Gunnison	81230
Hinsdale	Lake City	81235
Huerfano	Walsenburg	81089
Jackson	Walden	80480
Jefferson	Golden	80401
Kiowa	Eads	81036
Kit Carson	Burlington	80807
La Plata	Durango	81300
Lake	Leadville	80461
Larimer	Fort Collins	80521
Las Animas	Trinidad	81082
Lincoln	Hugo	80821
Logan	Sterling	80751
Mesa	Grand Junction	81501
Mineral	Creede	81130
Moffat	Craig	81625
Montezuma	Cortez	81321
Montrose	Montrose	81401
Morgan	Fort Morgan	80701
Otero	La Junta	81050
Ouray	Ouray	81427
Park	Fairplay	80440
Phillips	Holyoke	80734
Pitkin	Aspen	81611
Prowers	Lamar	81052
Pueblo	Pueblo	81000
Rio Blanco	Meeker	81641
Rio Grande	Del Norte	81132
Routt	Steamboat Springs	80477
Saguache	Saguache	81149
San Juan	Silverton	81433
San Miguel	Telluride	80737
Sedgwick	Julesburg	81435
Summit	Breckenridge	80424
Teller	Cripple Creek	80813
Washington	Akron	80720
Weld	Greeley	80631
Yuma	Wray	80758

Colorado Department of Public Health and Environment
Vital Records Section/HSVR-VR-A1
4300 Cherry Creek Drive South
Denver, Colorado 80246-1530
303-692-2200
http://www.cdphe.state.co.us/hs/cshom.html

Application for Certified Copy of Death Certificate

Colorado has death records for the entire state since 1900. Certified copies of certificates are also available in the county where death occurred.

Information about person whose death certificate is requested — *please type or print.*

Full name of deceased	First		Middle		Last	
Date of death	Month	Day	Year	Age at death		State of Birth
Place of death	City		County		State of Death Colorado	
Reason for Request						
Signature of Person Making Request			Your Relationship to deceased*		Date	
Address	City		State	Zip	Daytime Phone ( )	

*See other side

Ways to order:
- Order certificates online** at http://www.cdphe.state.co.us/hs/certs.html. Certificate(s) mailed on next work day.
- Fax your application with credit card information**: within continental USA fax 1-800-423-1108; outside continental USA fax: 1-303-691-9307. Certificate(s) mailed on next work day.
- Apply in person for same day service. Office hours are from 8:30 a.m. to 5 p.m.
- Mail in application with credit card information**, check or money order. Certificate(s) mailed within two weeks.

**Convenience charge to be added. See fees below.

Charges:
- $15 for first copy (or search of files when no record is found)
- $6 for each additional copy of the same record ordered at the same time
- $5 convenience charge for credit card orders only
- $10.75 shipping charge for return by Express Mail or Federal Express
- $5.00 **additional charge** per each index searched when date of death is unknown. Indices are grouped as follows:

1900-1925
1926-1950
1951-1975
1975-1999

Make check or money order payable to Vital Records Section. Please do not send cash.

Credit card orders:

Card Type: VISA ☐ MasterCard ☐ Discover ☐ American Express ☐

Cardholder name: _____

Card Number: | | | | | | | | | | | | | | | | | Exp. Date: _____ / _____

PLEASE COMPLETE THIS AREA

PRINT name and address of person to whom the certified copy is to be mailed to or issued to over the counter:

_____
Name

_____
Address

_____
City/State/Zip

Number copies ordered	_____
Searches where date of death is unknown ($5.00 each index search)	$_____
Cost of certificates ($15 for 1st copy; $6 for each additional copy of same record ordered at same time)	$_____
Convenience charge (credit card orders, $5)	$_____
Express Mail or FedEx ($10.75, circle one)	$_____
Total Charges	$_____

dthcert.p65 (Rev 7/99)

CONNECTICUT

Send your requests to:*

Connecticut State Department of Public Health
Vital Records Section
410 Capitol Avenue, First Floor
Hartford, Connecticut 06134

Tel. (860) 509-7897
Fax (860) 509-7964
E-mail: kelly.mcgarrity@po.state.ct.us
http://www.state.ct.us/dph/OPPE/vr-birth.html

The Vital Records Section has birth, marriage, and death records from January 1, 1897. Connecticut restricts access to birth records for the past 100 years (Public Act No. 96-258). All marriage and death certificates are open to the public.

*(Note: At the time of writing, these records were closed to the public while they were being microfilmed. Until this project is completed, all requests for certificates must be directed to the town clerk of the town or city of occurrence.)

Cost for a certified Birth Certificate	$5.00
Cost for a wallet-size Birth Certificate	$5.00
Cost for a certified Marriage Certificate	$5.00
Cost for a certified Death Certificate	$5.00

For earlier records write to:

Town Clerk
(Town), Connecticut

For Divorce Records write to:

Clerk
Superior Court

For Adoption Record information write to:

Office of Foster and Adoption Services
Department of Children and Families
Public Affairs and Information Office
505 Hudson Street
Hartford, Connecticut 06106-7107

Tel. (860) 550-6578
Fax (860) 550-3453
http://www.state.ct.us/dcf/foster.htm#SEARCH

The Connecticut State Library (231 Capitol Avenue; Hartford, CT 06106; 860-566-3692) has pre-1900 vital records and the Barbour Index to Connecticut Vital Records, which indexes records from the 1600s to the mid-1800s.

For further information see:

Acts of the State of Connecticut Relating to the Legislation of Births, Marriages and Deaths. Hartford, CT: State, 1856. 8p.
Handbook for Connecticut Town Clerks. Storrs, CT: University of Connecticut, Institute of Public Service, 1979. Loose-leaf.
_____. 1989. Loose-leaf.
Kemp, Thomas Jay. *Connecticut Researcher's Handbook.* Detroit, MI: Gale Research, 1981. 755p.
Morrison, Betty Jean. *Connecting to Connecticut.* East Hartford, CT: CT Society of Genealogists, 1995. 342p.

REQUEST FOR COPY OF BIRTH CERTIFICATE
VS-39B   Revised: 4/24/98

PLESE PRINT   **DO NOT MAIL CASH**

FULL NAME AT
BIRTH:_____
                        FIRST   MIDDLE   LAST NAME

DATE OF BIRTH: _____/_____/_____   PLACE OF BIRTH: _____
                MONTH DAY YEAR   TOWN/CITY

FATHER'S FULL NAME: _____
                              FIRST   MIDDLE   LAST NAME

MOTHER'S MAIDEN NAME: _____
                               FIRST   MIDDLE   MAIDEN NAME

PERSON MAKING THIS REQUEST:

NAME: _____
                FIRST   MIDDLE   LAST NAME

ADDRESS: _____
                    NUMBER   STREET

TOWN/CITY: _____   STATE: _____   ZIP CODE: _____

SIGNATURE: **X**_____

RELATION TO PERSON NAMED IN CERTIFICATE: _____

REASON FOR MAKING REQUEST: _____

CERTIFICATE SIZE: ☐   WALLET SIZE

                              ☐   FULL SIZE

ATTACH A COPY OF PICTURE IDENTIFICATION
FEE: $5.00 MONEY ORDER MADE PAYABLE TO THE TOWN/CITY OF BIRTH
MAIL THIS REQUEST WITH PAYMENT TO THE TOWN CLERK AT THE TOWN/CITY OF BIRTH
FOR TOWN CLERK ADDRESSES PLEASE CALL (860) 509-7897

ATTACH A COPY OF PICTURE IDENTIFICATION HERE:

REQUEST FOR COPY OF MARRIAGE CERTIFICATE

VS-39M   Revised: 5/15/98

PLEASE PRINT   **DO NOT MAIL CASH**

GROOM	FULL NAME	FIRST	MIDDLE	LAST
BRIDE	FULL NAME BEFORE MARRIAGE	FIRST	MIDDLE	LAST
DATE OF MARRIAGE (MONTH/DAY/YEAR)		PLACE OF MARRIAGE	TOWN	

PLEASE NOTE: ONLY THE BRIDE AND GROOM APPEARING ON THE MARRIAGE CERTIFICATE SHALL RECEIVE A CERTIFIED COPY OF SUCH CERTIFICATE INCLUDING THEIR SOCIAL SECURITY NUMBERS AS SPECIFIED IN PA 97-7.

ALL OTHER CERTIFIED COPIES WILL MASK THE SOCIAL SECURITY NUMBERS OF THE BRIDE AND GROOM TO COMPLY WITH THE PROVISIONS OF PA 97-7.

PERSON MAKING THIS REQUEST:

NAME: _____

          FIRST   MIDDLE   LAST NAME

ADDRESS: _____

              NUMBER   STREET

TOWN/CITY: _____   STATE: _____   ZIP CODE: _____

SIGNATURE: **X**_____

THE LEGAL FEE IS $5.00 PER COPY.

NUMBER OF COPIES WANTED: _____   AMOUNT ATTACHED: $_____

FEE: $5.00 PER COPY MONEY ORDER MADE PAYABLE TO THE TOWN/CITY OF MARRIAGE

MAIL THIS REQUEST WITH PAYMENT TO THE TOWN CLERK AT THE TOWN/CITY OF MARRIAGE

FOR TOWN CLERK ADDRESSES PLEASE CALL (860) 509-7897

REQUEST FOR COPY OF DEATH CERTIFICATE
VS-39D   Revised: 5/19/98

PLEASE PRINT   **DO NOT MAIL CASH**

DEATH CERTIFICATE OF:	FULL NAME FIRST MIDDLE LAST		SEX ☐ M ☐ F	DATE OF DEATH (OR LAST KNOWN TO BE ALIVE)
	PLACE OF DEATH (TOWN)	DATE OF BIRTH (MONTH/DAY/YEAR)	PLACE OF BIRTH (TOWN, STATE OR FOREIGN COUNTRY)	
	FATHER'S NAME	MOTHER'S NAME	IF MARRIED, SPOUSE'S NAME	

PLEASE NOTE: THE SOCIAL SECURITY NUMBER OF THE DECEDENT IS CONFIDENTIAL IN ACCORDANCE WITH PA 97-7. AS SUCH, ONLY SPECIFIC INDIVIDUALS, APPROVED BY THE DEPARTMENT OF PUBLIC HEALTH, WILL BE ISSUED CERTIFIED COPIES OF DEATH CERTIFICATES INCLUDING THE SOCIAL SECURITY NUMBER OF THE DECEDENT.

ALL OTHER CERTIFIED COPIES WILL MASK THE SOCIAL SECURITY NUMBER OF THE DECEDENT TO COMPLY WITH THE PROVISIONS OF PA 97-7.

PERSON MAKING THIS REQUEST:

NAME: _____
                FIRST   MIDDLE   LAST NAME

ADDRESS: _____
                NUMBER   STREET

TOWN/CITY: _____ STATE: _____ ZIP CODE: _____

SIGNATURE: **X**_____

THE LEGAL FEE IS $5.00 PER COPY.
NUMBER OF COPIES WANTED: _____ AMOUNT ATTACHED: $_____

FEE: $5.00 PER COPY MONEY ORDER MADE PAYABLE TO THE TOWN/CITY OF DEATH
MAIL THIS REQUEST WITH PAYMENT TO THE TOWN CLERK AT THE TOWN/CITY OF DEATH
FOR TOWN CLERK ADDRESSES PLEASE CALL (860) 509-7897

DELAWARE

Send your requests to:

Office of Vital Statistics
Division of Public Health
P.O. Box 637
Dover, Delaware 19903-0637

Tel. (302) 739-4721
Fax (302) 739-3008
http://www.state.de.us/dhss/irm/dph/dphhome.htm

The Office of Vital Statistics only handles requests for birth records less than 72 years old, and marriage and death records less than 40 years old. See below for information on earlier records. Divorce records from 1935 to the present are available for verification only. Expedited service is available (with payment by credit card) for an additional fee of $5.00, plus shipping.

Cost for a certified Birth Certificate	$6.00
Cost for a certified Marriage Certificate	$6.00
Cost for verification of Divorce for each 5 years searched	$6.00
Cost for a certified Death Certificate	$6.00
Cost for a duplicate copy, when ordered at the same time	$4.00

For Birth Records older than 72 years, and Marriage and Death Records older than 40 years write to:

The Hall of Records
P.O. Box 1401
Dover, DE 19903-1401

Tel. (302) 739-5318
http://www.lib.de.us/archives/index.htm

For Divorce Records after 1975 write to:

Kent County	**New Castle County**	**Sussex County**
Family Court Building	Family Court	Family Court
Divorce Section	Divorce Section	Divorce Section
P.O. Box 310	P.O. Box 2359	P.O. Box 609
Dover, DE 19903	Wilmington, DE 19899	Georgetown, DE 19947

For Divorce Records before 1975 write to:

Kent County	**New Castle County**	**Sussex County**
Prothonotary	Prothonotary	Prothonotary
Kent County Court House	Superior Court	Sussex County Court House
38 The Green	10th & King Streets	Race & Market Streets
Dover, DE 19901	Wilmington, DE 19801	Georgetown, DE 19801
(302) 739-3184	(302) 577-6484	(302) 856-5741

For Adoption Record information write to:

Kent County	**New Castle County**	**Sussex County**
Family Court	Family Court	Family Court
400 Court Street	900 King Street	22 The Circle
Dover, DE 19901-3730	Wilmington, DE 19801	Georgetown, DE 19947-1500
(302) 739-6500	(302) 577-2200	(302) 856-5601

The Family History Library of The Church of Jesus Christ of Latter-day Saints in Salt Lake City, Utah has microfilm copies of birth records and their indexes from 1861 to 1913; marriage records and indexes from 1680 to 1850; and death records and indexes from 1855 to 1910.

For further information see:

Vital Records Management for Delaware Local Governments. Dover, DE: DE Bureau of Archives and Records Management, DE Local Records Project, 1986. 5p.

**OFFICE OF VITAL STATISTICS
P. O. BOX 637
DOVER, DELAWARE 19903**

Today's Date _____

Number of Copies _____

APPLICATION FOR BIRTH CERTIFICATE
COMPLETE ALL ITEMS REQUESTED BELOW AS ACCURATELY AS POSSIBLE

_____
Full Name at Birth of Person Whose Record is Requested — If Name Has Ever Been Changed, Please Give Details on Back

_____   _____
Date of Birth (Month, Day, Year)   *Place of Birth (Hospital)*

_____
Full Maiden Name of Mother

_____
Full Name of Father

_____
If Known, Name of Doctor or Midwife

_____
For What Purpose Is Certificate Needed

***PLEASE COMPLETE
YOUR NAME AND
MAILING ADDRESS...***

_____
Name

_____
Street/Development/Rural Delivery/Box Number

_____
City/Town

_____
State   *Zip Code*

FEE — $6.00 for the first copy. $4.00 for each additional copy of same record requested at same time.

A certified copy of the original birth record has entered thereon the name, birthdate, birthplace, names of parents and personal particulars. This copy is used for all purposes.

Payable to the OFFICE OF VITAL STATISTICS.

If the record is not found the $6.00 will be retained for the search.

Insufficient fee being returned. _____

If a check with the incorrect fee is being returned do not alter, make another check.

Doc. No. 35-05-02-95-07-07

**OFFICE OF VITAL STATISTICS
P. O. BOX 637
DOVER, DELAWARE 19903**

Today's Date_____

Number of Copies _____

APPLICATION FOR MARRIAGE CERTIFICATE
COMPLETE ALL ITEMS REQUESTED BELOW AS ACCURATELY AS POSSIBLE

FULL NAME OF GROOM _____

FULL MAIDEN NAME OF BRIDE _____

PLACE OF MARRIAGE _____

DATE OF MARRIAGE _____

NAME OF OFFICIATING MINISTER _____

MAIL COPY TO...   NAME _____

STREET ADDRESS _____

TOWN _____

STATE _____ ZIP CODE _____

Fee for a certified copy is $6.00 for the first copy.

$4.00 for each additional copy of same record requested at same time.

Include fee with application - Make payable to the Office of Vital Statistics.

If the record is not found $6.00 will be retained as the search fee.

Insufficient fee being returned.

Doc. No. 35-05-02-95-07-05

OFFICE OF VITAL STATISTICS
P. O. BOX 637
DOVER, DELAWARE 19903

Today's Date _____

Number of Copies _____

APPLICATION FOR A CERTIFIED COPY OF A
DEATH CERTIFICATE
COMPLETE ALL ITEMS REQUESTED BELOW AS ACCURATELY AS POSSIBLE

_____   _____

Name of Decedent   *Race*

_____   _____

Date of Decease   *Place of Decease*

_____   _____

Full Name of Decedent's Father   *Full Maiden Name of Mother*

_____

For What Purpose Is Certificate Needed

_____

SEND COPY TO...   _____

                        Name

                        _____

                        Street/Development/Rural Delivery/Box Number

                        _____

                        City/Town

                        _____   _____

                        State   *Zip Code*

FEE — $6.00 for the first copy. $4.00 for each additional copy of same record requested at same time.

Payable to the OFFICE OF VITAL STATISTICS.

If the record is not found the fee will be retained for the search.

Insufficient fee being returned. _____

If a check with the incorrect fee is being returned do not alter. Make another check.

Doc. No. 35-05-02-95-07-06

DISTRICT OF COLUMBIA

Send your requests for Birth and Death Certificates to:

Vital Records Division
825 North Capitol Street, NE
Washington, DC 20002

Tel. (202) 442-9009
Fax (202) 783-0136
http://www.dcheath.com/vitalrecords.htm

Birth records are available from January 1, 1874, and death records from 1855 (except Civil War). Expedited service is available (with payment by credit card) for an additional fee of $8.50, plus shipping; call (202) 783-1809 to purchase certificates by credit card.

Cost for a certified Birth Certificate	$18.00
Cost for a computerized Short Form Birth Certificate	$12.00
Cost for a certified Marriage Certificate	$10.00
Cost for a certified Death Certificate	$12.00
Cost for an adoptee birth record, initial registration (includes a copy of the short form birth certificate)	$20.00

Send your requests for Marriage Records to:

The Superior Court of The District of Columbia
Marriage Bureau & Special Services
500 Indiana Avenue, NW
Washington, DC 20001

Tel. (202) 879-4804

Send your requests for Divorce Certificates (before September 1, 1956) to:

Clerk
U.S. District Court for the District of Columbia
333 Constitution Avenue, NW
Washington DC 20001-2802

Tel. (202) 273-0555

Send your requests for Divorce Certificates (after September 1, 1956) to:

District of Columbia Superior Court
Divorce Decrees—Room 4335
500 Indiana Avenue, NW
Washington, DC 20001

Tel. (202) 879-1418

The Family History Library of The Church of Jesus Christ of Latter-day Saints in Salt Lake City, Utah has microfilmed many of the original and published vital records and church registers of the District of Columbia. For details on their holdings please consult your nearest Family History Center.

Birth Certificate Request
For District of Columbia Occurrences Only
Mail-In Form

1. Certificate Holder's Name: (first)   (middle)   (last)
2. Birth Date: 3. Sex: Male   Female
4: Hospital: 5. City: WASHINGTON, D.C
6: Father's Name: (first)   (middle)   (last)
7. Mother's Maiden Name: (first)   (middle)   (last)
8a. No. of Original Certificate Form requested: @$18.00 ea.   Total Cost: $

8b.No. of Computer Certificate Short Form requested:.
              @$12.00 ea.
 	
                  Total Cost: $

8c. Total Amount Enclosed: $
9. Relationship to Certificate Holder: Self Mother   Father   Other
10. Signature of Requester: _____
MAKE CHECK/MONEY ORDER PAYABLE TO: **D.C. TREASURER**
Mail Certificate to:
11. Name:
12a. Address:
b. City: c. State: Zip:
13. Day Phone: (required)
Copy of Requester's Photo ID Required:
Government of the District of Columbia   **Department of Health**   **Vital Records Division**   **825 North Capitol Street N.E First Floor**   **Washington, D.C. 20002**   **202 442-9009**

1/7/98

We will be pleased to process your request upon payment of the required fees as follows. Please indicate the quantity for each service requested.

☐   A search of our records for the possible license and marriage between

_____ Age___ and _____ Age___ in this City

on or about _____ .

☒   A certified copy of this office's record regarding the application license and marriage between

_____ and _____

in this City on or about _____ , Certificate No. _____ (if known).

Please Indicate the Purpose for Request Below:

☐   Regular Certified Copy (Motor Vehicles, Social Security & Divorce)

☐   Embassy, Out of the Country, Immigration & Naturalization

☐   Number of Copies____$10.00 each

☐   Records Search (per year prior to 1921)____$10.00 each

☐   Number of Triple Seals ____$20.00 each

     All fees must be paid by **MONEY ORDER** made payable to the CLERK, SUPERIOR COURT OF THE DISTRICT OF COLUMBIA. **"NO PERSONAL CHECKS"**.

MAIL COPY TO:

Request for Death Certificates
For District of Columbia Occurrences Only
Mail-In Form

1. Name of Deceased
2. Social Security Number of Deceased 3. Sex: Male Female
4. Date of Death 5. Place of Death: WASHINGTON, D.C.
6. Death Certificate No. (If Known)
7a. Number of copies of certificate requested @$12.00 each 7a Amount enclosed $
8. Number of requested copies: (a) cause of death included: (b) cause of death omitted:
9. Relationship to Deceased: Mother Father   Spouse Other
10. Signature of Requester _____Date _____

MAKE CHECK/MONEY ORDER TO: D.C. TREASURER.

Mail Certificate(s) to:

11. Name
12a. Address 12b.CityState Zip
13. Day Phone(Required)

Copy of Requester's Photo ID Required

Government of the District of Columbia
Department of Health
Vital Records Division
825 North Capitol Street, N.E. 1st Floor
Washington, D.C. 20002
202 442-9009

05/00

Send your requests to:

Office of Vital Statistics
1217 Pearl Street
P.O. Box 210
Jacksonville, Florida 32231-0042

Tel. (904) 359-6900, ext. 1029
Fax (904) 359-6993
http://www.doh.state.fl.us/

The Office of Vital Statistics has birth records from April 1865; marriage and divorce records from June 6, 1927; and death records from August 1877. Expedited service is available (with payment by credit card) for an additional fee of $14.50.

Cost for a certified Birth Certificate	$9.00
Cost for a commemorative Birth Certificate	$34.00
Cost for a certified Marriage Certificate or Divorce Report	$5.00
Cost for a commemorative Marriage Certificate	$30.00
Cost for a certified Death Certificate	$5.00
Cost for a duplicate copy, when ordered at the same time	$4.00
Additional search fee	$2.00 per additional year searched, maximum $50.00

For earlier records write to:

County Clerk
County Court House
(County Seat), Florida

For Adoption Record information write to:

Florida Adoption Registry (PDCFR)
Vital Statistics Registry
Florida Department of Children and Families
1317 Winewood Blvd, Bldg 8, Room 100
Tallahassee, Florida 32399-0700

Tel. (904) 488-8000
http://www.state.fl.us/cf_web/adopt/main.html

Cost for initial filing with Adoption Reunion Registry	$35.00
Cost for updating information with Adoption Reunion Registry	$10.00

Florida Adoption Registry is a confidential service. It does not search for any persons involved in the adoption. Only those who register and authorize the release of information are notified. The Florida Department of Children and Families does provide non-identifying information for adoptees, adoptive and birth parents.

The Florida Bureau of Archives and Records Management (500 South Bronough Street; Talahassee, FL 32399-0250; 850-487-2073) holds microfilm copies of county marriage records and a few original registers of birth and death records.

For further information see:

Vital News, From the Sunshine State. (Serial). Quarterly. Jacksonville, FL: Office of Vital Statistics, Vol. 1, No. 1, 1988– .

State of Florida, Department of Health

APPLICATION FOR BIRTH RECORD FOR PERSON BORN IN FLORIDA

PLEASE TYPE OR PRINT CLEARLY

FULL NAME AT BIRTH (Registrant)	First	Middle	Last	
If name was changed since birth, indicate new name here ——→	First	Middle	Last	
BIRTH NUMBER (if known)			Social Security Number (if known)	Age
DATE OF BIRTH (required for search)	Month	Day	Year	Sex
PLACE OF BIRTH	Hospital	City	County	**FLORIDA**
FATHER'S NAME	First	Middle	Last	
MOTHER'S MAIDEN NAME (name before marriage)	First	Middle	Last (Maiden)	

MAIL THIS APPLICATION WITH PAYMENT TO VITAL STATISTICS, P.O. Box 210, Jacksonville, FL 32231-0042
FEES ARE NONREFUNDABLE and subject to change without notice.

A BIRTH RECORD SEARCH REQUIRES ADVANCE PAYMENT OF A NONREFUNDABLE SEARCH FEE OF $9.00*

This fee entitles the applicant to one computer certificate for births registered between 1963 and present, plus 1946 and 1947, or a photocopy for births from 1962 back to 1865, or a wallet size card on all the above years, or a certified no record statement if no record is found . . . . Record [ ]   Wallet Card [ ]

Additional computer certifications, photocopies, or cards are $4 each when ordered at the same time as the initial search . . . . Number of Records [ ]   No. of Cards [ ]

If a photocopy is requested for computer years (1963 to present, plus 1946 and 1947) instead of the computer certification, a fee of $14 is required; each additional photocopy at that time is $4 . . . . Number of Records [ ]

RUSH ORDERS: An additional $10 per application is required if you wish rush service. Your envelope must be marked "RUSH" . . . . YES [ ]   NO [ ]

COMMEMORATIVE CERTIFICATE NOW AVAILABLE: signed by the Governor of Florida; large size suitable for framing; $25 if ordered at the same time as certificate record, $34 if ordered separately, allow 4-6 weeks for delivery . . . . YES [ ]   NO [ ]

TOTAL ENCLOSED: Check or money order payable to U.S. dollars to Vital Statistics . . . . PLEASE DO NOT MAIL CASH   TOTAL ENCLOSED [ ]

Florida Law imposes an additional service charge of $15 for dishonored checks.

Applicant's Signature		Applicant's relationship to registrant
Home Phone Number	Work Phone Number	Name and Address for mailing, if different from residence
Residence Address	Apt. No.	
City, State	Zip Code	

DH 726, 6/97 (Replaces 9/96 edition which may be used)
(Stock Number: 5740-000-0726-8)

*$2 of this fee is for Crimes Against Children; $1.50 is for Child Welfare Training

Application for Commemorative Birth Certificate

REGISTRANT (person named on the record)

Full Name at Birth:_____Sex_____

Date of Birth: _____

City or County of Birth:_____

Father's Full Name:_____

Mother's Full Maiden Name:_____

MAILING ADDRESS(of registrant 18 or older OR of parent or guardian)

Name:_____

Reigstrant Name Change:_____
(if name is NOT the same as above birth name, explain: "Married", "legally changed", etc. Give date and place.)

Relationship to Registrant:_____
(If addressed to parent or guardian)

Street Address:_____Appt. No.:_____

City, State, Zip:_____

SENDER'S NAME & ADDRESS (if different from above)

Name:_____

Street Address:_____Appt. No.:_____

City, State, Zip:_____

Return this form to:

```
Commemorative Certificate
Office of Vital Statistics
Post Office Box 210
Jacksonville, FL 32231-0042
```

Include a check or money order for $34.00 made payable to the "Office of Vital Statistics"
The fee includes a search fee, one regular certificate, the commemorative certificate, and mailing
If the record is not located, a certified statement of that fact is issued along with a $25.00 refund.
The $9.00 search fee is not refundable.

State of Florida, Department of Health and Rehabilitative Services

APPLICATION FOR MARRIAGE RECORD FOR LICENSES ISSUED IN FLORIDA

HRS

	First	Middle	Last	Race
NAME OF GROOM				
NAME OF BRIDE	First	Middle	Last	Race
DATE OF MARRIAGE (approximate month & day)	Month	Day	Specify exact year or series of years to be searched	
PLACE LICENSE ISSUED	City or Town		County	FLORIDA

AVAILABILITY: Marriage records from June 6, 1927 are available at this office. Beginning with 1972, the marriage application is an integral part of the record issued here. Other marriage documents are obtainable only from the county court which issued them.

FIRST YEAR SEARCH FEE: (includes one certified record or a "no record found" statement) **$5.00**

ADDITIONAL YEARS: $2 per year. The maximum search fee is $55 regardless of the total number of years to be searched

ADDITIONAL RECORDS: when ordered at the same time. $4 each ....

RUSH ORDERS (optional): $10 per order. Envelope must be marked "RUSH" ....

FOR JACKSONVILLE PICKUP SERVICE OR FOR MASTERCARD OR VISA CHARGES, TELEPHONE (904) 359-6911
FEES ARE NON REFUNDABLE AND SUBJECT TO CHANGE WITHOUT NOTICE

COMMEMORATIVE CERTIFICATE NOW AVAILABLE: signed by the Governor of Florida; large size suitable for framing; $25
if ordered at the same time as a certified record, $30 if ordered separately, allow 4-6 weeks for delivery. ....

TOTAL ENCLOSED: Check or money order payable in U.S. dollars to Vital Statistics. .... PLEASE DO NOT MAIL CASH
Florida Law imposes an additional service charge of $15 for dishonored checks.

Applicant's Signature	Name and Address for mailing, if different from residence
Applicant's Name (must be typed or printed)	
Residence Address	Apt. No
City, State, Zip Telephone No.	

MAIL THIS APPLICATION TO VITAL STATISTICS, P.O. BOX 210, JACKSONVILLE, FL 32231-0042

HRS Form 261, Oct 90 (Obsoletes previous editions which may not be used)
(Stock Number: 5740-000-0261-4)

PLEASE TYPE OR PRINT CLEARLY

HRS

State of Florida, Department of Health and Rehabilitative Services
APPLICATION FOR DISSOLUTION OF MARRIAGE RECORD (DIVORCE OR ANNULMENT) GRANTED IN FLORIDA

	First	Middle	Last
NAME OF HUSBAND			
NAME OF WIFE	First	Middle	Last
DATE OF DISSOLUTION (approximate month & day)	Month	Day	Specify exact year or series of years to be searched
PLACE GRANTED	City or Town	County	FLORIDA

AVAILABILITY: Dissolution records from June 6, 1927 are available at this office. All other dissolution documents, including copies of final decrees, are obtainable only from the Clerk of the Circuit Court of the county where granted.

FIRST YEAR SEARCH FEE: (includes one certified record or a "no record found" statement) $5.00

ADDITIONAL YEARS: $2 per year. The maximum search fee is $55 regardless of the total number of years to be searched

ADDITIONAL RECORDS: when ordered at the same time. $4 each ......

RUSH ORDERS: $10 per order (optional). Envelope must be marked "RUSH" ......

FOR JACKSONVILLE PICKUP SERVICE OR FOR MASTERCARD OR VISA CHARGES, TELEPHONE (904) 359-6911

FEES ARE NON REFUNDABLE AND SUBJECT TO CHANGE WITHOUT NOTICE

TOTAL ENCLOSED: Check or money order payable in U.S. dollars to Vital Statistics ......
PLEASE DO NOT MAIL CASH

Florida Law imposes an additional service charge of $15 for dishonored checks.

Applicant's Signature	Name and Address for mailing, if different from residence
Applicant's Name (must be typed or printed)	
Residence Address	Apt. No.
City, State, Zip	Telephone No.

MAIL THIS APPLICATION TO VITAL STATISTICS, P.O. BOX 210, JACKSONVILLE, FL 32231-0042

HRS Form 260, Feb. 91 (Replaces Oct 90 edition which may be used)
(Stock Number: 5740-000-0260-6)

PLEASE TYPE OR PRINT CLEARLY

FLORIDA DEPARTMENT OF HEALTH

State of Florida, Department of Health
APPLICATION FOR DEATH RECORD FOR DEATH WHICH OCCURRED IN FLORIDA

NAME OF DECEASED (Registrant)	First	Middle	Last	Race
SOCIAL SECURITY NO. (If known)				Sex
DATE OF DEATH (approximate month & day)	Month	Day	Specify exact year or series of years to be searched	
PLACE OF DEATH	City or Town		County	FLORIDA
NAME OF FUNERAL DIRECTOR				

FEES ARE NONREFUNDABLE and subject to change without notice.

FIRST YEAR SEARCH FEE: (includes one certified record or a "no record found" statement) **$5.00**

ADDITIONAL YEARS: $2 per year. The maximum search fee is $55 regardless of the total number of years to be searched

ADDITIONAL RECORDS: when ordered at the same time. $4 each . . . .

RUSH ORDERS: $10 per order (optional). Envelope must be marked "RUSH" . . . .

FOR JACKSONVILLE PICKUP SERVICE OR FOR MASTERCARD, VISA, DISCOVER
OR AMERICAN EXPRESS CHARGES, TELEPHONE (904) 359-6911

TOTAL ENCLOSED: Check or money order payable in U.S. dollars to Vital Statistics . . . .

PLEASE DO NOT MAIL CASH

Florida Law imposes an additional service charge of $15 for dishonored checks.

Applicant's Name (must be typed or printed)		Applicant's Signature	
Home Phone Number	Work Phone Number	CAUSE OF DEATH REQUESTED (see back of form for eligibility) YES ☐ NO ☐	
Residence Address		Apt. No.	Relationship to deceased (must be completed when cause of death is requested)
City	State	Zip Code	

MAIL THIS APPLICATION TO VITAL STATISTICS, P.O. BOX 210, JACKSONVILLE, FL 32231-0042

DH 727, 6/97 (Replaces 2/97 edition which may be used)
(Stock Number: 5740-000-0727-6)

PLEASE TYPE OR PRINT CLEARLY

Send your requests to:

Georgia Department of Human Resources
Vital Records Service
Room 217-H, Health Building
47 Trinity Avenue, SW
Atlanta, Georgia 30334-5600

Tel. (404) 656-4750
E-mail: GDPHINFO@dhr.state.ga.us
http://www.ph.dhr.state.ga.us/epi/vitalrecords/

The Vital Records Service has birth and death records from January 1, 1919; marriage records and verification of divorces from June 9, 1952. Make payment in the form of a certified check or money order, made out to "Georgia Department of Human Resources." No personal checks are accepted. Expedited service is available (with payment by credit card) for an additional fee of $8.95, plus shipping.

Cost for a certified Birth Certificate	$10.00
Cost for a certified Birth Card	$10.00
Cost for a certified Marriage Certificate	$10.00
Cost for verification of Divorce Decree	$10.00
Cost for a certified Death Certificate	$10.00
Cost for a duplicate copy, when ordered at the same time	$5.00

For earlier records write to:

County Probate Court
(County Seat), Georgia

For Divorce Records write to:

Superior Court
(County Seat), Georgia

For Adoption Record information write to:

Georgia Department of Human Resources
Division of Family and Children Services
Two Peachtree Street, NW, Suite 13-400
Atlanta, Georgia 30303-3142

Tel. (404) 657-3550
Fax (404) 657-3624
http://www.state.ga.us/Departments/DHR/facadop.html

Georgia Department of Archives & History (300 Capitol Avenue, SE, Atlanta, GA 30334; 404-656-2393) has marriage and divorce records (years vary by county).

For further information see:

Instruction Manual for the Vital Records Registration System in Georgia. 2nd ed. Atlanta, GA: Georgia Department of Human Resources, Division of Physical Health, Vital Records Service, 1982. 243p.
A Manual for City Clerks in Georgia. Atlanta, GA: Georgia Municipal Clerks and Financial Officers Association, 1970. Unpgd.

Georgia Department of Human Resources
REQUEST FOR SEARCH OF <u>BIRTH</u> RECORDS
<u>GEORGIA BIRTH RECORDS ONLY</u>
COMPLETE ALL NUMBERED SPACES BELOW ..... PLEASE PRINT OR TYPE INFORMATION
NOTE: <u>THE $10.00 SEARCH FEE IS NOT REFUNDABLE</u>
<u>PAY FEE BY CERTIFIED CHECK OR MONEY ORDER IF REQUEST IS MAILED</u>

NOTE: Georgia Law Chapter 31-10-26 provides that certified copies of Birth Certificates shall be issued **ONLY** to registrant (the person whose Birth Certificate is being requested), or other persons authorized by law.

1 ENTER THE NUMBER OF CERTIFIED COPIES BELOW AND PAY TOTAL FEE

Full Size Copy - $10
☐ Each Additional Copy - $5.00

Wallet Size Copy - $10
☐ Each Additional Copy - $10.00

TOTAL COPIES REQUESTED ☐

2 FULL NAME _____
(First)   (Middle)   (Last) (If Married, enter MAIDEN Name)

3 DATE OF BIRTH _____
(Month)   (Day)   (Year)

4 PLACE OF BIRTH_____

5 CURRENT AGE _____ **6** SEX_____ **7** RACE _____

8 FULL NAME OF FATHER _____
(First)   (Middle)   (Last)

9 FULL NAME OF MOTHER _____
(First)   (Middle)   (Enter MAIDEN Name)

The above fees have been established in accordance with Chapter 31-10 of the Official Code of Georgia. Pursuant to O.C.G.A. Chapter 31-10; Section 31: Any person who willfully or knowingly supplies false information on this form to be used for any purpose of deception with intent to defraud; willfully uses or attempts to use any certificate of birth or copy of any record of birth knowing that such certificate was issued upon a record which was false or which relates to the birth of another person may be fined not more than $10,000 or imprisoned for not more than five (5) years, or both upon conviction.

10 SIGNATURE OF REQUESTER _____

Relationship *(if other than self)* _____

- -

ADDRESS CORRESPONDENCE TO:
Vital Records Service
Room 217-H, 47 Trinity Avenue, S.W.
Atlanta, Georgia 30334

(MAILING LABEL)

PRINT YOUR NAME AND ADDRESS BELOW (legibly and correctly)

_____
Name

_____
Street Name/Number   Apt. No.

_____
City   State   Zip

MARRIAGE CERTIFICATE REQUESTS

Please indicate below the type and number of copies requested and forward this form with either a money order or certified check for the correct amount, made payable to the Georgia Department of Human Resources.

[   ] Full size copy $10.00; Additional Copies are $5.00 each at this time   [   ] Total Number of Copies Requested

NOTE: Records prior to June 9, 1952 must be requested at the Office of the Probate Judge in the county where the license was issued. If you are requesting a marriage certificate prior to this date, complete this application and mail it to the County's Probate Court's Office in which the marriage was granted. Contact their office concerning their fee requirements, as their prices may differ from our prices.

COMPLETE ALL INFORMATION FOR THE MARRIAGE RECORD BEING REQUESTED:

Groom's Name_____

          (First)   (Middle)   (Last)

Bride's Name_____

          (First)   (Middle)   (Maiden)

Date of Marriage_____

          (Month)   (Day)   (Year)

Place of Marriage_____

          (City)   (County)   (State)

Signature of Requestor_____

Relationship (if other than Bride or Groom)_____

DIVORCE VERIFICATION REQUESTS ONLY

Please indicate below the type and number of verifications requested and forward this form with either a money order or certified check for the correct amount, made payable to the Georgia Department of Human Resources. Divorce records are kept for statistical purposes only; therefore, copies are never issued by the State Office.

[   ] One Certified Statement $10.00; Additional statements are $5.00 at this time   [   ] Total Number of Statements Requested

NOTE: Records prior to June 9, 1952 must be requested at the Clerk of the Superior Court in the county where the divorce was granted. If you are requesting a divorce record prior to this date, complete this application and mail it to the Clerk of the Superior Court in the county where the divorce was granted. Contact their office concerning their fee requirements, as their prices may differ from our prices.

COMPLETE ALL INFORMATION FOR THE DIVORCE VERIFICATION BEING REQUESTED:

Groom's Name_____

          (First)   (Middle)   (Last)

Bride's Name_____

          (First)   (Middle)   (Maiden)

Date of Divorce_____

          (Month)   (Day)   (Year)

Place of Divorce_____

          (City)   (County)   (State)

Signature of Requestor_____

Relationship (if other than Bride or Groom)_____

MAILING ADDRESS

List below the name and address of person to whom certificate is to be mailed; then, indicate relationship to the person whose name is on the certificate.

Name:_____   Relationship:_____

Address:_____

          (No. & Street)   (Apartment Number)

_____

          (City)   (State)   (Zip Code)

Georgia Department of Human Resources
Vital Records Service
Room 217-H, Health Building, 47 Trinity Avenue, S.W.
Atlanta, Georgia 30334
REQUEST FOR SEARCH OF DEATH RECORDS

The fee for searches of vital records has been established by the State Board of Human Resorces as ten dollars ($10.00), in accordance with Section 31-10-27 of the Georgia Code. The ten dollar fee includes a certified copy if the record is found. Each additional copy paid for at the same time is five dollars ($5.00). Eleven years are searched.

PLEASE INDICATE BELOW THE NUMBERS OF COPIES NEEDED AND FORWARD THIS FORM WITH EITHER A MONEY ORDER OR CHECK FOR THE CORRECT AMOUNT MADE PAYABLE TO THE GEORGIA DEPARTMENT OF HUMAN RESOURCES

Total Number of Copies   Amount Received $ _____

FILL IN INFORMATION BELOW CONCERNING PERSON WHOSE CERTIFICATE IS REQUESTED

Name_____ Date of Death _____
     (First)   (Middle)   (Last)

Age _____ Race _____ Sex_____

Place of Death_____
     (Hospital)   (City)   (County)   (State)

If Married, Name of Husband or Wife _____

Occupation of Deceased _____

Funeral Director's Name _____

Name of Doctor _____

Place of Burial _____

ADDRESS CORRESPONDENCE TO: (MAILING LABEL)
Vital Records Service
Room 217-H, 47 Trinity Avenue, S.W.
Atlanta, Georgia 30334

PRINT YOUR NAME AND ADDRESS BELOW (legibly and correctly)

_____
Name

_____
Street Name/Number   Apt. No.

_____
City   State   Zip

Send your requests to:

Hawaii Department of Health
Office of Health Status Monitoring
Vital Records Section
1250 Punchbowl Street, Room 103
P.O. Box 3378
Honolulu, Hawaii 96801-3378

Tel. (808) 586-4533
Fax (808) 586-4606
E-mail: vr-info@mail.health.state.hi.us
http://www.hawaii.gov/health/records/index.html

The Vital Records Section has birth, marriage, divorce, and death records from 1853. Hawaiian vital records are restricted for 75 years. Make money orders or cashiers' checks payable to "Hawaii State Department of Health."

Cost for a certified Birth Certificate	$10.00
Cost for a certified Marriage Certificate	$10.00
Cost for a certified Divorce Record	$10.00
Cost for a certified Death Certificate	$10.00
Cost for a duplicate copy, when ordered at the same time	$4.00

For Adoption Record information contact: http://www.hawaii.gov/jud/index.html *or write to:*

Family Court	**Family Court**	**Family Court**
First Circuit Court	Second Circuit	Third Circuit
Kaahumanu Hale	Hoapili Hale	5 Aupuni Street
777 Punchbowl Street	2145 Main Street	PO Box 1007
Honolulu, HI 96813	Wailuku, HI 96793	Hilo, HI 96721
Tel. (808) 539-4400	(808) 244-2770	(808) 934-5767
Fax (808) 539-4402	(808) 244-2777	(808) 961-6510

Indexes of birth records from 1896 to 1909 are available at the Hamilton Library of the University of Hawaii at Manoa. For more information call the Hawaii Collection (University of Hawaii at Manoa Library, 2550 The Mall, Honolulu, HI 96822; 808-956-2852, 808-956-8264).

The State Archives (Kekauluohi Building, Iolani Palace Grounds, Honolulu, Hawaii 96813; 808-586-0329) holds divorce records. The State Library of Hawaii (478 South King Street, Honolulu, Hawaii 96813; 808-586-3535) maintains indexes to all birth and marriage notices (1850–1950) and obituary notices (1836–1950) from Hawaiian newspapers.

The Family History Library of Salt Lake City, Utah has microfilm copies of the statewide birth and death registers that are 75 years older than the previous current year.

REQUEST FOR CERTIFIED COPY OF **BIRTH** RECORD

_____1_____ COPY AT $10.00*   = $10.00 _____

_____ ADDITIONAL COPIES AT $4.00 EACH   = $ _____

_____ TOTAL COPIES   TOTAL AMOUNT DUE   = $ _____

*(SEE BACK FOR IMPORTANT INFORMATION)

	FIRST	MIDDLE	LAST
NAME ON CERTIFICATE:			

	MONTH	DAY	YEAR		CITY OR TOWN	ISLAND
DATE OF BIRTH:				**PLACE OF BIRTH:**		

	FIRST	MIDDLE	LAST
FATHER'S NAME:			

	FIRST	MIDDLE	MAIDEN NAME
MOTHER'S NAME:			

RELATIONSHIP OF REQUESTOR TO PERSON NAMED ON CERTIFICATE	REASON FOR REQUESTING A CERTIFIED COPY

SIGNATURE OF REQUESTOR	TELEPHONE NUMBERS
	RES.:
PRINT NAME OF REQUESTOR:	BUS.:

ADDRESS OF REQUESTOR: NO. AND STREET OR P.O. BOX

CITY	STATE	ZIP

ALL ITEMS MUST BE COMPLETED IN FULL TO PERMIT THIS OFFICE TO COMPLY WITH THIS REQUEST. FOR THE PROTECTION OF THE INDIVIDUAL, CERTIFICATES OF VITAL EVENTS ARE NOT OPEN TO PUBLIC INSPECTION.

MAIL TO:

PLEASE COMPLETE ONLY IF MAILING TO PERSON OTHER THAN REQUESTOR.

NAME

NO. AND STREET OR P.O. BOX

CITY	STATE	ZIP

FOR OFFICE USE ONLY

____ ____ HBC

____ DBC

____ UNREC. BC

____ NR FILE

____ Pending:

Index Searched		Volumes Searched		Date Copy Prepared
From	To	From	To	
Year	Volume	Certificate		Receipt Number

STATE OF HAWAII, DEPARTMENT OF HEALTH
OFFICE OF HEALTH STATUS MONITORING

REQUEST FOR CERTIFIED COPY OF MARRIAGE RECORD

___1___	COPY AT $10.00*	= $10.00
_____	ADDITIONAL COPIES AT $4.00 EACH	= $ _____
_____	TOTAL COPIES TOTAL AMOUNT DUE	= $ _____

*(SEE BACK FOR IMPORTANT INFORMATION)

	FIRST	MIDDLE	LAST
GROOM'S NAME:			
	FIRST	MIDDLE	MAIDEN NAME
BRIDE'S NAME:			
	MONTH	DAY	YEAR
DATE OF MARRIAGE:			
	CITY OR TOWN		ISLAND
PLACE OF MARRIAGE:			

RELATIONSHIP OF REQUESTOR TO PERSON NAMED ON CERTIFICATE	REASON FOR REQUESTING A CERTIFIED COPY

SIGNATURE OF REQUESTOR	TELEPHONE NUMBERS
	RES.:
PRINT NAME OF REQUESTOR:	BUS.:

ADDRESS OF REQUESTOR: NO. AND STREET OR P.O. BOX

CITY	STATE	ZIP

ALL ITEMS MUST BE COMPLETED IN FULL TO PERMIT THIS OFFICE TO COMPLY WITH THIS REQUEST. FOR THE PROTECTION OF THE INDIVIDUAL, CERTIFICATES OF VITAL EVENTS ARE NOT OPEN TO PUBLIC INSPECTION.

MAIL TO:

PLEASE COMPLETE ONLY IF MAILING TO PERSON OTHER THAN REQUESTOR.

NAME

NO. AND STREET OR P.O. BOX

CITY	STATE	ZIP

FOR OFFICE USE ONLY

____ NR File

____ Pending:

Index Searched		Volumes Searched		Date Copy Prepared
From	To	From	To	
Year	Volume	Certificate		Receipt Number

OHSM 137 (REV. 7/1/97)   **COMPLETE ALL ITEMS**

STATE OF HAWAII, DEPARTMENT OF HEALTH
OFFICE OF HEALTH STATUS MONITORING

REQUEST FOR COPY OF **DIVORCE** RECORD

(ATTACH $10.00 FOR EACH COPY. DO NOT SEND CASH BY MAIL)

AMOUNT ATTACHED $ _____   NO. OF COPIES _____

	FIRST	MIDDLE	LAST
HUSBAND'S NAME:			

	FIRST	MIDDLE	MAIDEN
WIFE'S NAME:			

	MONTH	DAY	YEAR
DATE OF DIVORCE:			

	CITY OR TOWN	ISLAND
PLACE OF DIVORCE:		

RELATIONSHIP OF REQUESTOR TO PERSON NAMED ON CERTIFICATE	REASON FOR REQUESTING A CERTIFIED COPY

SIGNATURE OF REQUESTOR:	TELEPHONE NUMBERS RES:
PRINT NAME OF REQUESTOR:	BUS:

ADDRESS OF REQUESTOR: NO. AND STREET OR P.O. BOX

CITY	STATE	ZIP

ALL ITEMS MUST BE COMPLETED IN FULL TO PERMIT THIS OFFICE TO COMPLY WITH THIS REQUEST. FOR THE PROTECTION OF THE INDIVIDUAL, CERTIFICATES OF VITAL EVENTS ARE NOT OPEN TO PUBLIC INSPECTION.

MAIL TO: PLEASE COMPLETE ONLY IF MAILING TO PERSON OTHER THAN REQUESTOR.

NAME

NO. AND STREET OR P.O. BOX

CITY	STATE	ZIP

COMPLETE ALL ITEMS

FOR OFFICE USE ONLY

Index Searched		Volumes Searched		Date Copy Prepared
From	To	From	To	
Year	Volume	Certificate		Receipt Number

OHSM 138 (REV. 1/95)

6/3/95, 9:51 AM

STATE OF HAWAII, DEPARTMENT OF HEALTH
OFFICE OF HEALTH STATUS MONITORING

REQUEST FOR CERTIFIED COPY OF **DEATH** RECORD

_____1_____ COPY AT $10.00* = $ **10.00**_____

_____ ADDITIONAL COPIES AT $4.00 EACH = $ _____

_____ TOTAL COPIES TOTAL AMOUNT DUE = $ _____

*(SEE BACK FOR IMPORTANT INFORMATION)

	FIRST	MIDDLE	LAST
NAME OF DECEASED:			

	MONTH	DAY	YEAR
DATE OF DEATH:			

	CITY OR TOWN	ISLAND
PLACE OF DEATH:		

RELATIONSHIP OF REQUESTOR TO PERSON NAMED ON CERTIFICATE	REASON FOR REQUESTING A CERTIFIED COPY

SIGNATURE OF REQUESTOR:	TELEPHONE NUMBERS
	RES:
PRINT NAME OF REQUESTOR:	BUS:

ADDRESS OF REQUESTOR:	NO. AND STREET OR P.O. BOX

CITY	STATE	ZIP

ALL ITEMS MUST BE COMPLETED IN FULL TO PERMIT THIS OFFICE TO COMPLY WITH THIS REQUEST. FOR THE PROTECTION OF THE INDIVIDUAL, CERTIFICATES OF VITAL EVENTS ARE NOT OPEN TO PUBLIC INSPECTION.

MAIL TO:

PLEASE COMPLETE ONLY IF MAILING TO PERSON OTHER THAN REQUESTOR.

NAME
NO. AND STREET OR P.O. BOX

CITY	STATE	ZIP

FOR OFFICE USE ONLY

____ NR FILE

____ PENDING:

INDEX SEARCHED		VOLUMES SEARCHED		DATE COPY PREPARED
FROM	TO	FROM	TO	

YEAR	VOLUME	CERTIFICATE	RECEIPT NUMBER

OHSM 136 (Rev. 7/1/97) **COMPLETE ALL ITEMS**

IDAHO

Idaho Department of Health and Welfare   Tel. (208) 334-5980
Vital Statistics Unit   Tel. (208) 334-5988
450 West State Street, First Floor   Fax (208) 389-9096
P.O. Box 83720
Boise, Idaho 83720-0036   http://www.state.id.us/dhw/hwgd_www/health/vs/appmenu.html

The Vital Statistics Unit has birth records from July 1, 1911; marriage and divorce records from May 1, 1947; and death records from July 1, 1911. Expedited service is available (with request by fax and payment by credit card) for an additional fee of $10.00, plus shipping.

Cost for a certified Birth Certificate, computer-generated	$10.00
Cost for a certified Birth Certificate, photostat of the original	$15.00
Cost for a certified Birth Certificate, short form	$10.00
Cost for a certified Marriage or Divorce Certificate	$10.00
Cost for a certified Death Certificate	$10.00

For earlier records write to:

County Clerk
County Court House
(County Seat), Idaho

For Adoption Record information write to:

Voluntary Adoption Registry   Tel. (208) 334-5990
Department of Health and Welfare   Fax (208) 389-9096
Center for Vital Statistics and Health Policy   http://www2.state.id.us/dhw/hwgd_www/
450 West State Street, First Floor   health/vs/adop.var.html
P.O. Box 83720
Boise, Idaho 83720-0036

Cost for registering with the Voluntary Adoption Registry $10.00

The Idaho State Historical Society, which houses the State Archives (450 North Fourth Street, Boise, ID 83702-6027; 208-334-3356) has copies of early county records.

The Family History Library of Salt Lake City, Utah has microfilmed many of the original and published vital records and church registers of Idaho. For details on their holdings please consult your nearest Family History Center.

Idaho
Certificate Application

☐ **BIRTH**   ☐ **DEATH**

Birth/Death records have been filed since July 1911

Name on
Certificate_____
　　　　　(First)　　*(Middle)*　　*(Last)*

Place
of event_____ Sex_____
　　　　　(City)　　　　*(County)*

Date
of Event_____ _____ _____ File #_____
　　　(Month)　*(Day)*　*(Year)*　　*(If Known)*

Father's
Name_____
　　　　(First)　　*(Middle)*　　*(Last)*

Mother's Full **MAIDEN**

Name_____
　　　　(First)　　*(Middle)*　　*(Maiden)*

☐ **MARRIAGE**   ☐ **DIVORCE**

Marriage/Divorce records have been filed since May 1947

Husband_____
　　　　　(First)　　*(Middle)*　　*(Last)*

Wife_____
　　　　(First)　　*(Middle)*　　*(Last)*

Date
of Event_____ _____
　　　(Month)　　*(Day)*　　*(Year)*

Place
of Event_____
　　　　(City)　　　　*(County)*

File #_____
　　　(If Known)

WARNING: False application for a certified copy of a vital record is a felony punishable by a fine up to $5,000, five years in prison, or both (Title 39, Chapter 2, **Idaho Code**).

☞**ID Is Required** of the person that signs this request. HAVE READY TO SHOW **EITHER** a state issued ID *(with a signature)* **OR** TWO other things that have your signature. *(Please send photocopies of ID when mailing your request.)*

Quantity ordered:

#_____ **Certified Copy** - $10.00 each*. *Valid for all legal purposes.* (**If the record is not found, a no record letter will be issued.**)

#_____ **Legal Amendment Fee** - $10.00. *A filing fee is required to process paternity and adoption actions, court ordered name changes, and filing delayed certificates.* (*The fee does **NOT** include a certified copy.*)

Your Signature_____

Address_____
　　　　　(Street or PO Box)　　*(City)*　　*(State)*　　*(Zip)*
What will the certificate be used for?_____

Your Relationship to Person Named on Certificate *(Self, Mother, Spouse, etc.)*:_____

IF Legal Representative - State Legal Relationship_____

PLEASE SPECIFY if any additional services are requested:

☐ *Certified copies are computer-generated. Certified photostat copies are available: Fee - **$15.00**

☐ Add a **$5.00** special handling fee to orders requiring expedited processing and **sent to us** by special mailing *(express, priority, etc.)*

Cash or Check/Money Order payable to - **VITAL STATISTICS**, 450 W State St, 1st Fl, PO Box 83720, Boise, Idaho 83720-0036

(208) 334-5988　　http://www.state.id.us/dhw *(Rev 12/99)*

ILLINOIS

Send your requests for Birth and Death Certificates to:

Illinois Department of Public Health
Division of Vital Records
605 West Jefferson Street
Springfield, Illinois 62702-5097

Tel. (217) 782-6554
Fax (217) 523-2648
TTY (800) 547-0466
E-mail: mailus@idph.state.il.us
http://www.idph.state.il.us/vital/vitalhome.htm

The Division of Vital Records has birth and death records from January 1, 1916. The Division does not issue certified copies of marriage and divorce records; certified copies are available from the county clerk in the county where the event occurred. However, it can verify the facts of a marriage or divorce that has taken place from 1962 to the present. Expedited service is available (with request by fax and payment by credit card) for an additional fee of $6.00, plus shipping.

Cost for a certified Birth Certificate	$15.00
Cost for a certified short-form, computerized Birth Certificate	$10.00
Cost for a certified wallet-size Birth Card	$10.00
Cost for a verified Marriage or Divorce Record	$5.00
Cost for a certified Death Certificate	$17.00
Cost for a duplicate copy, when ordered at the same time	$2.00

For earlier records and Marriage or Divorce Certificates write to:

County Clerk
County Court House
(County Seat), Illinois

For Adoption Record information write to:

Illinois Adoption Registry
Illinois Department of Public Health
Division of Vital Records
605 West Jefferson Street
Springfield, Illinois 62702-5097

Tel. (217) 785-3189
http://www.idph.state.il.us/vital/forms/abhow.htm#info

Cost for registration in Illinois Adoption Registry $40.00

Illinois State Archives (Capitol Complex, Springfield, IL 62756-0001; 217-782-4682) has an index to births from 1877 and deaths from 1916–1938, and is in the process of preparing an index to marriages from the earliest records to 1900. Eighty-four counties are currently at least partially indexed (forty-three are completed). There is a $.50 charge per page of the index copied. The Illinois Regional Archives Depository (IRAD) system also has early records.

For further information see:

Handbook for Township Clerks. Springfield, IL: State Board of Elections, 1976. 75p.

Illinois Registrar's Digest. (Serial). Springfield, IL: State Department of Public Health, Bureau of Statistics, Vol. 1, No. 1, February 1967– .

A Summary Guide to Local Governmental Records in the Illinois Regional Archives. 2nd edition. Springfield, IL: Illinois State Archives, 1999. 265p.

Illinois Department of Public Health
APPLICATION FOR SEARCH OF BIRTH RECORD FILES
The state began recording birth records on January 1, 1916.

The Division of Vital Records offers you a choice between two types of certified copies of birth records. For $15.00, you can receive a certified copy (photocopy of original) or for $10.00 you can receive a certified computer generated abstract of the original record. The $10.00 version comes in two sizes and does not list parents names. One is approximately 6X8 1/2" and the other is wallet size.

All versions are certified by the state of Illinois and are acceptable for all legal purposes.

Additional copies of the same record requested at the same time are $2.00 each.

Please indicate below the type and number of copies requested and return this form with the proper fee.

CERTIFIED COPY $15.00 Each	CERTIFICATION $10.00 Each	BIRTH CARD (wallet size) $10.00 Each
Amount enclosed $_____ for_____copies	Amount enclosed $_____ for _____copies	Amount enclosed $_____ for_____copies

(DO NOT SEND CASH) Make check or money order payable to ILLINOIS DEPARTMENT OF PUBLIC HEALTH

FULL NAME	First	Middle	Last	

PLACE OF BIRTH	Hospital	City or Town	County	State

DATE OF BIRTH	Month	Day	Year	SEX	BIRTH NUMBER IF KNOWN

FATHER	First	Middle	Last

MOTHER	First	Middle	Maiden Name	Married Name

APPLICATION MADE BY

_____
NAME (written signature)

_____
STREET ADDRESS

_____
CITY   STATE   ZIP

_____
YOUR RELATIONSHIP TO PERSON

MAIL COPY TO (if other than applicant)

_____
NAME

_____
STREET ADDRESS

_____
CITY   STATE   ZIP

_____
INTENDED USE OF DOCUMENT

NOTE: Birth certificates are confidential records and copies can be issued only to persons entitled to receive them. The application must indicate the requester's relationship to the person and the intended use of the document.

MAIL TO	Illinois Department of Public Health, Division of Vital Records, 605 W. Jefferson St., Springfield, IL 62702-5097, 217-782-6553

Printed by Authority of the State of Illinois   P.O. #146005   30M   6/96

Illinois Department of Public Health

APPLICATION FOR VERIFICATION OF MARRIAGE RECORD FILES

Certified copies can only be obtained by writing to the county clerk where the marriage occurred. The Department began recording marriage information on January 1, 1962.

FURNISH ALL POSSIBLE INFORMATION

	First	Middle	Last
Name of GROOM			
MAIDEN name of BRIDE	First	Middle	Last
Place of MARRIAGE	City	County	State
Date of MARRIAGE	Month	Day	Year

The statutory fee for the search of the marriage record files of the Illinois Department of Public Health is $5.00. If a record is found, a verification of the marriage is furnished without further cost.

APPLICATION MADE BY

Name		
Street Address		
City	State	ZIP
Signature		

Mail To

Illinois Department of Public Health
Division of Vital Records
605 W. Jefferson St.
Springfield, IL 62702-5097

Printed by Authority of the State of Illinois   P.O. #146009   10M   6/96

Illinois Department of Public Health

APPLICATION FOR VERIFICATION OF DIVORCE RECORD FILES

Certified copies can only be obtained by writing to the circuit clerk where the divorce was filed. The Department began recording divorce information on January 1, 1962.

FURNISH ALL POSSIBLE INFORMATION

Name of HUSBAND	First	Middle	Last
MAIDEN name of WIFE	First	Middle	Last
Place of DIVORCE	City	County	State
Date of DIVORCE	Month	Day	Year

The statutory fee for the search of the divorce record files of the Illinois Department of Public Health is $5.00. If a record is found, a verification of the divorce is furnished without further cost.

APPLICATION MADE BY

Name		
Street Address		
City	State	ZIP
Signature		

Mail To

Illinois Department of Public Health
Division of Vital Records
605 W. Jefferson St.
Springfield, IL 62702-5097

Printed by Authority of the State of Illinois   P.O. #146010   10M   6/96

Illinois Department of Public Health
APPLICATION FOR SEARCH OF DEATH RECORD FILES
The State began recording death records on January 1, 1916.

The fee for a certified copy of the death record is $17.00. Additional copies of the same record ordered at the same time are $2.00 each. The fee for an uncertified (genealogical) copy is $10.00. Additional copies of the same record ordered at the same time are $2.00 each.

A certified copy is a sealed photographic copy of the original death certificate suitable for all legal purposes.

An uncertified genealogical copy is a photographic copy of the original death certificate not suitable for legal purposes.

CERTIFIED COPY $17.00 Each	GENEALOGICAL RESEARCH (Uncertified copy)
Amount enclosed $_____	Amount enclosed $_____
for_____copies	for_____copies

(DO NOT SEND CASH) Make check or money order payable to ILLINOIS DEPARTMENT OF PUBLIC HEALTH

FULL NAME OF DECEASED	First	Middle	Last	

PLACE OF DEATH	Hospital	City or Town	County	State

DATE OF DEATH	Month	Day	Year	SEX	RACE	OCCUPATION	SOCIAL SECURITY NUMBER

DATE LAST KNOWN TO BE ALIVE	Month	Day	Year	LAST KNOWN ADDRESS	MARITAL STATUS

DATE OF BIRTH	Month	Day	Year	BIRTHPLACE (City and State)	NAME OF HUSBAND OR WIFE

FULL NAME OF FATHER OF DECEASED	FULL MAIDEN NAME OF MOTHER OF DECEASED

APPLICATION MADE BY	MAIL COPY TO (if other than applicant)
NAME OR FIRM NAME (if any)	NAME OR FIRM NAME (in any)
STREET ADDRESS	STREET ADDRESS
CITY STATE ZIP	CITY STATE ZIP

MAIL TO	Illinois Department of Public Health, Division of Vital Records, 605 W. Jefferson St., Springfield, IL 62702-5097, 217-782-6553

Printed by Authority of the State of Illinois   P.O. #146006   30M   6/96

Send your requests for Birth and Death Certificates to:

Vital Records Department
Indiana State Department of Health
2 North Meridian Street
Indianapolis, Indiana 46204-3006

Tel. (317) 233-2700
(317) 233-1325
E-mail: webmaster@ai.org
http://www.state.in.us/isdh/bdcertifs/bdcert.html

The Vital Records Department has birth records from October 1907 and death records from January 1900 (death records from 1900 to 1918 are not indexed). There is a $4.00 search per county per five years searched from January 1958 to the present. Expedited service is available (with payment by credit card) for an additional fee.

For earlier birth and death records, contact the Local Health Department in the county where the event occurred (a list of Local Health Department addresses is available on the Vital Records Department web site). A marriage index from 1958 is also available; contact the county clerk for certificates.

Cost for a certified Birth Certificate	$6.00
Cost for an heirloom Birth Certificate	$30.00
Cost for a certified Death Certificate	$4.00
Cost for a duplicate copy, when ordered at the same time	$1.00

For Marriage and Divorce Certificates write to:

Clerk of the Court
County Court House
(County Seat), Indiana

For Adoption Records:
Tel. (317) 233-7523

Identifying Adoption information
Indiana Adoption History Registry
Indiana State Department of Health
Vital Statistics, Section B-4
2 North Meridian Street
Indianapolis, IN 46204-3006

Non-identifying Adoption information
32-22
Indiana Adoption History Registry
Indiana State Department of Health
P.O. Box 1964
1330 West Michigan Street
Indianapolis, IN 46206-1964

There is no charge for adoption registration and information.

Fred J. Reynolds Historical Genealogy Department of the Allen County Public Library (900 Webster Street, Fort Wayne, IN 46802-3899; 219-424-7241) has a substantial collection of Indiana published and microfilm materials.

For further information see:

Indiana Vital Statistics Newsletter. Indianapolis, IN: Indiana State Board of Health, 1977– .

APPLICATION FOR SEARCH AND CERTIFIED COPY OF BIRTH RECORD

State Form 49607 (5-00)
Approved by State Board of Accounts, 2000
INDIANA STATE DEPARTMENT OF HEALTH

BIRTH RECORDS IN THE STATE VITAL STATISTICS' OFFICE BEGAN WITH 1907. Prior to 1907, records of birth are filed ONLY with the local health department in the <u>county where the birth actually occurred</u>.

FEES ARE ESTABLISHED BY LAW (IC 16-37-1-11 and IC 16-37-1-11.5). Each search for a record costs $6.00. The fee is non-refundable. Included in one search is a 5-year period: the reported year of birth and, if the record is not found in that year, the 2 years before and after. A certified copy of the record, if found, is included in the search fee. Additional copies of the same record purchased at the same time are $1.00 each.

WARNING: FALSE APPLICATION, ALTERING, MUTILATING, OR COUNTERFEITING INDIANA BIRTH CERTIFICATES IS A CRIMINAL OFFENSE UNDER IC 16-37-1-12.

IDENTIFICATION IS REQUIRED according to IC 16-37-1-7 (*i.e., photocopy of driver's license, work identification card, etc.*). Birth requests sent without proper identification will be sent back to the requester without processing. Please complete <u>all</u> items below as required pursuant to IC 16-37-1-10 (a):

Full name at birth

Could this birth be recorded under any other name? If yes, please give name

Has this person ever been adopted? If yes, please give name AFTER adoption

Place of birth: City | Place of birth: County

Name of hospital

Date of birth | Age last birthday

Full name of father (*If adopted, give name of adopted father*)

Full name of mother including maiden name (*If adopted, give name of adopted mother*)

Purpose for which record is to be used:

Your relationship to the person whose birth record is requested:

Total certificates:
        Standard size: _____; Wallet size: _____ | Total fee(s)

Delivery preference:
☐ Regular Mail   ☐ Federal Express (*requires an additional Fed Ex fee*)   ☐ Pickup   ☐ Customer Waiting

Signature of applicant

Mailing address (*number and street, city, state, ZIP code*)

Daytime telephone number (*including area code*) | Today's date (*month, day, year*)

Send this application, check or money order payable to the Indiana State Department of Health, and a copy of your identification to: Vital Statistics, Indiana State Department of Health, PO Box 7125, Indianapolis, IN 46206-7125.

PRINT name and address of person to whom the certified copy is to be mailed if different than stated above.

Name

Mailing address (*number and street, city, state, ZIP code*)

FOR OFFICE USE ONLY

Date received (*month, day, year*) | Receipt number | Volume number

Certificate number | Application number | Initials of verifier

☐ Your fee of $ _____ was received and is being held pending return of information requested.

☐ Please remit additional fee of $ _____.

APPLICATION FOR SEARCH AND CERTIFIED COPY OF DEATH RECORD

State Form 49606 (5-00)
Approved by State Board of Accounts, 2000
INDIANA STATE DEPARTMENT OF HEALTH

DEATH RECORDS IN THE STATE VITAL STATISTICS' OFFICE BEGIN WITH 1900. Prior to 1900, records of death are filed ONLY with the local health department in the <u>county where the death actually occurred.</u> For deaths occurring from 1900 to 1917, the city and/ or county of death is required in order to locate the record.

FEES ARE ESTABLISHED BY LAW (IC 16-37-1-11). Each search for a record costs $4.00. The fee is non-refundable. Included in one search is a 5-year period; the reported year of death and, if the record is not found in that year, the 2 years before and after. For records prior to 1917, the search covers a 5-year period and only one county. A certified copy of the record, if found, is included in the search fee. Additional copies of the same record purchased at the same time are $1.00 each.

IDENTIFICATION IS REQUIRED according to IC 16-37-1-7, (*i.e., photocopy of driver's license, work identification card, etc.*) . DO NOT SEND ORIGINALS IN THE MAIL. Death records requests sent without proper identification will be sent back to the requester without processing. Please complete all items below as required pursuant to IC 16-37-1-10 (a):

Name of deceased *	Stillborn? ☐ Yes ☐ No

* (If decedent was a married, divorced, or widowed woman, ISDH must have her legal name at the time of death. Please do not give the maiden name of a woman who changed her name by marriage during her lifetime.)

Date of death

City of death	County of death

Total certificates	Total fee(s)

Delivery preference:
☐ Regular Mail   ☐ Federal Express (*requires an additional Fed Ex fee*)   ☐ Pickup   ☐ Customer Waiting

Date of birth of deceased (*if known*)

Name of father	Maiden name of mother

Your relationship to the person named on this record

Purpose for which the record is to be used

Signature of applicant

Printed name of applicant

Mailing address (*number and street, city, state, ZIP code*)

Daytime telephone number (*including area code*)	Today's date (*month, day, year*)

Send this application, check or money order payable to the Indiana State Department of Health, and a copy of your identification to: Vital Statistics, Indiana State Department of Health, PO Box 7125, Indianapolis, IN 46206-7125.

FOR OFFICE USE ONLY		
Date received (*month, day, year*)	Receipt number	Volume number
Certificate number	Application number	Initials of verifier

IOWA

Send your requests to:

Iowa Department of Public Health
Vital Records Bureau
Lucas State Office Building, 1st Floor
321 East 12th Street
Des Moines, Iowa 50319-0075

Tel. (515) 281-4944
E-mail: fdhs@dhs.state.ia.us
http://idph.state.ia.us/pa/vr.htm

The Vital Records Bureau has records of births, marriages, and deaths from July 1, 1880. To search marriage records 1880–1915, or death records 1880–1895, the county of occurrence and the year must be furnished. There is a $10 fee for each year and each county searched, for a total of $20 per search request. Expedited service is available (with payment by credit card) for an additional fee of $5.00, plus shipping.

Cost for a certified Birth Certificate	$10.00
Cost for a commemorative Birth Certificate	$35.00
Cost for a certified Marriage Certificate	$10.00
Cost for a commemorative Marriage Certificate	$35.00
Cost for a certified Death Certificate	$10.00
Phone orders (credit card handling fee)	$5.00

For earlier records write to:

Clerk
District Court
(County Seat), Iowa

At the county level, all vital records occurring in that county (excluding fetal death, adoptive records, and out-of-wedlock births prior to July 1, 1995) are open to the public for inspection. There may be a fee to inspect the records.

For Adoption Record information write to:

Adoption Program Manager
Iowa Department of Human Services
Hoover State Office Building, 5th Floor
Des Moines, Iowa 50319

Tel. (515) 281-5358
http://www.dhs.state.ia.us/HomePages/DHS/Adoption.htm

The State Historical Society of Iowa (600 East Locust, Des Moines, IA 50319-0290; 515-281-5111) has marriage records from the counties from 1880 to 1916.

The Family History Library of Salt Lake City, Utah has microfilmed many of the original and published vital records and church registers of Iowa. For details on their holdings please consult your nearest Family History Center.

APPLICATION FOR CERTIFIED COPY OF AN IOWA VITAL RECORD

- This application is for a certified copy of a birth, death or marriage record, if the event occurred in Iowa.
- If requesting a birth record, complete all items except 2(A).
- If requesting a death record, complete all items except 2(A) and 7.
- If requesting a marriage record, complete all items except 7.

1.	TYPE OF RECORD (Check one)	☐ BIRTH	☐ DEATH	☐ MARRIAGE	

2. **PERSON NAMED ON RECORD**

_____ _____ _____
FIRST   MIDDLE   SURNAME (Last)

2(A) **(Marriage Only) SPOUSE'S NAME**

_____ _____ _____
FIRST   MIDDLE   SURNAME (Last)

3. **DATE OF EVENT (birth, death, or marriage)**

_____ _____ _____
MONTH   DAY   YEAR

4. **PLACE OF EVENT (city and/or county)** _____

5. **MOTHER'S MAIDEN NAME**

_____ _____ _____
FIRST   MIDDLE   MAIDEN SURNAME (Last)

6. **FATHER'S NAME**

_____ _____ _____
FIRST   MIDDLE   SURNAME (Last)

7. **(Birth Only) WERE THE PARENTS MARRIED AT THE TIME OF BIRTH?**   ☐ Yes   ☐ No   ☐ Unknown

8. **LEGAL ACTIONS TO RECORD**   ☐ None   ☐ Adoption   ☐ Paternity   ☐ Name Change

8(A) PREVIOUS NAME, IF KNOWN _____

(NOTE: Marriage does NOT change the name on the birth record)

9. **APPLICANT'S RELATIONSHIP TO THE PERSON NAMED ON THE RECORD** _____

10. **PURPOSE FOR THIS COPY** _____   11. **NUMBER OF COPIES** _____

12. **APPLICANT'S SIGNATURE** _____

12 (A) APPLICANT'S DAYTIME TELEPHONE NUMBER _____

13. **NAME AND ADDRESS OF PERSON TO RECEIVE THIS COPY:**

NAME _____

STREET _____

CITY, STATE, ZIP CODE _____

14. **THIS COPY IS TO BE (Check one)**   ☐ Mailed   ☐ Picked up (for in-person application requests only)

15. **THIS COPY BEING PAID BY (Check one)**   ☐ Check   ☐ Cash   ☐ Money Order

16. **AMOUNT ENCLOSED** _____

APPLICATION FOR IOWA COMMEMORATIVE BIRTH CERTIFICATE

Please print clearly. Fill out completely.

Name on Record: _____
   (first)   (middle)   (last as it appears on the record)   (suffix, if any)

Date of Birth: _____   Place of Birth: _____
   (month, day, year)   (city or county)

Mother's Full Maiden Name: _____
   (first)   (middle)   (last as it appears on her birth certificate)

Father's Full Name: _____
   (first)   (middle)   (last)   (suffix, if any)

Has the name on the record ever been changed by a legal procedure?   ❑ Yes   ❑ No   ❑ Unknown

   If yes, what type?   ❑   Adoption   ❑   Paternity Action   ❑   Legal Name Change

   Previous name on the record: _____
                                    (first)   (middle)   (last)   (suffix, if any)

Applicant's relationship to the person named on the record: _____

   Recipient's relationship to the person named on the
   record, if recipient someone other than the applicant: _____

Number of copies requested: _____   Amount enclosed: _____

Applicant's full name: *(please print)* _____
                              (first)   (middle)   (last)   (suffix, if any)

Applicant's signature: _____

Applicant's daytime telephone number: (_____)_____--_____

Name and address of person to receive the copy by: ❑   Mail   ❑   Pick-up
(Please print clearly on lines below)

_____   Name

_____   Street Address or P.O. Box

_____   City, State, Zip Code

APPLICATION FOR IOWA COMMEMORATIVE MARRIAGE CERTIFICATE

Please print clearly. Fill out completely

Bride's Full Name: _____
                        (first)   (middle)   (maiden)   (last)

Groom's Full Name: _____
                        (first)   (middle)   (last)   (suffix, if any)

Date of Event: _____
                        (month)   (day)   (year)

Place of Event: _____
                        (city or county)

Officiant who performed the marriage ceremony _____

Witnesses who signed the marriage certificate   1. _____

                                            2. _____

Applicant's relationship to the person named on the record: _____

Recipient's relationship to the person named on the record,
if recipient someone other than the applicant: _____

Number of copies requested: _____   Amount enclosed: _____

Applicant's full name: *(please print)* _____
                        (first)   (middle)   (last)   (suffix, if any)

Applicant's signature: _____

Applicant's daytime telephone number: (_____) _____ -- _____

Name and address of person to receive the copy by: ❑ Mail ❑ Pick-up
(Please print clearly on lines below)

_____ Name

_____ Street Address or P.O. Box

_____ City, State, Zip Code

KANSAS

Kansas State Department of Health and Environment
Office of Vital Statistics
First Floor, Room 151
Landon State Office Building
900 S.W. Jackson
Topeka, Kansas 66612-2221

Tel. (785) 296-1400
Fax (785) 296-8075
E-mail: Vital.Records@kdhe.state.ks.us
http://www.kdhe.state.ks.us/vital/index.html

Birth certificates are on file at the Office of Vital Statistics beginning July 1, 1911, with a few delayed birth certificates dating back to the 1960s. Marriage records from May 1, 1913; divorce records from July 1, 1951; and death records from July 1, 1911 are also available. When ordering certificates, make checks or money orders payable to "Kansas Vital Statistics." Expedited service is available by phone (785-296-3253) or fax (785-357-4332), with payment by credit card, for an additional fee of $8.00, plus shipping. Genealogy requests are not considered urgent and must be requested through regular mail.

Cost for a certified Birth Certificate	$10.00
Cost for a wallet-size Birth Certificate	$10.00
Cost for a certified Marriage or Divorce Certificate	$10.00
Cost for a certified Death Certificate	$10.00
Cost for a duplicate copy, when ordered at the same time	$5.00

For earlier records write to:

County Clerk
County Court House
(County Seat), Kansas

For Adoption Record Information write to:

Adoption Program Consultant
Kansas Children and Family Services
300 SW Oakley Street, West Hall
Topeka, Kansas 66606

Tel. (913) 296-8138

Adult adoptees may receive copies of their records at age 18.

Kansas State Historical Society (6425 SW Sixth Avenue, Topeka, KS 66615-1099; 785-272-8681) holds early county marriage and divorce records.

The Family History Library of Salt Lake City, Utah has microfilmed many of the original and published vital records and church registers of Kansas. For details on their holdings please consult your nearest Family History Center.

For further information see:
Manual for the Clerks of the District Courts. Topeka, KS: State of Kansas, 1973. Looseleaf.

APPLICATION FOR CERTIFIED COPY OF BIRTH CERTIFICATE

BIRTH CERTIFICATES ARE ON FILE FROM July 1, 1911 to PRESENT

THIS REQUEST MAY BE REJECTED UNLESS ALL ITEMS ARE COMPLETED AND CORRECT FEES SUBMITTED

APPLICANT'S NAME (PLEASE PRINT) _____

APPLICANT'S MAILING ADDRESS _____

_____

_____
                    CITY   STATE   ZIP CODE

REASON FOR REQUEST (PLEASE BE SPECIFIC) _____

APPLICANT'S DAYTIME PHONE NUMBER _____

APPLICANT'S RELATIONSHIP TO PERSON NAMED ON CERTIFICATE _____

APPLICANT'S IDENTIFICATION NO. (SEE REVERSE SIDE) _____

NUMBER OF CERTIFICATES REQUESTED   FEE INFORMATION ON REVERSE SIDE

_____ CERTIFIED COPIES   _____ WALLET-SIZE   _____ TOTAL FEE
(No parental information on card)

NAME ON RECORD _____
              FIRST   MIDDLE   LAST

DATE OF BIRTH   _____ – _____ – _____   PRESENT AGE OF THIS PERSON _____   RACE _____
         MONTH DAY YEAR   DATE OF DEATH, IF APPLICABLE _____   SEX: M ☐ F ☐

PLACE OF BIRTH _____
        CITY   COUNTY   STATE   HOSPITAL

MOTHER'S NAME _____ BIRTHPLACE _____
      FIRST   MIDDLE   MAIDEN   SS# _____

FATHER'S NAME _____ BIRTHPLACE _____
      FIRST   MIDDLE   LAST   SS# _____

ADOPTED?   YES ☐   NO ☐   Is request for record before adoption?   YES ☐   NO ☐

ORIGINAL NAME, IF KNOWN _____

I hereby declare that as the applicant for a certified copy of the certificate described above, I have direct
interest in the matter recorded and the information therein contained is necessary for the determination of personal or property rights.

PURSUANT TO K.S.A. 65-2422d (c), CERTIFICATES ARE NOT OPEN TO PUBLIC INSPECTION.

SIGNATURE OF APPLICANT _____ TODAY'S DATE _____

FORM VS-235 REV. 2-1997   **(OVER)**

PLEASE ENCLOSE A SELF-ADDRESSED STAMPED ENVELOPE.

ONE IDENTIFICATION IS REQUIRED OF PERSON COMPLETING FORM

Examples of acceptable ID:

1. Driver's License (state and # or copy)
2. Picture ID Card (state and # or copy)
3. Social Services ID (state and #)
4. Employment ID (firm and #)
5. Payroll Stub

6. Social Security Card (# or copy)
7. Credit Card # (issuing company and #)
8. Voter's Registration (state and #)
9. Military ID (# or copy)

A copy of ID is acceptable; DO NOT send original item with application.

FEE INFORMATION
BIRTH CERTIFICATES ARE ON FILE FROM July 1, 1911 TO PRESENT
K.A.R. 28-17-6 requires the following fee(s).
$10.00 for 1 certified copy OR wallet size card and
$ 5.00 for each additional certified copy OR card of the same record ordered at the same time.
The correct fee must be submitted with request.

This fee allows a 5 year search of the records - the year indicated and two years before and two years after, or you may indicate the 5 year period you want searched.
IF THE CERTIFICATE IS NOT LOCATED THE $10.00 FEE MUST BE RETAINED FOR THE SEARCH.

Make checks or money orders payable to KANSAS VITAL STATISTICS. For your protection do not send cash.
Fees expire 12 months from date paid.

Multiple requests may be handled and mailed separately.
Please enclose a self-addressed stamped envelope.

NOTE: The birth registration card does not contain parental information nor an embossed seal (contains ink seal only).

If legal guardianship has been established through the courts, please send copy of guardianship papers.
If name change has occurred, please send copy of court order or proof of original name.

Once an adoption has occurred, the biological family does not have a legal right to the adoptee's record nor does the adoptee have a legal right to the biological family's records.

WARNING: DO NOT MAKE COPIES OF BIRTH RECORDS. It is a violation of K.S.A. 65-2422d (g) and K.S.A. 21-3830 for anyone to make a photocopy of a birth record for personal use, or for anyone to make, sell, or offer for sale, any birth record for false identification purposes. These offenses may be punishable by fine or imprisonment, or both.

KANSAS DEPARTMENT OF HEALTH AND ENVIRONMENT
OFFICE OF VITAL STATISTICS

APPLICATION FOR CERTIFIED COPY OF MARRIAGE CERTIFICATE
MARRIAGE RECORDS ARE ON FILE FROM MAY 1, 1913 TO PRESENT

THIS REQUEST MAY BE REJECTED UNLESS ALL ITEMS ARE COMPLETED AND CORRECT FEES SUBMITTED

I hereby declare that as the applicant for a certified copy of the certificate described below, I have direct interest in the matter recorded and that the information therein contained is necessary for the determination of personal or property rights, pursuant to K.S.A. 65-2422(c). FOR THE PROTECTION OF THE INDIVIDUAL, CERTIFICATES ARE NOT OPEN TO PUBLIC INSPECTION. Proof of legal representation, direct interest, or written authorization is required.

Signature of person
making request _____

Today's
date _____

Relationship to person
named on record _____

Daytime
phone no.(_____) _____

Reason for request
(Please be specific) _____

One identification is required of anyone requesting and/or picking up a vital record. (See reverse side for examples of acceptable ID)

Applicant's Identification No. _____

MARRIAGE INFORMATION (All items must be completed) **(PLEASE PRINT OR TYPE)**

Groom
(full name) _____

Date of
Birth _____

Bride (maiden and previous
married surname) _____

Date of
Birth _____

Date of marriage _____
　　　　　　　　　　　(Month)　　　　　　　(Day)　　　　　　(Year)

County in which marriage license was issued _____

City or town in which marriage took place _____

Print name & address of person to receive record(s)

_____
(Name)

FEE INFORMATION ON REVERSE SIDE

_____
(Street Address)

Number of certified
copies requested _____

_____
(City)　　　　　　(State)　　　　　(Zip)

TOTAL FEE: _____

PLEASE ENCLOSE A BUSINESS SIZE, SELF-ADDRESSED
STAMPED ENVELOPE

Fees expire 12 months from date paid

Form VS-237　Rev. 1993

WARNING: DO NOT MAKE COPIES. It is a violation of State and Federal laws for anyone to make, sell, or offer for sale any marriage record for false identification purposes and is a punishable offense.

IDENTIFICATION INFORMATION

Examples of acceptable ID:

1. Driver's License (state and # or copy)
2. Picture ID Card (state and # or copy)
3. Social Services ID (state and #)
4. Employment ID (firm and #)
5. Payroll Stub
6. Social Security Card (# or copy)
7. Credit Card # (issuing company and #)
8. Voter's Registration (state and #)
9. Military ID (# or copy)

A copy of ID is acceptable; DO NOT send original item with application.

FEE INFORMATION

K.A.R. 28-17-6 requires the following fee(s). Correct fee must be submitted with request.

$10.00 for one certified copy.
$ 5.00 for each additional certified copy of the same record ordered at the same time.

A FEE OF $10.00 MUST BE RETAINED FOR THE SEARCH IF THE CERTIFICATE IS NOT LOCATED. That fee allows a 5 year search of the records – the year indicated and two years before and two years after, or you may indicate the 5 year period you want searched.

Make checks or money orders payable to KANSAS VITAL STATISTICS. For your protection do not send cash.

Multiple requests may be handled and mailed separately.

MAILING ADDRESS

Office of Vital Statistics
Landon State Office Building
900 SW Jackson, Rm. 151
TOPEKA, KS 66612-2221

TELEPHONE
(913) 296-1400

CUSTOMER SERVICE HOURS
9:00 - 4:00, Monday through Friday

KANSAS DEPARTMENT OF HEALTH AND ENVIRONMENT
OFFICE OF VITAL STATISTICS

APPLICATION FOR CERTIFIED COPY OF DIVORCE CERTIFICATE
DIVORCE RECORDS ARE ON FILE FROM JULY 1, 1951 TO PRESENT

THIS REQUEST MAY BE REJECTED UNLESS ALL ITEMS ARE COMPLETED AND CORRECT FEES SUBMITTED

I hereby declare that as the applicant for a certified copy of the certificate described below, I have direct interest in the matter recorded and that the information therein contained is necessary for the determination of personal or property rights, pursuant to K.S.A. 65-2422(c). FOR THE PROTECTION OF THE INDIVIDUAL, CERTIFICATES ARE NOT OPEN TO PUBLIC INSPECTION. Proof of legal representation, direct interest, or written authorization is required.

Signature of person
making request _____

Today's
date _____

Relationship to person
named on record _____

Daytime
phone no. (_____) _____

Reason for request _____
(Please be specific)

One identification is required of anyone requesting and/or picking up a vital record. (See reverse side for examples of acceptable ID)

Applicant's Identification No. _____

DIVORCE INFORMATION (All items must be completed) **(PLEASE PRINT OR TYPE)**

Husband (full name) _____

Wife (maiden and married name) _____

Date divorce was granted _____
                              (Month)   (Day)   (Year)

County in which divorce was granted _____

Date of this marriage _____

Print name & address of person to receive record(s)

_____
(Name)

_____
(Street Address)

_____
(City)   (State)   (Zip)

FEE INFORMATION ON REVERSE SIDE

Number of certified
copies requested _____

TOTAL FEE: _____

PLEASE ENCLOSE A BUSINESS SIZE, SELF-ADDRESSED
STAMPED ENVELOPE

Fees expire 12 months from date paid

Form VS-238   Rev. 1993

WARNING: DO NOT MAKE COPIES. It is a violation of State and Federal laws for anyone to make, sell, or offer for sale any divorce record for false identification purposes and is a punishable offense.

IDENTIFICATION INFORMATION

Examples of acceptable ID:

1. Driver's License (state and # or copy)
2. Picture ID Card (state and # or copy)
3. Social Services ID (state and #)
4. Employment ID (firm and #)
5. Payroll Stub

6. Social Security Card (# or copy)
7. Credit Card # (issuing company and #)
8. Voter's Registration (state and #)
9. Military ID (# or copy)

A copy of ID is acceptable; DO NOT send original item with application.

FEE INFORMATION

K.A.R. 28-17-6 requires the following fee(s). Correct fee must be submitted with request.

$10.00 for one certified copy.
$ 5.00 for each additional certified copy of the same record ordered at the same time.

A FEE OF $10.00 MUST BE RETAINED FOR THE SEARCH IF THE CERTIFICATE IS NOT LOCATED. That fee allows a 5 year search of the records – the year indicated and two years before and two years after, or you may indicate the 5 year period you want searched.

Make checks or money orders payable to KANSAS VITAL STATISTICS. For your protection do not send cash.

Multiple requests may be handled and mailed separately.

MAILING ADDRESS

Office of Vital Statistics
Landon State Office Building
900 SW Jackson, Rm. 151
TOPEKA, KS 66612-2221

TELEPHONE
(913) 296-1400

CUSTOMER SERVICE HOURS
9:00 - 4:00, Monday through Friday

APPLICATION FOR CERTIFIED COPY OF DEATH CERTIFICATE

DEATH CERTIFICATES ARE ON FILE FROM July 1, 1911 to PRESENT

THIS REQUEST MAY BE REJECTED UNLESS ALL ITEMS ARE COMPLETED AND CORRECT FEES SUBMITTED

APPLICANT'S NAME (PLEASE PRINT) _____

APPLICANT'S MAILING ADDRESS _____

_____

| | CITY | STATE | ZIP CODE |

REASON FOR REQUEST (PLEASE BE SPECIFIC) _____

APPLICANT'S DAYTIME PHONE NUMBER _____

APPLICANT'S RELATIONSHIP TO PERSON NAMED ON CERTIFICATE _____

APPLICANT'S IDENTIFICATION NO. (SEE REVERSE SIDE) _____

| **NUMBER OF CERTIFICATES REQUESTED** | **FEE INFORMATION ON REVERSE SIDE** |
| _____ CERTIFIED COPIES | _____ TOTAL FEE |

FULL NAME OF DECEASED _____
FIRST   MIDDLE   LAST

PLACE OF DEATH _____
CITY   COUNTY   STATE

DATE OF DEATH ____ – ____ – ____   CHECK IF STILLBIRTH ☐   RACE _____
MONTH   DAY   YEAR   SEX: M ☐   F ☐

RESIDENCE AT DEATH _____   MARITAL STATUS AT DEATH _____

NAME OF SPOUSE (if applicable) _____

FATHER'S NAME/MOTHER'S MAIDEN NAME _____

AGE AT TIME OF DEATH (or birth date) _____   PLACE OF BIRTH _____

FUNERAL HOME _____

CITY/COUNTY WHERE BURIED _____
CITY   COUNTY

I hereby declare that as the applicant for a certified copy of the certificate described above, I have direct interest in the matter recorded and the information therein contained is necessary for the determination of personal or property rights.

PURSUANT TO K.S.A. 65-2422d (c), CERTIFICATES ARE NOT OPEN TO PUBLIC INSPECTION.

SIGNATURE OF APPLICANT _____   TODAY'S DATE _____

FORM VS-236 REV. 2-1997

(OVER)

PLEASE ENCLOSE A SELF-ADDRESSED STAMPED ENVELOPE.

ONE IDENTIFICATION IS REQUIRED OF PERSON COMPLETING FORM

Examples of acceptable ID:

1. Driver's License (state and # or copy)
2. Picture ID Card (state and # or copy)
3. Social Services ID (state and #)
4. Employment ID (firm and #)
5. Payroll Stub

6. Social Security Card (# or copy)
7. Credit Card # (issuing company and #)
8. Voter's Registration (state and #)
9. Military ID (# or copy)

A copy of ID is acceptable. DO NOT send original item with application.

FEE INFORMATION
DEATH RECORDS ARE ON FILE FROM July 1, 1911 TO PRESENT

K.A.R. 28-17-6 requires the following fee(s). See chart below.
$10.00 for 1 certified copy and $5.00 for each additional certified copy of the same record ordered at the same time.
The correct fee must be submitted with the request.

This fee allows a 5 year search of the records - the year indicated and two years before and two years after,
or you may indicate the 5 year period you want searched.
IF THE CERTIFICATE IS NOT LOCATED A $10.00 FEE MUST BE RETAINED FOR THE SEARCH.
Make checks or money orders payable to KANSAS VITAL STATISTICS. For your protection do not send cash.
Fees expire 12 months from date paid.

Multiple requests may be handled and mailed separately.
Please enclose a self-addressed stamped envelope.

WARNING: DO NOT MAKE COPIES OF DEATH RECORDS. It is a violation of K.S.A. 65-2422d (g), or for anyone to make a photocopy of a death record. These offenses may be punishable by fine or imprisonment, or both.

$10.00 for 1 certified copy and $5.00 for each additional certified copy of the same record ordered at the same time.

NUMBER OF CERTIFIED COPIES	FEE REQUIRED
1	$ 10.00
2	$ 15.00
3	$ 20.00
4	$ 25.00
5	$ 30.00
6	$ 35.00
7	$ 40.00
8	$ 45.00
9	$ 50.00
10	$ 55.00

KENTUCKY

Send your requests to:

Department for Health Services
Office of Vital Statistics
275 East Main Street

Tel. (502) 564-4212
Fax (502) 227-0032
http://publichealth.state.ky.us/vital.htm

The Office of Vital Statistics has birth and death records from January 1, 1911 and marriage and divorce records from June 1, 1958. Expedited service is available (with payment by credit card) for an additional fee of $5.00, plus shipping.

After 50 years death certificates are transferred to the Public Records Division of the Kentucky Department for Libraries and Archives (300 Coffee Tree Road, PO Box 537, Frankfort, KY 40602-0537; 502-564-8704). The Public Records Division has microfilm copies of vital records from 1852–1910, deaths from 1911–1944, and indexes to all vital records from 1911 to 1954.

The Online Kentucky Vital Records Index (http://ukcc.uky.edu/~vitalrec/) lists deaths from 1911 to 1992 and marriages and divorces from 1973 to 1993.

Cost for a certified Birth Certificate	$10.00
Cost for a certified Marriage Certificate	$6.00
Cost for a certified Divorce Record	$6.00
Cost for a certified Death Certificate	$6.00

For earlier records write to:

County Clerk
County Court House
(County Seat), Kentucky

For vital records from 1852–1862, 1872–1910:

Public Records Division
Kentucky Department for Libraries and Archives
300 Coffee Tree Road
P. O. Box 537
Frankfort, Kentucky 40602-0537

Tel. (502) 564-8704
E-Mail: rjohnson@ctr.kdla.state.ky.us
http://www.kdla.state.ky.us/arch/vitastat.htm

For Adoption Record information write to:

Adult Adoptees Program
Kentucky Department of Social Services
275 East Main Street, 6th Floor
Frankfort, Kentucky 40621

Tel. (502) 564-2147

Kentucky Historical Society (P.O. Box H, Frankfort, KY 40602) has records of births, marriages and deaths 1851 to 1861; 1874–1878 (microfilm); indexes for births, deaths 1911–1969 and 1911–1986 (microfiche). The Family History Library of Salt Lake City, Utah has (microfilm) births, 1874–1878, 1907–1910, 1939–1954; marriages, 1875–1878, 1906–1914; and deaths, 1874–1878, 1905–1910, 1939–1954; and an additional index to births and deaths from 1911–1954.

For further information see:

Duff, Jeffrey Michael. *A Guide to Kentucky Birth, Marriage and Death Records, 1852–1910.* Rev. ed. Frankfort, KY: Public Records Division KY Department for Libraries & Archives, 1988. 72p.

COMMONWEALTH OF KENTUCKY
STATE REGISTRAR OF VITAL STATISTICS

APPLICATION FOR BIRTH CERTIFICATE

Please Print Or Type All Information Required On This Form

Name on Certificate _____   Sex _____

Date of Birth _____   Kentucky County of Birth _____

Mother's Full Maiden Name _____

Father's Name _____

Hospital _____

_____   Phone: _____
(Signature of Applicant)   (Area Code)   (Number)

Relationship To Person Named On Certificate _____

Office Use Only
Vol _____
Cert _____
Year _____
Date _____
Initials _____

A $10.00 fee must accompany this application.
KRS 213.141 mandates that $3.00 of this fee be used toward the
prevention of child abuse and that $1.00 of this fee be used to provide
coverage for inherited metabolic disease products for uninsured children.

The $10.00 fee cannot be returned if the certificate is not found. If the certificate is on file you will receive one
copy. Additional copies are $10.00 each. Make check or money order payable to **"Kentucky State Treasurer"**.
When complete, mail the entire form to: **Vital Statistics, 275 East Main 1E-A, Frankfort, Kentucky 40621.**

....

Certified Copies - $10.00 Each Copy – Number of copies desired _____

Name and Mailing Address Required

_____

_____

_____

**If you have not received your certificate(s)
within 30 working days from the postmarked
date of mailing, please contact the Office of
VITAL STATISTICS at: 502-564-4212**

Applicant's Phone _____
(Area Code)   (Number)

VS-230
(Rev. 5/92)

COMMONWEALTH OF KENTUCKY
DEPARTMENT FOR HEALTH SERVICES
State Registrar of Vital Statistics

APPLICATION FOR MARRIAGE/DIVORCE CERTIFICATE

Please Print or Type All Information Requested on This Form.

Please Circle Type of Record Requested.

Full Name of Husband _____

Maiden Name of Wife _____

County In Which   (Marriage License)   (Divorce Decree)   Granted _____
                              (Circle One)

Date of   (Marriage)   (Divorce)   _____
                (Circle One)   (Mo.)   (Day)   (Year)

Name of Applicant _____

Address _____

The Information I Am Requesting Concerns
(Marriage)   (Divorce)
(Circle One)

Please Indicate Quantity Desired _____

Office Use Only	
Vol.	_____
Cert.	_____
Year	_____
Date	_____
Initials	_____

A $6.00 fee must accompany this application. The fee cannot be returned. If the certificate is on file you will receive one copy. Additional copies are $6.00 each. Make check or money order payable to "Kentucky State Treasurer". When complete, mail the entire form to Vital Statistics, 275 East Main Street, Frankfort, Kentucky 40621.

Print Name and Mailing Address of Person to Receive the Certificate.
This Portion is a Mailing Insert and Will be Used to Mail the Copy you
Have Requested.

_____
Name

_____
Street Number & Name

_____
City-State-Zip Code

VS-31
(Rev. 9/96)

APPLICATION FOR DEATH CERTIFICATE

Please Print Or Type All Information Required On This Form.

Full Name of Deceased _____

Date of Death _____   Ky. County in Which
(Mo.)   (Day)   (Year)   Death Occurred _____

Did Death Occur In a Hospital?   ❑ Yes   ❑ No   Age at Death _____

If "Yes" Give Name of Hospital _____

Name of Attending Physician _____

Name of Funeral Director _____

Address _____
(Street)   (City)   (State)

Name of Applicant_____

Address _____
(Street)   (City)   (State)

_____ Phone: _____
(Signature of Applicant)   (Area Code)   (Number)

A **$6.00** fee must accompany this application. The fee cannot be returned. If the certificate is on file you will receive a copy. Additional copies are **$6.00** each. Make check or money order payable to "Kentucky State Treasurer". When complete, mail the entire form to **Vital Statistics, 275 East Main Street, Frankfort, Kentucky 40621**.

Please Indicate Quantity Desired _____

- -

Print Name and Mailing Address of Person to Receive the Certificate.
This Portion is a Mailing Insert and will be used to Mail the Copy you
Have Requested.

_____
_____
_____

LOUISIANA

Send your requests to:

Louisiana Department of Health and Hospitals
Office of Public Health
Vital Records Registry
P.O. Box 60630
New Orleans, Louisiana 70160-0630

Tel. (504) 568-8353
Recording (504) 568-5152
Fax (504) 568-5391
http://www.dhh.state.la.us/oph/vital/Index.htm

The Vital Records Registry has records of births for the past 100 years, deaths for the past 50 years, and Orleans Parish marriage records for the past 50 years. Expedited service is available (with payment by credit card) for an additional fee of $15.50 to cover Federal Express shipping costs.

Cost for a certified Birth Certificate	$15.00
Cost for a wallet-size Birth Certificate	$9.00
Cost for a certified Marriage Certificate	$5.00
Cost for a certified Death Certificate	$5.00

For Marriage Records outside of Orleans Parish write to:

Clerk of Court
(Parish Seat), Louisiana

For Orleans Parish Birth Records over 100 years old, Marriage and Death records over 50 years old; and statewide Death Records over 50 years old, write to:

Louisiana State Archives
3851 Essen Lane
Baton Rouge, Louisiana 70809-2137

Tel. (504) 922-1206
http://www.sec.state.la.us/archives/archives/archives-index.htm

Orleans Parish was the only parish in Louisiana that maintained birth and death records prior to it being mandated by the state legislature in 1918. Records from Orleans Parish are filed separately from the combined statewide listing of all the other parishes in the state. Records prior to 1918 for other parishes are probably nonexistent unless the parish where the birth or death occurred kept such a record. If the person being researched was Catholic, his birth and death would probably be shown in the records of the church or diocese where that person lived.

For Adoption Record information write to:

Louisiana Voluntary Registry
P.O. Box 3318
Baton Rouge, Louisiana 70821

Tel. (504) 342-9922, (800) 259-2456
http://www.dss.state.la.us/offocs/html/registry.html

Cost for registering with the Voluntary Registry $25.00

The City Archives at the New Orleans Public Library (219 Loyola Avenue, New Orleans, LA 70112-2044; 504-596-2610) holds microfilm copies of New Orleans deaths, 1804–1915; death indexes 1804–1916, 1927–1929, 1957–1968; an index to death certificates for the State of Louisiana, 1971–1976; and the Jefferson City Register of Deaths, 1868–1870. It holds extensive collections of marriage records and indexes, including microfilmed county records from across the state. The Archives does not have birth certificates.

For further information see:

Hamer, Colin, Jr. *Genealogical Materials in the New Orleans Public Library*. New Orleans, LA: New Orleans Public Library.
Louisiana Handbook on Fetal Death Registration. New Orleans, LA: LA Divison of Records and Statistics, 1994. 31p.

DEPARTMENT OF HEALTH AND HOSPITALS
OFFICE OF PUBLIC HEALTH
VITAL RECORDS REGISTRY

PHS 520A   **APPLICATION FOR CERTIFIED COPY OF BIRTH/DEATH CERTIFICATE**   (Rev. 1/97)

FOR SERVICE BY MAIL: SUBMIT CHECK OR MONEY ORDER PAYABLE TO VITAL RECORDS. MAIL TO: VITAL RECORDS REGISTRY, P.O. BOX 60630, NEW ORLEANS, LA 70160. **PLEASE DO NOT SEND CASH.** IF NO RECORD IS FOUND, YOU WILL BE NOTIFIED AND FEES WILL BE RETAINED FOR THE SEARCH.

☐ BIRTHCARD   BIRTHCARD: $ 9.00
☐ BIRTH CERTIFICATE   BIRTH CERTIFICATE: $15.00
☐ DEATH CERTIFICATE   DEATH CERTIFICATE: $ 5.00

*See Note Below: _____
NAME AT BIRTH/DEATH (FIRST, MIDDLE, LAST)

_____   _____
DATE OF BIRTH/DEATH   SEX

_____   _____
CITY OF BIRTH/DEATH   PARISH OF BIRTH/DEATH

_____
FATHER'S NAME (FOR BIRTH RECORD ONLY)

_____
MOTHER'S MAIDEN NAME - BEFORE MARRIAGE (FOR BIRTH RECORD ONLY)

HOW ARE YOU RELATED TO THE PERSON WHOSE RECORD YOU ARE REQUESTING?_____

PRINT YOUR ADDRESS:
Name_____
Street or
Route No._____   Number of
City   Copies Requested: _____
and State_____
                                      ZIP CODE   Total Fees Due $_____
Home   Office
Phone No._____ Phone No._____

I AM AWARE THAT ANY PERSON WHO WILLFULLY AND KNOWINGLY MAKES ANY FALSE STATEMENT IN AN APPLICATION FOR A CERTIFIED COPY OF A VITAL RECORD IS SUBJECT UPON CONVICTION TO A FINE OF NOT MORE THAN $10,000 OR IMPRISONMENT OF NOT MORE THAN FIVE YEARS, OR BOTH.

Signature of Applicant _____

*PLEASE NOTE: Birth records **over 100 years** old and Death records **over 50 years** old are obtained by writing the Louisiana State Archives, P.O. Box 94125, Baton Rouge, LA 70804-9125. Please make check PAYABLE TO: Secretary of State.

CERTIFICATE TO BE MAILED TO:

Name_____
Street or
Route No. _____
City
and State_____
                                      ZIP CODE

SEARCH METHOD	EMPLOYEE	DATE
TRANSMITTAL:	_____	_____
COMPUTER:	_____	_____
MICROFILM:	_____	_____
BOOK INDICES:	_____	_____
CHARITY CARDS:	_____	_____
DELAY CARDS:	_____	_____
HAND SEARCHED:	_____	_____
OTHER (INDICATE)		
_____	_____	_____
_____	_____	_____
CERTIFICATE #	_____	

DEPARTMENT OF HEALTH AND HUMAN RESOURCES
OFFICE OF PREVENTIVE AND PUBLIC HEALTH SERVICES
VITAL RECORDS REGISTRY

APPLICATION FOR CERTIFIED COPY OF MARRIAGE CERTIFICATE

PHS 520C   (Rev. 9/87)

FOR SERVICE BY MAIL: SUBMIT CHECK OR MONEY ORDER PAYABLE TO VITAL RECORDS. MAIL TO: VITAL RECORDS REGISTRY, P.O. BOX 60630, NEW ORLEANS, LA 70160. **PLEASE DO NOT SEND CASH.** IF NO RECORD IS FOUND, YOU WILL BE NOTIFIED AND FEES WILL BE RETAINED FOR THE SEARCH.

MARRIAGE RECORD OF: FEE: $5.00 ea

Groom (First, Middle, Last)

Bride (First, Middle, Maiden Name)

Parish where License was Purchased

Date of Marriage

PLEASE NOTE: A MARRIAGE RECORD IS AVAILABLE FROM THE VITAL RECORDS REGISTRY ONLY IF THE MARRIAGE LICENSE WAS PURCHASED IN ORLEANS PARISH. OTHERWISE YOU MUST CONTACT THE CLERK OF COURT IN THE PARISH WHERE THE LICENSE WAS PURCHASED.

PRINT YOUR ADDRESS

Name _____   Number of Copies
                                            Requested _____

Street or
Route No. _____   Total Fees Due $_____

City and
State _____
                        Zip Code
Home   Office
Phone No. _____   Phone No. _____

- -

Certificate to be mailed to:

            Name _____

            Street or
            Route No. _____

            City
            and State _____
                            Zip Code

Louisiana Secretary of State
Birth/ Death/ Marriage Records
APPLICATION FOR A CERTIFIED COPY

You **must** check one of the following categories. Please print information clearly.

1. _____ Orleans Parish birth record (over 100 years old)*

2. _____ Orleans Parish/ Statewide death record (over 50 years old)*

_____
Name (First, Middle, Last)

_____
Date (If unknown, indicate three years to be researched)

_____
City   Parish

3. ____ Orleans Parish marriage record (over 50 years old)**

_____
Groom's Name (First, Middle, Last)

_____
Bride's Name (First, Middle, Maiden Name)

_____
Date (If unknown, indicate three years to be researched)

Submit check or money order to:
Secretary of State, Vital Records, P.O. Box 94125, Baton Rouge, LA 70804
Please do not send cash!

Name_____

Address_____

_____

City/State/Zip Code_____

Telephone number (day) including area code _____

Number of copies requested _____ Total fees due ($5 each) $_____

For more recent records, contact Vital Records Registry, P.O. Box 60630, New
Orleans, LA 70160; Phone (504) 568-5150 or 568-5152.

Send your requests from 1923 to the present to:

Maine Department of Human Services
Office of Vital Statistics
221 State Street
State House, Station #11
Augusta, Maine 04333-0011

Tel. (207) 287-3181
Fax (207) 287-1907

The Office of Vital Statistics has birth, marriage, divorce, and death records from January 1, 1923. Earlier records from the 1600s to 1955 and a marriage index from 1892 to 1966 are at the Maine State Archives. They provide certified or uncertified copies. Expedited service is available (with payment by credit card) for an additional fee of $5.00.

Cost for a certified Birth Certificate	$10.00
Cost for a certified Marriage or Divorce Certificate	$10.00
Cost for a certified Death Certificate	$10.00
Cost for an uncertified Vital Record	$ 6.00
Cost for a duplicate copy, when ordered at the same time	$ 4.00
Cost for registration in Adoption Reunion Registry	$20.00

For pre-1923 vital records write to:

Maine State Archives
State House Station 84
Augusta, Maine 04333-0084

Tel. (207) 287-5790
Fax (207) 287-5739
http://www.state.me.us/sos/arc/archives/genealog/genie.htm

Online Marriages Index, 1892–1966, 1977–1996:

http://thor.ddp.state.me.us/archives/plsql/archdev.Marriage_Archive.search_form

Online Deaths Index, 1960–1996:

http://thor.ddp.state.me.us/archives/plsql/archdev.death_archive.search_form

For Adoption Record information write to:

Maine Adoption Reunion Registry
Maine Department of Human Services
Office of Vital Statistics
(Same address as given above)

Tel. (207) 287-3181
Fax (207) 287-1907

The Family History Library of Salt Lake City, Utah has microfilms of births, marriages, and deaths from 1670 to 1922. They also have a bride's marriage index from 1895 to 1953.

For further information see:

Hospital Vital Statistics Handbook. Augusta, ME: ME Department of Human Services, Office of Data, Research and Vital Statistics, 1994.
A Manual for Clerks, Maine District Courts. Boston, MA: National Center for State Courts, Northeastern Regional Office, 1975. 283p.
Municipal Clerk's Vital Statistics Handbook. Augusta, ME: Department of Human Services, 1993.
The Vital Records Reporter. Augusta, ME: State of Maine, Department of Human Services, Office of Data, Research and Vital Statistics.

MAINE DEPARTMENT OF HUMAN SERVICES
OFFICE OF VITAL STATISTICS

APPLICATION FOR A SEARCH AND CERTIFIED COPY OF A VITAL RECORD

Applicant:

Please fill in the information in the appropriate box for the record you are requesting, the reason for requesting the record, and the name and address for mailing the certified copy. Enclose a check or money order payable to TREASURER, STATE OF MAINE and mail application to:

> DEPARTMENT OF HUMAN SERVICES
> OFFICE OF VITAL STATISTICS
> STATE HOUSE STATION 11
> AUGUSTA, MAINE 04333-0011

BIRTH RECORD

Full Name of Child
Date of Birth
Place of Birth
Farther's Full Name
Mother's Maiden Name

DEATH RECORD

Full Name of Decendent
Date of Death
Place of Death

MARRIAGE RECORD

Full Name of Groom
Full Maiden Name of Bride
Date of Marriage
Place of Marriage

DIVORCE RECORD

Full Name of Husband
Full Maiden Name of Wife
Date of Divorce or Annulment
Place Superior Court, County or District(Division)

Reason for requesting <u>Record:</u>

Print or type name and address to whom the record is to be sent.

Applicant signature: _____ _____

VS-107 R1/92

Applicant address: _____

MARYLAND

Send your requests to:

Maryland Department of Health & Mental Hygiene
Division of Vital Records
6550 Reisterstown Road Plaza
PO Box 68760
Baltimore, Maryland 21215-0020

Tel. (410) 764-3038
Recording (410) 318-6119
Inside Maryland (800) 832-3277
Fax (410) 358-0738
http://www.dhmh.state.md.us/html/vitalrec.htm

The Division of Vital Records has birth and death records from August 1, 1898; marriage records from June 1, 1951; divorce records from July 1, 1961; Baltimore birth and death records from January 1, 1875; and adoptions records pre-June 1, 1947 (earlier records require a court order). The office will provide divorce verification only. Certified copies of a divorce decree must be obtained from the Clerk of the Circuit Court in the county where the divorce was granted. Expedited service is available for an additional fee of $7.00 (with payment by credit card) by phoning (410) 764-3170 or faxing (410) 358-7381.

Cost for a certified Birth Certificate	$6.00
Cost for a commemorative Birth Certificate	$25.00
Cost for a certified Marriage Certificate	$6.00
Cost for verification of a Divorce	Free
Cost for a certified Death Certificate	$6.00

For Marriage Records before June 1, 1951 write to:

Clerk of the Circuit Court
(Town), Maryland

For Births, August 1, 1898–1978; Adoptions pre-June 1, 1947; Marriages pre-1914; Deaths, 1898–1987; Baltimore City Births 1875–1978 and Deaths, 1875–1987, write to:

Maryland State Archives
350 Rowe Boulevard
Annapolis, Maryland 21401-1602

Tel. (410) 974-3914
Fax (410) 974-3895
http://www.mdarchives.state.md.us/

The Archives also has divorce records for Baltimore City and several counties, into the 1980s for some jurisdictions.

For Adoption Record information write to:

Mutual Consent Voluntary Adoption Registry
Maryland Department of Human Resources
311 West Saratoga Street
Baltimore, Maryland 21201-3521

Tel. (410) 767-7423
E-mail: archives@mdarchives.state.md.us
http://www.gl.umbc.edu/~hickman/voladopr.htm

Cost to Register in Voluntary Adoption Registry $25.00

STATE OF MARYLAND
DEPARTMENT OF HEALTH & MENTAL HYGIENE
DIVISION OF VITAL RECORDS
P.O. BOX 68760
BALTIMORE, MARYLAND 21215-0020

Send Check or Money Order Payable to.
DIVISION OF VITAL RECORDS

APPLICATION FOR A COPY OR ABSTRACT OF BIRTH CERTIFICATE

PLEASE PRINT   Date:_____ ____

Full name at birth: _____
                        (First)   (Middle)   (Last)

Date of birth: _____ Sex _____
                  (Month)   (Day)   (Year)

Age last birthday: _____ Certificate No. (If known): _____

Place of birth: _____ County _____

Name of hospital (If known): _____

Full name of father: _____

Full maiden name of mother: _____

Your relationship to person on the certificate _____

NOTE: A non-refundable $6.00 fee is required for each certificate requested. You may apply in person
or by mail. **DO NOT SEND CASH OR STAMPS.** Birth records are on file beginning 1875 for
Baltimore City and 1898 for Maryland counties. For County birth records prior to 1898,
contact the Maryland State Archives.

<u>IMPORTANT</u>: **PLEASE INDICATE IN THE BOX BELOW THE NUMBER OF CERTIFICATES REQUESTED**
CERTIFIED COPY: This certificate can be used for all purposes.

[   ]   APPLICANT'S NAME (Print): _____

           APPLICANT'S SIGNATURE: _____

           MAILING ADDRESS: _____

           CITY AND STATE: _____

           ZIP CODE: _____ TELEPHONE # _____

*Any person who willfully uses or attempts to use the requested certificate(s) for fraudulent or
deceptive purposes is guilty of a misdemeanor and on conviction is subject to a fine not exceeding
$500.00 in accordance with MD Health-General Article, Annotated Code, Section 4-227.*

VR C-31

STATE OF MARYLAND
DEPARTMENT OF HEALTH AND MENTAL HYGIENE
DIVISION OF VITAL RECORDS
P.O. BOX 68760
BALTIMORE, MARYLAND 21215-0020

Send Check or Money Order Payable to:
DIVISION OF VITAL RECORDS

DO NOT WRITE IN ABOVE SPACE

APPLICATION FOR A COPY OF MARRIAGE CERTIFICATE

Date_____ _____

Groom's name_____
          (First)   (Middle)   (Last)

Bride's maiden name_____
          (First)   (Middle)   (Last)

Date of marriage_____
          (Month)   (Day)   (Year)

Place of marriage_____
          (Town)   (County)

Reason for request_____

Who do you represent_____

NOTE: A non-refundable $6.00 fee is required for each certificate requested. If the search provides no record, the $6.00 fee is not returned, and a certificate of no record will be issued. You may apply in person or by mail. When applying by mail, please enclose a self-addressed, stamped legal size envelope. **DO NOT SEND CASH OR STAMPS.** For marriages performed PRIOR TO JUNE 1, 1951, certified copies of certificates are available at the Circuit Court of the County in which the marriage took place and the Maryland State Archives, 350 Rowe Boulevard, Annapolis, Maryland 21401, 410-974-3914/3916.

IMPORTANT: **PLEASE INDICATE BELOW THE NUMBER OF COPIES REQUESTED.**

[ ]   **CERTIFIED PHOTOCOPY**

      APPLICANT'S NAME (Print):_____

      APPLICANT'S SIGNATURE_____

      ADDRESS_____

      CITY AND STATE_____

      ZIP CODE_____

VR C-80
DHMH 1937
REV. 9/98

STATE OF MARYLAND
DEPARTMENT OF HEALTH & MENTAL HYGIENE
DIVISION OF VITAL RECORDS
P.O.BOX 68760
BALTIMORE, MARYLAND 21215-0020

Send Check or Money Order Payable to:

DIVISION OF VITAL RECORDS   **DO NOT WRITE IN ABOVE SPACE**

★★

APPLICATION FOR A COPY OF DEATH CERTIFICATE

Date_____ ____

NOTE: A non-refundable $6.00 fee is required for each certificate requested. If the search provides no record, the $6.00 fee is not returned, and a certificate of No Record will be issued. You may apply in person or by mail. When applying by mail, please enclose a self-addressed, stamp envelope. **DO NOT SEND CASH OR STAMPS.** We do not issue records prior to 1969 for genealogical purposes. If you desire a death certificate for genealogical purposes, please contact the Maryland Hall of Records. 350 Rowe Boulevard, Annapolis, Maryland 21401, 410-974-3914/3916.

Name of deceased_____
                 (First)   (Middle)   (Last)

Sex _____ Date of death_____ Age at death_____
                 (Month)   (Day)   (Year)
Funeral home_____

Place of death regardless of residence_____
                                    (Town)   (County)

Reason for request_____

Your relation to deceased_____

IMPORTANT: PLEASE INDICATE BELOW THE NUMBER OF COPIES REQUESTED.

[   ] **CERTIFIED PHOTOCOPY (S)**

APPLICANT'S NAME(Print)_____

APPLICANT'S SIGNATURE_____

ADDRESS_____

CITY AND STATE_____

ZIP CODE_____TELEPHONE #_____

VR C-.34
DHMH 4326
REV. 9/98.

Send your requests to:

Massachusetts Executive Office of Health and Human Services   Tel. (617) 740-2600
Department of Public Health   http://www.magnet.state.ma.us/dph/rvr.htm
Registry of Vital Records and Statistics
150 Mt. Vernon Street, 1st floor
Dorchester, Massachusetts 02125-3105

The Registry of Vital Records and Statistics has records of births, deaths, and marriages from January 1, 1906. Every five years the earliest five years of records maintained at the Registry are transferred to the custody of the State Archives. The next transfer will occur in 2001. After the transfer any restrictions that may be on the transferred records will be removed. Expedited service is available for an additional fee (with payment by credit card) by phoning (617) 740-2606 or faxing (617) 825-7725. The cost of the certificates varies according to the method used to purchase the copy.

Cost for a certified Birth Certificate, in person	$6.00
Cost for a certified Birth Certificate, by mail	$11.00
Cost for a certified Birth Certificate, by expedited mail	$14.00
Cost for an heirloom Birth Certificate, in person	$25.00
Cost for an heirloom Birth Certificate, by mail	$30.00
Cost for a certified Marriage Certificate, in person	$6.00
Cost for a certified Marriage Certificate, by mail	$11.00
Cost for a certified Marriage Certificate, by expedited mail	$14.00
Cost for a certified Death Certificate, in person	$6.00
Cost for a certified Death Certificate, by mail	$11.00
Cost for a certified Death Certificate, by expedited mail	$14.00

For earlier records from 1841 to 1905 write to:

Massachusetts State Archives   Tel. (617) 727-2816
220 Morrissey Boulevard   http://www.magnet.state.ma.us/sec/arc/arcidx.htm
Boston, Massachusetts 02125-3384

The State Archives has records from 1841 to 1905. For pre-1841 records, write to the Town Clerk in the city or town where the event occurred. Births and deaths from 1906 are restricted.

For Adoption Record information write to:

Massachusetts Department of Social Services   Tel. (617) 748-2400
24 Farnsworth Street
Boston, Massachusetts 02210

The Family History Library of Salt Lake City, Utah has microfilmed many of the original and published vital records and church registers of Massachusetts including vital records from 1841 to 1899; corrections of the vital records made from 1893 to 1970, and of the indexes from 1891 to 1971. For details on their holdings please consult your nearest Family History Center.

MASSACHUSETTS DEPARTMENT OF PUBLIC HEALTH
REGISTRY OF VITAL RECORDS AND STATISTICS
150 MT. VERNON STREET, 1st Floor
DORCHESTER, MA 02125-3105
APPLICATION FOR VITAL RECORD
(Please print legibly.)

Please fill out and return this form to the address above, along with a stamped, self-addressed, business-letter-sized envelope and a personal check or money order for $11.00 for each record. Make checks payable to the Registry of Vital Records. Do not submit more than 5 requests per letter. DO NOT SEND CASH THROUGH THE MAIL.

BIRTH RECORD   Number of copies:_____

Name of Subject:_____
(first)   (middle)   (last)
Date of Birth:	City or Town of Birth:
Mother's Name:_____
(first)   (middle)   (maiden)   (last)
Father's Name:_____
(first)   (middle)   (last)

MARRIAGE RECORD   Number of copies:_____

Name of Groom:_____
(first)   (middle)   (last)
Name of Bride:_____
(first)   (middle)   (maiden)
Date of Marriage:	City or Town of Marriage:

DEATH RECORD   Number of copies:_____

Name of Deceased:_____
(first)   (middle)   (last)   (maiden, if applicable)
Spouse's Name:_____
(first)   (middle)   (last)   (maiden, if applicable)
Social Security Number (if known):
Date of Death:	City or Town of Death:
Father's Name:_____
(first)   (middle)   (last)
Mother's Name:_____
(first)   (middle)   (maiden)   (last)

Relationship of requestor to subject(s) named on record:_____

Mail record to:	
Address:	
City/State/ZIP Code:	
Your signature:	
Date of request:	

Send your requests to:

Michigan Department of Community Health
Vital Records Requests
3423 North Martin Luther King, Jr., Blvd.
P.O. Box 30195
Lansing, Michigan 48909-7535

Tel. (517) 335-8656
Fax (517) 321-5884
E-mail: PelmearJ@state.mi.us
http://www.mdch.state.mi.us/PHA/OSR/frame.htm

The Vital Records Offices has records of births, marriages, and deaths from 1867, and divorces from 1897. You can order a copy of a Michigan vital record from the Office's web site, using your credit card; expedited service (with payment by credit card) is also available by phone or fax. There is a $5.00 handling fee for all credit card orders, plus Federal Express shipping charges for expedited service. Michigan death records from 1867 to 1882 can be searched online at **http://www.mdch.state.mi.us/PHA/OSR/ gendis/index.htm**.

Cost for a certified Birth Certificate	$13.00
Cost for a wallet-size Birth Certificate	$13.00
Cost for a certified Marriage Certificate	$13.00
Cost for a certified Marriage Certificate	$13.00
Cost for a certified Death Certificate	$13.00
Cost for a duplicate copy, when ordered at the same time	$4.00

For earlier records write to:

County Clerk
County Court House
(County Seat), Michigan

For Adoption Record information write to:

Michigan Central Adoption Registry
Michigan Department of Social Services
P.O. Box 30037
Lansing, Michigan 48909

Tel. (517) 373-3513

The Family History Library of Salt Lake City, Utah has microfilmed many of the original and published vital records and church registers of Michigan. For details on their holdings please consult your nearest Family History Center.

For further information see:

Michigan County Clerks Genealogy Directory. Lansing, MI: State Archives of Michigan.

1989 Update, Survey of Vital Records Services Offered to Genealogists by Local Registrar's Offices. Lansing, MI: Office of the State Registrar and Center for Health Statistics, 1989. 23p.

Wilbour, Cressy Livingston. *Registration of Vital Statistics in Michigan*. Lansing, MI: Michigan State Medical Society, 1894. 17p.

REGISTRATION NUMBER

_____

APPLICATION FOR A CERTIFIED COPY OF A BIRTH RECORD

PRINT CLEARLY

1. Name at Birth or
   Adopted Name_____ Date of Birth_____

   First   Middle   Last   Month Day Year

2. Place of Birth_____

   Hospital (if known)   City   County

3. Mother's Maiden Name_____

   First   Middle   Last

4. Father's Name_____

   First   Middle   Last

5. Is the individual named in No. 1 adopted?   ☐ Yes   ☐ No   ☐ Maybe

   If the information is available and you are the individual named in No. 1, or if the record is being sent to the individual named in No. 1, do you wish to receive the name and location of the court where the adoption took place? ☐ Yes   ☐ No

6. | PLEASE PROVIDE IN THIS SPACE ANY ADDITIONAL INFORMATION THAT WOULD HELP US LOCATE THE RECORD SUCH AS A LEGAL CHANGE OF NAME, YEAR OF NAME CHANGE, OR COUNTY OF NAME CHANGE. |
   | --- |

7. Please place an "X" in the appropriate area and follow additional instructions.
   My relationship to the person in Line 1 is:

   ☐ Individual named in Line 1   ☐ Parent named on record   ☐ Legal guardian

   ☐ Legal Representative - Whom are you representing? _____

   ☐ Heir - Specify your relationship to the person in line 1 _____

   > IF YOU STATED YOUR RELATIONSHIP AS AN HEIR, PLEASE PROVIDE THE DATE AND PLACE OF DEATH OF THE PERSON NAMED IN LINE 1.
   >
   > _____
   > DATE OF DEATH
   >
   > _____
   > PLACE OF DEATH

8. Applicant's
   Signature_____

   Signature of Applicant   Date

   Applicant's
   Address_____

   Street   City State Zip Area Code Telephone Number

APPLICATION MUST BE SIGNED TO PROCESS YOUR REQUEST

PLEASE DO NOT REMOVE THIS STUB

THIS IS A MAILING INSERT AND WILL BE USED TO MAIL THE RECORD(S)

PRINT THE NAME AND MAILING ADDRESS OF THE
PERSON TO WHOM THE RECORD(S) ARE TO BE SENT ▽

9. Name_____

   Street_____

   City/State_____ Zip_____

PLEASE SEND THE FOLLOWING

	Fee	
☐ Certified Photocopy	@ $13.00 _____	
☐ *Senior Citizen Fee* Certified Photocopy 65 Years and Older For Self, 1st Copy	@ $ 5.00 _____	
_____ Additional Copies	@ $ 4.00 _____	per copy
_____ Additional Years Searched	@ $ 4.00 _____	per year
	TOTAL $ _____	

MAKE CHECK or MONEY ORDER PAYABLE TO STATE OF MICHIGAN

APPLICATION FOR A CERTIFIED COPY OF A MARRIAGE CERTIFICATE

We are required by Act 368 of 1978 as amended, to collect the statutory fee before a search may be made for any record. Fee schedule is itemized below. Please make check or money order payable to the **STATE OF MICHIGAN.**

Minimum fee for **ONE CERTIFIED COPY -- $13.00** minimum fee includes a 3 year search	
ADDITIONAL CERTIFIED COPIES of the same record ordered at the same time -- **$4.00 each**	

ADDITIONAL YEARS searched over 3 years -- **$4.00 each year**
     (when exact year is not known and more than a 3 year search
     is required, remit **$4.00 FOR EACH** additional year over the
     minimum 3 years searched)	

TOTAL	$

FEES PAID TO SEARCH THE FILES ARE NOT REFUNDABLE

When a record is not found, the applicant will receive notification that the record as requested is not on file in this office.

PLEASE PRINT

Please send me a certified copy of the marriage of:

Name of groom: _____

Name of bride at time of
application for marriage license _____

Date of marriage: _____
               (Month)   (Day)   (Year)

If exact year is unknown: _____
                            (Years to be searched)

Place where license was obtained: _____
                                     (County)

_____   _____
    (Applicant's Signature)   (Date)

(PLEASE DO NOT REMOVE THIS STUB)

ADDITIONAL INFORMATION

PRINT THE NAME AND MAILING ADDRESS OF THE PERSON TO WHOM THE RECORD(S) ARE TO BE SENT. THIS IS A MAILING INSERT AND WILL BE USED TO MAIL THE RECORD(S).

NAME: _____

STREET: _____

CITY: _____

STATE: _____ ZIP: _____

B-225C 7/97

MICHIGAN DEPARTMENT OF COMMUNITY HEALTH
Office of the State Registrar and Division of Health Statistics
3423 N. Martin Luther King Jr. Blvd.
P.O. Box 30195
Lansing, Michigan 48909

APPLICATION FOR A CERTIFIED COPY OF A DIVORCE OR ANNULMENT RECORD

We are required by Act 368 of 1978 as amended, to collect the statutory fee before a search may be made for any record. Fee schedule is itemized below. Please make check or money order payable to the **STATE OF MICHIGAN.**

Minimum fee for **ONE CERTIFIED COPY -- $13.00** minimum fee includes a 3 year search	
ADDITIONAL CERTIFIED COPIES of the same record ordered at the same time -- **$4.00 each**	
ADDITIONAL YEARS searched over 3 years -- **$4.00 each year** (when exact year is not known and more than a 3 year search is required, remit **$4.00 FOR EACH** additional year over the minimum 3 years searched)	
TOTAL	$

FEES PAID TO SEARCH THE FILES ARE NOT REFUNDABLE

When a record is not found, the applicant will receive notification that the record as requested is not on file in this office.

PLEASE PRINT

Please send me a certified copy of the divorce or annulment decree of:

Name of man: _____

Name of woman: _____

Date of decree: _____
                        (Month)   (Day)   (Year)

If exact year is unknown: _____
                                    (Years to be searched)

Place where divorce or annulment was granted: _____
                                                            (County)

_____   _____
        (Applicant's Signature)   (Date)

- -

(PLEASE DO NOT REMOVE THIS STUB)   ADDITIONAL INFORMATION

PRINT THE NAME AND MAILING ADDRESS OF THE PERSON TO WHOM THE RECORD(S) ARE TO BE SENT. THIS IS A MAILING INSERT AND WILL BE USED TO MAIL THE RECORD(S).

NAME: _____

STREET: _____

CITY: _____

STATE: _____ ZIP: _____

B-225D 7/97

MICHIGAN DEPARTMENT OF COMMUNITY HEALTH
Office of the State Registrar and Division of Health Statistics
3423 N. Martin Luther King Jr. Blvd.
P.O. Box 30195
Lansing, Michigan 48909

APPLICATION FOR A CERTIFIED COPY OF A DEATH CERTIFICATE

We are required by Act 368 of 1978 as amended, to collect the statutory fee before a search may be made for any record. Fee schedule is itemized below. Please make check or money order payable to the **STATE OF MICHIGAN.**

Minimum fee for **ONE CERTIFIED COPY -- $13.00** minimum fee includes a 3 year search	
ADDITIONAL CERTIFIED COPIES of the same record ordered at the same time -- **$4.00 each**	
ADDITIONAL YEARS searched over 3 years -- **$4.00 each year** (when exact year is not known and more than a 3 year search is required, remit **$4.00 FOR EACH** additional year over the minimum 3 years searched)	
TOTAL	$

FEES PAID TO SEARCH THE FILES ARE NOT REFUNDABLE

When a record is not found, the applicant will receive notification that the record as requested is not on file in this office.

PLEASE PRINT

Please send me a certified copy of the death certificate of:

Name of deceased: _____
　　　　　　　　　　　　　(First)　　　　　　　　　(Middle)　　　　　　　　(Last)

Date of death: _____
　　　　　　　　　　　　(Month)　　　　　　　　　(Day)　　　　　　　　(Year)

If exact year is unknown: _____
　　　　　　　　　　　　　　　　　(Years to be searched)

Place of death: _____
　　　　　　　　　　　(Township, Village or City)　　　　　　(County)

_____　　_____
　　　(Applicant's Signature)　　　　　　　　　(Date)

IF THE INFORMATION REQUESTED ABOVE IS NOT KNOWN, please indicate in the box below any data which may be used for identifying the record, such as marital status, name of husband or wife if married, parents' names, age or birthplace.

- -

(PLEASE DO NOT REMOVE THIS STUB)

PRINT THE NAME AND MAILING ADDRESS OF THE PERSON TO WHOM THE RECORD(S) ARE TO BE SENT. THIS IS A MAILING INSERT AND WILL BE USED TO MAIL THE RECORD(S).

NAME: _____

STREET: _____

CITY: _____

STATE: _____ ZIP: _____

ADDITIONAL INFORMATION

B-225B 7/97

MINNESOTA

Send your requests to:

Minnesota Department of Health
Attn: Vital Records
717 Delaware Street, SE
P.O. Box 9441
Minneapolis, Minnesota 55440-9441

Tel. (612) 676-5120
Fax (612) 331-5776
E-mail: chs1@health.state.mn.us
http://www.health.state.mn.us/divs/chs/data/bd_1.htm

The Minnesota Department of Health has birth records from January 1, 1900 and death records from January 1, 1908. It does not issue copies of certificates of marriage or divorce decrees, but will issue statements for marriages since 1958 and divorces since 1970 if a record of the event was found in a state index. Expedited service is available (with payment by credit card) for an additional fee of $5.00, plus $14.00 for FedEx shipping.

Cost for a certified Birth Certificate	$14.00
Cost for a duplicate Birth Certificate	$8.00
Cost for a certified Death Certificate	$11.00
Cost for a duplicate Death Certificate, when ordered at the same time	$5.00

Send your requests for Marriage, Divorce, and early vital records to:

Court Administrator
County District Court
(County Seat), Minnesota

A certified marriage certificate costs $8.00; the cost for a divorce decree varies.

Send your requests for:

Minneapolis & Hennepin County Births and Deaths from 1870:

Vital Records
Hennepin County Government Center
300 South Sixth Street
Minneapolis, Minnesota 55487

St. Paul Births from 1867 and Deaths from 1870:

St. Paul Bureau of Health
555 Cedar Street
St. Paul, Minnesota 55101

For Adoption Record information write to:

Adoption/Guardianship
Minnesota Department of Human Services
444 Lafayette Road
St. Paul, Minnesota 55155-3831

Tel. (651) 296-2795

The Minnesota Historical Society (345 Kellogg Blvd. West, St. Paul, MN 55102-1906; 612-296-2143) has a large library of published materials about Minnesota.

For further information see:

Handbook on Birth Registration and Fetal Death Reporting. St. Paul, MN: Minnesota Center for Health Statistics, 1995. 51p.

MINNESOTA BIRTH CERTIFICATE APPLICATION

PENALTIES:
Any person who willfully and knowingly makes false application for a birth certificate is guilty of a misdemeanor
or gross misdemeanor (MN Statutes, section 144.227, subdivision 1)

<table>
<tr><td rowspan="7">BIRTH INFORMATION</td><td>FIRST NAME</td><td colspan="2">MIDDLE NAME</td><td colspan="2">LAST (MAIDEN) NAME</td></tr>
<tr><td></td><td colspan="2"></td><td colspan="2"></td></tr>
<tr><td>SEX</td><td>MONTH</td><td>DAY</td><td>YEAR</td><td>CITY AND COUNTY OF BIRTH</td></tr>
<tr><td></td><td></td><td></td><td></td><td></td></tr>
<tr><td colspan="2">MOTHER'S FIRST NAME</td><td colspan="2">MIDDLE NAME</td><td>MAIDEN NAME</td></tr>
<tr><td colspan="2"></td><td colspan="2"></td><td></td></tr>
<tr><td colspan="2">FATHER'S FIRST NAME</td><td colspan="2">MIDDLE NAME</td><td>LAST NAME</td></tr>
</table>

If you are requesting multiple certificates, please put the number in the blank next to the type of certificate.

☐ $14.00 First Copy

☐ ____ $ 8.00 Each additional copy of the identical record issued at the same time as the first copy

☐ ____ $11.00 Non-Certified Copy

1.   ☐ I am the: ☐ subject   ☐ child of subject   ☐ parent of the subject   ☐ grandchild   ☐ grandparent   ☐ spouse

2.   ☐ I am the legal custodian or guardian of the subject.

3.   ☐ I am the personal representative of the estate of the subject or a successor to the subject. (MN Statutes, section 524.1201)

4.   ☐ I am a representative authorized by a person under # 1.

5.   ☐ I can demonstrate that the information from the record is necessary for the determination of protection of person or property.

6.   ☐ I represent a local, state, or federal governmental agency and it is necessary to secure a certified copy for authorized agency duties.

7.   ☐ I am presenting your office with a court order issued by a court of competent jurisdiction to release the above mentioned record.

8.   ☐ Other:

THE FOLLOWING INFORMATION IS ABOUT THE PERSON COMPLETING THIS APPLICATION:			
Your Name: (please print)			
Your Signature:		**Today's Date:**	
Your Address:			
City, State, Zip:		**Mail To (if different)**	
Daytime Phone Number:			

If paying by check or money order, make payable to *Minnesota Department of Health*

***CREDIT CARD ORDERS** (note: the "Your Name" and "Your Address" sections above must match the name and address registered for the card)	
*add $5.00	
Account number for Master Card, VISA, American Express or Discover Card:	
Expiration date:	

Choose a Mail Service Option:

☐   Regular Delivery

☐   Federal Express (add $13.50)

Return to: Minnesota Department of Health
            Attention: Vital Records
            717 Delaware Street Southeast
            P.O. Box 9441
            Minneapolis, MN 55440-9441

MINNESOTA DEATH CERTIFICATE APPLICATION

PENALTIES:
Any person who willfully and knowingly makes false application for a birth certificate is guilty of a misdemeanor
or gross misdemeanor (MN Statutes, section 144.227, subdivision 1)

<table>
<tr><td rowspan="8" style="writing-mode: vertical">DEATH INFORMATION</td><td colspan="2">FULL NAME OF DECEDENT</td><td>DATE OF DEATH</td></tr>
<tr><td colspan="2"></td><td></td></tr>
<tr><td>PLACE OF DEATH</td><td>(CITY, VILLAGE, TOWNSHIP)</td><td>COUNTY OF DEATH</td></tr>
<tr><td colspan="2"></td><td></td></tr>
<tr><td colspan="2">DECEDENT'S AGE/BIRTH DATE</td><td>DECEDENT'S OCCUPATION</td></tr>
<tr><td colspan="2"></td><td></td></tr>
<tr><td colspan="3">DECEDENT'S SPOUSE</td></tr>
<tr><td colspan="3"></td></tr>
</table>

If you are requesting multiple certificates, please put the number in the blank next to the type of certificate.

☐ $11.00 First Copy

☐ _____ $ 5.00 Each additional copy of the identical record issued at the same time as the first copy

☐ _____ $11.00 Uncertified Copy

1.   ☐ I am the: ☐ subject   ☐ child of subject   ☐ parent of the subject   ☐ grandchild   ☐ grandparent   ☐ spouse

2.   ☐ I was the legal custodian or guardian of the subject.

3.   ☐ I am the personal representative of the estate of the subject or a successor to the subject (MN Statutes, section 524.1201)

4.   ☐ I am a representative authorized by a person under # 1.

5.   ☐ I can demonstrate that the information from the record is necessary for the determination of protection of person or property.

6.   ☐ I represent a local, state, or federal governmental agency and it is necessary to secure a certified copy for authorized agency duties.

7.   ☐ Other:

THE FOLLOWING INFORMATION IS ABOUT THE PERSON COMPLETING THIS APPLICATION:

Your Name: (please print)			
Your Signature:		**Today's Date:**	
Your Address:			
City, State, Zip:		**Mail To:**	
Daytime Phone Number:		**(If different)**	

If paying by check or money order, make payable to *Minnesota Department of Health*

*CREDIT CARD ORDERS (note: the "Your Name" and "Your Address" sections above must match the name and address registered for the card)	
*add $5.00	
Account number for Master Card, VISA, American Express or Discover Card:	
Expiration date:	

Choose a Mail Service Option:

☐   Regular Delivery

☐   Federal Express (add $13.50)

Return to: Minnesota Department of Health
Attention: Vital Records
717 Delaware Street Southeast
P.O. Box 9441
Minneapolis, MN 55440-9441

MISSISSIPPI

Mississippi State Department of Health
Vital Records Office
571 Stadium Drive
P.O. Box 1700
Jackson, Mississippi 39215-1700

Tel. (601) 576-7960
Fax (601) 576-7505
E-mail: VRInfo@msdh.state.ms.us
http://www.msdh.state.ms.us/phs/index.htm

The Vital Records Office has birth records from November 1, 1912; marriage records from January 1, 1926 (records from July 1, 1938 to December 31, 1941 are at the circuit court in the county where the license was issued); and death records from November 1, 1912. For earlier records contact the county in which the event occurred. The Office will conduct genealogical research for a charge of $20.00 per hour.

Expedited service is available (with payment by credit card) for an additional fee of $5.00 plus shipping by phoning (601) 576-7988 or faxing (601) 352-0013.

Cost for a certified Birth Certificate	$12.00
Cost for a short form Birth Certificate	$7.00
Cost for a duplicate Birth Certificate ordered at the same time	$3.00
Cost for a certified Marriage Certificate	$10.00
Cost for a certified Death Certificate	$10.00
Cost for a duplicate Marriage or Death Certificate, when ordered at the same time	$2.00

For Marriage Records (July 1, 1938–December 31, 1941) and Divorce Records write to:

Circuit Court Clerk
County Circuit Court House
(County Seat), Mississippi

For Adoption Record information write to:

Adoption Unit
Mississippi Department of Human Services
P.O. Box 352
Jackson, Mississippi 39205

Tel. (601) 359-4907
(800) 821-9157

The Mississippi Department of Archives & History (100 South State Street, Capitol Green, P.O. Box 571, Jackson, MS 39205; 601-359-6876) has early marriage records in with the county records (dates vary by county) and Mississippi death records from November 1912 to December 1937. The Family History Library of Salt Lake City, Utah has microfilmed many of the original and published vital records and church registers of Mississippi.

For further information see:

Handbook on Registration and Reporting of Vital Events, Live Births, Deaths, Spontaneous Fetal Deaths, Induced Terminations of Pregnancy. Jackson, MS: Mississippi State Board of Health, 1989. 127p.

MISSISSIPPI STATE DEPARTMENT OF HEALTH

Vital Records
P.O. Box 1700
Jackson, Mississippi 39215-1700

APPLICATION FOR CERTIFIED COPY OF BIRTH CERTIFICATE

INFORMATION

1. Only births recorded after November 1, 1912, are on file.
2. Two types of certified birth certificates are available. The certified ABSTRACT (Short Form) may be obtained for $7.00 and each additional copy ordered at the same time is $3.00. This certified certificate shows child's name, date and county of birth, state file number, filing and issue dates, and is sufficient for proof of birth but will not satisfy claims requiring proof of dependency e.g. IRS, Social Security, Welfare. The certified COPY of the birth certificate (Long Form) is available for $12.00 for the first copy and $3.00 for each additional copy ordered at the same time. This type certified certificate will satisfy claims requiring proof of dependency and situations where for family, historical or legal reasons additional information is required.
3. A five year search of records on file will be made. If no record is found a certification of NOT-ON-FILE will be issued and a search fee of $7.00 will be retained.

NOTE: As required by Section 41-57-11 of the Mississippi Code of 1972, annotated, $1.00 for each requested copy is deposited to the Children's Trust Fund administered by the Department of Human Services to fund programs to prevent child abuse and neglect.

INSTRUCTIONS

1. Complete ALL the information sections of the form. PLEASE PRINT.
2. The application must be signed.
3. PAYMENT:

   Out-of-state: Remit a bank or postal money order or a bank cashier's check in the correct amount made payable to Mississippi State Department of Health.

   Mississippi Resident: In addition to the above methods of payment, personal checks are acceptable if drawn on a Mississippi bank; make payable to Mississippi State Department of Health.

   We accept no responsibility for cash sent through the mail.

   Request for adjustments or refunds will be honored only if received within six months of application.

4. Send completed application, appropriate fee and self-addressed stamped legal size envelope to the address at the top of this form.

BASIC INFORMATION: DOUBLE CHECK SPELLING AND DATE

DO NOT WRITE IN THIS SPACE

1. FULL NAME AT BIRTH	FIRST NAME	MIDDLE NAME	LAST NAME	STATE FILING NUMBER
2. DATE OF BIRTH	MONTH	DAY	YEAR	
3. PLACE OF BIRTH	COUNTY	CITY OR TOWN	STATE	FILING DATE

4. Has name ever been changed other than by marriage? ☐ Yes ☐ No | If so, what was original name?

ADDITIONAL INFORMATION REQUIRED

12 — 36

5. SEX	6. RACE	37 — 66

7. FULL NAME OF FATHER	FIRST NAME	MIDDLE NAME	LAST NAME	S.C.
8. FULL MAIDEN NAME OF MOTHER	FIRST NAME	MIDDLE NAME	LAST NAME	S.C.

ABOUT THE APPLICANT

S.C.

9. FEE

I AM ENCLOSING FEE OF $ _____ FOR _____ SHORT FORMS.

S.C.

I AM ENCLOSING FEE OF $ _____ FOR _____ LONG FORMS.

C.D.

10. RELATIONSHIP OF APPLICANT TO PERSON NAMED IN ITEM 1.

SUP.

11. PURPOSE FOR WHICH THIS COPY IS REQUESTED

P.

Pursuant to Section 41-57-2 of the Mississippi Code of 1972, Annotated, and as defined by Mississippi State Board of Health Rules and Regulations, I hereby certify that I have a legitimate and tangible interest in the birth record requested. I understand that obtaining a record under false pretenses may subject me to the penalty as described in Section 41-57-27 of the Mississippi Code of 1972, Annotated.

CWA.

12. SIGNATURE OF APPLICANT | DATE SIGNED

PRINT YOUR MAILING ADDRESS HERE

13.			Name
14.		Apt. No.	Street or Route
15.			City or Town State, ZIP Code

MISSISSIPPI STATE DEPARTMENT OF HEALTH
Vital Records
P O Box 1700
Jackson, Mississippi 39215-1700

APPLICATION FOR CERTIFIED COPY OF STATISTICAL RECORD OF MARRIAGE

INFORMATION

1. Marriage records have been kept by state and county officials since January 1, 1926. From July 1, 1938, to December 31, 1941, records were kept only by the circuit court clerk in the county in which the marriage license was issued.
2. The fee for a search of the records and a certified copy is $10.00. Additional copies ordered at the same time are $2.00 each.
3. A five year search of our records will be made. If the record is not on file, a search fee of $6.00 will be retained.

INSTRUCTIONS

1. Complete the required section of this form. PLEASE PRINT.
2. The application must be signed.
3. PAYMENT:

   Out-of-state: Remit a bank or postal money order or a bank cashier's check in the correct amount made payable to Mississippi State Department of Health.

   Mississippi Resident: In addition to the above methods of payment, personal checks are acceptable if drawn on a Mississippi bank; make payable to Mississippi State Department of Health.

   We accept no responsibility for cash sent through the mail. Request for adjustments or refunds will be honored only if received within six months of application.

4. Send completed application, appropriate fee and self-addressed stamped legal size envelope to the address at the top of this form.

INFORMATION ABOUT BRIDE AND GROOM WHOSE STATISTICAL RECORD OF MARRIAGE IS REQUESTED (Please Print)			
1. FULL NAME OF GROOM	FIRST NAME	MIDDLE NAME	LAST NAME
2. FULL NAME OF BRIDE	FIRST NAME	MIDDLE NAME	LAST NAME
3. DATE OF MARRIAGE	MONTH	DAY	YEAR
4. PLACE OF MARRIAGE	COUNTY	CITY OR TOWN	STATE
5. WHERE LICENSE WAS BOUGHT	COUNTY	CITY OR TOWN	STATE
PERSON REQUESTING CERTIFIED COPY			
6. PURPOSE FOR WHICH COPY IS TO BE USED			
7. RELATIONSHIP OR INTEREST OF PERSON REQUESTING CERTIFICATE			
8. FEE I AM ENCLOSING A FEE OF $ _____ FOR _____ CERTIFIED COPIES.			
9. SIGNATURE OF APPLICANT		10. DATE SIGNED	

PRINT OR TYPE YOUR MAILING ADDRESS HERE

11.	Name
12.	Street or Route
13.	City or Town State, ZIP Code

Mississippi State Department of Health
Vital Records
P O Box 1700
Jackson, Mississippi 39215-1700

APPLICATION FOR CERTIFIED COPY OF DEATH CERTIFICATE

INFORMATION

1. Only deaths recorded after November 1. 1912 are on file.
2. The death certificate is the most important legal document in the settlement of the estate and insurance. It is important that the information on the certificate is correct. When you receive copies of the death certificate, check particularly spelling of names and that dates are correct.
3. If there are incorrect items on the certificate and the death occurred less than one year ago, please notify the funeral director who filed the certificate.
4. If there are incorrect items on the certificate and the death occurred more than one year ago, a court order may be required. Please contact Vital Records at the above address for additional information.
5. The fee for a certified copy of a death certificate is $10.00. Each additional copy ordered at the same time is $2.00.
6. A five year search of our records will be made. If the record is not on file, a search fee of $6.00 will be retained.

INSTRUCTIONS

1. Complete the information sections of this form. **Please print.**
2. The application must be signed.
3. PAYMENT
   Out-of-state: Remit a bank or postal money order or a bank cashier's check in the correct amount made payable to Mississippi State Department of Health.
   Mississippi Resident: In addition to the above methods of payment, personal checks are acceptable if drawn on a Mississippi bank; make payable to Mississippi State Department of Health.

We accept no responsibility for cash sent through the mail. Request for adjustments or refunds will be honored only if received within six months of application.

4. Send completed application, appropriate fee and self-addressed stamped legal size envelope to the address at the top of this form.

INFORMATION ABOUT PERSON WHOSE DEATH CERTIFICATE IS REQUESTED (Type or Print)		
1. FULL NAME OF DECEASED — First Name	Middle Name	Last Name
2. DATE OF DEATH — Month	Day	Year
3. PLACE OF DEATH — County	City or Town	State
4. Sex	5. Race	6. Age at Death	7. State File Number if known
8. Name of Father		9. Name of Mother
10. FUNERAL DIRECTOR — Name		Address

11. PURPOSE FOR WHICH CERTIFIED COPY IS TO BE USED

12. RELATIONSHIP OR INTEREST OF PERSON REQUESTING CERTIFICATE

Pursuant to Section 41-57-2 of the Mississippi Code of 1972, Annotated, and as defined by Mississippi State Board of Health Rules and Regulations, I hereby certify that I have a legitimate and tangible interest in the death record requested. I understand that obtaining a record under false pretenses may subject me to the penalty as described in Section 41-57-27 of the Mississippi Code of 1972, Annotated.

13. SIGNATURE OF APPLICANT

14. DATE SIGNED

NO. OF COPIES. . . . . _____

VETERAN'S SERVICE OR VA CLAIM NO: _____

TOTAL. . . . . _____

FEE SUBMITTED. . . . . . . $ _____

PRINT OR TYPE YOUR MAILING ADDRESS HERE

15.		Name
16.		Street or Route
17.		City or Town / State, ZIP Code

Send your requests to:

Missouri Department of Health
Bureau of Vital Records
930 Wildwood Street
P.O. Box 570
Jefferson City, Missouri 65102-0570

Tel. (314) 751-6400
http://www.health.state.mo.us/BirthAndDeathRecords/
BirthAndDeathRecords.html

The Bureau of Vital Records has birth and death records from January 1, 1910, and marriage and divorce indexes from July 1, 1948.

Cost for a certified Birth Certificate	$10.00
Cost for a wallet-size Birth Certificate	$10.00
Cost for verification of a Marriage Record	$10.00
Cost for verification of a Divorce Record	$10.00
Cost for a certified Death Certificate	$10.00

Send your requests for Marriage Certificates to:

Recorder of Deeds
County Court House
(County Seat), Missouri

Send your requests for Divorce Records to:

Clerk of the Circuit Court
(County Seat), Missouri

Send your requests for Adoption Records to:

Missouri Division of Family Services
Adoption Information Registry
P.O. Box 88
Jefferson City, Missouri 65103-0088

Tel. (324) 751-2502

The Missouri State Archives (100 Industrial Drive, P.O. Box 778, Jefferson City, Missouri 65102; 314-751-3280) has microfilm copies of the records of the County Recorders, some dating from the early 1800s.

For further information see:

County Clerk's Records Manual. Jefferson City, MO: Missouri State Records Management & Archives Services, 1990. Unpgd.
A Guide to County Records on Microfilm. Jefferson City, MO: Missouri State Archives, 1990. Unpgd.
Manual for City Clerks in Fourth Class Cities. Jefferson City, MO: Missouri Municipal League, 1980. 152p.
Vitally Speaking. (Serial). Jefferson City, MO: State Bureau of Vital Records, September 1999–.

MISSOURI DEPARTMENT OF HEALTH
BUREAU OF VITAL RECORDS
APPLICATION FOR CERTIFIED COPY OF BIRTH CERTIFICATION

INSTRUCTIONS	COPIES REQUESTED	RECORDS ARE FILED BY YEAR OF THE EVENT AND THEN ALPHABETICALLY BY THE NAME OF THE PERSON AT THE TIME OF THE EVENT. THEREFORE, AT LEAST THE MONTH AND YEAR OF BIRTH AND THE FIRST AND LAST NAME OF THE REGIS-TRANT MUST BE GIVEN BEFORE A SEARCH CAN BE MADE.

Recording of births began in this office January 1, 1910. The law requires a fee of $10 for a 5 year search of the files. This fee entitles you to a certified copy, if available. Additional copies are $10 each. **Fee must accompany application.**
 	
NO CASH BY MAIL PLEASE. Make check or money order payable to *Missouri Department of Health.*
 	
Mail this application to:
    Missouri Department of Health
    Bureau of Vital Records
    P.O. Box 570
    Jefferson City, Missouri 65102-0570
	Birth Certification
	Certification of facts of birth contained in original record.
	
	How Many ☐
	<hr>**Amount of Money Enclosed** $	

AN UNAPPLIED REMITTANCE IS VALID ONLY ONE YEAR FROM THE DATE OF RECEIPT

INFORMATION ABOUT PERSON WHOSE BIRTH CERTIFICATE IS REQUESTED
(TYPE OR PRINT ALL ITEMS EXCEPT SIGNATURE)

1. FULL NAME OF PERSON*	FIRST NAME	MIDDLE NAME	LAST NAME (MAIDEN NAME)
	IF THIS BIRTH COULD BE RECORDED UNDER ANOTHER NAME, PLEASE INDICATE THE NAME		

2. DATE OF BIRTH	MONTH	DAY	YEAR	3. SEX	4. RACE

5. PLACE OF BIRTH	CITY OR TOWN	COUNTY	STATE
	HOSPITAL OR STREET NO.	ATTENDING PHYSICIAN	☐ PHYSICIAN ☐ MIDWIFE ☐ OTHER

6. FULL NAME OF FATHER	FIRST NAME	MIDDLE NAME	LAST NAME

7. FULL MAIDEN NAME OF MOTHER	FIRST NAME	MIDDLE NAME	LAST NAME (MAIDEN)

*IF NEWBORN, PLEASE WAIT 6 TO 8 WEEKS BEFORE REQUESTING

PERSON REQUESTING CERTIFIED COPY

8. PURPOSE FOR WHICH CERTIFIED COPY IS TO BE USED	9. RELATIONSHIP (MUST BE REGISTRANT, MEMBER OF IMMEDIATE FAMILY, LEGAL GUARDIAN, OR LEGAL REPRESENTATIVE) **IF LEGAL GUARDIAN OF REGISTRANT, SEND ALONG GUARDIANSHIP PAPERS.**

10. SIGNATURE OF APPLICANT ▶	DATE SIGNED

12. PRINTED APPLICANT NAME	NAME OF APPLICANT

13. ADDRESS OF APPLICANT **(TYPE OR PRINT)**	STREET ADDRESS		
	CITY OR TOWN	STATE	ZIP CODE

MISSOURI DEPARTMENT OF HEALTH
BUREAU OF VITAL RECORDS
APPLICATION FOR SEARCH OF MARRIAGE INDEXES

P.O. BOX 570
JEFFERSON CITY, MO 65102

FULL NAME OF GROOM (FIRST, MIDDLE, LAST)

FULL MAIDEN NAME OF BRIDE (FIRST, MIDDLE, LAST) | PREVIOUS MARRIED NAME

COUNTY ISSUING THE LICENSE

DATE OR APPROXIMATE DATE THE MARRIAGE OCCURRED

NOTE:

THESE INDEXES BEGIN ON JULY 1, 1948.
MARRIAGE INFORMATION PRIOR TO THAT DATE MAY BE OBTAINED ONLY FROM THE RECORDER OF DEEDS OF THE COUNTY THAT ISSUED THE LICENSE.

MO 580-0692 (3-92)   VS-705 (R3-92)

MISSOURI DEPARTMENT OF HEALTH
BUREAU OF VITAL RECORDS
APPLICATION FOR SEARCH OF DIVORCE
OR DISSOLUTION OF MARRIAGE INDEXES

P O BOX 570
JEFFERSON CITY MO 65102

FULL NAME OF HUSBAND (FIRST, MIDDLE, LAST)

FULL MAIDEN NAME OF WIFE (FIRST, MIDDLE, LAST) | PREVIOUS MARRIED NAME

COUNTY ISSUING THE DECREE

DATE OR APPROXIMATE DATE DEGREE WAS ISSUED

NOTE: THESE INDEXES BEGIN ON JULY 1, 1948.
INFORMATION PRIOR TO THAT DATE MAY BE OBTAINED ONLY FROM THE CIRCUIT CLERK OF THE COUNTY THAT ISSUED THE DECREE.

MO 580-0693 (8-92)   VS 803 (R8-92)

MISSOURI DEPARTMENT OF HEALTH
BUREAU OF VITAL RECORDS
APPLICATION FOR CERTIFIED COPY OF DEATH CERTIFICATION

INSTRUCTIONS

The law requires a $10.00 fee for a search of the files. This search fee also entitles you to one certification copy of the death record if it is available. Additional copies are $10.00 each. **The fee must accompany this application.**

No Cash Please. Make check or money order payable to:
Missouri Department of Health

Mail this application to:
Missouri Department of Health
Bureau of Vital Records
P.O. Box 570
Jefferson City, Missouri 65102-0570

COPIES REQUESTED

Death Certification
(Certification of facts of death contained in original record)

How Many

$10.00 EACH

Amount of Money Enclosed

THE RECORDING OF DEATHS BEGAN IN THIS OFFICE ON JAN. 1, 1910. RECORDS ARE FILED BY YEAR OF DEATH AND ALPHABETICALLY BY THE NAME OF THE DECEASED AT THE TIME OF DEATH. THEREFORE, AT LEAST THE APPROXIMATE YEAR OF DEATH OR LAST YEAR IN WHICH THE DECEASED WAS KNOWN TO BE ALIVE MUST BE GIVEN.

INFORMATION ABOUT PERSON WHOSE DEATH CERTIFICATE IS REQUESTED *(TYPE or PRINT all items EXCEPT SIGNATURE)*

1. FULL NAME OF DECEASED	FIRST NAME	MIDDLE NAME		LAST NAME AT TIME OF DEATH		
2. DATE OF DEATH	MONTH	DAY	YEAR	3. SEX	RACE	AGE
4. PLACE OF DEATH	CITY OR TOWN	COUNTY		STATE		
5. FULL NAME OF SPOUSE	FIRST NAME	MIDDLE NAME		LAST NAME		
6. FULL NAME OF FATHER	FIRST NAME	MIDDLE NAME		LAST NAME		
7. FULL MAIDEN NAME OF MOTHER	FIRST NAME	MIDDLE NAME		LAST NAME (MAIDEN)		

PERSON REQUESTING CERTIFIED COPY OF DEATH RECORD

8. PURPOSE FOR WHICH CERTIFIED COPY IS TO BE USED (PLEASE CHECK)	9. RELATIONSHIP TO REGISTRANT OR INTEREST OF PERSON REQUESTING CERTIFICATION
☐ INSURANCE CLAIM ON POLICY ISSUED WITHIN 2 YEARS OF DEATH ☐ OTHER INSURANCE CLAIMS ☐ OTHER (SPECIFY) ▶	

10. SIGNATURE OF APPLICANT ▶	DATE SIGNED

11. NAME AND ADDRESS WHERE COPIES ARE TO BE MAILED (TYPE OR PRINT)	NAME AND ADDRESS OF FUNERAL HOME		
	NAME OF INDIVIDUAL TO RECEIVE COPIES	STREET ADDRESS	
	CITY OR TOWN	STATE	ZIP CODE

THIS COUPON MUST BE COMPLETED AND WILL BE USED TO ADDRESS OUR REPLY

NAME OF PERSON CERTIFICATION IS REQUESTED FOR

PLEASE PRINT OR TYPE THE NAME AND ADDRESS OF THE PERSON TO WHOM THE RECORD IS TO BE RETURNED.

▶ NAME

ADDRESS (NUMBER AND STREET)

CITY   STATE   ZIP CODE

Montana Department of Public Health and Human Services   Tel. (406) 444-2685
Vital Records Office   Recording (406) 444-4228
PO Box 4210   Fax (406) 444-1803
111 North Sanders, Room 209   E-mail: kferlicka@state.mt.us
Helena, Montana 59604-4210   http://www.dphhs.state.mt.us

The Vital Records Office has birth and death records from 1907, with a few dating back to 1860, and marriage and divorce indexes from January 1, 1943. Copies of birth and death records less than 30 years old are restricted. Expedited service is available (with payment by credit card) for an additional fee of $5.00, plus shipping.

Cost for a certified Birth Certificate	$10.00
Cost for searching the Marriage Index	$10.00
Cost for searching the Divorce Index	$10.00
Cost for a certified Death Certificate	$10.00

Send your requests for Marriage and Death Certificates and early vital records to:

Clerk
County District Court
(County Seat), Montana

For Adoption Record information write to:

Montana Department of Public Health and Human Services   Tel. (406) 444-2685
P.O. Box 4210
Helena, Montana 59604

Adult adoptees may receive copies of their original birth certificate if the adoption was finalized more than 30 years ago. Those finalized less than 30 years require a court order for the certificate.

The Family History Library of Salt Lake City, Utah has microfilmed many of the original and published vital records and church registers of Montana. For details on their holdings please consult your nearest Family History Center.

MONTANA VITAL STATISTICS
111 N SANDERS RM 209
PO BOX 4210
HELENA, MONTANA 59604-4210
406-444-2685

APPLICATION FOR A COPY OF A BIRTH CERTIFICATE

We maintain birth certificates for births that occurred in Montana from 1907 to the present.

CERTIFIED copies of a birth certificate may be issued to the Certificate Holder, the Certificate Holder's Parent, Spouse, Child, Legal Guardian or Authorized Representative.

INFORMATIONAL copies of a birth certificate may be issued to anyone as long as the birth occurred 30 years prior to the date of application.

Please complete the following information.

Name on Birth Certificate: _____

Date of Birth: _____ Place of Birth: _____

Mother's Full **Maiden** Name: _____

Father's Full Name: _____

Your relationship to the certificate holder: _____

Reason the Birth Certificate is needed: _____ # of copies _____

> NOTICE: STATE LAW PROVIDES PENALTIES FOR PERSONS WHO WILLFULLY AND KNOWINGLY USE OR ATTEMPT TO USE THIS CERTIFICATE FOR ANY PURPOSE OF DECEPTION. (50-15-114, MCA)

Your Signature: _____

Ways to order:
✓ Fax your application with credit card information to 406-444-1803. Certificates are mailed the next working day.
✓ Mail the application with correct fee (check or money order*). Certificates are mailed within two weeks.
✓ Apply in person for same day service. Office hours are 8:00 am to 5:00 pm Monday through Friday.

* Make checks or money orders payable to **Montana Vital Records**.

What is the cost ?
✓ If the date of birth is known it is $10.00 per each copy requested.
✓ If the date is not known it is $10.00 for each 5 year period we search for the first copy then $10.00 for each additional copy.
✓ $5.00 shipping and handling fee when fees are charged to a major credit card.
✓ $11.50 for Federal Express weekday delivery in the continental United States.
✓ $22.00 for Federal Express weekday delivery to Alaska and Hawaii.

Method of Delivery: _____ Regular Mail _____ Federal Express (cannot be delivered to a PO BOX)
(package must be signed for)

Credit Card # _____ **Expiration Date** _____

Mailing or Delivery Address:

Name: _____

Address: _____

City, State, Zip: _____

Daytime Telephone Number: _____

APPLICATION FOR SEARCH OF MARRIAGE & DIVORCE INDEXES

Applicant's Name: _____

Mailing Address: _____

City: _____ State: _____ Zip Code: _____

❖❖❖

✔ **Please check type of search you want done - Marriage** _____ **Divorce** _____

$ FEE is $10.00 for each 5 year time period searched per type of search. Must be received before we can do the search.

<u>BRIDE/WIFE</u>:
  Complete **MAIDEN** name: _____

    Date and Place of Birth: _____

    Fathers Name: _____

    Mothers Full <u>Maiden</u> Name: _____

    Has she been married before? YES _____ NO _____

      If Yes, What was that married name? _____

    Dates You Wish to be Searched: _____

<u>GROOM/HUSBAND</u>:
  Complete name: _____

  Date and Place of Birth: _____

  Fathers Name: _____

  Mothers Full <u>Maiden</u> Name: _____

  Has he been married before? YES _____ NO _____

    If Yes, to whom? _____

  Dates You Wish to be Searched: _____

FOR STATE USE ONLY	
Date Received _____	File # _____
Receipt # _____	Amount Rcvd $ _____
Comments: _____	
No Find: _____	

APPLICATION FOR A COPY OF A DEATH CERTIFICATE

We maintain death certificates for deaths that occurred in Montana from 1907 to the present.

Please complete the following information.

Decedent's Name: _____

Date of Death (We need a date to begin searching if date is unknown): _____

Place of Death: _____ Age at time of death: _____

Spouse's Name: _____ Parents: _____

Do you need a certified or genealogy copy of the death certificate? _____

Number of copies needed: _____

NOTICE: STATE LAW PROVIDES PENALTIES FOR PERSONS WHO WILLFULLY AND KNOWINGLY USE OR ATTEMPT TO USE THIS CERTIFICATE FOR ANY PURPOSE OF DECEPTION. (50-15-114, MCA)

Your Signature: _____

Ways to order:
    ✓Fax your application with credit card information to 406-444-1803. Certificates are mailed the next working day.
    ✓Mail the application with correct fee (check or money order*). Certificates are mailed within two weeks.
    ✓Apply in person for same day service. Office hours are 8:00 am to 5:00 pm Monday through Friday.

* Make checks or money orders payable to **Montana Vital Records**.

What is the cost ?
    ✓If the date of death is known it is $10.00 per each copy requested.
    ✓If the date is not known it is $10.00 for each 5 year period we search for the first copy then $10.00 for each additional copy.
    ✓$5.00 shipping and handling fee when fees are charged to a major credit card.
    ✓$11.50 for Federal Express weekday delivery in the continental United States.
    ✓$22.00 for Federal Express weekday delivery to Alaska and Hawaii.

Method of Delivery: _____ Regular Mail _____ Federal Express (cannot be delivered to a PO BOX)
    (package must be signed for)

Credit Card # _____ **Expiration Date** _____

Mailing or Delivery Address:

    Name: _____

    Address: _____

    City, State, Zip: _____

    Daytime Telephone Number: _____

NEBRASKA

Send your requests to:

Nebraska Department of Health & Human Services
Vital Statistics
301 Centennial Mall South, Third Floor
P.O. Box 95065
Lincoln, Nebraska 68509-5065

Tel. (402) 471-2871
E-mail: vitalrecords@hhss.state.ne.us
http://www.hhs.state.ne.us/ced/cedindex.htm

The Vital Statistics Office has birth records from 1904, and marriage and divorce records from January 1, 1909. Make your check or money order payable to "Vital Records." Expedited service is available (with payment by credit card) for an additional fee of $8.00, plus shipping.

Cost for a certified Birth Certificate	$8.00
Cost for a certified Marriage Certificate	$7.00
Cost for a certified Divorce Record	$7.00
Cost for a certified Death Certificate	$7.00

For earlier vital records contact:

County Clerk
County Court House
(County Seat), Nebraska

For Adoption Record information write to:

Nebraska Department of Health & Human Services
P.O. Box 95065
Lincoln, Nebraska 68509-5026

Tel. (402) 471-0918

The Nebraska State Historical Society (1500 R Street, P.O. Box 82554, Lincoln, NE 68501; 402-471-4771) has a large collection of county marriage and divorce records.

The Family History Library of Salt Lake City, Utah has microfilmed many of the original and published vital records and church registers of Nebraska. For details please consult your nearest Family History Center.

APPLICATION FOR CERTIFIED COPY OF BIRTH CERTIFICATE

This office has been registering births occurring in Nebraska since <u>1904</u>.
PLEASE TYPE OR PRINT LEGIBLY

Full name at birth_____
(if adopted, list adoptive name)

Month, day, and year of birth_____

City or town of birth_____County of birth_____

Father's full name_____
(If adopted, list adoptive father's name)

Mother's full maiden name_____
(If adopted, list adoptive mother's name)

Is this the record of an adopted person?　　　☐ Yes　　　☐ No

For what purpose is this record to be used?_____

If this is not your record, how are you related?_____

> **Delayed Birth Certificate**--*Legislation passed in 1941 provides for the filing of delayed birth certificates for person who were born prior to 1904 OR for person whose births were not recorded at the time of birth.*
>
> Is this a delayed birth certificate?　　　☐ Yes　　　☐ No

WARNING: Section 71-649, Nebraska Revised Statutes: It is a felony to obtain, possess, use, sell, furnish, or attempt to obtain any vital record for purposes of deception.

SIGNATURE_____

Type or print name _____

Street address_____

City, State, ZIP_____

Phone number _____

Today's date_____

> Fees are subject to change without notice. Please call our
> 24-hour recorded message at (402) 471-2871 to verify fees.
>
> _____ x $8.00 each - $ _____
> Total

<u>Mail to:</u>　　　　**or**
Vital Records
PO Box 95065
Lincoln, NE 68509-5065

<u>Bring to:</u>
Vital Records
301 Centennial Mall South
Third Floor, West of Elevators
Lincoln, Nebraska

Please enclose a stamped, self-addressed, business size envelope.

APPLICATION FOR CERTIFIED COPY OF
MARRIAGE CERTIFICATE

This office has been registering marriage occurring in Nebraska since **1909**.

(For records occurring prior to 1909, contact the county clerk of the county in which the marriage license was issued or the State Historical Society, P.O. Box 82554, Lincoln, NE 68501. They both will require a file search fee.)

PLEASE TYPE OR PRINT LEGIBLY

Full name of groom_____

Full maiden name of bride_____
(Please list any other name bride may have used)

County in which license was issued_____

Month, day, and year of marriage_____

For what purpose is this record to be used?_____

If this not your marriage record, how are you related to the persons listed on the record?_____

WARNING: Section 71-649, Nebraska Revised Statutes: It is a felony to obtain, possess, use, sell, furnish, or attempt to obtain any vital record for purposes of deception.

SIGNATURE_____

Type or Print Name_____

Street Address_____

City, State, ZIP_____

Today's Date_____

Number of certified copies _____ x $7.00 each = _____

(Fees are subject to change without notice)

<u>Mail to:</u>   <u>Questions, call:</u> (402) 471-2871

Vital Records
PO Box 95065
Lincoln, NE 68509-5065

Please enclose a stamped, self-addressed, business size envelope.

APPLICATION FOR CERTIFIED COPY OF
DISSOLUTION OF MARRIAGE (DIVORCE) CERTIFICATE

This office has been registering dissolutions of marriage (divorces) occurring in Nebraska since **1909**.

(For records occurring prior to 1909 or if you wish to obtain the divorce __decree,__ contact the district court in the county where the divorce was granted.)

PLEASE TYPE OR PRINT LEGIBLY

Full name of husband_____

Full name of wife_____

City or county where granted_____

Month, day, and year granted_____

For what purpose is this record to be used?_____

If this not your divorce certificate,
how are you related to the persons listed on the record?_____

WARNING: Section 71-649, Nebraska Revised Statutes: It is a felony to obtain, possess, use, sell, furnish, or attempt to obtain any vital record for purposes of deception.

SIGNATURE_____

Type or Print Name_____

Street Address_____

City, State, ZIP_____

Today's Date_____

┌───┐
Number of certified copies _____ x $7.00 each = _____

(Fees are subject to change without notice)
└───┘

<u>Mail to:</u>   <u>Questions, call:</u> (402) 471-2871

Vital Records
PO Box 95065
Lincoln, NE 68509-5065

Please enclose a stamped, self-addressed, business size envelope.

APPLICATION FOR CERTIFIED COPY OF DEATH CERTIFICATE

This office has been registering deaths occurring in Nebraska since <u>1904</u>.

PLEASE TYPE OR PRINT LEGIBLY

Full name of deceased_____
(If female, list married name or any other name decedent may have used)

City or town of death_____County of death_____
(If exact place of death is not known, list last known address)

Month, day, and year of death_____
(If exact date of death is unknown, list date decedent was last known to be alive or indicate a span of years to search.)

How are you related to decedent?_____

For what purpose is this record to be used?_____
•••
The information in this section is option information to assist our office in locating and identifying the requested record:

Year of birth_____Birthplace_____

Spouse's full name_____Home address_____

Father's full name_____

Mother's full maiden name_____

Funeral Director_____City_____

WARNING: Section 71-649, Nebraska Revised Statutes: It is a felony to obtain, possess, use, sell, furnish, or attempt to obtain any vital record for purposes of deception.

SIGNATURE_____

Type or Print Name_____

Street Address_____

City, State, ZIP_____

Today's Date_____

Number of certified copies _____ x $7.00 each = _____
(Fees are subject to change without notice)

Name_____

Street Address_____

City, State, ZIP_____

<u>Mail to:</u>   Vital Records   <u>Questions, call:</u> (402) 471-2871
            PO Box 95065
            Lincoln, NE 68509-5065
Please enclose a stamped, self-addressed, business size envelope.

FOR OFFICE USE ONLY
☐ Check   ☐ MO   ☐ Cash
Amount Received_____
Date Received_____
By Whom Received_____
PROOF OF IDENTIFICATION:
_____

NEVADA

Send your requests to:

Nevada State Division of Health   Tel. (775) 684-4242
Office of Vital Records & Statistics   Recording (775) 684-4280
505 East King Street, Room 102   Fax (775) 684-4156
Carson City, Nevada 89701-4749

The Office of Vital Records has birth and death records from July 1, 1911; marriage and divorce indexes from 1968. Make checks or money orders payable to "Office of Vital Records." There is an additional $5.00 fee for credit card orders, plus a $15.50 Federal Express fee for urgent requests. Certified marriage and divorce certificates are not available from the state. Contact the county in which the marriage license or divorce decree was issued.

Cost for a certified Birth Certificate	$11.00
Cost for a wallet-size Birth Certificate	$11.00
Cost to search the Marriage or Divorce Index	$8.00
Cost for a certified Death Certificate	$8.00

Send your requests for Marriage Certificates and Divorce Records to:

County Recorder
County Court House
(County Seat), Nevada

For Adoption Record information write to:

Adoption Registry   Tel. (775) 684-4415
Nevada Department of Human Resources
Division of Child and Family Services
711 East Fifth Street
Carson City, Nevada 89710-1002

The Nevada State Library and Archives (100 N. Stewart Street, Carson City, NV 89701; 775-684-3360) has an index to marriages and divorces from 1968 to 1991. The Family History Library of Salt Lake City, Utah has microfilmed many of the original and published vital records and church registers of Nevada. For details please consult your nearest Family History Center.

STATE OF NEVADA

HEALTH DIVISION

BUREAU OF HEALTH PLANNING AND STATISTICS

OFFICE OF VITAL RECORDS AND STATISTICS

505 E. King Street, Room 102

Carson City, Nevada 89701-4749

Telephone (775) 684-4242 • Fax (775) 684-4156

BIRTH CERTIFICATE APPLICATION

☐ $11.00 Per Certified Copy...No. of Copies.....................................

☐ $ 8.00 Search Fee (when no record found)......................................No. of Searches.................................

☐ $ 8.00 Per Verification of a Record (no copy issued)......................No. Verified.....................................

Full Name at Birth ....

....

Date of Birth ....

Place of Birth ....

Father's Name..

Mother's *Maiden* Name ....

NRS 440.650 and NAC 440.070 requires that a **relationship** or a need to facilitate a **legal process** be established in order to receive a certified copy of a record. Please state your relationship and your legal need for this record:

....

....

Your Name and Address (please print) ....

....

....

Signature of Applicant ....

FOR OFFICE USE ONLY

Amount Received... Receipt Number...

No. of Copies Issued.. Date...

VITAL RECORDS & STATISTICS STATE OFFICES
DO NOT ISSUE COPIES OF THE MARRIAGE & DIVORCE RECORDS
The Vital Records & statistics State Index is used for verification purposes only

To obtain a certified copy of a Marriage Certificate you must write to the County Recorder's Office in the county where the license was purchased. To obtain a certified copy of a Divorce Record, write to the County Office where the divorce was granted. Please complete the following information and forward this to the appropriate county office listed below.

Marriage Certificate	$7.00 per copy	_____ Copy(ies)	
Marriage application	$4.00 per copy	_____ Copy(ies)	
Divorce Decree	$1.00 per pg. (average $6.00 per certification)	Copy(ies)	Total Payment Enclosed
Name of Bride/Female	Name of Groom/Male	City/County	Year/Date of Marriage

CARSON CITY COUNTY 885 E Musser St. Ste 1025 Carson City NV 89701 Marriage 775-887-2084 Message 775-887-2085 Divorce 775-887-2082 No Personal Checks Accepted Credit Card Request Not Available	**CHURCHILL COUNTY** 155 N Taylor Ste 131 Fallon NV 89404 Marriage 775-425-6001 Divorce 775-423-3080* Send to District Court 73 N Main Fallon NV 89406 Credit Card Request Not Available	**CLARK COUNTY** 500 S Grand Central Parkway Las Vegas NV 89155 Marriage 702-455-4415** **Web site www.co.clark.nv.us Divorce 702-455-2590* *Send to County Clerk Family Court 601 N Pecos Rd, Las Vegas NV 89101 Credit Card Request 702-455-4336
DOUGLAS COUNTY P O BOX 218 Minden NV 89423 Marriage 775 782-9024 Divorce 775-782-9820 Credit Card Request 775-782-9028	**ELKO COUNTY** 571 Idaho St. Rm 103 Elko NV 89801 Marriage 775-738-6526 Divorce 775-753-4600* *Attn County Clerk Annex (3rd Fl) Credit Card Request Not Available	**ESMERALDA COUNTY** P O Box 458 Goldfield NV 89013 Marriage 775-485-6337 Divorce 775-485-6367 Credit Card Request Not Available
EUREKA COUNTY P O Box 556 Eureka NV 89316 Marriage 775-237-5263 Divorce 775-237-5263 Credit Card Request Not Available	**HUMBOLDT COUNTY** 25 West 4th Street Winnemucca NV 89445 Marriage 775-623-6414 Divorce 775-623-6344* *50 W 5th St, Winnemucca NV Credit Card Request Not Available	**LANDER COUNTY** 315 S Humboldt St Battle Mountain NV 89820 Marriage 775-635-5173 Divorce 775-635-5738 Credit Card Request Not Available
LINCOLN COUNTY P O Box 218 Pioche NV 89043 Marriage 775-962-5495 Divorce 775-962-5390 Credit Card Request Not Available	**LYON COUNTY** P O Box 927 Yerington NV 89447 Marriage 775-463-6581 Divorce 775-463-6503* *P O Box 816 89447 (County Office) Credit Card Request Not Available	**MINERAL COUNTY** P O Box 1447 Hawthorne NV 89415 Marriage 775-945-3676 Divorce 775 945-2446* *Clerk Treasurer PO Box 1450 89415 Credit Card Request Not Available
NYE COUNTY P O Box 1111 Tonopah NV 89049 Marriage 775-482-8145/8116 Divorce 775-482-8127* *P O Box 1031 Tonopah NV 89040 Credit Card Request Not Available	**PERSHING COUNTY** P O Box 736 Lovelock NV 89419 Marriage 775-273-2408 Divorce 775-273-2408* *County Clerks Office P O Box 820, Lovelock NV 89419 Credit Card Request Not Available	**STOREY COUNTY** P O Box 493 B Street Courthouse Virginia City NV 89440 Marriage 775-847-0967 Divorce 775-847-0969* *Drawer D Clerks Office Virginia City NV 89440 Credit Card Request Not Available
WASHOE COUNTY P O Box 11130 Reno NV 89520-0027 Marriage 775-328-3660 Divorce 775-328-3110* *P O 30083 Reno NV 89520-3083 Credit Card Request Not Available	**WHITE PINE COUNTY** P O Box 68 Ely NV 89301 Marriage 775-289-4567 Divorce 775-289-2341 Credit Card Request Not Available	c:\word\stateoff's/7/99

STATE OF NEVADA

HEALTH DIVISION

BUREAU OF HEALTH PLANNING AND STATISTICS

OFFICE OF VITAL RECORDS AND STATISTICS

505 E. King Street, Room 102

Carson City, Nevada 89701-4749

Telephone (775) 684-4242 • Fax (775) 684-4156

DEATH CERTIFICATE APPLICATION

☐ $8.00 Per Certified Copy...No. of Copies.................................

☐ $8.00 Search Fee (when no record found)..No. of Searches...............................

☐ $8.00 Per Verification of a Record (no copy issued)..No. Verified.....................................

Full Name of Decedent ....

Date of Death ....Social Security No. ....

Place of Death ....

Decedent's Father's Name ....

Decedent's Mother's *Maiden* Name ....

Mortuary/Funeral Home in Charge of Arrangements..

....

NRS 440.650 and NAC 440.070 requires that a **relationship** or a need to facilitate a **legal process** be established in order to receive a certified copy of a record. Please state your relationship and your legal need for this record:

....

....

Signature of Applicant ....

Name and Mailing Address..

....

....

FOR OFFICE USE ONLY

Amount Received.. Receipt Number...

No. of Copies Issued.. Date...

NEW HAMPSHIRE

Send your requests to:

New Hampshire Division of Public Health Services
Department of Health and Human Services
Bureau of Vital Records & Health Statistics
6 Hazen Drive
Concord, New Hampshire 03301-6527

Tel. (603) 271-4650
Recording (603) 271-4654
Toll free tel. in NH 800-852-3345, ext. 4651
Fax (603) 271-3447
E-mail: vitalrecords@dhhs.state.nh.us

The Bureau of Vital Records has birth, marriage, and death records from 1640, and divorce records from 1808. Make check or money order payable to "State of New Hampshire." Certificates may be ordered by phone using a major credit card for an additional $6.00 fee.

Cost for a certified Birth Certificate by mail	$12.00
Cost for a certified Marriage Certificate by mail	$12.00
Cost for a certified Divorce Record by mail	$12.00
Cost for a certified Death Certificate by mail	$12.00
Cost for a duplicate certificate	$6.00

Vital records are also available from:

Town Clerk
Town Hall
(Town), New Hampshire

For Adoption Record information write to:

Adoption Unit
New Hampshire Division for Children, Youth & Families
6 Hazen Drive
Concord, New Hampshire 03301-6527

Tel. (603) 271-4707

The Family History Library of Salt Lake City, Utah has microfilms of birth, marriage and death records from 1640 to 1900 and an index to early town records from 1639 to 1910.

For further information see:

The Town Clerk in New Hampshire. Durham, NH: University of New Hampshire Bookstore, 1858. 45p.

BIRTHS

NUMBER: _____

REQUESTED: _____

ISSUED: _____

New Hampshire Division of Public Health Services
Bureau of Vital Records & Health Statistics
Health & Welfare Building, 6 Hazen Drive
Concord, New Hampshire 03301

APPLICATION FOR COPY OF BIRTH CERTIFICATE

PLEASE PRINT

Name
at Birth: _____
      FIRST   MIDDLE   LAST

Date
of Birth: _____
    MONTH   DAY   YEAR

Place
of Birth: _____

Father's
Name: _____
      FIRST   LAST

Mother's
Maiden Name: _____
      FIRST   LAST

Purpose for which
certificate is requested? _____

Your
Signature: _____

Your Relationship
to Registrant? _____

A FEE IS REQUIRED BY LAW FOR THE SEARCH OF THE FILE FOR ANY ONE RECORD.

Notice: *Any person shall be guilty of a Class B Felony if he/she willfully and knowingly makes any false statement in an application for a certified copy of a vital record. (RSA 126:24)*

MARRIAGES

DIVISION OF PUBLIC HEALTH SERVICES

BUREAU OF VITAL RECORDS & HEALTH STATISTICS

H&W BUILDING, HAZEN DRIVE

CONCORD, NEW HAMPSHIRE 03301

NUMBER
REQUESTED
ISSUED

APPLICATION FOR COPY OF MARRIAGE RETURN

PLEASE PRINT PLAINLY

GROOM'S
NAME ....
      (FIRST NAME)   (MIDDLE NAME)   (LAST NAME)

BRIDE'S
NAME ....
      (FIRST NAME)   (MIDDLE NAME)   (LAST NAME)

DATE OF
MARRIAGE ....
      (MONTH)   (DAY)   (YEAR)

PLACE OF
MARRIAGE ....
      (COUNTY)

PURPOSE FOR WHICH CERTIFICATE IS REQUESTED ....

BY WHOM .... RELATIONSHIP TO REGISTRANT ....

A FEE OF 12 DOLLARS IS REQUIRED BY LAW FOR THE SEARCH OF THE FILE FOR ANY ONE RECORD

NOTICE: ANY PERSON SHALL BE GUILTY OF A CLASS B FELONY IF HE/SHE WILLFULLY AND KNOWINGLY MAKE ANY FALSE STATEMENT IN AN APPLICATION FOR A CERTIFIED COPY OF A VITAL RECORD. (RSA 126:24)

VS B-1

DIVORCE

NUMBER
REQUESTED
ISSUED

DIVISION OF PUBLIC HEALTH SERVICES
BUREAU OF VITAL RECORDS & HEALTH STATISTICS
H&W BUILDING, HAZEN DRIVE
CONCORD, NEW HAMPSHIRE 03301

APPLICATION FOR COPY OF DIVORCE, LEGAL SEPARATION OR ANNULMENT RECORD

PLEASE PRINT PLAINLY

HUSBAND'S
NAME ....
      (FIRST NAME)   (MIDDLE NAME)   (LAST NAME)

WIFE'S
NAME ....
      (FIRST NAME)   (MIDDLE NAME)   (MAIDEN/LAST NAME)

DATE OF
DECREE ....
      (MONTH)   (DAY)   (YEAR)

PLACE OF
DECREE ....
      (COUNTY)

PURPOSE FOR WHICH CERTIFICATE IS REQUESTED ....

BY WHOM .... RELATIONSHIP TO REGISTRANT ....

A FEE OF 12 DOLLARS IS REQUIRED BY LAW FOR THE SEARCH OF THE FILE FOR ANY ONE RECORD

NOTICE: ANY PERSON SHALL BE GUILTY OF A CLASS B FELONY IF HE/SHE WILLFULLY AND KNOWINGLY MAKE ANY FALSE STATEMENT IN AN APPLICATION FOR A CERTIFIED COPY OF A VITAL RECORD.
(RSA 126:24)

VS L-1

DEATHS

DIVISION OF PUBLIC HEALTH SERVICES
BUREAU OF VITAL RECORDS & HEALTH STATISTICS
H&W BUILDING, HAZEN DRIVE
CONCORD, NEW HAMPSHIRE 03301

APPLICATION FOR COPY OF DEATH RETURN

PLEASE PRINT PLAINLY

NAME OF
DECEASED _____ _____ _____
         (FIRST NAME)   (MIDDLE NAME)   (LAST NAME)

DATE OF
DEATH _____ _____ _____
      (MONTH)   (DAY)   (YEAR)

PLACE OF
DEATH _____ _____
                          (COUNTY)

PURPOSE FOR WHICH CERTIFICATE IS REQUESTED _____

BY WHOM _____ RELATIONSHIP TO REGISTRANT _____

☐ ISSUED WITH CAUSE OF DEATH   ☐ ISSUED WITHOUT CAUSE OF DEATH

A FEE IS REQUIRED BY LAW FOR THE SEARCH OF THE FILE FOR ANY ONE RECORD.

NOTICE: ANY PERSON SHALL BE GUILTY OF A CLASS B FELONY IF HE/SHE WILLFULLY AND KNOW-
INGLY MAKE ANY FALSE STATEMENT IN AN APPLICATION FOR A CERTIFIED COPY OF A VITAL
RECORD.
(RSA 126:24)

New Jersey Department of Health and Senior Services   Tel. (609) 292-4087
Bureau of Vital Statistics   Fax (609) 392-4292
Health-Agriculture Building, Room 504   http://www.state.nj.us/health/vital/vital.htm
PO Box 370, Front and Market Streets
Trenton, New Jersey 08625-0370

Birth, marriage, and death records are available from June 1878. Expedited service is available (with payment by credit card) for an additional fee of $8.95, plus shipping.

Cost for a certified Birth Certificate	$4.00
Cost for a certified Marriage Certificate	$4.00
Cost for a certified Death Certificate	$4.00
Cost for a duplicate certificate, when ordered at the same time	$2.00

For Birth, Marriage, and Death Records from May 1848 to May 1878 write to:

Department of State   Tel. (609) 530-3200
New Jersey State Archives
PO Box 307, 185 West State Street
Trenton, New Jersey 08625-0307

For a paid-in-advance fee of $10.00 the Archives will conduct a search of up to five years and send a typed transcript of the record.

For Divorce Records write to:

Clerk of the Superior Court
Superior Court of New Jersey, Public Information Center
PO Box 967, 171 Jersey Street
Trenton, New Jersey 08625-0967

For Adoption Record information write to:

New Jersey Department of Human Services   Tel. (609) 292-8816
Division of Youth and Family Services   http://www.state.nj.us/humanservices/
Adoption Registry Coordinator   adoption/registry.htm
PO Box 717, 50 East State Street
Trenton, New Jersey 08625-0717

There is no charge for registration with the Adoption Registry.

The Family History Library of Salt Lake City, Utah has microfilmed many of the original and published vital records and church registers of New Jersey. For details please consult your nearest Family History Center.

For further information see:

Manual for Clerks of the County District Court. Trenton, NJ: State of New Jersey, Administrative Office of the Courts, 1973. 44p.
Manual of New Jersey Recording Acts. Newark, NJ: Historical Records Survey, 1940.

New Jersey Department of Health and Senior Services
APPLICATION FOR CERTIFIED COPY OF VITAL RECORD

Make Check or Money Order payable to "State Registrar."
Do Not Mail Cash or Stamps. Please Print or Type.

Name of Applicant	Date of Application	THIS COLUMN FOR STATE USE ONLY	
Street Address	Relationship to Person Named in Requested Record *(required)*	Cash	Check
City State Zip Code	Telephone No.		

Why is a Certified Copy Being Requested?

			MO.	V/C

- ☐ School/Sports
- ☐ Social Security ID Card
- ☐ Passport
- ☐ Driver License
- ☐ Genealogy
- ☐ Welfare
- ☐ Soc. Sec. Disability
- ☐ Other Soc. Sec. Benefits
- ☐ Medicare
- ☐ Veteran Benefits
- ☐ Other (specify)

_____

BIRTH

Full Name of Child at Time of Birth	No. of Copies Requested
Place of Birth (City, Town or Township)	County
Date of Birth (*) Name of Hospital, If Any	
Father's Name	
Mother's Maiden Name	
If Child's Name Was Changed, Indicate New Name And How It Was Changed	

MARRIAGE

Name of Husband	No. of Copies Requested
Maiden Name of Wife	
Place of Marriage (City, Township)	County
Date of Marriage	

DEATH

Name of Deceased	No. of Copies Requested
Place of Death (City, Town, Township, County)	Date of Death (*)
Residence if Different from Place of Death	Age at Death
Father's Name	
Mother's Maiden Name	

(*) For any death or birth record before 1903, a search cannot be made unless you can name the county where the event took place.

Address your envelope to:

STATE REGISTRAR - SEARCH UNIT:
N.J. DEPARTMENT OF HEALTH AND SENIOR SERVICES
PO BOX 370, TRENTON, N.J. 08625-0370

This will be used as a mailing label when we send the results of the search. Enter name and mailing address.

Dear Applicant:

The fee you paid is correct unless either block below is checked.

☐ An additional fee of $ _____ is due, since either additional years or another name was involved.

☐ You are entitled to refund check of $ _____ which will be forwarded within 45 days of _____ . If you have occasion to write about this matter, return this form with your letter.

REG-3
Revised 9/98

@ G6700

Department of State
NEW JERSEY STATE ARCHIVES
PO Box 307, 185 West State Street
Trenton, NJ 08625-0307

NEW JERSEY
NJSA
STATE ARCHIVES

VITAL RECORD
SEARCH REQUEST

The State Archives maintains all Birth, Marriage and Death records from **May 1848 through May 1878.** All requests for vital records information after May 1878 should be directed to: State Registrar-Search Unit, New Jersey State Department of Health, P.O. Box 370, Trenton, New Jersey 08625-0370.

For a **paid-in-advance fee of $10.00** per record requested, the Archives will conduct a search, and, if successful, send the requester a typed transcript of the record. The fee covers a search of up to five (5) years. *Each additional five years searched will cost an additional $10.00.* The search fee is nonrefundable whether or not the requested records are found. Advanced payment should be made in the form of check or money order only, payable to: ***New Jersey General Treasury.***

PLEASE PRINT OR TYPE

Requestor Name	Telephone Number	
Requestor Address	City	State	Zip Code

BIRTH SEARCH ($10.00)		STATE USE ONLY
Full Name of Child at Time of Birth	Birth Date	Date Received
Place of Birth (City, Town, Township)	County	Date Researched
Father's Name	Mother's Maiden Name	Date Answered

MARRIAGE SEARCH ($10.00)		NOTES
Name of Husband	Maiden Name of Wife	
Place of Marriage (City, Township)		
County of Marriage (Searches between 1848-1864)	Marriage Date	

DEATH SEARCH ($10.00)	
Deceased's Name	Date of Death
Place of Death (City, Town, Township or County)	Age at Death
Father's Name	
Mother's Maiden Name	

MAKE CHECKS PAYABLE TO: **NEW JERSEY GENERAL TREASURY**	NO. SEARCHES REQUESTED:
	TOTAL AMOUNT DUE X $10.00 =

Form No. NJSA1.PM5

NEW MEXICO

Bureau of Vital Records and Health Statistics
Department of Health
1105 St. Francis Drive
P.O. Box 26110
Santa Fe, New Mexico 87502

Tel. (505) 827-0121
Fax (505) 827-1751
http://www.health.state.nm.us/website.nsf/frames?ReadForm

The Vital Records Bureau has birth and death records from 1920, with delayed records from 1880. New Mexico birth records are restricted for 100 years, death records for 50 years. Expedited service is available (with payment by credit card) for an additional fee of $10.00 plus shipping by phoning (505) 827-2316 or faxing (505) 984-1048.

Cost for a certified Birth Certificate	$10.00
Cost for a certified Death Certificate	$5.00

For Marriage Certificates, Divorce Records, and earlier records write to:

County Clerk
County Court House
(County Seat), New Mexico

For Adoption Record information write to:

Adoption Unit
New Mexico Social Services Division
Children, Youth & Family Department
P.O. Drawer 5160
Santa Fe, New Mexico 87502

Tel. (505) 827-8400

The Family History Library of Salt Lake City, Utah has microfilmed many of the original and published vital records and church registers of New Mexico. For details on their holdings please consult your nearest Family History Center.

Search Application For BIRTH Record

Mail request with fee or bring to:

New Mexico Vital Records and Health Statistics
Office of Information Management
1105 St. Francis Drive
P.O. Box 26110
Santa Fe, New Mexico 87502-6110

**PUBLIC
HEALTH
DIVISION**

ID. Type _____

No. _____

Request No: _____

WARNING: False application for a birth certificate is a felony and punishable by fine and/or imprisonment. Requests submitted without street address or geographical location will not be processed.

PLEASE PRINT or TYPE

I. BIRTH CERTIFICATE OF

FULL NAME at BIRTH

DATE of BIRTH | SEX

PLACE of BIRTH *(city, county, state)*

II. PARENTS OF PERSON NAMED ON BIRTH CERTIFICATE

FATHER'S FULL NAME

MOTHER'S FULL MAIDEN NAME

ABOVE NAMED PARENTS ARE:
FATHER: ☐ Natural ☐ Adoptive   MOTHER: ☐ Natural ☐ Adoptive

III. PERSON MAKING THIS REQUEST

YOUR NAME: | Last | First | Initial

YOUR ADDRESS:
No. and Street (Physical Address)
Mailing Address/P.O. Box
Town/City | State | Zip

IV. NUMBER OF COPIES WANTED and FEE(S)

I am requesting:
_____ certified copy(ies)
Number

Date of Request _____

I am enclosing the Fee(s) of:
$10.00 non-refundable search fee,
includes one copy
($10.00 for each additional certified copy) $ _____

LEGAL NOTICE: For the protection of the individual, certificates of birth are NOT open to public inspection. In order to comply with this request, State Regulations require Section V to be completed.

V. STATEMENT OF REQUESTOR

Your relationship to person named in Certificate *(e.g., parent, attorney, etc.)*

For what purpose(s) do you need the copy(ies)?

Your signature

Daytime telephone number
(   )

NMVRHS 913   Revised 12/97

Search Application For DEATH Record

Mail request with fee or bring to:

New Mexico Vital Records and Health Statistics
Office of Information Management
1105 St. Francis Drive
P.O. Box 26110
Santa Fe, New Mexico 87502-6110

PUBLIC HEALTH DIVISION

State of New Mexico
DEPARTMENT OF HEALTH

I.D. Type _____

No. _____

Request No: _____

WARNING: False application for a death certificate is a felony and punishable by fine and/or imprisonment. Requests submitted without street address or geographical location will not be processed.

PLEASE PRINT or TYPE

I. DEATH CERTIFICATE OF

FULL NAME of DECEASED

FULL NAME of SPOUSE *(Maiden name, if wife)*

DATE of DEATH

SEX

DECEASED'S DATE of BIRTH or AGE at TIME of DEATH

PLACE of DEATH *(city, county, state)*

MORTUARY in CHARGE of FINAL ARRANGEMENTS

III. PERSON MAKING THIS REQUEST

YOUR NAME:

Last   First   Initial

YOUR ADDRESS:

No. and Street (Physical Address)

Mailing Address/P.O. Box

Town/City   State   Zip

IV. NUMBER OF COPIES WANTED and FEE(S)

I am requesting:

_____ certified copy(ies)
Number

Date of Request _____

I am enclosing the Fee(s) of:
$5.00 for each certified copy

$ _____

($5.00 Non-Refundable Search Fee)

LEGAL NOTICE: For the protection of the individual, whose name appears on the death certificate, and surviving family members, certificates of death are NOT open to public inspection.

V. STATEMENT OF REQUESTOR

Your relationship to person named in Certificate *(e.g., spouse, attorney, etc.)*

For what purpose(s) do you need the copy(ies)?

Your signature

Daytime telephone number

( )

NMVRHS 914   Revised 12/97

Send your requests for Birth and Death Records to:

Office of Vital Records
New York City Department of Health
125 Worth Street, Box 4, Room 133
New York, New York 10013-4093

Tel. (212) 788-4520
Fax (800) 908-9146
http://www.ci.nyc.ny.us/html/doh/html/vr/vr.html

The Office of Vital Records has birth certificates from 1910 for people who were born in one of the five boroughs of New York City (Manhattan, Brooklyn, Queens, The Bronx, or Staten Island), and death certificates from 1949 for people who died in the five boroughs. Expedited service is available (with payment by credit card) for an additional fee of $5.00, plus shipping.

Send your requests for Marriage Records to:

City Clerk of New York
Municipal Building
1 Centre Street, Room 252
New York, New York 10007

(212) 669-2400

The City Clerk has copies of marriage licenses from 1930 to the present. Divorce records are available from the Court Clerk in the county where the decree was granted.

Send your requests for earlier Birth, Marriage, and Death Records to:

Municipal Archives
Department of Records and Information Services (DORIS)
31 Chambers Street, Room 103
New York, New York 10007-1288

Tel. (212) 788-8580
http://www.ci.nyc.ny.us/html/
serdir/html/xdoris01.html

The Municipal Archives has the following records, which are filed and indexed according to the borough in which the event occurred: **Manhattan:** Births July 1847–1848, July 1853–1909; Marriages June 1847–1848, July 1853–1994; Deaths 1795, 1802–1804, 1808, 1812–1948. **Brooklyn:** Births 1866–1909; Marriages 1866–1994; Deaths 1847–1853, 1857–1948. **Bronx:** Births 1898–1909; Marriages 1899–1994; Deaths 1898–1948. **Queens:** Births 1898–1909; Marriages 1898–1994; Deaths 1898–1948; Town & Village Records 1847–1849, 1881–1897. **Staten Island:** Births 1898–1909; Marriages 1898–1994; Deaths 1898–1948; Town & Village Records 1847–1849, 1881–1897.

Fees for the Office of Vital Records:

Cost for a certified Birth Certificate	$15.00
Cost for a certified Marriage Certificate	$15.00
Cost for a certified Death Certificate	$15.00
Cost for a duplicate certificate ordered at the same time	$15.00

Fees for the Municipal Archives:

Cost for a certified Birth Certificate	$10.00
Cost for a certified Death Certificate	$10.00

Fees for City Clerk:

Cost for a copy of a Marriage License	$15.00

The Family History Library of Salt Lake City, Utah has microfilmed many of the original and published vital records and church registers of New York City. For details on their holdings please consult your nearest Family History Center.

THE CITY OF NEW YORK – DEPARTMENT OF HEALTH

OFFICE OF VITAL RECORDS
125 Worth Street, Box 4, Room 133
New York, N.Y. 10013

APPLICATION FOR A BIRTH RECORD
(Print All Items Clearly)

LAST NAME ON BIRTH RECORD	FIRST NAME	❏ FEMALE ❏ MALE

DATE OF BIRTH Month Day Year	PLACE OF BIRTH (NAME OF HOSPITAL, OR IF AT HOME, NO. AND STREET)	BOROUGH OF BIRTH

MOTHER'S **MAIDEN** NAME (NAME BEFORE MARRIAGE) FIRST LAST	CERTIFICATE NUMBER IF KNOWN

FATHER'S NAME FIRST LAST	*FOR OFFICE USE ONLY*
NO. OF COPIES	YOUR RELATIONSHIP TO PERSON NAMED ON BIRTH RECORD IF SELF, STATE "SELF"	
FOR WHAT PURPOSE ARE YOU GOING TO USE THIS BIRTH RECORD	

NOTE: Copy of a birth record can be issued only to persons to whom the record of birth relates, if of age, or a parent or other lawful representative. IF THIS REQUEST IS NOT FOR YOUR OWN BIRTH RECORD OR THAT OF YOUR CHILD, NOTARIZED AUTHORIZATION FROM THE PARENT OR THE PERSON NAMED ON THE CERTIFICATE MUST BE PRESENTED WITH THIS APPLICATION.

Section 3.19, New York City Health Code provides, in part: ". . . no person shall make a false, untrue or misleading statement or forge the signature of another on a certificate, application, registration, report or other document required to be prepared pursuant to this Code." Section 558 (e) of the New York City Charter provides that any violation of the Health Code shall be treated and punished as a misdemeanor.

SIGN / PRINT YOUR NAME AND RECORD YOUR ADDRESS BELOW

SIGNATURE	PRINT NAME	
STREET ADDRESS		APT. #
CITY	STATE	ZIP CODE
DAYTIME TELEPHONE NUMBER	Area Code — Telephone Number	

NOTE: PLEASE ATTACH A STAMPED SELF – ADDRESSED ENVELOPE

FEES

SEARCH FOR TWO CONSECUTIVE YEARS AND ONE COPY, OR A CERTIFIED "NOT FOUND STATEMENT"............$15.00
EACH ADDITIONAL COPY REQUESTED $15.00
EACH EXTRA YEAR SEARCHED (WITH THIS APPLICATION) ....$ 3.00

    1. Make money order or check payable to: N.Y.C. Department of Health. **CASH NOT ACCEPTED BY MAIL.**
    2. If from a foreign country, send an international money order or check drawn on a U.S. Bank.

VR 67 (REV. 8/96)

DEPARTMENT OF RECORDS & INFORMATION SERVICES
MUNICIPAL ARCHIVES
31 Chambers Street, New York, NY 10007, (212) 788-8580
APPLICATION FOR A SEARCH AND/OR
CERTIFIED COPY OF A BIRTH RECORD (PRE-1910)

	Fees
$10	Search of birth records in one year and one City/Borough for one name and issuance of one certified copy or "not found" statement.
$2	Per additional year to be searched in one City/Borough for same name.
$2	Per additional City/Borough to be searched in one year for same name.
$5	Per additional copy of record.
$5	Issuance of certified copy, when certificate number is provided.

- Enclose stamped, self-addressed envelope. Make check or money order payable to NYC Dept. of Records & Information Services.
- To expedite processing, please send each request separately with the required fee and a stamped addressed envelope.
- Manhattan birth records prior to 1857 are not indexed. You must supply the month, day, and year of the event in your search request.

PLEASE PRINT OR TYPE

Last name on birth record | First name | Female/Male

Date of birth

Month   Day   Year

Place of birth - if at home, house number and street | City/Borough

Father's name, if known | Mother's name, if known

Your relationship to person named above | Certificate no.

Purpose for which this record will be used | Number of copie

Your name (please print) | Signature

Address

City | State | Zip Code

DEPARTMENT OF RECORDS & INFORMATION SERVICES
MUNICIPAL ARCHIVES
31 Chambers Street, New York, NY 10007, (212) 788-8580
APPLICATION FOR A SEARCH AND/OR
CERTIFIED COPY OF A MARRIAGE RECORD (PRE-1938)

	Fees
$10	Search of marriage records in one year and one City/Borough for one groom and/or bride and issuance of one certified copy or "not found" statement.
$2	Per additional year to be searched in one City/Borough for same name.
$2	Per additional City/Borough to be searched in one year for same name.
$5	Per additional copy of record.
$5	Issuance of certified copy, when certificate number is provided.

- Enclose stamped, self-addressed envelope.
- Make check or money order payable to NYC Dept. of Records & Information Services.
- To expedite processing, please send each request separately with the required fee and a stamped addressed envelope.
- Please limit the date span of each marriage search application to FIVE years. If the record is "not found," you may submit a request for a continuation of the search at $2/year.
- Manhattan marriage records prior to 1866 are not indexed. You must supply the month, day, and year of the event in your search request.

PLEASE PRINT OR TYPE

Last name of groom | First name of grc

Last name of bride | First name of bri

Date of marriage

Month   Day   Year

Place of marriage | City/Borough

Your relationship to people named above | Certificate no.

Purpose for which this record will be used | Number of copie

Your name (please print) | Signature

Address

City | State | Zip Code

THE CITY OF NEW YORK – DEPARTMENT OF HEALTH

OFFICE OF VITAL RECORDS
125 Worth Street, Box 4, Room 133
New York, N.Y. 10013

APPLICATION FOR A COPY OF A DEATH RECORD
(Print All Items Clearly)

1. LAST NAME AT TIME OF DEATH	2. FIRST NAME	2.A ❏ FEMALE ❏ MALE
3. DATE OF DEATH Month Day Year	4. PLACE OF DEATH	5. BOROUGH	6. AGE

7. NO OF COPIES	8. SPOUSE'S NAME	9. OCCUPATION OF DECEASED
10. FATHER'S NAME		11. SOCIAL SECURITY NUMBER
12. MOTHER'S NAME (Name Before Marriage)		13. BURIAL PERMIT NUMBER (IF KNOWN)
14. FOR WHAT PURPOSE ARE YOU GOING TO USE THIS CERTIFICATE		15. YOUR RELATIONSHIP TO DECEDENT

NOTE: Section 205.07 of the Health Code provides, in part:" . . . The confidential medical report of death shall not be subject to subpoena or to inspection." Therefore, copies of the medical report of death cannot be issued.

SIGN YOUR NAME AND ADDRESS BELOW

NAME
ADDRESS   APT. NO.
CITY   STATE   ZIP CODE

DAYTIME TELEPHONE NUMBER   [   ][   ][   ]   [   ][   ][   ] — [   ][   ][   ][   ]

Area Code   Telephone Number

INFORMATION: APPLICATION SHOULD BE MADE IN PERSON AT 125 WORTH STREET OR BY MAIL TO THE ABOVE DIVISION.

NOTE: 1. CASH NOT ACCEPTED BY MAIL
2. PLEASE ATTACH A STAMPED SELF-ADDRESSED ENVELOPE

FEES

	(FOR OFFICE USE ONLY)

SEARCH FOR TWO CONSECUTIVE YEARS AND ONE COPY **$15.00**
EACH ADDITIONAL COPY REQUESTED **$15.00**
EACH EXTRA YEAR SEARCHED (WITH THIS APPLICATION) .... **$ 3.00**
IF RECORD IS NOT ON FILE, A CERTIFIED "NOT FOUND STATEMENT" WILL BE ISSUED.

1. Make check or money order payable to: Department of Health, N.Y.C.
2. If from a foreign country, send an international money order or check drawn on a U.S. Bank.
3. Stamps or foreign currency will not be accepted.

VR 66 (REV. 9/96)

DEPARTMENT OF RECORDS & INFORMATION SERVICES
MUNICIPAL ARCHIVES
31 Chambers Street, New York, NY 10007, (212) 788-8580
APPLICATION FOR A SEARCH AND/OR
CERTIFIED COPY OF A DEATH RECORD (PRE-1949)

	Fees
$10	Search of death records in one year and one City/Borough for one name and issuance of one certified copy or "not found" statement.
$2	Per additional year to be searched in one City/Borough for same name.
$2	Per additional City/Borough to be searched in one year for same name.
$5	Per additional copy of record.
$5	Issuance of certified copy, when certificate number is provided.

- Enclose stamped, self-addressed envelope.
- Make check or money order payable to NYC Dept. of Records & Information Services.
- To expedite processing, please send each request separately with the required fee and a stamped addressed envelope.
- Please limit the date span of each death search application to FIVE years. If the record is "not found," you may submit a request for a continuation of the search at $2/year.
- Please indicate the age, or approximate age (infant, child, adult, etc.) of the decedent, particularly if the exact date of death is not known.

PLEASE PRINT OR TYPE

Last name at time of death	First name	Middle name

Date of death	Cemetery, if known
Month Day Year	

Place of death	City/Borough	Age

Father's name, if known	Mother's name, if known

Your relationship to decedent	Certificate no.

Purpose for which this record will be used	Number of copie

Your name (please print)	Signature

Address

City	State	Zip Code

NEW YORK—NEW YORK STATE

Send your requests to:

Vital Records Section
New York State Department of Health
Corning Tower Building
Empire State Plaza
Albany, New York 12237-0023

Tel. (518) 474-3077
Fax (518) 474-9168
E-mail: nyhealth@health.state.ny.us
http://www.health.state.ny.us/nysdoh/consumer/vr.htm

The Vital Records Section has original records of births and marriages for the entire state from 1881, deaths from 1880, and divorces from 1963, except for birth and death records filed in Albany, Buffalo, and Yonkers prior to 1914 or marriage records in those cities prior to 1908. Applications for these cities should be made to the City Clerk, City Hall, in either Albany, NY 12207; Buffalo, NY 14202; or Yonkers, NY 10701. Birth records are restricted for 75 years; marriage and death records from 50 years. Expedited service is available (with payment by credit card) for an additional fee. *The Vital Records Section does not have any New York City records except for births occurring in Queens and Richmond counties for the years 1881–1897*. (See New York—New York City for record information.)

Cost for a certified Birth Certificate	$15.00
Cost for a genealogical Birth Certificate	$11.00
Cost for a certified Marriage Certificate	$5.00
Cost for a Dissolution of Marriage Record	$15.00
Cost for a genealogical Death Certificate	$11.00
Cost for a certified Death Certificate	$15.00

For earlier records write to:

Registrar of Vital Statistics
(Town or Township), New York

Certified Marriage and Death Certificates from the town/township are available for $5.00.

For Adoption Record information write to:

New York State Department of Health
Adoption Information Registry
P.O. Box 2602
Albany, New York 12237-2602

Tel. (518) 474-9600
http://www.health.state.ny.us/nysdoh/consumer/vr.htm#adoption

The State Vital Records Section has transferred to The New York State Archives (11th Floor, Cultural Education Center, Empire State Plaza, Albany, New York 12230; 518-474-8955) microfilm copies of its birth, marriage, and death indexes; these are open to the public at no charge.

The Family History Library of Salt Lake City, Utah has microfilmed many of the original and published vital records and church registers of New York. For details on their holdings please consult your nearest Family History Center.

For further information see:

Bowman, Fred Q. *Directory to Collections of New York Vital Records, 1726–1989.* Bowie, MD: Heritage Books, 1995. 91p.
Guide to Public Vital Statistics Records in New York State, including New York City. 1942. 3 vols.
Thompson, Isaac Grant. *The Assessors, Collectors and Town Clerks' Manual Containing a Full and Accurate Exposition of the Law Relating to the Powers and Duties of These Officers, with an Appendix of Forms.* Albany, NY: J.D. Parsdon, Jr., 1870. 223p.
Vital Records Registration Handbook, Birth, Death, Fetal Death. Albany, NY: New York State Department of Health, Office of Biostatistics, 1978. 75.p.

Application for Copy of Birth Record

PLEASE COMPLETE FORM AND ENCLOSE FEE

FEE: $15.00 per copy or No Record Certification.

Make money order or check payable to New York State Department of Health. Please do not send cash or stamps.

Send to: New York State Department of Health
Vital Records Section
Empire State Plaza
Albany, NY 12237-0223

PLEASE PRINT OR TYPE

Name:

First   Middle   Last

Date of Birth or Period Covered by Search:

Place of Birth:

Hospital (if not hospital, give street & number)   Village, town or city   County

Father:

First   Middle   Last

Maiden Name of Mother:

First   Middle   Last

Number of Copies Requested:

Standard Size _____   Wallet Size_____

Birth Certificate No. If Known _____

Local Registration No. If Known _____

Purpose for which
Record is Required
(Check one)

☐ Passport
☐ Social Security
☐ Retirement
☐ Employment
☐ Other (specify) _____

☐ Working papers
☐ School entrance
☐ Driver's license
☐ Marriage license

☐ Welfare assistance
☐ Veteran's benefits
☐ Court proceeding
☐ Entrance into Armed Forces

What is your relationship to person whose record is required? If self, state "self".

If attorney, given name and relationship of your client to person whose record is required.

This office requires written authorization of the person/parents whose record is requested before processing.

Signature of Applicant:

Date (mm/dd/yy):

Address of Applicant:

_____
(street)

_____
(city)   (state)   (zip)

Please print name and address where record should be sent:

_____
(name)

_____
(street)

_____
(city)   (state)   (zip)

DOH-296B

Application for Copy of Marriage Record

TYPE OF RECORD DESIRED (Check One)

Search and Certification ☐ Fee $5.00 per copy	Search and Certified Copy ☐ Fee $5.00 per copy
A Certification, an abstract from the marriage record issued under the seal of the Department of Health, includes the names of the contracting parties, their residence at the time the license was issued as well as date and place of birth of the bride and groom. A Certification may be used as proof that a marriage occurred.	A Certified Transcript includes all of the items of information occurring on the original record of the marriage. A Certified Transcript may be needed where proof of parentage and certain other detailed information may be required, such as for passports, veterans' benefits, court proceedings, or settlement of an estate.

PLEASE COMPLETE FORM AND ENCLOSE FEE

Make money order or check payable to New York State Department of Health. Please do not send cash or stamps. There is no fee for a record to be used for eligibility determination for social welfare or veterans' benefits.

Send to: New York State Department of Health
Vital Records Section
Empire State Plaza
Albany, NY 12237-0223

PLEASE PRINT OR TYPE

Name of Groom:	Name of Bride:
First Middle Last	First Middle Last
Groom's Age or Date of Birth:	Bride's Age or Date of Birth:
Residence of Groom: County State	Residence of Bride: County State
Date of Marriage or Period Covered by Search:	If Bride Previously Married, State Name Used at that Time:
Place Where License Was Issued:	Place Where Marriage Was Performed:
Purpose for which Record Is Required:	What is your relationship to person whose record is requested? If self, state "self".
In what capacity are you acting?	If attorney: Name and relationship of your client to the persons whose marriage record is required.

Signature of Applicant_____ Date Requested _____

| Address of Applicant:

Street_____

City _____State _____ Zip _____ | Please print name and address where record should be sent:

Name_____

Address_____

City_____ State_____ Zip_____ |

DOH-301

NEW YORK STATE DEPARTMENT OF HEALTH
Vital Records Section

Application for Copy of
Dissolution of Marriage Record

PLEASE COMPLETE FORM AND ENCLOSE FEE

FEE: $15.00 per copy or No Record Certification.
Make money order or check payable to New York State Department of Health. Please do not send cash or stamps.
Send to: New York State Department of Health
Vital Records Section
Empire State Plaza
Albany, NY 12237-0223

NOTE: Certificates of Dissolution of Marriage for divorce decrees granted prior to January 1, 1963, were not filed with the Department of Health. To obtain a record of the decree, contact the county clerk of the county in which the decree was granted.

PLEASE PRINT OR TYPE

Name of Husband:	Name of Wife:
First Middle Last	First Middle Last
Address at time of Decree (Husband):	Address at time of Decree (Wife):
Date of Marriage: Month Day Year	Place Marriage License Was Issued (city, town or village):
County in which Decree Was Filed:	Date of final Decree or Period to be Searched: Month Day Year
Purpose for which Record Is Required:	What is your relationship to the individuals named in the Decree?

If attorney, give name and relationship of your client to the individuals named in the Decree.

Signature of Applicant_____ Date Requested _____

Address of Applicant:
Street_____

City _____State _____ Zip_____

PLEASE PRINT NAME AND ADDRESS WHERE RECORD SHOULD BE SENT

Name_____

Address_____

City _____ State _____ Zip_____

DOH-295

Application for Copy of Death Record

PLEASE COMPLETE FORM AND ENCLOSE FEE

FEE: $15.00 per copy or No Record Certification.
Make money order or check payable to New York State Department of Health. Please do not send cash or stamps.

Send to: New York State Department of Health
Vital Records Section
Empire State Plaza
Albany, NY 12237-0223

PLEASE PRINT OR TYPE

Name of Deceased:

First   Middle   Last

Date of Death or Period to be Covered by Search:

Name of Father of Deceased:

First   Middle   Last

Social Security Number of Deceased:

Maiden Name of Mother of Deceased:

First   Middle   Last

Date of Birth of Deceased:

Month   Day   Year

Age at Death:

Place of Death:

Name of Hospital or Street Address   Village, town or city   County

Number of Copies Requested:

Enter Death No. If Known _____

Enter Local Registration No. If Known _____

Purpose for Which Record Is Required:

What is your relationship to person whose record is required?_____

In what capacity are you acting?_____

If attorney, name and relationship of your client to deceased_____

Signature of Applicant _____ Date_____

Address of Applicant _____

PLEASE PRINT NAME AND ADDRESS WHERE RECORD SHOULD BE SENT

Name_____

Address_____

City _____ State _____ Zip _____

DOH-294B

Information and Application for Genealogical Services

VITAL RECORDS COPIES CANNOT BE PROVIDED FOR COMMERCIAL PURPOSES

1. FEE: $11.00 includes search and uncertified copy or notification of No Record.
2. Original records of births and marriages for the entire state begin with 1881, deaths begin with 1880, EXCEPT for records filed in Albany, Buffalo and Yonkers prior to 1914. Applications for these cities should be made directly to the local office.
3. The New York State Department of Health does not have New York City records exceppt for births occurring in Queens and Richmond counties for the years 1881 through 1897.
4. Please read the Administrative Rule Summary on the reverse side of this sheet which specifies years available for genealogical research.

Send to: New York State Department of Health, Vital Records Section, Empire State Plaza, Albany, NY 12237-0023

TO INSURE A COMPLETE SEARCH, PROVIDE AS MUCH INFORMATION AS POSSIBLE.

BIRTH REQUEST

Name at birth _____	Name at birth _____
Date of birth _____	Date of birth _____
Place of birth _____	Place of birth _____
Father's name _____	Father's name _____
Mother's maiden name _____	Mother's maiden name _____

MARRIAGE REQUEST

Name of bride _____	Name of bride _____
Name of groom _____	Name of groom _____
Date of marriage _____	Date of marriage _____
Place of marriage and/or license _____	Place of marriage and/or license _____

DEATH REQUEST

Name at death _____	Name at death _____
Date of death _____ Age at death _____	Date of death _____ Age at death _____
Place of death _____	Place of death _____
Names of parents _____	Names of parents _____
Name of spouse _____	Name of spouse _____

For what purpose is information required?

What is your relationship to person whose record is requested?

In what capacity are you acting?

Signature of applicant _____ Date _____

Applicant's address _____

Please print name and address where record should be sent:	If requesting birth and marriage records, please sign the following statement:
Name _____	To the best of my knowledge, the person(s) named in the application are deceased.
Street _____	
City _____ State ____ Zip ____	SIGNATURE OF APPLICANT

DOH-1562

NORTH CAROLINA

Send your requests to:

North Carolina Department of Health and Human Services   Tel. (919) 733-3526
Vital Records Branch   http://hermes.schs.state.nc.us/SCHS/certificates/
225 North McDowell Street
1903 Mail Service Center
Raleigh, North Carolina 27699-1903

The Vital Records branch has birth records from 1913; death records from 1930; marriage records from 1962; and divorce records from 1958. Births and deaths have been registered in North Carolina only since 1913; prior to that the state did not use birth records or certificates of any kind. Expedited service is available (with payment by credit card) for an additional fee of $10.00, plus shipping.

For marriage records after 1868 contact the Register of Deeds in the county where the marriage was performed; fees vary. For divorce records not available at the Vital Records Branch, contact the Clerk of the Superior Court in the county where the divorce was granted.

Cost for a certified Birth Certificate	$10.00
Cost for a certified Marriage Certificate	$10.00
Cost for a certified Divorce Record	$10.00
Cost for a certified Death Certificate	$10.00
Cost for a duplicate copy, when ordered at the same time	$5.00

For earlier Death Records write to:

North Carolina Division of Archives & History   Tel. (919) 733-3952
109 East Jones Street   http://www.ah.dcr.state.nc.us/
4610 Mail Service Center
Raleigh, North Carolina 27699-4610

The State Archives also has a marriage bond index from 1741 to 1868.

For Adoption Record information write to:

Adoption Services   Tel. (919) 733-3801
North Carolina Division of Social Services
Department of Health and Human Resources
325 North Salisbury Street
Raleigh, North Carolina 27603

The Family History Library of Salt Lake City, Utah has a microfiche copy of the statewide marriage index.

For further information see:

North Carolina Registrar, Vital Records Newsletter. (Serial) Raleigh, NC: NC State Department of Health, Office of Vital Statistics. Vol. 1, 1991– .
Patterson, A. M. and F. D. Gatton. *The County Records Manual, 1970.* Raleigh, NC: State Department of Archives and History, 1970. 98p.
The Vital Record (Serial). Raleigh, NC: State Vital Records Section. Vol. 1, No. 1, February 1994– .

North Carolina Department of Health and Human Services
North Carolina Vital Records
1903 Mail Service Center • Raleigh, NC 27699-1903

Application for Copy of North Carolina Birth Certificate

North Carolina requires a $10 fee for the search of the records, whether the record is located or not. If located, the search fee includes one copy. Additional copies are available for $5 each if requested at the same time. **Make check or money order payable to North Carolina Vital Records.**

Please Print

Full Name on Certificate _____
First Name   Middle Name   Last Name

Date of Birth   __ __ | __ __ | __ __ __ __   Sex ☐ Male ☐ Female
Month   Day   Year

Place of Birth _____   Were parents married at time
City   County   of birth? ☐ Yes ☐ No

Full Name of Father _____
First Name   Middle Name   Last Name

Full Name of Mother _____
First Name   Middle Name   Maiden Name (Required)

Number of Copies Requested: Certified (Legally suitable for any purpose) _____

Uncertified (Suitable for research purposes) _____

Your Relationship to the Person Whose Certificate is Requested: *(Check one)*

1. ☐ Self   6. ☐ Grandparent   ☐ Other *(for non-family use only)*
2. ☐ Spouse (current)   7. ☐ Authorized agent, attorney
3. ☐ Brother/Sister   or legal representative of   Requestor _____
4. ☐ Child   the person listed in 1-6
5. ☐ Parent/Step-Parent   *(Proof Required)*   How do you plan to use this record?
                                                         _____

I hereby certify that all the above information is true to the best of my knowledge. **Note: It is a <u>felony violation</u> of North Carolina Law (G.S. 130A-26) to make a false statement on this application or to unlawfully obtain a certified copy of a birth certificate.**

_____   _____
Signature of Person Applying for Certificate   *Date*

_____
Street Address or P.O. Box

_____   ( ) _____
City, State and Zip Code   *Telephone Number*

Office Use Only: Volume _____   Page _____   Cartridge/Frame _____

Amount received: $_____   Identification furnished: _____

North Carolina Department of Health and Human Services
North Carolina Vital Records
1903 Mail Service Center • Raleigh, NC 27699-1903

Application for North Carolina Death, Marriage, or Divorce Record

North Carolina requires a $10 fee for the search of the records, whether the record is located or not. If located, the search fee includes one copy. Additional copies are available for $5 each if requested at the same time. **Make check or money order payable to North Carolina Vital Records.**

Please Print

Death Certificate   **Number of Copies Requested:**   Certified _____   Uncertified _____

Full Name of Deceased _____

Date of Death *(Month/Day/Year)* __ __ | __ __ | __ __ __ __   Age at Time of Death _____   Race _____

Location of Death *(City or County)* _____

Date of Birth *(Month/Day/Year)* __ __ | __ __ | __ __ __ __

Office Use Only:
Book _____
Page _____

Marriage Certificate   **Number of Copies Requested:**   Certified _____   Uncertified _____

Full Name of Groom _____

Full Maiden Name of Bride _____

Date of Marriage *(Month/Day/Year)* __ __ | __ __ | __ __ __ __

Location of Marriage *(City or County)* _____

Office Use Only:
Book _____
Page _____

Divorce Certificate   **Number of Copies Requested:**   Certified _____   Uncertified _____

Full Name of Husband _____

Full Name of Wife _____

Date of Divorce *(Month/Day/Year)* __ __ | __ __ | __ __ __ __

Location of Divorce *(City or County)* _____

Office Use Only:
Book _____
Page _____

Required for all Certificates Requested

Your Relationship to the Person Whose Certificate is Requested: *(Check one)*

1. ☐ Self
2. ☐ Spouse (current)
3. ☐ Brother/Sister
4. ☐ Child
5. ☐ Parent/Step-Parent

6. ☐ Grandparent
7. ☐ Authorized agent, attorney or legal representative of the person listed in 1-6 *(Proof Required)*

☐ Other *(for non-family use only)*

Requestor _____

How do you plan to use this record?

_____

I hereby certify that all the above information is true to the best of my knowledge. **Note: It is a <u>felony violation</u> of North Carolina Law (G.S. 130A-26) to make a false statement on this application or to unlawfully obtain a certified copy of a vital record.**

_____
Signature of Person Applying for Certificate

_____
Street Address or P.O. Box

_____
City, State and Zip Code

_____   (___) _____
Date   *Telephone Number*

Office Use Only

Identification Furnished

_____

_____

Amount Received $_____

NORTH DAKOTA

Send your requests to:

North Dakota Department of Health
Division of Vital Records
State Capitol
600 East Boulevard
Bismarck, North Dakota 58505-0200

Tel. (701) 328-2360
Fax (701) 328-1850
E-mail: vitalrec@state.nd.us
http://www.health.state.nd.us/ndhd/admin/vital/

The Division of Vital Records has birth records from 1870; marriage records from July 1, 1925; a divorce decrees index from July 1, 1949; and death records from 1881. Expedited service is available (with payment by credit card) for an additional fee of $5.00, plus shipping.

According to the Division, "the first law requiring registration of births and deaths in North Dakota became effective July 1, 1893, but was repealed in 1895 and not re-enacted until 1899. Even though registration was required by law, it was very poorly done and there are very few births or deaths recorded prior to 1900 or in the early 1900s. More events were recorded beginning about 1908, but it was not until about the 1920s that registration became about 90 percent complete."

Cost for a certified Birth Certificate	$7.00
Additional copy of Birth Certificate, when ordered at the same time	$4.00
Cost for a certified Marriage Certificate, ordered from the state office	$5.00
Additional copy of Marriage Certificate, ordered at the same time (state)	$2.00
Cost for a certified Death Certificate	$5.00
Additional copy of Death Certificate, when ordered at the same time	$2.00

For Divorce Records and earlier Marriage Certificates write to:

County Clerk of Court
District County Court
(County Seat), North Dakota
(For help in selecting correct county call 701-328-2360 or E-mail: msmail.vitalrec@state.nd.us)

Cost for a certified Marriage Certificate, ordered from a county district court	$10.00
Additional copy of Marriage Certificate, ordered at the same time (county)	$5.00

For Adoption Record information write to:

North Dakota Department of Human Services
Adoption Search/Disclosure
600 East Boulevard
Bismarck, North Dakota 58505-0250

Tel. (701) 328-2316
(800) 245-3736

The Family History Library in Salt Lake City, Utah has microfilmed many of the original and published vital records and church registers of North Dakota. For details on the holdings please consult your nearest Family History Center.

REQUEST FOR COPY OF BIRTH CERTIFICATE
NORTH DAKOTA DEPARTMENT OF HEALTH
DIVISION OF VITAL RECORDS
SFN 8140 (5-95)

PLEASE PRINT - ALL ITEMS MUST BE COMPLETED FOR US TO LOCATE AND IDENTIFY THE RECORD

1. Full Name at Birth	2. Sex ☐ Male ☐ Female

3. Date of Birth (Month, Day, Year)	4. Place of Birth (City or Township)	County

5. Residence of Parents at Time of this Birth (City & State)	6. Order of Birth (1st Child, 2nd, etc.)

7. Full Name of Father (First, Middle, Last)

8. Full Name of Mother (First, Middle, Maiden)

9. Certificate for An Adopted Child ☐ Yes ☐ No	10. Purpose of Requested Copy

11. Type of Copy Desired
☐ Paper Copy   ☐ Plastic Birth Card - (Birth card may not be acceptable for travel outside the U.S.)

12. Your Relationship to Person on Line 1*	13. Fee Enclosed (see schedule) $	No. of Copies

* Birth certificates relating to an out of wedlock birth can be furnished only to the parent of the child, the child's guardian, to the person to whom the record relates if that person is at least 18 years old, or upon order of a court of competent jurisdiction.

This Section Is To Be Completed By Person Making Request

Signature

Printed Name	Daytime Telephone Number ( )

Address	Apartment No.	City	State	Zip Code

If Copy Is To Be Mailed Elsewhere

Name

Address	Apartment No.	City	State	Zip Code

FEE SCHEDULE

The fee for a search of the files is $7.00; one search fee pays for one certified copy. Additional copies of the same certificate issued at the same time are $4.00 each. (Two dollars of this fee is used to support the Children's Trust Fund, a state fund for aiding in the prevention of child abuse and neglect.)

NOTE: Make all checks or money orders payable to "NORTH DAKOTA DEPARTMENT OF HEALTH".
Cash is sent at your own risk!

Mail Request with fee to:
**NORTH DAKOTA DEPARTMENT OF HEALTH
VITAL RECORDS
STATE CAPITOL
600 EAST BOULEVARD AVENUE
BISMARCK, ND 58505-0200**

WARNING: ND Century Code Chapter 23-02.1.32. Penalties. (c) Any person who willfully and knowingly uses or attempts to use or to furnish to another for use, for any purpose of deception, any certificate, record, report, or certified copy thereof so made, altered, amended, or mutilated shall be guilty of a class A misdemeanor.

THIS PORTION FOR VITAL RECORDS
OFFICE USE ONLY

REQUEST FOR COPY OF MARRIAGE RECORD
NORTH DAKOTA DEPARTMENT OF HEALTH
DIVISION OF VITAL RECORDS
SFN 8141 (12-97)

PLEASE PRINT - ALL ITEMS MUST BE COMPLETED FOR US TO LOCATE AND IDENTIFY THE RECORD

Full Name of Groom	Full Maiden Name of Bride	
Residence of Groom At Marriage (City & State)	Residence of Bride At Marriage (City & State)	
Date of Marriage (Mo/Day/Year) — County Where License Issued	City Where Married	County Where Married
For What Purpose is Copy Needed	Fee Enclosed (see schedule) $	
Your Relationship to Groom/Bride (e.g., self, parent, attorney-specify)	Number of Copies	

This Section Is To Be Completed By Person Making Request

Signature		
Printed Name	Daytime Telephone Number ( )	
Address — Apt. No. — City	State	Zip Code

THIS PORTION FOR VITAL RECORDS OFFICE USE ONLY

Original Licenses and Certificates of Marriage are filed in the office of the **Clerk of District Court** of the **COUNTY WHERE LICENSE WAS ISSUED.** It is recommended that requests for certified copies be directed to the custodian of the <u>original</u> record.

<u>The fee for the county offices is $10 for one copy</u> and $5 for each additional copy issued of the same certificate at the same time.

See reverse side of this form for a list of the North Dakota counties, respective county seats, addresses, and zip codes.

• •

Since July 1, 1925, copies of Licenses and Certificates of Marriage have been forwarded to the State Registrar for statistical purposes and for maintaining a state-wide index. The state office is also authorized to issue certified copies. For marriages which have occurred since July 1, 1925, you may secure copies from the County Office (as noted above) or from address listed below.

<u>The fee at the State Vital Records Office is $5 for one copy</u> and $2 for each additional copy issued of the same certificate at the same time.

Mail request with fee to:

**NORTH DAKOTA DEPARTMENT OF HEALTH
DIVISION OF VITAL RECORDS
STATE CAPITOL, 600 EAST BOULEVARD AVENUE
BISMARCK, NORTH DAKOTA 58505-0200**

REQUEST FOR COPY OF DEATH CERTIFICATE
NORTH DAKOTA DEPARTMENT OF HEALTH
DIVISION OF VITAL RECORDS
SFN 5531 (6-95)

PLEASE PRINT - ALL ITEMS MUST BE COMPLETED FOR US TO LOCATE AND IDENTIFY THE RECORD

Full Name of Deceased	Sex ☐ Male ☐ Female

Date of Death (Month, Day, Year)	Name of Spouse

Place of Death (Name of Hospital)	City	County

Your Relationship to the Deceased*	Name of Funeral Home

* The <u>cause of death</u> on death certificates is by law confidential and copies showing the cause of death are to be furnished only to a relative or personal representative of the deceased, to the attorney or the agent of a relative or personal representative of the deceased or upon order of a court of competent jurisdiction.

For what purpose is this copy requested?	Amount Enclosed (see fee schduled below) $	No. of Certified Copies

This Section Is To Be Completed By Person Making Request

Signature		
Printed Name		Telephone Number ( )
Address	City	State	Zip Code

If Copy Is To Be Mailed Elsewhere

Name		
Address	City	State	Zip Code

THIS PORTION FOR VITAL RECORD'S OFFICE USE ONLY

<u>The fee for a search of the files is $5</u>; one search fee pays for one certified copy. Additional copies of the same certificate issued at the same time are $2 each. NOTE: Make all checks or money orders payable to the "NORTH DAKOTA DEPARTMENT OF HEALTH". Cash is sent at your own risk!	

Mail request with fee to:

NORTH DAKOTA DEPARTMENT OF HEALTH
DIVISION OF VITAL RECORDS
STATE CAPITOL, 600 EAST BOULEVARD AVENUE
BISMARCK, NORTH DAKOTA 58505-0200

OHIO

Ohio State Department of Health
Vital Statistics Unit
35 East Chestnut Street
P.O. Box 15098
Columbus, Ohio 43215-0098

Tel. (614) 466-2531
http://www.odh.state.oh.us/Birth/birthmain.htm

The Vital Statistics Unit has birth records from December 20, 1908; marriage and divorce records from September 7, 1949; and death records from January 1, 1945. Copies of vital records cannot be ordered by telephone or e-mail. Other birth, death, and marriage records are available at the Ohio Historical Society (see below for address). The Historical Society also maintains an online index to Ohio death certificates 1913–1937.

Cost for a certified Birth Certificate	$9.00
Cost for an heirloom Birth Certificate	$25.00
Cost for a certified Marriage Certificate	$9.00
Cost for a certified Death Certificate	$9.00

For earlier Marriage, Birth, and Deaths Records write to:

County Probate Court
(County Seat), Ohio

For Death Records from December 20, 1908 through December 1944, write to:

Ohio Historical Society
1982 Velma Avenue
Columbus, Ohio 43211-2497

Tel. (617) 297-2300
http://www.ohiohistory.org

For Divorce Records write to:

Clerk of Courts
Court of Common Pleas
(County Seat), Ohio

For Adoption Record information write to:

Ohio Adoption Registry
Ohio Department of Health
Vital Statistics Unit, 35 East Chestnut Street
Post Office Box 15098
Columbus, Ohio 43215-0098

Tel. (614) 644-5635
http://www.odh.state.oh.us/Birth/adopt.htm

Adoption records pre-January 1, 1964 are open. Adoption Records from January 1, 1964 to September 18, 1996 are sealed and can only be opened with a court order. Adoptees over the age of 21 who were available for adoption after September 18, 1996 can request birth information. If they are over 18, the adoptive parents can request the information for them. There is no cost to register with the Adoption Registry; the fee for a copy of an adoption file is $20.00.

The Family History Library in Salt Lake City, Utah has microfilmed many of the original and published vital records and church registers of Ohio. For details on the holdings please consult your nearest Family History Center.

Ohio Department of Health • Bureau of Vital Statistics

Application for Certified Copies

Check appropriate box

☐ Birth Certificate — $9.00 each

☐ Death Certificate — $9.00 each

☐ Paternity Affidavit — $7.00 each

IMPORTANT!

Intended for Ohio records only. Each copy requested must have the required fee.

Enclose check or money order. Must be made payable to "Treasurer, State of Ohio", do not send cash.

Notice—Fee overpayment of $2.00 or less will not be refunded—ORC 3705.24

To be _printed_ below is information about requested certificate.

Full name	first	middle	last	Phone ( )
Present address	number and street	city, village or township	state	ZIP
Parents	mother's first		mother's maiden	
	father's first		father's last	
Place of event	county	city, village or township	Date of event	Age (last birthday)

Amount enclosed $ ☐ Cash ☐ Check ☐ Money order

Date of payment

To your knowledge has a copy of this record been obtained before? ☐ Yes ☐ No ☐ Unknown

Have any corrections/changes been made to this certificate? ☐ Yes ☐ No ☐ Unknown

Applicant's signature

Date

Do not detach

Print name and address of person to whom certificates(s) is (are) to be mailed in the space below. This is a mailing insert and will be used to mail the certified copy which you have requested. When the above application and the name and address in the section below have been completed please send the entire form to the preprinted address below:

Name		
Address		
City	State	ZIP

Ohio Department of Health
Bureau of Vital Statistics
P.O. Box 15098
Columbus. Ohio 43215-0098

HEA 2709 (Rev. 8/99)

5132.06

Heirloom Birth Certificate

Order Form

Name on record:

First_____ Middle_____

Last_____

Date of birth:

Sex ☐ M ☐ F

Month_____ Day_____ Year_____

Father's Name:

First_____ Middle_____

Last_____

Mother's Name:

First_____ Middle_____

Last_____

Name of person ordering certificate:

First_____ Last_____

Please indicate the size you are ordering.

☐ 8.5 x 11   or   ☐ 11 x 14

Your signature: _____

Telephone

(   ) _____

Mailing address for certificate:

Name_____

Address_____

City_____ State_____ Zip_____

Please note: All information must be completed. The fee for each birth certificate is $25. If the requested certificate cannot be found, a refund will be issued as prescribed by law .

Please enclose the cor rect fee with this application form. Make checks or money order payable to: T reasurer, State of Ohio. Please do not send cash! Mail to: Ohio Department of Health, Vital Statistics, P.O. Box 15098 Columbus, Ohio 43215-0098.

OKLAHOMA

Vital Records Service
Oklahoma State Department of Health
1000 Northeast 10th Street
P.O. Box 53551
Oklahoma City, Oklahoma 73152-3551

or

Vital Records Service
108 N. Greenwood Street
Tulsa, Oklahoma 74120

Tel. (405) 271-4040
http://www.health.state.ok.us/program/vital/brec.html

Tel. (918) 582-4973

The Vital Records Service has birth and death records from October 1908. Please include a self-addressed stamped envelope with your request. The County Clerks also maintain vital records, including many records from the 1800s.

Cost for a certified Birth Certificate	$5.00
Cost for a certified Death Certificate	$10.00

For Marriage Certificates write to:

County Clerk
County Court House
(County Seat), Oklahoma

For Divorce Records write to:

Clerk
District Court
(County Seat), Oklahoma

For Adoption Record information write to:

Oklahoma Mutual Consent Voluntary Registry
Oklahoma Department of Human Services
Adoption Section
P.O. Box 25352
Oklahoma City, Oklahoma 73125-9975

Tel. (405) 521-2475

The cost for registration in the Mutual Consent Voluntary Registry is $20.00.

The Family History Library of Salt Lake City, Utah has microfilmed many of the original and published vital records and church registers of Oklahoma. For details on their holdings please consult your nearest Family History Center.

Division of Vital Records, Oklahoma State Department of Health
1000 Northeast 10th Street, Post Office Box 53551
Oklahoma City, Oklahoma 73152-3551

APPLICATION FOR SEARCH AND CERTIFIED COPY OF BIRTH CERTIFICATE

Facts Concerning This Birth

Full name of child _____

Date of
birth _____ Place of
birth _____, OKLAH
    (Mo.) (Day) (Year)   (County) (City)

Full name of father _____

Full Maiden name of mother _____

Signature of person
making this application _____ Date of this
application _____

If both parents names are not indicated on the original certificate of birth and a "full copy" is desired it will be necessary to have the signature of the mother, or the registrant if of legal age, or if certificate is required for "adoption purposes" the signature of the attorney of record and a statement from him to that effect.

The above signature is by ( ) person himself-herself ( ) next-of-kin ( ) authorized agent

Purpose for which this copy is needed
( ) School ( ) Passport ( ) Employment ( ) Adoption ( ) Other (Please state) _____

Has copy of this persons birth certificate been received before? ( ) Yes ( ) No ( ) Unknown

PLEASE PRINT CORRECT MAILING ADDRESS BELOW:

Number of copies
wanted @ $5.00 _____

_____
(Name)

Fee enclosed $ _____

_____
(Street Address)

**ENCLOSE A STAMPED
SELF-ADDRESSED
ENVELOPE WITH THIS
APPLICATION**

_____
(City)   (State)   (Zip)

Division of Vital Records, Oklahoma State Department of Health
1000 Northeast 10th Street, Post Office Box 53551
Oklahoma City, Oklahoma 73152-3551

APPLICATION FOR SEARCH AND CERTIFIED COPY OF DEATH CERTIFICATE

Facts Concerning This Death

Full name of deceased _____ Race _____

Date of
death _____ Place of death _____, OKLAHOMA
     (Mo.) (Day) (Year)   (County) (City)

Check box if death was stillbirth or fetal death ☐
Funeral director
in charge _____ Address _____

Purpose for which this copy is needed _____

Signature of person
making this application _____ Date of application _____

PLEASE PRINT CORRECT MAILING ADDRESS BELOW:

_____
(Name)

Number of copies
wanted @ $10.00 _____

_____
(Street Address)

Fee enclosed $ _____

**ENCLOSE A STAMPED
SELF-ADDRESSED
ENVELOPE WITH THIS
APPLICATION**

_____
(City)   (State)   (Zip)

Request for a search of the records for a death certificate of any person who died in the State of Oklahoma should be submitted on this blank along with the required fee of $10.00. If the death certificate is on file a certified copy will be mailed.

The information requested above should be filled in carefully and accurately. It is the minimum needed to make a thorough search for a death record.

Send ten dollars ($10.00) in cash, money order or check for each copy desired. Cash is sent at sender's risk. Make checks or money orders payable to the State Department of Health.

A copy required to be submitted to the Veterans Administration or U.S. Commissioner of Pensions, in connection with a claim for military-service-connected benefits may be obtained without fee provided a signed statement is attached which sets forth these facts and requests that the copy be issued without fee. Members of the armed forces and veterans must pay regular fees for copies to be used for all other purposes.

VS150 R8-93

OREGON

Send your requests to:

Oregon Department of Human Resources
State Health Division
Vital Statistics Office
800 NE Oregon Street, Suite 205
P.O. Box 14050
Portland, Oregon 97293-0050

Tel. (503) 731-4108
Recording (503) 731-4095
Fax (503) 234-8417
http://www.ohd.hr.state.or.us/chs/certif/certfaqs.htm

The Vital Statistics Office has birth and death records from July 1903, marriage records from 1906, and divorce certificates (not decrees) from 1925. Expedited service is available (with payment by credit card) for an additional fee of $10, plus shipping. The Vital Statistics Office also provides pre-adoption birth records to adoptees 21 years or older (born in Oregon), or their legal representatives, for cases where the Office received an adoption report that sealed the original record and created a new record. Applicants requesting such records should use the Birth Record Order Form and clearly identify themselves as an "Adoptee seeking a pre-adoption birth record." More information and downloadable forms are available at **http://www.ohd.hr.state.or.us/chs. certif/preadopt.htm**.

Cost for a certified Birth Certificate	$15.00
Cost for an heirloom Birth Certificate	$40.00
Cost for a wallet-size Birth Certificate	$15.00
Cost for a certified Marriage or Divorce Certificate	$15.00
Cost for a certified Death Certificate	$15.00
Cost for a duplicate certificate, when ordered at the same time	$12.00

For earlier records write to:

County Clerk
County Court House
(County Seat), Oregon

For Adoption Record information write to:

Permanency and Adoption Services/Registry
State Office for Services to Children and Families
500 Summer Street, NE
Salem, Oregon 97310-1010

Tel. (503) 945-6643

Cost for registering for identifying Adoption information	$25.00
Cost for registering for non-identifying Adoption information	$45.00
Cost for an assisted search for Adoption information	$400.00

The Oregon State Archives (800 Summer Street, Salem, OR 97310; 503-373-0701) has some city and county vital records, as well as a statewide marriage index for 1906–1924 and 1946–1996; a divorce index for 1946–1996; death records for 1903–1947; and a death index for 1903–1996. Non-certified copies of death records older than 50 years are available for a small fee.

The Family History Library of Salt Lake City, Utah has a microfilm copy of the index to death records from 1903 to 1970.

State of Oregon
Department of Human Services
Health Division

BIRTH RECORD ORDER FORM
$15 first copy / $12 every additional copy/card

_____ Number of Certified Copies Requested
_____ Number of Certified Cards Requested

1. Name on Record _____

2. Date of Birth _____

3. Place of Birth _____

4. Father's Full Name _____

5. Mother's Full
   Maiden Name _____

6. Name of Person
   Ordering Record _____

7. Your Relationship To The
   Person Named on the Record _____

8. Daytime Telephone Number _____

9. Your Address _____

10. City/State/Zip _____

In accordance with law - ORS 432.120, access to birth records is restricted for 100 years to the registrant, immediate family members, legal representatives, government agencies, and persons licensed or registered under ORS 03.430. Legal guardians must enclose a copy of the legal document. If you are not eligible, enclose a written permission note with a notarized signature of an eligible person..

Send to: **OREGON VITAL RECORDS**
PO BOX 14050
PORTLAND OR 97293-0050

Make payment to Oregon Health Division

All fees are non-refundable search fees.
Do not sent cash.

Call (503) 731-4095 for record ordering information
Web Page: http://www.ohd.hr.state.or.us/chs

International customers: Only U.S. bank money orders or traveler's checks in U.S. dollars can be accepted.

NSF Check Processing Policy: In the event that your check is returned unpaid for insufficient or uncollected funds, we may present your check electronically. In the ordinary course of business, your check will not be provided to you with your bank statement, but a copy can be retrieved by other means

PLEASE ENTER YOUR MAILING ADDRESS BELOW

Name _____

Street _____

City/State/Zip _____

DO NOT DETACH
THIS IS YOUR MAILING LABEL

45/13birth/01/00

State of Oregon
Department of Human Services
Health Division

MARRIAGE RECORD ORDER FORM
$15 first copy / $12 every additional copy

_____ Number of Certified Copies Requested

ATTENTION:

CERTIFICATE #:

1. Full Name of Groom _____

2. Bride's Full Maiden Name _____

FILM _____

3. Date of Marriage _____

FILM (P) _____

4. Place License Issued _____

COMPUTER _____

5. Name of Person
   Ordering Record _____

INDEXES _____

INDEX (P) _____

6. Your Relationship To The
   Person Named on the Record _____
   Or Reason You Need Record

DF/CO _____

7. Daytime Telephone Number _____

REFUND: $ _____

Excess Fee: Out/State _____

8. Your Address _____

No Record: Uncompleted: _____

9. City/State/Zip _____

CHECK # _____

DATE: _____

In accordance with law -- ORS 432.120 -- access to statewide marriage records is restricted for 50 years to family members, legal representatives, government agencies, persons and organizations with a personal or or property right and persons licensed/registered under ORS 703.430. If you are not eligible, enclose a written permission note with a notarized signature of an eligible person. Note: marriage records may be ordered from the county office that issued the marriage license.

**Send to: OREGON VITAL RECORDS
PO BOX 14050
PORTLAND OR 97293-0050**

FOR OFFICE USE ONLY

File Date	Amendment Fee

Make money orders payable to Oregon Health Division
All fees are non-refundable search fees.
Do not sent cash.

Call (503) 731-4095 for record ordering information
World Wide Web Page: http://www.ohd.hr.state.or.us/chs

NRL/Ref Issued	Full Issued

Follow Up	Card Issued

International customers: Only U.S. bank money orders or traveler's checks in U.S. dollars can be accepted.

NSF Check Processing Policy: In the event that your check is returned unpaid for insufficient or uncollected funds, we may present your check electronically. In the ordinary course of business, your check will not be provided to you with your bank statement, but a copy can be retrieved by other means.

PLEASE ENTER YOUR MAILING ADDRESS BELOW

Name _____

Street _____

City/State/Zip _____

DO NOT DETACH

THIS IS YOUR MAILING LABEL

45/13Marriage/01/00

State of Oregon
Department of Human Services
Health Division

DIVORCE RECORD ORDER FORM
$15 first copy / $12 every additional copy

_____ Number of Certified Copies Requested

1. Full Name of Husband _____

2. Full Maiden Name of Wife _____

3. Date of Divorce _____

4. County Where Divorce Granted _____

5. Name of Person
   Ordering Record _____

6. Your Relationship To The
   Person Named on the Record _____
   Or Reason You Need Record

7. Daytime Telephone Number_____

8. Your Address_____

9. City/State/Zip_____

CERTIFICATE #: _____

_____
FILM _____
FILM (P) _____
COMPUTER _____
INDEXES _____
INDEX (P) _____
DF/CO _____

REFUND: $ _____
Excess Fee: _____ Out/State _____
No Record: _____ Uncompleted: ____
CHECK # _____

Date _____

In accordance with law -- ORS.432.120 -- access to statewide divorce records is restricted for 50 years to family members, legal representatives, government agencies, persons and organizations with a personal or property right and person's licensed/registered under ORS 703.430. If you are not eligible, enclose a written permission note with a notarized signature of an eligible person. Note: **Divorce decrees** are available from the county court that granted the divorce.

Send to: **OREGON VITAL RECORDS
PO BOX 14050
PORTLAND OR 97293-0050**

Make money orders payable to Oregon Health Division
All fees are non-refundable search fees.
Do not sent cash.

Call (503) 731-4095 for record ordering information
Web Page: http://www.ohd.hr.state.or.us/chs

International customers: Only U.S. bank money orders or traveler's checks in U.S. dollars can be accepted.

NSF Check Processing Policy: In the event that your check is returned unpaid for insufficient or uncollected funds, we may present your check electronically. In the ordinary course of business, your check will not be provided to you with your bank statement, but a copy can be retrieved by other means

PLEASE ENTER YOUR MAILING ADDRESS BELOW

Name _____

Street _____

City/State/Zip _____

DO NOT DETACH

THIS IS YOUR MAILING LABEL

45/13Divorce/01/00

State of Oregon
Department of Human Services
Health Division

DEATH RECORD ORDER FORM
$15 first copy / $12 every additional copy

ATTENTION:

_____ Number of certified copies requested
_____ Number of fact of death copies requested – does not include cause of death

CERTIFICATE #

_____

1. Name on Record _____

2. Spouse of Decedent _____

FILM _____

3. Date of Death _____

FILM (P) _____

4. Place of Death _____

COMPUTER _____

5. Name of Person
Ordering Record _____

INDEXES _____

INDEX (P) _____

6. Your Relationship To The
Person Named on the Record _____
Or Reason You Need Record

DF/CO _____

7. Daytime Telephone Number_____

REFUND: $ _____

Excess Fee: _____ Out/State _____

8. Your Address_____

No Record: _____ Uncompleted: ____

9. City/State/Zip_____

CHECK # _____

In accordance with law - ORS 432.120, access to death records is restricted for 50 years to family members, legal representatives, government agencies, persons licensed or registered under ORS 703.430 and persons with a personal or property right. Legal guardians must enclose a copy of the legal document. If you are not eligible, enclose a written permission note with a notarized signature of an eligible person.

DATE: _____

Send to: **OREGON VITAL RECORDS
PO BOX 14050
PORTLAND OR 97293-0050**

File Date   Amendment Fee

Make payment to Oregon Health Division
All fees are non-refundable search fees.
Do not sent cash

NRL/Ref Issued   Full Issued

Call (503) 731-4095 for record ordering information
Web Page: http://www.ohd.hr.state.or.us/chs

Follow Up

NSF Check Processing Policy: In the event that your check is returned unpaid for insufficient or uncollected funds, we may present your check electronically In the ordinary course of business, your check will not be provided to you with your bank statement, but a copy can be retrieved by other means

International customers: Only U.S. bank money orders or traveler's checks in U.S. dollars can be accepted.

PLEASE ENTER YOUR MAILING ADDRESS BELOW

Name _____

DO NOT DETACH

Street _____

THIS IS YOUR MAILING LABEL

City/State/Zip _____

45/13death/01/00

PENNSYLVANIA

Send your requests to:

Pennsylvania Department of Health
Division of Vital Records
101 South Mercer Street
P.O. Box 1528
New Castle, Pennsylvania 16103-1528

Tel. (724) 656-3100
Fax (724) 652-8951
http://www.health.state.pa.us/HPA/apply_bd.htm

The Division of Vital Records has birth and death records from January 1906. Include a self-addressed stamped envelope with your request. Expedited service is available by fax (with payment by credit card) for an additional fee of $7.00, plus shipping.

Requests for vital records may be made in person at the Vital Records offices in Erie, Harrisburg, Philadelphia, Pittsburgh, and Scranton, as well as at the New Castle office. The address of these other offices are as follows—**Erie:** 1910 West 26th Street; **Harrisburg:** Health & Welfare Building, Room 516, 7th & Forster; **Philadelphia:** 1400 West Spring Garden Street, Room 1009; **Pittsburgh:** 300 Liberty Avenue, Room 512; **Scranton:** 100 Lackawanna Avenue.

Cost for a certified Birth Certificate	$4.00
Cost for a certified Death Certificate	$3.00
Records of veterans, veterans' spouses and their minor children	No Charge

For Marriage or Divorce Certificates, or earlier Birth and Death Records write to:

County Clerk
County Court House
(County Seat), Pennsylvania

For Adoption Record information write to:

Adoption Exchange
Pennsylvania Department of Public Welfare
P.O. Box 2675
Harrisburg, Pennsylvania 17105-2675

Tel. (717) 772-7015
(800) 227-0225
Fax (717) 772-6857
http://www.dpw.state.pa.us/ocyf/ocyfas.asp

The Historical Society of Pennsylvania (1300 Locust Street, Philadelphia, PA 19107; 215-732-6200) has a large microfilm collection of Pennsylvania vital, county, and church records.

The Family History Library of Salt Lake City, Utah has microfilm copies of births from 1852 to 1854; marriages from 1852 to 1854 and 1885 to 1889; and deaths from 1774 to 1873.

H105.102 Rev. 3/97

PENNSYLVANIA DEPARTMENT OF HEALTH
VITAL RECORDS

APPLICATION FOR CERTIFIED COPY OF BIRTH OR DEATH RECORD

RECORDS AVAILABLE FROM 1906 TO THE PRESENT

If Veteran (✓)
See Other Side ☐

PRINT OR TYPE   ALL ITEMS MUST BE COMPLETED   OFFICE USE ONLY

INDICATE NUMBER OF COPIES IN BOX	☐ BIRTH $4.00	☐ DEATH $3.00	If social security number is known of deceased _ _ _ _		

1. Date of Birth **OR** Date of Death	2. Place of Birth **OR** Place of Death	County	Boro/City/Twp.	File No.

3. Name at Birth **OR** Name at Death		4. Sex	5. Age Now	Searched By

6. Father's Full Name	First	Middle	Last	Type By

7. Mother's Maiden Name	First	Middle	Last	File Date

8. Hospital	Funeral Director	Refund Ck. No.

9. **REASON FOR REQUEST. THIS ITEM MUST BE COMPLETED**

Date   Amt.

10. **HOW** ARE YOU RELATED TO PERSON IN NUMBER 3?

In accordance with §4904, Unsworn Falsification to Authorities, I state the above information is accurate. (If subject is under 18, parent must sign.)

11. Signature Required: Please sign here.

12. Mailing Address

13. City, State, Zip Code

14. Daytime Phone Number   Area Code: Number:

FEE FOR CERTIFIED COPIES ARE: BIRTHS $4.00   DEATHS $3.00
NOT REFUNDABLE

DO NOT SEND CASH
Make Check or Money Order Payable to   VITAL RECORDS

PLEASE ENCLOSE A LEGAL-SIZE SELF-ADDRESSED STAMPED ENVELOPE FOR RETURN OF COPIES
IF ALL ITEMS ARE NOT COMPLETED, APPLICATION MAY BE REJECTED

☐ Prev. Amend.   ☐ Adopt   ☐ Affidavit
☐ Usage   ☐ Court Order   ☐ Issue Affidavit

DO NOT REMOVE THIS STUB

If birth or death occurred in: Mail application to:

1) Philadelphia — Division of Vital Records, 1400 W. Spring Garden St., Room 1009, Philadelphia, PA 19130-4090
2) Pittsburgh — Division of Vital Records, 300 Liberty Ave., Room 512, Pittsburgh, PA 15222-1210
3) Erie — Division of Vital Records, 1910 West 26th St., Erie, PA 16508-1148
4) Scranton — Division of Vital Records, 100 Lackawanna Ave., Scranton, PA 18503-1928

Print or type name and address in the space below.

Name
Street
City, State, Zip Code

FOR ALL OTHER AREAS
MAIL COMPLETED APPLICATION TO:
PENNSYLVANIA DEPARTMENT OF HEALTH
DIVISION OF VITAL RECORDS
P.O. BOX 1528
NEW CASTLE, PA 16103-1528
or visit our public offices at
101 South Mercer Street, New Castle or
Room 129 Health & Welfare Bldg., Harrisburg

REQUIREMENTS FOR FREE COPIES

1. Records of Veterans, Veteran's Spouses, and their minor children will be issued free.
2. Rank, Branch of Service, Service Number, and mailing address of veteran or dependent must be supplied.

THIS PORTION TO BE COMPLETED BY VETERAN OR VETERAN'S DEPENDENT ONLY

Veteran's Name _____

Service Number _____

Rank and Branch of Service _____

Signature of Veteran or Spouse _____

Are You the Veteran? Yes ☐
                   No ☐

If Not, What is Your
Relationship?_____

Mailing Address of Veteran or Dependent _____

_____

Pennsylvania Vital Records
PO Box 1528, New Castle, PA 16103-1528
724-656-3100

FAX Application for Certified Copy of Birth or Death Record
(Records Available from 1906 to the Present)

To order by fax: **In addition to the cost of the certified copy(s), there is a $7.00 service and handling fee.**
Print or type this form and fax to: 724-652-8951

BIRTH: $4.00 each *(No genealogy requests)*

Name at Birth: _____

Number of
Copies: _____   (If name has changed since birth due to adoption, court order or any reason other than marriage, please list changed name here:

_____

Date of Birth: _____ Sex: ____ Male ____ Female   Age Now _____

Place of Birth: _____ Hospital: _____
(County/City in Pennsylvania)

Full Name of Father: _____

Full Maiden Name of Mother: _____

DEATH: $3.00 each *(No genealogy requests)*

Name at Death: _____

Number of
Copies: _____   Date of Death: _____   Sex: ____ Male ____ Female

Place of Death: _____   SS# __ __ __ - __ __ - __ __ __ __
(County/City in Pennsylvania)

Name of Requester: _____

Address: _____

City: _____ State: _____ Zip: _____

Daytime phone Number: (__ __ __) __ __ __ - __ __ __ __

Required Information

What is your relationship to the person named on the record? _____

Reason for Request: _____

In accordance with § 4904. Unsworn Falsification to Authorities, I state the above information is accurate.

Signature of Applicant: _____

(Required)   (If subject is under 18, parent must sign)   Date

Ship by: _____ Regular Mail   _____ Overnight Carrier   (Additional Fee. Specify ___Fed-X ___ UPS or ___ Express Mail)

Type of Card:	_____Master Card	_____ Discover	_____Visa	_____ American Express
Card #:				
Expiration Date:				

Mail to: Name:	
Address:	
City/State /Zip:	

RHODE ISLAND

Send your requests to:

Division of Vital Records   Tel. (401) 277-2812
Rhode Island Department of Health   TDD (401) 277-2506
Cannon Building, Room 101
3 Capitol Hill
Providence, Rhode Island 02908-5097

The Division of Vital Records has birth and marriage records from 1899, and death records from 1949. Make your payment payable to "General Treasurer, State of Rhode Island."

Cost for a certified Birth Certificate	$15.00
Cost for a certified Marriage Certificate	$15.00
Cost for a certified Death Certificate	$15.00
Cost for a duplicate copy, when ordered at the same time	$5.00
Cost of certificates issued to a veteran	No Charge

For older Birth, Death, and Marriage Records, and Divorce Records write to:

Town Clerk
Town Hall
(Town), Rhode Island

For Adoption Record information write to:

Rhode Island Department of Children, Youth and Families   Tel. (401) 457-5306
610 Mount Pleasant Avenue, Bldg. 2
Providence, Rhode Island 02908-1935

For early Rhode Island vital records you should consult James Newell Arnold's *Vital Records of Rhode Island 1636–1850.* Providence, RI: Narragansett Historical Publishing, Co., 1891–1912. 20 vols.

The Rhode Island Historical Society (121 Hope Street, Providence, Rhode Island 02906; 401-331-8575) has computerized indexes of marriages and deaths to 1900. The Rhode Island State Archives (337 Westminster Street, Providence, RI 02903) maintains the original statewide manuscript filings for births and marriages 1852–1898, and deaths 1853–1948.

The Family History Library of Salt Lake City, Utah has microfilmed many of the original and published vital records and church registers of Rhode Island. For details on their holdings please consult your nearest Family History Center.

R.I. DEPT. OF HEALTH, DIV. OF VITAL RECORDS, 3 CAPITOL HILL, PROVIDENCE, R.I. 02908-5097

APPLICATION FOR A CERTIFIED COPY OF A BIRTH RECORD

PLEASE COMPLETE ALL QUESTIONS 1-5

1. Please fill in the information below for the person whose birth record you are requesting.

   FULL NAME AT BIRTH _____ AGE _____

   DATE OF BIRTH _____ CITY/TOWN OF BIRTH _____ HOSPITAL _____

   MOTHER'S FULL MAIDEN NAME _____

   FATHER'S FULL NAME _____ (if listed on record)

2. Please complete __one__ of the following:

   I am applying for the birth record of: _____ MYSELF   _____ MY CHILD

   _____ MY MOTHER/FATHER   _____ MY GRANDPARENT   _____ MY BROTHER/SISTER

   _____ MY CLIENT. I'M AN ATTORNEY REPRESENTING: _____

   _____ OTHER PERSON (SPECIFY HOW YOU ARE RELATED): _____

3. Copies cost $15.00 for the first copy and $5.00 for additional copies of the same record.

   FULL COPY _____.   How many do you want? _____

   WALLET SIZE _____.   How many do you want? _____
   (A wallet size is not accepted by all offices)

4. Why do you need this record?   (We ask this question so that we can supply you with a
   certified copy which will be suitable for your needs.)

   SCHOOL _____   WIC _____   PASSPORT _____   SOCIAL SECURITY _____   LICENSE _____

   WORK _____   WELFARE _____   OTHER SPECIFY _____

5. I hereby state that the information supplied __above__ is true to the best of my knowledge, and
   that the signature on this application is my own.

   PLEASE SIGN _____   _____
                  (Signature of person completing this form)   Date signed
   YOUR
   ADDRESS _____
                  Street or mailing address   City/Town   State   Zip Code

************************** BELOW THIS LINE FOR STATE USE ONLY **************************

State File Number	Amount Received	Receipt Number	Date Sent	Initials
_____	_____	_____	_____	_____

	Birth	Death	Marriage
Number of First Copies	_____	_____	_____
Number of Add'l Copies	_____	_____	_____

Number of Searches _____ Add'l Yrs Searched _____ Del.Fil. Corr. Pat. Adop. Legit.

VS 82B REV 5/93

R.I. DEPT. OF HEALTH, DIV. OF VITAL RECORDS, 3 CAPITOL HILL, PROVIDENCE, R.I. 02908-5097

APPLICATION FOR A CERTIFIED COPY OF A MARRIAGE RECORD

1. Please fill in the information below for the persons whose marriage record you are requesting:

   FULL NAME OF GROOM _____

   FULL NAME OF BRIDE _____

   FULL MAIDEN NAME OF BRIDE (IF DIFFERENT)_____

   DATE OF MARRIAGE _____ PLACE OF MARRIAGE _____

2. What is your relationship to the Bride or Groom?

   ____ BRIDE OR GROOM   ____ GRANDPARENT

   ____ MOTHER OR FATHER   ____ BROTHER OR SISTER

   ____ MY CLIENT. I'M AN ATTORNEY REPRESENTING: _____

   ____ OTHER PERSON (SPECIFY HOW YOU ARE RELATED) _____

3. Why do you need this record?

   _____

4. Copies cost $15.00 for the first copy and $5.00 for additional copies of the same record. How many copies do you want? _____

5. PLEASE SIGN _____ _____
               (Signature of person completing this form)   Date signed

   YOUR ADDRESS _____
                Street or mailing address   City/Town   State   Zip Code

****************************BELOW THIS LINE FOR STATE USE ONLY***********************
State File   Amount   Receipt   Date   Initials
Number _____ Received _____ Number _____ Sent _____   _____

	Birth	Death	Marriage
Number of First Copies	_____	_____	_____
Number of Add'l Copies	_____	_____	_____

Number of Searches _____ Add'l Yrs Searched _____ Del.Fil. Corr. Pat. Adop. Legit.

VS 82M REV 5/93

R.I. DEPT. OF HEALTH, DIV. OF VITAL RECORDS, 3 CAPITOL HILL,
PROVIDENCE, R.I. 02908-5097

APPLICATION FOR A CERTIFIED COPY OF A DEATH RECORD

1. Please fill in the information below for the individual whose death record you are requesting:

FULL NAME _____

DATE OF DEATH _____ PLACE OF DEATH _____

NAME OF SPOUSE (IF MARRIED) _____

MOTHER'S FULL MAIDEN NAME _____

FATHER'S FULL NAME _____

2. How are you related to the person whose death record is being requested?

_____

3. Why do you need this record?

_____

4. Copies cost $15.00 for the first copy and $5.00 for additional copies of the same record. How many copies do you want? _____

5. PLEASE SIGN _____ _____
   (Signature of person completing this form)   Date signed

YOUR
ADDRESS _____
   Street or mailing address   City/Town   State   Zip Code

***************************BELOW THIS LINE FOR STATE USE ONLY***********************

State
File   Amount   Receipt   Date   Initials
Number _____ Received _____ Number _____ Sent _____ _____

                    Birth   Death   Marriage
Number of First Copies _____   _____   _____

Number of Add'l Copies _____   _____   _____

Number of Searches _____ Add'l Yrs Searched _____ Del.Fil. Corr. Pat. Adop. Legit.

VS 82D REV 5/93

Send your requests to:

South Carolina Department of Health and Environmental Control   Tel. (803) 898-3630
Office of Vital Records & Public Health Statistics   Fax (803) 799-0301
2600 Bull Street
Columbia, South Carolina 29201-1797

The Office of Vital Records has birth and death records from January 1, 1915; marriage records from July 1, 1950; and divorce records from January 1, 1962. Expedited service is available (with payment by credit card) for an additional fee of $5.00 plus shipping by phoning (803) 734-4831 or faxing (803) 799-0301.

Cost for a certified Birth Certificate	$12.00
Cost for a wallet-size Birth Certificate (available only from the county)	$12.00
Cost for a certified Marriage or Divorce Certificate	$12.00
Cost for a certified Death Certificate	$12.00
Cost for a duplicate copy, when ordered at the same time	$3.00

For pre-July 1, 1950 Marriage Certificates write to:

Probate Judge
Probate Court
(County Seat), South Carolina

For Divorce Decrees since 1911 write to:

Clerk of the Court
County Court
(County Seat), South Carolina

For Adoption Record information write to:

Adoption and Birth Parent Services   Tel. (803) 898-7601
South Carolina Department of Social Services   (800) 311-7220
P.O. Box 1520
Columbia, South Carolina 29202-1520

The South Carolina Department of Archives and History (P.O. Box 11669, Columbia, SC 29211-1669; 803-734-8577) has death records from 1915–1944. The Family History Library of Salt Lake City, Utah has microfilmed many vital records including state marriage records from 1785 to 1889.

For further information see:

Barton, Elizabeth R. *New Items on the South Carolina Birth Certificate, 1989 and 1990.* Columbia, SC: Division of Biostatistics, Office of Vital Records and Public Health Statistics, South Carolina Department of Health and Environmental Control, 1992. 41p.
Vital Times. (Newsletter). Columbia, SC: Office of Vital Records and Public Health Statistics, 1992– .

D H E C
PROMOTE PROTECT PROSPER

Application for Certified Copy of Birth Certificate
Office of Vital Records & Public Health Statistics
2600 Bull Street, Columbia SC 29201-1708

PLEASE READ BEFORE COMPLETING THIS APPLICATION

A. Only births recorded after January 1, 1915 in South Carolina are on file.

B. The application must be signed by the registrant, parent, guardian or their legal representative.

C. **WARNING: FALSE APPLICATION IS PUNISHABLE BY LAW.** (Section 44-63-161; S.C. Code of Laws, 1976, amended Feb. 24, 1988.)

D. S.C. Law requires a $12.00 fee for the search of the records. If located, the search fee includes issuance of one copy. If not located, search fee is not refundable. Checks and money orders should be made payable to DHEC.

E. Complete all of the information sections required on this form. **PLEASE PRINT.**

	First Name	Middle Name	Last Name (If married woman, please enter maiden surname)	OFFICE USE ONLY
1. FULL NAME				
2. DATE OF BIRTH	Month	Day	Year	Year—Cert. No.
3. PLACE OF BIRTH	County	Hospital and/or city/town	State SOUTH CAROLINA	Search 1st Date
4. SEX		5. RACE		2nd Date

	First Name	Middle Name	Last Name			
6. FULL NAME OF FATHER				Living ☐ Deceased ☐	Pending Sect. C Date
7. FULL MAIDEN NAME OF MOTHER	First Name	Middle Name	Last Name Before Marriage	Living ☐ Deceased ☐	D

8. WERE PARENTS MARRIED? Yes ☐ No ☐	9. NUMBER OF OLDER CHILDREN BORN TO THIS MOTHER _____ NUMBER OF YOUNGER CHILDREN BORN TO THIS MOTHER_____	A
10. NAME OF NEXT OLDER BROTHER OR SISTER, LIVING OR DEAD	DATE OF BIRTH	L
11. NAME OF NEXT YOUNGER BROTHER OR SISTER LIVING OR DEAD	DATE OF BIRTH	PR
12. HAS NAME EVER BEEN CHANGED OTHER THAN MARRIAGE? Yes ☐ No ☐	If so, what was the original name?	LOC
13. PURPOSE FOR WHICH THIS COPY IS REQUESTED?		Final Disposition
		Issue Date

FEE

14. I am enclosing $_____ for _____ certificates as follows: Specify Number and Type Certification

Control Number(s)

_____ Wallet size, short form certification — Accepted for all purposes except to establish relationship of parent to child. Does not include parents' names. Initial certification — $12.00. Additional short form certification ordered at same time — $3.00 each.

_____ Photocopy certification — Issued only by the state office and only to registrant if of legal age (18 yrs.), parent/guardian or their legal representative. Initial certification — $12.00. Additional photocopy certifications ordered at same time — $3.00 each.

☐ Refund
Refunded
Amount $_____

15. WRITTEN SIGNATURE OF registrant, parent/guardian or legal representative DO NOT PRINT _____	OFFICE USE ONLY IDENTIFICATION
Your relationship to registrant: Self____ Parent____ Guardian____ Other (specify) _____	SYS/36

NAME & ADDRESS OF APPLICANT (MUST BE COMPLETED)   PLEASE PRINT   CERTIFICATE TO BE MAILED TO:

PLEASE PRINT 16. NAME	PLEASE PRINT (If other than applicant) 19. NAME
17. NUMBER, P.O. BOX AND STREET	20. NUMBER, P.O. BOX AND STREET
18. CITY, STATE AND ZIP CODE	21. CITY, STATE AND ZIP CODE

DHEC 612 (06/1998)

D H E C

PROMOTE PROTECT PROSPER

APPLICATION FOR CERTIFIED COPY OF MARRIAGE RECORD
DIVISION OF VITAL RECORDS

INFORMATION

1. Only marriage licenses issued after July 1950 in South Carolina are on file.

2. S.C. Law requires an $12.00 fee for the search of a marriage record. If located, a certified copy of the marriage record will be issued to those entitled. Verification of the date and place of marriage will be provided if the applicant is not entitled to a copy of the record. Additional copies of the same record ordered at the same time are $3.00 each. If not located, search fee is not refundable.

3. S.C. Law (Section 44-63-86) provides that "Copies of marriage certificates...may be issued to the parties married..., their adult children, a present or former spouse of either party married..., or their respective legal representative."

4. If the marriage occurred prior to July 1950, or if a copy of the application is required, contact the probate judge of the county where the marriage license was issued.

5. WARNING: FALSE APPLICATION FOR A MARRIAGE CERTIFICATE IS PUNISHABLE BY LAW (Section 44-63-161, S.C. Code of Laws, 1976, Amended).

INSTRUCTIONS

1. Complete all of the information sections of the form. **PLEASE PRINT.**

2. An application for a certified copy of a marriage record must be signed by one of the married parties, their adult children, a present or former spouse, or the legal representative of one of these persons. Relationship must be stated.

3. Checks and money orders should be made payable to **SC DHEC.** Send completed application and appropriate fee to:

   Division of Vital Records
   South Carolina Department of Health and Environmental Control
   2600 Bull Street
   Columbia SC 29201-1708

						OFFICE USE ONLY
1 FULL NAME OF GROOM	First	Middle	Last			
2 DATE OF BIRTH	Month	Day	Year	Race		YEAR — CERT. NO.
3 FULL NAME OF BRIDE	First	Middle	Last			DNL DATE
4 DATE OF BIRTH	Month	Day	Year	Race		PROC. DATE
5 HAS BRIDE EVER USED ANY OTHER NAME? ☐ Yes ☐ No		If so, please list:				ISSUE DATE
6 DATE OF MARRIAGE	Month	Day	Year			CONTROL NO.
7 PLACE LICENSE ISSUED	City	County	State SOUTH CAROLINA			

8 FEE	I am enclosing a Fee of $_____ for _____ CERTIFIED COPIES	Refund Refunded Amount $_____
9a. WRITTEN SIGNATURE OF APPLICANT		IDENTIFICATION
9b. RELATIONSHIP: Self ☐ Adult Child ☐ Present/Former Spouse ☐ Legal Representative of: _____ ☐ Not Related ☐		

NAME & ADDRESS OF APPLICANT (MUST BE COMPLETED)   PLEASE PRINT   CERTIFICATE TO BE MAILED TO:

PLEASE PRINT **10 NAME**	PLEASE PRINT (if other than applicant) **13 NAME**
11 NUMBER, P.O. BOX AND STREET	**14 NUMBER, P.O. BOX AND STREET**
12 CITY, STATE AND ZIP CODE	**15 CITY, STATE AND ZIP CODE**

DHEC 0678 (06/1998)

APPLICATION FOR CERTIFIED COPY OF A DIVORCE OR ANNULMENT
DIVISION OF VITAL RECORDS

INFORMATION

1. Reports of divorce or annulments granted after July 1, 1962, in South Carolina are on file.

2. S.C. Law requires a $12.00 fee for the search of a report of a divorce or annulment. If located, a certified copy of the report will be issued to those entitled. Verification of the date and place of divorce will be provided if the applicant is not entitled to a copy of the record. Additional copies of the same record ordered at the same time are $3.00 each. If not located, search fee is not refundable.

3. S.C. Law (Section 44-63-86) provides that "Copies of...reports of divorce...may be issued to the parties...divorced, their adult children, a present or former spouse of either party...divorced, or their respective legal representative."

4. If a copy of the decree of divorce or annulment is required, or if the event occurred prior to July 1, 1962, a complete record can be obtained from the Clerk of Court of the county in which the decree was granted.

5. WARNING: FALSE APPLICATION FOR A REPORT OF DIVORCE OR ANNULMENT IS PUNISHABLE BY LAW (Section 44-63-161, S.C. Code of Laws, 1976, Amended).

INSTRUCTIONS

1. Complete all of the information sections of the form. **PLEASE PRINT.**

2. An application for a certified copy of a report of a divorce or annulment must be signed by one of the parties to the divorce or annulment, their adult children, a present or former spouse, or their respective legal representatives. Relationship must be stated.

3. Checks and money ordered should be made payable to **SC DHEC.** Send completed application and appropriate fee to:

   Division of Vital Records
   South Carolina Department of Health and Environmental Control
   2600 Bull Street
   Columbia SC 29201-1708

	First	Middle	Last	Race	OFFICE USE ONLY
1. FULL NAME OF HUSBAND					
2. MAIDEN NAME OF WIFE	First	Middle	Last	Race	YEAR — CERT. NO.
3. DATE OF DIVORCE OR ANNULMENT	Month	Day	Year		DNL DATE
4. PLACE DIVORCE GRANTED	City	County	State SOUTH CAROLINA		PROC. DATE

5. FEE   I am enclosing a Fee of $_____ for _____ CERTIFIED COPIES

ISSUE DATE

6a. WRITTEN SIGNATURE OF APPLICANT

CONTROL NO.

6b. RELATIONSHIP:
Self ☐   Adult Child ☐   Present/Former Spouse ☐   Legal Representative of: _____   Not Related ☐

Refund
Refunded Amount
$_____

IDENTIFICATION

NAME & ADDRESS OF APPLICANT (MUST BE COMPLETED)   PLEASE PRINT   CERTIFICATE TO BE MAILED TO:

PLEASE PRINT 7. NAME	PLEASE PRINT (if other than applicant) 10. NAME
8. NUMBER, P.O. BOX AND STREET	11. NUMBER, P.O. BOX AND STREET
9. CITY, STATE AND ZIP CODE	12. CITY, STATE AND ZIP CODE

DHEC 0679 (06/1998)

D H E C

PROMOTE PROTECT PROSPER

Application for Certified Copy of a Death Record
Division of Vital Records
2600 Bull Street, Columbia, SC 29201-1708

				OFFICE USE ONLY
1. FULL NAME OF DECEASED	First Name	Middle Name and/or Maiden	Last Name	
2. DATE OF DEATH	Month	Day	Year	YEAR — CERT. NO.
3. PLACE OF DEATH	Hospital/City	County	State **SOUTH CAROLINA**	DNL. DATE
4. SEX		5. RACE	6. AGE AT TIME OF DEATH	PROC. DATE
7. SOCIAL SECURITY NO. OF DECEASED (IF KNOWN)				
8. NAME OF FUNERAL DIRECTOR				ISSUE DATE
9. IF THE DECEASED WAS MARRIED, PLEASE LIST HUSBAND/WIFE			LIVING ☐ DEAD ☐	CONTROL. NO.
10. FATHER OF THE DECEASED	Last Name	First Name	Middle Name	
11. MOTHER OF THE DECEASED	Last Name	First Name	Middle Name	☐ Refund Refunded Amount $_____

12. FEE   I am enclosing a Fee of $_____ for _____ CERTIFIED COPIES.

	IDENTIFICATION
13a. WRITTEN SIGNATURE OF APPLICANT:	
13b. Relation of Applicant to the Deceased: Family Member ☐ ; Legal Rep. of a Family Member ☐ ; Not Related ☐	SYS/36
13c. If not a family member or the legal representative of a family member, state need for record.	

NAME & ADDRESS OF APPLICANT (MUST BE COMPLETED)   (PLEASE PRINT)   CERTIFICATE TO BE MAILED TO:

PLEASE PRINT 14. NAME	PLEASE PRINT (If other than applicant) 17. NAME
15. NUMBER, P.O. BOX AND STREET	18. NUMBER, P.O. BOX AND STREET
16. CITY, STATE AND ZIP CODE	19. CITY, STATE AND ZIP CODE

DHEC 0677 (06/1998)

SOUTH DAKOTA

Send your requests to:

South Dakota Department of Health
Vital Records
600 East Capitol Avenue
Pierre, South Dakota 57501-2536

Tel. (605) 773-4961
Fax (605) 773-5683
kathi.mueller@state.sd.us
http://www.state.sd.us/doh/VitalRec/

Vital Records has birth, death, marriage, and divorce records from July 1905. Make checks payable to the South Dakota Department of Health. Births more than 100 years old may be searched online at **http://www.state.sd.us/doh/VitalRec/ birthrecords/index.cfm**. Expedited service is available online or by phone (with payment by credit card) for an additional fee of $10.00 per request.

Cost for a certified Birth Certificate	$10.00
Cost for a certified Marriage Certificate	$7.00
Cost for a certified Divorce Record	$7.00
Cost for a certified Death Certificate	$10.00

Birth Records from January 1, 1951–present are also available at:

Clerk
County Register of Deeds
(County Seat), South Dakota

For copies of pre-1905 Marriage Certificates write to:

County Treasurer
County Court House
(County Seat), South Dakota

For Adoption Record information write to:

Adoption Unit
South Dakota Department of Social Services
700 Governors Drive
Pierre, South Dakota 57501

Tel. (605) 773-3227
Fax (605) 773-6834

There is no charge for registration in the Voluntary Adoption Registry.

The Family History Library of Salt Lake City, Utah has microfilmed many of the original and published vital records and church registers of South Dakota. For details on their holdings please consult your nearest Family History Center.

For further information see:

Manual for Clerks of the Circuit Court. Pierre, SD: State Court Administrator's Office, 1978. Loose-leaf.

DEPARTMENT OF HEALTH

ADMINISTRATION
600 East Capitol Avenue
Pierre, South Dakota 57501-2536
605/773-3361 FAX: 605/773-5683

BIRTH	FULL NAME ON THE BIRTH RECORD AT THIS TIME _____ HAS THE NAME ON THE RECORD EVER BEEN CHANGED BY A LEGAL PROCEDURE? (not marriage) YES _____ NO _____ UNK _____ IF YES, WHAT TYPE OF LEGAL PROCEDURE? ADOPTION _____ PATERNITY ACTION _____ LEGAL NAME CHANGE _____ IF YES, PREVIOUS NAME, ON RECORD IF KNOWN _____ (First) (Middle) (Last) DATE OF BIRTH (Month, Day & Year) _____ PLACE OF BIRTH (City & County) _____ FATHER'S FULL NAME _____ MOTHER'S FULL MAIDEN NAME _____ _____ (Signature of person requesting record)
DEATH	FULL NAME AT TIME OF DEATH _____ APPROXIAMTE DATE OF DEATH (Month, Day & Year) _____ PLACE OF DEATH (City & County) _____
MARRIAGE	FULL NAME OF GROOM _____ FULL NAME OF BRIDE _____ APPROXIAMTE DATE OF MARRIAGE (Month, Day & Year) _____ WHERE LICENSE WAS OBTAINED _____
DIVORCE	FULL NAME OF HUSBAND _____ FULL NAME OF WIFE _____ APPROXIAMTE DATE OF DIVORCE (Month, Day & Year) _____ PLACE OF DIVORCE _____

<u>PRINT OR TYPE</u> NAME AND ADDRESS OF PERSON TO WHOM CERTIFICATE IS TO BE SENT

_____
(Name)

_____
(Street or Box)

_____
(City, State and Zip+)

_____
(Phone Number)

TENNESSEE

Send your requests to:

Tennessee State Department of Health and Environment
Vital Records Office
Central Services Building, First Floor
421 5th Avenue North
Nashville, Tennessee 37247-0450

Tel. (615) 741-1763
Fax (615) 741-9860
http://www.state.tn.us/health/vr/index.html

The Vital Records Office has birth records from January 1, 1914 and death, marriage, and divorce records from the past 50 years. Some records of births that occurred in the major cities from 1881–1913 are also available. Expedited service is available (with payment by credit card), either online or by phone (615-741-0778) or fax (615-726-2559), for an additional fee of $10.00.

Cost for a certified Birth Certificate	$10.00
Cost for a short form Birth Certificate (1949–present only)	$5.00
Cost for a certified Marriage Certificate	$10.00
Cost for a certified Divorce Record	$10.00
Cost for a certified Death Certificate	$5.00
Cost for a duplicate copy, when ordered at the same time	$2.00

For earlier Birth, Marriage, and Death Records write to:

County Clerk
County Court House
(County Seat), Tennessee

For Divorce Records write to:

Clerk of the Court
(County Seat), Tennessee

For Adoption Record information write to:

Department of Children's Services
Post Adoption Unit
436 Sixth Avenue North
Nashville, Tennessee 37243-1290

Tel. (615) 532-5637

Adoptees 21 and over have open access to their adoption records. Non-identifying information is available at age 18.

The Tennessee State Library & Archives (403 Seventh Avenue North, Nashville, TN 37243; 615-741-2451) has birth records from 1908–1912; death records from 1908–1912 and 1914–1949; and many marriage and divorce records 1861–1949. Among its county records are Chattanooga births from 1879–1907 and deaths from 1872–1907; Knoxville births from 1881–1907 and deaths from 1881–1907; Nashville births from 1881–1907; and Memphis deaths from 1848–1907. There are no birth and death records for 1913 because the law had lapsed.

The Family History Library of Salt Lake City, Utah has microfilm copies of births 1908–1912 and deaths 1908–1912 and 1914–1925.

The Memphis Shelby County Library has online indexes to Memphis death registers 1848–1901 and Memphis and Shelby County death certificates from 1902–1945 at **http://www.memphislibrary.lib.tn.us/history/indmsd.htm.**

For further information see:

County Records Manual for the County Court Clerk. Knoxville, TN: University of Tennessee, County Technical Assistance Services, 1979. 55p.
Keeping Tennessee's Heritage, a self-evaluation guide for keepers of historical documents and public records. Nashville, TN: Tennessee State Library & Archives, 1999. 33p.

184

TENNESSEE DEPARTMENT OF HEALTH
Office Of Vital Records

APPLICATION FOR CERTIFIED COPY OF CERTIFICATE OF BIRTH

Date:_____

Full Name on Birth Certificate_____
First   Middle   Last

Has name ever been changed other than by marriage?_____

If yes, what was original name?_____

Date of Birth _____ Sex_____
Month   Day   Year

Place of Birth _____
City   County   State

Full Name of Father _____

Full Maiden Name of Mother _____

Last Name of Mother at Time of Birth _____

Hospital Where Birth Occurred _____

Next Older Brother or Sister _____ Younger_____

Signature of Person Making Request_____

Relationship _____

Purpose of Copy_____

Telephone number where you may be reached for additional information _____

Indicate number of each type of certificate desired and enclose appropriate fee:

For years 1949-Current:
____Short form--$5.00 first copy
Additional copies of same record purchased at same time-$2.00 each

Short form is a certified transcript showing child's name, birthdate, sex, county of birth, certificate number and file date (1976-current year also shows parents' names)

____Long form--$10.00 first copy
Additional copies of same record purchased at same time-$2.00 each

Long form is a certified copy showing all information.

For births before 1949:
(No short form available)

____First copy--$10.00
Additional copies of same record purchased at same time-$2.00 each

The above fees for the first copy are charged for the search of the records even if no record is on file in this office. A 3 year search is provided for the initial fee.

IT IS UNLAWFUL TO WILLFULLY AND KNOWINGLY MAKE ANY FALSE STATEMENT ON THIS APPLICATION. VIOLATORS WILL BE PROSECUTED.

All items must be completed and appropriate fees attached to process this request. Do not send cash. Send check or money order payable to the Tennessee Department of Health. If you have not received a response within 45 days, please write or call Tennessee Vital Records at (615) 741-1763.

PH-1654 (Rev. 05/97)   RDA N/A

- -

FILL OUT BELOW / DO NOT DETACH

PRINT name and address of person to whom the certified copy is to be mailed.

SEND TO:

_____

Name_____
Street or
Route_____
City and
State_____ Zip_____

Tennessee Vital Records
421 5th Avenue, North
1st Floor, Central Services Building
Nashville, Tennessee 37247-0450

PH-1654 (Rev. 05/97)   RDA N/A

TENNESSEE DEPARTMENT OF HEALTH
Office Of Vital Records

APPLICATION FOR A CERTIFIED COPY OF A CERTIFICATE OF MARRIAGE

Number of copies _____
First copy $10.00, each additional copy $2.00

Date_____

Name of Groom_____
           First   Middle   Last

Name of Bride at Birth_____
           First   Middle   Last

Place This License Was Issued_____
                  County   State

Date of Marriage_____
                  Month   Day   Year

Place of Marriage_____
                  City   County   State

Signature of Person Making Request_____

Relationship of Requestor_____

Purpose of Copy_____

Telephone number where you may be reached for additional information _____

IT IS UNLAWFUL TO WILLFULLY AND KNOWINGLY MAKE ANY FALSE STATEMENT ON THIS APPLICATION.

Records are filed in this office for the past 50 years. Records prior to this date are available in the county where the license was obtained.

A fee of $10.00 is charged for the search of the records even if no record is found, and includes one copy if the record is filed in this office. Do not send cash. Send check or money order made payable to the Tennessee Department of Health. If you have not received a response within 45 days, please write or call Tennessee Vital Records at (615) 741-1763.

PH-1670 (Rev. 05/97)   RDA N/A

FILL OUT BELOW / DO NOT DETACH

PRINT name and address of person to whom the certified copy is to be mailed.

SEND TO:

_____

Name_____

Street or

Route_____

City and

State_____ Zip_____

SEND TO:

Tennessee Vital Records
421 5th Avenue, North
1st Floor, Central Services Building
Nashville, Tennessee 37247-0450

PH-1670 (Rev. 05/97)   RDA N/A

TENNESSEE DEPARTMENT OF HEALTH
Office Of Vital Records

APPLICATION FOR A CERTIFIED COPY OF A CERTIFICATE OF DIVORCE OR ANNULMENT

Number of copies _____

Date_____   First copy $10.00, each additional copy $2.00

Name of Husband _____
                First   Middle   Last

Name of Wife _____
                First   Middle   Last

Date of Divorce _____
                Month   Day   Year

Place of Divorce _____
                City   County   State

Signature of Person Making Request _____

Relationship of Requestor _____

Purpose of Copy _____

Telephone number where you may be reached for additional information _____

IT IS UNLAWFUL TO WILLINGLY AND KNOWINGLY MAKE ANY FALSE STATEMENT ON THIS APPLICATION.)

Records are filed in this office for the past 50 years. Records prior to this date are available from the clerk of the court where the divorce was granted.

A fee of $10.00 is charged for the search of the records even if no record is found, and includes one copy if the record is filed in this office. Do not send cash. Send check or money order made payable to the Tennessee Department of Health. If you have not received a response within 45 days, please write or call Tennessee Vital Records at (615) 741-1763.

PH-1671 (Rev. 05/97)   RDA N/A

FILL OUT BELOW / DO NOT DETACH

PRINT name and address of person to whom the certified copy
is to be mailed.

SEND TO:

_____

Name _____

Street or
Route _____

City and
State _____ Zip_____

Tennessee Vital Records
421 5th Avenue, North
1st Floor, Central Services Building
Nashville, Tennessee 37247-0450

PH-1671 (Rev. 05/97)   RDA N/A

TENNESSEE DEPARTMENT OF HEALTH
Office Of Vital Records

APPLICATION FOR CERTIFIED COPY OF CERTIFICATE OF DEATH

Number of copies_____
Enclose $5.00 for each copy.

Date_____

Name of Deceased_____
First   Middle   Last

Date of Death_____
Month   Day   Year

Sex_____   Age_____

Place of Death_____
City   County   State

Name of Funeral Home_____

Location of Funeral Home_____
City   County   State

Signature of Person Making Request_____

Relationship to Deceased_____

Purpose of Copy_____

Do you want the cause of death to show?   ☐ Yes   ☐ No

Telephone number where you may be reached for additional information_____

IT IS UNLAWFUL TO WILLFULLY AND KNOWINGLY MAKE ANY FALSE STATEMENT ON THIS APPLICATION.

A fee of $5.00 is charged for the search of the records even if no record is found, and includes one copy if the record is filed in this office. Do not send cash. Send check or money order made payable to the Tennessee Department of Health. If you have not received a response within 45 days, please write or call Tennessee Vital Records at (615) 741-1763.

PH-1663 (Rev. 5/97)   RDA N/A

- -

FILL OUT BELOW/DO NOT DETACH

PRINT name and address of person to whom the certified copy is to be mailed.

SEND TO:

_____

Name _____
Street or
Route _____
City and
State _____ Zip _____

TENNESSEE VITAL RECORDS
421 5th Avenue, North
1st Floor, Central Services Building
Nashville, Tennessee 37247-0450

PH-1663 (Rev. 5/97)   RDA N/A

Send your requests to:

Texas Department of Health
Bureau of Vital Statistics
1100 West 49th Street
Austin, Texas 78711-2040
P.O. Box 12040

Tel. (512) 458-7111
Fax (512) 458-7711 (for expedited service)
E-mail: register@tdh.state.tx.us
http://www.tdh.state.tx.us/bvs/

The Bureau of Vital Statistics has birth and death records from January 1, 1903; birth records are restricted for 50 years, death records for 25 years. Certified copies of marriage licenses or divorce decrees are only available from the County or District Clerk in the county in which the event occurred. The Bureau of Vital Statistics can, however, verify marriages from January 1, 1966 and divorces from January 1, 1968. Expedited service is available (with payment by credit card) for an additional fee of $5.00, plus the cost of overnight return, if requested.

Cost for a certified Birth Certificate	$11.00
Cost for an heirloom Birth Certificate	$25.00
Cost for a wallet-size Birth Certificate	$11.00
Cost for the verification of a Marriage Certificate	$9.00
Cost for the verification of a Divorce Record	$9.00
Cost for a certified Death Certificate	$9.00
Cost for a duplicate record, when ordered at the same time	$3.00

For Marriage or Divorce Certificates write to:

County Clerk
County Court House
(County Seat), Texas

For Adoption Record information write to:

Central Adoption Registry
Mail Code Y-943
Texas Department of Protective and Regulatory
 Services
P.O. Box 149030
Austin, Texas 78714-9030

Tel. (512) 834-4485
E-mail: molinapp@austy944a.aust.tdprs.state.tx.us
http://www.tdh.state.tx.us/bvs/car/car.htm

The cost to register with the Central Adoption Registry is $20.00.

The Local Records Division of the Texas State Library (1201 Brazos Street, P.O. Box 12927, Austin, TX 78701-2927; 512-463-5463) has an extensive collection of Texas county vital records.

For further information see:

Texas Vital Statistics Law. Austin, TX: State Bureau of Vital Statistics, 1935.

BUREAU OF VITAL STATISTICS
TEXAS DEPARTMENT OF HEALTH
PO Box 12040
AUSTIN TEXAS 78711-2040
PHONE (512) 458-7111

APPLICATION FOR CERTIFIED COPY OF BIRTH OR DEATH CERTIFICATE

BIRTH ☐	DEATH ☐
# REQUESTED _____ CERTIFIED COPIES X $11.00 = _____ _____ WALLET-SIZE X $11.00 = _____ _____ HEIRLOOM X $25.00 = _____ ☐ FLAG ☐ STATE OUTLINE **TOTAL ENCLOSED = _____**	# REQUESTED _____ CERTIFIED COPY X $9.00 = _____ _____ EXTRA COPIES OF SAME RECORD X $3.00 = _____ **TOTAL ENCLOSED = _____**

1. Full Name of Person on Record	First Name	Middle Name		Last Name
2. Date of Birth or Death	Month	Day	Year	3. Sex
4. Place of Birth or Death	City or Town	County		State
5. Full Name of Father	First Name	Middle Name		Last Name
6. Full Maiden Name of Mother	First Name	Middle Name		Maiden Name

7. ADDITIONAL IDENTIFYING INFORMATION FOR <u>DEATH</u> CERTIFICATE.

SOCIAL SECURITY NUMBER OF DECEASED _____

BIRTH DATE _____ BIRTH PLACE, ETC. _____

8. APPLICANT'S NAME: _____ 9. TELEPHONE #: ( ) _____
(MON-FRI 8:00-5:00)

10. MAILING ADDRESS: _____
STREET ADDRESS | CITY | STATE | ZIP

11. RELATIONSHIP TO PERSON NAMED IN ITEM 1: _____

12. PURPOSE FOR OBTAINING THIS RECORD: _____

WARNING: THE PENALTY FOR KNOWINGLY MAKING A FALSE STATEMENT IN THIS FORM CAN BE 2-10 YEARS IN PRISON AND A FINE OF UP TO $10,000. (HEALTH AND SAFETY CODE, CHAPTER 195, SEC. 195.003)

_____ _____
SIGNATURE OF APPLICANT   DATE

IDENTIFICATION TYPE _____ NUMBER _____
ATTACH PHOTOCOPY Drivers License, I.D. Card, etc.   on Drivers License, I.D. Card, etc.

Fees are subject to change without notice (call 512-458-7111 for fee verification). For any search of the files where a record is not found the searching fee is non-refundable or transferable.

Birth records are confidential for 50 years and death records for 25 years; therefore, issuance is restricted. Please **attach a photocopy** of ID to application.

Administrative rules require that on restricted records, all identifying information (items 1-6), relationship (item 11), and purpose (item 12) be provided in order to issue the record.

VS-141 REV. 5/96

This application is to be used for MAIL-IN REQUESTS only. It will not be accepted for walk-in requests.

TEXAS DEPARTMENT OF HEALTH
BUREAU OF VITAL STATISTICS
P.O. BOX 12040
AUSTIN, TEXAS 78711-2040
PHONE (512) 458-7111

APPLICATION FOR VERIFICATION OF MARRIAGE OR DIVORCE

APPLICATION FOR MARRIAGE ___   REPORT OF DIVORCE ___
(SINCE JAN. 1, 1966)   (SINCE JAN. 1, 1968)

FEE: $9.00 FOR EACH SEARCH.
Fees are subject to change without notice.
The searching fee is non-refundable or transferable if a record cannot be found.

PLEASE PRINT

FULL NAME OF HUSBAND (IF KNOWN):_____

DATE OF BIRTH OR AGE OF HUSBAND:_____

FULL MAIDEN NAME OF WIFE (IF KNOWN):_____

DATE OF BIRTH OR AGE OF WIFE:_____

DATE OF EVENT:_____

IF DATE UNKNOWN, TIME PERIOD TO SEARCH:_____

COUNTY OF EVENT:_____

APPLICANT'S NAME:_____

STREET ADDRESS:_____

CITY:_____ STATE:_____ ZIP CODE:_____

DAYTIME TELEPHONE NUMBER:____(____)_____

APPLICANT'S

UTAH

Send your requests to:

Office of Vital Records and Statistics
Utah Department of Health
Cannon Health Building
288 North 1460 West
P.O. Box 141012
Salt Lake City, UT 84114-1012

Tel. (801) 538-6380
Recording (801) 538-6105
Fax (801) 538-9467
E-mail: vrequest@doh.state.us.us
http://hlunix.ex.state.ut.us/bvr/home.html

The Office of Vital Records has birth and death records from January 1, 1905, and can provide verifications of marriage records from 1978 to present, and of divorce records from 1978 to present. If you do not know the exact date that the event occurred there is a $50.00 fee for this search. Expedited service is available (with payment by credit card) for an additional fee of $15.00, plus shipping.

Cost for a certified Birth Certificate	$12.00
Cost for a Heritage Birth Certificate	$22.00
Cost for a certified Marriage Certificate, from County Clerk	$5.00
Cost for a Marriage application form	$9.00
Cost for a Divorce Record	$9.00
Cost for a certified Death Certificate	$9.00
Cost for a duplicate copy, when ordered at the same time	$5.00

For Marriage Certificates write to:

County Clerk
County Court House
(County Seat), Utah

For Adoption Records write to:

Mutual Consent Voluntary Adoption Reunion Registry
Bureau of Vital Records
288 North 1460 West
P.O. Box 141012
Salt Lake City, Utah 84114-1012

Tel. (801) 538-6363
http://www.archives.state.ut.us/reference/adopt.htm

The cost for registering in the Adoption Registry is $25.00.

The Utah State Archives Research Center (P.O. Box 141021, Salt Lake City, UT 84114-1021; 801-538-3013) can provide copies of Utah death certificates from 1904 to 50 years from the present, as well as microfilm copies of most of the birth and death registers for Utah counties 1898–1905; some divorce decrees 1852–1969; and adoption records more than 100 years old.

The Family History Library of Salt Lake City, Utah has microfilmed many of the original and published vital records and church registers of Utah. For details on their holdings please consult your nearest Family History Center.

UTAH DEPARTMENT OF HEALTH
OFFICE OF VITAL RECORDS AND STATISTICS
APPLICATION FOR CERTIFIED COPY OF A BIRTH CERTIFICATE

INFORMATION

Certificates for births that occurred in Utah since 1905 are on file in this office. Persons who were born in Utah and have no birth certificate on file may make application to file a Delayed Registration of Birth. Application forms for Delayed Registration of Birth must be obtained from this office. It is a violation of Utah State law for any person to obtain, possess, use, sell, or furnish for any purpose of deception, a birth certificate or certified copy thereof.

INSTRUCTIONS

1. An application must be completed for each birth requested.
2. There is a fee of $12.00 for each search of our files. Additional certified copies of this record ordered at the same time are $5.00 each.
3. Send the completed application and required fee to Office of Vital Records and Statistics, 288 North 1460 West, P O Box 141012, Salt Lake City, Utah 84114-1012.
4. If the applicant does not respond to a written request from Vital Records within 90 days, Vital Records may retain all monies paid.

IDENTIFYING INFORMATION

FULL NAME AS IT SHOULD APPEAR ON CERTIFICATE _____

DATE OF BIRTH_____

PLACE OF BIRTH (City) _____ (County) _____ (Hospital) _____

FULL NAME OF FATHER _____BIRTH DATE_____

BIRTHPLACE OF FATHER_____

FULL MAIDEN NAME OF MOTHER_____BIRTH DATE_____

BIRTHPLACE OF MOTHER_____

APPLICANT

RELATIONSHIP: **I am:** (Please circle one)   Self   Mother   Father   Sibling   Spouse   Child   Grandparent   Grandchild
Other (Specify)_____
If other, reason for requesting certificate:_____

Your Signature:_____Date_____

Printed Name_____Telephone Number_____

Your Address_____
(City, State & Zip)

NUMBER OF CERTIFIED COPIES REQUESTED

_____   Regular Certificate **OR** _____ Birth Card $ 12.00   +
_____   Additional Certified Copies ($5.00 each) $_____ +
_____   Additional Birth Cards ($5.00 each) $_____ +
TOTAL FEE $_____

(If this order is to be mailed, please **PRINT** the name and mailing address below)

_____

_____

_____

For OFFICE USE only (do not write below this line.)
PAID: CHECK   CASH   MONEY ORDER
Certified Paper

_____

Request #_____   **Clerks Initials**_____
UDOH-BVR-11 Revised 3/99

UTAH'S HERITAGE BIRTH CERTIFICATE

The Utah Heritage Birth Certificate combines significant art within the legal framework of a birth certificate. The art is the contributed work of the famous Utah artist Trevor Southey, and it clearly expressed the high value Utahns place on children and family. This high quality full color birth certificate is appropriate for framing and using as a gift for special occasions. In addition to providing Utahns with this outstanding commemorative certificate, it will also raise funds for the Children's Trust Fund. The Children's Trust Fund provides the money to support a comprehensive statewide Child Abuse Prevention Plan. The fee for Utah's Heritage Birth Certificate is $22.00. Seven dollars of that fee will be deposited in the Children's Trust Fund. That $7.00 is tax deductible. This is an opportunity to obtain a unique gift for your child or another loved one, and to make a contribution to the prevention of child abuse. The size is 12 x 18 inches.

Mail completed application to:
Bureau of Vital Records
Utah Department of Health
288 North 1460 West P O Box 141012
Salt Lake City, Utah 84114-1012

Make checks payable to:
Bureau of Vital Records
For more information call: (801) 538-6105

NAME OF CHILD

DATE OF BIRTH

PLACE OF BIRTH

MOTHER'S MAIDEN NAME

FATHER'S NAME

APPLICANT'S NAME,
ADDRESS AND PHONE

PACKAGE DEAL: The "package deal" gives you one certified copy of the birth certificate, one laminated wallet birth card, and the Heritage Birth Certificate for $32.00, individually a $46.00 cost.

UTAH DEPARTMENT OF HEALTH
OFFICE OF VITAL RECORDS AND STATISTICS
APPLICATION FOR MARRIAGE OR DIVORCE CERTIFICATION
INFORMATION

1. State Vital Records can only verify marriages (1978-1998) or divorces (1978-1997) taking place in Utah.

2. Records provided are certification summaries. They are not copies of the original records.

3. There is a fee of $9.00 for each search of our files.

4. If the applicant does not respond to a written request from Vital Records within 90 days, Vital Records may retain all monies paid.

MARRIAGE CERTIFICATION
IDENTIFYING INFORMATION

GROOM'S NAME : _____

BRIDE'S MAIDEN NAME: _____

MARRIAGE DATE: _____

MARRIAGE PLACE: _____

DIVORCE CERTIFICATION
IDENTIFYING INFORMATION

HUSBAND'S NAME : _____

WIFE'S NAME: _____

DATE OF DIVORCE: _____

PLACE OF DIVORCE: _____

DATE OF MARRIAGE: _____

PLACE OF MARRIAGE: _____

APPLICANT

RELATIONSHIP: **I am:** (circle one) Husband   Wife   Mother   Father   Sibling   Child   Grandparent   Grandchild

If other, reason for requesting certificate: _____

Your Signature_____ Date_____

Printed Name_____ Telephone Number_____

Your Address _____
                                                              (City, State & Zip)

NUMBER OF CERTIFIED COPIES REQUESTED

(If this order is to be mailed, please **PRINT** the name and mailing address below)

_____ Regular Certificate $ 9.00   +

_____ Additional Certified Copies ($5.00 each) $_____   +   _____

TOTAL FEE $_____   _____

_____

▼▼▼
For OFFICE USE only (do not write below this line.)
PAID: CHECK   CASH   MONEY ORDER

Certified Paper # _____

Request # _____

Revised 8/99

Clerks Initials _____

UTAH DEPARTMENT OF HEALTH
BUREAU OF VITAL RECORDS
APPLICATION FOR CERTIFIED COPY OF A DEATH CERTIFICATE

INFORMATION
Death certificates for deaths that occurred in Utah since 1905 are on file in this office.

INSTRUCTIONS
1. An application must be completed for each death certificate requested.
2. There is a fee of $9.00 for each search of our files. Additional certified copies of this record ordered at the same time are $5.00 each.
3. Send the completed application and required fee to the Office of Vital Records and Statistics, 288 North 1460 West, Box 141012, Salt Lake City, Utah 84114-1012.
4. If the applicant does not respond to a written request from the Office of Vital Records ad Statistics within 90 days, Vital records may retain all monies paid.

IDENTIFYING INFORMATION

FULL NAME OF DECEASED_____ SOCIAL SECURITY NO_____

DATE OF DEATH_____ (If not known, specify years to be searched)

PLACE OF DEATH (City)_____ (County)_____

BIRTHPLACE OF DECEDENT (State or County)_____ DATE OF BIRTH OF DECEDENT_____

USUAL RESIDENCE OF DECEDENT_____
                                                                    (City & State)
FULL NAME OF FATHER _____

FULL MAIDEN NAME OF MOTHER_____

IF DECEASED WAS MARRIED, NAME OF SPOUSE_____

APPLICANT
RELATIONSHIP: **I am:** (Please circle one) Mother   Father   Sibling   Spouse   Child   Grandparent   Grandchild
Other (Specify)_____
If other, reason for requesting certificate:_____

Your Signature_____Date_____
Printed Name_____Telephone Number_____
Your Address_____
                                                                    (City, State & Zip)

NUMBER OF CERTIFIED COPIES REQUESTED

_____   Regular Certificate $ 9.00   +
_____   Additional Certified Copies ($5.00 each) $_____ +

                    TOTAL FEE $_____

(If this order is to be mailed, please **PRINT** the name and mailing address below)

_____

_____

_____

For OFFICE USE only (do not write below this line.)

PAID: CHECK   CASH   MONEY ORDER
Certified Paper #_____
Request #_____

Clerks Initials_____

Revised 4/99

Send your request for records from the past 10 years to:

Vermont Department of Health
Vital Records
108 Cherry Street
P.O. Box 70
Burlington, Vermont 05402-0070

Tel. (802) 863-7275
Inside Vermont (800) 642-3323, ext. 7275

Checks should be made payable to the "Vermont Department of Health." There is no charge for a verification of a birth, marriage, divorce, or death record.

Send your request for records more than 10 years old to:

Vermont Public Records Division, Reference and Research
US Rte. 2-Middlesex, Drawer 33
Montpelier, Vermont 05633-7601

Tel. (802) 828-3286
http://www.state.vt.us/gsd/pubrec.htm

Cost for a certified Birth Certificate	$7.00
Cost for a certified Marriage Certificate	$7.00
Cost for a certified Divorce Record	$7.00
Cost for a certified Death Certificate	$7.00

For Adoption Record information write to:

Vermont Adoption Registry
Vermont Department of Social & Rehabilitation Services
103 South Main Street
Waterbury, Vermont 05671-2401

Tel. (802) 241-2122
http://www.state.vt.us/srs/
adoption/registry.html

Adoptees who were adopted before July 1, 1986 can obtain identifying information with the consent of both adoptee and birth parent. Adoptees can obtain identifying information if the adoption was finalized on or after July 1, 1986.

The Family History Library of Salt Lake City, Utah has microfilmed many of the original and published vital records and church registers of Vermont. They have microfilm copies of the vital records from 1760 to 1908. For details on their holdings please consult your nearest Family History Center.

Application for Vital Record
BIRTH CERTIFICATE

REQUEST FOR (CHECK ONE): ___ Certified Copy ___ Verification ___ Record Search

INSTRUCTIONS

NOTE: For records more than ten years old,contact:
General Services Center, Reference and Research,
US Rte. 2 - Middlesex, Drawer 33,
Montpelier, VT 05633-7601 (802) 828-3286

Type or print all information clearly.
Sign and date application and return it with
your check or money order (made payable to the
Vermont Department of Health) to the address
below. **Do not mail cash.**

FEES:
Certified Copy $7.00
Verification no charge
Record Search no charge

Amount enclosed _____

BIRTH INFORMATION

Name on birth certificate _____ Sex _____

Date of Birth _____ Town or city of birth _____

Name of father _____

Maiden name of mother _____

Your name _____

Address _____

Town _____ State _____ Zip _____

Phone number (____) _____

Your relationship to person on birth certificate _____

Intended use of certificate:

_____ Social Security   _____ School Enrollment

_____ Passport   _____ Driver's License

_____ Family History   _____ Other (Specify): _____

Signature _____ Date _____

Return to: Vermont Department of Health, Vital Records Unit
108 Cherry Street, PO Box 70, Burlington, VT 05402
Telephone: (802) 863-7275 or 1-800-439-5008

Application for Vital Record
MARRIAGE CERTIFICATE

REQUEST FOR (CHECK ONE): ___ Certified Copy ___ Verification ___ Record Search

INSTRUCTIONS

NOTE: For records more than ten years old, contact:
General Services Center, Reference and Research,
US Rte. 2 - Middlesex, Drawer 33,
Montpelier, VT 05633-7601 (802) 828-3286

Type or print all information clearly.
Sign and date application and return it with
your check or money order (made payable to the
Vermont Department of Health) to the address
below. **Do not mail cash.**

FEES:
Certified Copy $7.00
Verification   no charge
Record Search   no charge

Amount enclosed _____

MARRIAGE INFORMATION

Date of Marriage _____ Town of Marriage _____

Groom:
Name _____

Bride:
Name _____

Date of birth _____ Date of birth _____

Name of father _____ Name of father _____

Name of mother _____ Name of mother _____

APPLICANT INFORMATION

Your name _____

Address _____

Town _____ State _____ Zip _____

Phone number (____) _____

Your relationship to couple on marriage certificate _____

Intended use of certificate:

_____ Proof of Marriage _____ Family History

_____ Other (Specify): _____

Signature _____ Date _____

Return to: Vermont Department of Health, Vital Records Unit
108 Cherry Street, PO Box 70, Burlington, VT 05402
Telephone: (802) 863-7275 or 1-800-439-5008

Application for Vital Record
DIVORCE CERTIFICATE

REQUEST FOR (CHECK ONE): ___ Certified Copy ___ Verification ___ Record Search

INSTRUCTIONS

NOTE: For records more than ten years old, contact:
General Services Center, Reference and Research,
US Rte. 2 - Middlesex, Drawer 33,
Montpelier, VT 05633-7601   (802) 828-3286

Type or print all information clearly.
Sign and date application and return it with
your check or money order (made payable to the
Vermont Department of Health) to the address
below. **Do not mail cash.**

FEES:
Certified Copy $7.00
Verification   no charge
Record Search   no charge

Amount enclosed _____

DIVORCE INFORMATION

Husband's Name _____

Wife's Name _____

Date Divorce became final _____

County of Divorce _____

Date of Marriage _____

APPLICANT INFORMATION

Your name _____

Address _____

Town _____ State _____ Zip _____

Phone number (____) _____

Your relationship to people on certificate _____

Intended use of certificate:

____ Proof of Divorce   ____ Personal Use

____ Other (Specify): _____

Signature _____ Date _____

Return to: Vermont Department of Health, Vital Records Unit
108 Cherry Street, PO Box 70, Burlington, VT 05402
Telephone: (802) 863-7275 or 1-800-439-5008

Application for Vital Record
DEATH CERTIFICATE

REQUEST FOR (CHECK ONE): ___ Certified Copy ___ Verification ___ Record Search

INSTRUCTIONS

NOTE: For records more than ten years old, contact:
General Services Center, Reference and Research,
US Rte. 2 - Middlesex, Drawer 33,
Montpelier, VT 05633-7601 (802) 828-3286

Type or print all information clearly.
Sign and date application and return it with
your check or money order (made payable to the
Vermont Department of Health) to the address
below. **Do not mail cash.**

FEES:
Certified Copy $7.00
Verification   no charge
Record Search   no charge

Amount enclosed _____

DEATH INFORMATION

Name on death certificate _____ Sex _____

Date of death _____ Town or city of death _____

Date of birth _____ State of birth _____

Age at death _____ Name of spouse _____

Your name _____

Address _____

Town _____ State _____ Zip _____

Phone number (____) _____

Your relationship to person on death certificate _____

Intended use of certificate:

_____ Benefits   _____ Settlement of Estate

_____ Family History   _____ Other (Specify): _____

Signature _____ Date _____

Return to: Vermont Department of Health, Vital Records Unit
108 Cherry Street, PO Box 70, Burlington, VT 05402
Telephone: (802) 863-7275 or 1-800-439-5008

VIRGINIA

Send your requests to:

Virginia Department of Health
Division of Vital Records
James Madison Building
P.O. Box 1000
Richmond, Virginia 23218-1000

Tel. (804) 225-5000
Fax (804) 644-2550
http://www.vdh.state.va.us/misc/f_08.htm

Make check or money order out to "State Health Department." The Division of Vital Records has birth and death records from 1853–1896 and from June 1912–present; marriage records from 1853; and divorce records from 1918. Birth records are restricted for 100 years; death, marriage, and divorce records are restricted for 50 years.

Expedited service is available (with payment by credit card) for an additional fee of $22.20, which includes Federal Express shipping; phone (804) 644-2537 or (804) 644-2723 or fax (804) 644-2550.

Cost for a certified Birth Certificate	$8.00
Cost for a certified Marriage Certificate	$8.00
Cost for a Certified Divorce Record	$8.00
Cost for a Certified Death Certificate	$8.00

Vital records are also kept by:

County Clerk
County Court House
(County Seat), Virginia

For Adoption Record information write to:

Adoption Program Specialist
Virginia Department of Social Services
730 East Broad Street
Richmond, Virginia 23219-1849

Tel. (804) 692-1290
http://www.dss.state.va.us/family/adoption.html

The Library of Virginia (800 East Broad Street, Richmond, VA 23219-8000; 804-692-3500) has birth and death records from 1853 to 1896, and marriage records from 1853 to 1935.

The Family History Library of Salt Lake City, Utah has microfilmed original and published vital records and church registers of Virginia. For details on their holdings please consult your nearest Family History Center.

Application for Certification of a Vital Record

VS6 9/99

Virginia statutes require a fee of $8.00 be charged for each certification of a vital record or for a search of the files when no certification is made. Please make check or money order payable to **State Health Department**. There is a $20.00 service charge for returned checks.

Name of Requester: _____ Daytime Phone Number:(____)_____

Address:_____ City:_____ State: _____ Zip:_____

What is your relationship to the person named on the certificate?_____

If you are not the person named on the certificate, please state your direct and tangible interest in receiving this certificate:

_____

I understand that making a false application for a Vital Record is a **FELONY** under state and federal law.

Signature of Applicant:_____

BIRTH

Number of Copies:_____

Name at Birth:_____

If name has changed since birth due to adoption, court order, or any reason other than marriage please list changed name here:

_____

Date of Birth:_____ Race: _____ Sex:_____

Place of Birth :_____ Hospital of Birth:_____
(City/County in Virginia)

Full Maiden Name of Mother:_____

Full Name of Father:_____

DEATH

Number of Copies:_____

Name of Deceased_____

Date of Death:_____ Age at Death:_____ Race: _____ Sex:_____

Place of Death:_____Hospital Name:_____
(City/County in Virginia)

MARRIAGE

Number of Copies:_____

Full Name of Husband:_____

Full Name of Wife:_____

DIVORCE

Number of Copies:_____

Marriage - Date:_____ Place._____

Divorce - Date:_____ Place:_____
(City/County in Virginia)

If Marriage, place where license was issued:_____

Please include a **self-addressed stamped envelope.**

Please indicate the address you wish the certificate(s) mailed to in the box below. -- Please type or print clearly.

Name
Address
City/State/Zip

Send Completed Application To:

Division of Vital Records
P. O. Box 1000
Richmond, Va. 23218-1000
(804) 225-5000

WASHINGTON

Send your requests to:

Washington State Department of Health
Center for Health Statistics
P.O. Box 9709
Olympia, Washington 98507-9709

Tel. (360) 236-4300
Fax (360) 352-2586
http://www.doh.wa.gov/EHSPHL/CHS/cert.htm

The Center for Health Statistics has birth and marriage records from July 1, 1907, and marriage and divorce records from January 1, 1968. Make checks or money orders payable to "Department of Health." Expedited service is available (with payment by credit card) for an additional fee of $24.00, plus shipping.

Cost for a certified Birth Certificate	$13.00
Cost for an heirloom Birth Certificate	$25.00
Cost for a certified Marriage Certificate	$13.00
Cost for a certified Divorce Record	$13.00
Cost for a certified Death Certificate	$13.00

Send your requests for pre-1968 Marriage Certificates to:

County Auditor
County Court House
(County Seat), Washington

For Adoption Record information write to:

Adoption Program Manager
Washington State Department of Social & Health Services
Division of Children & Family Services—Adoptions
P.O. Box 45713
Olympia, Washington 98504-5713

E-mail: Children@dshs.wa.gov
http://www.wa.gov/dshs/ca/ca3ov.html

The Washington State Archives (1120 Washington Street, P.O. Box 40238, Olympia, WA 98504; 360-586-1492) has an index to death records from 1907 to 1986; an index birth records from 1907 to 1920; and marriage and divorce indexes from 1968 to 1997.

The Family History Library of Salt Lake City, Utah has microfilmed many of the original and published vital records and church registers of Washington. They have microfilm copies of birth records and indexes from 1907 to 1959, death records from 1907 to 1952, and death indexes from 1907 to 1949.

 **Health**

Center for Health Statistics
WASHINGTON STATE VITAL RECORDS APPLICATION

Name and Address Required
(Certified copy(ies) will be sent to the address you specify below)

NAME	TELEPHONE (DAYTIME)

MAILING ADDRESS

CITY	STATE	ZIP

REQUESTED DOCUMENT (S)

_____ Birth
(Exact Information Required)

INDICATE NUMBER/QUANTITY REQUESTED

_____ Certified Copy(ies) @ $13 Each   _____ Adoption Sealed File @ $15 Each

_____ Heirloom Copy(ies)@ $25 Each   _____ Paternity Sealed File @ $15 Each

Was this person adopted? ☐ Yes ☐ No | Have you received a copy before? ☐ Yes ☐ No

NAME ON RECORD FIRST	MIDDLE	LAST

DATE OF BIRTH (MONTH/DAY/YEAR)	PLACE OF BIRTH CITY	COUNTY	HOSPITAL

FATHER'S FULL NAME FIRST IF NOT NAMED, WRITE "NOT NAMED"	MIDDLE	LAST

MOTHER'S **FULL MAIDEN** NAME FIRST	MIDDLE	LAST

REQUESTED DOCUMENT(S)   **INDICATE NUMBER OF COPY(IES) @ $13.00**
FOR EACH TEN-YEAR INDEX PERIOD SEARCHED.   _____ **Death**   _____ **Marriage**   _____ **Divorce**

NAME ON RECORD FIRST	MIDDLE	LAST

SPOUSE FIRST	MIDDLE	LAST

DATE OF EVENT (MONTH/DAY/YEAR - OR 10 YEAR PERIOD)	PLACE EVENT FILED

REQUESTOR'S NAME (IF DIFFERENT THAN THE ABOVE ADDRESS)	TELEPHONE (DAYTIME)

REQUESTOR'S ADDRESS

DOH 110-039 FRONT(REV 4/99)

For State Use Only - Do Not Write Below This Line
(DO NOT DETACH BOTTOM PORTION. SUBMIT ENTIRE FORM)

QTY _____ Birth Copy @ $13 Ea (28 0005)   QTY _____ Adoption Sealed File @ $15 Ea (31 0007)   Refund

QTY _____ Heirloom Copy @ $25 Ea (30 0006)   QTY _____ Paternity Sealed File @ $15 Ea (32 0008)   Amount $ _____

QTY _____ Death (28 00021)   QTY _____ Marriage (28 00039)   QTY _____ Divorce (28 00047)

Name _____

☐ SIE   001 04 41 28 X 8
        02K 04 21 03 X 5
☐ OP   001 04 41 28
☐ H   001 04 41 30 X 14.5
        04 41 28 X 10.5
☐ AS   001 04 41 31 X 15
☐ PS   001 04 41 32 X 15
☐ NR   02K 04 21 03 X 5

WEST VIRGINIA

Bureau for Public Health
Vital Registration Program
Room 165
350 Capitol Street
Charleston, West Virginia 25301-3701

Tel. (304) 558-2931
Fax (304) 558-1051
http://www.wvdhhr.org/bph/oehp/hsc/vr/birtcert.htm

Make check or money order payable to "Vital Registration." The Vital Registration office has birth and death records from January 1, 1917; marriage records from January 1, 1921; and divorce records from 1968. For earlier records contact the County Clerk. Expedited service is available (with payment by credit card) for an additional fee.

Cost for a certified Birth Certificate	$5.00
Cost for a certified Marriage Certificate	$5.00
Cost for a certified Death Certificate	$5.00

Certificates are also issued by:

County Clerk
County Court House
(County Seat), West Virginia

For Adoption Record information write to:

West Virginia Department of Health and Human Services
Office of Social Services
Mutual Consent Voluntary Adoption Registry
350 Capitol Street, Room 691
Charleston, West Virginia 25301-3704

Tel. (304) 558-7980
Fax (304) 558-4563

There is no cost for registration with the Voluntary Adoption Registry.

The Family History Library of Salt Lake City, Utah has microfilmed many of the original and published vital records and church registers of West Virginia. They have microfilm copies of vital records from 1853 to 1860. For details on their holdings please consult your nearest Family History Center.

Application for Certified Copy of West Virginia Birth Certificate

Please print except where signature is required.

The following pertains to information that would be found on the certificate being requested.

Name of person on the certificate

_____

First   Middle   Last

Date of Birth

_____

Month/Day/Year

Place of Birth

City _____ County _____ State _____

Hospital _____

Mother's Maiden Name

_____

First   Middle   Last

Sex:

☐ Male   ☐ Female

Father's Name

_____

First   Middle   Last

The information below pertains to the person requesting the certificate.

Requestor's Relationship: Parent ☐   Guardian or agent ☐   Grandparent ☐

Record for self ☐   Spouse ☐

By my signature, I certify that the above marked relationship is true.

_____   _____

Signature (Required)   Printed Name (Required)

Enclosed is $_____ for _____ copies ($5.00 per copy). Please send check or money order.
Please do not send cash. Make checks payable to: Vital Registration

Send copies to: Print your address below.

_____

_____

_____   (_____) _____

_____   Area Code   Your daytime telephone number:

City   State   Zip

Submit form with check or money order to:

Vital Registration
Room 165
350 Capitol Street
Charleston, WV 25301-3701

Telephone: (304) 558-2931

Last Revised 05/05/00

Application for Copy of West Virginia Death Certificate

Please print except where signature is required.

The following pertains to information that would be found on the certificate being requested.

Name of person on the certificate

_____

First   Middle   Last

City _____ County _____

Hospital _____

Date of Death

_____

Month/Day/Year

State _____

Sex:

☐ Male   ☐ Female

The information below pertains to the person requesting the certificate.

Requestor's Relationship: Parent ☐   Guardian or agent ☐   Grandparent ☐

Child of decedent ☐   Spouse ☐

Other ☐ (Describe)

_____

_____

_____

_____

By my signature, I certify that the above marked relationship is true.

_____   _____

Signature (Required)   Printed Name (Required)

Reason for request: _____

_____

_____

Enclosed is $_____ for _____ copies ($5.00 per copy). Please send check or money order.
Please do not send cash. Make checks payable to: Vital Registration

Send copies to: **Print** your address below.

_____

_____

_____   (_____)_____

_____   Area Code   Your daytime telephone number:

_____

City   State   Zip

Submit form with check or money order to:

Vital Registration
Room 165
350 Capitol Street
Charleston, WV 25301-3701

Telephone: (304) 558-2931

Last Revised 05/05/00

WISCONSIN

Send your requests to:

Wisconsin Department of Health and Family Services
Vital Records
1 West Wilson Street
P.O. Box 309
Madison, Wisconsin 53701-0309

Tel. (608) 266-1373
Recording (608) 266-1371
Genealogical Research (608) 267-7820
http://www.dhfs.state.wi.us/vitalrecords/index.htm

Send check or money order to "Vital Records." Birth, marriage, and death records are Incomplete prior to January 1, 1907, although some go back as far as 1814; there are no divorce records prior to 1907. Expedited service is available (with payment by credit card) for an additional fee.

Cost for a certified Birth Certificate	$12.00
Cost for a certified Marriage Certificate	$7.00
Cost for a certified Divorce Record	$7.00
Cost for a certified Death Certificate	$7.00
Cost for a duplicate certificate, when ordered at the same time	$2.00

Vital records are also kept by:

County Clerk
County Court House
(County Seat), Wisconsin

For Adoption Record information write to:

Adoption Records Search Program
Wisconsin Department of Health and Family Services
P.O. Box 8916
Madison, Wisconsin 53708-7163

Tel. (608) 266-7163
http://www.dhfs.state.wi.us/Children/
adoption/adsearch.htm

The Family History Library of Salt Lake City, Utah has microfilmed many of the original and published vital records and church registers of Wisconsin. They have microfilm copies of birth records from 1852 to 1907; delayed birth records from 1937 to 1941; an index to marriage records from 1852 to 1907; and death records from 1862 to 1907. For details on their holdings please consult your nearest Family History Center.

For further information see:

Krueger, Ed K. *Handbook for Township Officials*. Shawano, WI: Wisconsin Towns Association, 1978. 350p.
A Manual for City and Village Clerks in Wisconsin. Madison, WI: League of Wisconsin Municipalities, 1942. 144p.

DEPARTMENT OF HEALTH AND FAMILY SERVICES
Division of Health Care Financing
HCF5291 (Rev. 04/00)

STATE OF WISCONSIN
Chap. 69.21 (1a), (2b), Wis.Stats.

WISCONSIN BIRTH CERTIFICATE APPLICATION

Please complete this form and return it to the following address with a self-addressed stamped envelope and appropriate fee.
Please make check or money order payable to: **VITAL RECORDS.**
Mail to: Vital Records, P. O. Box 309, Madison WI 53701-0309.

PENALTIES: Any person who willfully and knowingly makes false application for a birth certificate shall be fined not more than $10,000 or imprisoned not more than 3 years or both.

THE FOLLOWING INFORMATION IS ABOUT THE PERSON COMPLETING THIS APPLICATION

APPLICANT INFORMATION

YOUR Name (Please Print)

YOUR Signature | Today's Date

YOUR Daytime Telephone Number
(   )

YOUR Street Address | Mail To Address (if different)

City/State/Zip | City/State/Zip

RELATIONSHIP TO PERSONS NAMED ON THE CERTIFICATE

According to Wisconsin State Statute, a CERTIFIED copy of a BIRTH record is only available to a person with a "Direct and Tangible Interest". If you do not meet the criteria for boxes A – F, you can only receive an uncertified copy.

Please check one box which indicates YOUR RELATIONSHIP to the PERSON NAMED on the record:

☐ A. I AM the person NAMED on the record.

☐ B. I am the PARENT of the person NAMED on the record, and my parental rights have not been terminated. Note: In the case of a non-marital birth, the father's rights must have been established by a court or by a Voluntary Paternity Acknowledgement before he may obtain a copy of the record under this category.

☐ C. I am the Legal Custodian or Guardian of the person NAMED on the record.

☐ D. I am a member of the immediate family of the person NAMED on the record.
PLEASE CIRCLE ONE: (Only those listed below qualify as immediate family)
Spouse   Child   Brother   Sister   Grandparent

☐ E. I am a representative authorized, in writing, by any of the aforementioned (A through D).
Specify whom you represent:_____

☐ F. I can demonstrate that the information from the record is necessary for the determination or protection of a personal or property right for myself/my client/my agency.
Specify interest:_____

☐ Other: Uncertified copy only. Copy will not be valid for identification purposes.

FEES

☐ $12.00 First copy
☐ $2.00 Each additional copy of the same record, issued at the same time as the first copy.
Note: The fee is for a search and first copy. The fee is NOT REFUNDABLE if no record is found.

BIRTH INFORMATION

FIRST NAME	MIDDLE NAME	LAST NAME AT BIRTH	

SEX	MONTH	DAY	YEAR	CITY	COUNTY

MOTHER'S MAIDEN NAME	FIRST NAME	MIDDLE NAME

FATHER'S LAST NAME	FIRST NAME	MIDDLE NAME

CERTIFICATE NUMBER IF KNOWN

Below is FOR OFFICE USE ONLY

File Date | Mother's County

FAX REQUEST FOR WISCONSIN BIRTH CERTIFICATE

Fax this completed form to the following number: **608-255-2035**

PENALTIES: Any person who willfully and knowingly makes false application for a birth certificate shall be fined not more than $10,000, or imprisoned not more than 3 years or both.

All Fax requests will be shipped by Federal Express. The shipping and handling fee is $21.00.

SHIP TO: Name: _____

Address: _____ Daytime Phone Number: _____

City: _____ State: _____ Zip Code: _____

Credit Card Number: _____ Expires: _____
        (Visa, MasterCard, American Express or Discover)

_____   _____
            Applicant's Signature   Date

(We do not accept credit card payments through the mail.)

NUMBER OF COPIES REQUESTED:

_____ $12.00 First Copy (This fee is for a search and first copy. This fee is NOT REFUNDABLE if no record is found.)

_____ $2.00 Each additional copy of the same record issued at the same time as the first copy.
        Plus shipping fee of $21.00. Fee for one copy plus shipment $33.00

Relationship to person on the record: ☐Self   ☐Mother   ☐Father   ☐Child
        ☐Sister   ☐Brother   ☐Spouse   ☐Grandparent
        Only the above requesters may receive a certified copy of a birth certificate.

Purpose for requesting the certificate:
_____

Note: Genealogy requests will not be accepted by fax. Genealogy requests must be mailed.

Requests sent by mail must have fee enclosed.

INFORMATION ABOUT REQUESTED CERTIFICATE:

Full Name at Birth: _____ Sex: ☐Male ☐Female
        First Name   Middle Name   Last Name (Maiden)

Date of Birth: _____ Place of Birth: _____
        Month   Day   Year   City/Village/Township   County

Mother's Maiden Name: _____
                First Name   Middle Name   Last Name

Father's Name:
_____
                First Name   Middle Name   Last Name

| **OFFICE USE ONLY** | | |
| Certificate Number _____ | File Date _____ | Mom Res. _____ |

VitalChek Network, Inc. For more information call toll free (800) 255-2414. Web address: http://www.vitalchek.com

DEPARTMENT OF HEALTH AND FAMILY SERVICES
Division of Health Care Financing
HCF5291 (Rev. 04/00)

STATE OF WISCONSIN
Chap. 69.21 (1a), (2b), Wis.Stats.

WISCONSIN MARRIAGE CERTIFICATE APPLICATION

Please complete this form and return it to the following address with a self-addressed stamped envelope and appropriate fee.
Please make check or money order payable to: **VITAL RECORDS.**
Mail to: Vital Records, P. O. Box 309, Madison WI 53701-0309.

PENALTIES: Any person who willfully and knowingly makes false application for a marriage certificate shall be fined not more than $10,000 or imprisoned not more than 3 years or both.

THE FOLLOWING INFORMATION IS ABOUT THE PERSON COMPLETING THIS APPLICATION

APPLICANT INFORMATION

YOUR Name (Please Print)

YOUR Signature | Today's Date

YOUR Daytime Telephone Number
(   )

YOUR Street Address | Mail To Address (if different)

City/State/Zip | City/State/Zip

RELATIONSHIP TO PERSONS NAMED ON THE CERTIFICATE

According to Wisconsin State Statute, a CERTIFIED copy of a MARRIAGE record is only available to a person with a "Direct and Tangible Interest". If you do not meet the criteria for boxes A – F, you can only receive an uncertified copy.

Please check one box which indicates YOUR RELATIONSHIP to one of the PERSONS NAMED on the record:

☐ A. I AM one of the persons NAMED on the record.

☐ B. I am the PARENT of one of the persons NAMED on the record.

☐ C. I am the Legal Custodian or Guardian of one of the persons NAMED on the record.

☐ D. I am a member of the immediate family of one of the persons NAMED on the record.
PLEASE CIRCLE ONE: (Only those listed below qualify as immediate family)

Spouse   Child   Brother   Sister   Grandparent

☐ E. I am a representative authorized, in writing, by any of the aforementioned (A through D).
Specify whom you represent:_____

☐ F. I can demonstrate that the information from the record is necessary for the determination or protection of a personal or property right for myself/my client/my agency.
Specify interest:_____

☐ Other: Uncertified copy only. Copy will not be valid for identification purposes.

FEES

☐ $7.00 First copy
☐ $2.00 Each additional copy of the same record, issued at the same time as the first copy.
Note: The fee is for a search and first copy. The fee is NOT REFUNDABLE if no record is found.

MARRIAGE INFORMATION

FULL NAME OF GROOM

FULL MAIDEN NAME OF BRIDE

PLACE OF MARRIAGE | **CITY, VILLAGE, TOWNSHIP** | **COUNTY**

DATE OF MARRIAGE

FAX REQUEST FOR WISCONSIN MARRIAGE CERTIFICATE

Fax this completed form to the following number: **608-255-2035**

PENALTIES: Any person who willfully and knowingly makes false application for a marriage certificate shall be fined not more than $10,000, or imprisoned not more than 3 years or both.

All Fax requests will be shipped by Federal Express. The shipping and handling fee is $21.00.

SHIP TO: Name: _____

Address: _____ Daytime Phone Number: _____

City: _____ State: _____ Zip Code: _____

Credit Card Number: _____ Expires: _____
(Visa, MasterCard, American Express or Discover)

_____   _____
        Applicant's Signature   Date

(We do not accept credit card payments through the mail.)

NUMBER OF COPIES REQUESTED:

_____ $7.00 First Copy (This fee is for a search and first copy. This fee is NOT REFUNDABLE if no record is found.)

_____ $2.00 Each additional copy of the same record issued at the same time as the first copy.
Plus shipping fee of $21.00. Fee for one copy plus shipment $28.00

Relationship to person on the record ☐ Self   ☐ Mother   ☐ Father   ☐ Sister
☐ Brother   ☐ Spouse   ☐ Child   ☐ Grandparent
Only the above requesters may receive a certified copy of a marriage certificate.

Purpose for requesting the certificate:

_____

Note: Genealogy requests will not be accepted by fax. Genealogy requests must be mailed.

Requests sent by mail must have fee enclosed.

INFORMATION ABOUT REQUESTED CERTIFICATE:

Full Name of Groom: _____
                          First Name   Middle Name   Last Name

Full Maiden Name of Bride: _____
                          First Name   Middle Name   Last Name

Place of Marriage:

_____
                City/Village/Township   County

Date of Marriage: _____
                        Month   Day   Year

```
OFFICE USE ONLY

Certificate Number _____
```

VitalChek Network, Inc. For more information call toll free (800) 255-2414. Web address: http://www.vitalchek.com

DEPARTMENT OF HEALTH AND FAMILY SERVICES
Division of Health Care Financing
HCF5291 (Rev. 04/00)

STATE OF WISCONSIN
Chap. 69.21 (1a), (2b), Wis.Stats.

WISCONSIN DIVORCE CERTIFICATE APPLICATION

Please complete this form and return it to the following address with a self-addressed stamped envelope and appropriate fee.
Please make check or money order payable to: **VITAL RECORDS.**
Mail to: Vital Records, P. O. Box 309, Madison WI 53701-0309.

PENALTIES: Any person who willfully and knowingly makes false application for a divorce certificate shall be fined not more than $10,000 or imprisoned not more than 3 years or both.

THE FOLLOWING INFORMATION IS ABOUT THE PERSON COMPLETING THIS APPLICATION

APPLICANT INFORMATION

YOUR Name (Please Print)

YOUR Signature

Today's Date

YOUR Daytime Telephone Number
(   )

YOUR Street Address

Mail To Address (if different)

City/State/Zip

City/State/Zip

RELATIONSHIP TO PERSONS NAMED ON THE CERTIFICATE

According to Wisconsin State Statute, a CERTIFIED copy of a divorce record is only available to a person with a "Direct and Tangible Interest". If you do not meet the criteria for boxes A – F, you can only receive an uncertified copy.

Please check one box which indicates YOUR RELATIONSHIP to one of the PERSONS NAMED on the record:

☐ A. I AM one of the persons NAMED on the record.

☐ B. I am the PARENT of one of the persons NAMED on the record.

☐ C. I am the Legal Custodian or Guardian of one of the persons NAMED on the record.

☐ D. I am a member of the immediate family of one of the persons NAMED on the record.
PLEASE CIRCLE ONE: (Only those listed below qualify as immediate family)

Spouse   Child   Brother   Sister   Grandparent

☐ E. I am a representative authorized, in writing, by any of the aforementioned (A through D).

Specify whom you represent:_____

☐ F. I can demonstrate that the information from the record is necessary for the determination or protection of a personal or property right for myself/my client/my agency.

Specify interest _____

☐ Other: Uncertified copy only. Copy will not be valid for identification purposes.

FEES

☐ $7.00 First copy

☐ $2.00 Each additional copy of the same record, issued at the same time as the first copy.
Note: The fee is for a search and first copy. The fee is NOT REFUNDABLE if no record is found.

DIVORCE INFORMATION

FULL NAME OF HUSBAND

FULL MAIDEN NAME OF WIFE

PLACE OF DIVORCE	CITY, VILLAGE, TOWNSHIP	COUNTY

DATE OF DIVORCE

FAX REQUEST FOR WISCONSIN DIVORCE CERTIFICATE

Fax this completed form to the following number: **608-255-2035**

PENALTIES: Any person who willfully and knowingly makes false application for a divorce certificate shall be fined not more than $10,000, or imprisoned not more than 3 years or both.

All Fax requests will be shipped by Federal Express. The shipping and handling fee is $21.00.

SHIP TO: Name: _____

Address: _____ Daytime Phone Number: _____

City: _____ State: _____ Zip Code: _____

Credit Card Number: _____ Expires: _____
             (Visa, MasterCard, American Express or Discover)

_____   _____
             Applicant's Signature   Date

(We do not accept credit card payments through the mail.)

NUMBER OF COPIES REQUESTED:

_____ $7.00 First Copy (This fee is for a search and first copy. This fee is NOT REFUNDABLE if no record is found.)

_____ $2.00 Each additional copy of the same record issued at the same time as the first copy.
     Plus shipping fee of $21.00. Fee for one copy plus shipment $28.00

Relationship to person on the record ☐ Self   ☐ Mother   ☐ Father   ☐ Sister
              ☐ Brother   ☐ Spouse   ☐ Child   ☐ Grandparent
     Only the above requesters may receive a certified copy of a divorce certificate.

Purpose for requesting the certificate:
_____
Note: Genealogy requests will not be accepted by fax. Genealogy requests must be mailed.

Requests sent by mail must have fee enclosed.

INFORMATION ABOUT REQUESTED CERTIFICATE:

Full Name of Husband: _____
              First Name   Middle Name   Last Name

Full Maiden Name of Wife: _____
              First Name   Middle Name   Last Name

Place of Divorce: _____
              City/Village/Township   County

Date of Divorce: _____
              Month Day Year

┌───┐
│ **OFFICE USE ONLY**   │
│   │
│ Certificate Number _____   │
└───┘

VitalChek Network, Inc. For more information call toll free (800) 255-2414. Web address: http://www.vitalchek.com

DEPARTMENT OF HEALTH AND FAMILY SERVICES
Division of Health Care Financing
HCF 5291 (Rev. 04/00)

STATE OF WISCONSIN
Chap. 69.21 (1a), (2b), Wis.Stats.

WISCONSIN DEATH CERTIFICATE APPLICATION

Please complete this form and return it to the following address with a self-addressed stamped envelope and appropriate fee.
Please make check or money order payable to: **VITAL RECORDS.**
Mail to: Vital Records, P. O. Box 309, Madison WI 53701-0309.

PENALTIES: Any person who willfully and knowingly makes false application for a death certificate shall be fined not more than $10,000 or imprisoned not more than 3 years or both.

APPLICANT INFORMATION

THE FOLLOWING INFORMATION IS ABOUT THE PERSON COMPLETING THIS APPLICATION

YOUR Name (Please Print)

YOUR Signature

Today's Date

YOUR Daytime Telephone Number
(   )

YOUR Street Address

Mail To Address (if different)

City/State/Zip

City/State/Zip

RELATIONSHIP TO PERSON NAMED ON THE CERTIFICATE

According to Wisconsin State Statute, a CERTIFIED copy of a DEATH record is only available to a person with a "Direct and Tangible Interest". If you do not meet the criteria for boxes A – E, you can only receive an uncertified copy.

Please check one box which indicates YOUR RELATIONSHIP to the PERSON NAMED on the record:

☐ A. I am a PARENT of the person NAMED on the record.

☐ B. I am the Legal Custodian or Guardian of the person NAMED on the record.

☐ C. I am a member of the immediate family of the person NAMED on the record.
PLEASE CIRCLE ONE: (Only those listed below qualify as immediate family.)

Spouse   Child   Brother   Sister   Grandparent

☐ D. I am a representative authorized, in writing, by any of the aforementioned (A through C).
Specify whom you represent:_____

☐ E. I can demonstrate that the information from the record is necessary for the determination or protection of a personal or property right for myself/my client/my agency.

Specify interest _____

☐ Other: Uncertified copy only. Copy will not be valid for identification purposes.

FEES

☐ $7.00 First copy
☐ $2.00 Each additional copy of the same record, issued at the same time as the first copy.
Note: The fee is for a search and first copy. The fee is NOT REFUNDABLE if no record is found.

DEATH INFORMATION

FULL NAME OF DECEDENT

PLACE OF DEATH   **CITY, VILLAGE, TOWNSHIP**   **COUNTY**

DATE OF DEATH   **DECEDENT'S SOCIAL SECURITY NUMBER**

DECEDENT'S AGE/ BIRTHDATE   **DECEDENT'S OCCUPATION**

NAME OF DECEDENT'S SPOUSE   **NAME OF DECEDENT'S PARENTS**

FAX REQUEST FOR WISCONSIN DEATH CERTIFICATE

Fax this completed form to the following number: **608-255-2035**

PENALTIES: Any person who willfully and knowingly makes false application for a death certificate shall be fined not more than $10,000, or imprisoned not more than 3 years or both.

All Fax requests will be shipped by Federal Express. The shipping and handling fee is $21.00.

SHIP TO: Name: _____

Address: _____ Daytime Phone Number: _____

City: _____ State: _____ Zip Code: ____ _____

Credit Card Number: _____ Expires: _____
   (Visa, MasterCard, American Express or Discover)

_____   _____
    Applicant's Signature   Date

(We do not accept credit card payments through the mail.)

NUMBER OF COPIES REQUESTED:

_____ $7.00 First Copy (This fee is for a search and first copy. This fee is NOT REFUNDABLE if no record is found.)

_____ $2.00 Each additional copy of the same record issued at the same time as the first copy.
   Plus shipping fee of $21.00. Fee for one copy plus shipment $28.00

Relationship to person on the record: ☐ Mother ☐ Father ☐ Child ☐ Sister
   ☐ Brother ☐ Spouse ☐ Grandparent
   Only the above requesters may receive a certified copy of a death certificate.

Purpose for requesting the certificate:

_____

Note: Genealogy requests will not be accepted by fax. Genealogy requests must be mailed.

Requests sent by mail must have fee enclosed.

INFORMATION ABOUT REQUESTED CERTIFICATE:

Full Name of Decedent: _____
            First Name   Middle Name   Last Name

Date of Death: _____ **Place of Death** _____
         Month Day Year   City/Village/Township   County

Full Name of Spouse** _____
            First Name   Middle Name   Last Name

Decedent's Parents**

_____
            Father's Name   and/or   Mother's Name

Decedent's Age/Birthdate** _____ **Decedent's Social Security Number**** _____

****Information helpful to search, but not necessary

+------------------------------------+
| **OFFICE USE ONLY** |
| Certificate |
| Number_____ |
+------------------------------------+

VitalChek Network, Inc. For more information call toll free (800) 255-2414. Web address: http://www.vitalchek.com

WYOMING

Send your requests to:

Wyoming Department of Health
Vital Records Services
Hathaway Building
Cheyenne, Wyoming 82002

Tel. (307) 777-7591
Fax (307) 635-4103
TTY (307) 777-5648
http://wdhfs.state.wy.us/vital_records/

Vital Records has birth and death records from July 1909, and marriage and divorce records from May 1941. Birth records in Wyoming are restricted for 100 years; other records for 50 years. Expedited service is available (with payment by credit card) for an additional fee of $5.00, plus shipping.

For Marriage, Divorce, and Death records more than 50 years old write to:

Records Management & Micrographics Services
Wyoming State Archives
2301 Central Avenue
Barrett Building
Cheyenne, Wyoming 82002

Tel. (307) 777-7826
Fax (307) 777-7044
E-mail: wyarchive@state.wy.us
http://spacr.state.wy.us/CR/Archives

Current records, from Wyoming State Vital Records Services:

Cost for a certified Birth Certificate	$12.00
Cost for a certified Marriage Certificate	$12.00
Cost for a certified Divorce Record	$12.00
Cost for a certified Death Certificate	$9.00

Records more than 50 years old, from Wyoming State Archives:

Cost for a certified Marriage Certificate	$3.50
Cost for a non-certified Marriage Certificate	$.50
Cost for a certified Divorce Record	$3.50
Cost for a non-certified Divorce Record	$.50
Cost for a Certified Death Certificate	$3.50
Cost for a non-certified Death Certificate	$.50

Vital records are also kept by:

County Clerk
County Court House
(County Seat), Wyoming

For Adoption Record information write to:

Confidential Adoption Intermediary Services
Wyoming Department of Family Services
Division of Programs and Policy
Hathaway Building, 3rd floor
2300 Capitol Avenue
Cheyenne, Wyoming 82002

Tel. (307) 777-3570
Fax (307) 777-3693

For further information see:

Rules and Regulations, Vital Records Services, State of Wyoming. Cheyenne, WY: Wyoming State, Department of Health and Social Services, 1973. 26p.

STATE OF WYOMING
APPLICATION FOR CERTIFIED COPY OF BIRTH CERTIFICATE

A request for a certified copy of a birth certificate should be submitted on this form along with the fee of $12.00 per copy. Money orders or a personalized check from the person making the request should be made payable to VITAL RECORDS SERVICES. Please enclose a self-addressed, stamped envelope with the application.

Send to:
Vital Records Services
Hathaway Building
Cheyenne, WY 82002
(307) 777-7591

If you do not have a birth record on file, you will be sent instructions for filing a Delayed Birth Certificate, and your $12.00 fee will be retained as a searching fee.

Enclosed is $ _____ for _____ certified copy(s).

Full Name at Birth	First	Middle	Last (Maiden Name)
If this birth could be recorded under another name, please list that name here:			
Sex	Date of Birth (Month, Day and Year)		City or County of Birth
Mother's Maiden Name	First	Middle	Maiden Last Name
Father's Name	First	Middle	Last

Signature of person whose certificate is being requested or parent named on certificate. (If under 18 years of age, signature of parent or legal guardian required. Legal guardian must submit a copy of guardianship papers.)

► _____

Address to which copy is to be mailed: _____

_____

_____

W.S. 35-1-428 requires Vital Records Services to collect a $5.00 surcharge on all certified copies and searches of the files to be deposited in the Wyoming Children's Trust Fund. This surcharge is included in the fee listed above. The fund is used to establish programs for the prevention of child abuse and neglect.

STATE OF WYOMING
APPLICATION FOR CERTIFIED COPY OF MARRIAGE OR DIVORCE CERTIFICATE

A request for a certified copy of a marriage or divorce certificate should be submitted on this form along with the fee of $12.00 per copy. A money order or a personalized check from the person making the request should be made payable to VITAL RECORDS SERVICES. Please enclose a self-addressed, stamped envelope with the application.

Send to:
Vital Records Services
Hathaway Building
Cheyenne, WY 82002
(307) 777-7591

If a record is not located, your $12.00 fee will be retained as a searching fee.

Type of record requested: (check one) Marriage _____ Divorce _____

Enclosed is $ _____ for _____ certified copy(s).

Name of Husband - First	Middle	Last
Name of Wife - First	Middle	Surname at time of Marriage
Date of occurrence (month, day, year)	Place of Occurrence - City or County	
Signature of Husband or Wife Named on Certificate ▶ _____		

Address to which copy is to be mailed: _____

_____

_____

W.S. 35-1-428 requires Vital Records Services to collect a $5.00 surcharge on all certified copies and searches of the files to be deposited in the Wyoming Children's Trust Fund. This surcharge is included in the fee listed above. The fund is used to establish programs for the prevention of child abuse and neglect.

STATE OF WYOMING
APPLICATION FOR CERTIFIED COPY OF DEATH CERTIFICATE

A request for a certified copy of a death certificate should be submitted on this form along with the fee of $9.00 per copy. If the date of death is unknown, a searching fee of $12.00 for every five years searched is charged, which includes either a certified copy or verification of the record if one is found. A money order or a personalized check from the person making the request should be made payable to VITAL RECORDS SERVICES. Please enclose a self-addressed, stamped envelope with the application.

Send to:

Vital Records Services
Hathaway Building
Cheyenne, WY 82002
(307) 777-7591

If a death record is not located, your fee will be retained as a searching fee.

Enclosed is $ _____ for _____ certified copy(s).

Full Name of Deceased - First	Middle Name	Last Name
Date of Death	Place of Death - City or County	
Name of Surviving Spouse		
Signature of person requesting certificate ▶ _____		
Relationship to Deceased (If funeral director or attorney, state the relationship of the person for whom you are obtaining the copies. Ex: Attorney for spouse)	Purpose for Which Copy is Needed	

Address of applicant: _____

_____

Address to which copy is to be mailed: _____
   (if different)

_____

_____

W.S. 35-1-428 as amended by the 52nd Legislature requires Vital Records Services to collect a $5.00 surcharge on all certified copies and searches of the files to be deposited in the Wyoming Children's Trust Fund. This surcharge is included in the fee listed above. The fund is used to establish programs for the prevention of child abuse and neglect.

2. U.S. Trust Territories

AMERICAN SAMOA

Send your requests to:

Registrar of Vital Statistics
Vital Statistics Section
Health Services Department
LBJ Tropical Medical Center
Pago Pago, American Samoa 96799

Tel. (011) (684) 633-1222
(011) (684) 633-1406

Make money order payable to "ASG Treasurer"; personal checks are not accepted. The Vital Statistics Section has birth, marriage, and death records from 1900. For divorce records write to: High Court of American Samoa, Tutuila, AS 96799.

Cost for a certified Birth Certificate	$5.00
Cost for a certified Marriage Certificate	$5.00
Cost for a certified Divorce Record	$1.00
Cost for a certified Death Certificate	$5.00

The Family History Library of Salt Lake City, Utah has microfilmed original and published vital records and church registers of American Samoa. For details on their holdings please consult your nearest Family History Center.

TO: _____

_____

_____

REFERENCE: _____

I REQUEST A CERTIFIED COPY OF MY BIRTH CERTIFICATE BE SENT TO THE ABOVE ADDRESS TO ESTABLISH BIRTH IN THE UNITED STATES. THIS BIRTH CERTIFICATE MUST HAVE A RAISED OR MULTI-COLORED STATE SEAL ON IT. THE FOLLOWING INFORMATION IS PROVIDED TO ASSIST YOUR OFFICE IN LOCATING MY BIRTH CERTIFICATE.

_____
SIGNATURE

NAME I WAS BORN UNDER: _____
                FIRST   MIDDLE   MAIDEN   LAST

PLACE OF BIRTH: _____
        CITY OR TOWN   COUNTY   STATE

DATE OF BIRTH: _____
        MONTH   DAY   YEAR

SEX: _____ RACE: _____

FATHER'S NAME: _____
      FIRST   MIDDLE   LAST

MOTHER'S MAIDEN NAME: _____
      FIRST   MIDDLE   LAST

NAME OF HOSPITAL: _____

ENCLOSED FIND A MONEY ORDER IN THE AMMOUNT OF $_____

Office of Vital Statistics   Tel. (011) (671) 734-2931
Department of Public Health and Social Services
P.O. Box 2816
Agana, Guam 96910

The Office of Vital Statistics has birth, marriage, and death records from October 1901. Money orders should be made payable to "Treasurer of Guam"; personal checks are not accepted. For divorce records write to: write to: Clerk, Superior Court of Guam, Agana, GU 96910.

Cost for a certified Birth Certificate	$5.00
Cost for a certified Marriage Certificate	$5.00
Cost for a certified Death Certificate	$5.00

Send your requests for Adoption Records to:

Superior Court of Guam
Guam Judicial Center
120 West O'Brien Drive
Agana, Guam 96910

The Family History Library of Salt Lake City, Utah has microfilmed original and published records of Guam. For details on their holdings please consult your nearest Family History Center.

OFFICE OF VITAL STATISTICS
Department of Public Health and Social Services
P.O. Box 2816
Agana, Guam 96910

APPLICATION FOR A COPY OF Birth ☐ Death ☐ Marriage ☐

INFORMATION FOR APPLICANT: It is absolutely essential that the name be accurately spelled and that the **exact date** - month, day and year - the exact place of birth, name of hospital be fully given in every application.

PRINT ALL ITEMS CLEARLY

1. NAME _____
              (First name)   (Middle)   (Last name at time of birth)

2. DATE OF BIRTH _____   DATE OF DEATH _____
              (Month)   (Day)   (Year)   DATE OF MARRIAGE _____

3. PLACE OF BIRTH _____   PLACE OF DEATH _____
              (Name of Hospital or village)

4. FATHER'S NAME _____
                     (First)   (Middle)   (Last)

5. MOTHER'S MAIDEN NAME _____
                            (First)   (Middle)   (Last)

6. NUMBER OF COPIES DESIRED _____ Certificate. NUMBER, IF KNOWN _____

7. _____
         Relationship to person named in Item one above. If self, state "SELF"

NOTE: Copy of a birth or death record can be issued only to persons to whom the record relates, if of age, or a parent or other lawful representative.

IF THIS REQUEST IS NOT FOR YOUR OWN BIRTH RECORD OR THAT OF YOUR CHILD, PROPER WRITTEN AUTHORIZATION FROM THE PERSON MUST BE PRESENTED WITH THIS APPLICATION.

SIGN YOUR NAME AND ADDRESS BELOW

NAME _____

ADDRESS _____

CITY _____ STATE _____ ZIP CODE _____

FEE

PURSUANT TO PUBLIC LAW 10-44, Section 9324, a fee of $5.00 is now being charged for each certified copy issued.

APPLICANTS ARE ADVISED NOT TO SEND CASH BY MAIL. Fees must be paid at time application is made.   Money order should be made payable to the Treasurer of Guam. Stamps and foreign currency cannot be accepted.

PANAMA CANAL ZONE

Send your requests to:

Vital Statistics Unit
Panama Canal Commission
Unit 2300
APO AA, 34011-5000

Tel. (011) (507) 52-7854
Fax (011) (507) 52-2122

Make international money orders (a regular money order will be returned) payable to "Treasurer, Panama Canal Commission." The Vital Statistics Unit has birth, marriage, and death records from 1904 to September 30, 1979. On that date the Panama Canal Treaty became effective and the Canal Zone Government ceased to exist.

Cost for a certified Birth Certificate	$4.00
Cost for a certified Marriage Certificate	$4.00
Cost for a certified Death Certificate	$4.00

The United States District Court for the District of the Canal Zone was closed on March 31, 1982. All records of the court are at the National Archives Records Center in Suitland, Maryland. For divorce information write to the Panama Canal Commission, which will send you the information needed by the Records Center to process the request. All certified copies are provided only by the National Archives.

The Family History Library of Salt Lake City, Utah has microfilmed original and published records about the Panama Canal Zone. For details on their holdings please consult your nearest Family History Center.

COMISION DEL CANAL DE PANAMA

La Comisión del Canal de Panamá cobra $4 por cada copia entregada de certificado de nacimiento, defunción o matrimonio. Sírvase llenar esta solicitud y enviarla junto con la suma correspondiente a la dirección que aparece en la parte de abajo. Se girará todo giro postal a favor del TESORERO, Comisión del Canal de Panamá.

Solamente los certificados de nacimiento, defunción o matrimonio ocurridos en la antigua Zona del Canal reposan en los archivos de esta oficina. Para los casos de nacimientos, defunciones o matrimonios ocurridos en la República de Panamá, diríjase al Registro Civil, Apartado 5281, Panamá 5, República de Panamá.

....
(Fecha)

COMISION DEL CANAL DE PANAMA
División Administrativa
Oficina de Estadística Demográfica
Unit 2300
APO AA 34011

REGISTRADOR:

Por favor entregue ....copia(s) en ☐ inglés ☐ español del certificado de ☐ nacimiento ☐ defunción ☐ matrimonio, solicitado a continuación. Adjunto $........................ (giro postal).

Certificado de Nacimiento:

Nombre en el Certificado.............................

Fecha de Nacimiento ....

Lugar de Nacimiento ....

Nombre completo del Padre ....

Nombre de soltera de la Madre ....

Certificado de Defunción:

Nombre del Difunto ....

Fecha de Defunción ....

Lugar de Defunción ....

Certificado de Matrimonio:

Nombre de los Contrayentes: Masculino .... Femenino...........................

Fecha de Matrimonio........................... Nº de la Licencia...........................

Lugar de Matrimonio .... Balboa........................... Cristóbal.

....
Firma del solicitante

....
Parentesco

Motivo de la solicitud.................................

Dirección—Llénese solamente si el certificado se ha de enviar por correo.

PUERTO RICO

Puerto Rico Department of Health   Tel. (787) 767-9120
Demographic Registry
P.O. Box 11854, Fernandez Juncos Station
San Juan, Puerto Rico 00910

The Puerto Rico Department of Health has some vital records as early as 1885. The majority of the records are since June 22, 1931. They hold divorce records since 1962. Make money order payable to Secretary of the Treasury. Personal checks are not accepted. Copies of earlier records may be obtained by writing to the local Registrar (Registrador Demografico) in the municipality where the event occurred or by writing to the central office for information.

Cost for a certified Birth Certificate	$5.00
Cost for a certified Marriage Certificate	$5.00
Cost for a certified Divorce Certificate	$5.00
Cost for a certified Death Certificate	$5.00

The Family History Library of Salt Lake City, Utah has microfilmed original and published vital records and church registers of Puerto Rico. For details on their holdings please consult your nearest Family History Center.

J- 225
DD 5/87

COMMONWEALTH OF PUERTO RICO
DEPARTMENT OF HEALTH
DEMOGRAPHIC REGISTRY

BIRTH CERTIFICATE APPLICATION BY MAIL

PART I: INFORMATION ABOUT REGISTRANT'S

1- Name at Birth:		
Father's Last Name	Mother's Last Name	First Name
2- Date of birth:(month/day/year)		3- Place of birth:(Town and Hospital)
4- Father's Name:		5- Mother's Maiden Name:
6- This certificate will be used for:		7- Number of Copies:

PART II: APPLICANT'S INFORMATION

1- Applicant's Name:			2- Relationship:**
Father's Last Name	Mother's Last Name	First Name	
3- Applicant's Address:		4- Address where you want the certificate to be sent:	
5- Applicant's Identification: ___Driving License ___Work ___Passport ____Other		6- Applicant's Signature and Date:	

IMPORTANT :

For "Rush" mail: Quisqueya St. #171 Hato Rey, PR 00917

1- If event occurred from June 22,1931 to present you can apply with us to the following address: Department of Health, Demographic Registry, P.O. Box 11854, San Juan, Puerto Rico 00910.

2- If event occurred from 1885 to June 21,1931 you must write to the Municipality where the event occurred.

3- Please send a photocopy of an IDENTIFICATION WITH PHOTOGRAPHY OF APPLICANT.

4- Applicant in Puerto Rico, please send a $5.00 Internal Revenue Stamp for each copy requested. Additional copies ordered at the same time $4.00 each of the same person.

5- Applicant out of Puerto Rico please send a $5.00 Money Order for each copy you need payable to SECRETARY OF THE TREASURY. Additional copies ordered at the same time $4.00 each of the same person.

6- Please send us a pre-addressed envelope to mail your certificate.

* Applicant - Means registrant, parents, their sons or legal representatives.

** Relationship   relation between the applicant and the registrant. This blank will be filled if the applicant and the registrant are not the same person.

RD-226
ROD 5/87

COMMONWEALTH OF PUERTO RICO
DEPARTMENT OF HEALTH
DEMOGRAPHIC REGISTRY

MARRIAGE CERTIFICATE APPLICATION BY MAIL

PART I: INFORMATION ABOUT MARRIED COUPLE

1- Husband's Name:		
Father's Last Name	Mother's Last Name	First Name
2- Spouse's Maiden Name:		
Father's Last Name	Mother's Last Name	First Name

3- Date of Marriage: (month/day/year/)	4- Place of Marriage:

5- This certificate will be used for:	6- Number of Copies:

PART II: APPLICANT'S * INFORMATION

1- Applicant's Name:			2- Relationship: **
Father's Last Name	Mother's Last Name	First Name	

3- Applicant's Address:	4- Address where you want the certificate to be sent:

5- Applicant's Identification:	6- Applicant's Signature and Date:
__Driving License __Work __Passport __Other	

IMPORTANT:

1 If event occurred from June 22, 1931 to present you can apply with us to the following address:
   Department of Health, Demographic Registry, P.O. Box 11854, San Juan, Puerto Rico 00910.

2- IF event occurred from 1885 to June 21, 1931 you must write to the Municipality where the event occurred.

3- Please send a photocopy of an IDENTIFICATION WITH PHOTOGRAPHY OF APPLICANT.

4- Applicant in Puerto Rico please send a $5.00 Internal Revenue Stamp for each copy requested.
   Additional copies ordered at the same time $4.00 each of the same person.

5- Applicant out of Puerto Rico send a $5.00 Money Order for each copy you need payable to
   SECRETARY OF TREASURY. Additional copies ordered at the same time $4.00 each of the
   same person.

6- Please send us a pre-addressed envelope to mail your certificate.

* Applicant -Means contracting parties, parents, child or legal representative.

** This blank will be filled by applicant if other than Husband or Wife.

RD- 227
MOD 5/87

DEATH CERTIFICATE APPLICATION BY MAIL

PART I: INFORMATION ABOUT DECEASED

1- Deceased Name:

Father's Last Name	Mother's Last Name	First Name

2- Date of Death: (month/day/year)

3- Place of Death: (Town and Hospital)

PART II: APPLICANT'S * INFORMATION

1- Applicant's Name:

Father's Last Name	Mother's Last Name	First Name

2- Relationship.

3- This certificate will be used for:

4- Number of Copies:

5- Applicant's Address:

6- Address where you want the certificate to be sent:

7- Applicant's Identification:
___ Driving License ___ Work ___ 'assport ___ Other

8- Applicant's Signature and Date:

IMPORTANT:

1- If event occurred from June 22, 1931 to present you can apply with us to the following address:
Department of Health, Demographic Registry, P.O. Box 11854, San Juan, Puerto Rico 00910.

2- If event occurred from 1885 to June 21, 1931 you must write to the Municipality where the event occurr

3- Please send a photocopy of an IDENTIFICATION WITH PHOTOGRAPHY OF APPLICANT.

4- Applicant in Puerto Rico, please send a $5.00 Internal Revenue Stamp for each copy requested.
Additional copies ordered at the same time $4.00 each of the same person.

5- Applicant out of Puerto Rico, please send a $5.00 Money Order for each copy you need payable to
SECRETARY OF TREASURY. Additional copies ordered at the same time $4.00 each of the same
person.

6- Please send us a pre-addressed envelope to mail your certificate.

* Applicant - Means the funeral home, parents, sons, or legal representative.
** Relationship - relation between the applicant and the deceased.

VIRGIN ISLANDS—St. Croix

Send your requests to:

Virgin Islands Department of Health   Tel. (809) 773-4050
Office of the Registrar of Vital Statistics
Charles Harwood Memorial Hospital
P.O. Box 520
Christiansted, St. Croix, Virgin Islands 00820

The Office has birth and death records from 1919. Current registration is considered to be complete.

Send your requests for Marriage Certificates and Divorce Records to:

Chief Deputy Clerk   Tel. (809) 778-3350
Territory Court of the Virgin Islands
P.O. Box 929
Christiansted, St. Croix, Virgin Islands 00820

Cost for a certified Birth Certificate	$10.00
Cost for a short form Birth Certificate	$5.00
Cost for a certified Marriage Certificate	$10.00
Cost for a certified Divorce Record	Varies
Cost for a certified Death Certificate	$10.00
Cost for a verification of Death	$5.00

The Family History Library of Salt Lake City, Utah has microfilmed original and published records of the Virgin Islands and the region. For details on their holdings please consult your nearest Family History Center.

VIRGIN ISLANDS—St. Thomas and St. John

Send your requests to:

Virgin Islands Department of Health
Office of the Registrar of Vital Statistics
St. Thomas, Virgin Islands 00802

Tel. (809) 774-1734

The Office has birth records from July 1, 1906 and death records from January 1, 1906. Current registration is considered to be complete. The Registrar will do genealogical research for a base charge of $50.00.

Send your requests for Marriage Certificates to:

Chief Deputy Clerk
Territory Court of the Virgin Islands
P.O. Box 70
Charlotte Amalie, St. Thomas, Virgin Islands 00801

Tel. (809) 774-6680

Cost for a certified Birth Certificate	$10.00
Cost for a short form Birth Certificate	$5.00
Cost for a certified Marriage Certificate	$10.00
Cost for a certified Divorce Record	Varies
Cost for a certified Death Certificate	$10.00
Cost for a verification of Death	$5.00

The Family History Library of Salt Lake City, Utah has microfilmed original and published records of the Virgin Islands and the region. For details on their holdings please consult your nearest Family History Center.

VIRGIN ISLANDS OF THE UNITED STATES

DEPARTMENT OF HEALTH
OFFICE OF THE REGISTRAR OF VITAL STATISTICS

HD-ve   St. — — — — — — — — — — — — —, Virgin Islands

APPLICATION FOR BIRTH RECORD

PLEASE PRINT OR TYPE: FAILURE TO COMPLETE THIS FORM PROPERLY MAY DELAY SERVICE TO YOU.

TYPE OF RECORD DESIRED (Check one)

VERIFICATION

A verification is a statement as to the date of birth and name of the child. A verification is used when it is necessary to prove age only.

CERTIFIED COPY

A certified copy is an abstract from the original birth certificate. It gives the name sex, date and place of birth, certificate number, as well as the names of the parents.

An application for a certified copy of birth must be signed by the person named in the original certificate if 18 years or more or by a parent or legal representative of that person.

FEES: Send money order or check payable to the VIRGIN ISLANDS DEPARTMENT OF HEALTH.
                         (Please do not send cash)

FULL NAME	DATE OF BIRTH Or period to be searched.
PLACE OF BIRTH (City and Island)	
NAME FATHER	MAIDEN NAME MOTHER
AGE AT BIRTH	AGE AT BIRTH
BIRTHPLACE	BIRTHPLACE
ADDRESS (At time of birth)	ADDRESS (At time of birth)
PURPOSE FOR WHICH RECORD IS REQUIRED	SOCIAL SECURITY NUMBER

Your relationship to person whose record is required? If self, state "SELF." _____

If attorney give name and relationship of your client to person whose record is required. _____

TO WHOM SHALL RECORD BE SENT?

Name_____

Address_____

City_____ State _____

Signature of Applicant_____

Address of Applicant_____

_____

Date _____

Sworn to and subscribed before me this _____ day of _____ 19_____ .

_____
(Signature and Seal of Notary Public)

VIRGIN ISLANDS OF THE UNITED STATES

DEPARTMENT OF HEALTH

OFFICE OF THE REGISTRAR OF VITAL STATISTICS

St. ————————————, Virgin Islands

HD-vf

●

APPLICATION FOR DEATH RECORD

PLEASE PRINT OR TYPE: FAILURE TO COMPLETE THIS FORM PROPERLY MAY DELAY SERVICE TO YOU.

TYPE OF RECORD DESIRED (Check one)

VERIFICATION	CERTIFIED COPY ☐ Fee
A verification is a statement as to the date of death and name of decedent. A verification is used as proof that the event occurred.	A certified copy is a replica of the original death certificate.
Anyone may apply for a verification of death.	Anyone who can establish that the record is needed for proof of parentage, social security and other benefits, settlement of estate, or for judicial or other proper purpose may apply for a certified copy.

FEES: Send money order or check payable to the VIRGIN ISLANDS DEPARTMENT OF HEALTH.
(PLEASE DO NOT SEND CASH)
No fee is charged when the certificate is required by a local, state or federal government agency.

NAME OF DECEDENT	DATE OF DEATH OR PERIOD TO BE SEARCHED
PLACE OF DEATH (CITY AND ISLAND)	
NAME OF FATHER OF DECEDENT	MAIDEN NAME OF MOTHER OF DECEDENT
NUMBER OF COPIES DESIRED	CERTIFICATE NUMBER, IF KNOWN
PURPOSE FOR WHICH RECORD IS REQUIRED	

What is your relationship to decedent? _____

In what capacity are you acting? _____

If attorney, give name and relationship
of your client to decedent. _____

TO WHOM SHALL RECORD BE SENT?	
Name _____	Signature of Applicant _____
Address _____	Address of Applicant _____
City _____ State _____	_____
	Date _____

3. International

Send your requests to:

Department of Population, Registration and Vital Statistics
Ministry of the Interior
Sharinow, Kabul, Afghanistan

Afghanistan has required all males to register for identification cards since 1952. Efforts have been made to strengthen the registration of vital records in Afghanistan since 1977, but with limited success. Given the limited number of vital records and the ongoing transition of government authority, this is a difficult time to obtain information from the government. Afghanistan handles adoption under Islamic law. Children are placed within families.

Cost for a certified Birth Certificate	Free
Cost for a certified Marriage Certificate or Divorce Record	Free
Cost for a certified Death Certificate	Free

For additional assistance contact:

Charaii I Malik
(Kabul Library)
Asghar, Kabul, Afghanistan

Library
Pohantoon e Kabul
(Kabul University)
Pohantoon, Kabul, Afghanistan

For further information see:

Bhan, B. L. *Study of a Civil Registration System of Births and Deaths, an Experiment in Afghanistan.* IIVRS Technical Papers, No. 26. Bethesda, MD: International Institute for Vital Registration and Statistics, 1983. 6p.

ALBANIA

Send your requests to:

Drejtoria Qendore e Statistikave
Keshili i Ministrave [Kryemistrial]
Bulevardi Deshmoret e Kombit
Tirana, Albania

Registration is required of all residents.

Cost for a certified Birth Certificate	Lek 2.10
Cost for a certified Marriage Certificate	Lek 2.10
Cost for a certified Death Certificate	Lek 2.10

Send your requests for Adoption Records to:

Albanian Adoption Committee   Tel. (202) 223-4942
Embassy of the Republic of Albania
1511 K Street, NW, Suite 1010
Washington, DC 20005

For additional assistance contact:

Central Directorate of Statistics
Bulevardi Deshmoret e Kombit
Tirana, Albania

Central Archives   Tel. (011) (355) (42) 238 43
Tirana, Albania

Biblioteka Kombëtare   Tel. (011) (355) (42) 258 87
(National Library)
Sheshi Skenderbe
Tirana, Albania

Biblioteka e Shtetit
(Elbassan Public Library)
Elbassan, Albania

Send your requests to:

> Service d'État Civil des Communes
> Ministère de l'Intérieur
> B.P. 5516000 Algiers, Algeria

Vital registration began in Algeria in 1882 and included principally Muslims in the North. By 1905 coverage also included Muslims in the South. Today the registration of vital records is not considered to be comprehensive.

Cost for a certified Birth Certificate	Free
Cost for a certified Marriage Certificate	Free
Cost for a certified Death Certificate	Free

For additional assistance contact:

> Directeur General
> Office National des Statistiques
> Perhat Boussad
> B.P. 202
> 16000 Algiers, Algeria

> Embassy of Algeria   Tel. (202) 265-2800
> 2118 Kalorama Road, NW
> Washington, DC 20008

The Family History Library of Salt Lake City, Utah has microfilmed some material about Algeria and Africa. For further details on their holdings please consult your nearest Family History Center.

For further information see:

Methods and Problems of Civil Registration Practices and Vital Statistics Collection in Africa. IIVRS Technical Papers, No. 16. Bethesda, MD: International Institute for Vital Registration and Statistics, 1981. 27p.

Organization and Status of Civil Registration in Africa and Recommendations for Improvement. IIVRS Technical Papers, No. 31. Bethesda, MD: International Institute for Vital Registration and Statistics, 1988. 15p.

Organization and Status of Civil Registration in the Arab Countries. IIVRS Technical Papers, No. 33. Bethesda, MD: International Institute for Vital Registration and Statistics, 1988. 6p.

ANGOLA

Send your requests to:

Direccao Nacional dos Registos
Notariado e Identificacao
Ministerio de Justicia
Luanda, Angola

Vital registration began for Europeans from earlier in this century and efforts have been made to expand registration throughout the country. The civil strife there has made this an impractical goal for the nation.

Cost for a certified Birth Certificate	Kz 2.50
Cost for a certified Marriage Certificate	Kz 2.50
Cost for a certified Death Certificate	Kz 2.50

For additional assistance contact:

Director
National Statistical Institute
C.P. 1215
Luanda, Angola

Biiblioteca Nacional de Angola
(National Library)
Ave. Norton de Matos
C.P. 2915
Luanda, Angola

Centro Nacional de Documentação a Investigação Histórico
C.P. 1267-C
Luanda, Angola

Embassy of Angola   Tel. (202) 785-1156
1615 M Street, NW, Suite 900
Washington, DC 20036

For further information see:

Methods and Problems of Civil Registration Practices and Vital Statistics Collection in Africa. IIVRS Technical Papers, No. 16. Bethesda, MD: International Institute for Vital Registration and Statistics, 1981. 27p.

Organization and Status of Civil Registration in Africa and Recommendations for Improvement. IIVRS Technical Papers, No. 31. Bethesda, MD: International Institute for Vital Registration and Statistics, 1988. 15p.

ANTIGUA and BARBUDA

Registrar General's Office   Tel. (268) 462-0609
High Court
High Street
St. John's, Antigua and Barbuda

Antigua was discovered by Columbus in 1493 and became independent in 1967. The Registrar General has records from August 1, 1856. The local churches also have their own records. No application forms are required or provided by this office.

Cost for a certified Birth Certificate	US$1.20 Ec$3.00
Cost for a certified Marriage Certificate	US$3.80 Ec$10.00
Cost for a certified Death Certificate	US$1.20 EC$3.00

For additional assistance contact:

Chief
Statistics Division
Ministry of Finance
Upper Redcliffe Street
St. John's, Antigua and Barbuda

St. Johns Public Library
St. John's, Antiqua and Barbuda

Embassy of Antigua and Barbuda   Tel. (202) 362-5122
3216 New Mexico Avenue, NW, Suite 4M
Washington, DC 20866

For further information see:

Registration of Vital Events in the English-Speaking Caribbean. IIVRS Technical Papers, No. 32. Bethesda, MD: International Institute for Vital Registration and Statistics, 1988. 10p.

ARGENTINA

Director of Civil Registration
Office of Civil Registration
Buenos Aires, Argentina

http://www.RegistroCivil.gov.ar

Director General del Registro del Estado Civil y Capacidad
de Las Personas de la Ciudad de Buenos Aires
Uruguay 753
1015 Buenos Aires, Argentina

Argentina's twenty-three provinces, Federal Capital Territory, and the National Territory maintain the vital records and issue national identification card forms. Vital registration began on August 1, 1886 and is considered to be 90 percent complete. Adoption records are kept by the court with jurisdiction over the domicile of the adoptive parents. Adoptees have access to records at age eighteen.

Cost for a certified Birth Certificate	A$15.00
Cost for a certified Marriage Certificate	A$15.00
Cost for a certified Death Certificate	A$15.00
Cost for a certified Adoption Record	A$15.00
Cost for a Household Registration (Libreta de Familia)	A$20.00
Cost for a duplicate Household Registration (Libreta de Familia)	A$30.00

For additional assistance contact:

Embassy of the Argentine Republic
1600 New Hampshire Avenue, NW
Washington, DC 20009

Tel. (202) 238-6400

For further information see:

Arancel de la Escribania de Gobierno. Tasas de Autorización e Inspección de Sociedades Anonimas, Pasaportes y Otras Documentaciones de Identidad Personal. Arancel de los Boletines Oficial y Judicial, Derechos del Registro de la Propiedad. Buenos Aires, Argentina: Pesce y Cia, 1938. 24p.

Civil Registration in the Republic of Argentina. IIVRS Technical Papers, No. 5. Bethesda, MD: International Institute for Vital Registration and Statistics, 1979. 8p.

Diagnostico del Registro Civil Latinoamericano, enero de 1980. Montevideo, Uruguay: UN Fund for Population Activities, 1982. 142p.

Macchi, Manuel E. *Registros Civiles Precursores en Argentina, Buenos Aires 1833; Santa Fe 1867; Colón, Entre Ríos 1873.* Santa Fe, Argentina: Libreria y Editorial Castellvi, SA. 100p.

Report on the First Latin American Training Centre on Statistics and Censuses Held at Mexico City from 2 September to 10 December 1948 by the Food and Agriculture Organization of the UN and the Government of the United States of Mexico with the Cooperation of the Statistical Office of the UN and the InterAmerican Statistical Institute. Lake Success, NY: Statistical Office of the UN, 1948. 33p.

Zinny, Mario Antonio. *El Acto Notarial, Dación de Fe.* Buenos Aires, Argentina: Depalma, 1990. 136p.

Send your requests to:

Chief
Department of Civil Registry
Ministry of Justice
8 Khorderdaran Street
Yerevan 375010, Armenia

Cost for a certified Birth Certificate	$25.00
Cost for a certified Marriage Certificate	$25.00
Cost for a certified Death Certificate	$25.00

For additional assistance contact:

Chairman
State Committee of Armenia on Statistics
3, Don Pravitelstva
Yerevan 375010, Armenia

Armianskaia Biblioteka
(National Library)
ul. Teriana 72
Yrevan, 375009 Armenia

Embassy of Armenia   Tel. (202) 319-1976
2225 R Street, NW
Washington, DC 20008

The Family History Library of Salt Lake City, Utah has microfilmed records of Armenia and the former Soviet Union. For further details on their holdings please consult your nearest Family History Center.

AUSTRALIA — AUSTRALIAN CAPITAL TERRITORY

Office of the Registrar General of Births, Deaths & Marriages   Tel. (011) (61) (6) 207-0460
Allara House   Fax (011) (61) (6) 207-0455
Allara Street   http://www.act.gov.au/services/law/births.html
G.P.O. Box 788
Canberra City, ACT 2601, Australia

The Registrar General holds records from January 1, 1930.

Cost for a certified Birth Certificate	Au$27.00
Cost for a certified Marriage Certificate	Au$27.00
Cost for a certified Death Certificate	Au$27.00

For Adoption Record information contact:

Adoption Information Service
Callum Office
Easty Street
Phillip, ACT 2606, Australia

The Family History Library of Salt Lake City, Utah has microfilmed original and published vital records and church registers of the area. For further details on their holdings please consult your nearest Family History Center.

Australian Capital Territory

OFFICE OF THE REGISTRAR BIRTHS, DEATHS, AND MARRIAGES

APPLICATION FOR BIRTH CERTIFICATE

RECORD OF FEES PAID

FEES — to be prepaid:

Full Certificate ... ...

Extract ... ...

PARTICULARS OF BIRTH
(Please use block letters)

Given (Christian) Names

Surname

Date of Birth

Age last Birthday (if applicable)

Place of Birth   A.C.T.

Father's full Given (Christian) Names

Mother's full Given (Christian) Names

Mother's full MAIDEN Surname

FOR OFFICE USE ONLY

Reg. No. ....

No. of Certified Copies ....

No. of Extracts ....

Total No. of Certificates ....

No. to be posted ....

No. to be collected ....

Date for Collection ....

Date Posted ....

Date Collected ....

Purpose for which certificate is required ....

Name of Applicant (Block Letters) Mr Mrs Miss ....

....

Relationship to person registered ....

Address in full ....

.... Postcode ....

Telephone No. .... Date of Application ....

Signature ....

Post to — The Registrar,
Births, Deaths & Marriages,
P.O. Box 788
CANBERRA CITY. 2601

Deliver to — Births, Deaths & Marriages Office.
Allara House,
Allara Street
CANBERRA CITY. A.C.T.

Australian Capital Territory
OFFICE OF THE REGISTRAR BIRTHS, DEATHS, AND MARRIAGES

APPLICATION FOR MARRIAGE CERTIFICATE

FEES — to be prepaid:
Full Certificate ... ...
Extract ... ...

APPLICANT TO FURNISH PARTICULARS OF MARRIAGE (Please use block letters)		FOR OFFICE USE ONLY
Bridegroom's given names		
Surname		Reg. No. ....
Bride's given names		No. of Certified Copies ....
		No. of Extracts ....
Surname before Marriage		Total No. of Certificates ....
		No. to be posted ....
		No. to be collected ....
		Date for Collection ....
Date of Marriage	/ /19	
Place of Marriage	A.C.T.	Date Posted ....
		Date Collected ....

Purpose for which certificate is required ....

Name of Applicant *(Block Letters)* Mr
Mrs ....
Miss

....

Relationship to bride/groom ....

Address in full ....

.... Postcode ....

Telephone No. .... Date of Application ....

Signature ....

Post to — The Registrar,
Births, Deaths & Marriages,
P.O. Box 788
CANBERRA CITY, 2601

Deliver to — Births, Deaths & Marriages Office,
Allara House,
Allara Street,
CANBERRA A.C.T.

BDM

Australian Capital Territory

OFFICE OF THE REGISTRAR BIRTHS, DEATHS, AND MARRIAGES

APPLICATION FOR DEATH CERTIFICATE

RECORD OF FEES PAID

FEES— to be prepaid:
Full Certificate · · · ·
Extract · · · ·

APPLICANT TO FURNISH PARTICULARS OF DECEASED (Please use block letters)		FOR OFFICE USE ONLY
Given (Christian) Names		
Surname		
Husband/Wife of		Reg. No. ....
Date of Death		No. of Certified Copies ....
		No. of Extracts ....
Place of Death	A.C.T.	Total No. of Certificates ....
		No. to be posted ....
Age last Birthday	years	No. to be collected ....
		Date for Collection ....
Father's full Names (Including surname)		
Mother's full Given (Christian) Names and Maiden Surname		Date posted ....
		Date Collected ....

Purpose for which certificate is required ....

Name of Applicant (*Block Letters*) Mr Mrs Miss ....

....

Relationship to deceased ....

Address in full ....

....Postcode..........

Telephone No. .... Date of Application ....

Signature ....

Post to— The Registrar
Births, Deaths & Marriages,
P.O. Box 788
CANBERRA CITY

Deliver to— Births, Deaths & Marriages Office,
Allara House,
Allara Street
CANBERRA CITY A C T

AUSTRALIA — NEW SOUTH WALES

Registry of Births, Deaths & Marriages
191 Thomas Street
G.P.O. Box 30
Sydney, New South Wales 2001, Australia

Tel. (011) (61) (2) 9243-8585
Fax (011) (61) (2) 9243-8530
E-mail: bdm_mail@agd.nsw.gov.au
http://www.bdm.nsw.gov.au/

The Registrar has records from March 1, 1856. Payment must be made in Australian dollars using an international money order or bank draft made payable to the "Registry of Births, Deaths and Marriages." There is an international shipping fee of Au$2.00. Expedited service is available (with payment by credit card) for an additional fee of Au$41.00, plus Au$10.00 for shipping.

Cost for a certified Birth Certificate	Au$26.00
Cost for a commemorative Birth Certificate	Au$36.00
Cost for a certified Marriage Certificate	Au$26.00
Cost for a certified Death Certificate	Au$26.00

The Family History Library of Salt Lake City, Utah has microfilmed original and published vital records and church registers of New South Wales. For further details on their holdings please consult your nearest Family History Center.

Certificate Order Form

Note: This form is to be printed out and sent by mail to the address below. The Registry does not accept online applications or applications via email due to our <u>identification requirements</u>.

Registry of Births, Deaths and Marriages,
GPO Box 30, Sydney NSW 2001
191 Thomas Street, Haymarket 2000
Tel: 1300-655-236 Fax: (02) 9243 8530.
Office Hours: Monday to Friday 8.00 am to 4.30 pm

☐ Non Urgent $26.00 Australian Dollars

☐ Family History $20.00 Australian Dollars (with Index Number provided)

☐ Urgent $41.00 Australian Dollars

☐ International Express Post $10 Australian Dollars

☐ Air Mail $2.00 Australian Dollars

☐ Express Post $3.00 Australian Dollars (the Express Post option is not available in some countries)

Details of certificate required

Certificate Type: ☐ Birth ☐ Death ☐ Marriage

Full family name (essential)	
Given names (essential)	
Any known alias	
Date of birth	
Place of birth	
Current age	
Date of marriage	
Place of marriage	
Place of death	
Age at death	
Years to be searched	
Mother's name	
Father's name	
Spouse's name	
Name of Funeral Director	
Number in Index	

Your details

Your name	
Mailing address	
Town or Suburb or City	
State or County	
Postcode	
Country	
Email address	
Telephone (Work):	
Telephone (Home):	
Fax:	
Relationship to person registered	
Reason certificate is required	

Payment options

☐ Non Urgent $26.00 Australian Dollars

☐ Urgent $41.00 Australian Dollars

☐ Family History $20.00 Australian Dollars (with index number)

☐ International Express Post $10.00 Australian Dollars

☐ Air Mail $2.00 Australian Dollars

Payment by credit card

You may pay in advance by Visa, American Express, Mastercard or Bankcard.

Credit card details

Name of cardholder	
Credit card type	☐ Visa
	☐ Mastercard
	☐ Bankcard
	☐ American Express
Credit card number	
Credit card expiry date	
Applicants Signature	

Please print using block letters and complete all sections. Payment by credit card is accepted. (Bankcard, American Express, Mastercard or Visa only). Personal cheques will not be accepted for Urgent Applications. You must send identification with your application.

AUSTRALIA — NORTHERN TERRITORY

Office of the Registrar of Births, Deaths & Marriages   Tel. (011) (61) (8) 899-6119
Department of Law   http://www.ke.com.au/bdmaus/bdmnt/index.html
Nichols Place
G.P.O. Box 3021
Darwin, Northern Territory 0801, Australia

The Registrar has birth records from August 24, 1870, marriage records from 1871, and death records from 1872. Expedited service is available (with payment by credit card) for an additional fee of Au$10.00. In addition to the office in Darwin, there is also one in Alice Springs.

Cost for a certified Birth Certificate	Au$25.00
Cost for a certified Marriage Certificate	Au$25.00
Cost for a certified Death Certificate	Au$25.00

The Family History Library of Salt Lake City, Utah has microfilmed original and published vital records and church registers of the Northern Territory. For further details on their holdings please consult your nearest Family History Center.

APPLICATION FOR A BIRTH, DEATH OR MARRIAGE CERTIFICATE

Northern Territory Registry of Births, Deaths and Marriages

Fax this form to:
(08) 8999 6324 Darwin
(08) 8951 5340 for Alice Springs registrations only

Further Information

I wish to make an application for a:

FULL BIRTH CERTIFICATE	__	DEATH CERTIFICATE	__
BIRTH EXTRACT	__	MARRIAGE CERTIFICATE	__

APPLICANTS DETAILS (Please use BLOCK LETTERS)

Applicants name:	Signature of Applicant:
Applicants address:	Postcode:
Postal address if different to above:	Postcode:
Daytime telephone No.:	
Reason document is required:	Relationship of Applicant:

CREDIT CARD DETAILS (Please complete)

Enclosed is a cheque/money order for $.................... or debit my Bankcard __ Mastercard __ Visa __ for $...................

Card Number: __ __ __ __ - __ __ __ __ - __ __ __ __ - __ __ __ __   Expiry Date of card: ..../..........

Name of Cardholder: Signature of Cardholder:

DETAILS FOR BIRTH CERTIFICATE (Complete only if you want a birth certificate)

Registration No.: *(if known)*	Place of birth: *City/Suburb/Town*
----------------------- Date of birth:	*Day/Month/Year* ..../........../..........
Family name (at birth):	Christian or given names:
Other family name used:	Present age:
Fathers name - Family name:	Fathers name - Christian or given names:
Mothers name - Family name:	Mothers name - (maiden): Christian or given names:

DETAILS FOR DEATH CERTIFICATE (Complete only if you want a death certificate)

Registration No.: *(if known)*	Place of death: *City/Suburb/Town*
----------------------- Date of death:	*Day/Month/Year:* ..../.........../...........
Family name:	Christian or given names:
Fathers name - Family name:	Fathers name - Christian or given names:

Mothers name:	Family name (maiden): Christian or given names:
Age at death:	Name of spouse:

DETAILS FOR MARRIAGE CERTIFICATE (Complete only if you want a marriage certificate)

Registration No. *(if known)*	Place of marriage *City/Suburb/Town*
------------------------ Date of marriage:	*Day/Month/Year* ..../.........../..........
Bridegrooms name:	Family name - Christian or given names:
Brides name:	Family name (maiden): Christian or given names:

AUSTRALIA — QUEENSLAND

Send your requests for records 1890-present to:

Registrar of Births, Deaths and Marriages
P.O. Box 188
Brisbane Albert Street
Queensland 4002, Australia

Tel. (011) (61) (7) 3247-9203
Fax (011) (61) (7) 3247-5803
http://www.ke.com.au/bdmaus/bdmqld/index.html

Send your requests for records 1829–1899 to:

Queensland State Archives
435 Compton Road
Runcorn
Queensland 4113, Australia
(mailing address: P.O. Box 1397, Sunnybank Hills,
Queensland 4109, Australia)

Tel. (011) (61) (7) 3875-8755
Fax (011) (61) (7) 3875-8764

Birth records after 1905, marriage records for the past 75 years, and death records for the past 50 years are restricted. When writing to the Office of the Registrar General please make the international bank draft in Australian dollars and made payable to the "Registrar General." Expedited service is available (with payment by credit card) for an additional fee.

Certificates Requested from the Registrar General

Cost for a certified Birth Certificate	Au$21.50
Cost for a certified Marriage Certificate	Au$21.50
Cost for a certified Death Certificate	Au$21.50

Certificates Requested from the Queensland State Archives

Cost for a certified Birth Certificate	Au$7.50
Cost for a certified Marriage Certificate	Au$7.50
Cost for a certified Death Certificate	Au$7.50

The Family History Library of Salt Lake City, Utah has microfilmed many of the original and published vital records and church registers of Queensland. For further details on their holdings please consult your nearest Family History Center.

APPLICATION FOR A BIRTH, DEATH OR MARRIAGE CERTIFICATE
Registry of Births, Deaths and Marriages, PO Box 188, Brisbane Albert Street, Qld 4002

FAX this form to (07) 3247 5803.   Further Information

I wish to make an application for (please tick) NON URGENT __ URGENT __ (priority fee payable) Certificate __ Extract __

APPLICANT'S DETAILS (Details of person applying)

Applicant's Name:	
Postal Address:	Postcode:
Reason Certificate is Required: (eg. passport, school enrolment)	Relationship to Person/s Registered: (eg. self, mother)
Signature of Applicant:	Daytime Telephone Number: ( )

PAYMENT DETAILS

Enclosed is a cheque/money order for $..................... or debit my Bankcard __ Mastercard __ Visa __ for $....................

Card Number: __ __ __ __ - __ __ __ __ - __ __ __ __ - __ __ __ __	Expiry Date of card: ..../..........
Name of Cardholder:	Signature of Cardholder:

BIRTH CERTIFICATE

Surname at Birth	Date of Birth ..../........../..........
Given Names:	Present Age:

If date unknown period to be searched:	From:	To:
Place of Birth:	(Town/City):	(State):

Father's Full Name:	
Mother's Given Names:	Mother's Maiden Surname:

DEATH CERTIFICATE

Surname:	Date of Death: ..../........../..........

Given Names:		
If date unknown period to be searched:	From:	To:
Place of Death: (Town/City)	(State)	

Father's Full Name:	
Mother's Given Names:	Mother's Maiden Surname:

MARRIAGE CERTIFICATE

GROOM'S Surname:	Given Names:
BRIDE'S Surname: (before marriage)	Given Names:

Date of Marriage: ..../........../..........	If date unknown,period to be searched - From:	To:
Place of Marriage: (Town/City)	(State)	

AUSTRALIA — SOUTH AUSTRALIA

Send your requests to:

Principal Registrar of Births, Deaths & Marriages
Department of Public & Consumer Affairs
Edmund Wright House
59 King William Street
G.P.O. Box 1351
Adelaide, South Australia 5001, Australia

Tel. (011) (61) (8) 8204-9599
http://www.ocba.sa.gov.au/births.htm

The Registrar has records from July 1, 1842. Enclose an additional Au$2.00 per certificate for air mail postage. If your request is urgent there is a priority charge of Au$52.00. Please make your international bank draft in Australian dollars payable to the "Principal Registrar." Adoption records and original birth certificates are open upon request.

Cost for a certified Birth Certificate	Au$30.00
Cost for a certified Marriage Certificate	Au$30.00
Cost for a certified Death Certificate	Au$30.00

For Adoption Record information write to:

Adoption and Family Information Service
Citicentre
9th Floor, Hindmarsh Square
Adelaide, South Australia 5001, Australia

Tel. (011) (618) 8226-6694

The Family History Library of Salt Lake City, Utah has microfilmed original and published vital records and church registers of South Australia. For further details on their holdings please consult your nearest Family History Center.

Births Deaths and Marriages Registration Office
59 King William Street
ADELAIDE 5000

BIRTH

BIRTH OF ....

G.P.O. Box 1351
ADELAIDE 5001
This Receipt MUST be produced when collecting documents

Received amount printed by cash register

(Tick appropriate boxes)

☐ **EXTRACT**

☐ **PRIORITY SERVICE**

☐ **CERTIFICATE**

COMPLETE IN <u>BLOCK</u> LETTERS. Incorrect information may result in a No-Record Result. Additional Fee Payable for a further search.

You are advised that a certified copy includes **any former married name(s) of the mother.** A copy MAY be supplied omitting this information. Please indicate if you wish this information to be omitted.

☐ place tick in box

SURNAME (1.) .... (2.) ....
(At Birth)   (At Present)

Given Names ....

Date of Birth .... Age Last Birthday .... Sex ....

Place of Birth ....
(Suburb/Town/City)

Father's Name (in full) ....

Mother's Name (in full) ....
(Include any previous surnames)

NOTE:—If Birth occurred within 6 months of application, state at which hospital

....

Reg. No.

Book .... Page ....

1. Name and address of person completing this form

....

....

Contact Telephone ....

2. Relationship to person named above (e.g. self, mother, brother, etc.) ....

3. Purpose for which document is required (e.g. passport, pension, employment, etc.) ....

4. Signed ....

OFFICE USE ONLY

PLEASE COMPLETE THIS SECTION IF DOCUMENT IS TO BE <u>POSTED</u>.

Name
Address and
Postcode

....

....

....

H6550

Births Deaths & Marriages Registration Office
59 King William Street
ADELAIDE 5000

MARRIAGE

G.P.O. Box 1351
ADELAIDE 5001
This Receipt MUST be produced when collecting documents

(Tick appropriate boxes)

☐ EXTRACT

☐ CERTIFICATE   ☐ PRIORITY SERVICE

COMPLETE IN BLOCK LETTERS. Incorrect information may result in a No-Record result. Additional fee payable for a further search.

Groom

SURNAME...

Given Names..

Bride

SURNAME (Prior to Marriage)...

Given Names..

Place of Marriage..

Date of Marriage...

1. Name and address of person completing this form

....

....

Telephone:..

2. Relationship to person named above (e.g. bride, groom, broker,

etc.)...

3. Purpose for which document is required (e.g. passport, real estate,

legal, etc.)..

4. Signed..

COMPLETE IN BLOCK LETTERS.

SURNAMES OF PARTIES

...........................AND........................

Received amount printed by cash register

Note:—If Marriage occurred within 6 months of application, state name of celebrant

....

Reg. No.

Book...........................Page...........................

OFFICE USE ONLY

PLEASE COMPLETE THIS SECTION IF DOCUMENT IS TO BE POSTED.

Name
Address and
Postcode

....

....

....

H6536

Births Deaths & Marriages Registration Office
59 King William Street
ADELAIDE 5000

DEATH

G.P.O. Box 1351
ADELAIDE 5001
This Receipt MUST be produced when collecting documents

(Tick appropriate boxes)

☐ **EXTRACT**

☐ **CERTIFICATE**   ☐ **PRIORITY SERVICE**

COMPLETE IN BLOCK LETTERS. Incorrect information may result in a No-Record result. Additional fee payable for a further search.

SURNAME..

Given Names..

Date of Death...

Place of Death..

Age at Death..

Usual Residence...

1. Name and address of person completing this form

....

....

2. Relationship to person named above (e.g. widow, solicitor, son, etc.)..

3. Purpose for which document is required (e.g. estate purposes, pension, etc.)..

4. Signed...

SURNAME OF DECEASED

....

Received amount printed by cash register

Note:—If Death occurred within last 6 months, state name of funeral director

....

Reg. No.

Book ....Page........................

OFFICE USE ONLY

PLEASE COMPLETE THIS SECTION IF DOCUMENT IS TO BE POSTED.

Name
Address and
Postcode

....

....

....

STATE PRINT R1073

AUSTRALIA — TASMANIA

Send your requests to:

Registrar General of Births, Deaths & Marriages
15 Murray Street
G.P.O. Box 198
Hobart, Tasmania 7001, Australia

Tel. (011) (61) (3) 62 333793
Fax (011) (61) (3) 62 336444
http://www.justice.tas.gov.au/bdm/

The Registrar has records from 1803 now that church registers from1803 to 1838 have been added to the Registrar's records.

Cost for a certified Birth Certificate	Au$25.00
Cost for a decorative Birth Certificate	Au$40.00
Cost for a certified Marriage Certificate	Au$25.00
Cost for a certified Death Certificate	Au$25.00
Cost for an extract of the above certificates	Au$15.00

For Adoption Record information write to:

Adoption Information Service
Department of Community and Health Services
G.P.O. 1434
Hobart, Tasmania 7001, Australia

Tel. (011) (61) (3) 62 33801

Adoptees may request their records at age 18.

The Family History Library of Salt Lake City, Utah has microfilmed original and published vital records and church registers of Tasmania. For further details on their holdings please consult your nearest Family History Center.

Application for Search

BIRTH — TASMANIA

To: Registrar General,
    Registrar.

I hereby apply for:- (Tick appropriate box)

EXTRACT search ☐   CERTIFICATE search ☐   EXTENDED search ☐

of birth on the following information:—

Christian names ....

Surname at birth (Maiden name) ....

Birthplace (City or Town) ....

Date of birth ..../................./................. (Age ....) OR if not known

years to be searched..................to................. inclusive.

Full names natural adoptive parents: (delete as necessary)

Father: ....

Mother: ....(Maiden name ....)

Purpose for which Extract or Certificate is required ....

Name of Applicant Mr
(Block Letters)   Mrs ....
               Ms
               Miss

Relationship to person registered ....

Address in full ....

.... Postcode ....

Telephone No. .... Date ....

I enclose the amount of $ .... as payment for search.

PLEASE POST THE RESULT OF SEARCH TO ME.

(Tick One)

I WILL COLLECT THE RESULT OF SEARCH.

Signature ....

FOR OFFICE USE ONLY
Collected ....
Posted ....

K4781

Application for Search

MARRIAGE — TASMANIA

To: REGISTRAR-GENERAL, GPO Box 198, Hobart TAS 7001

I hereby apply for:— (Tick appropriate box)

EXTRACT search ☐   CERTIFICATE search ☐   EXTENDED search ☐

of marriage on the following information:—

Full names of parties:—

    Bridegroom: ....

    Bride (prior to marriage): ....

    Date of marriage ..../ ..../ .... OR if not known

        years to be searched.................to................. inclusive.

    Place of Marriage: ....in Tasmania.

    Purpose for which Extract or Certificate is required ....

    ....

Name of Applicant   Mr
(Block Letters)   Mrs ....
                Ms
                Miss

Relationship to person registered ....

    Address in full ....

    .... Postcode ....

    Telephone No. .... Date ....

I enclose the amount of $ .... as payment for search.

PLEASE POST THE RESULT OF SEARCH TO ME.

(Tick One)

I WILL COLLECT THE RESULT OF SEARCH.

Signature ....

<table>
<tr><td colspan="2" align="center">FOR OFFICE USE ONLY</td></tr>
<tr><td>Collected ....</td></tr>
<tr><td>Posted ....</td></tr>
</table>

K2772

Application for Search

DEATH — TASMANIA

To: Registrar General,
   Registrar.

I hereby apply for:— (Tick appropriate box)

EXTRACT search ☐   CERTIFICATE search ☐   EXTENDED search ☐

of death on the following information:—

Full Names: ....

Place of Death: ....in Tasmania.

Date of Death ..../......................./....................... OR if not known

years to be searched .... to .... inclusive.

Purpose for which Extract or Certificate is required: ....

Name of Applicant Mr
(Block Letters)   Mrs ....
                    Ms
                    Miss

Relationship to person registered ....

Address in full ....

.... Postcode ....

Telephone No. .... Date ....

I enclose the amount of $ .... as payment for search.

PLEASE POST THE RESULT OF SEARCH TO ME.

(Tick One)

I WILL COLLECT THE RESULT OF SEARCH.

Signature ....

K3995

AUSTRALIA — VICTORIA

Send your requests to:

Registry of Births, Deaths & Marriages
589 Collins Street
P.O. Box 4332
Melbourne, Victoria 3001, Australia

Tel. (011) (61) (3) 9603-5880
http://www.justice.vic.gov.au

With the incorporation of early church records, the Registrar has records from 1837. Vital registration began on July 1, 1853. If your request is urgent there is a charge of Au$26.00.

Cost for a certified Birth Certificate	Au$17.00
Cost for an heirloom Birth Certificate	Au$37.00
Cost for a certified Marriage Certificate	Au$17.00
Cost for a certified Death Certificate	Au$17.00
Additional fee for international mail	Au$10.00

For Adoption Record information write to:

Adoption Information Service
Department of Human Services
Melbourne, Victoria 3001, Australia

Tel. (011) (61) (3) 9616-2822

The Family History Library of Salt Lake City, Utah has microfilmed many of the original and published vital records and church registers of Victoria. For further details on their holdings please consult your nearest Family History Center.

Registry of Births, Deaths and Marriages

Office Use Only

APPLICATION FOR BIRTH CERTIFICATE

IN PERSON : Take the form to   589 Collins Street, Melbourne   8.30 am - 4.30 pm Monday to Friday
POST this form to   GPO Box 4332, Melbourne, Victoria, 3001, Australia
Fax this form to   (03) 9603 5880 (Outside Australia: {your country's exit IDD code} 61 3 96035880)

I wish to make application for a

☐ **STANDARD FULL BIRTH CERTIFICATE**

☐ **STANDARD ABRIDGED BIRTH CERTIFICATE**

Is certificate to be posted?   ☐ No   ☐ Yes   If YES, is Express Post required?   ☐ No   ☐ Yes

PLEASE USE BLOCK LETTERS

APPLICANTS DETAIL (Please complete)

Applicant's name		Signature of applicant	
Applicants address		Postcode	Daytime telephone No
Postal address if different to above		Postcode	Fax No.
Reason certificate is required		Relationship of Applicant	

PAYMENT DETAILS (Please complete)

Enclosed is a Cheque/money order for $ ....

or debit my   ☐ bankcard (Australia only)   ☐ Visa   ☐ Mastercard   ☐ Amex   for $ ....

Card Number	☐☐☐☐ ☐☐☐☐ ☐☐☐☐ ☐☐☐☐	Expiry Date /
Name of Cardholder		Signature of Cardholder	

DETAILS FOR BIRTH CERTIFICATE

Registration No. (if known)		Place of birth *City / Suburb / Town*	
Date of Birth	Day Month Year / /	Or years to be searched	From .... to ....
Family name (at birth)		Given names	
Other family name used		Present age	
Father's name	Family name Given names		
Mother's name	Family name (maiden) Given names		

Registry of Births, Deaths and Marriages

Office Use Only

APPLICATION FOR A COMMEMORATIVE BIRTH CERTIFICATE

IN PERSON : Take the form to   589 Collins Street, Melbourne 8.30 am - 4.30 pm Monday to Friday
POST this form to   GPO Box 4332, Melbourne, Victoria, 3001, Australia
Fax this form to   (03) 9603 5880   (Outside Australia: {your country's exit IDD code} 61 3 96035880)

Please Supply

CERTIFICATE STYLE	Qty		Total
Classic		$37	
Australian Blue		$37	
Australian Pink		$37	
'Victorian' Bird		$37	
'Victorian' Flora		$37	
'Victorian' Fauna		$37	

One standard full birth certificate is supplied with each order of a Commerative Certificate unless otherwise requested

☐   **STANDARD BIRTH CERTIFICATE** ☐   *Full* ☐   *Abridged*

APPLICANTS DETAIL (Please complete)   PLEASE USE BLOCK LETTERS

Applicant's name		Signature of applicant	
Applicants address	Postcode		Daytime telephone No
Postal address if different to above	Postcode		Fax No.
Reason certificate is required		Relationship of Applicant	

PAYMENT DETAILS (Please complete)

Enclosed is a Cheque/money order for $ ....

or debit my   ☐   bankcard (Australia only)   ☐   Visa   ☐   Mastercard   ☐   Amex   for $ ....

Card Number	☐☐☐☐ ☐☐☐☐ ☐☐☐☐ ☐☐☐☐	Expiry Date /
Name of Cardholder		Signature of Cardholder

DETAILS OF PERSON ON COMMEMORATIVE BIRTH CERTIFICATE

Registration No. (if known)		Place of birth *City / Suburb / Town*	
Date of Birth	Day Month Year / /	Or years to be searched	From .... to ....
Family name (at birth)		Given names	
Other family name used		Present age	
Father's name	Family name	Given names	
Mother's name	Family name (maiden)	Given names	
Address		Postcode	

AUTHORISATION

If the person named on the certificate is **not a member of your immediate family**, (ie. child, grandchild, mother, father, brother or sister) the certificate will be sent to that person. If you wish to have the certificate **sent to you**

I, ... authorise .... to request a copy of my birth certificate
        (person named on certificate)   (person requesting certificate)

Signature ....   Date: ....

Registry of Births, Deaths and Marriages

Office Use Only

APPLICATION FOR MARRIAGE CERTIFICATE

IN PERSON : Take the form to   589 Collins Street, Melbourne   8.30 am - 4.30 pm Monday to Friday
POST this form to   GPO Box 4332, Melbourne, Victoria, 3001, Australia
Fax this form to   (03) 9603 5880 (Outside Australia: {your country's exit IDD code} 61 3 96035880)

Is certificate to be posted?   ☐ No   ☐ Yes   If YES, is Express Post required?   ☐ No   ☐ Yes

PLEASE USE BLOCK LETTERS

APPLICANTS DETAIL (Please complete)

Applicant's name		Signature of applicant	
Applicant's address		Postcode	Daytime telephone No
Postal address if different to above		Postcode	Fax No.
Reason certificate is required		Relationship of Applicant	

PAYMENT DETAILS (Please complete)

Enclosed is a Cheque/money order for $ ....
or debit my   ☐ bankcard (Australia only)   ☐ Visa   ☐ Mastercard   ☐ Amex   for $ ....

Card Number	☐☐☐☐ ☐☐☐☐ ☐☐☐☐ ☐☐☐☐	Expiry Date /
Name of Cardholder		Signature of Cardholder

DETAILS FOR MARRIAGE CERTIFICATE

Registration No. (if known) .		Place of marriage *City / Suburb / Town*	Victoria
Date of Marriage	Day Month Year / /	Or years to be searched	From .... to ....
Bridegroom's name	Family name	Given names	
Bride's name	Family name at time of marriage	Given names	

DEPARTMENT OF
JUSTICE
VICTORIA

Registry of Births, Deaths and Marriages

Office Use Only

APPLICATION FOR DEATH CERTIFICATE

IN PERSON : Take the form to   589 Collins Street, Melbourne   8.30 am - 4.30 pm Monday to Friday
POST this form to   GPO Box 4332, Melbourne, Victoria, 3001, Australia
Fax this form to   (03) 9603 5880 (Outside Australia: {your country's exit IDD code} 61 3 96035880)

Is certificate to be posted?	☐ No	☐ Yes	If YES, is Express Post required?	☐ No ☐ Yes

PLEASE USE BLOCK LETTERS

APPLICANTS DETAIL (Please complete)

Applicant's name		Signature of applicant	
Applicant's address		Postcode	Daytime telephone No.
Postal address if different to above		Postcode	Fax No.
Reason certificate is required		Relationship of Applicant	

PAYMENT DETAILS (Please complete)

Enclosed is a Cheque/money order for $ ....
or debit my   ☐   bankcard (Australia only)   ☐   Visa   ☐   Mastercard   ☐   Amex   for $ ....

Card Number	☐☐☐☐ ☐☐☐☐ ☐☐☐☐ ☐☐☐☐	Expiry Date /
Name of Cardholder		Signature of Cardholder

DETAILS FOR DEATH CERTIFICATE

Registration No. (if known)		Place of death *City / Suburb / Town*	
Date of Death	Day Month Year / /	Or years to be searched	From .... to ....
Family name (at death)		Given names	
Other family name used		Age at death	
Father's name	Family name Given names		
Mother's name	Family name (maiden) Given names		

Send your requests to:

Registry of Births, Deaths & Marriages
Level 10
141 St. Georges Terrace
P.O. Box 7720, Cloisters Square
Perth, Western Australia 6850, Australia

Tel. (011) (61) (8) 9264-1555
Fax (011) (61) (8) 9264-1599
E-mail: rgoperth@justice.wa.gov.au
http://www.moj.wa.gov.au/

The Registry has records from September 9, 1841. Birth records less than 75 years old, death records less than 10 years old, and marriage records less than 40 years old are restricted. Priority service is available for an additional fee of Au$17.00.

Cost for a certified Birth Certificate	Au$27.00
Cost for a commemorative Birth Certificate	Au$37.00
Cost for a certified Marriage Certificate	Au$27.00
Cost for a certified Death Certificate	Au$27.00

The Family History Library of Salt Lake City, Utah has microfilmed original and published vital records and church registers of Western Australia. For further details on their holdings please consult your nearest Family History Center.

BIRTH, DEATH OR MARRIAGE CERTIFICATE APPLICATION FORM

Registry of Births, Deaths & Marriages - 141 St Georges Tce, Perth or PO Box 7720 Cloisters Square, Perth 6850 Tel (08) 9264 1555

- • BIRTH CERTIFICATE
- • BIRTH EXTRACT
- • DEATH CERTIFICATE
- • DEATH EXTRACT
- • MARRIAGE CERTIFICATE
- • MARRIAGE EXTRACT
- • URGENT CERTIFICATE (ADDITIONAL FEE PAYABLE)

Please print clearly

BIRTH

Surname at birth		Given name(s)	
Any other surname used			Male • OR Female •
Date of birth	Day / Month / Year	Present age	
Place of birth *Suburb/Town/City*		Registration number (If known)	
Father's name	Surname	Given name(s)	
Mother's name	Maiden surname	Given name(s)	

DEATH

Surname		Given name(s)	
Date of death	Day / Month / Year	Age at death	
Any other surname used		Name of spouse	
Place of death *Suburb/Town/City*		Registration number (if known)	
Father's name	Surname	Given name(s)	
Mother's name	Maiden surname	Given name(s)	

MARRIAGE

Bridegroom's name	Surname	Given name(s)	
Bride's name	Surname at time of marriage	Given name(s)	
Date of marriage	Day / Month / Year		
Place of marriage *Suburb/Town/City*		Registration number (If known)	

APPLICANTS DETAILS

Applicant's name			
Postal address		Postcode	
Reason document required		How are you related to this person?	
Signature		Daytime telephone number	

PAYMENT DETAILS

Enclosed is a cheque/money order for $.................. OR debit my Bankcard • Mastercard • Visa • for $..................

Card Number ●●●●	●●●●	●●●●	●●●●	Expiry Date ●●	/●●
Name of cardholder		Signature of cardholder			

Standesamt
(Town), Austria

There is no central office for vital records in Austria. To obtain copies of birth, marriage, and death certificates, write to the Civil Registration District Office in the town where the event occurred. Vital records are on file from 1784. Current vital registration is considered to be comprehensive.

Cost for a certified Birth Certificate	Price Varies
Cost for a certified Marriage Certificate	Price Varies
Cost for a certified Death Certificate	Price Varies

Send Your Requests for Adoption Records to:

State Youth Welfare Office
(Provincial Capitol), Province, Austria

Adoption decrees (*Beschluss)* are issued by the local court where the adoption was granted.

For additional assistance contact:

Department for Personal Registration
Federal Ministry of the Interior
Herrengasse 7
1014 Vienna, Austria

Chief Department of Population Statistics
Austrian Central Statistical Office
Hintere Zollamtsstrasse 2b
1033 Vienna, Austria

Embassy of Austria   Tel. (202) 895-6700
3524 International Court, NW
Washington, DC 20008

AZERBAIJAN

For information write to:

Chairman
State Committee of Azerbaijan on Statistics
10 Chapaena Street
37008 Baku, Azerbaijan

Azerbaidzhanskaia Respublikanskaia Biblioteka
(Azerbaijan Republic Library)
ul. Khagani 29
370601 Baku, Azerbaijan

Bakinskij Gosudarstvennyj Universitet
(Bakin University)
ul. P. Lumumba 23
370073, Baku, Azerbaijan

Embassy of Azerbaijan   Tel. (202) 842-0001
927 15th Street, NW, Suite 700
Washington, DC 20005

The Family History Library of Salt Lake City, Utah has microfilmed records of Azerbaijan and the former Soviet Union. For further details on their holdings please consult your nearest Family History Center.

Send your requests to:

Registrar General's Office
Office of the Attorney General
P.O. Box N-532
Nassau, NP, Bahamas

Tel. (242) 322-3316

The Registrar has birth and death records from January 1, 1850 and marriage records from January 1, 1799. Current vital registration is considered to be comprehensive for the country. The Registrar provides no application form for marriage and death certificates.

Cost for a certified Birth Certificate	$2.50
Cost for a certified Marriage Certificate	$5.00
Cost for a certified Death Certificate	$2.50
Cost for a duplicate copy, when ordered at the same time	$2.00

Send your requests for Adoption Records to:

Bahamas Department of Social Services
Nassau, NP, Bahamas

For additional assistance contact:

Director of Statistics
Department of Statistics
Cabinet Office
P.O. Box N-3904
Nassau, NP, Bahamas

Nassau Public Library
P.O. Box N-3210
Nassau, NP, Bahamas

Embassy of Bahamas
2220 Massachusetts Avenue, NW
Washington, DC 20008

Tel. (202) 319-2660

The Family History Library of Salt Lake City, Utah has microfilmed original and published records of the Bahamas. For further details on their holdings please consult your nearest Family History Center.

REGISTRAR GENERAL'S DEPARTMENT

P.O. Box N532   Nassau, Bahamas

To: Registrar General
Nassau, Bahamas

APPLICATION FOR BIRTH CERTIFICATE

I desire to have a search made for and* _____ copy/ies supplied
of the Register of Birth of

_____
(Enter All Names)

A.

Born at _____

on the Island of _____

Date of Birth _____

Father's full name _____

Mother's full name _____

Mother's maiden name _____

Signature of Applicant _____

*

Insert number of copies required.

_____

OFFICE USE ONLY

B.

Period searched _____ By _____

Period checked _____ By _____

Certified copies made _____ By _____

Examined by _____

Copies received by _____

Registration found in year _____ At page _____

C.

_____ (a) No record of Birth can be found on file.

_____ (b) Birth Record shows information given above to be correct.

_____ (c) Birth of male/female child recorded without name.

_____ (d) Father's name not recorded.

Indicate with (   ) where appropriate at (a), (b), (c) or (d).

Send your requests to:

Registrar of Births and Deaths
Ministry of Health
Manama, Bahrain

Registration is not considered to be complete. Bahrain handles adoption under Islamic law. Children are placed within families.

Cost for a certified Birth Certificate	2bd
Cost for a certified Marriage Certificate	2bd
Cost for a certified Death Certificate	2bd

For additional assistance contact:

Head
Population and Social Statistics Section
Central Statistics Organization
P.O. Box 5835
Manama, Bahrain

Library   Tel. (011) (973) 44-9266
University of Bahrain
P.O. Box 32038
Manama, Bahrain

Manama Central Library
P.O. Box 43
Manama, Bahrain

Bahrain Historical and Archeological Society
P.O. Box 5087
Manama, Bahrain

Embassy of Bahrain   Tel. (202) 342-0741
3502 International Drive, NW
Washington, DC 20008

For further information see:

Organization and Status of Civil Registration in the Arab Countries. IIVRS Technical Papers, No. 33. Bethesda, MD: International Institute for Vital Registration and Statistics, 1988. 6p.

BANGLADESH

Send your requests to:

Bangladesh Demographic Survey and Vital Registration System
Bangladesh Bureau of Statistics
Gana Bhavan Extension Block-1
Sher-A-Bangla Nagar
Dhaka, 7, Bangladesh

While some records exist from 1873, and modern vital registration in Bangladesh began in 1960, current registration is not comprehensive. Marriages and divorces are filed with the Ministry of Law and Parliamentary Affairs. Bangladesh does not currently approve adoptions. Guardianship is permitted and is handled by the Family Court for the area where the child lived.

Cost for a certified Birth Certificate	Tk. 7.50/-
Cost for a certified Marriage Certificate	Tk. 7.50/-
Cost for a certified Death Certificate	Tk. 7.50/-

For Guardianship Records contact:

Family Court
(City), Bangladesh

Ministry of Home Affairs
School Building
2nd and 3rd Floors
Bangladesh Secretariat
Dhaka, 7, Bangladesh

For additional assistance contact:

Embassy of the Peoples Republic of Bangladesh   Tel. (202) 342-8372
2201 Wisconsin Avenue, NW
Washington, DC 20007

For further information see:

Bangladesh Demographic Survey and Vital Registration System. A Short Description and Summary Findings, 1980–85
Dhaka, Bangladesh: Bangladesh Bureau of Statistics, Ministry of Planning, 1986. 23p.

BARBADOS

Send your requests to:

Registrar   Tel. (246) 426-3461
Registration Office
Supreme Court of Barbados
Law Courts
Coleridge Street
Bridgetown, Barbados, WI

The Registrar has birth records from January 1, 1890; marriage records from 1637; and death records from January 1, 1925. The Registrar also holds baptismal records before 1890 and burial records before 1925. These may be requested by using the appropriate birth and death certificate application forms. Vital registration is considered to be comprehensive.

Cost for a certified Birth Certificate	BD$5.00
Cost for a certified Marriage Certificate	BD$5.00
Cost for a certified Death Certificate	BD$5.00
Cost of all certificates if the requestor is over 60 years of age	BD$1.00

For additional assistance contact:

Barbados Statistical Service
National Insurance Building
Fairchild Street
Bridgetown, Barbados

Barbados National Library Service   Tel. (246) 436-6081
Coleridge Street
Bridgetown, Barbados

Embassy of Barbados   Tel. (202) 939-9200
2144 Wyoming Avenue, NW
Washington, DC 20008

For further information see:

Registration of Vital Events in the English-Speaking Caribbean. IIVRS Technical Papers, No. 32. Bethesda, MD: International Institute for Vital Registration and Statistics, 1988. 10p.

APPLICATION FOR BIRTH CERTIFICATE

SURNAME	CHRISTIAN NAMES

Date of Birth:	Day	Month	Year

Place of Birth:

Place of Baptism:

PARENTS NAMES

	SURNAME	CHRISTIAN NAMES
Father		
Mother		

OFFICE USE ONLY

References:

REGISTRATION OFFICE

APPLICATION FOR DEATH CERTIFICATE

SURNAME	CHRISTIAN NAMES

Date of Death:

Place of Death:

FOR OFFICE USE ONLY.

Reference

Send your requests to:

Russian American Genealogical Archival Service (RAGAS)
1929 18th Street, NW
Washington, DC 20009

E-mail: ragas@cityline.ru
ragas@dgs.dgsys.com

By an agreement between the United States National Archives and the Archives of Russia Society this agency will receive and process requests for vital records in Belarus. For a preliminary search to establish whether records exist for your subject it is $50.00. If indications are good and you wish to pursue a fuller request there is a non-refundable deposit of $100.00 to initiate the search.

For Adoption Record information contact:

City District Executive Committee (Raispolkom)
(City), Belarus

For additional assistance contact:

Chairman
State Committee of the Republic of Belarus on Statistics and Analysis
12 Partizansky Avenue
Minsk 220658, Belarus

Belarusskaia Gosudarstvennaia Biblioteka
(Belarus State Library)
Krasnoarmeiskaia 9
220636 Minsk, Belarus

Tel. (011) (375) (0172) 275-463

Embassy of the Republic of Belarus
1619 New Hampshire Avenue, NW
Washington, DC 20009

Tel. (202) 986-1604
Fax (202) 986-1805

The Family History Library of Salt Lake City, Utah has microfilmed records of Belarus and the former Soviet Union. For further details on their holdings please consult your nearest Family History Center.

RAGAS INFORMATIONAL REQUEST FORM:

RAGAS
1929 18th St., NW
Washington, DC 20009

A $50.00 non-refundable fee is required to complete this preliminary report. You will have a reply from RAGAS/Moscow office within one-two months to inform you whether a search is feasible and which sources are available. The reply will include a detailed description of archival records, the current address of each archive which will be useful to you for your research, and an estimate of actual costs to complete a full search. You may also be advised that it is not possible to accept a request for this area. With this information you will then be able to determine whether you wish to submit a request for a fuller search. In the case of some archives it may require additional travel and research expense for a special investigation.

Please type or print:

1. PLACE:

It is essential for any search to be successful to have as a starting point the exact geographic location. Many regions have several towns with the same name. Include the name of the region, district, town, village or rural area.

2. TIME FRAME:

Please give dates a report should cover and, if specific dates for individual events are known, include them within the time frame.

3. Please enclose a stamped self-addressed envelope.

SPECIFIC INFORMATION FORM

RAGAS
1929 18th St., NW
Washington, DC 20009

PLEASE PRINT OR TYPE (пожалуйста, пишите печатными буквами)

It is realized that you may not have answers to some questions. Fill in to the best of your knowledge.
(Возможно, Вы не сможете ответить на все вопросы. Постарайтесь ответить как можно более подробно)

Search for information about a specific event or a specific document.

Record to be searched:	☐ **Birth** Рождение	☐ **Baptism** Крещение	☐ **Marriage** Брак	☐ **Death** Смерть

☐ Military Service Records   ☐ Civil Service Records   ☐ Property Records
О Военной Службе   О Гражданской Службе   Об Имущественной Собственности

Approximate date (within 5 years) & place of event (guberniya/region, district, town, village, parish; in large cities - ward, quarter, parish, street, house)
Дата (приблизительно – в пределах 5 лет) и место события (губерния/область, уезд /район, волость, стан, округаж город, село, деревня, церковный приход, синагога; в крупных городах – район, участок=. церковный приход, улица, дом)

First name Имя	Patronymic Отчество	Last name Фамилия	Sex Пол

All other names used at any time (including maiden name if married) Другие имена (включая девичью фамилию)

Variant spelling Возможные разночтения фамилии, имени, отчества

Citizenship Гражданство	Ethnic group Национальность	Religion Вероисповедание	Class: Сословие ☐ Nobility Дворянство ☐ Clergy Духовенство ☐ Middle Class Мещанство ☐ Merchant class Купечество ☐ Peasantry Крестьянство ☐ Working class Рабочий класс ☐ Foreign national working in Russia Иностранцы на русской службе

P A R E N T S (РОДИТЕЛИ)

Father ОТЕЦ	Full name Фамилия, имя, отчество	Date of birth Дата рождения	Place of birth Место рождения	Other information Дополнительная информация
Mother МАТЬ	Full name Фамилия, имя, отчество	Date of birth Дата рождения	Place of birth Место рождения	Other information Дополнительная информация

FULLER GENEALOGICAL SEARCH FORM
PLEASE PRINT OR TYPE (пожалуйста, пишите печатными буквами)

It is realized that you may not have answers to some questions. Fill in to the best of your knowledge. (Возможно, Вы не сможете ответить на все вопросы. Постарайтесь ответить как можно более подробно)

FOCUS OF SEARCH: ☐ To link several generations (Установить связи между несколькими поколениями)

ЦЕЛЬ ПОИСКА ☐ To link family members within a generation (Установить связи между членами семьи одного поколения)

☐ To confirm several events in the life of a single individual (Подтвердить определенные события из жизни одного человека)

First name Имя	Patronymic Отчество	Last name Фамилия	Sex Пол	Date of birth Дата рождения

All other names used at any time (including maiden name if married) Другие имена	Place of birth Место рождения
Variant spelling Возможные разночтения фамилии, имени, отчества	

Citizenship Гражданство	Ethnic group Национальность	Religion Вероисповедание	Class: Сословие ☐ Nobility Дворянство ☐ Clergy Духовенство ☐ Middle Class Мещанство ☐ Merchant class Купечество ☐ Peasantry Крестьянство ☐ Working class Рабочий класс ☐ Foreign national working in Russia Иностранцы на русской службе Transfer from one class to another Переход из одного класса в другой

P A R E N T S (РОДИТЕЛИ)

Father ОТЕЦ Full name Фамилия, имя, отчество	Date of birth Дата рождения	Place of birth Место рождения	Other information Дополнительная информация
Mother МАТЬ Full name Фамилия, имя, отчество	Date of birth Дата рождения	Place of birth Место рождения	Other information Дополнительная информация

B R O T H E R S A N D S I S T E R S (БРАТЬЯ И СЕСТРЫ)

Name including maiden name Фамилия, имя, отчество (включая девичью фамилию)	Sex Пол	Date of Birth Дата рождения	Place of Birth Место рождения	Other information Дополнительная информация

SPOUSE(S) OF PERSON TO BE SEARCHED (МУЖЬЯ, ЖЕНЫ)

Name including maiden name Фамилия, имя, отчество (включая девичью фамилию)	Date of birth Дата рождения	Place of birth Место рождения	Other information Дополнительная информация

BROTHERS AND SISTERS (БРАТЬЯ И СЕСТРЫ)

Name including maiden name Фамилия, имя, отчество (включая девичью фамилию)	Sex Пол	Date of Birth Дата рождения	Place of Birth Место рождения	Other information Дополнительная информация

SPOUSE(S) OF PERSON TO BE SEARCHED (МУЖЬЯ, ЖЕНЫ)

Name including maiden name Фамилия, имя, отчество (включая девичью фамилию)	Date of birth Дата рождения	Place of birth Место рождения	Other information Дополнительная информация

CHILDREN (ДЕТИ)

Name Имя	Date of birth Дата рождения	Place of birth Место рождения	Other information Дополнительная информация

PLACES OF RESIDENCE (МЕСТО ЖИТЕЛЬСТВА)

	Place of residence Место жительства	~~Time~~ Время проживания
1.		
2.		

NAME AND ADDRESS OF THE REQUESTER

ФАМИЛИЯ И АДРЕС ЗАЯВИТЕЛЯ

RAGAS
1929 18th St., NW
Washington, DC 20009

CHILDREN (ДЕТИ)

Name Имя	Date of birth Дата рождения	Place of birth Место рождения	Other information Дополнительная информация

PLACES OF RESIDENCE (МЕСТО ЖИТЕЛЬСТВА)

	Place of residence Место жительства	Date Время проживания
1.		
2.		

OTHER INFORMATION (ДОПОЛНИТЕЛЬНАЯ ИНФОРМАЦИЯ)

Education (Name and address of institution)
Образование (Название и адрес учебного заведения)

Place of service or work
Место службы или работы

Titles, Ranks, Awards
Звания, чины, награды

Real estate ownership
Земельные владения

Adoption, guardianship
Усыновление, опекунство

Legal actions
Нахождение под судом

Place and date of emigration
Место и дата эмиграции

Membership in organizations (cultural, fraternal)
Членство в организациях (культурных, общественных)

Military service (rank, organization, dates)
Военная служба (звание, название части, время службы)

Other information that might help in identification
Дополнительная информация, которая могла бы облегчить поиски

NAME AND ADDRESS OF THE REQUESTER
ФАМИЛИЯ И АДРЕС ЗАЯВИТЕЛЯ ....

RAGAS
1929 18th St., NW
Washington, DC 20009

BELGIUM

Send your requests to:

> Registres de l'État Civil
> (Town), Belgium

There is no central office for vital records in Belgium. To obtain copies of birth, marriage, and death certificates write to the town where the event occurred. Vital records are on file from 1796, and the current registration is considered to be comprehensive.

Cost for a certified Birth Certificate	Price Varies
Cost for a certified Marriage Certificate	Price Varies
Cost for a certified Death Certificate	Price Varies

For additional assistance contact:

> Directeur General
> Registre National des Personnes Physiques
> Ministère de l'Intérieur
> rue de la Regence, 66
> 1000 Brussels, Belgium

> Directeur General
> Institut National de Statistiques
> Ministère des Affaires Économiques
> rue de Louvain, 44
> 1000 Brussels, Belgium

> Embassy of Belgium   Tel. (202) 333-6900
> 3330 Garfield Street, NW
> Washington, DC 20008

The Family History Library of Salt Lake City, Utah has microfilmed many of the original and published vital records and church registers of Belgium's cities and regions. For further details on their holdings please consult your nearest Family History Center.

For further information see:

Stichelbaudt, Leon. *Manuel de l'État Civil*. 2nd ed. Brussels, Belgium: La Charte, 1959.

BELIZE

Send your requests to:

Registrar General
Vital Statistics Unit
Corner Eyre & Houston Streets
Belize City, Belize

Tel. (011) (501) 02-35625
Fax (011) (501) 02-35635

Formerly British Honduras, Belize became independent in 1964. The Vital Statistics Unit has birth and death records from 1885, and marriage records from 1881. The Unit also will provide adoption certificates. Original adoption orders are kept by the Supreme Court of Belize, Supreme Court Building, Belize City, Belize (Tel. 011-501-77-256; Fax 011-501-70-181).

Cost for a certified Birth Certificate	Bze$4.00
Cost for a certified Marriage Certificate	Bze$5.00
Cost for a certified Divorce Record	Bze$19.00
Cost for a certified Death Certificate	Bze$4.00
Cost for a certified Adoption Record	Bze$4.00

For additional assistance contact:

Chief Statistician
Central Statistical Office
Ministry of Economic Development
New Administrative Building
Belmopan, Belize

Tel. (011) (501) (8) 22-169
Fax (011) (501) (8) 22-886

Embassy of Belize Consular Section
2535 Massachusetts Avenue, NW
Washington, DC 20008

Tel. (202) 332-9636

For further information see:

Report on the First Latin American Training Centre on Statistics and Censuses Held at Mexico City from 2 September to 10 December 1948 by the Food and Agriculture Organization of the UN and the Government of the United States of Mexico with the Cooperation of the Statistical Office of the UN and the InterAmerican Statistical Institute. Lake Success, NY: Statistical Office of the UN, 1948. 33p.

APPLICATION FOR BIRTH CERTIFICATE

A fee of $3.00 is payable for each certified copy and $1.00 for a search in connection therewith.

I desire to have a search made for, and if found .... copy/copies of the Register of Birth for:—

Name of Person ....

Born at ....

In the District of ....

on the .... *Day of* .... *19* ....

Registered on the .... *Day of* .... *19* ....

Age last Birthday ....

Father's Name ....

Mother's Name ....

Mother's Maiden Name ....

the sum of .... *to cover cost.*

Applicant's Name ....

Address ....

....

Date ....

Date ....

For Official Use Only

R.C.R. No. ....

Entry No. ....

Typed By ....

Checked By ....

Signed By ....

APPLICATION FOR MARRIAGE CERTIFICATE

A fee of $3.00 is payable for each certified copy and $2.00 for a search in connection therewith.

I desire to have a search made for, and if found .... copy/copies of the Register of Marriage for:

Name of Husband ....

Maiden Name of Wife ....

Married at ....

In the District of ....

on the .... *day of* .... *19* ....

Witnesses ....

Marriage Officer ....

I enclose the sum of $ .... *to cover cost.*

    Applicant's Name ....

    Address ....

    ....

    Date ....

    Received by ....

    Date ....

For Official Use Only

R.C.R. No. ....

Entry No. ....

Typed By ....

Checked By ....

Signed By ....

APPLICATION FOR DEATH CERTIFICATE

A fee of $3.00 is payable for each certified copy and $1.00 for a search in connection therewith.

I desire to have a search made for, and if found ....copy/copies of the Register of Death for:

Name of Person ....

Place of Death ....

In the District of ....

on the .... *Day of* .... *19* ....

Registered on the .... *Day of* .... *19* ....

I enclose the sum of $ .... *to cover cost.*

Applicant's Name ....

Address ....

....

Received by ....

Date ....

_____

For Official Use Only

R.C.R. No. ....

Entry No.. ....

Typed By ....

Checked By ....

Signed By ....

BENIN

Send your requests to:

Directeur General
Institut National de la Statistique et de l'Analyse Économique
B.P. 323
Cotonou, Benin

Vital registration began in Benin, formerly known as Dahomey, in 1933 and included mostly French citizens and foreigners. By 1950 registration included most residents within 15 miles of a registration center. Benin became independent on August 1, 1960. Currently registration is not considered to be comprehensive.

Cost for a certified Birth Certificate	Price Varies
Cost for a certified Marriage Certificate	Price Varies
Cost for a certified Death Certificate	Price Varies

For additional assistance contact:

Directeur des Affaires Intérieurs
Pour la Reforme de l'État Civil
B.P. 929
Cotonou, Benin

Archives Nationales de la République Populaire de Bénin
(National Archives of Benin)
B.P. 3
Porto Novo, Benin

Bibliothéque Nationale
(National Library)
B.P. 401
Porto Novo, Benin

Embassy of Benin   Tel. (202) 232-6656
2737 Cathedral Avenue, NW
Washington, DC 20008

For further information see:

Methods and Problems of Civil Registration Practices and Vital Statistics Collection in Africa. IIVRS Technical Papers, No. 16. Bethesda, MD: International Institute for Vital Registration and Statistics, 1981. 27p.

Organization and Status of Civil Registration in Africa and Recommendations for Improvement. IIVRS Technical Papers, No. 31. Bethesda, MD: International Institute for Vital Registration and Statistics, 1988. 15p.

Some Observations on Civil Registration in French-Speaking Africa. IIVRS Technical Papers, No. 39. Bethesda, MD: International Institute for Vital Registration and Statistics, 1990. 13p.

BERMUDA

Send your requests to:

Registry General
Ministry of Labour & Home Affairs
Government Administration Building
30 Parliament Street
Hamilton, HM12, Bermuda

Tel. (441) 295-5151

The Registry has birth and marriage records from 1866, and death records from 1865 to the present. The registration is considered to be comprehensive. The Registry provides no forms for requesting copies of vital records. You may send payment by an international money order payable in U.S. currency.

Cost for a certified Birth Certificate	US$23.00
Cost for a certified Marriage Certificate	US$25.00
Cost for a certified Death Certificate	US$23.00

For additional assistance contact:

Bermuda Library
13 Queen Street
Hamilton, HM 11, Bermuda

Tel. (441) 295-2905

The Family History Library of Salt Lake City, Utah has microfilmed original and published vital records and church registers of Bermuda. For further details on their holdings please consult your nearest Family History Center.

BHUTAN

Send your requests to:

Director
Registration, Census and Immigration Division
Department of Registration
Ministry of Home Affairs
Thimphu, Bhutan

Vital registration is considered to be 70 percent complete in Bhutan.

Cost for a certified Birth Certificate	Nu. 2
Cost for a certified Marriage Certificate	Nu. 2
Cost for a certified Death Certificate	Nu. 2

For additional assistance contact:

Central Statistical Office
Planning Commission
P.O. Box 338
Thimphu, Bhutan

Embassy of Bhutan   Tel. (212) 826-1919
2 United Nations Plaza
27th Floor
New York, NY 10017

The Family History Library of Salt Lake City, Utah has microfilmed records of Bhutan and the region. For further details on their holdings please consult your nearest Family History Center.

BOLIVIA

Send your requests to:

Dirección Nacional de Registro Civil
Ministerio del Interior, Migración, y Justicia
Av. Arce No. 2409
La Paz, Bolivia

While some records exist from 1898, modern vital registration in Bolivia didn't begin until July 1, 1940. The current registration is not considered to be comprehensive. Adoptions are approved by the Bolivian Juvenile Courts and the Regional Directorates for Minors.

Cost for a certified Birth Certificate	$B 25
Cost for a certified Marriage Certificate	$B 25
Cost for a certified Death Certificate	$B 25

For more Adoption Record information contact:

Aseroria Juridica
Vice-Ministerio de Asuntos de Genero Generacionales y Familia
Casilla 5960
La Paz, Bolivia

Tel. (011) (591) (2) 376-862
Fax (011) (591) (2) 366-763

For additional assistance contact:

Biblioteca y Archivo Nacional de Bolivia
Bolivar
Casilla 338
Sucre, Bolivia

Embassy of Bolivia
Consular Section
3014 Massachusetts Avenue, NW
Washington, DC 20008

Tel. (202) 483-4410

For further information see:

Coca Echeverria, Alfonso. *Compilacion de Lleyes sobre Registro Civil y Guia Practica para Su Ensenanza*. Santa Cruz de la Sierra, Bolivia: El Horcon, 1989. 171p.

Diagnostico del Registro Civil Latinoamericano, enero de 1980. Montevideo, Uruguay: UN Fund for Population Activities, 1982. 142p.

Report on the First Latin American Training Centre on Statistics and Censuses Held at Mexico City from 2 September to 10 December 1948 by the Food and Agriculture Organization of the UN and the Government of the United States of Mexico with the Cooperation of the Statistical Office of the UN and the InterAmerican Statistical Institute. Lake Success, NY: Statistical Office of the UN, 1948. 33p.

BOSNIA and HERZEGOVINA

Civil Registration Office
(Town), Bosnia and Herzegovina

This country has no central office for vital records. To obtain copies of birth, marriage, and death certificates write to the Civil Registration District Office in the town where the event occurred. Vital records are on file from 1946. Records before that were kept by the local churches.

Cost for a certified Birth Certificate	Price Varies
Cost for a certified Marriage Certificate	Price Varies
Cost for a certified Death Certificate	Price Varies

Send your requests for Adoption Records to:

The Center for Social Work
(Town), Bosnia and Herzegovina

For additional assistance contact:

Embassy of Bosnia and Herzegovina   Tel. (202) 337-1500
2109 E Street, NW
Washington, DC 20037

Send your requests to:

Registrar
Division of Civil Registration
Ministry of Labor and Home Affairs
Private Bag 002
Gaborone, Botswana

The Registrar has birth records from 1915, marriage records from 1895, and death records from 1904. Botswana became independent in 1966 and vital registration became compulsory in 1969. It is not considered to be comprehensive.

Cost for a certified Birth Certificate	Pula .85
Cost for a certified Marriage Certificate	Pula .85
Cost for a certified Death Certificate	Pula .85

Send your requests for Divorce Records to:

High Court of Botswana   Fax (011) (267) 332-317
Private Bag 1
Lobatse, Botswana

For additional assistance contact:

Central Statistical Office
Private Bag 0024
Gaborone, Botswana

Embassy of Botswana   Tel. (202) 244-4990
1531-3 New Hampshire Avenue, NW
Washington, DC 20036

For further information see:

Busang, L. and G. Tukula. *New Strategies for Improving Civil Registration-Based Vital Statistics in Botswana.* Paper Presented at the 51st International Statistical Institute, Istanbul, Turkey, 1997.

Methods and Problems of Civil Registration Practices and Vital Statistics Collection in Africa. IIVRS Technical Papers, No. 16. Bethesda, MD: International Institute for Vital Registration and Statistics, 1981. 27p.

Organization and Status of Civil Registration in Africa and Recommendations for Improvement. IIVRS Technical Papers, No. 31. Bethesda, MD: International Institute for Vital Registration and Statistics, 1988. 15p.

BRAZIL

Send your requests to:

> State Archives
> (Town, State), Brazil

Vital registration began September 9, 1870. Records are kept at the State Archives. Divorces are at the State Archives and also on file at the court where the decree was issued. Adoption records are not centralized. Adoptions can be approved by the local, state and federal courts; send your requests for adoption records to the court that issued the adoption decree.

Cost for a certified Birth Certificate	Price Varies
Cost for a certified Marriage Certificate	Price Varies
Cost for a certified Death Certificate	Price Varies

For additional assistance contact:

> Chefe do Departamento de Populacao
> Fundacao Instituto Brasilerio de Geographia e Estatística (IBGE)
> Rua Visconde de Niteroi, 1246
> Bloco B-8 Andar CEP 20943-001
> Rio de Janiero, Brazil

> Embassy of Brazil   Tel. (202) 238-2700
> 3006 Massachusetts Avenue, NW
> Washington, DC 20008

For further information see:

Arquivos Cartorários de Curitiba. Curitiba, Brazil: Universidade Federal do Paraná, Departamento de História, 1971. 90p.

Bussada, Wilson. *Nascimento, Casamento, Óbiot, Emancipaçâo Interdiçâo, Aeséncia e o Registro Civil.* Catanduva, Brazil: Irmâos Boso, 1963. 1,045p.

Ceneviva, Walter. *Lei dos Registros Publicos Comentada.* 5th ed. Sao Paulo, Brazil: Ediotora Saraiva, 1986. 687p.

Diagnostico del Registro Civil Latinoamericano, enero de 1980. Montevideo, Uruguay: UN Fund for Population Activities, 1982. 142p.

Oliva, Jero. *Registro Civil das Pessoas Juridicas, Legislacao, Doutrina, Jurisprudencia, Contratos e Estatutos de Sociedades Civis.* Belo Horizonte, Brazil: Editora Forense, 1969. 400p.

Registros Publicos. Sao Paulo, Brazil: Ediotra Saraiva, 1982. 196p.

Report on the First Latin American Training Centre on Statistics and Censuses Held at Mexico City from 2 September to 10 December 1948 by the Food and Agriculture Organization of the UN and the Government of the United States of Mexico with the Cooperation of the Statistical Office of the UN and the InterAmerican Statistical Institute. Lake Success, NY: Statistical Office of the UN, 1948. 33p.

Serpa Lopes, Miguel Maria de. *Tratado dos Registros Publicos em Comentario ao Decreto no. 4.857, de 9 de Vovembro de 1939, com as Alteracoes Introduzidas pelo Decreto no. 5.318, de 29 de novembro de 1940 e Legislacao Posterior em Conexao com o Direito Privado Brasileiro.* 3rd. ed. Rio de Janeiro, Brazil: Livraria Freitas Bastos, 1955–57. 4 vols.

Send your requests to:

Registrar of Births and Deaths
Medical and Health Department
Ministry of Health
Bandar Seri Begawan 2062
Brunei Darussalam

Vital registration in Brunei began in 1923 for births and deaths, and in 1948 for marriages. Current registration is considered to be comprehensive. The registration is considered to be more than 90 percent complete.

Cost for a certified Birth Certificate	B2.10
Cost for a certified Marriage Certificate	B2.10
Cost for a certified Death Certificate	B2.10

For additional assistance contact:

Chief Registrar of the Supreme Court
Awang Kifrawi bin
P.O. Box 2231
Bandar Seri Begawan 2056
Brunei Darussalam

Director
Economic Planning Unit
Ministry of Finance
Bandar Seri Begawan 2012
Brunei Darussalam

Embassy of Brunei   Tel. (202) 342-0159
2600 Virginia Avenue, NW
Washington, DC 20037

The Family History Library of Salt Lake City, Utah has microfilmed original and published materials about Brunei. For further details on their holdings please consult your nearest Family History Center.

BULGARIA

Send your requests to:

Executive Committee
Town Council
(Town), Bulgaria

Civil registration began in 1881, and current registration in Bulgaria is considered to be more than 90 percent complete. Church registers are available before that time. It should be noted that Bulgaria is one of the most closed of the Eastern European countries.

Cost for a Certified Birth Certificate	Price Varies
Cost for a Certified Marriage Certificate	Price Varies
Cost for a Certified Death Certificate	Price Varies

Send your requests for Adoption Records to:

Ministry of Justice
Blvd. Dondukov 2
1000 Sofia, Bulgaria

Adoptions of children three years old and younger are approved by the Ministry of Health. Adoptions of older children are approved by the Ministry of Education. All adoptions must be finalized by the Ministry of Justice.

For additional assistance contact:

Natsionalna biblioteka Kiril i Metodii   Tel. (011) (359) (2) 882-811
(National Library)
bul. Vassil Levski 11
1504 Sofia, Bulgaria

Library
Sofiiski universitet Kliment Ohridski
(University of Sofia)
Blvd. Ruski 5
1000 Sofia, Bulgaria

Embassy of the Republic of Bulgaria   Tel. (202) 387-7969
1621 22nd Street, NW   Fax (202) 234-7973
Washington, DC 20008

BURKINA FASO

Send your requests to:

> Center for the Civil Status
> (Town), Burkina Faso

Vital registration in Burkina Faso, formerly known as Upper Volta, began in 1933 for French citizens and expanded in 1950 to include all residents living within 15 miles of registration centers. Currently the registration is not considered to be comprehensive.

Cost for a certified Birth Certificate	Price Varies
Cost for a certified Marriage Certificate	Price Varies
Cost for a certified Death Certificate	Price Varies

For additional assistance contact:

> Directeur General
> Institut National de la Statistique et de la Demographie
> Ministère de Plan et de la Cooperation
> 17, Blvd. de la Révolution
> 01-B.P. 374
> Ouagadougou 01, Burkina Faso

> Embassy of Burkina Faso   Tel. (202) 332-5577
> 2340 Massachusetts Avenue, NW
> Washington, DC 20008

For further information see:

Methods and Problems of Civil Registration Practices and Vital Statistics Collection in Africa. IIVRS Technical Papers, No. 16. Bethesda, MD: International Institute for Vital Registration and Statistics, 1981. 27p.

Organization and Status of Civil Registration in Africa and Recommendations for Improvement. IIVRS Technical Papers, No. 31. Bethesda, MD: International Institute for Vital Registration and Statistics, 1988. 15p.

Some Observations on Civil Registration in French-Speaking Africa. IIVRS Technical Papers, No. 39. Bethesda, MD: International Institute for Vital Registration and Statistics, 1990. 13p.

BURUNDI

Send your requests to:

Chef
Service National de l'État Civil
B.P. 174, Gitega
Bujumbura, Burundi

Vital registration for the entire nation began in 1922. Even though efforts have been made to include all areas, the registration is not considered to be comprehensive.

Cost for a certified Birth Certificate	13 BF
Cost for a certified Marriage Certificate	13 BF
Cost for a certified Death Certificate	13 BF

For additional assistance contact:

Directeur
Département de la Population
B.P. 160 Gitega
Bujumbura, Burundi

Bibliothéque Publique
B.P. 960
Bujumbura, Burundi

Embassy of Burundi   Tel. (202) 342-2574
2233 Wisconsin Avenue, Suite 212
Washington, DC 20007

For further information see:

Methods and Problems of Civil Registration Practices and Vital Statistics Collection in Africa. IIVRS Technical Papers, No. 16. Bethesda, MD: International Institute for Vital Registration and Statistics, 1981. 27p.

Organization and Status of Civil Registration in Africa and Recommendations for Improvement. IIVRS Technical Papers, No. 31. Bethesda, MD: International Institute for Vital Registration and Statistics, 1988. 15p.

Send your requests to:

Director
National Institute of Statistics
Ministry of Planning
Phnom Penh, Cambodia

Send your requests for Adoption Records to:

Ministry of Social Action
Phnom Penh, Cambodia

Adoptions are approved by the Ministry of Social Action.

For additional assistance contact:

Embassy of Cambodia   Tel. (202) 726-7742
4500 16th Street, NW
Washington, DC 20011

CAMEROON

Send your requests to:

Ministère de l'Administration Territoriale
B.P. 7854
Yaoundé, Cameroon

Vital registration began for Western Cameroon in 1917. By 1935 registration also included Eastern Cameroon. Currently registration is not considered to be comprehensive.

Cost for a certified Birth Certificate	250f CFA
Cost for a certified Marriage Certificate	250f CFA
Cost for a certified Death Certificate	250f CFA

For additional assistance contact:

Chef
Section de l'Explotation et de l'Agalyse des Statistiques d'État Civil
Direction de la Statistique et de la Comptabilité Nationale
B.P. 660
Yaoundé, Cameroon

Embassy of Cameroon
2349 Massachusetts Avenue, NW
Washington, DC 20008

Tel. (202) 265-8790

The Family History Library of Salt Lake City, Utah has microfilmed records about Cameroon and Africa. For further details on their holdings please consult your nearest Family History Center.

For further information see:

An Evaluation of Vital Registers as Sources of Data for Infant Mortality Rates in Cameroon. IIVRS Technical Papers, No. 59. Bethesda, MD: International Institute for Vital Registration and Statistics, 1994. 6p.

Civil Status Registration, Ordinance No. 81-02 of 29 June 1981. Organization de l'Etat Civil. 2nd ed. Yaounde, Cameroon: l'Impr. Nationale, 1981. 28p.

Comparative Analysis of Deaths Registered in the Civil Registration of Cameroon, the Case of the Mayoralities of Yaoundé (1986–1993). IIVRS Technical Papers, No. 62. Bethesda, MD: International Institute for Vital Registration and Statistics, 1995. 17p.

Methods and Problems of Civil Registration Practices and Vital Statistics Collection in Africa. IIVRS Technical Papers, No. 16. Bethesda, MD: International Institute for Vital Registration and Statistics, 1981. 27p.

Organization and Status of Civil Registration in Africa and Recommendations for Improvement. IIVRS Technical Papers, No. 31. Bethesda, MD: International Institute for Vital Registration and Statistics, 1988. 15p.

Some Observations on Civil Registration in French-Speaking Africa. IIVRS Technical Papers, No. 39. Bethesda, MD: International Institute for Vital Registration and Statistics, 1990. 13p.

Send your requests to:

Government Services, Alberta Registries
Vital Statistics
10130, 112th Street
Box 2023
Edmonton, Alberta T5J 4W7
Canada

Tel.(780) 427-7013
Fax (403) 422-9117
E-mail: vs@gov.ab.ca
http://www2.gov.ab.ca/gs/services/vpe/

To apply for a certified copy of a vital record, an applicant who is a resident of Alberta must apply through a registry agent. Those who are not residents of Alberta may apply through a registry agent or from the Vital Statistics Office. Vital Statistics has birth records from 1853, marriage records from 1898, and death records from 1893. Birth records are restricted for 100 years. Make payment payable to "Provincial Treasurer."

Cost for a certified Birth Certificate	Can$20.00
Cost for a certified Marriage Certificate	Can$20.00
Cost for a certified Death Certificate	Can$20.00

The Family History Library of Salt Lake City, Utah has microfilmed many of the original and published vital records and church registers of Alberta. For further details on their holdings please consult your nearest Family History Center.

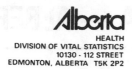

Alberta

HEALTH
DIVISION OF VITAL STATISTICS
10130 - 112 STREET
EDMONTON, ALBERTA T5K 2P2

APPLICATION FOR CERTIFICATE
(BIRTH, MARRIAGE, OR DEATH)
PLEASE PRINT ALL INFORMATION CLEARLY, ACCURATELY AND
IN FULL TO AVOID ANY DELAYS IN PROCESSING THIS APPLICATION

SHADED AREAS FOR
OFFICE USE ONLY!

Name:

If Company, Attention.

Your Reference No (if applicable).

Apt. No   Street Address.

City: Province: (Country)   Postal Code:

I require these certificates for the following purpose
(give date of departure if for passport).

State your Relationship to person named on certificate

Signature of Applicant: Phone No. (During Office Hours)

Number of Certificates x _____   **= Total Fee Enclosed** _____

FOR OFFICE USE ONLY

☐ CHEQUE   Amount $ Mail Clerk: Cashier:
☐ CASH

Remarks:

Surname (if certificate is for a married woman surname required only)	(Given Names)	Sex. ☐ M ☐ F	Quantity	Size
				Wallet
Date of Birth. Month by Name Day Year	Place of Birth (city, town, or village) **ALBERTA** Name of Hospital Where Birth Occurred.			Framing
Surname of Father: (Given Names)	Birthplace of Father			Certified Copy
Maiden Surname of Mother: Any Other Surname Known By Given Names	Birthplace of Mother			Genealogical
Date of Registration: Place of Registration Amendment Number Registration Number		Searched	Double Searched	Verified

---

Surname of Groom (Given Names)	Birthplace of Groom	Quantity	Size
			Wallet
Surname of Bride (prior to this marriage) (Given Names)	Birthplace of Bride		Framing
Date of Marriage Month by Name Day Year	Place of Marriage (city, town or village) **ALBERTA**		Certified Copy
			Genealogical
Date of Registration Place of Registration Amendment Number Registration Number		Searched	Double Searched	Verified

---

Surname of Deceased (Given Names)	Age	Sex ☐ M ☐ F	Quantity	Size
Date of Death Month by Name Day Year	Place of Death (city, town or village) **ALBERTA**		Marital Status ☐ Never married	Framing
			☐ Married	Certified Copy
Usual Residence of Deceased Prior to Death (city, town or village)	Date of Birth Month by Name Day Year		☐ Widowed ☐ Divorced	Genealogical
Date of Registration Place of Registration Amendment Number Registration Number		Searched	Double Searched	Verified

DVS-32A (92/06)

CANADA — BRITISH COLUMBIA

Send your requests to:

Province of British Columbia
Ministry of Health
Division of Vital Statistics
818 Fort Street
P.O. Box 9657 STN PROV GOVT
Victoria, British Columbia V8W 9P3
Canada

Tel. (250) 952-2681
Fax (250) 952-2527
http://www.hlth.gov.bc.ca/vs/menu.html

The British Columbia Ministry of Health has vital records from 1872 and some baptismal registers from 1849. Birth certificates are issued only to the individual, parents of the child, or an authorized agent. Marriage certificates are issued only to the individuals married or to an authorized agent. Death certificates are issued to anyone who has a valid reason. If your request is urgent there is a Can$60.00 charge for 24-hour service (phone 250-952-2557 or 888-876-1633; or fax 250-952-2182). Adoption records are available to adoptees at age 19, unless a party to the adoption has filed a "disclosure veto."

Genealogists should request a genealogy verification extract for birth and marriage certificates. There is a Can$50.00 charge for an extended genealogical search.

Cost for a certified Birth Certificate	Can$27.00
Cost for a commemorative Birth Certificate	Can$50.00
Cost for a genealogy verification abstract of Birth Certificate	Can$50.00
Cost for a certified Marriage Certificate	Can$27.00
Cost for a genealogy verification abstract of Marriage Certificate	Can$50.00
Cost for a certified Death Certificate	Can$27.00
Cost for a genealogy verification abstract of Death Certificate	Can$50.00
Cost for an Adoption Record	Can$50.00

The Family History Library of Salt Lake City, Utah has microfilmed many of the original and published vital records and church registers of British Columbia. For further details on their holdings please consult your nearest Family History Center.

For further information see:

Milestone, a Communication Link from Vital Statistics. (Serial). Victoria, BC: BC Ministry of Health, Vital Statistics. Vol. 1, No. 1, December 1992– .

BRITISH COLUMBIA

Ministry of Health and
Ministry Responsible for Seniors
BRITISH COLUMBIA
VITAL STATISTICS AGENCY

APPLICATION FOR BIRTH
CERTIFICATE OR REGISTRATION PHOTOCOPY

MAILING ADDRESS INFORMATION

NOTE: Please PRINT your name, address and identifying information clearly. This portion will be used when mailing your service or correspondence.

NAME

GIVEN NAMES

MAILING ADDRESS

CITY, PROVINCE/STATE, COUNTRY

POSTAL CODE

HOME NUMBER

WORK NUMBER

FACSIMILE NUMBER

SHADED AREAS FOR OFFICE USE ONLY

APPLICANT'S CLIENT NUMBER
(FOR CORPORATE OR GOVERNMENT CLIENTS)

BIRTH DETAILS

SURNAME

NOTE: If application is for the birth certificate of a married person, the surname at birth must be provided, not the surname from marriage

GIVEN NAMES & SEX — First | Middle Names | ☐ MALE ☐ FEMALE

DATE & PLACE OF BIRTH — Month (abbreviated) | Day | Year | City | Province **BRITISH COLUMBIA**

FATHER DETAILS

SURNAME

GIVEN NAMES — First | Middle Names

BIRTH PLACE — City | Province/State | Country

MOTHER DETAILS

SURNAME*

* NOTE: Mother's Maiden Surname (Surname before marriage)

GIVEN NAMES — First | Middle Names

BIRTH PLACE — City | Province/State | Country

NUMBER OF SERVICES REQUIRED *(see reverse for fee information)*

☐ Certificate (Large) } regular service - $27.00 per certificate
☐ Certificate (Small) } *(average 10 day processing time)*

☐ Registration Photocopy, regular service - $50.00 per photocopy
☐ Registration Photocopy, rush 24 hour service - $60.00 per photocopy

☐ Certificate (Small) } rush 24 hour service - $60.00 per certificate
☐ Certificate (Large) }

NOTE: All services, other than rush services, will be mailed. Rush services are <u>generated</u> within 24 hours of receipt of request, and courier returned.

PAYMENT METHOD   SUBMITTED BY

☐ Cheque .... ☐ Mail ☐ In Person

☐ Money Order .... ☐ Mail ☐ In Person

☐ Credit Card *(complete Credit Card section on the right)*

* Interac/Cash payment may be made in person at one of our four offices

AMOUNT ENCLOSED $_____

CREDIT CARD   SUBMITTED BY

☐ Visa .... } ☐ Mail
☐ MasterCard .... } ☐ Phone _____
☐ American Express .... } ☐ Fax _____

My credit card number is: # _____

Name exactly as shown on credit card _____

Expiry date _____ _____
                               Card holder signature

NOTE: The additional cost for credit card transactions (**$5.95**) is collected by Vital Chek for shipping and handling fees.

YOUR SIGNATURE *(written)* : _____

YOUR RELATIONSHIP TO BIRTH

☐ Self ☐ Mother ☐ Father ☐ Spouse ☐ Other _____

Reason Certificate Required _____

NOTE: If the above particulars are not completed in full, or if the correct payment per service requested is not enclosed, your request will be returned by mail.

HLTH 430b (fax) REV 98/02/03

APPLICATION FOR MARRIAGE OR DEATH
CERTIFICATE OR REGISTRATION PHOTOCOPY

BRITISH COLUMBIA
Ministry of Health and
Ministry Responsible for Seniors
BRITISH COLUMBIA
VITAL STATISTICS AGENCY

MAILING ADDRESS INFORMATION

NOTE: Please PRINT your name, address and identifying information clearly. This portion will be used when mailing your service or correspondence.

SURNAME	GIVEN NAMES

MAILING ADDRESS

CITY, PROVINCE/STATE, COUNTRY	POSTAL CODE

HOME NUMBER	WORK NUMBER	FACSIMILE NUMBER

SHADED AREAS FOR OFFICE USE ONLY

APPLICANT'S CLIENT NUMBER
(FOR CORPORATE OR GOVERNMENT CLIENTS)

MARRIAGE

Groom's Details

DATE & PLACE OF MARRIAGE	Month (abbreviated)	Day	Year	City	Province **BRITISH COLUMBIA**

GROOM'S SURNAME	

GIVEN NAMES	First	Middle Names

BIRTH PLACE	City	Province/State	Country

Bride's Details

BRIDE'S SURNAME *	*NOTE: SURNAME BEFORE MARRIAGE

GIVEN NAMES	First	Middle Names

BIRTH PLACE	City	Province/State	Country

DEATH

Death Details

NOTE: ONLY LARGE SIZE DEATH CERTIFICATES ARE AVAILABLE

SURNAME	

GIVEN NAMES & SEX	First	Middle Names	AGE	☐ MALE ☐ FEMALE

DATE & PLACE OF DEATH	Month (abbreviated)	Day	Year	City	Province **BRITISH COLUMBIA**

PERMANENT RESIDENCE BEFORE DEATH	City	Province/State	Country	Place of Birth (City, Province/State, Country)

NUMBER OF SERVICES REQUIRED *(see reverse for fee Information)*

☐ Certificate (Small) } regular service - $27.00 per certificate
☐ Certificate (Large) } *(average 10 day processing time)*

☐ Certificate (Small) } rush 24 hour service - $60.00 per certificate
☐ Certificate (Large) }

☐ Marriage Registration Photocopy, regular service - $50.00 per photocopy
☐ Marriage Registration Photocopy, rush 24 hour service - $60.00 per photocopy

NOTE: All services, other than rush services, will be mailed. Rush services are generated within 24 hours of receipt of request, and courier returned.

PAYMENT METHOD   SUBMITTED BY

☐ Cheque .... ☐ Mail ☐ In Person

☐ Money Order .... ☐ Mail ☐ In Person

☐ Credit Card *(complete Credit Card section on the right)*

Interac/Cash payment may be made in person at one of our four offices

AMOUNT ENCLOSED $_____

CREDIT CARD   SUBMITTED BY

☐ Visa ....   ☐ Mail
☐ MasterCard .... } ☐ Phone _____
☐ American Express .... ┘ ☐ Fax _____

Credit Card number: # _____

Card holder name as shown on Credit Card _____

Expiry date _____ _____
                              Card holder signature

NOTE: The additional cost for credit card transactions ($5.95) is collected by Vital Chek for shipping and handling fees.

YOUR RELATIONSHIP TO EVENT   ☐ Self   ☐ Mother   ☐ Father   ☐ Spouse   ☐ Other: _____

REASON CERTIFICATE REQUIRED: _____

YOUR SIGNATURE *(written)* : _____

HLTH 430m Rev.98/07/09

BRITISH COLUMBIA

Ministry of Health and
Ministry Responsible for Seniors
BRITISH COLUMBIA
VITAL STATISTICS AGENCY

APPLICATION FOR
GENEALOGY CERTIFICATE

MAILING ADDRESS INFORMATION	SHADED AREAS FOR OFFICE USE ONLY
NOTE: Please PRINT your name, address and identifying information clearly. This portion will be used when mailing your service or correspondence.	

SURNAME	GIVEN NAMES

MAILING ADDRESS

CITY, PROVINCE/STATE, COUNTRY	POSTAL CODE

HOME NUMBER	WORK NUMBER	FACSIMILE NUMBER

APPLICANT'S CLIENT NUMBER
(FOR CORPORATE OR GOVERNMENT CLIENTS)

PLEASE INDICATE TYPE AND NUMBER
OF CERTIFICATE(S) REQUIRED ⟶ ▼

BIRTH

SURNAME (IF FOR MARRIED WOMAN MAIDEN/BIRTH SURNAME)	(GIVEN NAMES)	SEX

DATE OF BIRTH — MONTH DAY YEAR	PLACE OF BIRTH (CITY, TOWN OR VILLAGE)	BRITISH COLUMBIA

SURNAME OF FATHER	(GIVEN NAMES)	BIRTHPLACE OF FATHER (CITY, PROV/STATE, COUNTRY)

MAIDEN SURNAME OF MOTHER	(GIVEN NAMES)	BIRTHPLACE OF MOTHER (CITY, PROV/STATE, COUNTRY)

Standard Certificates
☐ Genealogy Certificate Dogwood
☐ Special Edition - Happy Birthday

Commemorative Certificates
☐ Flowers
☐ Birds
☐ Animals
☐ Classic Style
☐ New Born

MARRIAGE

SURNAME OF GROOM	(GIVEN NAMES)	BIRTHPLACE OF GROOM (CITY, PROV/STATE, COUNTRY)

SURNAME OF BRIDE PRIOR TO MARRIAGE	(GIVEN NAMES)	BIRTHPLACE OF BRIDE (CITY, PROV/STATE, COUNTRY)

DATE OF MARRIAGE — MONTH DAY YEAR	PLACE OF MARRIAGE (CITY, TOWN OR VILLAGE)	BRITISH COLUMBIA

☐ Genealogy Certificate Dogwood

☐ Special Anniversary

DEATH

SURNAME OF DECEASED	(GIVEN NAMES)	DATE OF DEATH — MONTH DAY YEAR	SEX	AGE

PLACE OF DEATH (CITY, TOWN OR VILLAGE)	BRITISH COLUMBIA	PLACE OF BIRTH (CITY, PROV/STATE, COUNTRY)

☐ Genealogy Certificate Dogwood

PAYMENT METHOD   *SUBMITTED BY*

☐ Cheque .... ☐ Mail ☐ In Person

☐ Money Order .... ☐ Mail ☐ In Person

☐ Credit Card *(complete Credit Card section on the right)*

Interac/Cash payment may be made in person at one of our four offices

AMOUNT ENCLOSED $_____
($50.00 per certificate)

CREDIT CARD   *SUBMITTED BY*

☐ Visa ....   ☐ Mail
☐ MasterCard .... } ☐ Phone _____
☐ American Express ....   ☐ Fax _____

Credit Card number: # _____

Card holder name as shown on Credit Card _____

Expiry date _____
_____
Card holder signature

NOTE: The additional cost for credit card transactions ($5.95) is collected by Vital Chek for shipping and handling

---

YOUR RELATIONSHIP TO EVENT   ☐ Self   ☐ Mother   ☐ Father   ☐ Spouse   ☐ Other: _____

YOUR SIGNATURE *(written)* : _____

REASON CERTIFICATE REQUIRED: _____

_____

VSA013 98/06

BRITISH COLUMBIA

Ministry of Health and
Ministry Responsible for Seniors
VITAL STATISTICS AGENCY

APPLICATION FOR SEARCH
OF WILLS NOTICE

APPLICANT'S INFORMATION	SHADED AREAS FOR OFFICE USE ONLY

APPLICANT'S PERSONAL HEALTH NUMBER

APPLICANT'S DATE OF BIRTH
MONTH   DAY   YEAR

APPLICATION FOR SERVICE NUMBER

SURNAME

GIVEN NAMES

APPLICANT'S MAILING ADDRESS

APPLICANT'S CLIENT NUMBER

CITY, PROV./STATE, COUNTRY

POSTAL CODE

(FOR CORPORATE OR GOVERNMENT CLIENTS)

IF COMPANY,

ATTENTION:

HOME NUMBER

WORK NUMBER

FACSIMILE NUMBER

Complete either Section A or Section B, then complete Section C

SECTION A APPLICATION FOR WILLS SEARCH	SECTION B SOLICITORS OR NOTARIES ONLY

A certificate of death or statutory declaration proving to the satisfaction of the Director of Vital Statistics that the person named as Testator had died and the search fee must accompany this application.

I, _____ am;

☐ (a) a solicitor of the Supreme Court of British Columbia
☐ (b) a member of the society of Notaries Public of British Columbia

1) acting on behalf of the below listed individual I request a Living Will Search ☐ or,

2) after due investigation, I believe the below named individual, died on _____

at _____

_____
Written signature of applicant

_____
Written signature of solicitor/notary

SECTION C SEARCH REQUEST DETAILS OF DECEASED PERSON

		FEE
Date of birth _____ Place of birth _____		
Full name *(Surname, Given Names)* _____		$20.00
Also known as *(Surname, Given Names)* _____		+ $5.00
Also known as *(Surname, Given Names)* _____		+ $5.00
Also known as *(Surname, Given Names)* _____		+ $5.00
	TOTAL:	_____

SPACE BELOW FOR VITAL STATISTICS AND COURT USE ONLY

FOR COURT REGISTRY USE ONLY

WILLS NOTICE No. :

PLACE OF ISSUANCE:

DATE OF ISSUANCE:

DATE OF WILL:

COURT REGISTRY No. :

_____   _____

_____   _____

_____   _____

_____   _____

_____   _____

HLTH 532 REV 96/05

CANADA — MANITOBA

Send your requests to:

Vital Statistics Agency
Manitoba Consumer and Corporate Affairs
254 Portage Avenue
Winnipeg, Manitoba R3C 0B6
Canada

Tel. (204) 945-3701
Fax (204) 948-3128
E-mail: vitalstats@cca.gov.mb.ca

The Vital Statistics Agency has records from 1882. Make checks payable to "Minister of Finance." If your request is urgent there is a Can$55.00 fee for 24-hour rush service within Canada (including courier fee), Can$60.00 for rush service within the United States (including courier fee).

Cost for a certified Birth Certificate	Can$25.00
Cost for a wallet-size Birth Certificate	Can$25.00
Cost for a certified Marriage Certificate	Can$25.00
Cost for a wallet-size Marriage Certificate	Can$25.00
Cost for a certified Death Certificate	Can$25.00
Cost for Courier Delivery within Canada	Can$8.00
Cost for Courier Delivery to U.S.	Can$20.00

The Family History Library of Salt Lake City, Utah has microfilmed many of the original and published vital records and church registers of Manitoba. For further details on their holdings please consult your nearest Family History Center.

Govt of Manitoba

Formule de demande

Vital Statistics   État civil

Name/Nom

Address/Adresse   Apt. No./N° app.

English/Anglais

City/Ville   Province   Postal Code/Code postal   French/Français

Please print all information clearly./Prière d'écrire clairement en lettres moulées. ($25.00 each/25$ ch.)

Birth / Naissance

Surname (if married woman, maiden surname) Nom de famille (nom de jeune fille si vous êtes mariée)	Given Name(s)/Prénom(s)		Size/Format	Quantity Quantité
Date of Birth/Date de naissance — month/mois / day/jour / year/anné	Place of Birth/Lieu de naissance	Sex/Sexe	Wallet/Format Portefeuille / Frame/Cadre	
Surname of Father/Nom de famille du père	Given Name(s)/Prénom(s)		Restricted/Usage Limité See note 4 on reverse/ Voir note 4 au verso	
Maiden Surname of Mother/Nom de jeune fille de la mère	Given Name(s)/Prénom(s)			

Marriage / Mariage

Surname of groom/nom de famille du marié	Given Name(s)/Prénom(s)	Size/Format	Quantity Quantité
Surname of bride at time of marriage/Nom de famille de l'épouse dès le mariage	Given Name(s)/Prénom(s)	Wallet/Format Portefeuille	
Date of Marriage/Date du mariage — Month/mois / day/jour / year/anné	Place of Marriage/Lieu du mariage	Frame/Cadre	
		Restricted/Usage Limité See note 4 on reverse/ Voir note 4 au verso	

Death / Décès

Surname of Deceased/Nom de famille du défunt	Given Name(s)/Prénom(s)	Sex/Sexe	Size/Format	Quantity Quantité
			Frame/Cadre	
Date of Death/Date du décès — Month/mois / day/jour / Year/Anné	Place of Death/Lieu de décès	AGE/AGE	Restricted/Usage Limité See note 4 on reverse/ Voir note 4 au verso	

Reason for Application/Raison de la demande	Relationship to Person Named/Liens de parenté avec la personne nommée	Telephone No.-Business/N° de téléphone-Bureau	FEE ENCLOSED/ MONTANT INCLUS
	SIGNATURE OF APPLICANT/SIGNATURE DU DEMANDEUR X	Telephone No. – Home / N° de téléphone-domicile	$

VITAL STATISTICS - PLEASE CHARGE MY: ☐ MASTERCARD OR ☐ VISA THE AMOUNT OF:

☐ $25   For Regular Service processed within 15 business days and then mailed back

☐ $ 8   For Courier Delivery Within Canada, If Applicable

☐ $20   For Courier Delivery To U.S.A., If Applicable

☐ $55   For 24-HOUR RUSH SERVICE Including Courier Fee Within Canada

☐ $60   For 24-HOUR RUSH SERVICE Including Courier Fee To U.S.A.

MY CARD NUMBER IS:_____ THE EXPIRY DATE IS:_____

CARDHOLDER'S NAME (PLEASE PRINT): _____

CARDHOLDER'S SIGNATURE: _____

IMPORTANT INFORMATION	RENSEIGNEMENTS IMPORTANTS
1. Certificates contain information extracted from the	1. Les certificats contiennent des renseignements tirés

CANADA — NEW BRUNSWICK

Send your requests to:

Department of Health and Community Services
Vital Statistics Office
Box 6000
Fredericton, New Brunswick E3B 5H1
Canada

Tel. (506) 453-2385
Fax (506) 453-3245
http://www.gov.nb.ca/hcs-ssc/english/services/vital_statistics/

The Vital Statistics Office has records from January 1888. If your request is for genealogical purposes, you may obtain a non-certified extract of the birth, marriage, or death record.

Cost for a certified Birth Certificate	Can$25.00
Cost for a wallet-size Birth Certificate	Can$20.00
Cost for a certified Marriage Certificate	Can$25.00
Cost for a wallet-size Marriage Certificate	Can$20.00
Cost for a certified Death Certificate	Can$25.00

The Family History Library of Salt Lake City, Utah has microfilmed many of the original and published vital records and church registers of New Brunswick. For further details on their holdings please consult your nearest Family History Center.

APPLICATION FOR CERTIFICATE OF BIRTH, MARRIAGE OR DEATH

DEPARTMENT OF HEALTH AND COMMUNITY SERVICES
VITAL STATISTICS
P.O. BOX 6000, FREDERICTON, N.B.
E3B 5H1

New Nouveau
Brunswick

DEMANDE DE CERTIFICAT DE NAISSANCE, DE MARIAGE OU DE DÉCÈS

MINISTÈRE DE LA SANTÉ ET DES SERVICES COMMUNAUTAIRES
STATISTIQUES DE L'ÉTAT CIVIL
C.P. 6000, FREDERICTON (N.-B.)
E3B 5H1

Please print all information clearly.
Complete in full and return to the office above

35-2262 (4/91)

Prière d'écrire clairement en lettres moulées
Veuillez remplir en entier et renvoyer à l'adresse ci-dessus

Name And Mailing Address of Applicant / Nom et l'adresse postale du demandeur	Name / Nom		Address / Adresse	
	City / Ville	Province	Postal Code postal	

If Birth Certificates Required, Complete This Section / Pour obtenir un (des) certificat(s) de naissance, veuillez remplir

Surname (if married woman, maiden surname) / Nom de famille ou nom de jeune fille si vous êtes mariée	Given Names / Prénoms	Medicare No. / N° d'assurance-maladie
Birth Date / Date de naissance — Yr. / Année Month / Mois Day / Jour	Sex / Sexe Place of Birth / Lieu de naissance County / Comté	NB
Surname of Father / Nom de famille du père	Given Names / Prénoms	
Maiden Surname of Mother / Nom de jeune fille de la mère	Given Names / Prénoms	

If Marriage Certificates Required, Complete This Section / Pour obtenir un (des) certificat(s) de mariage, veuillez remplir cette partie

Surname of Bridegroom / Nom de famille de l'époux	Given Names / Prénoms	Medicare No. / N° d'assurance-maladie
Maiden Surname of Bride / Nom de jeune fille de l'épouse	Given Names / Prénoms	Medicare No. / N° d'assurance-maladie
Date of Marriage / Date du mariage — Yr. / Année Month / Mois Day / Jour	Place of Marriage / Lieu du mariage	NB

If Death Certificates Required, Complete This Section / Pour obtenir un (des) certificat(s) de décès, veuillez remplir cette partie

Surname of Deceased / Nom de famille du défunt	Given Names / Prénoms	Sex / Sexe	Medicare No. / N° d'assurance-maladie
Date of Death / Date du décès — Yr. / Année Month / Mois Day / Jour	Place of Death / Lieu du décès		NB
If deceased was married give name of spouse / Si le défunt était marié, indiquez le nom du conjoint			
Name of Father of Deceased / Nom de famille du père du défunt	Maiden Name of Mother of Deceased / Nom de jeune fille de la mère du défunt		

Indicate the Type and Number of Certificates Required / Indiquez le genre et le nombre de certificats requis

		Certified / Certifié	Wallet Size / Format-poche	Photographic Print / Épreuve photographique	Genealogical Statement / Déclaration Généalogique	Relationship to Person Named / Liens de parenté avec le personne nommée
	Birth / Naissance			/////		Reason for Application / Raison de la demande
	Marriage / Mariage					Telephone / Téléphone
	Death / Décès		/////	/////		

☐ In English / en anglais
☐ In French / en français

Fee Enclosed / Montant inclus $

Signature of Applicant / Signature du demandeur

OFFICE USE ONLY / A L'USAGE DU BUREAU SEULEMENT	Registration Number / Numero d'enregistrement	Date Issued / By / Date d'émission / Par	Checked By / Verifié par

APPLICATION FOR
GENEALOGICAL RESEARCH
VITAL STATISTICS
P.O. BOX 6000, FREDERICTON, N.B.
E3B 5H1

New — Nouveau
Brunswick

35-3723 (4/92)

APPLICATION POUR RECHERCHE
GENEALOGIQUE
STATISTIQUES DE L'ÉTAT CIVIL
C.P. 6000, FREDERICTON N.-B.
E3B 5H1

I,
Je soussigné, _____
(Name of Applicant / Nom du demandeur)

of
de _____
(Address / Adresse)

DO HEREBY MAKE APPLICATION FOR INFORMATION / SEARCHES
OF THE REGISTRATION RECORD OF

FAIS APPLICATION POUR INFORMATION / RECHERCHE POUR
DOSSIER SUR L'ENREGISTREMENT DE

☐ Birth
   Naissance

☐ Marriage
   Mariage

☐ Death
   Décès

of
de _____
(Complete Name of Person / Nom au complet de la personne)

who is my
qui est _____

and who was
et était

☐ Born
   née

☐ Married
   marié

☐ Deceased
   décédé

on
le _____ 19 ___ at
à _____ , New Brunswick
, Nouveau-Brunswick

ADDITIONAL INFORMATION   ## INFORMATION ADDITIONNELLE

A) Name of Mother (Maiden Surname)
   Nom de la mère, (jeune fille) _____

B) Name of Father
   Nom du père _____

C) If a married woman give maiden surname
   Si femme mariée, nom de jeune fille _____

D) If marriage record requested, give full name of Groom
   Si un dossier de mariage, nom complet du marié _____

E) If marriage record requested, give full name used by Bride prior to marriage.
   Si un dossier de mariage, nom complet de la mariée avant le mariage _____

F) If request is for death record, give name of spouse, if married
   Si dossier de décès demandé, donner le nom de l'époux ou l'épouse, si marié _____

Date _____ 19 ___

Signature of Applicant
Signature du demandeur _____

FOR OFFICE USE ONLY   ## POUR L'USAGE DU BUREAU SEULEMENT

INFORMATION WHICH MAY BE PROVIDED (If on Vital Statistics
Records) are:

INFORMATION QUI PEUT ÊTRE DÉVOILÉ (Si sur les dossiers des
Statistiques de l'état civil) est:

1. Registered name	10. Names of Father and Mother
2. Type of Event	11. Birthplace of Parents
3. Date of Event	12. Birthdate of Parents
4. Place of Event	13. Age of Parents
5. Date of Registration	14. Place of Disposition
6. Registration Number	15. Funeral Director
7. Sex	16. Occupation
8. Age	17. Attending Physician
9. Marital Status	18. Addresses

1. Nom enregistre	10. Nom du père et de la mère
2. Type d'événement	11. Lieu de naissance des parents
3. Date d'événement	12. Date de naissance des parents
4. Lieu d'événement	13. Âge des parents
5. Date d'enregistrement	14. Lieu de disposition
6. Numéro d'enregistrement	15. Directeur Funéraire
7. Sexe	16. Occupation
8. Âge	17. Médecin traitant
9. État matrimonial	18. Adresses

OFFICE USE ONLY A L'USAGE DU BUREAU SEULEMENT	Registration Number Numéro d'enregistrement	Date Issued / By Date d'émission / Par	Checked By Verifié par

CANADA — NEWFOUNDLAND

Send your requests to:

Vital Statistics Division
Government Service Centre
Department of Government Services and Land
5 Mews Place
P.O. Box 8700
St. John's, Newfoundland A1B 4J6
Canada

Tel. (709) 729-3308
Fax (709) 729-0946
http://www.gov.nf.ca/gsl/gslvfaq.htm

The Newfoundland Vital Statistics Division has records from 1892. There is a Can$4.00 charge for each three-year period searched. Make checks payable to "Newfoundland Exchequer Account."

Cost for a certified Birth Certificate	Can$20.00
Cost for a certified Marriage Certificate	Can$20.00
Cost for a certified Death Certificate	Free

The Family History Library of Salt Lake City, Utah has microfilmed many of the original and published vital records and church registers of Newfoundland. For further details on their holdings please consult your nearest Family History Center.

GOVERNMENT SERVICE CENTRE

VITAL STATISTICS DIVISION

APPLICATION FOR SERVICE

Department of Government Services and Lands
P.O. Box 8700
St. John's NF A1B 4J6
Telephone: (709) 729-3308
Facsimile: (709) 729-0946

MAILING ADDRESS: PLEASE PRINT YOUR NAME AND ADDRESS CLEARLY

NAME

MAILING ADDRESS

ADDRESS(con't)	CITY& PROVINCE	POSTAL CODE
HOME TELEPHONE	BUS. TELEPHONE	FAX NO.
SIGNATURE OF APPLICANT	RELATIONSHIP TO PERSON NAMED	

REASON CERTIFICATE IS REQUIRED	[ ] SEND CERTIFICATE BY MAIL [ ] WILL PICKUP CERTIFICATE

BIRTH CERTIFICATE(S) REQUIRED COMPLETE THIS SECTION(PLEASE PRINT)

SURNAME(IF FOR MARRIED WOMAN,STATE BIRTH SURNAME) (GIVEN NAMES)	SEX [ ] FEMALE [ ] MALE
DATE OF BIRTH (MONTH/DAY/YEAR)	PLACE OF BIRTH (CITY OR TOWN)	CERTIFICATE REQUIRED [ ] PAPER [ ] WALLET

SURNAME AND GIVEN NAMES OF FATHER

SURNAME AND GIVEN NAMES OF MOTHER

FOR OFFICE USE ONLY			
	INITIALS	DATE	RECORD NO.
SEARCH			DATE OF REGISTRATION
SECOND SEARCH			CERTIFICATE NO.
ISSUED			FILE NO.
VERIFIED			RECEIPT NO.
MAILED			AMOUNT RECEIVED
			REFUND

METHOD OF PAYMENT:

[ ]CASH   [ ]CHEQUE   [ ]MONEY ORDER   [ ]VISA   [ ]MASTERCARD   EXPIRY DATE_____

CREDIT CARD NUMBER_____ SIGNATURE_____

GOVERNMENT SERVICE CENTRE

VITAL STATISTICS DIVISION

APPLICATION FOR SERVICE

Department of Government Services and Lands
P.O. Box 8700
St. John's NF A1B 4J6
Telephone: (709) 729-3308
Facsimile: (709) 729-0946

MAILING ADDRESS: PLEASE PRINT YOUR NAME AND ADDRESS CLEARLY

NAME

MAILING ADDRESS

ADDRESS(con't)	CITY& PROVINCE	POSTAL CODE

HOME TELEPHONE	BUS. TELEPHONE	FAX NO.

SIGNATURE OF APPLICANT	RELATIONSHIP TO PERSON NAMED

REASON CERTIFICATE IS REQUIRED	[ ] SEND CERTIFICATE BY MAIL [ ] WILL PICKUP CERTIFICATE

MARRIAGE CERTIFICATE(S) REQUIRED COMPLETE THIS SECTION(PLEASE PRINT)

SURNAME AND GIVEN NAMES OF GROOM	BIRTHPLACE OF GROOM

SURNAME OF BRIDE PRIOR TO MARRIAGE	BIRTHPLACE OF BRIDE

DATE OF MARRIAGE	PLACE OF MARRIAGE(CITY/TOWN)

FOR OFFICE USE ONLY			
	INITIALS	DATE	RECORD NO.
SEARCH			DATE OF REGISTRATION
SECOND SEARCH			CERTIFICATE NO.
ISSUED			FILE NO.
VERIFIED			RECEIPT NO.
MAILED			AMOUNT RECEIVED
			REFUND

METHOD OF PAYMENT:

[ ] CASH   [ ] CHEQUE   [ ] MONEY ORDER   [ ] VISA   [ ] MASTERCARD   EXPIRY DATE_____

CREDIT CARD NUMBER_____   SIGNATURE_____

GOVERNMENT SERVICE CENTER

VITAL STATISTICS DIVISION

Department of Government Services and Lands
P.O. Box 8700
St. John's NF A1B 4J6
Telephone: (709) 729-3308
Facsimile: (709) 729-0946

APPLICATION FOR SERVICE

MAILING ADDRESS: PLEASE PRINT YOUR NAME AND ADDRESS CLEARLY

NAME

MAILING ADDRESS

ADDRESS(con't)	CITY& PROVINCE	POSTAL CODE

HOME TELEPHONE	BUS. TELEPHONE	FAX NO.

SIGNATURE OF APPLICANT	RELATIONSHIP TO PERSON NAMED

REASON CERTIFICATE IS REQUIRED	[ ] SEND CERTIFICATE BY MAIL [ ] WILL PICKUP CERTIFICATE

DEATH CERTIFICATE(S) REQUIRED COMPLETE THIS SECTION(PLEASE PRINT)

SURNAME OF DECEASED GIVEN NAMES	SEX [ ] FEMALE [ ] MALE

DATE OF DEATH (MONTH/DAY/YEAR)	PLACE OF DEATH	PLACE OF BIRTH

PERMANENT RESIDENCE OF DECEASED PRIOR TO DEATH	DATE OF BIRTH (MONTH/DAY/YEAR)

FOR OFFICE USE ONLY			
	INITIALS	DATE	RECORD NO.
SEARCH			DATE OF REGISTRATION
SECOND SEARCH			CERTIFICATE NO.
ISSUED			FILE NO.
VERIFIED			RECEIPT NO.
MAILED			AMOUNT RECEIVED
			REFUND

METHOD OF PAYMENT:
[ ] CASH   [ ] CHEQUE   [ ] MONEY ORDER   [ ] VISA   [ ] MASTERCARD   EXPIRY DATE_____
CREDIT CARD NUMBER_____   SIGNATURE_____

CANADA — NORTHWEST TERRITORIES

Send your requests to:

Registrar General
Vital Statistics
Department of Health & Social Services
Government of the Northwest Territories
Bag 9
Inuvik, NT X0E 0T0
Canada

Tel. (867) 777-7420
Fax (867) 777-3197

The Northwest Territories Registrar General has records from 1925.

Cost for a certified Birth Certificate	Can$10.00
Cost for a certified Marriage Certificate	Can$10.00
Cost for a certified Death Certificate	Can$10.00

The Family History Library of Salt Lake City, Utah has microfilmed many of the original and published vital records and church registers of the Northwest Territories. For further details on their holdings please consult your nearest Family History Center.

Northwest Territories

APPLICATION FOR CERTIFICATE OF
DEMANDE D'EXTRAIT D'ACTE DE

☐ BIRTH
NAISSANCE   ☐ MARRIAGE
MARIAGE   ☐ DEATH
DECES

CERTIFICATE TYPE – GENRE D'EXTRAIT

QTY – QUANTITÉ

BIRTH NAISSANCE	☐ PAPER PAPIER	☐ WALLET PORTEFEUILLE	☐ RESTRICTED PHOTOCOPY PHOTOCOPIE À USAGE RESTREINT	▶
MARRIAGE MARIAGE	☐ PAPER PAPIER	☐ WALLET PORTEFEUILLE	☐ RESTRICTED PHOTOCOPY PHOTOCOPIE À USAGE RESTREINT	▶
DEATH DECES	☐ PAPER ONLY (81/2" x 11") PAPIER SEULEMENT (81/2" x 11")			▶

BIRTH – NAISSANCE

SURNAME (if married woman, maiden surname) – NOM DE FAMILLE (si mariée, nom de jeune fille)   GIVEN NAME(S) – PRÉNOM(S)

SEX – SEXE ☐ MALE MASCULIN ☐ FEMALE FÉMININ

DATE OF BIRTH / DATE DE NAISSANCE   Y–A M–M D–J   PLACE OF BIRTH: (city, town or village) / LIEU DE NAISSANCE: (ville ou village)

CERTIFICATE TYPE – GENRE D'EXTRAIT
SPECIFY TYPE AND QUANTITY ABOVE.
SPÉCIFIER GENRE ET QUANTITÉ CI-DESSUS.

OFFICE USE ONLY À L'USAGE DU BUREAU
REGISTR. DATE – DATE D'ENREGISTR.

FATHER SURNAME – NOM DE FAMILLE DU PÈRE   GIVEN NAME(S) – PRÉNOM(S)

MOTHER'S MAIDEN SURNAME – NOM DE JEUNE FILLE DE LA MÈRE   GIVEN NAME(S) – PRÉNOM(S)

REGISTRATION No. – Nº D'ENREGISTR.

MARRIAGE – MARIAGE

BRIDEGROOM SURNAME – NOM DE FAMILLE DU MARIÉ   GIVEN NAME(S) – PRÉNOM(S)

OFFICE USE ONLY À L'USAGE DU BUREAU
REGISTR. DATE – DATE D'ENREGISTR.

BRIDE'S MAIDEN SURNAME – NOM DE JEUNE FILLE DE LA MARIÉE   GIVEN NAME(S) – PRÉNOM(S)

DATE OF MARRIAGE / DATE DU MARIAGE   Y–A M–M D–J   PLACE OF MARRIAGE: (city, town or village) / LIEU DU MARIAGE: (ville ou village)

CERTIFICATE TYPE – GENRE D'EXTRAIT
SPECIFY TYPE AND QUANTITY ABOVE.
SPÉCIFIER GENRE ET QUANTITÉ CI-DESSUS.

REGISTRATION No. – Nº D'ENREGISTR.

DEATH – DÉCÈS

SURNAME OF DECEASED – NOM DE FAMILLE DE LA PERSONNE DÉCÉDÉE   GIVEN NAME(S) – PRÉNOM(S)

AGE–ÂGE SEX – SEXE ☐ MALE MASCULIN ☐ FEMALE FÉMININ

DATE OF DEATH / DATE DU DÉCÈS   Y–A M–M D–J   PLACE OF DEATH: (city, town or village) / LIEU DU DÉCÈS: (ville ou village)

CERTIFICATE – EXTRAIT
SPECIFY QUANTITY ABOVE (PAPER ONLY).
SPÉCIFIER QUANTITÉ CI-DESSUS (PAPIER SEULEM.)

OFFICE USE ONLY À L'USAGE DU BUREAU
REGISTR. DATE – DATE D'ENREGISTR.

PERMANENT RESIDENCE OF DECEASED PRIOR TO DEATH – ADRESSE PERMANENTE DE LA PERSONNE DÉCÉDÉE

MARITAL STATUS – ÉTAT CIVIL   IF MARRIED, SPOUSE MAIDEN SURNAME – SI MARIÉ, NOM DE FAMILLE DU CONJOINT   GIVEN NAME(S) – PRÉNOM(S)

REGISTRATION No. – Nº D'ENREGISTR.

NAME OF FATHER OF DECEASED – NOM DU PÈRE DE LA PERSONNE DÉCÉDÉE   MAIDEN NAME OF MOTHER OF DECEASED – NOM DE JEUNE FILLE DE LA MÈRE

RAISON(S) FOR REQUESTING CERTIFICATE(S) – RAISON(S) DE CETTE DEMANDE D'EXTRAIT(S) D'ACTE(S)

I require these certificate(s) for the following reason(s):
J'ai besoin de cet (ces) extrait(s) d'acte(s) pour les raisons suivantes:

X
APPLICANT'S SIGNATURE – SIGNATURE DU DEMANDEUR   DATE

RELATIONSHIP TO PERSON NAMED – LIEN AVEC LA PERSONNE CITÉE   PHONE No. (BUS.) – Nº DE TÉLÉPHONE (TRAV.)
( )

NUMBER OF CERTIFICATE(S)
NOMBRE D'EXTRAITS D'ACTE(S)   ☐ (FEE NEEDED) x $10.00 $ (MONTANT REQUIS)   FEE ENCLOSED: MONTANT INCLUS: $

PHONE No. (RES.) – Nº DE TÉLÉPHONE (DOM.)
( )

PRINT CLEARLY, THIS IS YOUR MAILING ADDRESS LABEL
IMPRIMER CLAIREMENT CAR CECI EST VOTRE ÉTIQUETTE POSTALE

NAME – NOM

MAILING ADDRESS – ADRESSE POSTALE

POSTAL CODE – CODE POSTAL

OFFICE USE ONLY À L'USAGE DU BUREAU

AMOUNT RECEIVED: MONTANT REÇU: $

REFUND/RETURN: REMB./RETOUR: $

Return BOTH COPIES of form and PAYMENT to:

Registrar General, Vital Statistics
Government of the N.W.T.
Bag 9
Inuvik, N.W.T.
X0E 0T0

Retourner les DEUX COPIES du formulaire avec votre PAIEMENT au:

Bureau de l'état civil
Gouvernement des T.N.-O.
Bag 9
Inuvik, T.N.-O.
X0E 0T0

NOTES:

NWT 5243/0389

CANADA — NOVA SCOTIA

Send your requests for records after October 1, 1908 to:

Deputy Registrar General
1690 Hollis Street
P.O. Box 157
Halifax, Nova Scotia B3J 2M9
Canada

Tel. (902) 424-4.0381
Recording (902) 424-8380
http://www.gov.ns.ca/bacs/vstat/

The Deputy Registrar General has birth and death records from October 1, 1908, and marriage records from 1907 to 1918, depending on the county in which the marriage occurred. Older records as well as church registers have been placed in the Public Archives of Nova Scotia (see below). Payment should be made by money order or check, made payable to the "Deputy Registrar General." The Registrar does not accept credit cards.

Cost for a certified Birth Certificate	Can$25.00
Cost for a wallet-size Birth Certificate	Can$20.00
Cost for a certified Marriage Certificate	Can$25.00
Cost for a wallet-size Marriage Certificate	Can$20.00
Cost for a certified Death Certificate	Can$25.00
Cost for a short form Death Certificate	Can$20.00
Cost for a 3-year genealogical search	Can$15.00; Can$10.00 for any 3-year period thereafter

Send your requests for earlier records to:

Public Archives of Nova Scotia
6016 University Avenue
Halifax, Nova Scotia B3H 1W4
Canada

The Family History Library of Salt Lake City, Utah has microfilmed many of the original and published vital records and church registers of Nova Scotia. For further details on their holdings please consult your nearest Family History Center.

CERTIFICATE APPLICATION
Birth, Marriage, Death

Please see fees and instructions on the reverse side of this form.

Applicant's Name:	
Full Address:	**Date:**
Regarding:	
Signature of Applicant:	Have you written to this office regarding this request? ❑ Yes ❑ No

BIRTH CERTIFICATE

Full Name at birth:

Full Date of Birth:

Full Place of Birth:

Father's Full Name:

Mother's Full Maiden Name:

Specific Reason for Request:

Relationship to Person Named:

Please Check Certificate Required:
❑ Wallet ❑ Long Form (restricted, subject to Vital Statistics Act)

MARRIAGE CERTIFICATE

Full Name of Groom:

Full Maiden name of Bride:

Full Date of Marriage:

Full Place of Marriage:

Specific Reason for Request:

Relationship to Person Named:

Please Check Certificate Required:
❑ Wallet ❑ Long Form (restricted, subject to Vital Statistics Act)

DEATH CERTIFICATE

Full Name of Person Deceased:

Full Date of Death:

Full Place of Death:

Permanent Residence of Deceased Prior to Death:

Specific Reason for Request:

Relationship to Person Named:

Please Check Certificate Required:
❑ Short Form ❑ Long Form (restricted, subject to Vital Statistics Act)

06/96

Send your requests to:

Office of the Registrar General
189 Red River Road
P.O. Box 4600
Thunder Bay, Ontario P7B 6L8
Canada

Tel (416) 325-8305
Fax (807) 343-7459
http://www.ccr.gov.on.ca/mccr/orgindex.htm

The Office of the Registrar General has birth records for the past 95 years, marriage records for the past 80 years, and death records for the past 70 years. Birth and marriage records are restricted by the Registrar. Earlier records are at the Archives of Ontario (see below). Requests may be submitted in person at the Office of the Registrar General or at the Land Registry Offices throughout Ontario. Anyone may request a letter confirming that the birth, marriage, or death record is on file.

Cost for a Birth Certificate	Can$22.00
Cost for a wallet-size Birth Certificate	Can$15.00
Cost for a Marriage Certificate	Can$22.00
Cost for a wallet-size Marriage Certificate	Can$15.00
Cost for a Death Certificate	Can$22.00

Send your requests for earlier records to:

Vital Statistics Reference Archivist
Archives of Ontario
77 Grenville Street
Toronto, Ontario, M7A 2R9
Canada

Tel. (416) 327-1593

The Family History Library of Salt Lake City, Utah has microfilmed many of the original and published vital records and church registers of Ontario. For further details on their holdings please consult your nearest Family History Center.

Ministry of Consumer and Commercial Relations
Office of the Registrar General

 Ontario

Request for Birth, Marriage or Death Certificates

1. To be mailed to:

You can only use this form to get certificates for births, marriages or deaths that happened in Ontario. We keep records of births for 95 years, marriages for 80 years and deaths for 70 years. If you need older records, contact the Archives of Ontario. You can find more information on the opposite page.

Your name (First, middle, last)

Street number and name | Apartment

City, town or village

Province | Postal code

Please PRINT clearly in blue or black ink and sign Section 4.

If you have any questions, please contact the **Office of the Registrar General at 1-800-461-2156 or 416-325-8305**

2. What documents do you want?

Please read the opposite page to find out if you're entitled to receive the information you're asking for.

Birth certificate

Name on birth certificate (Last, first, middle – if married, use last name at birth) | Date of birth — day / month / year

Place of birth (City, town or village) | Sex | Father's name (Last, first, middle)

Mother's name at birth (Last/Maiden name, first, middle) | Any other last name used by mother

How many copies of each type of certificate do you want? Print number in the appropriate box. (There is a charge for **each** certificate.)

☐ Certificate (includes basic information, such as name, date and place of birth) ☐ Long form (contains all registered information, including parents' information and signatures) ☐ Confirmation letter (a letter saying the birth is on file)

Marriage certificate

Name of groom (Last, first, middle)

Name of bride (Last name before marriage, first, middle) | Any other last name used

Date of marriage — day / month / year | Place of marriage (City, town or village)

How many copies of each type of certificate do you want? Print number in the appropriate box. (There is a charge for **each** certificate.)

☐ Certificate (includes basic information, such as names, date and place of marriage) ☐ Long form (contains all registered information, including signatures) ☐ Marriage letter (usually needed to get married in some countries)

Death certificate

Name of deceased (Last, first, middle) | Date of death — day / month / year | Sex | Age

Place of death (City, town or village) | If the person was married or in a common-law or same-sex relationship, name of spouse or partner

Father's name (Last, first, middle) | Mother's name (Last name before marriage, first, middle)

How many copies of each type of certificate do you want? Print number in the appropriate box. (There is a charge for **each** certificate.)

☐ Certificate (includes basic information, such as name, date and place of death) ☐ Long form (contains all registered information, including signatures)

3. Fees and payment

Please read the *Fees and payment* section on the opposite page to find out how much you have to pay.

How are you paying?

☐ Cheque or money order. Please make payable to: Minister of Finance **OR** ☐ VISA or ☐ MasterCard

Total amount enclosed $

Name of cardholder: | Signature of cardholder | Card number | Expiry date (m/y)

4. Important information and signature

By signing below, you are stating that you are entitled to, and authorize the Office of the Registrar General to issue, the requested information.

If you have asked someone to obtain the information on your behalf, print the persons name here ▶ _____

Why are you requesting the certificate? | What is your relationship to the person named on the certificate? (eg: self, mother, father)

Signature of entitled person
X | Date signed — day / month / year | Home telephone number ( ) | Work telephone number ( )

11076(02/00)

CANADA—PRINCE EDWARD ISLAND

Send your requests to:

Department of Health & Social Services
Vital Statistics Division
P.O. Box 3000
Montague, Prince Edward Island C0A 1R0
Canada

Tel. (902) 838-0880
Fax (902) 838-0883

The Division of Vital Statistics has records from 1906. Make check or money order payable to "Provincial Treasurer, P.E.I."

Cost for a certified Birth Certificate	Can$30.00
Cost for a wallet-size Birth Certificate	Can$20.00
Cost for a plastic wallet-size Birth Certificate	Can$20.00
Cost for a certified Marriage Certificate	Can$30.00
Cost for a wallet-size Marriage Certificate	Can$20.00
Cost for a certified Death Certificate	Can$30.00

The Family History Library of Salt Lake City, Utah has microfilmed original and published vital records and church registers of Prince Edward Island. For further details on their holdings please consult your nearest Family History Center.

Form 11
P.E.I. Vital Statistics, Dept. of Health & Social Services
PO Box 3000, Montague, PE C0A 1R0
Telephone: (902) 838-0880 FAX: (902) 838-0883

APPLICATION FOR SERVICE
[Section 32 of the Act]

Name of Applicant:_____

Method of payment (must accompany application):
Cash/Debit Card □   **Cheque** □   **Account** □
Visa □   **MasterCard** □ **Card #:**_____
Exp. Date:_____ **Signature:**_____

Mailing Address:_____

City/Province:_____ **Postal/Zip code**_____

Phone.: (H) _____ **(W)**_____ **Relationship to person named on certificate:**_____

Specific reason certificate is required:_____

If BIRTH certificate required, complete this section (PLEASE PRINT)

Last name(give maiden name if certificate is for a married woman):_____

Male □
Given names:_____ **Female** □ **Date of birth:**_____ /___/___
Month (written out)   day   year

Place of birth (city, town or village)_____, **PRINCE EDWARD ISLAND**

Last name of Father:_____ **Given names:**_____ **Birthplace:**_____

Maiden Name of mother:_____ **Given names:**_____ **Birthplace:**_____

Type:	**Wallet** □	**Framing** □	**Certified Copy** □	**Search** □

If MARRIAGE certificate required, complete this section (PLEASE PRINT)

Last name of groom:_____ **Given names:**_____ **Birthplace:**_____

Last (maiden)name of bride:_____ **Given names:**_____ **Birthplace:**_____

Date of marriage:_____ /____/____ **Place of marriage (city/town/village):**_____, **PEI**
Month (written out)   Day   Year

Type:	**Wallet** □	**Framing** □	**Certified Copy** □	**Search** □

If DEATH certificate(s) required, complete this section (PLEASE PRINT)

Surname of deceased:_____ **Given names:**_____

Male □
Date of death:_____ /___/___ **Female** □ **Age:** _____ **Date of birth:**_____ /___/___
Month(written out)   Day   Year   Month(written out)   Day   Year

Place of death:_____ , **PEI** **Usual Residence prior to death:**_____

Marital Status: **Single** □   **Married** □   **Widow** □   **Divorced** □

Type:	**Certificate of Death** □	**Search** □

X _____   _____
     Signature of applicant   **Date of application**

FOR OFFICE USE ONLY
Receipt No._____ **Invoice No.**_____ **Certificate typed by:**_____ **Date Issued:**_____

Registration Date:_____ **Registration No.**_____ **Certificate No.**_____ **Fee Chg'd:**_____

Send your requests to:

Le Directeur de l'état civil
Service à la clientèle
205, rue Montmagny
Quebec, Quebec G1N 2Z9
Canada

Tel. (418) 643-3900
Fax (418) 646-3255
http://www.etatcivil.gouv.qc.ca/

Certificates can be paid for by credit card, money order, or checks, made payable to "Le Directeur de l'état civil." There is a CAN$35.00 rush charge (plus shipping) for certificates issued within 24 hours of application. The Archives Nationales du Quebec and the Bibliothéque de la Ville de Montreal have extensive collections of vital records.

Cost for a certified Birth Certificate	Can$15.00
Cost for a certified Marriage Certificate	Can$15.00
Cost for a certified Death Certificate	Can$15.00

Send your requests for records before 1885 to:

Archives Nationales du Quebec
Regional Centre
1210 Ave de Seminaire
St. Foy, Quebec G1V 4N1
Canada

Tel. (418) 643-1322

Genealogy Department
Bibliothéque de la Ville de Montreal
1210 Sherbrooke East
Montreal, Quebec H2L 1L9
Canada

Tel. (514) 872-5923

The Family History Library of Salt Lake City, Utah has microfilmed original and published vital records and church registers of Quebec. For further details on their holdings please consult your nearest Family History Center.

Gouvernement du Québec
Le Directeur de l'état civil

Request for certificate

- READ THE INFORMATION OVERLEAF CAREFULLY BEFORE COMPLETING THE FORM.
- This declaration must be completed using block letters.

SPACE RESERVED FOR THE OFFICE OF THE REGISTRAR OF CIVIL STATUS — Request No.

APPLICANT — Person to whom the document(s) is(are) to be sent

Surname	Given name(s)	Telephone No. (home)	Area code
Address (no., street)	Apt.	Telephone No. (office)	Area code
	Municipality, province		Postal code

Complete this section when applying for any document.

Registration number if known 1 1 9 _ 0 4

1. Surname according to the Act of Birth	2. Given name(s) according to the Act of Birth Underline usual name.

BIRTH

3. Sex ☐ M ☐ F
4. Date of birth Year Month Day
5. Place of birth (hospital and municipality)

For births prior to 1994:
- If the person was **baptized**:
  - 6. Name of parish
  - 7. Name of municipality, county and province
- If the person was **civilly registered**:
  - 8. Name of municipality, county and province

9. Surname of father
10. Given name(s)
11. Surname of mother according to her act of birth
12. Given name(s)

Complete this section when applying for a document concerning marriage, AFTER FILLING BIRTH SECTION.

Registration number if known 1 1 9 _ 0 4

BIRTH/SPOUSE

13. Surname of SPOUSE according to birth certificate
14. Given name of SPOUSE according to birth certificate Underline usual name

15. Sex ☐ M ☐ F
16. Date of birth (SPOUSE) Year Month Day
17. Place of birth (hospital and municipality)

For births prior to 1994:
- If the person was **baptized**:
  - 18. Name of parish
  - 19. Name of municipality, county and province
- If the person was **civilly registered**:
  - 20. Name of municipality, county and province

21. Surname of father according to birth certificate
22. Given name(s)
23. Surname of mother according to birth certificate
24. Given name(s)

MARRIAGE

Registration number if known 2 1 9 _ 0 4

25. Date of marriage Year Month Day

If the marriage was solemnized in a church prior to 1994:
- 26. Name of parish
- 27. Name of municipality, county and province

For a civil marriage solemnized before 1994:
- 28. Name of municipality, county and province (Court house)

Complete this section when applying for a document concerning death. ALSO COMPLETE THE BIRTH SECTION, AND, IF APPLICABLE, THE MARRIAGE SECTION.

Registration number if known 3 1 9 _ 0 4

DÉCÈS

29. Place of death
30. Name of religious parish where the burial was registered

Status at time of death
- ☐ Single
- ☐ Married
- ☐ Widowed
- ☐ Divorced

31. Date of death Year Month Day

For deaths prior to 1994:
- 32. Name of municipality, county and province
- 33. Name of cemetery or crematorium

When ordering, please specify in appropriate box the number of certificates or copies requested.

	BIRTH			MARRIAGE		DEATH		CIVIL STATUS	
	Pocket-sized certificate	Full-sized certificate	Copy of act*	Full-sized certificate	Copy of act*	Full-sized certificate	Copy of act*	Full-sized certificate	Total amount
	34. ☐ X $15	35. ☐ X $15	36. ☐ X $20	37. ☐ X $15	38. ☐ X $20	39. ☐ X $15	40. ☐ X $20	41. ☐ X $25	= 42. $

☐ RUSH: Processing the request within 24 hours → $35 (includes the document)

* 43. Justification of interest of person applying for a copy of an act

Form of payment

44.
1. ☐ Cash (in person)
2. ☐ Personalized cheque
3. ☐ Bank/postal money order

4 ☐ Credit card number – Master Card
Issue date Year Month Expiry date Year Month

5 ☐ Credit card number – Visa
Issue date Year Month Expiry date Year Month

- DEC-150A (98-03)

45. Signature of applicant

46. Date of application

IMPORTANT:

Please write the correct date and place of birth or place of civil registration.

Correct and complete information will enable us to provide you with a better service.

REQUEST FOR EXTRACT
OF REGISTERS OF CIVIL STATUS

Gouvernement du Québec
Ministère de la Justice
Archives de l'État civil
Civil Status Records

Name	
Address	
City	Province
Country	Postal Code

INSTRUCTIONS
— **COMPLETE IN BLOCK LETTERS**
— **ONLY ONE REQUEST PER FORM**
— **FILL IN THE SECTION CORRESPONDING TO YOUR REQUEST**

☐ I WILL COME TO YOUR OFFICE FOR THE DOCUMENT

☐ PLEASE SEND THE DOCUMENT BY MAIL

NAME AND ADDRESS OF THE PERSON(S) TO WHOM THE DOCUMENT(S) WILL BE SENT — IN BLOCK LETTERS

THIS PART MUST BE COMPLETED BY THE PERSON MAKING THE REQUEST

Surname of requesting person	First Name(s)	Number of copies
Address (No., Street, Apt., Town, Province, Country)		
	Postal Code	Home telephone No.	Work telephone No.

BIRTH

Surname at birth	First Name(s) (most frequently used)	Sex M F
Place of birth		Date of birth Year Month Day
Name of father		
Mother's maiden name		
Name of Church, Congregation and municipality where the person was baptized or registered	Religion	
Municipality where birth was registered	☐ Plastic card ☐ Extract 21.5 cm X 35.5 cm	

MARRIAGE

Surname of husband	First Name(s)	
Maiden name of wife	First Name(s)	Date of marriage Year Month Day
Name of Church, Congregation or Court-house where marriage was solemnized	Religion	
Municipality where marriage was solemnized	☐ Plastic card ☐ Extract 21.5 cm X 35.5 cm	

BURIAL

Surname of deceased person (in the case of a married woman, indicate her maiden name)	First Name(s)
Surname of husband or maiden name of wife	First Name(s)
Surname of father	First Name(s)
Mother's maiden name	First Name(s)
Name of cemetery or crematorium	Date of death Year Month Day
Name of Church or Congregation where this burial was registered	Religion
Municipality where burial was registered	

THERE IS A FEE OF $ 8 FOR EACH EXTRACT PAYABLE BY CERTIFIED CHEQUE OR MONEY ORDER MADE TO THE ORDER OF THE MINISTER OF FINANCE.

PLEASE SEND YOUR REQUEST TO THE BUREAU D'ARCHIVES DE L'ÉTAT CIVIL (CIVIL STATUS RECORDS OFFICE) WHERE THE BIRTH, MARRIAGE OR BURIAL TOOK PLACE.

SJ-365A (90-06)

CANADA — SASKATCHEWAN

Vital Statistics
Saskatchewan Department of Health
1942 Hamilton Street
Regina, Saskatchewan S4P 3V7
Canada

Tel. (306) 787-3092

The Saskatchewan Department of Health has records from 1878. Genealogical photocopies may be requested for marriage and death certificates. Same-day service is available for an additional charge of Can$30.00.

Cost for a certified Birth Certificate	Can$25.00
Cost for a certified Marriage Certificate	Can$25.00
Cost for a certified Death Certificate	Can$25.00

The Family History Library of Salt Lake City, Utah has microfilmed original and published vital records and church registers of Saskatchewan. For further details on their holdings please consult your nearest Family History Center.

Government of Saskatchewan
Department of Health
Vital Statistics

APPLICATION FOR CERTIFICATE

1942 Hamilton Street
Regina, Saskatchewan S4P 3V7
Telephone: 306-787-3092
Toll Free 1-800-458-1179 (In Sask Only)
Fax: 306-787-2288

THE FOLLOWING MUST BE COMPLETED
Note: Please PRINT your name and address.

MAILING ADDRESS

Name

Address

City, Province/State, Country | Postal Code

Home Number | Work Number | Certificates will be:
☐ Picked Up ☐ Mailed

Relationship to Person Named on Certificate(s) | Signature of Applicant
X

Reason Why Certificate(s) is (are) Required

NOTE: If application is for the birth certificate of a married person, the surname at birth must be Provided, NOT the surname from marriage.

PAYMENT METHOD

☐ Cheque ☐ Money Order ☐ Visa ☐ Mastercard

Credit card # _____

Name on credit card _____

Expiry date _____ Amount Enclosed/Authorized $ _____

Signature X _____

For Office Use Only

Date Signed

BIRTH

Surname (Give **MAIDEN** name if certificate is for a Married Woman) Given Name(s)				Sex	Quantity	Size
						Small ($20 each) 9.5cm x 6.4 cm
Date of Birth Month	Day	Year	Place of Birth **Saskatchewan**			Framing size with Parental Information ($20 each) 21.6 cm x 17.8 cm
Surname of Father		Given Name(s)				Certified Photocopy Of Registration ($25 each) (Long Form)
MAIDEN Surname of Mother		Given Name(s)				Genealogical Photocopy ($25 each)
For Office Use Only						Reg. No.
						Date of Reg.

MARRIAGE

Surname of Groom		Given Name(s)		Quantity	Size
					Small ($20 each) 9.5cm x 6.4 cm
MAIDEN Surname of Bride		Given Name(s)			Framing Size ($20 each) 21.6 cm x 17.8 cm
Date of Marriage Month	Day	Year	Place of Marriage **Saskatchewan**		Certified Photocopy Of Registration ($25 each)
					Genealogical Photocopy ($25 each)
For Office Use Only					Reg. No.
					Date of Reg.

DEATH

Surname of Deceased		Given Name(s)			Quantity	Size
Death Month	Day	Year	Place of Death **Saskatchewan**			Framing Size ($20 each) 21.6 cm x 17.8 cm
Residence Prior to Death				Age Sex		Certified Photocopy Of Registration ($25 each)
Marital Status		Spouse's **MAIDEN** Name, If Applicable				Genealogical Photocopy ($25 each)
Father – Surname and Given Name(s)		Mother – Maiden Surname and Given Name(s)				
For Office Use Only						Reg. No.
						Date of Reg.

CANADA — YUKON

Send your requests to:

Yukon Health and Human Resources
Division of Vital Statistics
P.O. Box 2703
Whitehorse, Yukon, Y1A 2C6
Canada

Tel. (867) 667-5207
Fax (867) 393-6486

The Division of Vital Statistics has some birth records from 1898 and complete records from 1925. Birth and marriage certificates are issued in a wallet size and framing size. The framing size is a more complete document. A photocopy of the original birth or marriage certificate is also available, but it is a restricted document. Rush service is available for an additional fee. Make checks payable to "Registrar of Vital Statistics."

Cost for a certified Birth Certificate	Can$10.00
Cost for a wallet-size Birth Certificate	Can$10.00
Cost for a certified Marriage Certificate	Can$10.00
Cost for a wallet-size Marriage Certificate	Can$10.00
Cost for a certified Death Certificate	Can$10.00

The Family History Library of Salt Lake City, Utah has microfilmed many of the original and published vital records and church registers of the Yukon. For further details on their holdings please consult your nearest Family History Center.

APPLICATION FOR
CERTIFICATE OR SEARCH

Health and Social Services
DIVISION OF VITAL STATISTICS
BOX 2703
WHITEHORSE, YUKON Y1A 2C6
PH. (403) 667-5207

PLEASE INDICATE
TYPE & NUMBER
OF CERTIFICATES
REQUIRED ↓

IF BIRTH CERTIFICATE(S) REQUIRED COMPLETE THIS SECTION (PLEASE PRINT)

QUANTITY/SIZE

BIRTH

SURNAME (IF MARRIED SURNAME AT BIRTH)	(GIVEN NAMES)	SEX

WALLET

YEAR	MONTH BY NAME	DAY	PLACE OF BIRTH (CITY, TOWN OR VILLAGE)	PROVINCE/TERRITORY

FRAMING

SURNAME OF FATHER	(GIVEN NAMES)	BIRTHPLACE OF FATHER

RESTRICTED PHOTOCOPY

SURNAME OF MOTHER AT BIRTH	(GIVEN NAMES)	BIRTHPLACE OF MOTHER

DATE OF REGISTRATION	PLACE OF REGISTRATION	REGISTRATION NUMBER
SEARCHED	RESEARCHED	VERIFIED	CERT. NO.	AMENDMENT NO.

IF MARRIAGE CERTIFICATE(S) REQUIRED COMPLETE THIS SECTION (PLEASE PRINT)

QUANTITY/SIZE

MARRIAGE

SURNAME OF GROOM	(GIVEN NAMES)	BIRTHPLACE OF GROOM

WALLET

SURNAME OF BRIDE AT BIRTH	(GIVEN NAMES)	BIRTHPLACE OF BRIDE

FRAMING

YEAR	MONTH BY NAME	DAY	PLACE OF MARRIAGE (CITY, TOWN OR VILLAGE)	PROVINCE/TERRITORY

RESTRICTED PHOTOCOPY

DATE OF REGISTRATION	PLACE OF REGISTRATION	REGISTRATION NUMBER
SEARCHED	RESEARCHED	VERIFIED	CERT. NO.	AMENDMENT NO.

IF DEATH CERTIFICATE(S) REQUIRED COMPLETE THIS SECTION (PLEASE PRINT)

QUANTITY/SIZE

DEATH

SURNAME OF DECEASED	(GIVEN NAMES)	AGE	SEX

YEAR	MONTH BY NAME	DAY	PLACE OF DEATH (CITY, TOWN OR VILLAGE)	PROVINCE/TERRITORY

FRAMING

PERMANENT RESIDENCE OF DECEASED PRIOR TO DEATH	MARITAL STATUS

DATE OF REGISTRATION	PLACE OF REGISTRATION	REGISTRATION NUMBER
SEARCHED	RESEARCHED	VERIFIED	CERT. NO.	AMENDMENT NO.

PLEASE INDICATE THE REASON FOR APPLICATION:

STATE RELATIONSHIP TO PERSON NAMED:

SIGNATURE OF APPLICANT:

FOR OFFICE USE ONLY

REMARKS

X

DATE YR.	MO.	DAY	FEE ENCLOSED WITH THIS APPLICATION $

NAME

MAILING ADDRESS

STREET ADDRESS

REFUND

DATE MAILED

CITY   PROVINCE   POSTAL CODE

CAPE VERDE

Send your requests to:

Direccao Geral dos Registos e Notariado
Ministerio de Justiça
C.P. 204
Praia, Cape Verde

While records date back to 1803, modern registration has been considered more than 90 percent comprehensive only since independence in 1975.

Cost for a certified Birth Certificate	15.00$
Cost for a certified Marriage Certificate	15.00$
Cost for a certified Death Certificate	15.00$

For additional assistance contact:

Director Geral de Estatística
Direccao Geral de Estatística
C.P. 116
Praia, Cape Verde

Embassy of Cape Verde   Tel. (202) 965-6820
3415 Massachusetts Avenue, NW
Washington, DC 20007

The Family History Library of Salt Lake City, Utah has microfilmed records about Cape Verde and the region. For further details on their holdings please consult your nearest Family History Center.

CAYMAN ISLANDS

Send your requests to:

Registrar General   Tel. (345) 949-7900
Tower Building
George Town
Grand Cayman, Cayman Islands, BWI

Vital registration in the Cayman Islands is considered to be comprehensive. Payment should be made by certified check payable to the "Government of the Cayman Islands." No forms are required to apply for copies of vital records.

Cost for a certified Birth Certificate	US $3.75
Cost for a certified Marriage Certificate	US $8.75
Cost for a certified Death Certificate	US $3.75

For additional assistance contact:

Government Statistician
Statistics Unit
Government Administration Building
George Town
Grand Cayman, Cayman Islands, BWI

The Family History Library of Salt Lake City, Utah has microfilmed many of the original and published vital records and church registers of the Cayman Islands. For further details on their holdings please consult your nearest Family History Center.

CENTRAL AFRICAN REPUBLIC

Send your requests to:

Service de l'État Civil et du Recensement Demographique
B.P. 689
Bangui, Central African Republic

Vital registration began in 1940 in the Central African Republic for French citizens and foreigners. By 1966 registration expanded to the entire population. Currently the registration is not considered to be comprehensive.

Cost for a certified Birth Certificate	Price Varies
Cost for a certified Marriage Certificate	Price Varies
Cost for a certified Death Certificate	Price Varies

For additional assistance contact:

Directeur de la Statistique Generale
B.P. 696
Bangui, Central African Republic

Embassy of Central African Republic   Tel. (202) 483-7800
1618 22nd Street, NW
Washington, DC 20008

For further information see:

Methods and Problems of Civil Registration Practices and Vital Statistics Collection in Africa. IIVRS Technical Papers, No. 16. Bethesda, MD: International Institute for Vital Registration and Statistics, 1981. 27p.

Organization and Status of Civil Registration in Africa and Recommendations for Improvement. IIVRS Technical Papers, No. 31. Bethesda, MD: International Institute for Vital Registration and Statistics, 1988. 15p.

Some Observations on Civil Registration in French-Speaking Africa. IIVRS Technical Papers, No. 39. Bethesda, MD: International Institute for Vital Registration and Statistics, 1990. 13p.

CHAD

Send your requests to:

Registrar
Direction de la Statistique, des Études Économiques et Demographiques
B.P. 453
N'Djamena, Chad

Modern vital registration of births, marriages, and deaths in Chad began in 1961. Divorce records are kept by the court that issued the decree. Registration in Chad is not comprehensive.

Cost for a certified Birth Certificate	75F CFA
Cost for a certified Marriage Certificate	75F CFA
Cost for a certified Death Certificate	75F CFA

For additional assistance contact:

Chef
Division de la Population
Sous-Direction de la Statistique
B.P. 453
N'Djamena, Chad

Embassy of Chad   Tel. (202) 462-4009
2002 R Street, NW
Washington, DC 20009

For further information see:

Methods and Problems of Civil Registration Practices and Vital Statistics Collection in Africa. IIVRS Technical Papers, No. 16. Bethesda, MD: International Institute for Vital Registration and Statistics, 1981. 27p.

Organization and Status of Civil Registration in Africa and Recommendations for Improvement. IIVRS Technical Papers, No. 31. Bethesda, MD: International Institute for Vital Registration and Statistics, 1988. 15p.

Some Observations on Civil Registration in French-Speaking Africa. IIVRS Technical Papers, No. 39. Bethesda, MD: International Institute for Vital Registration and Statistics, 1990. 13p.

CHILE

Send your requests to:

Director General del Servicio de Registro Civil e Identificación   Tel. (011) (56) (2) 698-2546
Ministerio de Justicia   http://santiago.ciudad.cl/registro.htm
Huérfanos 1570
Santiago, Chile

Church registers date from the 1500s, while vital registration began January 1, 1885 and is considered to be 75 percent complete. The Family Court approves adoptions; amended birth certificates are issued by the Registro Civil.

Cost for a certified Birth Certificate	Ps 300
Cost for a certified Marriage Certificate	Ps 300
Cost for a certified Death Certificate	Ps 300

Send your requests for Adoption Records to:

Family Court
(City), Chile

For additional assistance contact:

SENAME   Tel. (011) (56) (2) 696-8151
Ministry of Justice
Compania 1111
Santiago, Chile

Instituto Nacional de Estadísticas
Av. Bulnes 418
Casilla, 7597, Correo 3
Santiago, Chile

Biblioteca Nacional
Av. Bernardo O'Higgins 651
Santiago, Chile

Embassy of Chile   Tel. (202) 785-1746
Consular Section
1732 Massachusetts Avenue, NW
Washington, DC 20036

For further information see:

Fueyo Laneri, Fernando. *Teoria General De Los Registros*. Buenos Aires, Argentina: Editorial Astrea, 1982. 248p.

Report on the First Latin American Training Centre on Statistics and Censuses Held at Mexico City from 2 September to 10 December 1948 by the Food and Agriculture Organization of the UN and the Government of the United States of Mexico with the Cooperation of the Statistical Office of the UN and the InterAmerican Statistical Institute. Lake Success, NY: Statistical Office of the UN, 1948. 33p.

CHINA

Send your requests to:

Population Registration
Ministry of Public Security
(City), China

Section Chief
Administrative Division for Population Registration
Third Bureau
Ministry of Public Security
14 Dong Chang An Jie
Beijing, China

China uses a household registration system to record and identify each person in China. China has kept family registers for the past 4,000 years. Currently this is handled by the local police office and is considered to be 90 percent complete.

Cost for a certified Birth Certificate	Price Varies
Cost for a certified Marriage Certificate	Price Varies
Cost for a certified Death Certificate	Price Varies

For direct assistance with Chinese genealogical research contact:

Genealogical Research Center
Shanghai Library
1555 Huaihaizhong Road
Shanghai 200031, China

Send your requests for Adoption Records to:

China Center for Adoption Affairs
103 Beiheyan Street
Dongcheng District
Beijing 100006, China

Tel. (011) (86) (10) 6522-3102
Fax (011) (86) (10) 6522-3102

Adoptions in China are approved by the Civil Affairs Bureau, (Capitol City), Province, China and are under the direction of the Ministry of Civil Affairs, No. 147 Beiheyan Street, Beijing, 100032 China.

For additional assistance contact:

Embassy of the People's Republic of China
Consular Section
2300 Connecticut Avenue, NW
Washington, DC 20008

Tel. (202) 328-2500

The Family History Library of Salt Lake City, Utah has microfilmed original and published Chinese family records.

For further information see:

Loi Sur l'État-Civil Promulguée le 12 décembre 1931, entrée en Vigueur le 1 juillet 1934. Texte Chinois et Traduction Française. Tientsin, China: Hautes Études, 1934. 34p.

(用于涉外公证)

出 生 公 证 申 请 表

证号（　）沪　　字第　　　号

填 表 须 知

　　填表人必须如实填写本表所列各栏。如发现有不真实内容，除拒绝办理公证外，将根据情节和后果，建议有关部门作必要处理。

申请公证用途,画✓表示	定居	探亲	留学	工作	公证书使用于	国家或地区

申请人	姓　名	曾用名、别名	外文名	性别	出生日期	工作单位和地址（或原）
	住　　　　　　　　址			联系电话	邮政编码	居民身份证编号

申请人已住境外者，出境年月日		出境前户籍所在地	
住境外者回沪临时住址		过去办过何种公证	

申请人出生地点（详填门牌号码或医院）	

	姓　名	出生日期	健在否	现 住 址 或 生 前 住 址
生父				
生母				

	生父母现住境外的，在沪最后户籍所在地及离沪日期	生父母出境前若住外省市的地址
生父		
生母		

代申请人	姓　名	性别	出生日期	与申请人关系	联 系 地 址	邮政编码	电话

申请人提供由公证处收下证件登记，原件画（〇）、复印件及其他材料画（✓）表示

身份证	户口本	护照	出入境通行证	境外身份证	委托书（信）	单位证明	照　片
							寸张

填表人：　　　　　　　　　　　19　　年　　月　　日

接待人　　　　　　　　　　　　　　上海市司法局公证管理处制(91)表十八

（用于涉外公证）

结婚（　　）离婚（　　）未婚（　　）未再婚（　　）公证申请表

（申请公证事项应在以上事项的括号内划"✓"表示　　　　证号（　　）沪　字第　　号

填 表 须 知

填表人必须如实填写本表所列各栏，如发现有不真实内容，除拒绝办理公证外，将根据情节和后果，建议有关部门必要处理。

申请公证用途，画✓表示	定居	探亲	留学	工作	公证书使用于			国家或地区

申请人	姓名	曾用别名	外文名	性别	出生日期	工作单位和地址（或原单位）		
	住 址			联系电话	邮政编码	居民身份证编号		

申请人已住境外者，出境年月		出境前户籍所在地址	

现婚姻状况，画✓表示	未婚	结婚	离婚	丧偶	未再婚	过去办过何公证

结婚情况	结婚日期	年 月 日	结婚地点		登记或批准机关	
	配偶姓名	外文名		出生日期	住 址	

离婚情况·	离婚日期	年 月 日	离婚地点		登记或批准机关	
	原配偶姓名	出生日期		住 址		

丧偶情况	配偶姓名	出生日期		死亡日期、地点	
	生前住址		原结婚日期、地点		

代申请人	姓名	性别	出生日期	与申请人关系	联 系 地 址	邮政编码	电话

申请人提供由公证处收下证件登记，原件画（○）复印件及其他证明材料画（✓）表示

身份证	户口本	护照	出入境通行证	境外身份证	委托书	未婚证明	结婚证明	离婚证或判决调解书	死亡证明	未再婚证明	其 他
（　份）	（　份）										

填表人：　　　　　　　　　　　　　　19　年　月　日

接待人：　　　　　　　　　　　　　上海市司法局公证管理处制（91）表二十

公 证 申 请 表

证号（　　）沪　　字第　　号

	姓名		性别	出生日期		文化程度	工作单位及地址		
申请人	住址				电话		邮编	身份证号码	
	姓名		性别	出生日期		文化程度	工作单位及地址		
	住址				电话		邮编	身份证号码	
	姓名		性别	出生日期		文化程度	工作单位及地址		
	住址				电话		邮编	身份证号码	
代申请人	姓名		性别	出生日期		文化程度	工作单位及地址		
	住址				电话		邮编	身份证号码	

申请公证的目的、用途		代申请人与申请人关系	
申请公证的内容			
需要说明的情况			

申请人提供由公证处收下证件登记：

填表人：　　　　　　　　　　　　　　　19　　年　　月　　日

接待人：　　　　　　　　　　　上海市司法局公证管理处制（91）表一

CHINA — HONG KONG SPECIAL ADMINISTRATIVE REGION

Send your requests to:

Immigration Department
Personal Documentation Branch
Registration of Persons Sub-division
General Register Office
3/F, Low Block
Queensway Government Offices
66 Queensway
Hong Kong (HKSAR), China

Tel. (011) (852) 2867-2785; (011) (852) 2824-6111
http://www.info.gov.hk/immd/

Church registers date from the colonial period, while vital registration in Hong Kong began in 1872. The Sub-division maintains seven birth registries and four death registries. Per the Sub-division, "marriages may take place at any of the ten marriage registries, or at the 220 places of public worship licensed for celebration of marriage."

Requests for certificates are a two-step process. For births and adoptions use form BDR 40 to search for a record and form BDR 87 to request a copy of the located record. For deaths use search form BDR 41 and copy request form BDR 62. Requests for searches and copies of marriage records require only one form, MR 10.

Personal identification cards have been issued since 1949. On July 1, 1987 special, "Hong Kong Permanent Identity Cards," were issued as a guarantee of the "right of abode in Hong Kong." Each person receives an identity card at age 11. Currently the aged, blind, infirm, and Vietnamese refugees are excluded from receiving an identity card.

Cost for a certified Birth Certificate	(In Person) HK$140.00	(Overseas) HK$275.00
Cost for a certified Marriage Certificate	(In Person) HK$140.00	(Overseas) HK$275.00
Cost for a certified Divorce Record	(Overseas) HK$140.00	(Overseas) HK$275.00
Cost for a certified Death Certificate or missing person entry	(In Person) HK$140.00	(Overseas) HK$275.00
Cost for a certified Adoption Certificate	(In Person) HK$140.00	(Overseas) HK$275.00

For direct assistance with Chinese genealogical research contact:

Genealogical Research Center
Shanghai Library
1555 Huaihaizhong Road
Shanghai 200031, China

Send your requests for Adoption Records to:

Adoption Unit
Social Welfare Department
38, Pier Road
4/F Harbour Building
Central, Hong Kong, China

Tel. (011) (852) 2852-3107

For further information see:

Annual Report. Commissioner of Registration of Persons. Hong Kong: Commission.

Shum, Donna. *Vital Statistics Data Collection and Compilation System, Hong Kong.* IIVRS Technical Papers, No. 14. Bethesda, MD: International Institute for Vital Registration and Statistics, 1981. 9p.

香港特別行政區政府
入境事務處
生死登記處
Births and Deaths Registry
Immigration Department
The Government of the Hong Kong Special Administrative Region
出生登記紀錄內記項的核證副本申請書
Application for a certified true copy of an entry in the births registers
在填寫本表格前，請參看說明事項
Please read guidance notes before completing this form.

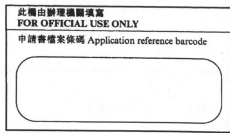

出生登記記項持有人資料 Particulars of the Birth Entry Holder

出生登記編號 Birth registration no.		登記日期 Date of registration	日 Day	月 Month	年 Year

姓（英文）
Surname

名（英文）
Other names in full

中文姓名 Name in Chinese	別名（如有者） Alias (if any)

中文姓名電碼（如適用者）
C.C.C. number (if applicable)

性別 Sex	男 Male ☐	女 Female ☐	香港身分證號碼（如有者） Hong Kong identity card no. (if any)	（ ）

出生日期 Date of birth	日 Day	月 Month	年 Year	申請張數 Copies applied for	

申請人資料 Particulars of Applicant

申請人姓名
Name of applicant

香港身分證／旅行證件號碼 HK identity card/travel document no.	日間電話號碼 Daytime telephone no.

地址
Address

與出生證明書持有人的關係
Relationship with the birth certificate holder

日期 Date	申請人簽署 Signature of applicant

確認 Acknowledgement

我，_____，已經查閱過出生登記記項核證副本上的資料，並沒有需要修改的地方。
I, _____ , have checked and found the certified true copy(ies) of birth entry in order.

簽署 Signed _____	（申請人） (Applicant)	日期 Date _____

☐ 請在適當方格內填上「√」號 Tick as appropriate

BDR 87 (1/98)

香港特別行政區政府
入境事務處
生死登記處
Births and Deaths Registry
Immigration Department
The Government of the Hong Kong
Special Administrative Region

ᗑ

翻查出生登記紀錄申請書
Application for Search of Record of Birth

在填寫本表格前，請參看説明事項
Please read guidance notes before completing this form

翻查資料 Search Information	特定查冊 Particular Search ☐	一般查冊 General Search ☐

姓（英文）
Surname

名（英文）
Other names in full

中文姓名 Name in Chinese	別名（如有者）Alias (if any)	性別 Sex	男 Male ☐	女 Female ☐

中文姓名電碼（如適用者）
C.C.C. number (if applicable)

（特定查冊者適用）For Particular Search	（一般查冊適用者）For General Search
出生日期 ＊西曆／農曆 （日／月／年）Date of birth ＊Gregorian/Lunar (Day/Month/Year)	查冊年期 Period for the search: 由（日／月／年）From (Day/Month/Year) _____ 至（日／月／年）To (Day/Month/Year) _____

出生地址或醫院 Address of birth or hospital	香港身分證號碼（如有者）Hong Kong identity card no. (if any)	（　）

父親姓名
Name of father

母親姓名
Name of mother

助產士姓名（如適用者）
Name of midwife (if applicable)

出生登記編號 Birth registration no.	登記日期 Date of registration	日 Day	月 Month	年 Year

其他資料
Additional information

申請人資料 Particulars of Applicant

申請人姓名
Name of applicant

香港身分證／旅行證件號碼 HK identity card/travel document no.	日間電話號碼 Daytime telephone no.

地址
Address

日期 Date	申請人簽署 Signature of applicant

☐ 請在適當方格內填上「✓」號 Tick as appropriate　　＊ 請將不適用者刪去 Delete where inapplicable

BDR 40 (1/98)

香港特別行政區政府
入境事務處
生死登記處

ᗑ

Births and Deaths Registry
Immigration Department
The Government of the Hong Kong
Special Administrative Region

翻查出生登記紀錄結果 Result of Birth Search	特定查冊 Particular Search ☐	一般查冊 General Search ☐

姓名 Name	性別 Sex	申請檔案號碼 Application reference no.

出生日期 Date of birth 日 Day 月 Month 年 Year	或查冊日期 or period for the search 由（日／月／年）From (Day/Month/Year) 至（日／月／年）To (Day/Month/Year)	B｜S｜— ... — ... （　）

☐ 出生登記編號 Birth registration no.　　　登記日期 Date of registration

☐ 有相似的醫院／留產所紀錄但出生未經登記
Similar hospital/midwife record found but birth not yet registered.

☐ 據查並無紀錄
No record found on information provided.

☐ 紀錄遺失 #
Record lost.#

日期 Date	生死登記官員 （代行）for Registrar of Births & Deaths

BDR 40 (1/98)

香 港 特 別 行 政 區 政 府
入 境 事 務 處
生 死 登 記 處
Births and Deaths Registry
Immigration Department
The Government of the Hong Kong Special Administrative Region
死 亡 登 記 紀 錄 內 記 項 的 核 證 副 本 申 請 書
Application for a certified true copy of an entry in the deaths registers
在填寫本表格前，請參看說明事項
Please read guidance notes before completing this form.

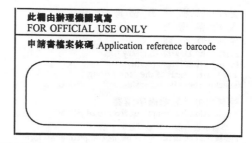

死者資料 Particulars of the Deceased

死亡登記編號 Death registration no.		登記日期 Date of registration	日 Day　月 Month　年 Year

姓 (英文) Surname

名 (英文) Other names in full

中文姓名 Name in Chinese	別名 (如有者) Alias (if any)	性別　男　　女 Sex　Male □　Female □

中文姓名電碼 (如適用者) C.C.C. number (if applicable)

死亡日期 Date of death	日 Day　月 Month　年 Year	香港身分證號碼 (如有者) Hong Kong identity card no. (if any)	( )

申請張數 Copies applied for	

申請人資料 Particulars of Applicant

申請人姓名 Name of applicant

香港身分證／旅行證件號碼 HK identity card/travel document no.	日間電話號碼 Daytime telephone no.

地址 Address

與死者關係 Relationship with the deceased

日期
Date _____

申請人簽署
Signature of applicant _____

確認 Acknowledgement

我，_____ ，已經查閱過死亡登記記項核證副本上的資料，並沒有需要修改的地方。
I, _____ , have checked and found the certified true copy(ies) of death entry in order.

簽署
Signed _____

(申請人)
(Applicant)

日期
Date _____

□ 請在適當方格內填上「√」號 Tick as appropriate

BDR 62 (4/98)

香港特別行政區政府
入境事務處
生死登記處
Births and Deaths Registry
Immigration Department
The Government of the Hong Kong
Special Administrative Region
翻查死亡登記紀錄申請書
Application for Search of Record of Death

在填寫本表格前，請參看說明事項。
Please read guidance notes before completing this form.

翻查資料 Search Information　☐ 特定查冊 Particular Search　☐ 一般查冊 General Search

姓（英文） Surname	
名（英文） Other names in full	

中文姓名　Name in Chinese ｜ 別名（如有者）Alias (if any) ｜ 性別 Sex　男 Male ☐　女 Female ☐

中文姓名電碼（如適用者）
C.C.C. number (if applicable)

（特定查冊者適用）For Particular Search
死亡日期　*西曆／農曆　（日／月／年）
Date of death *Gregorian/Lunar (Day/Month/Year)

香港身分證號碼（如有者）
Hong Kong identity card no. (if any)　（　）

（一般查冊者適用）For General Search
查冊年期　　由（日／月／年）　　　　　　　至（日／月／年）
Period for the search:　From (Day/Month/Year)＿＿＿　To (Day/Month/Year)＿＿＿

死亡地址或醫院　Address of death or hospital ｜ 死時年齡 Age at death ｜ 國籍 Nationality

死亡登記編號　Death registration no. ｜ 登記日期 Date of registration　日 Day　月 Month　年 Year

其他資料（例如：土葬／火葬紙編號）
Additional information (e.g. burial/cremation order no.)

申請人資料　Particulars of Applicant

申請人姓名
Name of applicant

香港身分證／旅行證件號碼　　　　　　　　　日間電話號碼
HK identity card/travel document no.　　　　Daytime telephone no.

地址
Address

日期　　　　　　　　　　申請人簽署
Date　　　　　　　　　　Signature of applicant

☐ 請在適當方格內填上「✓」號 Tick as appropriate　　　* 請將不適用者劃去 Delete where inapplicable

BDR 41 (1/98)

- -

香港特別行政區政府
入境事務處
生死登記處

Births and Deaths Registry
Immigration Department
The Government of the Hong Kong
Special Administrative Region

翻查死亡登記紀錄結果　**Result of Death Search**　☐ 特定查冊 Particular Search　☐ 一般查冊 General Search

姓名 Name ｜ 性別 Sex ｜ 申請檔案號碼 Application reference no.

死亡日期 Date of Death　日 Day 月 Month 年 Year ｜ 或查冊年期 or period for the search
由（日/月/年）＿＿　至（日/月/年）＿＿
From (Day / Month / Year)　To (Day / Month / Year) ｜ **D S** — ＿＿＿ — ＿＿（　）

☐ 死亡登記編號
Death registration no. ｜ 登記日期
Date of registration

☐ 據查並無紀錄
No record found on information provided.

☐ 紀錄遺失 #
Record lost.#　｜　日期
Date　｜　生死登記官員　（代行）
for Registrar Ol Births & Deaths

BDR 41 (1/98)

CHINA — MACAU

Gavineti dos Asuntos de Justiça
Secretario-Adjunto para a Administracao
Rua da Praia Grande, No. 26
Edificio B.C.M., 8,9,10
Andares, Macau, China

Church registers date from the colonial period, while vital registration in Macau began in 1887. The Office has birth records from 1890 and marriage, death, and church records from 1900 to the present. In May 1987 two separate departments were created: the Birth & Death Register, and the Marriage Register.

Cost for a certified Birth Certificate	MOP 20.00
Cost for a certified Marriage Certificate	MOP 35.00
Cost for a certified Death Certificate	MOP 35.00

For direct assistance with Chinese genealogical research contact:

Genealogical Research Center
Shanghai Library
1555 Huaihaizhong Road
Shanghai 200031, China

For additional assistance contact:

Director
Direccao de Servicos de Estatística e Censos
C.P. 3022
Seaview Gardens, Macau, China

CHINA — TAIWAN

Send your requests to:

Civil Registration Service
Department of Civil Affairs
Taipei City Government Offices
39 Chang An West Road
Taipei, Taiwan
Republic of China

Tel. (011) (886) (2) 383-2741

China uses a household registration system to record and identify each person in China. China has kept famiy registers for the past 4,000 years. Currently this is handled by the local registration office and is considered to be comprehensive.

Cost for a certified Birth Certificate	NT$10.00
Cost for a certified Marriage Certificate	NT$10.00
Cost for a certified Death Certificate	NT$10.00
Cost for a certified Household Registration	NT$10.00

For direct assistance with Chinese genealogical research contact:

Genealogical Research Center
Shanghai Library
1555 Huaihaizhong Road
Shanghai 200031, China

For additional assistance contact:

National Central Library
20 Chungshan South Road
Taipei, Taiwan
Republic of China

Tel. (011) (886) (2) 361-9132

The Family History Library of Salt Lake City, Utah has microfilmed original and published Chinese family records.

For further information see:

Loi Sur l'État-Civil Promulguée le 12 décembre 1931, entrée en Vigueur le 1 juillet 1934. Texte Chinois et Traduction Française. Tientsin, China: Hautes Études, 1934. 34p.

戶 001

80. 4. 4,000本

出生登記申請書

本冊申請書
之順序號數

戶號

欄位	內容

出生者 姓名　統一號碼

生　胎次　第　胎　胎別

出生地點　省市　縣市　鄉鎮區市　村里

出生別　（　）男1　（　）女2
遠腹子1　接生身分3　非婚生已認領3　非婚生未認領4　養兒5　出生身分　同胎次多3　雙2　單1
醫院診所1　助產士院2　自宅3　其他4
出生日期　民國　年　月　日　出生時重　公克　出生別　同生本籍2　同生本籍1　其他　懷胎週數　週

生父　姓名　統一號碼　本籍　省市　縣市　鄉鎮區市　村里
行業　職業　出生日期　民國　年　月　日　教育程度

生母　姓名　統一號碼　本籍　省市　縣市　鄉鎮區市　村里　同申請人住址　不同而是
行業　職業　出生日期　民國　年　月　日　教育程度

生父母結婚（同居）日期　民國　年　月　日

戶長姓名及其關係　戶長之關係

記事

附繳證件　出生證明書　出生（接生）調查證明　出生　其他

申請人與出生者之關係　出生者之

申請日期　民國　年　月　日
申請人住址　台北市　區　里　鄰　路街　段　巷　弄　號　樓之

申請人　承辦人

戶籍登記簿　民國　年　月　日登記
戶口查察簿　民國　年　月　日登理遷並村里收件
戶口卡片　民國　年　月　日註記

主任

填寫說明：1. 出生別、出生日期、出生時重、填胎週數、出生證重、出生地點、生父母結婚日期及申請日期各欄應使用阿拉伯數字清晰填寫；戶號及統一號碼一號一碼兩欄婚使用英文大寫字母
　　及阿拉伯數字填寫。
　　2. 出生別、胎別、胎次、同胎次多寡、出生身分、設定本籍、接生者身分、本籍及附繳證件各欄註在適當項「□」內以「√」選擇之，或加填適當文字。
　　3. 教育程度、行業、職業等欄請依實際情形填寫，至其填寫方法可參照背面所示小欄註由戶政事務所承人填註其代號。

戶 002

本頁申請書
之順序編號

死亡登記申請書
死亡宣告

役別			死 亡 或 死 亡 宣 告 書			
	戶號					
	姓名		統一號碼		出生別 □男 1 ( )女 2	婚姻狀況 □	配偶 未婚 □1 有配偶 □2 喪偶 □3 離婚 □4	配偶姓名
	出生日期	民前 民國 年 月 日			死亡或推定死亡地點	醫院 診所 □1 自宅 □2 其他 □3
	教育程度		死亡或推定死亡日期	行業 職業 年 月 日	死亡原因 (直接原因) (死亡原因)	
				藏業 鄰 里 村		
			戶長姓名			
死 亡 宣 告 書	本籍	□同申請人住址 不同 而是	省 市 縣 市	鄉鎮 區市 村 里	路 街	鄰 段 巷 弄	附繳證件 □死亡診斷書 □死亡宣告裁判書 □軍方死亡通報文件 □見證相驗書 □死亡事實證明書 □其他
	戶籍所在地址	□同申請人住址 不同 而是	台北市 區	里	段	就 樣之
	記事					
	申請日期	民國 年 月 日	申請人與死亡者之關係	死亡者之	戶籍登記簿 戶口查察簿 戶口卡片	本人住址
	申請人住址	省 市 縣 市 ( )	鄉鎮 區市 ( )	村 里 ( )	鄰 路 街	段 巷 弄	就 樣之
					申請人	(簽章)
	主任			承辦人	事核	戶籍登記 民國 年 月 日 登記 村里收件 年 月 日 註記	校對 審查 年 月 日 登記

78. 8. 1,200本

填寫說明：1.出生日期、死亡日期及申請日期各欄均應使用阿拉伯數字清晰地填寫；戶號及統一號碼兩欄應使用英文大寫字母及阿拉伯數字填寫。
　　　　　2.出生別、婚姻狀況、死亡地點、本籍及附繳證件各欄請在所在「□」內以「✓」選擇之，或加填適當文字。
　　　　　3.教育程度、行業及死亡原因等欄請按實際情形填寫，至其後面兩小欄則由戶政事務所之承辦人標註代號。
　　　　　4.死亡宣告登記應在記事欄內填寫經法院裁判之時間及文號。

結婚登記申請書

戶 003

本件申請書之順序編號

81. 9. 1,500本

夫妻現別	原戶號				

結婚當事人

夫

姓名	統一號碼		出生日期	民國 年 月 日	出生別 ( )男
教育程度	行業				
婚前婚後狀況	未婚1 夫偶2 離婚3 重婚4	婚前住址	□同申請人住址 □不同兩者→	省市 縣市 鄉鎮市區 村里 路街 段 巷 弄 號	
生父姓名		婚後住址	□同申請人住址 □不同兩者→	省市 縣市 鄉鎮市區 村里 路街 段 巷 弄 號	
生母姓名	原配偶姓名				

女

姓名	統一號碼		出生日期	民國 年 月 日	出生別 ( )女
教育程度	行業				
婚前婚後狀況	未婚1 夫偶2 離婚3 重婚4	婚前住址	□同申請人住址 □不同兩者→	省市 縣市 鄉鎮市區 村里 路街 段 巷 弄 號	
生父姓名		婚後住址	□同申請人住址 □不同兩者→	省市 縣市 鄉鎮市區 村里 路街 段 巷 弄 號	
生母姓名	原配偶姓名				

結婚日期	民國 年 月 日		結婚儀式 及舉行地點	1.約定事項：□冠夫（妻）姓 □不冠夫（妻）姓			
夫之原戶長及其關係	姓名 省市 縣市 鄉鎮市區 ( )村里 ( )	與本籍戶長 姓名 關係		結婚儀式 自宅1 飯店2 教堂3 法院4 其他5			
妻之原戶 長及其關 係	姓名 省市 縣市 鄉鎮市區 ( )村里 ( )	與戶長之 關係	證人 姓名 1. 2.	婚姻類別 □普通 婚姻1 □招贅 婚姻2	附 繳證件	□結婚證書 □軍人結婚報告表 □其他	

申請日期	民國 年 月 日				
申請人 住址	省市 縣市 ( )村里 ( ) 路街 段 巷 弄 號			(簽章)	

主任		承辦人	書橫	戶籍登記簿 戶口查察簿 戶口卡片	民國 年 月 日 日登記 民國 年 月 日登理訖 民國 年 月 日註記	村里收件

填寫說明：1.出生日期、結婚日期及申請日期各欄應使用阿拉伯數字清晰地填寫；戶籍及戶籍登記字號一號及阿拉伯數字母填寫。

2.婚前婚後狀況、婚前及婚後住址、婚前及婚後行地點、結婚儀式舉行住址、約定事項及附繳證件各欄請在適當項目"□"內以"∨"選擇之，或加填適當文字。

3.教育程度、行業、職業等各欄請按實際情形填寫，至其後兩小欄則由戶政事務所人員註記代號。

役別

離婚登記申請書

本冊申請書之順序編號

戶號

夫

	統一號碼	姓名	出生日期 民國 年 月 日	出生別 ( ) 男
教育程度		職業 行業	原配偶姓名及存歿欄
生父姓名			稱 路 街 段 巷 弄 號
生母姓名			稱 路 街 段 巷 弄 號

離婚前住址 □同申請人住址 □不同而是→ 省市 縣市 鄉鎮區市 村里

離婚後住址 □同離婚前住址 □不同而是→ 省市 縣市 鄉鎮區市 村里

妻

	統一號碼	姓名	出生日期 民國 年 月 日	出生別 ( ) 男
教育程度		職業 行業	原配偶姓名及存歿欄
生父姓名			稱 路 街 段 巷 弄 號
生母姓名			稱 路 街 段 巷 弄 號

離婚前住址 □同申請人住址 □不同而是→ 省市 縣市 鄉鎮區市 村里

離婚後住址 □同離婚前住址 □不同而是→ 省市 縣市 鄉鎮區市 村里

離婚當事人

結婚日期	民國 年 月 日
離婚日期	民國 年 月 日
本次婚姻生育子女數	男 女
離婚種類	協議 判決
戶長姓名	
附繳證件	□離婚協議書 □法院判決書及判決確定證明書 □其他

記事：□1.由夫監護之子女姓名：□2.由妻監護之子女姓名：

| 申請人 | 姓名 | 申請日期 民國 年 月 日 | |
| | □3.撤冠夫(妻)姓 □4.其他 | | |

申請人住址 省市 縣市 ( ) 鄉鎮區市 村里 ( ) 路街 段 巷 弄 號

戶籍登記簿			日登記
戶口查察簿			日整理訖
戶口卡片			日註冊

| 主任 | 審核 | 承辦人 | 村里收件 號 |

填寫說明：1.出生日期：結婚日期、出生別、生育子女數、離婚日期等欄應使用阿拉伯數字清晰地填寫；戶號及統一號碼二號兩欄應使用英大寫及阿拉伯數字填寫。
2.離婚前(後)本籍、離婚前(後)住址、附繳證件及記事各欄請在適合欄內以"✓"選擇之，或加填適當文字。
3.教育程度、行業、職業等欄請查對資料詳盡情形填寫，至其後面兩小欄附由戶政事務所承人標註代號。

戶籍謄本登記簿閱覽申請書

申請日期：民國　年　月　日

申請人（受託人）姓名住址	姓名　　　　簽章　　縣市　鄉鎮市區　里村　鄰　街路　段　巷　弄　號　樓之
被申請者姓名住址	姓名　　　　縣市　鄉鎮市區　里村　鄰　街路　段　巷　弄　號　樓之　等　名
戶長	□同申請人住址　□不同而是↓　里村　鄰　街路　段　巷　弄　號　樓之　等　名
申請種類	□現行戶籍謄本　□民國　年除戶謄本　□閱覽戶籍登記簿　□據時期調查簿謄本
申請份數	□全部謄本　　份　□部分謄本　　份　合計張數（由本所填寫）　　張
委託申請	委託人：　地址：　身分證統一號碼：　蓋章：
附繳證件	
備註	
規費	新台幣　百　拾　元
收據號碼	
發文字號	年　月　日辦理登記
核審	
複印或抄錄	
受理	
主任	

81.10.8,000本

說明：

一、被申請者姓名住址、申請種類及申請份數各欄，請在適當項目「□」內劃「✓」號，或加填適當文字。

二、附繳證明文件欄，請領本人之謄本者免填。委託申請欄，親自申請者免填。

三、合計張數、發文字號、規費及收據號碼等欄由戶政事務所人員填寫。

四、如辦理籍別、出生、認領、收養、結婚、離婚、死亡、遷入、變更、更正或撤銷登記後，即時申請戶籍謄本時，應在申請書備註欄註明其登記類別及日期。

COLOMBIA

Send your requests to:

Superintendente de Notariado y Registro Civil
Ministerio de Justicia
Calle 26 #13-49, Int 201
Santa Fe de Bogota, DC, Colombia

http://www.minijusticia.gov.co

Church registers date from the 1500s, vital records from June 3, 1852. Current vital registration is considered to be 75 percent complete for births and 65 percent complete for deaths.

Cost for a certified Birth Certificate	$20.00
Cost for a certified Marriage Certificate	$20.00
Cost for a certified Death Certificate	$20.00

Send your requests for Adoption Records to:

Colombian Family Welfare Institute (ICBF)
Bienestar Familiar
Grupo Nacional De Adopciones
Apartado Aereo 18116; Santa Fe de Bogota, DC, Colombia

Tel. (011) (57) (1) 231-4558

For additional assistance contact:

Embassy of Colombia
2118 Leroy Place, NW
Washington, DC 20008

Tel. (202) 387-8338

For further information see:

Angarita Gomez, Jorge. *Estado Civil y Nombre de la Persona Natural*. Medellin, Colombia: Libreria Juridica Sanchez, 1995. 389p.

Bastidas Villota, Antonio. *Cartilla del Registador Municipal, Suplemento a la Compilación Electoral de 1949. Aplicacion Practicá de Legislacion sobre Cedula de Cuidadania*. Bogota, Colombia: Impr. Nacional, 1949. 46p.

Buelvas Acosta, Pedro. *Registro de Instumentos Publicos, Indice Tematico, Disposiciones Afines, Complementarias.* Bogota, Colombia: Colegio de Registradores de Instrumentos Publicos de Colombia, 1988. 177p.

Colombia. Departamento de Justicia. *Registro del Estado Civil de las Personas, Instrucciones a los Notarios, Alcaldes, Corregidores o Inspectores de Policía y Cónsules de Colombia en el Exterior sobre el Modo de Llevarlo*. Bogota, Colombia: Imprenta Nacional, 1940. 115p.

Diagnostico del Registro Civil Latinoamericano, enero de 1980. Montevideo, Uruguay: UN Fund for Population Activities, 1982. 142p.

Infolios. Bogota, Colombia: Superintendencia de Notariado y Registro, 1978– .

Manual para el Diligenciamiento del Nuevo Folio De Registro de Defunción. Bogota, Colombia: Superintendencia de Notariado y Registro, 1988. 61p.

Martinez Pardo, Hector. *Registro del Estado Civil de las Personas, Teoria y Practica.* Bogota, Colombia: Juridicas Wilches, 1987. 268p.

Notariado y Registro, Legislacion y Doctrina sobre Notariado. Bogota, Colombia: Editorial Temis, 1960. 289p.

Registro del Estado Civil de las Personas, Instrucciones a los Notarios, Alcaldes, Corregidores o Inspectores de Policia y Consules de Colombia en el Exterior sobre el Modo de Llevarlo. Bogota, Colombia: Imprenta Nacional, 1940.

Report on the First Latin American Training Centre on Statistics and Censuses Held at Mexico City from 2 September to 10 December 1948 by the Food and Agriculture Organization of the UN and the Government of the United States of Mexico with the Cooperation of the Statistical Office of the UN and the InterAmerican Statistical Institute. Lake Success, NY: Statistical Office of the UN, 1948. 33p.

Zuluaga Gil, Francisco. *Death Registration and Mortality Statistics in Colombia*. IIVRS Technical Papers, No. 54. Bethesda, MD: International Institute for Vital Registration and Statistics, 1993. 12p.

ANEXO Nº 2

PRIMER APELLIDO

SEGUNDO APELLIDO

NOMBRES

DANE

REPUBLICA DE COLOMBIA
REGISTRO CIVIL
SERVICIO NACIONAL DE INSCRIPCION

INDICE ALFABETICO

IDENTIFICACION Nº

CLASE DE REGISTRO	INDICATIVO SERIAL
NACIMIENTO	
MATRIMONIO	
DEFUNCION	
VARIOS	

CONTINUA AL RESPALDO

OHS

RESPALDO

CLASE DE REGISTRO	INDICATIVO SERIAL

COMOROS

Send your requests to:

Registrar General
Moroni, Comoros

Previously under French control, Comoros became independent in 1975. Its official language is Arabic. Vital registration in Comoros is not considered to be comprehensive.

Cost for a certified Birth Certificate	200F CFA
Cost for a certified Marriage Certificate	200F CFA
Cost for a certified Death Certificate	200F CFA

For additional assistance contact:

Directeur   Tel. (011) (269) (73) 2277
Ministry of Public Health
B.P. 42
Moroni, Comoros

Centre National de Documentation et de Recherche Scientifique
B. P. 169
Moroni, Comoros

Mission of Comoros   Tel. (212) 972-8010
336 East 45th Street
New York, NY 10017

For further information see:

Methods and Problems of Civil Registration Practices and Vital Statistics Collection in Africa. IIVRS Technical Papers, No. 16. Bethesda, MD: International Institute for Vital Registration and Statistics, 1981. 27p.

Organization and Status of Civil Registration in Africa and Recommendations for Improvement. IIVRS Technical Papers, No. 31. Bethesda, MD: International Institute for Vital Registration and Statistics, 1988. 15p.

CONGO

Send your requests to:

Directeur Nationale de l'État Civil
Ministère de l'Intérieur
B.P. 880
Brazzaville, Congo

Vital registration began in 1922 for all residents of the Congo. The registration is not considered to be comprehensive.

Cost for a certified Birth Certificate	60F CFA
Cost for a certified Marriage Certificate	60F CFA
Cost for a certified Death Certificate	60F CFA

For additional assistance contact:

Directeur
Statistiques Demographiques et Sociales
Centre National de la Statistique et des Études Économiques
B.P. 2031
Brazzaville, Congo

Service des Archives Nationales
Ministère de la Culture et des Arts, du Patrimoine National Chargé
    du Tourisme et de l'Environnement
Direction du Livre, des Bibliothèques d'Archives et de Documentation
B.P. 1489
Brazzaville, Congo

Embassy of Congo   Tel. (202) 726-5500
4891 Colorado Avenue, NW
Washington, DC 20011

For further information see:

Methods and Problems of Civil Registration Practices and Vital Statistics Collection in Africa. IIVRS Technical Papers, No. 16. Bethesda, MD: International Institute for Vital Registration and Statistics, 1981. 27p.

Organization and Status of Civil Registration in Africa and Recommendations for Improvement. IIVRS Technical Papers, No. 31. Bethesda, MD: International Institute for Vital Registration and Statistics, 1988. 15p.

Some Observations on Civil Registration in French-Speaking Africa. IIVRS Technical Papers, No. 39. Bethesda, MD: International Institute for Vital Registration and Statistics, 1990. 13p.

DEMOCRATIC REPUBLIC OF CONGO (former Zaire)

Send your requests to:

État Zairois
Ministere de l'Administration du Territoire
Kinshasa, Democratic Republic of Congo

Vital registration in the Democratic Republic of Congo, formerly Zaire, began in 1958. Currently the registration is not considered to be comprehensive.

Cost for a certified Birth Certificate	Free
Cost for a certified Marriage Certificate	Free
Cost for a certified Death Certificate	Free

For additional assistance contact:

Directeur
Institut National de la Statistique
B.P. 20
Kinshasa, Democratic Republic of Congo

Embassy of the Democratic Republic of Congo   Tel. (202) 234-7690
1800 New Hampshire Avenue, NW
Washington, DC 20009

For further information see:

Methods and Problems of Civil Registration Practices and Vital Statistics Collection in Africa. IIVRS Technical Papers, No. 16. Bethesda, MD: International Institute for Vital Registration and Statistics, 1981. 27p.

Organization and Status of Civil Registration in Africa and Recommendations for Improvement. IIVRS Technical Papers, No. 31. Bethesda, MD: International Institute for Vital Registration and Statistics, 1988. 15p.

Some Observations on Civil Registration in French-Speaking Africa. IIVRS Technical Papers, No. 39. Bethesda, MD: International Institute for Vital Registration and Statistics, 1990. 13p.

COSTA RICA

Send your requests to:

Dirección de Registro Civil y Notariado
Tribunal Supremo de Elecciones
AP 10218-1000
San José, Costa Rica

Tel. (011) (506) 287-5451; (011) (506) 287-5452
Fax (011) (506) 287-5559
http://www.tse.go.cr/

Church registers date from 1594, while modern vital registration began in the 1880s and is currently considered to be comprehensive. The *Registro del Estado Civil* was estabished December 1, 1881 and was later divided into four sections: Births, Marriages, Deaths, and Citizenship. In 1888 the office became a part of the Postal Service (*Administración General de Correos*) and on December 9, 1949 it became a part of the *Tribunal Supremo de Elecciones*. It now has twenty-eight regional offices. Costa Rica began issuing identity cards in 1937. In 1946 these cards were issued by the *Registro Electoral* (Registrar of Voters). This system was expanded April 7, 1949. Personal identification numbers were added beginning October 25, 1956. Computerized identity cards have been issued since 1960. Adoptions are finalized by local Family Court judges and the final decrees are registered with the local *Registro Civil*. Amended birth certificates are issued.

Cost for a certified Birth Certificate	Colon 15.50
Cost for a certified Marriage Certificate	Colon 15.50
Cost for a certified Divorce Record	Colon 15.50
Cost for a certified Death Certificate	Colon 15.50

Send your requests for Adoption and Divorce Records to:

Oficina de Actos Jurídicos
Registro Civil
Tribunal Supremo de Elecciones
San José, Costa Rica

Tel. (011) (506) 287-5467

For additional assistance contact:

Patronato Nacional de La Infancia (PANI)
P.O. Box 5000
San Jose, Costa Rica

Embassy of Costa Rica
2114 S Street, NW
Washington, DC 20008

Tel. (202) 234-2945

For further information see:

Palacios Echevarria, Ivan. *Derecho Notarial y Registral de Costa Rica*. 4th ed. 1990. 2 vols.

Report on the First Latin American Training Centre on Statistics and Censuses Held at Mexico City from 2 September to 10 December 1948 by the Food and Agriculture Organization of the UN and the Government of the United States of Mexico with the Cooperation of the Statistical Office of the UN and the InterAmerican Statistical Institute. Lake Success, NY: Statistical Office of the UN, 1948. 33p.

Salas Marrero, Oscar. *Teorica y Critica del Registro Publico en Costa Rica*. Ciudad Universitario, 1969. 82p.

Salazar Gamboa, Carlos E. *El Registro Publico de Costa Rica, Su Organizacion y Procedimiento Interno*. San Jose, Costa Rica: Registro Publico de Costa Rica, 1973. 158p.

Send your requests to:

Civil Registration Office
(Town), Croatia

This country has no central office for vital records. To obtain copies of birth, marriage, and death certificates write to the Civil Registration District Office in the town where the event occurred. Vital records are on file from 1946. Records before that were kept by the local churches.

Cost for a certified Birth Certificate	Price Varies
Cost for a certified Marriage Certificate	Price Varies
Cost for a certified Death Certificate	Price Varies

For additional assistance contact:

Director
Central Bureau of Statistics
Il ica 3
410000 Zagreb, Croatia

Ministry of Public Administration
Savska Cesta 41
41000 Zagreb, Croatia

Tel. (011) (385) (1) 53-7622
Fax (011) (385) (1) 53-6321

Croatian Archival Society
Marulićev trg 21
10000 Zagreb, Croatia

Tel. (011) (385) (1) 48-01-930
Fax (011) (385) (1) 48-29-000

Embassy of Croatia
2343 Massachusetts Avenue, NW
Washington, DC 20008

Tel. (202) 588-5899

The Family History Library of Salt Lake City, Utah has microfilmed original and published records of the former Yugoslavia and the region. For further details on their holdings please consult your nearest Family History Center.

CUBA

Send your requests to:

Director Registros y Notarias
Registro Civil
Ministerio de Justicia
13 Calle: O No. 216
3/23 y 25, Vedado
Havana, Cuba

While church registers date from the 1500s, modern vital registration in Cuba didn't begin until 1885. Vital registration currently is compulsory and is considered to be comprehensive.

Cost for a certified Birth Certificate	15c
Cost for a certified Marriage Certificate	15c
Cost for a certified Death Certificate	15c

For additional assistance contact:

US/Cuba Interest Section
315 Lexington Avenue and 38th Street
New York, NY 10016

Tel. (212) 689-7215

Archivo Nacional
Calle Compostela N° 906 esq.
San Isidro, Habana Vieja
10100 Havana, Cuba

The Family History Library of Salt Lake City, Utah has microfilmed original and published vital records and church registers of Cuba.

For further information see:

Ley de las Notarias Estatales, Reglamento de la Ley de las Notarias Estatales, Ley del Registro del Estado Civil, Reglamento de la Ley del Registro del Estado Civil. Havana, Cuba: Ministry of Justice, 1986. 177p.

Ley del Registro Civil y Reglamento para su Ejecución, concordados con la Constitución Cubana y Organica del Servicio Diplomatico y Consular, Ordenes del Govierno Militar y Disposiciones que han Modificado o Aclarado Algunos de sus Preceptos. Havana, Cuba: Impr. De Rambla y Bouza, 1903. 90p.

Treinta Años en el Registro Civil. Havana, Cuba: Editorial Selecta, 1991. 992p.

Report on the First Latin American Training Centre on Statistics and Censuses Held at Mexico City from 2 September to 10 December 1948 by the Food and Agriculture Organization of the UN and the Government of the United States of Mexico with the Cooperation of the Statistical Office of the UN and the InterAmerican Statistical Institute. Lake Success, NY: Statistical Office of the UN, 1948. 33p.

Send your requests to:

Registrar
District Office
(Town), Cyprus

Civil registration began in Cyprus in 1895 for births and deaths, and in 1923 for marriages. Current registration is considered to be 85 percent complete for births and 45 percent complete for deaths.

Cost for a certified Birth Certificate	Price Varies
Cost for a certified Marriage Certificate	Price Varies
Cost for a certified Death Certificate	Price Varies

Registration Officer
Registration Service
Ministry of the Interior
Nicosia, Cyprus

For additional assistance contact:

Director
Department of Statistics and Research
Ministry of Finance
Byron Avenue 13
162 Nicosia, Cyprus

State Archives
Ministry of Justice and Public Order
1461 Nicosia, Cyprus

Severios Bibliotheki
(National Library Service)
P.O. Box 34
Nicosia, Cyprus

Embassy of Cyprus   Tel. (202) 462-5772
2211 R Street, NW
Washington, DC 20008

CZECH REPUBLIC

Send your requests to:

Ministry of the Interior
Archivni Sprava
Tridadr. Milady Horákové 133
166 21 Prague, Czech Republic

Civilne Spravni Usek
Odbor Statniho Obcanstvi
U Obecniho domu 3
110 00 Prague 1, Czech Republic

The Czech Republic and Slovakia were created in January 1993. The Archives charges an hourly fee. Church records are available in the Czech Republic and Slovakia from 1785, but modern civil registration did not begin until 1919.

Cost for a certified Birth Certificate	$15
Cost for a certified Marriage Certificate	$15
Cost for a certified Death Certificate	$15

Send your requests for Adoption Records to:

Department of Youth (Where the Child Resided)
(Town), Czech Republic

Ministerstvo Spravedinosti CR
Wysehradska 16
128 00 Prague 2, Czech Republic

For additional assistance contact:

Census & Population Statistics Division
Czech Statistical Office
Sokolovska 142
186 13 Prague 8, Czech Republic

Embassy of the Czech Republic
3900 Spring of Freedom Street, NW
Washington, DC 20008

Tel: (202) 274-9100
Fax (202) 966 8540

Lutheran Pastor
(Town), Denmark

You can obtain copies of birth, marriage, and death certificates by writing to the local Lutheran pastor. Church registers are on file from the 1600s. Divorce records are kept in the County Archives (Amtsarkiver). Vital records more than 30 years old are kept at the respective Provincial Archives.

The Danish government created the system of local municipal registers in 1924 and required the local Lutheran pastors to file copies of vital records with the registrars. In 1968 with the passage of the National Registration Act, each person in Denmark received a personal identification number and identity card. The system is now completely computerized and can be searched by the local registrars. Information is kept on all persons who have lived in Denmark since 1968, citizens, permanent resident aliens, and Danish citizens who are living outside of Denmark. Genealogists should note that each registration includes the names of the individual's parents, thus extending the reach of the register back 100 years. All births, adoptions, marriages, divorces, changes of name, and deaths are centralized in the national register. There are currently 8 million entries in the system.

Cost for a certified Birth Certificate	Dkr. 256.60
Cost for a certified Marriage Certificate	Dkr. 256.60
Cost for a certified Divorce Record	Dkr. 256.60
Cost for a certified Death Certificate	Dkr. 256.60

Send your requests for Adoption Records to:

Civilretsdirektoratet
Æbeløgade1
DK 2100, København Ø, Denmark

Adoption records are closed for 80 years.

For additional assistance contact:

Central Office of Civil Registration
Ministry of the Interior
Datavej 20
P.O. Box 269
3460 Birkerød, Denmark

Tel. (011) (45) 82 72 00
Fax (011) (45) 93 03 07
E-mail: cpr@cpr.dk

Royal Danish Embassy
3200 Whitehaven Street, NW
Washington, DC 20008

Tel. (202) 234-4300

The Family History Library of Salt Lake City, Utah has microfilmed many of the original and published vital records and church registers of Denmark. For further details on their holdings please consult your nearest Family History Center.

For further information see:

The Civil Registration System in Denmark. IIVRS Technical Papers, No. 66. Bethesda, MD: International Institute for Vital Registration and Statistics, 1996. 10p.

DEN DANSKE FOLKEKIRKE   Personnr. _____

FØDSELS- og DÅBSATTEST
for

Efternavn: _____

For- og mellemnavne: _____

Registreringssted for fødslen (sogn og kommune):	
Fødselsår og -dag:	
Kirken, hvori dåben eller fremstillingen efter hjemmedåb har fundet sted:	
Dåbsår og -dag samt – ved fremstilling efter hjemmedåb – år og dag for fremstillingen:	
Forældrenes eller adoptiv-forældrenes fulde navne:	
Anmærkning angående optagelse i eller udtrædelse af folkekirken:	

Overensstemmelsen med ministerialbogen bevidnes

_____
Sted og dato

_____

Embedsstempel

Ki 22 (1-1-1988)

DEN DANSKE FOLKEKIRKE

VIELSESATTEST

Vielsesår og -dag	Vielsessted

KVINDEN

Efternavn

Eget efternavn

For- og mellemnavne

Registreringssted for fødslen (sogn og kommune)

Personnummer el. fødselsår og -dag

Anvender eget efternavn som mellemnavn foran giftenavn

Nej ☐   Ja ☐

MANDEN

Efternavn

Eget efternavn

For- og mellemnavne

Registreringssted for fødslen (sogn og kommune)

Personnummer el. fødselsår og -dag

Anvender eget efternavn som mellemnavn foran giftenavn

Nej ☐   Ja ☐

Overensstemmelsen med ministerialbogen bevidnes

_____
Sted og dato

_____
Embedsstempel

Ki 26 (1-1-1988)

DEN DANSKE FOLKEKIRKE

DØDS- og BEGRAVELSESATTEST

Efternavn:	
Eget efternavn:	
For- og mellemnavne:	
Registreringssted for fødslen (sogn og kommune):	
Personnummer eller fødselsår og -dag:	

Registreringssted for døds- faldet (sogn og kommune):	
Dødsår og -dag:	
År og dag for jordpåkastelsen:	
Begravelsesstedet:	

Efterlevende eller tidligere afdøde ægtefælles fulde navn:	
Ægtefællens personnummer eller fødselsår og -dag:	

Overensstemmelsen med ministerialbogen bevidnes

_____
Sted og dato

Embedsstempel

K. 28 (1-1-1988)

DJIBOUTI

Send your requests to:

Direction de la Population
Ministère de l'Intérieur et de la Decentralisation
Postes et Telecommunications
B.P. 3911
Djibouti, Djibouti

Formerly known as French Somalia and later as the French Territory of the Affars and the Issas, Djibouti became independent in 1977. Vital registration in Djibouti is not considered to be comprehensive.

Cost for a certified Birth Certificate	90FD
Cost for a certified Marriage Certificate	90FD
Cost for a certified Death Certificate	90FD

For additional assistance contact:

Direction Nationale de la Statistique
Ministre de l'Economie et du Commerce
B.P. 1846
Djibouti, Djibouti

Institut Supérieur d'Études et de Recherches Scientifiques et Techniques (ISERST)
B.P. 486
Djibouti, Djibouti

Embassy of Djibouti   Tel. (202) 331-0270
1156 15th Street, NW, Suite 515
Washington, DC 20005

For further information see:

Methods and Problems of Civil Registration Practices and Vital Statistics Collection in Africa. IIVRS Technical Papers, No. 16. Bethesda, MD: International Institute for Vital Registration and Statistics, 1981. 27p.

Organization and Status of Civil Registration in Africa and Recommendations for Improvement. IIVRS Technical Papers, No. 31. Bethesda, MD: International Institute for Vital Registration and Statistics, 1988. 15p.

DOMINICA

Send your requests to:

Registrar General
Registrar General's Office   Tel. (767) 448-2401
Supreme Court
Bay Front
P.O. Box 304
Rouseau, Commonwealth of Dominica
West Indies

This former British colony became independent in 1978. The Registrar General has records from April 2, 1861. The local churches also have their own records. The Registry was burned by a fire in June 1979, resulting in the destruction of many records. The current vital registration is considered to be comprehensive.

Cost for a certified Birth Certificate	US $2.00
Cost for a certified Marriage Certificate	US $3.00
Cost for a certified Death Certificate	US $2.00

Send your requests for Adoption Records to:

Supreme Court of the Windward and Leeward Islands
Bay Front
P.O. Box 304
Rouseau, Commonwealth of Dominica
West Indies

For additional assistance contact:

Public Library of Dominica
National Documentation Centre
Victoria Street
Roseau, Commonwealth of Dominica
West Indies

For further information see:

Registration of Vital Events in the English-Speaking Caribbean. IIVRS Technical Papers, No. 32. Bethesda, MD: International Institute for Vital Registration and Statistics, 1988. 10p.

REQUEST FOR BIRTH CERTIFICATE

To the Registrar General

Please issue_____ copy/copies of
the Birth Certificate of _____

Date of Birth _____

Place of Birth _____

Name of Mother _____

The amount of $_____ is enclosed.

Please issue the Certificate(s) to _____

or someone with written authority from me.

Signature _____

Name _____

Address _____

Tel. No. _____

Date _____

NOTE: The Registrar General accepts no liability if the particulars of
birth are not accurately entered in the Register of Births.

Received by:_____   Date:_____
        REGISTRAR GENERAL

CCertificate(s) received by_____
Delivered by _____
Date _____

ZREMARKS
(for Official use only)

REQUEST FOR MARRIAGE CERTIFICATE

To The Registrar of Marriages

Please issue _____ copy/copies of the

Marriage Certificate of _____ and

_____

Date of Marriage _____

Place of Marriage _____

The amount of $_____ is enclosed.

Please issue the Certificate(s) to _____

or someone with written authority from me.

Signature _____

Name _____

Address _____

Telephone No. _____

Date _____

NOTE: The Registrar of Marriages accept no liability if the

particulars of the Marriage are not properly entered.

Received by _____   Date _____
           REGISTRAR OF MARRIAGES

Certificate(s) received by _____

Delivered by _____

Date _____

REMARKS

(for Official use only)

REQUEST FOR DEATH CERTIFICATE

To the Registrar General

Please issue _____ copy/copies of

Death Certificate of _____

Date of Death _____

Place of Death _____

The amount of $_____ is enclosed.

Please issue the Certificate(s) to _____

or someone with written authority from me.

Signature _____

Name _____

Address _____

Telephone NO. _____

Date _____

NOTE: The Registrar General accepts no liability if the

particulars of death are not accurately entered.

Received by

_____   Date _____

REGISRAR GENERAL

Certificate(s) received by _____

Delivered by _____

Date _____

REMARKS

(for official use only)

DOMINICAN REPUBLIC

Send your requests to:

Sección de Actas del Estado Civil
Junta Central Electoral
Avenida Luperon
Santo Domingo, Dominican Republic

Send your requests for records before 1930 to:

Archivo General de la Nación
Cesar Nicolas Penson 91
Plaza de la Cultura
Santo Domingo, Dominican Republic

Church registers date from the 1500s, and vital registration began January 1, 1828. It is not considered to be comprehensive. The Dominican Republic became independent in 1844.

Cost for a certified Birth Certificate	RD$.50
Cost for a certified Marriage Certificate	RD$.50
Cost for a certified Death Certificate	RD$.50

Send your requests for Adoption Records to:

Secretaria de Estado de Salud Publica y Asistencia Social   Tel. (809) 565-3218
Avenida San Cristobal esq. Avenida Tiradentes
Ensanche La Fe
Santo Domingo, Dominican Republic

Adoptions are finalized by the local District Court and the decree is registered with both the local and national Registro Civil.

For additional assistance contact:

Embassy and Consulate of the Dominican Republic   Tel. (202) 332-6280
1715 22nd Street, NW
Washington, DC 20008

For further information see:

Diagnostico del Registro Civil Latinoamericano, enero de 1980. Montevideo, Uruguay: UN Fund for Population Activities, 1982. 142p.

Report on the First Latin American Training Centre on Statistics and Censuses Held at Mexico City from 2 September to 10 December 1948 by the Food and Agriculture Organization of the UN and the Government of the United States of Mexico with the Cooperation of the Statistical Office of the UN and the InterAmerican Statistical Institute. Lake Success, NY: Statistical Office of the UN, 1948. 33p.

Symposium sobre Registro Civil, Realizado en Santo Domingo, Republica Dominicana, en Abril de 1967. Montevideo, 1968. 45p.

ECUADOR

Send your requests to:

Director General de Registro Civil, Identificación y Cedulación
Ministerio de Gobierno
Av. Amazonas 743 y Veintimilla
Ed. Espinosa, 3er Piso
Quito, Ecuador

Send your requests for earlier records to:

Archivo Municipal
National Museum Building
Quito, Ecuador

While church registers date from the 1500s, modern vital registration in Ecuador didn't begin until January 1, 1901.

Cost for a certified Birth Certificate	S/1000
Cost for a certified Marriage Certificate	S/1000
Cost for a certified Death Certificate	S/1000

Send your requests for Adoption Records to:

National Directorate for the Protection of Minor Children
Dirección Nacional de Protección de Menores
Quito, Ecuador

Adoptions are finalized by the Juvenile Court, Tribunal de Menores.

For additional assistance contact:

Embassy of Ecuador   Tel. (202) 234-7200
Consular Section
2535 15th Street, NW
Washington, DC 20009

For further information see:

Diagnostico del Registro Civil Latinoamericano, enero de 1980. Montevideo, Uruguay: UN Fund for Population Activities, 1982. 142p.

Plaza de Garcia, Norma. **Practica Notarial en el Ecuador**. Guayoquil, Ecuador: Luis Pérez Larrain, 1985. 104p.

Report on the First Latin American Training Centre on Statistics and Censuses Held at Mexico City from 2 September to 10 December 1948 by the Food and Agriculture Organization of the UN and the Government of the United States of Mexico with the Cooperation of the Statistical Office of the UN and the InterAmerican Statistical Institute. Lake Success, NY: Statistical Office of the UN, 1948. 33p.

EGYPT

Civil Registration Department
Ministry of Interior
Abassia, Cairo, Egypt

While Egypt had the world's first vital records registration program, dating from the period of Ramses II in 1250 BC, modern civil registration didn't begin until 1839. Only births and deaths are registered. Marriage records are kept by the denomination that performed the wedding and divorce records are kept by the court issuing the decree. The registration is considered to be comprehensive. Egypt does not permit the adoption of Muslim children but has permitted the adoption of non-Muslim children since 1938. Under Islamic law, children are placed within families.

Cost for a certified Birth Certificate	£E.70
Cost for a certified Marriage Certificate	£E.70
Cost for a certified Death Certificate	£E.70

For additional assistance contact:

Director General
Population & Labor Statistics
Central Agency for Public Mobilization and Statistics
P.O. Box 2086
Nasr City, Cairo, Egypt

Embassy of Egypt   Tel. (202) 895-5400
3521 International Court, NW
Washington, DC 20008

For further information see:

Askar, Garnal. *The Development of the Vital Statistics System in Egypt.* IIVRS Technical Papers, No. 13. Bethesda, MD: International Institute for Vital Registration and Statistics, 1981. 4p.

El Deeb, Bothaina. *Towards a New Strategy to Improve Vital Statistics in Egypt.* Paper Presented at the 51st International Statistical Institute, Istanbul, Turkey, 1997.

Estimating the Completeness of Under-5 Death Registration in Egypt. IIVRS Technical Papers, No. 71. Bethesda, MD: International Institute for Vital Registration and Statistics, 1997. 14p.

Methods and Problems of Civil Registration Practices and Vital Statistics Collection in Africa. IIVRS Technical Papers, No. 16. Bethesda, MD: International Institute for Vital Registration and Statistics, 1981. 27p.

Organization and Status of Civil Registration in Africa and Recommendations for Improvement. IIVRS Technical Papers, No. 31. Bethesda, MD: International Institute for Vital Registration and Statistics, 1988. 15p.

Organization and Status of Civil Registration in the Arab Countries. IIVRS Technical Papers, No. 33. Bethesda, MD: International Institute for Vital Registration and Statistics, 1988. 6p.

Send your requests to:

Dirección General de Estadística y Censos   Tel. (011) (503) 23-1520
Ministerio de Economia
43a. Avenida Norte y la. Calle Ponient
A.P. 2670
San Salvador, El Salvador

Church registers date from the 1500s, while vital registration began January 1, 1879. Divorces are recorded on the original marriage certificate. Copies of the certificates are forwarded on to the Dirección General de Estadística y Censos. Current vital registration is considered to be comprehensive.

Cost for a certified Birth Certificate	Ce 1.25
Cost for a certified Marriage Certificate	Ce 1.25
Cost for a certified Divorce Record	Ce 1.25
Cost for a certified Death Certificate	Ce 1.25

Send your requests for Adoption Records to:

Jefe de Sección de Adopciones   Tel. (011) (503) 222-4444
Procuradoria General de la Republica
Centro de Gobierno
San Salvador, El Salvador

Adoptions are finalized by the National Institute for the Protection of Minors (INPM) and the Procurado General's Office (Procuradoria). Adoptions are noted in the margin of the original birth certificate and in a separate adoption register, both kept at the local Registro Civil.

For additional assistance contact:

Embassy of El Salvador   Tel. (202) 265-9671
Consular Section
2308 California Street NW
Washington, DC 20008

For further information see:

Diagnostico del Registro Civil Latinoamericano, enero de 1980. Montevideo, Uruguay: UN Fund for Population Activities, 1982. 142p.
Ley de la Dirección General de Registros. Botetin No. 41. San Salvador, El Salvador: Banco Hipotecario de El Salvador, 1976. 20p.
_____. San Salvador, El Salvador, 1980. 20p.
Olmado Sosa, Enrique. *Status of Civil Registration and Vital Statistics in El Salvador.* Bethesda, MD: International Institute for Vital Registration and Statistics, 1982. 4p.
Report on the First Latin American Training Centre on Statistics and Censuses Held at Mexico City from 2 September to 10 December 1948 by the Food and Agriculture Organization of the UN and the Government of the United States of Mexico with the Cooperation of the Statistical Office of the UN and the InterAmerican Statistical Institute. Lake Success, NY: Statistical Office of the UN, 1948. 33p.

EQUATORIAL GUINEA

Send your requests to:

Chief Vital Statistics Section
Directorate General of Statistics
Secretarial of State for Planning & Economic Development
Malabo, Equatorial Guinea

Equatorial Guinea, the only Spanish-speaking nation in Africa, became independent in 1968.

Cost for a certified Birth Certificate	140 E
Cost for a certified Marriage Certificate	140 E
Cost for a certified Death Certificate	140 E

For additional assistance contact:

Embassy of Equatorial Guinea   Tel. (202) 296-4174
1721 I Street, NW, Suite 410
Washington, DC 20006

For further information see:

Methods and Problems of Civil Registration Practices and Vital Statistics Collection in Africa. IIVRS Technical Papers, No. 16. Bethesda, MD: International Institute for Vital Registration and Statistics, 1981. 27p.

Organization and Status of Civil Registration in Africa and Recommendations for Improvement. IIVRS Technical Papers, No. 31. Bethesda, MD: International Institute for Vital Registration and Statistics, 1988. 15p.

Send your requests to:

Ministry of Health P.O. Box 212 Asmara, Eritrea	Tel. (011) (291) (1) 11-2877
Ministry of Local Government P.O. Box 225 Asmara, Eritrea	Tel. (011) (291) (1) 11-3066

Cost for a certified Birth Certificate	Free
Cost for a certified Marriage Certificate	Free
Cost for a certified Death Certificate	Free

For additional assistance contact:

Embassy of Eritrea
1708 New Hampshire Avenue, NW
Washington, DC 20009

Tel. (202) 319-1991

For further information see:

Methods and Problems of Civil Registration Practices and Vital Statistics Collection in Africa. IIVRS Technical Papers, No. 16. Bethesda, MD: International Institute for Vital Registration and Statistics, 1981. 27p.

Organization and Status of Civil Registration in Africa and Recommendations for Improvement. IIVRS Technical Papers, No. 31. Bethesda, MD: International Institute for Vital Registration and Statistics, 1988. 15p.

ESTONIA

Send your requests to:

> Director General
> State Registry Office of Estonia (Perekonnaseisuamet)
> Ministry of Justice
> 1 Lossi Plats, Toompea
> Tallinn, 15163, Estonia

Cost for a certified Birth Certificate	100 EEK
Cost for a certified Marriage Certificate	100 EEK
Cost for a certified Divorce Certificate	300 EEK
Cost for a certified Death Certificate	100 EEK

Send your requests for Adoption Records to:

> Ministry of Social Affairs
> Gonsiori 29
> Tallinn, 0104, Estonia

Adoptions are regulated by the Minister of Social Affairs.

For additional assistance contact:

> Director
> State Statistical Office
> 15 Endia Street
> Tallinn, Estonia

> Estonian Archives Department
> Central Directorate
> Maneeźi 4
> Tallinn, 15019-0100, Estonia

> Eesti Rahvusraamatukogu
> (National Library of Estonia)
> Tónismägi 2
> Tallinn, 15189, Estonia

> Embassy of Estonia   Tel. (202) 588-0101
> 2131 Massachusetts Avenue, NW   Fax (202) 588-0108
> Washington, DC 20008

Send your requests to:

Registrar
Ministry of Works and Urban Development
P.O. Box 3386
Addis Ababa, Ethiopia

Tel. (011) (251) (1) 150000

Vital registration is not considered to be comprehensive in Ethiopia.

Cost for a certified Birth Certificate	Free
Cost for a certified Marriage Certificate	Free
Cost for a certified Death Certificate	Free

For additional assistance contact:

Head, Population and Social Statistics Department
P.O. Box 1143
Addis Ababa, Ethiopia

Ethiopian National Archives and Library
P. O. Box 717
Addis Ababa, Ethiopia

Embassy of Ethiopia
1030 15th Street, NW
Washington, DC 20005

(202) 789-0320

For further information see:

Methods and Problems of Civil Registration Practices and Vital Statistics Collection in Africa. IIVRS Technical Papers, No. 16. Bethesda, MD: International Institute for Vital Registration and Statistics, 1981. 27p.

Organization and Status of Civil Registration in Africa and Recommendations for Improvement. IIVRS Technical Papers, No. 31. Bethesda, MD: International Institute for Vital Registration and Statistics, 1988. 15p.

FIJI

Send your requests to:

Registrar General
Office of the Registrar General
Office of the Attorney General
Crown Law Office
Box 2213
Suva, Fiji

Tel. (011) (679) 211-598

Vital registration began in Fiji in 1874. Current vital registration is considered to be 93 percent complete for births and 83 percent complete for deaths.

Cost for a certified Birth Certificate	Fiji $1.00
Cost for a certified Marriage Certificate	Fiji $1.00
Cost for a certified Death Certificate	Fiji $1.00

For additional assistance contact:

Government Statistician
Bureau of Statistics
Government Buildings
P.O. Box 2221
Suva, Fiji

National Archives of Fiji
P.O. Box 2125
Government Buildings
Suva, Fiji

Embassy of Fiji
2233 Wisconsin Avenue, NW
Washington, DC 20008

Tel. (202) 337-8320

The Family History Library of Salt Lake City, Utah has microfilmed original and published records of Fiji. For further details on their holdings please consult your nearest Family History Center.

Send your requests to:

> Pastor
> Lutheran Church
> (Town), Finland
> *or*
> Registrar
> District Registrar
> (Town), Finland

Over 90 percent of Finland's vital records are registered by the Lutheran Church. Non-Lutherans were allowed to register with their respective churches or the government after 1917. These records are forwarded to the Population Register Center and *are not open to public inspection*. A file is kept on every resident of Finland, immigrant or citizen, as well as on those who have emigrated from Finland. Current registration is considered to be comprehensive. Church registers date back to 1686.

Cost for a certified Birth Certificate	Price Varies
Cost for a certified Marriage Certificate	Price Varies
Cost for a certified Death Certificate	Price Varies

For additional assistance contact:

> Väestörekisterikeskus
> Population Register Centre
> Ministry of the Interior
> P.O. Box 7 (Kellosilta 4), þ
> 00521 Helsinki, Finland

Tel. (011) (358) (9) 229-161
http://www.vaestorekisterikeskus.fi/

> Embassy of Finland
> 3301 Massachusetts Avenue, NW
> Washington, DC 20008

Tel. (202) 298-5800

The Family History Library of Salt Lake City, Utah has microfilmed many of the original and published vital records and church registers of Finland.

For further information see:

Luntiala, Hannu Veikko. *The Population Information System, a Basic Administrative Register to Be Utilized Widely in Society.* Paper Presented at the 51st International Statistical Institute, Istanbul, Turkey, 1997.

Tulkki, Hannu. *General Description of Population Registration in Finland.* Bethesda, MD: International Institute for Vital Registration and Statistics, 1983. 10p.

Vaestonkirjanpidon jarjestelytoimikunta. *Vaestokirjanpidon Jarjestelytoimikunnan Mietinto. Betankande avgivet av Kommissionen for organisering av folkbokforing.* Helsinki, Finland: Valtion painatuskeskus, 1980. 221p.

FRANCE

Send your requests to:

Le Marie
(Town), France

There is no central office for vital records in France. Vital records are on file from the late 1700s. Current registration is considered to be comprehensive.

Cost for a certified Birth Certificate	Price Varies
Cost for a certified Marriage Certificate	Price Varies
Cost for a certified Death Certificate	Price Varies

For additional assistance contact:

Director
Centre Français sur la Population et le Development
15, rue de l'École de Medicine
75270 Paris, Cedex 06, France

Chief
Demographic Department
Institute National de la Statistique et des Études Économiques
18, Boulevard Adolphe Pinard
75675 Paris, Cedex 14, France

Embassy of France   Tel. (202) 944-6000
4101 Reservoir Road, NW
Washington, DC 20007

The Family History Library of Salt Lake City, Utah has microfilmed many of the original and published vital records and church registers of France.

For further information see:

Dardy, Claudine. *Identités de Papiers*. Paris, France: Lieu Commun, 1990. 187p.

Fleury, Michel. *Nouveau Manuel de Dépouillement et d'Exploitation de l'État Civil Ancien*. Paris, France: Éditions de l'Institute National d'Etudes Démographiques, 1965. 183p.

Gernigon, Jean Dominique. *De l'origine des registres paroissiaux a l'etablissement de l'état civil en Maine et en Anjou*. Sable, France: Impr. Coconnier, 1961. 196p.

Hebert, Jean Baptiste. *Expose complet d'un systeme general d'immatriculation des personnes, des immeubles et des titres. 4e livr. contenant, outre l'expose du systeme, son application, 1. a reforme du regime hypothecaire, en vertu d'une ordonnance royaleseulement, 2. au recensement de la population, 3. a la classification des pieces, etc., etc.* Paris, France: Imprimerie de E. Briere, 1847. 300p. ·

Instruction Generale Relative a l'État Civil. Paris, France: Ministre de la Justice; Journaux Officiels, 1975. 320p.

Send your requests to:

Chef de Service des Mouvements de la Population et de l'État Civil
Ministère de la Plannification et de l'Amendagement du Territoire
Direction Generale de la Statistique et des Études Économiques
B.P. 2119
Libreville, Gabon

Vital registration in Gabon, formerly French Equatorial Africa, began in 1940 for French citizens and in 1972 for the entire population. Gabon became independent in 1960. Currently the registration is not considered to be comprehensive.

Cost for a certified Birth Certificate	100F
Cost for a certified Marriage Certificate	100F
Cost for a certified Death Certificate	100F

For additional assistance contact:

Directeur de la Protection Civile
Ministre de l'Administration du Territoire
B.P. 1112
Libreville, Gabon

Direction générale des Archives nationales, de la Bibliothèque nationale
  et de la Documentation gabonaise (DGABD)
B. P. 1188
Libreville, Gabon

Embassy of Gabon   Tel. (202) 797-1000
2034 20th Street, NW, Suite 200
Washington, DC 20009

For further information see:

Methods and Problems of Civil Registration Practices and Vital Statistics Collection in Africa. IIVRS Technical Papers, No. 16. Bethesda, MD: International Institute for Vital Registration and Statistics, 1981. 27p.

Organization and Status of Civil Registration in Africa and Recommendations for Improvement. IIVRS Technical Papers, No. 31. Bethesda, MD: International Institute for Vital Registration and Statistics, 1988. 15p.

Some Observations on Civil Registration in French-Speaking Africa. IIVRS Technical Papers, No. 39. Bethesda, MD: International Institute for Vital Registration and Statistics, 1990. 13p.

THE GAMBIA

Send your requests to:

Medical Officer of Health   Tel. (011) (220) 227-872
Statistics Section   Fax (011) (220) 228-505
Medical and Health Department
Ministry of Health, Labour and Social Welfare
The Quadrangle
Banjul, Gambia

The Gambia, formerly under British control, became independent in 1970. Vital registration is considered to be 50 percent complete for births and only 10 percent complete for deaths.

Cost for a certified Birth Certificate	D 1.10
Cost for a certified Marriage Certificate	D 1.10
Cost for a certified Death Certificate	D 1.10

For additional assistance contact:

National Records Service
c/o Personnel Management Office
The Quadrangle
Banjul, Gambia

Embassy of The Gambia   Tel. (202) 785-1399
1155 15th Street, NW, Suite 1000
Washington, DC 20005

For further information see:

Methods and Problems of Civil Registration Practices and Vital Statistics Collection in Africa. IIVRS Technical Papers, No. 16. Bethesda, MD: International Institute for Vital Registration and Statistics, 1981. 27p.

Organization and Status of Civil Registration in Africa and Recommendations for Improvement. IIVRS Technical Papers, No. 31. Bethesda, MD: International Institute for Vital Registration and Statistics, 1988. 15p.

Send your requests for Adoption Records to:

Ministry of Education
380002, Tibilisi
Uznadze 52, Republic of Georgia

Tel. (011) (995) (32) 95-88-86
Fax (011) (995) (32) 77-60-73

For other information contact:

Department of Labour and Population Statistics
Committee for Social and Economic Information
4, K. Gamsakhourdia Avenue
Toillsi 380085, Georgia

Gruzinskaia Gosudarstvennaia Respublikanskaia Biblioteka
(National Library)
ul Ketskhoveli 5
38007 Tibilisi, Georgia

Embassy of Georgia
1511 K Street, NW Suite 400
Washington, DC 20005

Tel. (202) 393-5959

The Family History Library of Salt Lake City, Utah has microfilmed records of Georgia and the former Soviet Union. For further details on their holdings please consult your nearest Family History Center.

GERMANY

Standesamt
(Town), Germany

There is no central office for vital records in Germany. To obtain copies of birth, marriage, and death certificates write to the Civil Registration District Office or the parish church in the town where the event occurred. Vital records are on file from as early as 1809 but usually from 1875. Current registration is considered to be comprehensive.

Cost for a certified Birth Certificate	Price Varies
Cost for a certified Marriage Certificate	Price Varies
Cost for a certified Death Certificate	Price Varies

Send your requests for Adoption Records to:

Children's Court (Jugendgericht) (Where the Adoption Was Approved).
(City), Germany
or
Local Court (Amtsgericht) (Where the Adoption was Finalized)
(City), Germany

Adoptions are approved by the Children's Court, Jugendgericht, and finalized by the Local Court, Amtsgericht.

For additional assistance contact:

Chief Population Censuses
Federal Statistical Office
Gustav Stresemann, Ring 11
6580 Wiesbaden, Germany

Embassy of the Federal Republic of Germany   Tel. (202) 298-4000
4645 Reservoir Road, NW   Fax (202) 298-4249
Washington, DC 20007

For further information see:

Kempner, Robert Max Wasilii. *The German National Registration System*. Lansdowne, PA: 1943. 4p.

Send your requests to:

Registrar of Births and Deaths
Central Registry Office
Ministry of Local Government
P.O. Box M.270
Accra, Ghana

Ghana, formerly the Gold Coast and Togoland, became independent in 1960. While a system for vital records registration dates from 1888 in Accra and Christianborg and was expanded to other principal towns in 1912, registration for the entire nation was not begun until 1965. The Registrar has birth records from 1912 and death records from 1888. Ghana is still developing a comprehensive national program and the registration is considered to be less than 50 percent complete.

Cost for a certified Birth Certificate	Free
Cost for a certified Marriage Certificate	Free
Cost for a certified Death Certificate	Free

For additional assistance contact:

Demography Division
Ghana Statistical Service
P.O. Box 1098
Accra, Ghana

National Archives of Ghana
P. O. Box 3056
Accra, Ghana

Embassy of Ghana   Tel. (202) 686-4520
3512 International Drive, NW
Washington, DC 20008

For further information see:

Mehta, D. C. and J. B. Assie. *A Programme for Measurement of Life and Death in Ghana*. IIVRS Technical Papers, No. 1. Bethesda, MD: International Institute for Vital Registration and Statistics, 1979. 11p.

Methods and Problems of Civil Registration Practices and Vital Statistics Collection in Africa. IIVRS Technical Papers, No. 16. Bethesda, MD: International Institute for Vital Registration and Statistics, 1981. 27p.

Organization and Status of Civil Registration in Africa and Recommendations for Improvement. IIVRS Technical Papers, No. 31. Bethesda, MD: International Institute for Vital Registration and Statistics, 1988. 15p.

BIRTHS AND DEATHS REGISTRY
APPLICATION FOR CERTIFIED COPY OF ENTRY IN BIRTH
REGISTER

Full Name: ....

Relationship to the child:...

Postal Address:..

B. PARTICULARS OF THE BIRTH

Entry Number..

Full Name and Sex:...

Date and Place of Birth:...

Date and Place of Registration:..

Mother's Full Name:..

Mother's Maiden Name:,,,

Father's Full Name:..

Purpose of search..

Date:...

....
SIGNATURE OF APPLICANT

C FOR OFFICE USE

Type of Search:..

Number of copies required:...

Date of collection:..

Amount paid and C.R.No: ....

Date:...

....
SIGNATURE OF OFFICER

Report of Search:..

Extract(s) prepared, checked and sealed for signature

on: ....

....

BIRTHS AND DEATHS REGISTRY
APPLICATION FOR CERTIFIED COPY OF ENTRY IN DEATH REGISTER

A. APPLICANT

1. Full Name:...

2. Postal Address and Telephone No: ....

B. PARTICULARS OF DEATH

3. Full Name of Deceased...

4. Sex...................5: Date of Death......................................

6. Place of Death: ....
....
(State Town/Village, Local Authority Area and Region)

7. Date of Registration: ....

8. Place of Registration..
....
(State Town/Village, Local Authority Area and Region)

9. Date of Burial:..

10. Place of Burial:..
(Give Name of Cemetery and Town/Village)

C. DOCUMENTARY EVIDENCE AND DECLARATION

11. Applicant's Relationship to the Deceased: ....

12. Purpose of request for Extract, Search...................................
....

13. Number of copies of Extract Requested....................................

14. Documentary Evidence, Authority, Declarations etc. attached(to be
    listed...
....

15. Date...............-...

SIGNATURE OR MARK OF APPLICANT

D. FOR OFFICE USE

16. Type of Search:..

17. Date of collection: ....

18. Amount paid and C.R.No...

19. Date:....................

SIGNATURE OF SEARCH OFFICER

20. Report of Search...

21. Extract(s) prepared, checked and sealed for signature on:...........

22. Extract(s) signed..

GIBRALTAR

Send your requests for Birth, Marriage, and Death Records to:

Registrar General
Registry of Births, Deaths and Marriages
Supreme Court
277 Main Street
Gibraltar

Tel. (011) (350) 7-2289

Send your requests for Divorce Records to:

Registrar
Supreme Court of Gibraltar
277 Main Street
Gibraltar

The Registrar General has birth records from October 3, 1848; stillbirth records from November 24, 1951; marriage records from April 10, 1862; and death records from September 1, 1859. Registration was not compulsory for births until January 20, 1887; marriages July 17, 1902; and deaths until January 1, 1869. Current vital registration is considered to be more than 90 percent complete. The Supreme Court has divorce records on file from November 6, 1890. Payment must be made by certified check payable to "Gibraltar Government Account."

Cost for a certified Birth Certificate	£5.00
Cost for a certified Marriage Certificate	£5.00
Cost for a certified Divorce Certificate	£5.00
Cost for a certified Death Certificate	£5.00

For additional assistance contact:

Government Statistician
Statistics Office
Treasury Building
John Mackintosh Square
Gilbraltar

The Family History Library of Salt Lake City, Utah has microfilmed some materials about Gibraltar. For further details on their holdings please consult your nearest Family History Center.

Send your requests to:

Registrar
Civil Registry Office
(Town), Greece

Department of Civil Registry
Ministry of Internal Affairs
Stadiou 27 & Dragatsaniou 2
Klafthmonos Square
101 83 Athens, Greece

Tel. (011) (30) (1) 324-5152
Fax (011) (30) (1) 331-0091

Vital registration started in 1924. Current registration is considered to be comprehensive. Before contacting the Department of Civil Registry, you should consult the local church registers. The National Library's address is: Odos El Venizelu 32; 106 79 Athens, Greece.

Cost for a certified Birth Certificate	Price Varies
Cost for a certified Marriage Certificate	Price Varies
Cost for a certified Death Certificate	Price Varies

Send your requests for Adoption Records to:

Ministry of Social Services
Children's Protection Section
Athens, Greece

Adoptions are finalized by the Third Members Court of the area of residence of either the adoptive parents or the adoptee.

For additional assistance contact:

General Secretary
National Statistical Service of Greece
14-16, rue Lykourgou
101 66 Athens, Greece

Embassy of Greece
2221 Massachusetts Avenue, NW
Washington, DC 20008

Tel. (202) 939-5800
Fax (202) 939-5824

The Family History Library of Salt Lake City, Utah has microfilmed original and published records of Greece. For further details on their holdings please consult your nearest Family History Center.

GRENADA

Registrar General
Registrar General's Office   Tel. (473) 440-2030
Ministry of Health
Church Street
St. George's, Grenada
West Indies

The Registrar General has records from January 1, 1866. Current vital registration is considered to be comprehensive. The local churches also have their own records. In addition to the below fees, the Office charges a $2.00 search fee and a $5.00 stamp fee per document.

Cost for a certified Birth Certificate	$20.00
Cost for a certified Marriage Certificate	$20.00
Cost for a certified Divorce Certificate	$20.00
Cost for a certified Death Certificate	$20.00
Cost for a certified Adoption Certificate	$10.00

For additional assistance contact:

Embassy of Grenada   Tel. (202) 265-2561
1701 New Hampshire Avenue, NW
Washington, DC 20009

The Family History Library of Salt Lake City, Utah has microfilmed records of Grenada and the West Indies. For further details on their holdings please consult your nearest Family History Center.

For further information see:

Registration of Vital Events in the English-Speaking Caribbean. IIVRS Technical Papers, No. 32. Bethesda, MD: International Institute for Vital Registration and Statistics, 1988. 10p.

GRENADA

Application for a Search and Certificate Extract from Register of Births, Deaths and Marriages

_____

The Registrar General

PLEASE cause a search to be made for the Birth/Death/Marriage of

.... which took place on or about

.... in the parish of ....

and furnish me with a certified copy of the entry under your hand and seal.

In the case of an application for a Birth Certificate the following particulars are required:

Father's Name ....

Mother's Name ....

Where Born ....

Date of Birth ....

Mother's Name (before Marriage) ....

....

Date ....

Address ....

....

B 56.

GUATEMALA

Director
Registro Civil
Municipalidad de Guatemala
21 Calle 6-77 Zona 1
Guatemala City, Guatemala

Cost for a certified Birth Certificate	Price Varies
Cost for a certified Marriage Certificate	Price Varies
Cost for a certified Death Certificate	Price Varies

While church registers date from the 1500s, vital registration in Guatemala didn't begin until January 1, 1877. Current vital registration is considered to be comprehensive.

Send your requests for Adoption Records to:

Procuraduríía General de la Nación
Acisclo
Guatemala City, Guatemala

Final adoption decrees are filed with the Procuraduríía General de la Nación. Juvenile Courts, Juzgado de Menores, certify that a child is an orphan or abandoned.

For additional assistance contact:

Embassy of Guatemala   Tel. (202) 745-4952
Consular Section
2220 R Street, NW
Washington, DC 20008

For further information see:

Diagnostico del Registro Civil Latinoamericano, enero de 1980. Montevideo, Uruguay: UN Fund for Population Activities, 1982. 142p.

Prado, Gerardo. *The Supreme Electoral Tribunal and the Population Register: a New Strategy.* Paper Presented at the 51st International Statistical Institute, Istanbul, Turkey, 1997.

Report on the First Latin American Training Centre on Statistics and Censuses Held at Mexico City from 2 September to 10 December 1948 by the Food and Agriculture Organization of the UN and the Government of the United States of Mexico with the Cooperation of the Statistical Office of the UN and the InterAmerican Statistical Institute. Lake Success, NY: Statistical Office of the UN, 1948. 33p.

Send your requests to:

Chef de la Division
Recensement et Statistiques de la Population
Ministère de l'Intérieur et de la Sécurité
B.P. 3495
Conakry, Guinea

Registration began in 1979 and is not comprehensive.

Cost for a certified Birth Certificate	Price Varies
Cost for a certified Marriage Certificate	Price Varies
Cost for a certified Death Certificate	Price Varies

For additional assistance contact:

Archives nationales
B.P. 1005
Conakry, Guinea

Embassy of Guinea   Tel. (202) 483-9420
Consular Section
2212 Leroy Place, NW
Washington, DC 20008

GUINEA–BISSAU

Send your requests to:

Direction Generale de l'Identification et du Registre Civile
Ministère de la Justice
Bissau, Guinea-Bissau

Vital registration began in 1976 and is not comprehensive.

Cost for a certified Birth Certificate	20P
Cost for a certified Marriage Certificate	20P
Cost for a certified Death Certificate	20P

For additional assistance contact:

Direccao Geral de Estadística
C.P. 6
Bissau, Guinea-Bissau

Institut national d'études et de recherches (INER)
Archives historiques
B. P. 112, Bairro Cobornel
Complexo Escolar 14 de Novembro
Bissau, Guinea-Bissau

Embassy of Guinea-Bissau   Tel. (202) 872-4222
918 16th Street, NW, Mezzanine Suite
Washington, DC 20006

For further information see:

Methods and Problems of Civil Registration Practices and Vital Statistics Collection in Africa. IIVRS Technical Papers, No. 16. Bethesda, MD: International Institute for Vital Registration and Statistics, 1981. 27p.

Organization and Status of Civil Registration in Africa and Recommendations for Improvement. IIVRS Technical Papers, No. 31. Bethesda, MD: International Institute for Vital Registration and Statistics, 1988. 15p.

Send your requests to:

Registrar-General
General Register Office
Ministry of Home Affairs
G.P.O. Building
Robb Street
Georgetown, Guyana

Church registers date from the 1500s, while vital registration in Guyana began in 1880. Current vital registration is not comprehensive.

Cost for a certified Birth Certificate	$.50
Cost for a certified Marriage Certificate	$.50
Cost for a certified Death Certificate	$.50

Send your requests for Adoption Records to:

Magistrate Court
(City), Guyana

For additional assistance contact:

Health Statistics Unit
Ministry of Health
Brickdam
Georgetown, Guyana

Embassy of Guyana   Tel. (202) 265-6900
Consular Section
2490 Tracy Place, NW
Washington, DC 20008

For further information see:

Diagnostico del Registro Civil Latinoamericano, enero de 1980. Montevideo, Uruguay: UN Fund for Population Activities, 1982. 142p.

Report on the First Latin American Training Centre on Statistics and Censuses Held at Mexico City from 2 September to 10 December 1948 by the Food and Agriculture Organization of the UN and the Government of the United States of Mexico with the Cooperation of the Statistical Office of the UN and the InterAmerican Statistical Institute. Lake Success, NY: Statistical Office of the UN, 1948. 33p.

BIRTH CERTIFICATE APPLICATION FORM
General Register Office — Government of Guyana

ACCESSION/ FILE NO.	B
CERT. NO.	B

DO NOT WRITE IN SHADED AREAS ON THIS FORM — WRITE ALL INFORMATION CLEARLY IN INK — IN SECTIONS 1 TO 8 PROVIDE ALL INFORMATION ABOUT THE PERSON FOR WHOM THE BIRTH CERTIFICATE IS TO BE ISSUED.

1 LAST NAME (SURNAME)

2 FIRST NAME

3 OTHER NAMES

4 DATE OF BIRTH — DAY | MONTH | YEAR — NS ☐ OS ☐

5 SEX — MALE ☐ FEMALE ☐

6 PLACE OF BIRTH — HOSPITAL ☐ OTHER ☐
NAME OF HOSPITAL OR INSTITUTION
NUMBER | STREET OR DAM | WARD OR VILLAGE | LOCATION | TOWN OR COUNTY | REGION | REGION

7 MOTHER'S MAIDEN NAME — LAST NAME | FIRST NAME | OTHER NAMES

8 FATHER'S NAME — LAST NAME | FIRST NAME | OTHER NAMES

9 NAME AND LOCAL ADDRESS TO WHICH CERTIFICATE IS TO BE SENT — NAME | ADDRESS

10 POST OFFICE USE ONLY

POST OFFICE	DATE RECV.	TRANSMITTAL NO.	ITEM NO.	RECEIPT NO.	NO. COPIES	INITIAL

11 GRO USE ONLY

	RECV.		OPER.		TRANS.		DESP.	
	H	F	H	P	H	P	H	P
ADV								
CLK								
DI								
DO								

RMK | IC ☐ | ANE ☐ | TD ☐ | ENT ☐ | DES ☐ | CERT ☐ | NOT ☐

AFFIX POSTAGE STAMP HERE

Systems Design Under Contract: Guyana Management Institute, 1986

MARRIAGE CERTIFICATE APPLICATION FORM

General Register Office — Government of Guyana

ACCESSION/FILE NO.	M							
CERT. NO.	M							

DO NOT WRITE IN SHADED AREAS ON THIS FORM — WRITE ALL INFORMATION CLEARLY IN INK — IN SECTIONS 1 TO 12 PROVIDE ALL INFORMATION ABOUT THE PERSONS FOR WHOM THE MARRIAGE CERTIFICATE IS TO BE ISSUED.

PARTICULARS OF CONTRACTING PARTIES

HUSBAND (SECTIONS 1 – 5)

1 LAST NAME (SURNAME)/

2 FIRST & OTHER NAMES

3 ADDRESS

4 DATE OF BIRTH — DAY | MONTH | YEAR

5 OCCUPATION

WIFE (SECTIONS 6 – 10)

6 LAST NAME (SURNAME)

7 FIRST & OTHER NAMES

8 ADDRESS

9 DATE OF BIRTH — DAY | MONTH | YEAR

10 OCCUPATION

11 DATE OF MARRIAGE — DAY | MONTH | YEAR

12 PLACE OF MARRIAGE

13 NAME AND LOCAL ADDRESS TO WHICH CERTIFICATE IS TO BE SENT — NAME | ADDRESS

14 POST OFFICE USE ONLY

POST OFFICE	DATE RECV.	TRANSMITTAL NO.	ITEM NO.	RECEIPT NO.	NO. COPIES	INITIAL

	RECV.		OPER.			TRANS.			DESP.		
	H	P	H	P		H	P		H	P	
ADV											
CLK											
DI											
DO											

RMK IC ☐ ANE ☐ TD ☐ ENT ☐ DES ☐ CERT ☐ NOT ☐

AFFIX POSTAGE STAMP HERE

Systems Design Under Contract: Guyana Management Institute, 1986

Printed by G.N.P.L./R.V.

DEATH CERTIFICATE APPLICATION FORM
General Register Office — Government of Guyana

ACCESSION/FILE NO.	D						
CERT. NO.	D						

DO NOT WRITE IN SHADED AREAS ON THIS FORM—WRITE ALL INFORMATION CLEARLY IN INK—IN SECTIONS 1 TO 9 PROVIDE ALL INFORMATION ABOUT THE PERSON FOR WHOM THE DEATH CERTIFICATE IS TO BE ISSUED.

1. LAST NAME (SURNAME)

2. FIRST NAME

3. OTHER NAMES

4. DATE OF DEATH — DAY — MONTH — YEAR — NS — OS

5. SEX — MALE — FEMALE

6. PLACE OF DEATH — HOSPITAL — OTHER — NAME OF HOSPITAL OR INSTITUTION — LOCATION — REGION — NUMBER — STREET OR DAM — WARD OR VILLAGE — TOWN OR COUNTY — REGION

7. MAIDEN NAME

8. YEAR OF BIRTH

9. PLACE OF BIRTH — WARD OR VILLAGE — TOWN OR COUNTY

10. NAME AND LOCAL ADDRESS TO WHICH CERTIFICATE IS TO BE SENT — NAME — ADDRESS

11. POST OFFICE USE ONLY

POST OFFICE	DATE RECV.	TRANSMITTAL NO.	ITEM NO.	RECEIPT NO.	NO. COPIES	INITIAL

12. GRO USE ONLY

	RECV.		OPER.		TRANS.		DESP.	
ADV	H	P	H	P	H	P	H	P
CLK								
DI								
DO								

RMK — IC ☐ — ANE ☐ — TD ☐ — ENT ☐ — DES ☐ — CERT ☐ — NOT ☐

AFFIX POSTAGE STAMP HERE

Systems Design Under Contract: Guyana Management Institute, 1986

Send your requests to:

Chef de Service
Service National de l'Inspection et de Controle de l'État Civil
Ministère de la Justice
Avenue Charles Sumner, No. 18
Port au Prince, Haiti

Church registers date from the 1500s, while vital registration in Haiti began in 1880. Current vital registration is not comprehensive.

Cost for a certified Birth Certificate	1G
Cost for a certified Marriage Certificate	1G
Cost for a certified Death Certificate	1G

Send your requests for Adoption Records to:

Ministry of Social Affairs   Tel. (011) (509) (1) 22-2450
Institut du Bien Être Social et de Recherches
18 Avenue des Marguerites
Port au Prince, Haiti

Adoptions are approved by the *Institut du Bien Être Social et de Recherches* and finalized by the local *Tribunal Civil* of the area where the child resided.

For additional assistance contact:

Directeur General
Institute Haitian de Statistique et d'Informatique
Boulevard Harry Truman
Port au Prince, Haiti

Embassy of Haiti   Tel. (202) 332-4090
Consular Section
2311 Massachusetts Avenue, NW
Washington, DC 20008

For further information see:

Bistoury, Andre F. *Code et Guide de l'État Civil a l'Usage des Ministres des Coltes*. Port au Prince, Haiti: Les Presses Libres, 1956. 172p.
_____. 2nd ed. 1966. 142p.
Petit Guide à l'usage des Officiers de l'État Civil. Port au Prince, Haiti: Ministère de la Justice, 1984. 120p.

HONDURAS

Send your requests to:

Registro Civil
(Town), Honduras

Archivo Nacional de Honduras
6a Avenida 408
Tegucigalpa, Honduras

Church registers date from the 1500s, while vital registration in Honduras began January 1, 1881. Current vital registration is not considered to be comprehensive. There are no standard forms, registers, or fees. The records from 1906 to the present are kept at the Honduras National Archives.

Cost for a Certified Birth Certificate	L.50
Cost for a Certified Marriage Certificate	L.50
Cost for a Certified Death Certificate	L.50

For additional assistance contact:

Director General
Dirección General de Estadística y Censos
6a, Av. 8a, Calle
Comayaguela, DC, Honduras

Embassy of Honduras   Tel. (202) 966-7702
3007 Tilden Street, NW
Washington, DC 20008

The Family History Library of Salt Lake City, Utah has microfilmed original vital records and church registers of Honduras. For further details on their holdings please consult your nearest Family History Center.

For further information see:

Diagnostico del Registro Civil Latinoamericano, enero de 1980. Montevideo, Uruguay: UN Fund for Population Activities, 1982. 142p.

Report on the First Latin American Training Centre on Statistics and Censuses Held at Mexico City from 2 September to 10 December 1948 by the Food and Agriculture Organization of the UN and the Government of the United States of Mexico with the Cooperation of the Statistical Office of the UN and the InterAmerican Statistical Institute. Lake Success, NY: Statistical Office of the UN, 1948. 33p.

HUNGARY

Send your requests to:

Civil Registration Office
(Town), Hungary

There is no central office for vital records in Hungary. To obtain copies of birth, marriage, and death certificates write to the Civil Registration District Office in the town where the event occurred. Vital records are on file from 1895. Current vital registration in Hungary is considered to be comprehensive. Early records are available from the local parish church. The National Office of Personal Registration (H-Budapest PF 81, 1450 Hungary) also maintains files on residents of Hungary as part of the national identity card system. Divorces are approved by the local district courts. Adoptions are approved by the Children Care and Welfare Institute (GYIVI) and finalized by the local County Public Administration Office. The local Civil Registration Office issues an amended birth certificate.

Cost for a certified Birth Certificate	1.500 Forints
Cost for a certified Marriage Certificate	1.500 Forints
Cost for a certified Death Certificate	1.500 Forints

For earlier records contact:

County Archives (Megyei Levéltár)
(County Seat) Hungary

For additional assistance contact:

Embassy of the Republic of Hungary   Tel. (202) 362-6730
3910 Shoemaker Street, NW   Fax (202) 686-6412
Washington, DC 20008

ICELAND

Send your requests to:

Hagstofa Islands Pjooskra
The National Registry
Skuggasund 3
151 Reykjavik, Iceland

Tel. (011) (354) (1) 609-800
Fax (011) (354) (1) 623-312

The National Registry has records from 1953 on all residents of Iceland. They maintain these records as part of a national identity system. Prior to this time records were kept by the local, usually Lutheran, church. These church registers go back to 1785. The current vital registration is considered to be comprehensive.

Cost for a certified Birth Certificate	US $6.50
Cost for a certified Marriage Certificate	US $6.50
Cost for a certified Death Certificate	US $6.50

For additional assistance contact:

Director
The Statistical Bureau of Iceland
Skuggasund 3
105 Reykjavik, Iceland

National Archives of Iceland
P.O. Box R5-5390
Laugavegur 162
105 Reykjavik, Iceland

Embassy of Iceland
1156 15th Street, NW
Washington, DC 20005

Tel. (202) 265-6653

The Family History Library of Salt Lake City, Utah has microfilmed original and published records of Iceland. For further details on their holdings please consult your nearest Family History Center.

Fæðingarvottorð óskast

Fullt nafn _____

Fæðingardagur _____

Fæðingarstaður _____

Fullt nafn föður _____

Fullt nafn móður _____

Ísland

Iceland / Islande / IJsland

Hagstofa Íslands - Þjóðskrá
The National Registry
Skuggasundi 3
150 Reykjavík

Sími /tel. +354-1-609800
Telefax: +354-1-623312

Fæðingarvottorð

Fødselsattest / Extract of the register of births / Auszug aus dem Geburtsregister / Extrait des registres de l'état civil concernant une naissance / Extracto del registro de nacimientos / Estratto del registro delle nascite / Uittreksel uit de geboortearchieven

Nafn
navn / name / Name / nom / nombre
/ nome / naam

Fæðingardagur
fødselsdato / date of birth /
Geburtsdatum / date de naissance /
fecha de nacimiento / data di nascita
/ geboortedatum

Kyn
køn / sex / Geschlecht / sexe / sexo /
sesse / geslacht

Fæðingarstaður
fødested / place of birth / Geburtsort
/ lieu de naissance / lugar de
nacimiento / luogo di nascito /
geboorteplaats

Nafn föður
faders navn / name of the father /
Name des Vaters / nom du père /
nombre del padre / nome del padre /
naam van de vader

Nafn móður
moders navn / name of the mother /
Name der Mutter / nom de la mère /
nombre de la madre / nome della
madre / naam van de moeder

Dagsetning, undirskrift og stimpill embættis
udgivelsesdato, underskrift og myndigheds stempel
date of issue, signature and seal of keeper
Ausstellungsdatum, Unterschrift und Dienstsiegel des Registerführers
Date de délivrance, signature et sceau du dépositaire
fecha de expedición, firma y sello del depositario
data in cui è stato rilasciato l'atto, con firma e bollo dell'ufficio
afgiftedatum, handtekening en ambtelijk stempel

Reykjavík,

D2451 Gutenberg

Hjónavígsluvottorð óskast

Fullt nafn karls _____

Fæðingardagur hans _____ Fæðingarstaður _____

Fullt nafn konu _____

Fæðingardagur hennar _____ Fæðingarstaður _____

Hjónavígsludagur _____ Hjónavígslustaður _____

Ísland

Iceland / Islande / IJsland

Hagstofa Íslands - Þjóðskrá
The National Registry
Skuggasund 3   Sími / tel. +354-1-609800
150 Reykjavík   Telefax: +354-1-623312

Hjúskaparvottorð

Vielsesattest / Extract of the register of marriages / Auszug aus dem Eheregister / Extrait des registres de l´état civil concernant un mariage / Extracto del registro de matrimonios / Estratto del registro dei matrimoni / Uittreksel uit huwelijksarchieven

Nafn brúðguma brudgommens navn / name of the bridegroom / Name des Bräutigam / nom du marié/ nombre del novio / nome dello sposo / naam van de echtgenoot	
Fæðingardagur fødselsdato / date of birth / Geburtsdatum / date de naissance / fecha de nacimiento / data di nascita / geboortedatum	
Fæðingarstaður fødested / place of birth / Geburtsort / lieu de naissance / lugar de nacimiento / luogo di nascito / geboorteplaats	
Nafn brúðar brudens navn / name of the bride / Name der Braut / nom de la mariée / nombre de la novia / nome della sposa / naam van de echtgenote	
Fæðingardagur fødselsdato / date of birth / Geburtsdatum / date de naissance / fecha de nacimiento / data di nascita / geboortedatum	
Fæðingarstaður fødested / place of birth / Geburtsort / lieu de naissance / lugar de nacimiento / luogo di nascito / geboorteplaats	
Hjónavígsludagur og -staður sted og dato for vielsen / date and place of the marriage / Datum und Ort der Eheschließung / date et lieu du mariage / fecha y lugar del matrimonio / data e luogo della celebration del matrimonio / datum en plaats van het huwelijk	

Dagsetning, undirskrift og stimpill embættis

udgivelsesdato, underskrift og myndigheds stempel
date of issue, signature and seal of keeper
Ausstellungsdatum, Unterschrift und Dienstsiegel des Registerführers
Date de délivrance, signature et sceau du dépositaire
fecha de expedición, firma y sello del depositario
data in cui è stato rilasciato l´atto, con firma e bollo dell´ufficio
afgiftedatum, handtekening en ambtelijk stempel

Reykjavík, _____

02450 Standardsprent Gutenberg ??

Beiðni um staðfestingu á dánardegi

Nafn hins látna _____

Fæðingardagur og -ár _____ Hjúskaparstétt _____

Lögheimili _____

Dánardagur _____

Ísland	Hagstofa Íslands - Þjóðskrá
	The National Registry
	Skuggasundi 3
Iceland / Islande / IJsland	150 Reykjavík Sími / tel. (9)1 - 609800

D á n a r v o t t o r ð

Dødsattest / Extract of the register of deaths / Auszug aus dem Todesregister / Extrait des registres de l´état civil concernant un décès / Extracto del registro de defunciones / Estratto del registro delle morti / Uittreksel uit het overlijdensarchief

Nafn navn / name / Name / nom / nombre / nome / naam	
Fæðingardagur og -staður fødselsdato og fødested / date and place of birth / Geburtsdatum und Geburtsort / date et lieu de naissance / fecha y lugar de nacimiento / data e luogo di nascita / geboortedatum en geboorteplaats	
Kyn køn / sex / Geschlecht / sexe / sexo / sesse / geslacht	
Hjúskaparstaða civilstand / marital status / Familienstand / situation de famille / estado civil / stato di civile / burgerlijke staat	
Heimilisfang sidste bopæl / last residence / letzter Wohnsitz / dernier domicile / ultimo domicilio / ultimo domicilio / laatste woonplaats	
Dánardagur dødsdato / date of death / Todesdatum / date de décès / fecha de fallecimiento / data della morte / datum van overlijden	
Dánarstaður dødested / place of death / Todesort / lieu de décès / lugar de fallecimiento / luogo della morte / plaats van overlijden	
Dagsetning, undirskrift og stimpill embættis udgivelsesdato, underskrift og myndigheds stempel date of issue, signature and seal of keeper Ausstellungsdatum, Unterschrift und Dienstsiegel des Registerführers Date de délivrance, signature et sceau du dépositaire fecha de expedición, firma y sello del depositario data in cui è stato rilasciato l´atto, con firma e bollo dell´ufficio afgiftedatum, handtekening en ambtelijk stempel	Reykjavík, _____ _____

INDIA

Send your requests for Birth, Death and Hindu Marriage and Adoption certificates to:

Chief Registrar of Births, Deaths & Marriages
(Capital City; State, Union or Territory), India

Send your requests for records of British Nationals in pre-Independent India to:

Oriental and India Office Collections
British Library
96 Euston Road
London NW1 2DB, England

Tel. (011) (44) (20) 7412 7873
Fax (011) (44) (20) 7412 7641

The Bengal Births and Deaths Registration Act was passed in 1873, and in 1886 the Births, Deaths and Marriages Registration Act went into effect in British India. Compliance has been uneven outside of the major cities and states. The Indian Christian Marriage Act first took effect in 1872. Registration of non-Hindu marriages is not compulsory. For marriage records you should also contact the denomination where the wedding occurred. Registration of marriages and divorces is required in only a few states. Records of British residents in India are at the Oriental and India Office Collections in the British Library (see address above). They will issue certificates for an exact date and place for £13; if a search is needed, it will cost £23.

Non-Indians are not permitted to adopt children in India. Under the Guardian and Wards Act of 1890, they could obtain legal custody of a child who would then be adopted in another country. Hindu adoptive parents file adoption deeds with the Office of Sub-Registrar of Births, Deaths & Marriages in the capital city of the state, union, or territory where the adoption was finalized.

Fees Vary from State to State, Representative Fees are Given Below

Cost for a certified Birth Certificate	Rs.5/-
Cost for a certified Marriage Certificate, under the Special Marriage Act, 1954	Rs.5/-
Cost for a certified Marriage Certificate, under the Hindu Marriage Act, 1955	Rs.20/-
Cost for a certified Marriage Certificate, under the Christian Marriage Act, 1955	Rs.1/-
Cost for a certified Marriage Certificate, under the Parsee Marriage Act, 1936	Rs.2/-
Cost for a certified Death Certificate	Rs.5/-

For additional assistance contact:

Registrar General's Office
West Block 1, P.K. Puram
New Delhi 110066, India

Karnataka State Archives
Room No. 11, Ground Floor
Vidhana Soudha
Bangalore 560001, Karnataka, India

Andhra Pradesh State Archives
Taranaka
Hyderabad 500007, Andhra Pradesh
India

National Archives of India
Janpath
New Delhi 110001, India

State Archives of West Bengal
6 Bhowani Dutta Lane
Calcutta 700073, West Bengal, India

Kerala State Archives
Directorate of Archives
Nalanda-Trivandrum 3, Kerala, India

For further information see:

Awasthi, S. K. *The Registration Act, 1908, along with U.P. Rules under the Registration Act, 1908 as Amended up to Date.* Allahabad, India: Alia Law Agency, 1986. 418p.

Gardner, James Louis, and Melvin P. Thatcher. *Historical Population Records for India on Microfilm at the Genealogical Society of Utah.* http://www.library.upenn.edu/vanpelt/collections/sasia/salnaq/oct99/mormon.html

Handbook on Civil Registration. Delhi, India: Office of the Registrar General, 1981. 115p.

India. Directorate General of Health Services. *Review of the Registration System of Births and Deaths in India.* Delhi, Indian: Author, 1959. 191p.

India. Vital Statistics Division. *Civil Registration System in India; a Perspective.* New Delhi, India: Author, 1972. 213 p.

Karnataka (India). Dept. of Law and Parliamentary Affairs. *The Karnataka Registration Rules, 1965, and the Table of Registration Fees, as Amended up to 31st March 1977.* Bangalore, Karnataka, India: Author, 1977. 204p.

Lingner, Joan W., and H. Bradley Wells. *Organization and Methods of the Dual Record System in India.* Chapel Hill, NC: International Program of Laboratories for Population Statistics, 1973. 33p.

The Madras Registration Manual/Tamil Nadu Registration Manual. Madras, India: Superintendent, Govt. Press, 1957–1974. 2 vols.

Maharajistrara ki Patrika/Registrar General's News Letter. (Serial). New Delhi, India: Office of the Registrar General.

The Maharashtra Registration Manual. Bombay, India: Director, Govt. Print. and Stationery, 1974. Unpgd.

Padmanabha, P. *Organization of Civil Registration and Vital Statistics System in India.* Bethesda, MD: International Institute for Vital Registration and Statistics, 1980. 12p.

A Paper on Registration of Marriages in Karnataka. Bangalore, Karnataka, India: Directorate of Economics & Statistics, 1992. 16.

Pathak, Kunj Bihari. *Completeness of Civil Registration in India and Some Major States.* Bombay, India: International Institute for Population Sciences, 1994. 38p.

Registration Rules under Section 69 (2) of the Indian Registration Act, 1908 (XVI of 1908). Trivandrum, Kerala: Government of Kerala, 1959. 65p.

Sethi, Raghbirlal Bhagatram, and Lal, Jagdish. *Indian Registration Act, 1908. Sanjiva Row's The Registration Act, Act No. XVI of 1908, as Amended up to Date, Being an Exhaustive and Critical Commentary on the Act, with State Amendments and Tables of Registration Fees of Almost All the States.* 6th ed. Allahabad, India: Delhi Law House, 1978. 946p.

INDONESIA

Send your requests for Birth, Christian Marriages, and Death Certificates to:

Civil Registration Office
(Town), Indonesia

It was in 1815, during the British period, that population registers were introduced. The Dutch began vital registration of all Indonesians in Jakarta in 1929. Marriage and divorce records can be found in the records of the denomination, recorded at the vital registration office, and in the Indonesian Department of Religious Affairs. Under the direction of the Minister of Internal Affairs, all births and deaths must also be registered in each town on individual forms called *triplikats*. Both registrations should be consulted.

Cost for a certified Birth Certificate	Price Varies
Cost for a certified Marriage Certificate	Price Varies
Cost for a certified Death Certificate	Price Varies

Send your requests for Adoption Records to:

Yayasan Sayap Ibu Foundation   Tel. (011) (62-21) 722-1763
Jalan Barito II/55
Jakarta, Indonesia

For additional assistance contact:

Director
Bureau for Social and Population Statistics
Central Bureau of Statistics
8, Jalan Dokter Sutomo
P.O. Box 3
Jakarta, Indonesia

Embassy of Indonesia   Tel. (202) 775-5200
2020 Massachusetts Avenue, NW
Washington, DC 20036

For further information see:

Konsep dan Definisi Operasional Baku Statistik Sosial Dan Kependudukan. Jakarta, Indonesia: Biro Pusat Statistik, 1985. 94 p.

Laporan Hasil Penelitian Sistem Pencatatan dan Pelaporan Peristiwa Vital de Propinsi Sulawesi Selatan. Ujung Pandand, Indonesia: Propinsi Sulawesi Selatan, 1981. 34p.

Tim Teknis. **Sample Registrasi Penduduk.** *Analysis and Evaluation of the First Year Result of the Sample Vital Registration Project*. Jakarta, Indonesia: Biro Pusat Statistik, 1976. 259p.

Send your requests to:

Deputy, Ministry of the Interior and Head of Civil Registration
Civil Registration Organization
Eman Khomaini Street
Central Building No. 184
Tehran, Iran 11374

Identification cards have been required for Iranian men since 1918. Currently each Iranian is registered and receives an ID card. Marriage and divorce records are also kept by the Notarial Office and Court of Justice where the event occurred. Registration is considered to be 90 percent comprehensive. In 1994 the Registration Organization computerized its records for 80 million Iranians who have lived and are living in Iran over the past 100 years.

Cost for a certified Birth Certificate	Free
Cost for a certified Marriage Certificate	Free
Cost for a certified Death Certificate	Free

IRAQ

Send your requests to:

Director of Vital and Health Statistics
Ministry of Health
Alwiyah, Baghdad, Iraq

Vital records registration of births and deaths has been compulsory in Iraq since 1947. The nation also requires an identity card for each individual, which is issued by the Director General of the Office of Civil Status. Marriages are recorded by the denomination that performed the wedding and divorces are kept by the court that issued the decree. The registration is not considered to be comprehensive. Iraq handles adoption under Islamic law. Children are placed within families.

Cost for a certified Birth Certificate	.30d
Cost for a certified Marriage Certificate	.30d
Cost for a certified Death Certificate	.30d

For further information see:

Organization and Status of Civil Registration in the Arab Countries. IIVRS Technical Papers, No. 33. Bethesda, MD: International Institute for Vital Registration and Statistics, 1988. 6p.

Registration of Vital Events in Iraq. IIVRS Technical Papers, No. 10. Bethesda, MD: International Institute for Vital Registration and Statistics, 1980. 5p.

Send your requests to:

General Register Office (GRO)   Tel. (011) (353) (1) 6354000
Joyce House   http://www.groireland.ie/
8–11 Lombard Street East
Dublin 2, Ireland

The GRO has records from January 1, 1864. Vital registration is considered to be comprehensive. The County Heritage Centres provide direct access to many of Ireland's earliest vital records.

Cost for a certified Birth Certificate	Ire £5.50
Cost for a short form Birth Certificate	Ire £3.50
Cost for a certified Marriage Certificate	Ire £5.50
Cost for a certified Death Certificate	Ire £5.50
Cost for a duplicate copy, when ordered at the same time	Ire £4.00

Send your requests for Adoption Records to:

Adoption Board (An Bord Uchtala)   Tel. (011) (353) (1) 6671392
Shelbourne House   Fax (011) (353) (1) 6671438
Shelbourne Road
Ballsbridge
Dublin 4, Ireland

For additional assistance contact:

The Irish Family History Foundation   http://www.irishroots.net/

The Irish Family History Foundation is the co-ordinating body for a network of government-approved genealogical research centers in the Republic of Ireland and in Northern Ireland which have computerized tens of millions of Irish ancestral records of different types.

The Family History Library of Salt Lake City, Utah has microfilmed many of the original and published vital records and church registers of Ireland's cities and counties. For further details on their holdings please consult your nearest Family History Center.

For further information see:

An Act for the registration of Births and Deaths in Ireland, Passed 20th April, 1863; An Act to Amend the Law in Ireland Relating to the Registration of Births and Deaths in Ireland, Passed 2nd August 1880. Dublin, Ireland: A. Thom, 1880. 95p.

OIFIG AN ARD CHLÁRAITHEORA

Joyce House
8/11 Lombard St. East,
Dublin, 2.

APPLICATION FOR SEARCH

AND/OR CERTIFICATE OF A   **BIRTH**

Name in full of person
Whose Birth record is desired_____

Date of Birth or approximate age_____

Place of Birth
(if in a town, name of Street to be given)_____

Father's Name and Surname_____

Mother's Name and Maiden Surname_____

No. of Certificates required_____*short/*full *Delete whichever is not
applicable

Has the person whose birth record is desired been legally adopted?   Yes / No

*NAME AND ADDRESS BELOW IN BLOCK LETTERS

FOR FEES PLEASE GO TO   *Applicant_____ _ _____
FEES PAGE ON WEB SITE
                                 *Address_____
CHEQUES, ETC. SHOULD BE
MADE PAYABLE TO THE   _____
REGISTRAR GENERAL
                                 Phone No._____
CHEQUES SHOULD BE
ACCOMPANIED BY A
CURRENT BANKER'S CARD   FOR OFFICE USE ONLY

Tá leagan Gaeilge den fhoirm seo ar
Fail ach é a iarraidh.

OIFIG AN ARD CHLÁRAITHEOR

Joyce House,
8/11 Lombard St. East,
Dublin, 2.

APPLICATION FOR SEARCH

AND/OR CERTIFICATE OF A　　　MARRIAGE

Name and Surname of the Parties Married
(to be given in full in each case)_____

Date of Marriage, or if the date is not
known, approximate date of Marriage_____

Where Married_____

No. of Certificates required_____

---

*NAME AND ADDRESS BELOW IN BLOCK LETTERS

FOR FEES PLEASE GO TO
FEES PAGE ON WEB SITE

*Applicant_____

*Address_____

_____

CHEQUES ETC. SHOULD BE
MADE PAYABLE TO THE

Phone No._____

CHEQUES SHOULD BE
ACCOMPANIED BY A
CURRENT BANKER'S CARD

FOR OFFICE USE ONLY

Tá leagan Gaeilge den fhoirm soe ar
Fail ach é a iarraidh.

OIFIG AN ARD CHLÁRAITHEORA,

Joyce House,
8/11, Lombard St. East,
Dublin, 2.

APPLICATION FOR SEARCH
AND/OR CERTIFICATE OF A   DEATH

NAME in full and SURNAME
of deceased_____

Date of Death, or if date is not
kown, approximate date of death_____

Place of Death
(if in a town, name of Street to be given_____

Condition as to Marriage_____

Age of Deceased_____Occupation of Deceased_____

No. of Certificates required_____

---

*NAME AND ADDRESS BELOW IN BLOCK LETTERS

*Applicant_____

*Address_____

_____

Phone No._____

FOR FEES PLEASE GO TO
FEES PAGE ON WEB SITE

CHEQUES, ETC. SHOULD BE
MADE PAYABLE TO THE
REGISTRAR GENERAL   FOR OFFICE USE ONLY

Tá leagan Gaeilge den fhoirm seo ar
Fail ach é a iarraidh.

Send your requests to:

Registrar
Immigration Services and Population Registration
Ministry of the Interior
P.O. Box 2420
Jerusalem, Israel

Current registration is considered to be comprehensive.

Cost for a certified Birth Certificate	Price Varies
Cost for a certified Marriage Certificate	Price Varies
Cost for a certified Death Certificate	Price Varies

Send your requests for Marriage Certificates to:

Rabbinate
(Town), Israel

Send your requests for Adoption Records to:

Ministry of Social Welfare
Jerusalem, Israel

Adoption records are finalized by the local District Courts and supervised by the Ministry of Social Welfare.

For additional assistance contact:

Yad Vashem   Tel. (011) (972-2) 675-1611
P.O. Box 3477
Jerusalem, 91034, Israel

Embassy of Israel   Tel. (202) 364-5500
3514 International Drive, NW
Washington, DC 20008

ITALY

Send your requests to:

Stato Civile
(Town), Italy

There is no central office for vital records in Italy. To obtain copies of birth, marriage, and death certificates write to the town where the event occurred. Vital records are on file for most areas from the early 1800s, but are more generally available from 1870 to the present. Older records are often on deposit at the State Archives. Current vital registration is considered to be comprehensive.

Cost for a Certified Birth Certificate	Price Varies
Cost for a Certified Marriage Certificate	Price Varies
Cost for a Certified Death Certificate	Price Varies

For additional assistance contact:

Istituto Centrale di Statistica
Via Cesare Balbo 16
00184 Rome, Italy

Ufficio Centrale Beni Archivistici
Ministero per i Beni Culturali e Ambientali
Via Gaeta 8A
00185 Rome, Italy

Embassy of Italy   Tel. (202) 328-5500
1601 Fuller Street, NW
Washington, DC 20009

The Family History Library of Salt Lake City, Utah has microfilmed original and published records of Italy. For further details on their holdings please consult your nearest Family History Center.

For further information see:

Cafari Panico, Ruggiero. *Lo Stato Civile ed il Diritto Internazionale Privato.* Padova, Italy: CEDAM, 1992. 215p.
L'anagrafe della Popolazione Nella Legislazione Italiana. Empoli, Italy: Tipocomuni, 1960. 181p.

Send your requests to:

Registrar
Ministries of Interior and Justice
Abidjan 01, Ivory Coast

Vital registration began in 1933 for French citizens, was expanded in 1950 to include residents within 15 miles of registration centers, and was extended in 1964 to the entire nation. Currently the registration is not considered to be comprehensive.

Cost for a certified Birth Certificate	75f
Cost for a certified Marriage Certificate	75f
Cost for a certified Death Certificate	75f

For additional assistance contact:

Directeur
Institut National de la Statistique
01 B.P. V55
Abidjan 01, Ivory Coast

Embassy of the Ivory Coast   Tel. (202) 797-0300
3421 Massachusetts Avenue, NW
Washington, DC 20007

For further information see:

Methods and Problems of Civil Registration Practices and Vital Statistics Collection in Africa. IIVRS Technical Papers, No. 16. Bethesda, MD: International Institute for Vital Registration and Statistics, 1981. 27p.

Organization and Status of Civil Registration in Africa and Recommendations for Improvement. IIVRS Technical Papers, No. 31. Bethesda, MD: International Institute for Vital Registration and Statistics, 1988. 15p.

Some Observations on Civil Registration in French-Speaking Africa. IIVRS Technical Papers, No. 39. Bethesda, MD: International Institute for Vital Registration and Statistics, 1990. 13p.

JAMAICA

Send your requests for Births, Marriages, and Deaths to:

Registrar General
Registrar General's Office
Island Record Office
Spanish Town, Jamaica

Tel. (876) 984-3041-5

While church registers were kept from colonial times, modern vital registration began January 1, 1878 in Jamaica. When writing to the Registrar General the fee must also include postage. Current vital registration is considered to be comprehensive.

Send your requests for Adoption Records to:

Adoption Board
10a Chelsea Avenue
Kingston 10, Jamaica

Send your requests for Divorce Records to:

The Supreme Court
Public Building E
134 Tower Street
Kingston, Jamaica

Cost for a certified Birth Certificate	$Jam 100
Cost for a certified Marriage Certificate	$Jam 100
Cost for a certified Divorce Decree	$Jam 21.25
Cost for a certified Death Certificate	$Jam 100
Cost for a certified Adoption Certificate	$Jam 100
Additional cost if a search of the records is needed	$Jam 70
Additional cost for duplicate certificate if ordered at the same time	$Jam 35

For additional assistance contact:

Embassy of Jamaica
1520 New Hampshire Avenue, NW
Washington, DC 20036

Tel. (202) 452-0660

For further information see:

McCaw Binns, A.M., K. Fox, K.E. Foster-Williams, and B. Irons. "Registration of Births, Stillbirths and Infant Deaths in Jamaica." *International Journal of Epidemiology*. Vol. 25, 1996, pp. 807-813.

_____. IIVRS Technical Papers, No. 72. Bethesda, MD: International Institute for Vital Registration and Statistics, 1998. 10p.

Registration of Vital Events in the English-Speaking Caribbean. IIVRS Technical Papers, No. 32. Bethesda, MD: International Institute for Vital Registration and Statistics, 1988. 10p.

GOVERNMENT OF JAMAICA

REGISTRAR GENERAL'S DEPARTMENT

APPLICATION FOR A CERTIFIED COPY OF A BIRTH REGISTRATION

Please Print All Information In **BLOCK CAPITAL LETTERS**. The more information provided, the better the chance for prompt and accurate service.

I hereby apply for _____ Certified Copy(s) of the Birth Certificate for the following child:
Number

Child's Name _____   _____   _____

Date of Birth: _____ / _____ / _____   Sex: _____ Male _____ Female
  Day   Month   Year

Place _____
  Hospital Name or Home Address

of
Birth: _____   _____
  Parish   *District*

Date of Registration: _____ / _____ / _____   Registration (Birth Entry) Number: _____
  Day   Month   Year

Place of Registration: _____   _____
  Parish   *District*

Mother's Names _____   _____   _____
  Christian (First)   *Surname*   *Surname before Marriage*

Father's Names _____   _____   _____
  Christian (First)   *Middle*   *Surname*

Applicant's Names _____   _____   _____
  Christian (First)   *Middle*   *Surname*

Applicant's Signature _____

Street Address _____

Town _____   Parish _____

Applicant's Relationship to child: _____   Signature: _____

Date of Application: _____ / _____ / _____   Telephone Number: _____
  Day   Month   Year

Special Instructions _____

=============== For Use by RGD Only ===============

Cert. Loc.	Copy	Sealed	Signed	Deliv.	Mailed
Date: _____	Date: _____	Date: _____	Date: _____	Date: _____	Date: _____
By: _____	By: _____	By: _____	By: _____	By: _____	By: _____

GOVERNMENT OF JAMAICA

REGISTRAR GENERAL'S DEPARTMENT

APPLICATION FOR CERTIFIED COPY OF MARRIAGE CERTIFICATE

Please Print All Information In **BLOCK CAPITAL LETTERS**. The more information provided, the better the chances for prompt, accurate service.

I hereby apply for _____ copy(s) of the Marriage Certificate issued for:
Number

Husband's Names _____ _____ _____
　　　　　　　　　　　Christian (First)　　　　　　*Middle*　　　　　　　*Surname*

Wife's Names _____ _____ _____
　　　　　　　　　　Christian (First)　　　　　　*Surname*　　　　*Surname before Marriage*

Date of Marriage: _____ / _____ / _____
　　　　　　　　　　Day　　*Month*　　*Year*

Place (Church Name, Home Address, etc.) of Marriage:

_____

_____　　_____
　　　　　　　Street or District　　　　　　　　　　　　　*Parish*

Marriage Officer's Name: _____

Applicant's Names _____ _____ _____
　　　　　　　　　　　Christian (First)　　　　　　*Middle*　　　　　　　*Surname*

Street Address _____

Town _____　Parish _____

Date of Application: _____ / _____ / _____
　　　　　　　　　　　Day　　*Month*　　*Year*

----------------------------- **For Use by RGD Only** -----------------------------

Recvd.	Payment	Cert. Loc.	Copy	Sealed	Deliv.
Date: _____	Date: _____	Date: _____	Date: _____	Date: _____	Date: _____
By: _____	Amt.: _____	By: _____	By: _____	By: _____	By: _____

APPLICATION FORM FOR

CERTIFIED COPIES

OF DECREE ABSOLUTE

ADDRESS ....

....

....

....

DATE ....19...

The Court Administrator

Supreme Court

King Street

Kingston

Dear Madam,

I hereby apply for .... Certified Copies of Decree Absolute in the

matter of .... vs. ....

The Suit number is F.D.   /

I will be very grateful for your kind assistance as I need same for ....

Thank you.

Yours sincerely,

....
APPLICANT

GOVERNMENT OF JAMAICA

REGISTRAR GENERAL'S DEPARTMENT

APPLICATION FOR CERTIFIED COPY OF DEATH CERTIFICATE

Please Print All Information In **BLOCK CAPITAL LETTERS**. The more information provided, the better the chances for prompt, accurate service.

I hereby apply for _____ copy(s) of the Death Certificate issued for:
Number

Deceased's
Names _____ _____ _____
         Christian (First)   *Middle*   *Surname*

Place _____
         Hospital, District, Street Address, etc.
of
Death _____ _____
        Parish   *District*

Date of Death: _____ / _____ / _____   Sex of Deceased (Tick One):
        Day   *Month*   *Year*   _____ Male _____ Female

How did the Person Die?   (Tick [ ] the box that applies):

[ ] Violently   [ ] Suddenly   [ ] Accidentally [ ] Of Natural Causes

Place of Registration: _____ _____
of Death   *Parish*   *District*

Date of Registration: _____ / _____ / _____
        Day   *Month*   *Year*

Registration Number: _____

Applicant's
Names   _____ _____ _____
         Christian (First)   *Middle*   *Surname*

Street Address _____

Town _____ Parish _____

Applicant's Relationship to Deceased: _____

Date of Application: _____ / _____ / _____
        Day   *Month*   *Year*

=============== **For Use by RGD Only** ===============

Recvd.	Payment	Cert. Loc.	Copy	Sealed	Deliv.
Date: _____	Date: _____	Date: _____	Date: _____	Date: _____	Date: _____
By: _____	Amt. _____	By: _____	By: _____	By: _____	By: _____

Send your requests to:

Director General
Civil Affairs Bureau
Ministry of Justice
1-1-1 Kasumigaseki, Chiyoda-ku
Tokyo 100, Japan

Japan instituted its current system of *Koseki* or Family Registers in March 1868. These registers began as early as 451AD. The system has its roots in the Chinese tradition of keeping famiy registers for the past 4,000 years. Current registration is computerized and considered to be comprehensive. Any person may request a copy of the Family Register for any family in Japan. Each resident is required to have a national identification card.

Send your requests for Adoption Records to:

Family Court
(Town), Japan

Cost for a certified Birth Notation	¥350
Cost for a certified Divorce Notation	¥350
Cost for a certified Marriage Notation	¥350
Cost for a certified Death Certificate	¥350
Cost for a certified Adoption Notation	¥350
Cost for a certified Family Registration Form	¥450
Cost for a copy using the "old form"	¥500
Cost for a copy using rice paper	¥10,000

For additional assistance contact:

Vital Statistics Division
Statistics and Information Department
Ministry of Health and Welfare
7-3 Honmura-cho, Ichigaya
Shinjuku-ku
Tokyo 162, Japan

For further information see:

Bunmei, Sato. ***Koseki.*** *Tokyo*, Japan: Gendai Shokan, 1981. 173p.

Koseki to Mibun Toroku. ***Hikaku Kazokushi Gakkai Kanshu, Toshitani Nobuyoshi, Kamata Hiroshi, Hiramatsu Hiroshihen.*** Tokyo, Japan: Waseda Daigaku Shuppanbu, 1996. 297p.

Koseki Jiho. Tokyo, Japan: Nihon Kajo Shuppan, 1958– .

Mazzei, Franco. ***I Moduli Sociali di base nel Giappone Antico, Struttura e Funzioni Delle Famiglie (KO) dei Registri Anagrafici Conservati Nello Shosoin.*** Napoli, Italy: Istituto Orientale di Napoli, 1977. 87p.

Nanbu, Noboru. ***Nihon Kodai Koseki no Kenkyu.*** Tokyo, Japan: Yoshikawa Kobunkan, 1994. 475p.

Sakakibara, Fujiko. ***Josei to Koseki, Fufu Betsusei Jidai ni Mukete.*** Tokyo, Japan: Akashi Shoten, 1992. 259p.

Sawada, Shozo. ***Fufu Betsu Shiron to Koseki Mondai.*** Tokyo. Japan: Gyosei, 1990. 194p.

Ueda, Kozo, and Masasuke Omori. ***Vital Statistics System of Japan.*** IIVRS Technical Papers, No. 2. Bethesda, MD: International Institute for Vital Registration and Statistics, 1979. 12p.

◎夜の12時は「午前0時」、昼の12時は「午後0時」と書いてください。

死亡診断書（死体検案書）

氏　名		1男 2女	生年月日	明治 大正 昭和 平成　　年　　月　　日
(13) 発病年月日	平成　　年　　月　　日			
死亡年月日時分	平成　　年　　月　　日　午前・午後　　時　　分			
(14) 死亡したところ及びその種別（注意(1)参照）	1病院 2診療所 3老人保健施設 4助産所 5自宅 6その他			
死亡したところ			番地 番　号	
(15) 死亡の種類	1病死及び自然死 2不慮の外因死（3その他の災害 4自殺 5他殺 6その他及び不詳） 7その他の外因死及び不詳			
死亡の原因	I イ（直接死因） ロ（イ）の原因 ハ（ロ）の原因		発病から死亡までの期間	
	II その他の身体的状況（注意(2)参照）			
(16)（イ）(ロ)(ハ)の直接医学的関係の明らかな関係を書いてください	手術 手術の年月日		平成　年　月　日	
	解剖 主要所見			
(17) 外因死追加事項	傷害発生年月日時分	平成　年　月　日　午前・午後　時　分		
	手段及び状況			
	傷害発生の場所（注意(3)参照）	市区町村		
	場所名の具体的記載欄			
(18) 生後168時間未満で死亡した場合の追加事項（注意(4)参照）	妊娠・分娩時における母体の状況			
(19) 上記の通り診断（検案）する（病院、診療所若しくは老人保健施設の名称及び所在地又は医師の住所） 氏名　　医師			平成　年　月　日 番地 番　号　　印	

記入の注意

鉛筆や消えやすいインキで書かないでください。

死亡したことを知った日からかぞえて7日以内に出してください。

死亡者の本籍地でない役場に出すときは、2通出してください。

「筆頭者の氏名」には、戸籍のはじめに記載されている人の氏名を書いてください。

内縁のものはふくまれません。

□には、あてはまるものに☑のようにしるしをつけてください。

死亡について書いてください。

死亡診断書記入の注意

(1) 死亡の場所の種別は、老人ホームにおいて死亡した場合において、住民票に記載された老人ホームであるときは15を、その他のときは6を丸で囲んで下さい。

(2) I欄には、I欄記載の原因と直接の関係はないが、I欄記載の原因に影響を与えると思われる身体の状況を書いてください。なお妊娠中の死亡には「妊娠満何週」、分娩中の死亡には「妊娠満何週の分娩中」、産

後42日以内の死亡には「妊娠満何週産後何日」と書いてください。

(3) 傷害発生の場所名はたとえば「自宅の風呂場」、「小川の中」、「鉱山の坑内」のように具体的に書いてください。

(4) 妊娠・分娩中の母体の状況は、この死亡者の出生にも立ち会った医師又はこの死亡者が同一の病院・診療所で出生した場合のみこの欄に書いてください。

死亡届

平成　　年　　月　　日届出

　　　　　　　長　殿

	受理	平成　　年　　月　　日 第　　　　　号	発送	平成　　年　　月　　日 第　　　　　号
	送付	平成　　年　　月　　日 第　　　　　号		長印
	書類調査	戸籍記載	記載調査	調査票	附票	住民票	通知

(1)	氏　名		名	□男 □女
(2)				
(3)	生年月日	平成　　年　　月　　日（生まれてから30日以内に死亡したときは生まれた時刻も書いてください）午前・午後　時　分		
(4)	死亡したとき	平成　　年　　月　　日　午前・午後　　時　　分		
(5)	死亡したところ		番地 番　号	
(6)	住　所（住民登録をしているところ）		番地 番	
	世帯主の氏名			
(7)	本　籍（外国人のときは国籍だけを書いてください）		番地 番	
	筆頭者の氏名			
(8)	死亡した人の夫または妻	□いる（満　　歳）　□いない（□未婚 □死別 □離別）		
(9)	死亡した人の届出生	（生まれてから8日以内に死亡したときだけ書いてください）都道府県　役所や役場に届出		
(10)	死亡したときの世帯のおもな仕事と	□1.農業だけまたはその他の仕事を持っている世帯 □2.農業とその他の仕事を持っている世帯 □3.店や企業などを自分でしている世帯 □4.官公庁・事務・教員・販売・外交・医療保健技術者・旧制専門学校卒業以上の技術者などの勤労者世帯（日々または1年未満の契約の雇用者は6） □5.4にあてはまらない勤労者世帯（日々または1年未満の契約の雇用者は6） □6.その他の世帯		
(11)	世帯のおもな仕事と			
(12)	職業・産業	（国勢調査の年…の4月1日から翌年3月31日までに死亡したときだけ書いてください）職業　　産業		

その他	
届出人	□1.同居の親族 □2.同居していない親族 □3.同居者 □4.家主 □5.地主 □6.家屋管理人 □7.土地管理人
	住所　　　　　　　番地 番　号
	本籍　　　　　　　番地 番　号
	署名　　　　　　　印　　平成　　年　　月　　日生
事件簿番号	

離婚届

婚姻届

この届は、あらかじめ用意して、結婚式をあげる日または同居を始める日に出すようにしてください。その日が日曜日や祝日でも届けることができます。（この場合、宿直等で取扱うので、前日までに戸籍担当係で調べて下さい。）
夫になる人または妻になる人の本籍地に出すときは2通、その他のところに出すときは3通提出して下さい。
この届書を本籍地でない役場に出すときは、戸籍謄本が必要ですから、あらかじめ用意してください。（謄本でもけっこうです。）

証　人

署名押印	印	印
生年月日	年　月　日	年　月　日
住所	番地号	番地号
本籍	番地番	番地番

「筆頭者の氏名」には、戸籍のはじめに記載されている人の氏名を書いてください。

父母が離婚しているときは、母の氏は離婚のときのときだけを書いてください。

養父母については同じように書いてください。

□には、あてはまるものに□のようにしるしをつけてください。

外国人と婚姻する人が、まだ戸籍の筆頭者となっていない場合には、新しい籍がつくられますので、希望する本籍を書いてください。

再婚のときは、直前の婚姻について書いてください。
内縁のものはふくまれません。

◎ 署名は必ず本人が自署してください
◎ 印は各自別々の印を押してください
◎ 届出人の印を御持参下さい

連絡先
電話（　）
自宅・勤務先・呼出

平成　　年　　月　　日届出

受理　平成　　年　　月　　日
第　　　　　号
送付　平成　　年　　月　　日
第　　　　　号

	夫になる人	妻になる人
(1) 氏名		
生年月日	年　月　日	年　月　日
(2) 住所（住民登録をしているところ） 世帯主の氏名	番地番号	番地番号
(3) 本籍（外国人のときは国籍だけを書いてください） 筆頭者の氏名	番地番	番地番
父母の氏名 父母との続き柄（他の養父母はその他の欄に書いてください） 父　母	続き柄　男	続き柄　女
(4) 婚姻後の夫婦の氏・新しい本籍	□夫の氏　□妻の氏　新本籍	番地番
(5) 同居を始めたとき	年　月（結婚式をあげたとき、または同居を始めたときのうち早いほうを書いてください）
(6) 初婚・再婚の別	□初婚　□再婚（□死別 □離別 年月日）	□初婚　□再婚（□死別 □離別 年月日）
(7) 同居を始める前の夫妻のそれぞれの世帯のおもな仕事と	1. 農業だけまたは農業とその他の仕事を持っている世帯 2. 自由業・商工業・サービス業等を個人で経営している世帯 3. 企業・個人商店等（官公庁は除く）の常用勤労者世帯で勤め先の従業者数が1人から99人までの世帯 4. 3にあてはまらない常用勤労者世帯及び会社団体の役員の世帯 5. 1から4にあてはまらないその他の仕事をしている者のいる世帯 6. 仕事をしている者のいない世帯
(8) （国勢調査の年…年…の4月1日から翌年3月31日までに届出をするときだけ書いてください） 夫の職業		妻の職業

その他

届出人署名押印	夫　　　　　印　　妻　　　　　印
事件簿番号	

◎夜の12時は「午前0時」、昼の12時は「午後0時」と書いてください。

出生証明書

						グラム
(10)	子の男女の別、氏名及び体重	1 男 2 女	氏名		体重	
(11)	生まれた子の数の場合	双子以上	1 第一子 2 第二子 3 第三子 4 第四子以上（第　　子）	出産順位		
		1 双子 2 三つ子 3 四つ以上（子）				
(12)	出生の年月日時分	平成　　年　　月　　日　午前 午後　　時　　分				
	出生の場所	1 病院 2 診療所 3 助産所 4 自宅 5 その他	番地 番 号			
			(1.2.3の名称 ）			
(13)	妊娠週数及び母の氏名	妊娠 満 週	母の氏名			
(14)	この母の出産した子の数	出生子（この出生子及び出生後に死亡した子を含む）人 死産児（妊娠満20週以後の死産児）胎				
(15)	上記のとおり記入の日時場所で出生したことを証明する。	住所		番地 番 号		
	平成　　年　　月　　日	1 医師 2 助産婦 3 その他	氏名 押印	印		

出生証明書記入の注意

出生証明書(10)欄の体重は、立会者が医師又は助産婦以外の者で、わからなければ書かなくてもかまいません。

出生証明書(14)欄のこの母の出産した子の数は、当該母又は家人などから聞いて書いてください。

この出生証明書の作成者は、この出生の立会者が例えば医師・助産婦とともに立会った場合には医師が書くように1、2、3の順序に従って書いてくだ

記入の注意

鉛筆や消えやすいインキで書かないでください。

子が生まれた日からかぞえて14日以内に届出してください。

子の本籍地でない役場に出すときは、2通出してください（役場が相当と認めたときは、1通で足りることもあります。）。2通の場合でも、出生証明書欄は、原本1通と写し1通でさしつかえありません。

子の名は、常用漢字、人名用漢字、かたかな、ひらがなで書いてください。

よみかたは、戸籍には記載されません。住民票の処理上必要ですから書いてください。

□には、あてはまるものに✓のようにしるしをつけてください。

筆頭者の氏名には、戸籍のはじめに記載されている人の氏名を書いてください。

子の父または母が、まだ戸籍の筆頭者となっていない場合は、新しい戸籍がつくられますので、この欄に希望する本籍を書いてください。

◎母子健康手帳と届出人の印をご持参下さい。

連絡先
電話（　　）　　　番
自宅・勤務先・呼出　　　方

出生届

平成　　年　　月　　日届出

		受理 平成 年 月 日	発送 平成 年 月 日				長印
		第　　号	第　　号				
	氏名	送付 平成 年 月 日					印
		第　　号					
		書類調査	戸籍記載	記載調査	調査票	附票	住民票
(1)	子の氏名	名			□男 □女		
(2)	生まれたとき	平成 年 月 日 午前 午後 時 分					
(3)	生まれたところ	番地 番 号					
(4)	住所（住民登録をする）	世帯主の氏名	番地 番 号		世帯主と子の続き柄		
(5)	父母の氏名 生年月日	父	母		子が生まれたときの父母の年齢（満 歳）		
(6)	本籍	筆頭者の氏名	番地 番				
(7)	同居を始めたとき	平成 年 月（結婚式をあげたとき、または、同居を始めたときのうち早いほうを書いてください）					
(8)	子が生まれたときの世帯のおもな仕事と						
(9)	父母の職業	父の職業	母の職業				
	その他						
届出人	□1.父 □2.法定代理人（　　）□3.同居者 □4.医師 □5.助産婦 □6.その他の立会者						
	住所	番地 番 号					
	本籍	番地 番		筆頭者の氏名			
	署名	印		平成 年 月 日生			

事件簿番号

本		氏
籍		名

	父	
	母	
	出生	

	父	
	母	
	出生	

	父	
	母	
	出生	

Send your requests to:

Registrar
Department of Civil Status
Ministry of the Interior
P.O. Box 2740
Amman, Jordan

Jordan instituted vital registration in 1926. Today, vital registration is considered to be comprehensive for births and about 60 percent for deaths. Adoption is rare in Jordan. Orphaned children are raised by relatives.

Cost for a certified Birth Certificate	1JD
Cost for a certified Marriage Certificate	1JD
Cost for a certified Death Certificate	1JD

For additional assistance contact:

Department of Libraries, Documentation and Archives
P.O. Box 6070
Amman, Jordan

Amman Public Library
P.O. Box 182181
Amman, Jordan

Embassy of Jordan   Tel. (202) 966-2664
3504 International Drive, NW
Washington, DC 20008

For further information see:

Organization and Status of Civil Registration in the Arab Countries. IIVRS Technical Papers, No. 33. Bethesda, MD: International Institute for Vital Registration and Statistics, 1988. 6p.

KAZAKHSTAN

For information contact:

Kazakhskaia Biblioteka   Tel. (011) (7) (327) 69-6586
(National Library)
ul. Abaia 14
480013 Alma-Ata, Kazakhstan

Embassy of Kazakhstan   Tel. (202) 232-5488
1401 16th Street, NW
Washington, DC 20036

The Family History Library of Salt Lake City, Utah has microfilmed records of Kazakhstan and the former Soviet Union. For further details on their holdings please consult your nearest Family History Center.

KENYA

Send your requests to:

Principal Civil Registrar
P.O. Box 30031
Nairobi, Kenya

Tel. (011) (254) (2) 7461

While church registers were kept from colonial times, modern vital registration for Europeans didn't begin until 1904. Registration was expanded to include Asians in 1906 and the entire population by 1971. Currently registration is not considered to be comprehensive. The Registrar will accept an international bank draft payable in U.S. dollars. Kenya is divided into districts, and it is at the District Registry where the original birth and death certificates are kept. Duplicates are sent to the Central Registry.

Cost for a certified Birth Certificate	KSh. 10.00
Cost for a short form Birth Certificate	KSh. 5.00
Cost for a certified Marriage Certificate	KSh. 10.00
Cost for a certified Death Certificate	KSh. 10.00

For additional assistance contact:

Population Statistics
Central Bureau of Statistics
P.O. Box 30266
Nairobi, Kenya

Embassy of Kenya
2249 R Street, NW
Washington, DC 20008

Tel. (202) 387-6101

The Family History Library of Salt Lake City, Utah has microfilmed records of Kenya and Africa. For further details on their holdings please consult your nearest Family History Center.

For further information see:

Gil, Benjamin, and J. K. Rowah. *The Kenya Civil Registration Demonstration Project (CRDP), a Strategy for a Rapidly Developing Country in Africa*. Nairobi, Kenya: Government Printer, 1985. 568p.

A Guide to the Private (Local) Archives. Nairobi, Kenya: Kenya National Archives, 1987. 17p.

Kannisto, Vaino.*Civil Registration and Vital Statistics in the Africa Region, Lessons Learned from the Evaluation of UNFPA Assisted Projects in Kenya and Sierra Leone*. New York, NY: UN Fund for Population Activities, 1984.

Methods and Problems of Civil Registration Practices and Vital Statistics Collection in Africa. IIVRS Technical Papers, No. 16. Bethesda, MD: International Institute for Vital Registration and Statistics, 1981. 27p.

Munene, Francis. *Kenyan Experiences and Challenges in Demographic Data Collection and Utilization*. Paper Presented at the 51st International Statistical Institute, Istanbul, Turkey, 1997.

Organization and Status of Civil Registration in Africa and Recommendations for Improvement. IIVRS Technical Papers, No. 31. Bethesda, MD: International Institute for Vital Registration and Statistics, 1988. 15p.

REPUBLIC OF KENYA

No. . . . .

APPLICATION FOR A BIRTH/MARRIAGE/ DEATH CERTIFICATE

Insert name and
address of
applicant.

I, ...

of . . . .

Delete as
necessary.

hereby apply for Certificate(s) of Birth / Marriage / Death particulars whereof are given below.

I attach the sum of Sh. . . . . being the prescribed fee payable at the rate of

Sh. 10 for each certificate required.

Full Name	Where Born, Married or Died	Date of Birth, Marriage or Death	Entry No. (To be completed at District Registry)
. . . .	. . . .	. . . .	. . . .
. . . .	. . . .	. . . .	. . . .
. . . .	. . . .	. . . .	. . . .
. . . .	. . . .	. . . .	. . . .

(For use in Registrar's Department only)

Date   *Initials*

Application received
with fee as above . . . .

Certificate issued . . . .

TO THE REGISTRAR-GENERAL
P.O. BOX 30031,
NAIROBI.

Send your requests to:

Registrar General of Births, Deaths and Marriages
Civil Registration Office
P.O. Box 55
Bairiki, Tarawa, Kiribati

Civil registration began in the 19th century and is not comprehensive. All records through 1989 have been microfilmed. Current vital registration is considered to be 70 percent complete for births and 60 percent complete for deaths. Kiribati uses the Australian dollar as currency.

Cost for a certified Birth Certificate	A$2.00
Cost for a certified Marriage Certificate	A$2.00
Cost for a certified Death Certificate	A$2.00

For additional assistance contact:

Republic Statistician
Ministry of Finance and Economic Planning
P.O. Box 67
Bairiki, Tarawa, Kiribati

National Archives and Library   Tel. (011) (686) 21-337
P.O. Box 6   Fax (011) (686) 28-222
Bairiki, Tarawa, Kiribati

The Family History Library of Salt Lake City, Utah has microfilmed original and published records and registers of Kiribati. For further details on their holdings please consult your nearest Family History Center.

For further information see:

The Laws of the Gilbert Islands Enacted before 1st January 1977, Revised Edition 1977. Chapter 5, Births, Deaths and Marriages Registration. London, England: Eyre & Spottswoode, Ltd., 1979. 34p.

The Laws of the Gilbert Islands Enacted before 1st January 1977, Revised Edition 1977. Chapter 54, Marriage. London, England: Eyre & Spottswoode, Ltd., 1979. 16p.

KOREA — NORTH

Family household registers are maintained by:

Police Department
(Town), North Korea

Korea has maintained national population registers from the time of the United Silla Kingdom (668–935 AD). In 1896 a law on population registration was issued that required the registers to be updated annually. Currently individuals register and update their family listings with the local police department.

Cost for a certified Birth Certificate	Free
Cost for a certified Marriage Certificate	Free
Cost for a certified Death Certificate	Free

The Family History Library of Salt Lake City, Utah has microfilmed original and published records of Korea. For further details on their holdings please consult your nearest Family History Center.

Send your requests for copies of Household Registrations to:

Registrar
Ministry of Home Affairs
(Town of current residence), Korea

Send your requests for copies of Household/Individual Census Records to:

Director General
Bureau of Registry
Ministry of Court Administration
37, Sosomoon-dong, Chung-ku
Seoul, 110-310, Korea

Korea has maintained national population registers from the time of the United Silla Kingdom (668–935 AD). In 1896 a law on population registration was issued that required the registers to be updated annually. Currently individuals may register and update their family listings at either the Ministry of Home Affairs office where they currently live or at the Ministry of Court Administration's offices in the family's recognized "hometown" or "ancestral home." This dual registration system means that both registers need to be searched for copies of vital records.

Cost for a copy of a Household Registration (Ministry of Home Affairs)	400 Won
Cost for a Census Record, (Ho Juk, Deung Bon) for the entire family	400 Won
Cost for a Census Record, (Ho Juk, Cho Bon) for an individual	300 Won

Send your requests for Adoption Records to:

Ministry of Health and Social Affairs
1 Jungang-dong
Gwachon City, Kyonggi
Korea

Tel. (011) (82) (2) 503-7524
Fax (011) (82) (2) 504-6418

More Korean children have been adopted by American families than children from any other country. While the procedure has been that the child is formally adopted in U.S. courts after residing in the U.S. for one year, copies of these records are kept permanently by the Korean adoption agency that arranged for the adoption.

For additional assistance contact:

Director
Population Statistics Division
National Statistical Office
90, Gyeongun-dong, Jongro-gu
Seoul 110-310, Korea

Embassy of Korea
Consular Section
2450 Massachusetts Avenue, NW
Washington, DC 20008

Tel. (202) 939-5600

(양식 제1호)

출 생 신 고

장 귀하   19   년   월   일

①	출	본 적				읍면동 접수
			호주성명		호주와의 관계	
②	생	주 소				세대별주민등록표정리 월 일(인)
			세대주성명		새대주와의 관계	개인별주민등록표작성 월 일(인)
③		성 명	( )본		혼인중의 자 / 혼인외의 자 ①남②여 / ①남②여	주민등록번호 부여
④	자	출생년월일	년 월 일 시 분			대장정리 월 일(인)
⑤		출생장소			①자택 ②병원 ③기타	번 호
⑥	부모성명	부 본 모 본				주민등록지관할시구청송부 월 일(인)
⑦	기타사항					
⑧	신고인	본 적			호주성명	관할시구청접수
		주 소		전화	자격	
		기명날인		출생년월일		
				주민등록번호		

인 구 동 태 사 항

⑨	부모의 출생년월일	부 년 월 일	모 년 월 일		본적지송부 월 일(인)
⑩	부모의직업	부	모		본적지접수
⑪	부모의 교육정도	부 ①불취학 ②국민학교 ③중학교 ④고등학교 ⑤대학이상	모 ①불취학 ②국민학교 ③중학교 ④고등학교 ⑤대학이상		
⑫	부모의결혼년월일	년 월 일부터 동거			호적부정리 월 일(인)
⑬	임신월수 및 태수	임신 만 개월 / 태수 ①단태아 ②쌍태아(쌍둥이) ③3태아 이상	신생아체중 kg		호적부에주민등록번호개재 월 일(인)
⑭	모의 출산아수	총출산 명 생존 명 사망 명			주민등록지통보 월 일(인)
⑮	조산자	①의사 ②조산원 ③기타			인구동태신고서 송부 월 일(인)

◎ 뒷면의 기재요령에 의하여 기재하여 주시기 바랍니다.

기 재 요 령

1. 본적지에 신고할 경우에는 신고서 2통, 본적지가 아닌 곳에서 신고할 경우에는 3통을 작성 제출하여야 합니다.

2. 신고서는 한글과 아라비아 숫자로 기재합니다. 다만, 출생자 성명과 본은 한자로 기재하고 성명의 한글표기를 ( )안에 기재합니다. 출생자의 이름에 사용하는 한자는 대법원규칙이 정하는 범위내의 것이어야 합니다.

3. 제1란 본적에는 출생자가 들어가야 할 가(家)의 본적을 기재합니다.

4. 제3란 남녀 구분은 해당번호에 ○표시를 하고, 제5란 출생장소에는 실제 출산한 장소를 기입하고 해당번호에 ○표시를 합니다.(예 : ①)

5. 혼인외의 출생자를 모가 신고하는 경우에는 제6란 부(父)의 성명과 본은 기재하지 않습니다.

6. 재혼금지기간중에 재혼한 여자가 재혼 성립후 200일 이내에 출산했거나 혼인 종료후 300일 이후에 출산하여 모가 출생신고를 하는 경우에는 제6란 부(父)의 성명란에 "부미정"이라 기재합니다.

7. 출생신고서에는 의사 조산사 기타 분만에 관여한 자의 **출생증명서를 첨부하여야** 하며, 부득이한 사유로 첨부하지 못하는 때에는 그 취지를 기타사항란에 기재합니다.

8. 제7란 기타사항에는 다음과 같은 사항을 기재합니다.

   가. 혼인이외의 출생자를 부(父)가 신고하는 경우에는 모의 본적 및 호주와의 관계.

   나. 출생자가 출생신고에 의하여 일가를 창립하는 경우에는 그 취지, 원인과 창립장소.

   다. 선순위자(부모)가 출생신고를 할 수 없는 경우에는 그 선순위자의 성명, 출생년월일, 본적 및 신고할 수 없는 이유

   라. 기타 호적에 기재하여야 할 사항을 명료하게 하는데 특히 필요한 사항.

9. 제8란 중 자격란에는 부, 모, 호주, 동거하는 친족, 분만관여의사 등 신고인의 자격을 명시하여야 합니다.

10. 제9란 부모의 생년월인은 호적창 생년월일과 실제의 생년월일이 다른 경우에는 실제의 생년월일을 기재합니다.

11. 제10란 부모의 직업을 구체적·서술적으로 상세히 기재하여야 합니다.

    (예 : 운동화를 제조하는 ○○주식회사의 영업부 판촉담당사원)

12. 제11란은 해당번호에 ○표시를 합니다.(예 : ③)

13. 제12란 부모의 결혼년월일은 호적상 혼인신고일과는 관계없이 실제로 **결혼생활을 시작한 년월일을** 기재합니다.

14. 제13란 중 태수란, 제15란은 해당번호에 ○표시를 합니다.(예 : ①)

15. 제14란은 모가 재혼인 경우에는 전·후혼 또는 혼인외의 출산아도 기재합니다.

혼 인 신 고

장   귀하   19 년 월 일

①	구 분			남 편			처		
②	당	본 적	호 주 성 명		호 주 와 의 관계		호 주 성 명		호 주 와 의 관계
③	사	주 소	세대주 성 명		세대주 의 관계		세대주 성 명		세대주와 의 관계
④	자	성 명	(	)	본		(	)	본
⑤		출 생 년 월 일		주민등 록번호				주민등 록번호	
⑥	부모성명 및 본 적	부	본 적				본 적		
			성 명				성 명		
		모	본 적				본 적		
			성 명				성 명		
⑦	양친성명 및 본 적	양 부	본 적				본 적		
			성 명				성 명		
		양 모	본 적				본 적		
			성 명				성 명		

⑧	혼인해소년월일	
⑨	신 본 적	

⑩	수 반 입 적 자	성 명	출생년월일	부 모 성 명	분가자와의관계
		( )			
		( )			

⑪	폐 가 할 가	
⑫	기 타 사 항	

⑬	증	본 적		기 명 날 인		
		주 소		출생년월일		주민등록번호
	인	본 적		기 명 날 인		
		주 소		출생년월일		주민등록번호

(뒷면계속)

⑭ 동 의 자	남편의 부 기명날인			출 생 년 월 일		
	남편의 모 기명날인			출 생 년 월 일		
	처 의 부 기명날인			출 생 년 월 일		
	처 의 모 기명날인			출 생 년 월 일		
⑮ 신 고 인	남 편 기명날인		전 화		처 기명날인	전 화

인 구 동 태 사 항

⑯ 실제결혼년월일	서기 년 월 일부터 동거	
⑰ 성 혼 과 정	1 자유(연애) 2 중 매 3 절 충	
⑱ 혼 인 장 소	1 자 택 2 예식장 3 종교시설 4 기 타	
⑲ 직 업	남편 처	
⑳ 교 육 정 도	남편 [1 불취학 2 국민학교 3 중학교 4 고등학교 5 대학이상]	처 [1 불취학 2 국민학교 3 중학교 4 고등학교 5 대학이상]
㉑ 혼 인 종 류	남편 [1 초혼 2 사별후 재혼 3 이혼후 재혼]	처 [1 초혼 2 사별후 재혼 3 이혼후 재혼]

기 재 요 령

1. 남편 또는 처의 본적지에 신고할 경우에는 신고서 3통, 기타의 곳에 신고할 경우에는 4통을 작성 제출하고, 법정분가할 자일 경우에는 각1통을 추가작성 제출하고 남편과 처의 호적등본 각1통을 첨부하여야 합니다.

2. 신고서는 **한글과 아라비아 숫자**로 기재합니다. 다만 사건본인의 **성명**과 **본**은 **한자**로 기재하고 성명의 한글 표기를 (   )안에 기재합니다.

3. 처의 가(家)에 입적하는 혼인인 경우에는 그 사실을 신고명칭에 기재합니다.

4. 제9란 신본적에는 법정분가 장소를 기재합니다.

5. 제11란은 여호주가 폐가하고 혼인하는 경우에 기재합니다.

6. 제12란 기타사항은 다음과 같은 사항을 기재합니다.

   가. 혼인당사자들이 동성동본이나 동일혈족이 아닌 때에는 "혼인당사자들은 각 시조를 달리함"이라는 취지.

   나. 당사자의 일방이 혼가로부터 재혼하는 때에는 친가의 호주성명, 호주와의 관계 및 그 본적.

   다. 재혼금지기간 내에 재혼하는 여자가 전혼관계의 종료후 해산을 하였거나 임신하지 아니한 증명을 하여 혼인신고하는 경우에는 그 사유.

   라. 처의 가(家)에 입적하는 혼인인 경우에는 그 취지.

   마. 여호주가 폐가하고 혼인하는 경우에는 그 취지.

   바. 기타 호적에 기재하여야 할 사항을 명료하게 하는데 필요한 사항.

7. 제17란, 제18란, 제20란, 제21란은 해당번호에 ○표시를 합니다. (예 : ③)

8. 제20란의 "교육정도"는 교육부장관이 인정한 모든 정규교육기관을 기준으로 기재하되 각급 학교의 재학, 중 퇴자도 해당학교의 번호에 ○표시를 합니다.

9. 제19란의 직업은 실제 결혼당시의 **직업을 구체적, 서술적으로 기재**하여야 합니다. (예 : 전화기를 제조하는 ○○회사 경리사원)

이혼(친권자지정)신고

장　　귀하　　　　　　　　　　　　　　　　19 년 월 일

①	구　분		남　편			처		
②	당사자	본　적	호주성명		호주와의 관계	호주성명		호주와의 관계
③		주　소	세대주성명		세대주와의 관계	세대주성명		세대주와의 관계
④		성　명	(	)	본	(	)	본
⑤		출생년월일		주민등록번호			주민등록번호	
⑥	부모성명 및 본적	부	본적			본적		
			성명			성명		
		모	본적			본적		
			성명			성명		
⑦	양친성명 및 본적	양부	본적			본적		
			성명			성명		
		양모	본적			본적		
			성명			성명		
⑧	복적할가		본적			호주성명		
⑨	신　본　적							
⑩	일가창립원인			장　소				
⑪	부　흥　장　소							

⑫	수반입적자	성　명	출생년월일	부모성명	분가자와의관계
		( )			
		( )			

⑬	기　타　사　항				
⑭	재판확정년월일		법　원　명		

⑮	친권자지정	미성년자성명	(	)	미성년자성명	(	)
		본적		호주	본적		호주
		주소			주소		
		생년월일	주민등록번호		생년월일	주민등록번호	
		친권행사자			친권행사자		
		년월일	원인		년월일	원인	

(뒷면계속)

⑯ 증 인	본 적			기 명 날 인		
	주 소			출생년월일	주민등록번호	
	본 적			기 명 날 인		
	주 소			출생년월일	주민등록번호	

⑰ 동 의 자		출생년월일	
	남편의 부 기명날인	출생년월일	
	남편의 모 기명날인	출생년월일	
	처의 부 기명날인	출생년월일	
	처의 모 기명날인	출생년월일	

⑱ 신 고 인	남 편 기명날인		전 화	처 기명날인		전 화	

인 구 동 태 사 항

⑲	실제결혼년월일	서기 년 월 일 부터 동거		
⑳	실제이혼년월일	서기 년 월 일 부터 이혼		
㉑	성 혼 과 정	① 자 유 (연애)	② 중 매	③ 절 충
㉒	20세미만자녀수	명 이혼의 종류	① 협 의	② 재 판
㉓	이 혼 사 유	① 부부불화 ② 가족간 불화 ③ 건강상 ④ 경제문제 ⑤ 기 타		
㉔	교 육 정 도	남편 ① 불취학 ② 국민학교 ③ 중학교 ④ 고등학교 ⑤ 대학이상	처 ① 불취학 ② 국민학교 ③ 중학교 ④ 고등학교 ⑤ 대학이상	

기 재 요 령

1. 신고명칭중 해당하지 아니하는 사항을 삭제합니다.
2. 본적지에 신고할 경우에는 신고서 3통, 본적지 아닌 곳에 신고할 경우에는 4통을 작성, 제출하여야 합니다.
3. 복적을 원할 경우 협의이혼일 경우에는 처가 복적할 가(家)의 호적등본 1통과 협의이혼의사확인서 1통을 첨부하여야 하고 재판에 의한 이혼일 경우에는 처가 복적할 가(家)의 호적등본 1통과 이혼심판정본 및 그 확정증명 각 1통을 첨부하여야 합니다.
4. 신고서는 **한글과 아라비아 숫자**로 기재합니다. 다만, 사건본인의 **성명**과 **본**은 **한자**로 기재하고 성명의 한글 표기를 (   )안에 기재합니다.
5. 제9란 신본적은 법정분가 장소를 기재합니다.
6. 혼가를 떠나는 자가 복적하고자 할 경우에는 제8란을, 일가창립하고자 할 경우에는 제10란을, 친가부흥하고자 할 경우에는 제11란을 각 기재합니다.
7. 제13란 기타사항에는 다음과 같은 사항을 기재합니다.
   가. 혼가를 떠나는 자가 일가를 창립하는 경우에는 그 사유.
   나. 친가를 부흥하는 때에는 그 취지.
   다. 신고사건으로 인하여 신분의 변경이 있게되는 자가 있을 경우에 그 자의 성명, 출생년월일, 본적 및 신분변경의 사유
   라. 친권을 행사할 자가 정해진 때에는 그 취지.
   마. 재판상이혼의 신고시 호적법 제79조 제1항 제1호 내지 제4호의 사항을 기재할 수 없다는 취지 및 친가가 없거나 본적불명일 때의 그 취지.
   바. 기타 호적에 기재하여야 할 사항을 명료하게 하는데 특히 필요한 사항.
8. 제14란은 이혼판결(화해, 조정)에 의한 경우에만 기재하고, 협의이혼의 경우에는 이를 기재하지 아니합니다.
9. 제15란은 민법 제909조 제4항의 규정에 의하여 친권을 행사할 자가 정하여진 때에 기재하고, 그 내용을 증명하는 서면을 첨부하여야 합니다.
10. 제19란과 제20란은 호적상 신고일이나 재판확정일과는 상관없이 **실제로 결혼생활을 시작한 날**과 사실상 **이혼한 년월일**을 기재합니다.
11. 제21란, 제22란중 이혼의 종류란, 제23란, 제24란은 해당번호에 ○표시를 합니다(예 : ③)

(양식 제15호)

사망(호주승계)신고

장   귀하

19   년   월   일

① 사망자	본 적				
		호주성명		호주와의 관계	
②	주 소				
		세대주 성명		세대주와의 관계	
③	성 명	( )	성별	① 남 ② 여	주민등록번호
④ 사망년월일시		년 월 일 시 분			
⑤ 사 망 장 소				① 자택 ② 병원 ③ 기타	
⑥ 기 타 사 항					
⑦ 호주승계인	본 적				
	성 명	( )	전호주와의 관계		
⑧ 신고인	본 적			호주성명	
	주 소		자격	전화	
	기명날인	출생년월일		주민등록번호	

인 구 동 태 사 항

⑨ 사망전직업(발병당시)	
⑩ 사망진단자	① 의사 ② 한의사 ③ 기 타
⑪ 혼 인 상 태	① 미혼 ② 유배우 ③ 이혼 ④ 사별
⑫ 교 육 정 도	① 불취학 ② 국민학교 ③ 중학교 ④ 고등학교 ⑤ 대학이상
⑬ 사망의종류	① 병 사 ② 외인사 (㉮ 교통사고 ㉯ 불의의 중독 ㉰ 불의의 사고 ㉱ 자 살 ㉲ 타 살 ㉳ 기 타)
⑭ 사 망 원 인	① 직 접 사 인
	② 중간선행사인 (① 의 원인)
	③ 선 행 사 인 (② 의 원인)

오른쪽 처리란:

읍면동접수	
세대별주민등록표정리	월 일(인)
개인별주민등록표작성	월 일(인)
주민등록증회수	월 일(인)
주민등록지관할시구청송부	월 일(인)
관할시구청접수	
본적지송부	월 일(인)
본적지접수	
호적부정리	월 일(인)
병적정리	월 일(인)
주민등록지통보	월 일(인)
인구동태신고서 송부	월 일(인)

◎ 뒷면의 기재요령에 의하여 기재하여 주시기 바랍니다

기 재 요 령

1. 사망자의 본적지에서 신고할 경우에는 신고서 2통, 기타의 곳에서 신고하는 경우에는 3통을 작성 제출하여야 합니다.

2. 신고서는 한글과 아라비아 숫자로 기재합니다. 다만, 사망자와 호주승계인의 성명은 한자로 기재하고 한글표기를 ( )안에 기재합니다.

3. 신고명칭중 해당하지 아니하는 사항을 삭제합니다.

4. 제3란 중 성별란, 제5란 중 장소구분란, 제10란, 제11란, 제12란, 제13란은 해당번호에 ○표시를 합니다. (예 : ③)

5. 제3란 중 주민등록번호는 반드시 사망자의 주민등록번호를 정확히 기재합니다.

6. 제6란에는 다음과 같은 사항을 기재합니다.

   가. 호주승계인이 전호주와 호적을 달리하는 경우 그 취지.

   나. 선순위의 호주승계인이 호주승계권을 포기한 경우 그 취지 및 포기자의 성명과 본적.

   다. 기타 호적에 기재하여야 할 사항을 명료하게 하는데 특히 필요한 사항.

7. 제7란 호주승계인란은 호주승계인이 전호주의 사망신고와 호주승계신고를 동시에 할 때에만 기재합니다.

8. 제8란 중 자격란에는 동거하는 친족, 호주, 친족, 동거자, 사망장소를 관리하는 자 등 신고인의 해당자격을 기재하고 호주승계를 동시에 신고할 경우에는 "호주승계인"이라 기재합니다.

9. 제9란 사망전 직업은 사망전 또는 사망의 원인이 되는 질병이 발생한 때의 직업을 구체적, 서술적으로 상세히 기재하여야 합니다. (예 : 운동화를 제조하는 ○○회사의 경리사원)

10. 제12란 교육정도는 문교부장관이 인정하는 모든 정규교육기관을 기준으로 기재하되 각급학교의 재학 또는 중퇴자도 해당학교의 번호에 ○표시를 합니다.

11. 제13란과 제14란의 기재는 사망진단서 또는 검안서에 기재된 내용과 동일하게 기재하여야 합니다.

민 원 접 수 표

접수번호 :

'9. . .				
신청민원	지적도 (임야도)	도시계획 확인원	토지(임야)대장	건축물 관리대장
			호 적	호 적 제 적
		토(임아) 대장	호 분	호 분 초 분
			호 초 본	동 등 본
통 수				번지 호
신청주소	아파트 (연립)	동 번지 호	호 분 주	
			번지	호
		신 청 인		초본자 호
접 수 수				

※ 신청민원에 따라 따로따로 작성하여 구입시요.

접 수 증

'9. . . .

접수번호 (   )

성 명 :

주민등록표 열람·등·초본 교부신청서

신청인	주　소		제출처	
	성　명	㉺		
	주민등록번호			
등·초본 교부 대상자	주　소		교부 매수	
	성　명			
	주민등록번호			
활용용도 및 목적				
관계 입증 자료				

주민등록법시행령 제45조에 의하여 주민등록표열람 등·초본교부를 신청합니다.

년　　월　　일

동장　귀하

KUWAIT

Send your requests to:

Department of Central Civil Registration
Ministry of Public Health
P.O. Box 5286
13053 Safat, Kuwait

The Department has birth, marriage, divorce, and death records from 1964. A new system of national identity cards was instituted in 1988 by the Department. All citizens and permanent residents of Kuwait are required to hold a personal identity card. Over 70 percent of the population is non-Kuwaiti. According to Nasra Shah (see below), five copies are made of each birth and death record. The Central Registration Office has the permanent copy. The second copy is on file with the Authority for Civil Information for the issuance (or deletion) of a civil identification card; the third is sent to the Division for Vital and Health Statistics, the national office which prepares demographic data; the fourth copy is given to the family; and the fifth copy is kept by the hospital or clinic where the event occurred. Hospitals are only required to keep these records for five years. Kuwait handles adoption under Islamic law. Children are placed within families.

Cost for a certified Birth Certificate	Free
Cost for a certified Marriage Certificate	Free
Cost for a certified Death Certificate	Free

For additional assistance contact:

Director General
Public Authority for Civil Information
P.O. Box 6634
32041 Hawalli, Kuwait

Census Department & Population Census Statistics
Ministry of Planning
PO. Box 26188
13122 Safat, Kuwait

For further information see:

Organization and Status of Civil Registration in the Arab Countries. IIVRS Technical Papers, No. 33. Bethesda, MD: International Institute for Vital Registration and Statistics, 1988. 6p.

Shah, Nasra M., Ali Mohammad Al-Sayed and Makhdoom A. Shah. *Completeness and Reliability of Birth and Death Notifications in Kuwait*. IIVRS Technical Papers, No. 49. Bethesda, MD: International Institute for Vital Registration and Statistics, 1992. 12p.

Send your requests to:

Chief
Registry Office
Ministry of Justice of Kyrgyz Republic
140 Kalina Street
Bishkek, Kyrgyz Republic

For additional assistance contact:

National Ministry of Health   Tel. (011) (7) (3272) 22-86-97
Moskovskaya   Fax (011) (7) (3272) 22-84-24
720005 Bishkek, Kyrgyz Republic

State Committee on Statistics
374, Frunze Street
720884 Bishkek, Kyrgyz Republic

Gosudarstvennaia Respublikanskaia Biblioteka
(National Library)
ul. Ogonbaeva 242
720873 Bishkek, Kyrgyz Republic

Embassy of the Kyrgyz Republic   Tel. (202) 338-5141
1732 Wisconsin Avenue, NW
Washington, DC 20007

LAOS

Send your requests to:

National Ministry of Health
Vientiane, Laos

For additional assistance contact:

Bibliothèque nationale
B.P. 122
Vientiane, Laos

Embassy of Laos
2222 S Street, NW
Washington, DC 20008

Tel. (202) 332-6416
Fax (202) 332-4923

Send your requests to:

Civil Registration Department
Latvian Ministry of Justice
24 Kalku Street
Riga 1050, Latvia

Latvian adoption and vital records are maintained by the Civil Registration Department.

For additional assistance contact:

State Committee for Statistics of the Republic of Latvia
I, Lacplesa Street
Riga 1301, Latvia

Latvijas Valsts Arhivs
The State Archives of Latvia
Bezdelîgu 1
Riga 1007, Latvia

Latvijas Nacionâlâ Bibliotçka
Latvian National Library
K. Barona iela 14
Riga 1423, Latvia

Tel. (011) (371) 7289 874
Fax (011) (371) 7280 851
http://portico.bl.uk/gabriel/en/countries/latvia.html

Embassy of Latvia
4325 17th Street, NW
Washington, DC 20011

Tel. (202) 726-8213
Fax (202) 726-6785

LEBANON

Send your requests to:

Central Ministry of Public Health   Tel. (011) (961) (1) 309 843
Shiah
Beirut, Lebanon

Send your requests for Adoption Records to:

Surete General   Tel. (011) (961) (1) 38 4243
rue Sami Solh
Beirut, Lebanon

Only the adoption of Christian children is permitted. Islamic authorities administer adoption needs of Muslim youth by Islamic law.

For additional assistance contact:

Central Statistical Office
Ministry of Planning
Beirut, Lebanon

Centre des Archives Nationales
(National Archives)
rue Hamra
P.O. Box 6378/113
Beirut, Lebanon

National Library
Place de l'Etoile
Beirut, Lebanon

Embassy of Lebanon   Tel. (202) 939-6300
2560 28th Street, NW   Fax (202) 939-6324
Washington, DC 20008

Send your requests to:

Registrar General
The Law Office
Office of the Prime Minister
P.O. Box 33
Maseru 100, Lesotho

Vital registration began in 1880. Currently the registration is not comprehensive.

For additional assistance contact:

Director
Department of Chieftanship and Rural Development
Ministry of Home Affairs
P.O. Box 174
Maseru 100, Lesotho

Social and Demographic Statistics
Bureau of Statistics
P.O. Box 455
Maseru 100, Lesotho

National Archives
P.O. Box 52
Maseru 100, Lesotho

Lesotho National Library Service
Ministry of Education
Kingsway
P.O. Box 985
Maseru 100, Lesotho

Embassy of Lesotho   Tel. (202) 797-5533
2511 Massachusetts Avenue, NW
Washington, DC 20008

For further information see:

Methods and Problems of Civil Registration Practices and Vital Statistics Collection in Africa. IIVRS Technical Papers, No. 16. Bethesda, MD: International Institute for Vital Registration and Statistics, 1981. 27p.

Organization and Status of Civil Registration in Africa and Recommendations for Improvement. IIVRS Technical Papers, No. 31. Bethesda, MD: International Institute for Vital Registration and Statistics, 1988. 15p.

Sembajwe, Israel Serwano Lubwama. *The Evaluation of the Vital Registration System in Lesotho, the Case of Mantseba.* Roma, Lesotho: Demography Unit, Dept. of Statistics, National University of Lesotho, 1990. 39p.

LIBERIA

Send your requests to:

Bureau of Health and Vital Statistics
Ministry of Health and Social Welfare
P.O. Bag 3762
Monrovia, Liberia

Liberia gained its independence in 1847. While the system of vital registration has been worked on for years, including a United Nations project to improve the process, the registration is not considered to be comprehensive, with limited records available for the past 20 years.

For additional assistance contact:

Centre for National Documents & Records Agency
Tubman Library
P.O. Box 36
Maryland
Harpor, Liberia

Liberia National Library
Ashmun Street
Monrovia, Liberia

Embassy of Liberia   Tel. (202) 723-0437
5201 16th Street, NW
Washington, DC 20011

For further information see:

Lingner, Joan W. *Organization and Methods of the Dual Report System in Liberia*. Scientific Series, No. 5 Chapel Hill, NC: International Program for Laboratories for Population Statistics, University of North Carolina, 1972. 21p.

Methods and Problems of Civil Registration Practices and Vital Statistics Collection in Africa. IIVRS Technical Papers, No. 16. Bethesda, MD: International Institute for Vital Registration and Statistics, 1981. 27p.

Organization and Status of Civil Registration in Africa and Recommendations for Improvement. IIVRS Technical Papers, No. 31. Bethesda, MD: International Institute for Vital Registration and Statistics, 1988. 15p.

Send your requests to:

Vital Statistics
Census and Statistics Department
Secretariat of Planning
P.O. Box 600
Tripoli, Libya

In Libya there are no records of vital registration for the period of Turkish rule. During the period of Italian rule, vital registration began in urban areas. Modern vital registration began in 1968. Currently births and deaths are computerized and are not considered to be comprehensive. Marriage and divorce records are kept by both the religious law courts and the Municipal Registration Office.

Each household in Libya is required to keep a family registration certificate, which gives the vital information on each person in the family. These booklets have serial numbers and are copied and registered at the local Civil Records Office. All changes in the household, address changes, etc. must be recorded with the government.

Send your requests for Marriage and Divorce Records to:

Municipal Registration Office
(Town), Libya

For additional assistance contact:

National Archives
Castello
Tripoli, Libya

For further information see:

Methods and Problems of Civil Registration Practices and Vital Statistics Collection in Africa. IIVRS Technical Papers, No. 16. Bethesda, MD: International Institute for Vital Registration and Statistics, 1981. 27p.

Organization and Status of Civil Registration in Africa and Recommendations for Improvement. IIVRS Technical Papers, No. 31. Bethesda, MD: International Institute for Vital Registration and Statistics, 1988. 15p.

Sattar, Abdus. ***The Vital Registration and Statistics Systems in Libya and Its Improvement***. IIVRS Technical Papers, No. 47. Bethesda, MD: International Institute for Vital Registration and Statistics, 1991. 14p.

LIECHTENSTEIN

Send your requests to:

Amtsvorstand/Zivilstandsamt des Furstentums Liechtenstein
St. Florinsgasse 3
9490 Vaduz, Liechtenstein

Vital records in Liechtenstein are available from 1878. Current vital registration is considered to be comprehensive. Church records date back to the 1600s.

For additional assistance contact:

Liechtenstein National Archives
Liechtensteinisches Landesarchiv
Städtle 51
9490 Vaduz, Liechtenstein

Tel. (011) (41) (75) 66111

Liechtenstein National Library
Liechtensteinische Landesbibliothek
Gerberweg 5
Postfach 385
9490 Vaduz, Liechtenstein

Tel. (011) (41) (75) 236 63 62
Fax (011) (41) (75) 233 14 19
http://portico.bl.uk/gabriel/en/countries/liechtenstein.html

Send your requests for records of the past 75 years to:

Civil Registry Department
K. Kalinausko 21
Lt 2600
Vilnius, Lithuania

Tel. (011) (370) 2 634 720

Lithuanian adoption and vital records are kept at the Civil Registry Office. Adoptions are finalized by the District Court where the child resides. If you require the certificate within one month the fee is 40 litas, and if within 10 days the fee is 60 litas.

Cost for a certified Birth Certificate	20 litas
Cost for a certified Marriage Certificate	20 litas
Cost for a certified Divorce Certificate	20 litas
Cost for a certified Death Certificate	20 litas

For earlier records contact:

Lithuanian State Historical Archives
Gerosios Vilties 10
2015 Vilnius, Lithuania

General Directorate of Lithuanian Archives
Lietuvos Archyvu Generaline Direkcija
Mindaugo 8
2600 Vilnius, Lithuania

For more Adoption information contact:

Children's Rights Protective Service
Vaiku Teisiu Apsaugos Tarnyba
Juozapaviciaus 10A
Vilnius, Lithuania

For additional assistance contact:

Martynas Mažvydas National Library of Lithuania
Lietuvos nacionaline Martyno Mazvydo biblioteka (LNB)
Gedimino pr. 51
2635 Vilnius, Lithuania

Tel. (011) (370) 2 629 023
Fax (011) (370) 2 627 129
http://lnb.lrs.lt/index.html

Embassy of Lithuania
2622 16th Street, NW
Washington, DC 20009

Tel. (202) 234-5860

For further information see:

Bulavas, Vladas. "The Lithuanian Library Network." *LIBER Quarterly*, No. 3 (1993) pp. 258–274.

Lietuvos Nacionaline Martyno Mazvydo biblioteka. Vilnius, Lithuania: Martynas Mazvydas National Library of Lithuania, 1993. 36p.

LUXEMBOURG

Registrars of the Civil Status
(Town), Luxembourg

Luxembourg State Archives
Plateau du Saint-Esprit
B.P. 6
2010 Luxembourg, Luxembourg

Tel. (011) (352) 478 6661
Fax (011) (352) 47 46 92
E-mail: archives.nationales@mc.etat.lu

Vital records are generally on file from 1795. Current vital registration is considered to be comprehensive.

Directeur
Service Centrale de la Statistique et des Études Économiques
B.P. 304
2013 Luxembourg, Luxembourg

Archives nationales
B.P. 6
Plateau du Saint-Esprit
Chemin de la Corniche
2010 Luxembourg, Luxembourg

National Library of Luxembourg
Bibliothèque nationale Luxembourg
37, boulevard F.D. Roosevelt
2450 Luxembourg, Luxembourg

Tel. (011) (352) 22 97 55-1
Fax (011) (352) 47 56 72
http://portico.bl.uk/gabriel/fr/countries/lux.html

Embassy of Luxembourg
2200 Massachusetts Avenue, NW
Washington, DC 20008

Tel. (202) 265-4171

MACEDONIA

Send your requests to:

Civil Registration Office
(Town), Macedonia

This country has no central office for vital records. To obtain copies of birth, marriage, and death certificates write to the Civil Registration District Office in the town where the event occurred. Vital records are on file from 1946. Earlier records were kept by the local churches.

Cost for a certified Birth Certificate	Free
Cost for a certified Marriage Certificate	Free
Cost for a certified Death Certificate	Free

For additional assistance contact:

Statistical Office of Macedonia, Vital Statistics
Dame Gruev 4
91000, Skopje, Macedonia

Archives of Macedonia
Arhiv na Makedonija   Tel. (011) (389) 91 11-6571
Gligor Prličev 3   Fax (011) (389) 91 11-5827
91000, Skopje, Macedonia

Narodna i Universitetska Biblioteka
bul. Goce Delčev br 6
P.O. Box 566
91000, Skopje, Macedonia

Embassy of Macedonia   Tel. (202) 337-3063
3050 K Street, NW, Suite 210   Fax (202) 337-3093
Washington, DC 20007   E-mail: macedonia@aol.com

MADAGASCAR

Send your requests to:

Chef de Division des Affairs Administratives
Ministère de l'Intérieur
Antananarivo, 101, Madagascar

Vital registration began for the entire nation by decree in July 1878. Currently registration coverage is estimated to be about 80 percent for births and 50 percent for deaths.

Cost for a certified Birth Certificate	Free
Cost for a certified Marriage Certificate	Free
Cost for a certified Death Certificate	Free

For additional assistance contact:

Directeur du Recensement General de la Population et de l'Habitat
Institut National de la Statistique
B.P. 485
Antananarivo, 101, Madagascar

Service Statistiques Sanitaires et Demographiques
Ministère de la Santé
B.P. 568
Antananarivo, 101, Madagascar

Embassy of Madagascar   Tel. (202) 265-5525
2374 Massachusetts Avenue, NW
Washington, DC 20008

For further information see:

Kannisto, Vaino. *Civil Registration and Vital Statistics in the Africa Region, Lessons Learned from the Evaluation of UNFPA Assisted Projects in Kenya and Sierra Leone.* New York, NY: UN Fund for Population Activities, 1984.

Methods and Problems of Civil Registration Practices and Vital Statistics Collection in Africa. IIVRS Technical Papers, No. 16. Bethesda, MD: International Institute for Vital Registration and Statistics, 1981. 27p.

Organization and Status of Civil Registration in Africa and Recommendations for Improvement. IIVRS Technical Papers, No. 31. Bethesda, MD: International Institute for Vital Registration and Statistics, 1988. 15p.

Some Observations on Civil Registration in French-Speaking Africa. IIVRS Technical Papers, No. 39. Bethesda, MD: International Institute for Vital Registration and Statistics, 1990. 13p.

Send your requests to:

Registrar General
Ministry of Justice
P.O. Box 100
Blantyre, Malawi

The Registrar General has birth and death records from 1886, marriage records from 1903, and divorce records from 1905. These early records are mostly from Europeans living in Malawi. Currently the registration is not considered to be comprehensive.

Cost for a certified Birth Certificate	Free
Cost for a certified Marriage Certificate	Free
Cost for a certified Death Certificate	Free

For additional assistance contact:

Commissioner for Census and Statistics
Ministry of Economic Planning and Development
National Statistical Office
P.O. Box 333
Zomba, Malawi

Embassy of Malawi   Tel. (202) 797-1007
2408 Massachusetts Avenue, NW
Washington, DC 20008

For further information see:

Chiotha, Lidia Chiwa. **Arrangement and Description of Archives and Manuscripts with Special Reference to the National Archives of Malawi.** MA, Thesis, University of London, 1988.

Kannisto, Vaino. **Civil Registration and Vital Statistics in the Africa Region, Lessons Learned from the Evaluation of UNFPA Assisted Projects in Kenya and Sierra Leone.** New York, NY: UN Fund for Population Activities, 1984.

Methods and Problems of Civil Registration Practices and Vital Statistics Collection in Africa. IIVRS Technical Papers, No. 16. Bethesda, MD: International Institute for Vital Registration and Statistics, 1981. 27p.

Najira, Dick Doctor. "A Brief Guide to the Contents of the Library of the National Archives of Malawi." Vol. 1, No. 2, (1979) **MALA Bulletin,** pp. 30–34.

Organization and Status of Civil Registration in Africa and Recommendations for Improvement. IIVRS Technical Papers, No. 31. Bethesda, MD: International Institute for Vital Registration and Statistics, 1988. 15p.

Uta, J.J. **Directory of Malawi Libraries.** Zomba, Malawi: Government Printer, 1990.

MALAYSIA

Send your requests to:

National Registration Department   Tel. (011) (60) (3) 757-4524
Jabatan Pendaftaran Negara   Fax (011) (60) (3) 757-2028
Ministry of Home Affairs
Wisma Pendaftaran
Jalan Persiaran Barat
46551 Petaling Jaya
Selangor, Malaysia

Malaysia, as a Commonwealth nation, has had vital registration laws from the late 1800s. The National Registration Department was organized in 1948 and requires all individuals twelve and older to carry a national identity card. This system was computerized in 1990. Marriage and divorce records are handled differently according to the requirements of the religion that performed the marriage. These laws and customs are administered differently in different parts of the country.

Cost for a certified Birth Certificate	2.00R
Cost for a certified Marriage Certificate	2.00R
Cost for a certified Death Certificate	2.00R

For additional assistance contact:

Department of Statistics
Jalan Cendera Sari
50541 Kuala Lumpur, Malaysia

National Archives of Malaysia   Tel. (011) (60) (3) 651 0688
Ministry of Culture, Arts and Tourism   Fax (011) (60) (3) 651 5679
50568 Kuala Lumpur, Malaysia   http://arkib.gov.my/

Embassy of Malaysia   Tel. (202) 328-2700
2401 Massachusetts Avenue, NW
Washington, DC 20008

For further information see:

Aris, Normah Mohamed. ***Systems for the Improving the Collection of Vital Statistics in Malaysia, the Case of Sabah and Sarawak.*** Paper Presented at the 51st International Statistical Institute, Istanbul, Turkey, 1997.

Keeth, Kent H. ***A Directory of Libraries in Malaysia.*** Kuala Lumpur, University of Malaya Library, 1965. 163p.

Send your requests to:

Health Information Unit
Ministry of Health   Tel. (011) (960) 323-138
Ghaazee Building   Fax (011) (960) 328-889
Ameer Ahmed Magu
Male, 20-05, Maldives

Birth and death records are kept by the Ministry of Health. While vital registration began in the 1500s, the modern system did not begin until the 1950s.

Send your requests for Marriage and Divorce Records to:

Registrar   Tel. (011) (960) 322-303
Ministry of Justice   Fax (011) (960) 324-103
Justice Building
Orchid Magu
Male, 20-05, Maldives

Cost for a certified Birth Certificate	1.25R
Cost for a certified Marriage Certificate	1.25R
Cost for a certified Death Certificate	1.25R

For additional assistance contact:

Ministry of Information, Arts and Culture
Bururuzu Magu
Male 20-04, Maldives

Gaumi Kathub Khana
(National Library)
59 Majeedi Magu, Galolhu
Male 20-24, Maldives

Permanent Mission of the Republic of Maldives   Tel. (212) 599-6195
820 Second Avenue, Suite 800C
New York, NY 10017

MALI

Direction Nationale de l'Administration Territoriale   Tel (011) (223) 22-3937
Ministère d'État Charge de l'Administration
Territoriale et de la Sécurité Intérieur
B.P. 78
Bamako, Mali

Vital registration began in 1938. Currently the registration is not comprehensive.

Cost for a certified Birth Certificate	Free
Cost for a certified Marriage Certificate	Free
Cost for a certified Death Certificate	Free

For additional assistance contact:

Directeur General Adjoint
Direction Nationale de la Statistique et de l'Informatique
B.P. 6020
Bamako, Mali

National Archives
Archives Nationales   Tel. (011) (223) 22-5844
B.P. 159   Fax (011) (223) 22-5070
Koulouba
Bamako, Mali

Embassy of Mali   Tel. (202) 332-2249
2130 R Street, NW
Washington, DC 20008

For further information see:

Kannisto, Vaino. *Civil Registration and Vital Statistics in the Africa Region, Lessons Learned from the Evaluation of UNFPA Assisted Projects in Kenya and Sierra Leone.* New York, NY: UN Fund for Population Activities, 1984.

Methods and Problems of Civil Registration Practices and Vital Statistics Collection in Africa. IIVRS Technical Papers, No. 16. Bethesda, MD: International Institute for Vital Registration and Statistics, 1981. 27p.

Organization and Status of Civil Registration in Africa and Recommendations for Improvement. IIVRS Technical Papers, No. 31. Bethesda, MD: International Institute for Vital Registration and Statistics, 1988. 15p.

Send your requests to:

Director
Public Registry
Ministry of Justice and Parliamentary Affairs
197, Merchants Street
Valletta, Malta

The Public Registry has records beginning in 1863. Current vital registration is considered to be comprehensive. No separate divorce records are kept. Divorce information is annotated onto the marriage certificate.

Cost for a certified Birth Certificate	£M 2.00
Cost for a certified Marriage Certificate	£M 2.00
Cost for a certified Death Certificate	£M 2.00

For additional assistance contact:

Central Office of Statistics
Auberg d'Italie
Merchants Street
Valletta, Malta

National Library of Malta
36 Old Treasury Street
Valletta, Malta

Tel. (011) (356) 23 65 86
Fax (011) (356) 23 59 92
http://portico.bl.uk/gabriel/en/countries/malta.html

Embassy of Malta
2017 Connecticut Avenue, NW
Washington, DC 20008

Tel. (202) 462-3611

MALTA GOVERNMENT

Name & Surname of Applicant ....

Address ....

....

Director of Public Registry
197, Merchants Street,
Valletta, MALTA.

APPLICATION FOR A BIRTH CERTIFICATE

Name & Surname (person's required Certificate) ....

Place of Birth ....

Exact Date of Birth ....

Father's Name ....

Mother's name & Maiden surname ....

MALTA GOVERNMENT

Name & Surname of Applicant ....

Address ....

....

Director of Public Registry
197, Merchants Street,
Valletta - MALTA

APPLICATION FOR A MARRIAGE CERTIFICATE

Name & Surname of Husband ....

Name & Maiden Surname of wife ....

Date of Marriage ....

Place of Marriage ....

MALTA GOVERNMENT

Name & Surname of Applicant   ....

Address   ....

....

Director of Public Registry
197, Merchants Street
Valletta - MALTA

APPLICATION FOR A DEATH CERTIFICATE

Name & Surname of Deceased Person   ....

Place of Death .... Date of Death   ....

Name & Surname of Father   ....

Name & Maiden Surname of Mother   ....

If married (Name & Surname of Spouse)   ....

MARSHALL ISLANDS

Send your requests to:

Chief Clerk of Supreme Court
Republic of the Marshall Islands
Majuro, Marshall Islands

Records begin November 12, 1952, with some earlier records at the Hawaii State Bureau of Vital Statistics.

Cost for a certified Birth Certificate	$.25
Cost for a certified Marriage Certificate	$.25
Cost for a certified Death Certificate	$.25

For additional assistance contact:

Advisor
Office of Planning and Statistics
P.O. Box 7
Majuro, Marshall Islands 96960

Alele Museum of the Marshall Islands, Library & National Archives
P.O. Box 629
Majuro, Marshall Islands 98960

Tel. (011) (692) 625-3550
Fax (011) (692) 625-3226

Embassy of Marshall Islands
2433 Massachusetts Avenue, NW
Washington, DC 20008

Tel. (202) 234-5414

Send your requests to:

> Administrateur
> Secretariat d'État Charge de l'État Civil
> B.P. 195
> Nouakchott, Mauritania

Vital registration began in 1933 for French citizens as well as all residents within 15 miles of the registration centers. Currently the registration is not considered to be comprehensive.

For additional assistance contact:

> Chef
> Départément des Statistiques
> Demographiques et Sociales
> Office National de la Statistiques
> B.P. 240
> Nouakchott, Mauritania

> National Archives
> Archives Nationales
> B.P. 77
> Nouakchott, Mauritania

> Embassy of Mauritania   Tel. (202) 232-5700
> 2129 Leroy Place, NW
> Washington, DC 20008

For further information see:

Jereib, Saleck Ould. *New Strategies for the Improvement of Vital Statistics in Mauritania.* Paper Presented at the 51st International Statistical Institute, Istanbul, Turkey, 1997.

Kannisto, Vaino. *Civil Registration and Vital Statistics in the Africa Region, Lessons Learned from the Evaluation of UNFPA Assisted Projects in Kenya and Sierra Leone.* New York, NY: UN Fund for Population Activities, 1984.

Methods and Problems of Civil Registration Practices and Vital Statistics Collection in Africa. IIVRS Technical Papers, No. 16. Bethesda, MD: International Institute for Vital Registration and Statistics, 1981. 27p.

Organization and Status of Civil Registration in Africa and Recommendations for Improvement. IIVRS Technical Papers, No. 31. Bethesda, MD: International Institute for Vital Registration and Statistics, 1988. 15p.

MAURITIUS

Registrar General
Civil Status Office
Prime Minister's Office
Emmanuel Anquetil Building, 6th Level
Port Louis, Mauritius

The Registrar General has birth and death records from 1539, marriage records from 1579, and divorce records from 1793. The law of April 1667 formally established registration there. Mauritius is one of the few countries in Sub-Saharan Africa where the modern registration of births and deaths is considered to be comprehensive.

For additional assistance contact:

Commissioner for Statistics
Department of Statistics
Central Bureau of Statistics
Ministry of Economic Planning and Development
LIC Centre
John Kennedy Avenue
Port Louis, Mauritius

Embassy of Mauritius   Tel. (202) 244-1491
4301 Connecticut Avenue, NW, Suite 441
Washington, DC 20008

For further information see:

The Evaluation of the Completeness of Death Registration in the Presence of High Net Out-Migration, the Case Example of Mauritius. IIVRS Technical Papers, No. 61. Bethesda, MD: International Institute for Vital Registration and Statistics, 1995. 10p.

Kannisto, Vaino. *Civil Registration and Vital Statistics in the Africa Region, Lessons Learned from the Evaluation of UNFPA Assisted Projects in Kenya and Sierra Leone.* New York, NY: UN Fund for Population Activities, 1984.

Methods and Problems of Civil Registration Practices and Vital Statistics Collection in Africa. IIVRS Technical Papers, No. 16. Bethesda, MD: International Institute for Vital Registration and Statistics, 1981. 27p.

Organization and Status of Civil Registration in Africa and Recommendations for Improvement. IIVRS Technical Papers, No. 31. Bethesda, MD: International Institute for Vital Registration and Statistics, 1988. 15p.

Some Observations on Civil Registration in French-Speaking Africa. IIVRS Technical Papers, No. 39. Bethesda, MD: International Institute for Vital Registration and Statistics, 1990. 13p.

Registro Civil
(Town, State), Mexico

While church registers date from the 1500s, vital registration in Mexico didn't begin until the mid-1800s. Mexico currently requires each resident to have a national identity card. This office also registers all births, marriages, divorces, and deaths. Vital records have been computerized since 1982. The registration is considered to be 90 percent comprehensive for births and 72 percent for deaths. Adoption laws vary in each of Mexico's states.

Cost for a certified Birth Certificate	(In Mexico) Mex 13.50
	(Overseas) Mex 380.30
Cost for a certified Marriage Certificate	(In Mexico) Mex 13.50
	(Overseas) Mex 380.30
Cost for a certified Divorce Record	(In Mexico) Mex 13.50
	(Overseas) Mex 380.30
Cost for a certified Death Certificate	(In Mexico) Mex 13.50
	(Overseas) Mex 380.30
Cost for a certified Adoption Record	(In Mexico) Mex 13.50
	(Overseas) Mex 380.30

For additional assistance contact:

Director General
Dirección General del Registro Nacional de
    Población e Identificación Personal
Albaniles No. 18, Col. Ampliación Penitenciaria
15350 Mexico D.F., Mexico

Tel. (011) (52) (5) 789-5331
Fax (011) (52) (5) 789-5250

Archivo General de la Nación
(National Archives)
Eduardo Molina y Albaniles
15350 Mexico City, Mexico

Embassy of Mexico
Consular Section
2827 16th Street, NW
Washington, DC 20009-4260

Tel. (202) 736-1000

The State System for the Full Development of the Family
Desarrollo Integral de la Familia
Mexico City, Mexico

For further information see:

Archivos Estatales y Municipales de Mexico. Mexico City, Mexico: Archivo General de la Nación. Series.

Baz, Juan Jose. *Ley de 12 de Julio de 1859 que Nacionalizo los Bienes Llamados Eclesiasticos, Manifiesto del Gobierno Constitucional a la Nación y Circular del Ministerio de Justicia con Ocasion de la Misma. Ley de Cementerios, Circulates Aclaratorias de la Ley de 12 de Julio y Diversos Artículos de la Bandera Roja sobre Estas Materias y Sobre Matrimonio y Registo Civil.* Morelia, Mexico: Tip. de O. Ortiz, 1859. 175p.

Archundia Becerril, Oswaldo, Roberto Gomez Collado, and Fernando RIvera Arteaga. *El Registro Civil en Mexico.* Mexico City, Mexico: Centro de Documentación y Publicaciones de Registro Civil, 1981. 159p.

Carral y de Teresa, Luis. *Derecho Notarial y Derecho Registral.* Mexico, 1965. 266p.

Chavez, Jose Carlos. *Cien Años de Registro Civil en Chihuahua.* Chihuahua, Mexico: Ediciones del Gobierno del Estado, 1961. 11p.

Código Civil para E.L. y S. de Chiapas. Reglamento del Registro Público de la Propriedad, Reglamento del Registro del Estado Civil, con Sus Reformas. Puebla, Mexico: Ediotrial Cajica, 1968. 474p.

Diagnostico del Registro Civil en Mexico, 1980. Mexico City, Mexico: Secretaria de Gobernacion, Dirección General del Registro Nacional de Poblacion e Identificacion Personal, 1982. 80p.

Diagnostico del Registro Civil Latinoamericano, enero de 1980. Montevideo, Uruguay: UN Fund for Population Activities, 1982. 142p.

Generation of Vital Statistics in Mexico. IIVRS Technical Papers, No. 11. Bethesda, MD: International Institute for Vital Registration and Statistics, 1980. 5p.

López, Ricardo Garcia. *Guía de Instrumentos Públicos, 1795–1804, Investigación y Recopilación.* San Luis Postosi, SLP, Mexico: Archivo Historico del Estado de San Luis Potosi, 458p.

Padilla, Juan Carlos. *Demographic Information from Vital Registration Offices in Mexico, 1982.* IIVRS Technical Papers, No. 23. Bethesda, MD: International Institute for Vital Registration and Statistics, 1983. 8p.

Pavon Salinas, Cesar. *El Sistema Registral Mexicano.* MA Thesis, Universidad Nacional Autonoma de Mexico, 1963. 240p.

El Registro Civil en Mexico, Antecedentes Historico-Legislativos, Aspectos Juridicos y Doctrinarios. 2nd ed. Mexico City, Mexico: Secretaria de Gobernacion, Dirección General del Registro Nacional de Población e Identificación Personal, 1982. 181p.

Romero Arce, Jose Nicolas. *Breves Comentarios Sobre el Registro Civil.* Thesis, MA. Universidad Nacional Autonoma de Mexico, 1964. 67p.

Report on the First Latin American Training Centre on Statistics and Censuses Held at Mexico City from 2 September to 10 December 1948 by the Food and Agriculture Organization of the UN and the Government of the United States of Mexico with the Cooperation of the Statistical Office of the UN and the InterAmerican Statistical Institute. Lake Success, NY: Statistical Office of the UN, 1948. 33p.

Sanchez Marquez, Tirso. *El Registro Civil.* Puebla, Mexico, 1971. 118p.

Sinaloa. Secretaria de Govierno. *Formulario para los Oficiales del Registro Civil.* Culiacan, Mexico: Tip. de J.C. Arce, 1906. 44p.

MICRONESIA — Federated States of Micronesia

Send your requests to:

Clerk of Courts
State of Losrae
Lelu, Losrae, ECI 96944

Clerk of Courts
State of Truk, FSM
Moen, Truk, ECI 96942

Clerk of Courts
State of Pohnpei, FSM
P.O. Box 1449
Kolonia, Pohnpei, ECI 96941

Clerk of Courts
State of Yap, FSM
Colonia, Yap WCI 96943

The Court has records from November 12, 1952. Some earlier records are at the Hawaii State Bureau of Vital Statistics. In requesting certificates, personal checks are not accepted. There is also a typing charge of $.10 per every 100 words.

Cost for a certified Birth Certificate	$.25
Cost for a certified Marriage Certificate	$.25
Cost for a certified Death Certificate	$.25

For additional assistance contact:

Director of Health Services
Trust Territory of the Pacific Islands
Saipan, Northern Mariana Islands 96950

Embassy of Micronesia
1725 N Street, NW
Washington, DC 20036

Tel. (202) 223-4383

MOLDOVA

For information contact:

Biblioteca Nationala al Republicii Moldova   Tel. (011) (3732) 22-14-75; (3732) 24-04-18
(National Library)   Fax: (011) (3732) 22-14-75
str.31 August 1989 nr. 78 A   E-mail: mus@nlib.un.md
Chisinau, Moldova, cod 2012

Send your requests for Adoption Records to:

Committee on Adoption   Tel. (011) (7-0422) 23-3135
Ministry of Science and Education   Fax (011) (7-0422) 23-3474
277033 Chisinau
Pata Marii
Adunari Nationale, Moldova

For additional assistance contact:

Embassy of the Republic of Moldova   Tel. (202) 667-1130
2101 S Street, NW   Fax (202) 667-1204
Washington, DC 20008

MONACO

Send your requests to:

Mairie de Monaco
Bureau of the Civil Status
Monte Carlo, Monaco

Monaco began vital registration in 1793. Current vital registration is considered to be comprehensive.

Cost for a certified Birth Certificate	10.00F
Cost for a certified Marriage Certificate	10.00F
Cost for a certified Death Certificate	10.00F

For additional assistance contact:

Directeur du Service des Statistiques et des Études Économiques
4, rue des Iris
Monte Carlo, Monaco

Archives du Palais Princier
B.P. 518
Monte Carlo, Monaco 98015

MONGOLIA

Send your requests to:

State Center of Civil Registration
203 Ibmut Building
Ulaanbaatar 210646, Mongolia

Mongolia uses a household registration system to record and identify each person in the country. Current vital registration is considered to be 85 percent complete.

Cost for a certified Birth Certificate	Free
Cost for a certified Marriage Certificate	Free
Cost for a certified Death Certificate	Free

For further assistance contact:

Chairman
State Statistical Office
7 Erhuu Street
P.O. Box 49/207
Ulaanbaatar 210646, Mongolia

National Archives of Mongolia   Fax (011) (976) (1) 324533
Ulaanbaatar 210646, Mongolia

Embassy of Mongolia   Tel. (202) 333-7117
2833 M Street, NW
Washington, DC 20007

Send your requests to:

Civil Registration Office
(Town), Montenegro

This country has no central office for vital records. To obtain copies of birth, marriage, and death certificates, write to the Civil Registration District Office in the town where the event occurred. Vital records are on file from 1946. Records before that were kept by the local churches.

Cost for a certified Birth Certificate	Price Varies
Cost for a certified Marriage Certificate	Price Varies
Cost for a certified Death Certificate	Price Varies

For further assistance contact:

Narodna Biblioteka
(National Library)
P.O. Box 57
81250 Cetinje, Montenegro

The Family History Library of Salt Lake City, Utah has microfilmed original and published records of the former Yugoslavia and the region. For further details on their holdings please consult your nearest Family History Center.

MONTSERRAT

Registrar General's Office   Tel. (011) (664) 491-2129
Judicial Department
P.O. Box 22
Plymouth, Montserrat

The Registrar General's Office has records from February 12, 1862. The local churches also have their own records. No application forms are provided by this office, but they request that you give the complete details and indicate in which of the three districts of Montserrat the event occurred. The registration is considered to be comprehensive.

There is an additional charge of US $1.15 for postage to mail the certificates to the United States. If you are requesting a "general search" of the records, the charge is EC$20.00.

Cost for a certified Birth Certificate	EC$5.00
Cost for a certified Marriage Certificate	EC$5.00
Cost for a certified Death Certificate	EC$5.00

For further assistance contact:

Chief Statistician
Statistics Office
P.O. Box 292
Plymouth, Montserrat

The Family History Library of Salt Lake City, Utah has microfilmed original and published records and church registers of Montserrat. For further details on their holdings please consult your nearest Family History Center.

For further information see:

Registration of Vital Events in the English-Speaking Caribbean. IIVRS Technical Papers, No. 32. Bethesda, MD: International Institute for Vital Registration and Statistics, 1988. 10p.

Send your requests to:

Division d'État Civil au Ministère de l'Intérieur
Inspection Generale de l'État Civil
Ministère de l'Intérieur
Rabat, Morocco

Vital registration began in Morocco in 1915 for the French and foreign population. In 1931 it was extended to include all Moroccans. With independence in 1956 registration became formalized, and in 1987 there was a major effort to computerize all of Morocco's vital records. Currently vital registration is not considered to be comprehensive. Marriages and divorces are recorded by the denomination or court that had jurisdiction. Formal adoption is rare in Morocco—children are usually placed within extended families.

Cost for a certified Birth Certificate	Free
Cost for a certified Marriage Certificate	Free
Cost for a certified Death Certificate	Free

For additional assistance contact:

Ministère Charge de la Population
B.P. 178
Rabat, Morocco

Embassy of Morocco   Tel. (202) 462-7979
1601 21st Street, NW
Washington, DC 20009

For further information see:

Fellegi, Ivan P. *Some Aspects of the Survey Design for the Moroccan Dual Record Experimental Study.* Chapel Hill, NC: International Program of Laboratories for Population Statistics, 1974. 25p.

Gonzalez Diaz, Violeta. *Reforms in the Civil Registration and Vital Statistics Systems in Morocco.* IIVRS Technical Papers, No. 44. Bethesda, MD: International Institute for Vital Registration and Statistics, 1991. 9p.

Kannisto, Vaino. *Civil Registration and Vital Statistics in the Africa Region, Lessons Learned from the Evaluation of UNFPA Assisted Projects in Kenya and Sierra Leone.* New York, NY: UN Fund for Population Activities, 1984.

Methods and Problems of Civil Registration Practices and Vital Statistics Collection in Africa. IIVRS Technical Papers, No. 16. Bethesda, MD: International Institute for Vital Registration and Statistics, 1981. 27p.

Mghari, Mohamed. *Evaluation of Civil Registration in Morocco after the Reform of 1991.* Paper Presented at the 51st International Statistical Institute, Istanbul, Turkey, 1997.

Organization and Status of Civil Registration in Africa and Recommendations for Improvement. IIVRS Technical Papers, No. 31. Bethesda, MD: International Institute for Vital Registration and Statistics, 1988. 15p.

Organization and Status of Civil Registration in the Arab Countries. IIVRS Technical Papers, No. 33. Bethesda, MD: International Institute for Vital Registration and Statistics, 1988. 6p.

Rachidi, Mohamed. *Les Donnees et la Recherche Demographiques au Maroc.* Chapel Hill, NC: International Program of Laboratories for Population Statistics, 1974. 21p.

El Youb, Ali. *The Reform of 1991, a Strategy for Improvement of Statistics from the Moroccan Civil Registry.* Paper Presented at the 51st International Statistical Institute, Istanbul, Turkey, 1997.

MOZAMBIQUE

Send your requests to:

Direccao Nacional dos Registros e Notoriados
Av. Vladimir Lenine n. 565, 2 Andar
C.P. 2157
Maputo, Mozambique

Vital registration is not considered to be comprehensive.

Cost for a certified Birth Certificate	Free
Cost for a certified Marriage Certificate	Free
Cost for a certified Death Certificate	Free

For additional assistance contact:

Arquivo Historico de Moçambique
(National Archives)
Av. Filipe Magaia, 717 r/c
C.P. 2033
Maputo, Mozambique

Biblioteca National de Moçambique
(Mozambique National Library)
C.P. 141
Maputo, Mozambique

Embassy of Mozambique   Tel. (202) 293-7146
1990 M Street, NW, Suite 570
Washington, DC 20036

For further information see:

Kannisto, Vaino.*Civil Registration and Vital Statistics in the Africa Region, Lessons Learned from the Evaluation of UNFPA Assisted Projects in Kenya and Sierra Leone.* New York, NY: UN Fund for Population Activities, 1984.

Methods and Problems of Civil Registration Practices and Vital Statistics Collection in Africa. IIVRS Technical Papers, No. 16. Bethesda, MD: International Institute for Vital Registration and Statistics, 1981. 27p.

Organization and Status of Civil Registration in Africa and Recommendations for Improvement. IIVRS Technical Papers, No. 31. Bethesda, MD: International Institute for Vital Registration and Statistics, 1988. 15p.

Send your requests to:

Registrar
Health Department
Ministry of Health
Rangoon, Myanmar

Formerly known as Burma, Myanmar has a centralized vital registration program that is considered to be comprehensive.

Cost for a certified Birth Certificate	Free
Cost for a certified Marriage Certificate	Free
Cost for a certified Death Certificate	Free

For additional assistance contact:

Vital Statistics Section
Central Statistical Organization
186 Mahabandoola Street
Pasunmdamp PO
Rangoon, Myanmar

National Archives Department
Ministry of Planning and Finance
114 Pyidaungsu Yeiktha Road
Rangoon, Myanmar

Embassy of Myanmar   Tel. (202) 332-9044
2300 S Street, NW
Washington, DC 20008

The Family History Library of Salt Lake City, Utah has microfilmed records of Myanmar and the region. For further details on their holdings please consult your nearest Family History Center.

NAMIBIA

Send your requests to:

Subdivision of Births, Deaths and Marriages   Tel. (011) (264) (61) 22-1361
Ministry of Home Affairs   Fax (011) (264) (61) 22-3817
Cohen Building
Kasino Street
Private Bag 13200
Windhoek, Namibia

Namibia became independent in 1990. Vital registration follows the model of South Africa.

Cost for a certified Birth Certificate	Free
Cost for a certified Marriage Certificate	Free
Cost for a certified Death Certificate	Free

For additional assistance contact:

National Archives
4 Luderitz Street
P.M.B. 13250
Windhoek 9000, Namibia

National Library
Estorff House
Peter Muller Avenue and Michael Scott Street
P.M.B. 13349
Windhoek 9000, Namibia

Embassy of Namibia   Tel. (202) 986-0540
1605 New Hampshire Avenue, NW
Washington, DC 20009

For further information see:

Kannisto, Vaino.*Civil Registration and Vital Statistics in the Africa Region, Lessons Learned from the Evaluation of UNFPA Assisted Projects in Kenya and Sierra Leone.* New York, NY: UN Fund for Population Activities, 1984.

Methods and Problems of Civil Registration Practices and Vital Statistics Collection in Africa. IIVRS Technical Papers, No. 16. Bethesda, MD: International Institute for Vital Registration and Statistics, 1981. 27p.

Organization and Status of Civil Registration in Africa and Recommendations for Improvement. IIVRS Technical Papers, No. 31. Bethesda, MD: International Institute for Vital Registration and Statistics, 1988. 15p.

Send your requests to:

Registrar General
Republic of Nauru
Nauru Island

Nauru's current vital registration is considered to be comprehensive. Nauru uses the Australian dollar as currency.

Cost for a certified Birth Certificate	A$.50
Cost for a certified Marriage Certificate	A$.50
Cost for a certified Death Certificate	A$.50

The Family History Library of Salt Lake City, Utah has microfilmed records of Nauru and the region. For further details on their holdings please consult your nearest Family History Center.

NEPAL

Registrar
Vital Registration Section
Ministry of Local Development
Pulchowk, Lalitpur, Nepal

While there are earlier records from the colonial period, modern vital registration has been nearly comprehensive only in the past 10 years. The "Village Panchayat Law" passed in 1962 and expanded in 1976 requires the registration of births, marriages, divorces, deaths, and changes of residence. Births and deaths are generally on file from 1973; marriages began to be kept centrally in 1983 and divorces in 1985. It is estimated that 40 of Nepal's 75 registration districts are actively keeping records.

Cost for a certified Birth Certificate	Rs3.00
Cost for a certified Marriage Certificate	Rs3.00
Cost for a certified Death Certificate	Rs3.00

For additional assistance contact:

Director General
Central Bureau of Statistics
National Planning Commission
Kathmandu, Nepal

Nepal Rashtriya Pustakalaya   Tel. (011) (977) (1) 52-1132
(National Library)
Harihar Bhawan
Pulchowk, Lalitpur, Nepal

Embassy of Nepal   Tel. (202) 667-4550
2131 Leroy Place, NW
Washington, DC 20008

For further information see:

Acharya, Rajeshwar. *Registration of Vital Statistics in Nepal: An Overview.* Kathmandu, Nepal: Centre for Economic Development and Administration, Tribhuvan University, 1987. 58p.

THE NETHERLANDS

Send your requests to:

Burgerlijke Stand
(Town), The Netherlands

There is no central office for vital records in The Netherlands; however, the earliest records are usually deposited in the Provincial or Municipal Archives. To obtain copies of birth, marriage, and death certificates write to the Civil Registration District Office (Burgerlijke Stand) in the town where the event occurred. Vital records are on file from 1811. Current vital registration is considered to be comprehensive.

Cost for a certified Birth Certificate	Varies Dfl 13,75 - Dfl 14.55
Cost for a certified Marriage Certificate	Varies Dfl 13,75 - Dfl 14.55
Cost for a certified Divorce Record	Varies Dfl 13,75 - Dfl 14.55
Cost for a certified Death Certificate	Varies Dfl 13,75 - Dfl 14.55

For additional assistance contact:

Director General
Central Bureau of Statistics
428 Prinses Beatixlaan
2270 AZ Voorburg, The Netherlands

Director
Central Bureau of Statistics
Fort Amsterdam
Curaçao, Netherlands Antilles

Algemeen Rijksarchief
General State Archives
Prinz Willem-Alexanderhof 20
2595 BE The Hague, The Netherlands

Royal Netherlands Embassy   Tel. (202) 244-5300
4200 Linnean Avenue, NW
Washington, DC 20008

The Family History Library of Salt Lake City, Utah has microfilmed many of the original and published vital records and church registers of The Netherlands. For further details on their holdings please consult your nearest Family History Center.

For further information see:

Kraan, C. A. *De Authentieke Akte, Proeve van een Onderzoek naar de Authenticiteit van Akten.* Arnhem, Netherlands: Gouda Quint, 1984. 215p.

Netherlands

Aan de ambtenaar van de burgerlijke stand te.
To the clerk of the office of vital statistics.

Stad of Provincie _____
City or Province

Hierbij verzoek ik u mij toe te zenden een uittreksel uit het register van.
Please send me an abstract of the registration of:

☐ Geboorten - *Birth*	Ten name van - *In the name of*
☐ Huwelijken - *Marriage*	
☐ Echtscheidingen - *Divorce*	**Voornaan** **Middel** **Achternaam**
☐ Overlijden - *Death*	*First* *Middle* *Last*

☐ Geboren - *Born*	**Op** _____
	on
☐ Gehuwd - *Married*	**Dag** **Maand** **Jaar**
☐ Gescheiden - *Divorced*	*Day* *Month* *Year*
☐ Overleden - *Died*	

Dit uittreksel is nodig voor _____
This abstract is needed for   Reden - *Reason*

En kan worden toegezonden aan
And can be sent to

Name _____

Adres: _____
address

Stad of Provincie: _____
City / State

Land _____
Country

☐ Voor kosten van leges en toezending gelieve u hierbij een girobetaalkaart c.q. bankcheque
van ƒ 14,55 aan te treffen. *
To cover the cost, please find enclosed a international bank check or money order for 14.55 Guilders (Dƒl).

☐ U gelieve mij te berichten op welke wijze de betaling kan geschieden. *
Please inform me how you prefer payment.

* S.V.P. doorhalen wat niet van toepassing is.
Choose your option

De aanvrager - *Applicant*
_____
Handtekening - *Signature*
_____
Naam in blokletters - *Print name*

NEW ZEALAND

Send your requests to:

Central Registry
Births, Deaths and Marriages
191 High Street
P.O. Box 31-115
Lower Hutt, New Zealand

Tel. (011) (64) (4) 474-8000
Fax (011) (64) (4) 566-5311
E-mail: centralregistry@dia.govt.nz
http://www.bdm.govt.nz/

The Central Registry has birth and death records from January 1, 1848, and marriage records from 1854. Current vital registration is considered to be comprehensive. Payment can be made by credit card or by check or bank draft in New Zealand dollars, made payable to "The Department of Internal Affairs."

For the Cook Islands:
Registrar of Births and Deaths
P.O. Box 111
Rarotonga, Cook Islands

Statistics Officer
Statistics Office
P.O. Box 125
Rarotonga, Cook Islands

For Niue Births and Deaths:
Registrar General's Office
Department of Administration
P.O. Box 67
Alofi, Niue

For Niue Marriages and Divorces:
Registrar of Marriages
Department of Justice
Alofi, Niue

For New Zealand

Cost for a certified Birth Certificate

NZ $20.15 (from N. America)
NZ$21.00 (from inside New Zealand)

Cost for a certified Marriage Certificate

NZ $20.15 (from N. America)
NZ$21.00 (from inside New Zealand)

Cost for a certified Death Certificate

NZ $20.15 (from N. America)
NZ$21.00 (from inside New Zealand)

For Niue

Cost for a certified Birth Certificate — NZ $14.00
Cost for a short form Birth Certificate — NZ $6.00
Cost for a certified Marriage Certificate — NZ $14.00
Cost for a certified Death Certificate — NZ $14.00

For additional assistance contact:

National Archives of New Zealand
10 Mulgrave Street
PO Box 12-050
Wellington, New Zealand

Tel. (011) (64) (4) 499-5595
Fax (011) (64) (4) 495-6210
http://www.archives.govt.nz/index.html

Embassy of New Zealand
37 Observatory Circle, NW
Washington, DC 20008

Tel. (202) 328-4800

The Family History Library of Salt Lake City, Utah has microfilmed original and published records and registers of New Zealand.

BDM 94

REQUEST FOR NEW ZEALAND BIRTH, DEATH OR MARRIAGE CERTIFICATE

THE DEPARTMENT OF INTERNAL AFFAIRS

Te Tari Taiwhenua

Applicant's name	
Address where certificate is to be posted/couriered* to:	
Applicant's telephone no.	

PAYMENT DETAILS: (*If certificate is required to be sent by courier, please include self-addressed courier pack)

For prices, please check Certificate Fees page on our Website: http://www.bdm.govt.nz

I enclose a $NZ cheque/bankdraft (payable to: Department of Internal Affairs) for $NZ.......................

OR

Please debit my: ☐ VISA ☐ MASTERCARD ☐ BANKCARD for $NZ.......................

Credit Card No: ☐☐☐☐ ☐☐☐☐ ☐☐☐☐ ☐☐☐☐ Expiry Date: ☐☐ ☐☐

Cardholder Name: [   ]

Fax to: ++64 4 566-5311 OR

Post to: Central Registry PO Box 31-115, Lower Hutt, New Zealand

BIRTH CERTIFICATE

	(Certificate #1)	(Certificate #2)
Surname/family name at birth		
Given/first names		
Date and/or year of birth		
Place of birth		
(Mother's surname/family name)		
(Mother's given/first names)		
(Mother's birth surname/family name)		
(Father's surname/family name)		
(Father's given/first names)		

DEATH CERTIFICATE

Surname/family name		
Given/first names		
Date and/or year of death		
Place of death		

MARRIAGE CERTIFICATE

Wife's surname/family name		
Given/first names		
Husband's surname/family name		
Given/first names		
Date and/or year of marriage		
Place of marriage		

NOTES: If details are not known, customers should make written application to Central Registry, PO Box 31-115, Lower Hutt, giving as many details as are known. A search may have to be made, which attracts fees. Bulk Requests are not able to be processed by this method at present. Please make written application to Central Registry, PO Box 31-115, Lower Hutt.

Dirección General del Registro
Ministerio de Justica
Managua, Nicaragua

While church registers date from the 1500s, vital registration in Nicaragua didn't begin until 1867.

Cost for a certified Birth Certificate	Free
Cost for a certified Marriage Certificate	Free
Cost for a certified Death Certificate	Free

For Adoption Record information write to:

Social Security and Welfare Institution (INSSBI)
Managua, Nicaragua

For additional assistance contact:

Director General
Instituto Nacional de Estadísticas y Censos
AP 4031
Managua, Nicaragua

Archivo Nacional de Nicaragua
(Nicaragua National Archives)
Ministerio de Cultura
A.P. C-186
Del Cine Cabrera 2 1/2 c. al lago
Managua, Nicaragua

Embassy of Nicaragua   Tel. (202) 939-6570
1627 New Hampshire Avenue, NW
Washington, DC 20009

The Family History Library of Salt Lake City, Utah has microfilmed original and published vital records and church registers of Nicaragua.

For further information see:

Diagnostico del Registro Civil Latinoamericano, enero de 1980. Montevideo, Uruguay: UN Fund for Population Activities, 1982. 142p.

Report on the First Latin American Training Centre on Statistics and Censuses Held at Mexico City from 2 September to 10 December 1948 by the Food and Agriculture Organization of the UN and the Government of the United States of Mexico with the Cooperation of the Statistical Office of the UN and the InterAmerican Statistical Institute. Lake Success, NY: Statistical Office of the UN, 1948. 33p.

NIGER

Directeur National de l'État Civil et de la Population
Ministère de l'Intérieur et de l'Amenagement du Territoire
c/o Representant a.1., UNDP
B.P. 11207 Maison del'Afrique
Niamey, Niger

Tel. (011) (227) 72-21-76

Formal vital registration began in 1933 for French citizens. It was expanded to include residents within 15 miles of the registration centers in 1950. Currently the registration is not considered to be comprehensive.

Cost for a certified Birth Certificate	60f
Cost for a certified Marriage Certificate	60f
Cost for a certified Death Certificate	60f

For additional assistance contact:

Directeur de la Statistique et des Comptes Nationaux
Ministère du Plan
B.P. 467
Naimey, Niger

Direction des Archives Nationales
B. P. 550
Niamey, Niger

Embassy of Niger
2204 R Street, NW
Washington, DC 20008

Tel. (202) 483-4224

For further information see:

Kannisto, Vaino.*Civil Registration and Vital Statistics in the Africa Region, Lessons Learned from the Evaluation of UNFPA Assisted Projects in Kenya and Sierra Leone.* New York, NY: UN Fund for Population Activities, 1984.

Methods and Problems of Civil Registration Practices and Vital Statistics Collection in Africa. IIVRS Technical Papers, No. 16. Bethesda, MD: International Institute for Vital Registration and Statistics, 1981. 27p.

Organization and Status of Civil Registration in Africa and Recommendations for Improvement. IIVRS Technical Papers, No. 31. Bethesda, MD: International Institute for Vital Registration and Statistics, 1988. 15p.

Some Observations on Civil Registration in French-Speaking Africa. IIVRS Technical Papers, No. 39. Bethesda, MD: International Institute for Vital Registration and Statistics, 1990. 13p.

Send your requests to:

Vital Registration Department
National Population Commission
Babs Animashaun Road
P.M.B. 12628
Lagos, Nigeria

Vital registration in Nigeria began in 1867 for Lagos Island, and was expanded in 1901 to include Ebute, Metta, and the island of Iddo. By 1903 it included Southern Nigeria. The Laws of 1918 and 1979 have worked to improve coverage, but registration is still not considered to be comprehensive throughout the country. Nigeria became independent in 1960. Adoption in Nigeria is rare. Orphaned and abandoned children are usually placed within extended families and no formal records are kept.

Cost for a certified Birth Certificate	15k
Cost for a certified Marriage Certificate	15k
Cost for a certified Death Certificate	15k

For additional assistance contact:

National Archives Department
Federal Ministry of Information and Culture
Ikoyi Road
P.M.B. 12897
Lagos, Nigeria

Embassy of Nigeria   Tel. (202) 986-8400
1333 16th Street, NW
Washington, DC 20036

For further information see:

Kannisto, Vaino. *Civil Registration and Vital Statistics in the Africa Region, Lessons Learned from the Evaluation of UNFPA Assisted Projects in Kenya and Sierra Leone.* New York, NY: UN Fund for Population Activities, 1984.

Methods and Problems of Civil Registration Practices and Vital Statistics Collection in Africa. IIVRS Technical Papers, No. 16. Bethesda, MD: International Institute for Vital Registration and Statistics, 1981. 27p.

Organization and Status of Civil Registration in Africa and Recommendations for Improvement. IIVRS Technical Papers, No. 31. Bethesda, MD: International Institute for Vital Registration and Statistics, 1988. 15p.

NORTHERN MARIANA ISLANDS

Send your requests to:

Office of Vital Statistics
Superior Court
Commonwealth of the Northern Mariana Islands
P.O. Box 307
Saipan, Northern Mariana Islands 96950

Tel. (670) 234-6401
Fax (670) 234-8010

The Superior Court has birth and death records from 1945, and marriage records from 1954. Some records are at the Hawaii State Bureau of Vital Statistics. Money orders or cashier's checks should be made payable to the "CNMI Treasury."

Cost for a certified Birth Certificate	$10.00
Cost for a certified Marriage Certificate	$10.00
Cost for a certified Divorce Decree	$2.50, plus $.50/page copied
Cost for a certified Death Certificate	$10.00

For additional assistance contact:

Director of Health Services
Trust Territory of the Pacific Islands
Saipan, Northern Mariana Islands 96950

Send your requests for Birth Certificates to:

Folkeregister
Local Population Register
(Town), Norway

Send your requests for Marriage and Death Certificates to:

District Court
(Town), Norway

Send your requests for Adoption and Divorce Records to:

Flykesmann
(County Commissioner)
(County Seat, County), Norway

Government Adoption Office
P.O. Box 8036, Dep
0030 Oslo, Norway

Church records date from the 1600s. Modern vital registration began in 1906. Adoptees may obtain copies of their records at age 18.

Cost for a certified Birth Certificate	Free
Cost for a certified Marriage Certificate	Free
Cost for a certified Divorce Record	Free
Cost for a certified Death Certificate	Free
Cost for a certified Adoption Record	Free

For additional assistance contact:

Statistisk Sentralbyrå
Office of the National Registrar
Directorate of Taxes
P.O. Box 8131 Dep.
0033, Oslo, 7, Norway

Det Norske Utvandrersenteret   Tel. (011) (47) (4) 501-274
Norwegian Emigration Center   Fax: (011) (47) (4) 501-290
Bergjelandsgate 30
4012 Stavanger, Norway

Embassy of Norway   Tel. (202) 333-6000
2720 34th Street, NW
Washington, DC 20008

The Family History Library of Salt Lake City, Utah has microfilmed original records of Norway's cities and regions. For further details on their holdings please consult your nearest Family History Center.

For further information see:

Norway. Statistisk sentralbyra. *Lov, Forskrifter og Overenskomst om Folkeregistrering.* Oslo, Norway: Statistisk sentralbyra, 1971. 40p.

OMAN

Send your requests to:

Director General of Health Affairs
Ministry of Health
P.O. Box 803, PC 112
Muscat, Oman

The registration is not considered to be comprehensive.

Cost for a certified Birth Certificate	Free
Cost for a certified Marriage Certificate	Free
Cost for a certified Death Certificate	Free

For additional assistance contact:

Director General of National Statistics
Development Council Technical Secretariat
P.O. Box 881
Muscat, Oman

Ministry of National Heritage
P.O. Box 668
Muscat, Oman

Embassy of Oman
2535 Belmont Road, NW
Washington, DC 20008

Tel. (202) 387-1980

For further information see:

Organization and Status of Civil Registration in the Arab Countries. IIVRS Technical Papers, No. 33. Bethesda, MD: International Institute for Vital Registration and Statistics, 1988. 6p.

Send your requests to:

Director General of Registration
Civil Registration Organization
18-D, Blue Area
Islamabad, Pakistan

While vital registration has existed since 1863, modern Pakistan has required the registration of all persons 18 years of age and older, as well as of all citizens out of the country, since 1973. Birth, marriage, divorce, and death records are kept by the Directorate of General Registration. Vital registration is not considered to be comprehensive. Pakistan handles adoption under Islamic law. Children are placed within families.

Cost for a certified Birth Certificate	R4.00
Cost for a certified Marriage Certificate	R4.00
Cost for a certified Death Certificate	R4.00

For additional assistance contact:

Joint Census Commissioner
Population Census Organization
Statistics Division
16, Civic Centre, G/6
P.O. Box 1026
Islamabad, Pakistan

Embassy of Pakistan   Tel. (202) 939-6200
2315 Massachusetts Avenue, NW
Washington, DC 20008

For further information see:

Abernathy, James R. *Organization and Methods of the Dual Report System in Pakistan.* Chapel Hill, NC: International Program of Laboratories for Population Statistics, 1972. 24p.

Chaudhary, Zafar Hussain. *Latest and Most Up-to-date Commentary, Registration Act (XVI of 1908) with Registration Rules & Registration Manual.* Lahore, Pakistan: Lahore Law Times Publications, 1981. 150p.

Hanif, Ch Muhammad. *The Registration Act, 1908, with Registration Rules, 1929, and Provincial Amendments Bal[uchistan], N.W.F.P., Panjab & Sind.* Lahore, Pakistan: Lahore Law Times Publications, 1974. 128p.

PANAMA

Send your requests to:

Dirección General del Registro Civil   http://www.tribunal-electoral.gov.pa/regcivil/index.htm
Betania, La Gloria, Calle I No. 195
A.P. 5281
Panama 5, Panama

Church registers date from the 1500s and vital registration began in 1914. It is considered to be comprehensive for births and 75 percent complete for deaths. Money orders should be made payable to the "Tesoro Nacional." General adoptions are handled by the Minor's Court (Tribunal Tutelar de Menores). If the child was given by the natural parents for adoption it is handled by the Circuit Court (Juzgado Circuito). Once approved by the court the adoption is registered with the Registro Civil.

Cost for a certified Birth Certificate	US $15.00
Cost for a certified Marriage Certificate	US $15.00
Cost for a certified Death Certificate	US $15.00

For additional assistance contact:

Director de Estadística y Censo
Conroloria General de la Republica
AP 5213
Panama 5, Panama

Panama Embassy   Tel. (202) 483-1407
2862 McGill Terrace, NW
Washington, DC 20008

The Family History Library of Salt Lake City, Utah has microfilmed original and published records of Panama. For further details on their holdings please consult your nearest Family History Center.

For further information see:

Diagnostico del Registro Civil Latinoamericano, enero de 1980. Montevideo, Uruguay: UN Fund for Population Activities, 1982. 142p.

El Registro Publico en Panama, Centro deInvestigacion Juridica. 2nd ed. Panama: Universidad de Panama, Facultad de Derecho y Ciencias Politicas, 1985. 194p.

Report on the First Latin American Training Centre on Statistics and Censuses Held at Mexico City from 2 September to 10 December 1948 by the Food and Agriculture Organization of the UN and the Government of the United States of Mexico with the Cooperation of the Statistical Office of the UN and the InterAmerican Statistical Institute. Lake Success, NY: Statistical Office of the UN, 1948. 33p.

TRIBUNAL ELECTORAL

REGISTRO CIVIL

SOLICITUD DE CERTIFICADO   No. _____

Nombre _____

Fecha de: Defunción _____ Día _____ Mes _____ Año
           Nacimiento)
           Matrimonio)

Lugar _____

PROVINCIA _____ TOMO _____ FOLIO _____ ASIENTO _____

Fecha _____ 19 _____ Recibido por: _____

Fecha de reclamo _____

Llene los dos primeros renglones - subraye el certificado deseado.

PAPUA NEW GUINEA

Send your requests to:

Registrar General of Births, Deaths and Marriages
Department of Justice
P.O. Box 21
Gerehu, NCD, Port Moresby, Papua New Guinea

Vital registration began in British New Guinea in 1892, but with a limited registration organization, there is a large under-registration of vital records. Registration outside of the National Capital District is almost nonexistent; only births and deaths occurring at hospitals are registered. Marriages performed by provincial secretaries and churches are reported. Traditional or "customary marriages," as stipulated by the national Marriage Act, Part II, paragraph 3, are binding and require no registration. The care of orphans is generally taken care of by extended families and communities. Court-approved adoptions are rare. In the case of a child registered with the Registrar, an amended birth certificate is prepared with names of the new parents substituted for the birth parents.

Cost for a certified Birth Certificate	K.50
Cost for a certified Marriage Certificate	K.50
Cost for a certified Death Certificate	K.50

Send your requests for Divorce Records to:

Registrar of the Court
National Court of Justice
Port Moresby, Papua New Guinea

For additional assistance contact:

Health Statistician
Department of Health
P.O. Box 3991
Boroko, Port Moresby, Papua New Guinea

Embassy of Papua New Guinea   Tel. (202) 745-3680
1779 Massachusetts Avenue, NW, Suite 805
Washington, DC 20036

For further information see:

Bakker, M. L. *The Status of Civil Registration and the Collection of Vital Statistics through Alternative Sources in Papua New Guinea.* IIVRS Technical Papers, No. 30. Bethesda, MD: International Institute for Vital Registration and Statistics, 1987. 14p.

Handbook on Health Statistics, Papua New Guinea. Port Moresby, Papua New Guinea: Ministry of Health, Policy Planning and Research Division.

PARAGUAY

Send your requests to:

Director
Oficina de Registro del Estado Civil de las Personas
Ministerio de Justicia y Trabajo
Herrera 875
Asunción, Paraguay

While church registers date from the 1500s, vital registration in Paraguay began September 26, 1880.

Cost for a certified Birth Certificate	50G
Cost for a certified Marriage Certificate	50G
Cost for a certified Death Certificate	50G

For additional assistance contact:

Director General
Dirección General de Estadística y Censos
Humaita, 463
Asunción, Paraguay

Embassy of Paraguay   Tel. (202) 483-6960
2400 Massachusetts Avenue, NW
Washington, DC 20008

The Family History Library of Salt Lake City, Utah has microfilmed original and published vital records and church registers of Paraguay. For further details on their holdings please consult your nearest Family History Center.

For further information see:

Diagnostico del Registro Civil Latinoamericano, enero de 1980. Montevideo, Uruguay: UN Fund for Population Activities, 1982. 142p.

Registro del Estado Civil, Su Organización. Asunción, Paraguay: Talleres Nacionales de H. Kraus, 1899. 91p.

Report on the First Latin American Training Centre on Statistics and Censuses Held at Mexico City from 2 September to 10 December 1948 by the Food and Agriculture Organization of the UN and the Government of the United States of Mexico with the Cooperation of the Statistical Office of the UN and the InterAmerican Statistical Institute. Lake Success, NY: Statistical Office of the UN, 1948. 33p.

PERU

Send your requests to:

Registro Civil
District Office
(Town), Peru

Church registers date from the 1500s and civil registration began in 1852. Adoptions, legitimizations, and recognition of illegitimate children are recorded in the Birth Registers. Divorces are recorded in the Marriage Registers and the Minor's Court that finalized the action, as well as in the National Adoption Registry. Amended birth certificates note the court, case date, and number. Copies of the vital records are kept at the district level.

Cost for a certified Birth Certificate	S/. 6.00
Cost for a certified Marriage Certificate	S/. 6.00
Cost for a certified Death Certificate	S/. 6.00

For more Adoption Record information write to:

Technical Secretariat for Adoptions
Secretaria Tecnica de Adopción
Lima 1, Peru

For additional assistance contact:

Dirección General de Registro Civil   Tel. (011) (51-1) 33-4223
Instituto Nacional de Estadística e Informatica (INEI)
Presidencia del Consejo de Ministros
Av. 28 de Julio 1056
Lima 1, Peru

Embassy of Peru   Tel. (202) 833-9860
Consular Section
1700 Massachusetts Avenue, NW
Washington, DC 20036

For further information see:

Diagnostico del Registro Civil Latinoamericano, enero de 1980. Montevideo, Uruguay: UN Fund for Population Activities, 1982. 142p.

Herrera Cavero, Victorino. *Derecho Registral y Notorial.* 3rd ed. Lima, Peru: Raisol, 1987. 328p.

Pini Rodolfi, Francesco. *Registro Civil y Estadísticas Vitales en Lima Metropolitana, Problemas y Perspectivas.* Lima, Peru: Centro de Estudios de Población y Desarrollo, 1980. 188p.

Registros del Estado Civil. Lima, Peru: Dirección General de Demografía, 1984. 46p.

Report on the First Latin American Training Centre on Statistics and Censuses Held at Mexico City from 2 September to 10 December 1948 by the Food and Agriculture Organization of the UN and the Government of the United States of Mexico with the Cooperation of the Statistical Office of the UN and the InterAmerican Statistical Institute. Lake Success, NY: Statistical Office of the UN, 1948. 33p.

Send your requests to:

Civil Registrar General
National Statistics Office
Ramon Magsaysay Boulevard
P.O. Box 779, Sta. Mesa
Manila, Philippines
or
Local Civil Registrar
Municipal Building
(Town) Philippines

Tel. (011) (63-2) 893-5766
Tel. (011) (63-2) 857-8367
Fax (011) (63-2) 840-3663
E-mail: C.Lalicon@mail.census.gov.ph
http://www.census.gov.ph/data/civilreg/index.html

Send your requests for Adoption Records to:

Philippine Department of Social Welfare and Development (DSWD)
Constitution Hills
Quezon City
Metro Manila, Philippines
or
389 San Rafael Street
Legarda
Metro Manila, Philippines

Tel. (011) (63-2) 931-7916
Fax (011) (63-2) 741-6939

Tel. (011) (63-2) 732-6022

Vital registration began in 1898 and is now centrally administered by the Civil Registry and Vital Statistics Division of the National Statistics Office. Adoption, birth, marriage, divorce, and death records are kept. The original name of the child is used on the adoption decree and retained on the birth certificate.

Cost for all certificates requested by mail within the Philippines	PhP 50.00
Cost for all certificates requested in person	PhP 40.00
Cost for a certified Birth Certificate	(Overseas By Mail) US $15.00
Cost for a certified Marriage Certificate	(Overseas By Mail) US $15.00
Cost for a Divorce Record	(Overseas By Mail) US $15.00
Cost for a certified Death Certificate	(Overseas By Mail) US $15.00
Cost for a certified Adoption Record	(Overseas By Mail) US $15.00

For additional assistance contact:

National Library & Archives
T.M. Kalaw Street
Manila, Philippines

Tel. (011) (63-2) 491-114

For further information see:

La Dual Record System in a Rural Philippine Family Planning Project. Tagbilaran City, Philippines: Bohol Province Maternal Health Care/ Family Planning Project, 1977. 28p.

Legal Aspects of Civil Rgistration in the Philippines. IIVRS Technical Papers, No. 70. Bethesda, MD: International Institute for Vital Registration and Statistics, 1997. 18p.

Manual of Civil Registration. Manila, Philippines: National Census and Statistics Office, 1975. 153p.

☐ RUSH
☐ ORDINARY

For Birth Certificate Only

For NSO use only

Application No.   : _____

Date of filing   . _____

Number of copies   : _____

Date of release   : _____

O. R. Number   : _____

Amount paid   : _____

Verification Status

To be filled up by applicant
(Print all entries)

Name   : _____
                    First   Middle   Last

Date of Birth   : _____

Place of Birth   : _____
                                            (Town)   (Province)

Name of Father : _____

Name of Mother : _____

Registered late?

☐   Yes,   When : _____ _____

☐   No

Requested by   : _____

Address   : _____ Tel. No.: _____

Purpose   : _____
(If for travel, specify country/countries.)
_____

Received by   : _____

NOTE:

1. AUTHORIZATION and ID of the document owner ARE REQUIRED if the person is NOT any of the following:

    a. the owner of the document
    b. his parents
    c. his spouse
    d. his direct descendants
    e. his guardian/institution in charge, if minor

2. This office may or may not have the document being requested.

Republic of the Philippines
NATIONAL STATISTICS OFFICE
Manila

☐ RUSH

☐ ORDINARY   For Marriage Certificate Only

For NSO use only

Application No.	_____
Date of filing	_____
Number of copies	_____
Date of release	_____
O. R. Number	_____
Amount paid	_____

Verification Status

To be filled up by applicant
(Print all entries)

Name of Husband : _____
                     First   Middle   Last

Name of Wife : _____
                     First   Middle   Last

Date of Marriage : _____

Place of Marriage : _____
                        (Town)   (Province)

Requested by : _____

Address : _____

Purpose : _____
(If for travel, specify country/countries.)

_____

Received by : _____

NOTE:

This office may or may not have the document being requested.

DOCUMENT/CERTIFICATION NOT CLAIMED WITHIN THIRTY (30) WORKING DAYS FROM DATE OF RELEASE WILL BE DISPOSED OF

Republic of the Philippines
NATIONAL STATISTICS OFFICE
Manila

☐ **RUSH**

☐ **ORDINARY**

For Death Certificate Only

For NSO use only

Application No.   : _____

Date of filing   : _____

Number of copies   : _____

Date of release   : _____

O. R. Number   : _____

Amount paid   : _____

Verification Status

To be filled up by applicant
(*Print all entries*)

Name of Deceased   : _____
                          First   *Middle*   *Last*

Date of Death   : _____

Place of Death   : _____
                              (Town)   *(Province)*

Requested by   : _____

Address   : _____ Tel. No.: _____

Purpose   : _____
(*If for travel, specify country/countries.*)

_____

Received by   : _____

NOTE:

This office may or may not have the document being requested.

DOCUMENT/CERTIFICATION NOT CLAIMED WITHIN THIRTY (30) WORKING DAYS FROM DATE OF RELEASE WILL BE DISPOSED OF.

Send your requests to:

Urzad Stanu Cywilnego
(Civil Registration Office)
(Town), Poland

There is no central office for vital records in Poland. Records are kept in the town where the event occurred. Vital records are on file from 1809, with many older vital records at the National Archives.

Cost for a certified Birth Certificate	Price Varies
Cost for a certified Marriage Certificate	Price Varies
Cost for a certified Death Certificate	Price Varies

Send your requests for Adoption Records to:

Central Adoption Commission
Publiczny Osrodek Adopcyjno Opiekunczy
ulica Nowogrodzka #75
02-018 Warsaw, Poland

For additional assistance contact:

Department of Citizen Affairs
Ministry of the Interior
Pawinskiego 17/21
01-107 Warsaw, Poland

National Archives
Naczelnik Wydziahu Wspolpracy z Zagranica
Archiwow Pantswowych
ul. Dɫuga 6
Skrytka Pocztowa 1005
00-950 Warsaw, Poland

Embassy of Poland   Tel. (202) 234-3800
2640 16th Street, NW
Washington, DC 20009

For further information see:

Albiniak, Maria. *Prawo o Aktach Stanu Cywilnego, Z Objaśnieniami.* Warsaw: Wydawnictwo Prawnicze, 1989. 155p.
Litwin, Jozef. *Prawo o Aktach Stanu Cywilnego, Komentarz.* Warsaw: Dawnictwe Prawnicze, 1961. 667p.

PORTUGAL

Send your requests to:

Los Registos Civiles
(Town), Portugal

Their work is directed by:

Direccao-Geral dos Registos e do Notariado
Ministry of Justice
Av. Almirante Reis, 101
197 Lisbon Codex, Portugal

To obtain copies of birth, marriage, and death certificates write to the town where the event occurred. Vital records are on file from 1911. Some local registrars have records back to 1832. It is estimated that the current birth registrations are only 85 percent complete and that earlier records are even less so. Older records have been transferred to the District Archives.

Cost for a certified Birth Certificate	200$00
Cost for a certified Marriage Certificate	200$00
Cost for a certified Death Certificate	200$00

For additional assistance contact:

President
Conselho de Direccao
Instituto Nacional de Estatística
Avenida Antonio Jose de Almeida
1078 Lisbon Codex, Portugal

Embassy of Portugal   Tel. (202) 328-8610
2125 Kalorama Road, NW
Washington, DC 20008

The Family History Library of Salt Lake City, Utah has microfilmed records of Portugal. For further details on their holdings please consult your nearest Family History Center.

For further information see:

Codigo do Registo Civil, Actualizado, Portaria No. 795/84 de 11 de Outubro. Coimbra, Portugal: Livraria Almedina, 1986. 293p.
_____. Coimbra, Portugal: Livraria Almedina, 1991. 1,139p.
Sousa Pinto, F. *Código do Registo Civil.* Coimbra, Portugal: Livraria Almedina, 1986. 293p.

Send your requests for Birth Certificates since 1959 to:

> Chief
> Vital Statistics and Household Survey Section
> Central Statistical Organization
> P.O. Box 7283
> Doha, Qatar

Send other requests for Birth information to:

> Age Estimation Committee
> Ministry of Public Health
> Qatar

Births have been recorded by the government in Qatar since 1959. Marriages are recorded by the denomination performing the wedding. It is interesting to note that in Qatar the standard practice is to petition the government's Age Estimation Committee to determine a person's age. The registration is considered to be comprehensive. Qatar handles adoption under Islamic law. Children are placed within families.

Cost for a certified Birth Certificate	Free
Cost for a certified Marriage Certificate	Free
Cost for a certified Death Certificate	Free

For additional assistance contact:

> Ministry of Public Health
> P.O. Box 9374
> Doha, Qatar

> Embassy of Qatar   Tel. (202) 274-1600
> 4200 Wisconsin Avenue, NW, Suite 200
> Washington, DC 20016

For further information see:

Organization and Status of Civil Registration in the Arab Countries. IIVRS Technical Papers, No. 33. Bethesda, MD: International Institute for Vital Registration and Statistics, 1988. 6p.

Taj El Din, Sayed A. *Age Estimation Committee in Qatar.* IIVRS Technical Papers, No. 12. Bethesda, MD: International Institute for Vital Registration and Statistics, 1980. 7p.

ROMANIA

Send your requests to:

Civil Registration Office
(Town), Romania

There is no central office for vital records in Romania. To obtain copies of birth, marriage, and death certificates write to the Civil Registration District Office in the town where the event occurred. Vital records are on file from 1865 and in many areas begin much earlier. Current vital registration is considered to be comprehensive.

Cost for a certified Birth Certificate	Price Varies
Cost for a certified Marriage Certificate	Price Varies
Cost for a certified Death Certificate	Price Varies

Send your requests for Adoption Records to:

Romanian Adoption Committee
Bucharest, Romania

Tel. (011) (40) 1-614-3400, ex. 1096
Fax (011) (40) 1-312-7474

For additional assistance contact:

Archives nationales
(National Archives)
Bd. Mihail Kogălniceanu 29
Sector 5
70602 Bucharest, Romania

Biblioteca Naţională
(National Library)
Str. Ion Ghica nr. 4
Bucharest, Romania

Biblioteca Centrală Universitară din Bucureşti
(Bucharest Public Library)
Str. Transilvaniei nr. 6
Sector 1
70778 Bucharest, Romania

Embassy of Romania
1607 23rd Street, NW
Washington, DC 20008

Tel. (202) 332-4848

Send your requests to:

RAGAS, Russian American Genealogical Archival Service
1929 18th Street, NW
Washington, DC 20009

E-mail: ragas@cityline.ru
ragas@dgs.dgsys.com

Through an agreement between the United States National Archives and the Archives of Russia Society, RAGAS will receive and process requests for vital records in Russia. It costs $50.00 to establish whether records exist for your subject. If indications are good and you wish to pursue a fuller request, there is a non-refundable deposit of $100.00 to initiate the search. Adoptions in Russia are approved by local courts in the area where the child resides. Currently the Ministry of Education is the central contact agency for adoptions.

Send your requests for Adoption Records to:

Ministry of Education
Chistoprundny bul 6
101856 Moscow, Russia

Tel. (011) (7) (095) 924-84-68
Fax (011) (7) (095) 924-69-89

For additional assistance contact:

Moscow City Association of Archives
Profsoyuznaya, 80
117393 Moscow, Russia

Federal Archival Service of Russia
Ilynka, 12
103132 Moscow, Russia

State Committee of the Russian Federation on Statistics
39 Miasnitskaya Str.
Moscow 103450, Russia

Embassy of the Russian Federation
2650 Wisconsin Avenue, NW
Washington, DC 20007

Tel. (202) 298-5700
Fax (202) 298-5749

RAGAS INFORMATIONAL REQUEST FORM:

RAGAS
1929 18th St., NW
Washington, DC 20009

(© copyright 1997 Russian-American Genealogical Archival Service)

A $50.00 non-refundable fee is required to complete this preliminary report. You will have a reply from RAGAS/Moscow office within one-two months to inform you whether a search is feasible and which sources are available. The reply will include a detailed description of archival records, the current address of each archive which will be useful to you for your research, and an estimate of actual costs to complete a full search. You may also be advised that it is not possible to accept a request for this area. With this information you will then be able to determine whether you wish to submit a request for a fuller search. In the case of some archives it may require additional travel and research expense for a special investigation.

Please type or print:

1. PLACE:

It is essential for any search to be successful to have as a starting point the exact geographic location. Many regions have several towns with the same name. Include the name of the region, district, town, village or rural area.

2. TIME FRAME:

Please give dates a report should cover and, if specific dates for individual events are known, include them within the time frame.

3. Please enclose a stamped self-addressed envelope.

SPECIFIC INFORMATION FORM
PLEASE PRINT OR TYPE (пожалуйста, пишите печатными буквами)

RAGAS
1929 18th St., NW
Washington, DC 20009

It is realized that you may not have answers to some questions. Fill in to the best of your knowledge.
(Возможно, Вы не сможете ответить на все вопросы. Постарайтесь ответить как можно более подробно)

Search for information about a specific event or a specific document.

Record to be searched:	☐ Birth Рождение	☐ Baptism Крещение	☐ Marriage Брак	☐ Death Смерть
	☐ Military Service Records О Военной Службе	☐ Civil Service Records О Гражданской Службе	☐ Property Records Об Имущественной Собственности	

Approximate date (within 5 years) & place of event (guberniya/region, district, town, village, parish; in large cities – ward, quarter, parish, street, house)
Дата (приблизительно – в пределах 5 лет) и место события (губерния/область, уезд /район, волость, стан, округаж город, село, деревня, церковный приход, синагога; в крупных городах - район, участок=, церковный приход, улица, дом)

First name Имя	Patronymic Отчество	Last name Фамилия	Sex Пол

All other names used at any time (including maiden name if married) Другие имена (включая девичью фамилию)

Variant spelling Возможные разночтения фамилин, имени, отчества

Citizenship Гражданство	Ethnic group Национальность	Religion Вероисповедание	Class: Сословие
			☐ Nobility Дворянство ☐ Clergy Духовенство ☐ Middle Class Мещанство
			☐ Merchant class Купечество ☐ Peasantry Крестьянство ☐ Working class Рабочий класс
			☐ Foreign national working in Russia Иностранцы на русской службе

PARENTS (РОДИТЕЛИ)

	Full name Фамилия, имя, отчество	Date of birth Дата рождения	Place of birth Место рождения	Other information Дополнительная информация
Father ОТЕЦ				
Mother МАТЬ				

RAGAS
1929 18th St., NW
Washington, DC 20009

FULLER GENEALOGICAL SEARCH FORM
PLEASE PRINT OR TYPE (пожалуйста, пишите печатными буквами)

It is realized that you may not have answers to some questions. Fill in to the best of your knowledge. (Возможно, Вы не сможете ответить на все вопросы. Постарайтесь ответить как можно более подробно)

FOCUS OF SEARCH: ☐ To link several generations (Установить связи между несколькими поколениями)

ЦЕЛЬ ПОИСКА ☐ To link family members within a generation (Установить связи между членами семьи одного поколения)

☐ To confirm several events in the life of a single individual (Подтвердить определенные события из жизни одного человека)

First name Имя	Patronymic Отчество	Last name Фамилия	Sex Пол	Date of birth Дата рождения

All other names used at any time (including maiden name if married) Другие имена	Place of birth Место рождения
Variant spelling Возможные разночтения фамилии, имени, отчества	

Citizenship Гражданство	Ethnic group Национальность	Religion Вероисповедание	Class: Сословие ☐ Nobility Дворянство ☐ Clergy Духовенство ☐ Middle Class Мещанство ☐ Merchant class Купечество ☐ Peasantry Крестьянство ☐ Working class Рабочий класс ☐ Foreign national working in Russia Иностранцы на русской службе Transfer from one class to another Переход из одного класса в другой

PARENTS (РОДИТЕЛИ)

Father ОТЕЦ	Full name Фамилия, имя, отчество	Date of birth Дата рождения	Place of birth Место рождения	Other information Дополнительная информация
Mother МАТЬ	Full name Фамилия, имя, отчество	Date of birth Дата рождения	Place of birth Место рождения	Other information Дополнительная информация

BROTHERS AND SISTERS (БРАТЬЯ И СЕСТРЫ)

Name including maiden name Фамилия, имя, отчество (включая девичью фамилию)	Sex Пол	Date of Birth Дата рождения	Place of Birth Место рождения	Other information Дополнительная информация

SPOUSE(S) OF PERSON TO BE SEARCHED (МУЖЬЯ, ЖЕНЫ)

Name including maiden name Фамилия, имя, отчество (включая девичью фамилию)	Date of birth Дата рождения	Place of birth Место рождения	Other information Дополнительная информация

B R O T H E R S   A N D   S I S T E R S (БРАТЬЯ И СЕСТРЫ)

Name including maiden name Фамилия, имя, отчество (включая девичью фамилию)	Sex Пол	Date of Birth Дата рождения	Place of Birth Место рождения	Other information Дополнительная информация

SPOUSE(S) OF PERSON TO BE SEARCHED (МУЖЬЯ, ЖЕНЫ)

Name including maiden name Фамилия, имя, отчество (включая девичью фамилию)	Date of birth Дата рождения	Place of birth Место рождения	Other information Дополнительная информация

C H I L D R E N (ДЕТИ)

Name Имя	Date of birth Дата рождения	Place of birth Место рождения	Other information Дополнительная информация

P L A C E S   O F   R E S I D E N C E (МЕСТО ЖИТЕЛЬСТВА)

	Place of residence Место жительства	~~Time~~ Время проживания
1.		
2.		

NAME AND ADDRESS OF THE REQUESTER

ФАМИЛИЯ И АДРЕС ЗАЯВИТЕЛЯ

RAGAS
1929 18th St., NW
Washington, DC 20009

C H I L D R E N (ДЕТИ)

Name Имя	Date of birth Дата рождения	Place of birth Место рождения	Other information Дополнительная информация

P L A C E S   O F   R E S I D E N C E (МЕСТО ЖИТЕЛЬСТВА)

	Place of residence Место жительства	Date Время проживания
1.		
2.		

O T H E R   I N F O R M A T I O N (ДОПОЛНИТЕЛЬНАЯ ИНФОРМАЦИЯ)

Education (Name and address of institution)
Образование (Название и адрес учебного заведения)

Place of service or work
Место службы или работы

Titles, Ranks, Awards
Звания, чины, награды

Real estate ownership
Земельные владения

Adoption, guardianship
Усыновление, опекунство

Legal actions
Нахождение под судом

Place and date of emigration
Место и дата эмиграции

Membership in organizations (cultural, fraternal)
Членство в организациях (культурных, общественных)

Military service (rank, organization, dates)
Военная служба (звание, название части, время службы)

Other information that might help in identification
Дополнительная информация, которая могла бы облегчить поиски

NAME AND ADDRESS OF THE REQUESTER
ФАМИЛИЯ И АДРЕС ЗАЯВИТЕЛЯ

RAGAS
1929 18th St., NW
Washington, DC 20009

Send your requests to:

Direction Generale des Affaires Politiques et Administratives
Ministère de l'Intérieur et du Developpement Communal
B.P. 446
Kigali, Rwanda

Vital registration began May, 4 1895. It is not comprehensive.

Cost for a certified Birth Certificate	50 Frws.
Cost for a certified Marriage Certificate	50 Frws.
Cost for a Divorce Certificate	600 Frws.
Cost for a certified Death Certificate	600 Frws.

For additional assistance contact:

Directeur General de la Statistique
Ministère du Plan
B.P. 46
Kigali, Rwanda

Division des Archives nationales
(National Archives)
Ministère de l'Enseignement Supérieur, de la Recherche et de la Culture
B.P. 624
Kigali, Rwanda

Embassy of Rwanda   Tel. (202) 232-2882
1714 New Hampshire Avenue, NW
Washington, DC 20009

For further information see:

Kannisto, Vaino. *Civil Registration and Vital Statistics in the Africa Region, Lessons Learned from the Evaluation of UNFPA Assisted Projects in Kenya and Sierra Leone.* New York, NY: UN Fund for Population Activities, 1984.

Methods and Problems of Civil Registration Practices and Vital Statistics Collection in Africa. IIVRS Technical Papers, No. 16. Bethesda, MD: International Institute for Vital Registration and Statistics, 1981. 27p.

Organization and Status of Civil Registration in Africa and Recommendations for Improvement. IIVRS Technical Papers, No. 31. Bethesda, MD: International Institute for Vital Registration and Statistics, 1988. 15p.

Some Observations on Civil Registration in French-Speaking Africa. IIVRS Technical Papers, No. 39. Bethesda, MD: International Institute for Vital Registration and Statistics, 1990. 13p.

ST. KITTS AND NEVIS

Send your requests to:

Registrar General's Office   Tel. (869) 465-2521
Health Department
P.O. Box 236
Basseterre, St. Kitts-Nevis

The Registrar General's Office has records from St. Kitts from January 1, 1859 and Nevis from August 1, 1869. Current vital registration is considered to be comprehensive. Adoptions are finalized by the Judicial Court. Copies of adoption certificates are obtained from the Registrar General.

Cost for a certified Birth Certificate   US $2.00
Cost for a certified Marriage Certificate   US $2.00
Cost for a certified Death Certificate   US $2.00

For additional assistance contact:

Embassy of St. Kitts and Nevis   Tel. (202) 686-2636
3216 New Mexico Avenue, NW
Washington, DC 20016

For further information see:

Registration of Vital Events in the English-Speaking Caribbean. IIVRS Technical Papers, No. 32. Bethesda, MD: International Institute for Vital Registration and Statistics, 1988. 10p.

Executive Officer
Registry Department
Castries, St. Lucia, West Indies

Tel. (758) 452-1257

The Registry Department has records from January 1, 1869. Current registration is considered to be comprehensive. The local churches also have their own records.

Cost for a certified Birth Certificate   US $2.55
Cost for a certified Marriage Certificate   US $2.55
Cost for a certified Death Certificate   US $2.55

For additional assistance contact:

Director of Statistics
Government Statistics Department
Ministry of Finance, Statistics & Negotiating
New Government Building
John Compton Highway
Castries, St. Lucia, West Indies

Saint Lucia National Archives
P.O. Box 3060
Castries, St. Lucia, West Indies

Central Library of St. Lucia
P.O. Box 103
Castries, St. Lucia, West Indies

Embassy of St. Lucia
3216 New Mexico Avenue, NW
Washington, DC 20016

Tel. (202) 364-6792

For further information see:

Registration of Vital Events in the English-Speaking Caribbean. IIVRS Technical Papers, No. 32. Bethesda, MD: International Institute for Vital Registration and Statistics, 1988. 10p.

ST. VINCENT and the GRENADINES

Send your requests to:

Registrar General's Office Tel. (784) 457-1424
Registry Department
Courthouse
Kingstown, St. Vincent and the Grenadines

The Registrar General's Office has records from July 1, 1874. Current registration is considered to be comprehensive. The local churches also have their own records. No application forms are provided by this office. Adoptions are arranged by the Adoption Board and finalized by the local court. The adoption decree is then filed with the Registrar General, who amends the birth certificate.

Cost for a certified Birth Certificate US$1.75
Cost for a certified Marriage Certificate US$1.75
Cost for a certified Death Certificate US$1.75

For more Adoption Record information contact:

Adoption Board
Kingstown, St. Vincent and the Grenadines

For additional assistance contact:

Demographic Statistics Tel. (784) 456-1111
Ministry of Finance
Kingstown, St. Vincent and the Grenadines

Department of Libraries, Archives and Documentation Services Fax (784) 457-2022
Granby Street
Kingstown, St. Vincent and the Grenadines

Embassy of St. Vincent and the Grenadines Tel. (202) 364-6730
3216 New Mexico Avenue, NW
Washington, DC 20016

For further information see:

Registration of Vital Events in the English-Speaking Caribbean. IIVRS Technical Papers, No. 32. Bethesda, MD: International Institute for Vital Registration and Statistics, 1988. 10p.

Parish Priest
(Parish), San Marino

Vital records are available from the Roman Catholic parish churches in San Marino. Current vital registration is considered to be comprehensive.

Cost for a certified Birth Certificate	Free
Cost for a certified Marriage Certificate	Free
Cost for a certified Death Certificate	Free

For additional assistance contact:

Archivio Pubblico dello Stato
(State Archives)
Contrada Omerelli 23
47031 San Marino

San Marino Mission to the U.N.   Tel. (212) 751-1234
327 East 50th Street
New York, NY 10022

The Family History Library of Salt Lake City, Utah has microfilmed records of San Marino and the region. For further details on their holdings please consult your nearest Family History Center.

SÃO TOMÉ AND PRÍNCIPE

Send your requests to:

Departamento do Registo Civil
Ministerio de Justicia e Funcao Publica
C.P. 4
São Tomé, São Tomé and Príncipe

São Tomé and Príncipe were under Portugese control until independence in 1975. Vital registration here is considered to be comprehensive.

Cost for a certified Birth Certificate	Dobra .45
Cost for a certified Marriage Certificate	Dobra .45
Cost for a certified Death Certificate	Dobra .45

For additional assistance contact:

Arquivo Historico
(National Archives)
C.P. 87
São Tomé, São Tomé and Príncipe

Mission of São Tomé and Príncipe   Tel. (212) 317-0533
400 Park Avenue, 7th Floor
New York, NY 10022

For further information see:

Kannisto, Vaino.*Civil Registration and Vital Statistics in the Africa Region, Lessons Learned from the Evaluation of UNFPA Assisted Projects in Kenya and Sierra Leone.* New York, NY: UN Fund for Population Activities, 1984.

Methods and Problems of Civil Registration Practices and Vital Statistics Collection in Africa. IIVRS Technical Papers, No. 16. Bethesda, MD: International Institute for Vital Registration and Statistics, 1981. 27p.

Organization and Status of Civil Registration in Africa and Recommendations for Improvement. IIVRS Technical Papers, No. 31. Bethesda, MD: International Institute for Vital Registration and Statistics, 1988. 15p.

Send your requests to:

Registrar
Department of Preventive Medicine
Ministry of Health
Airport Road
Riyadh 11176, Saudi Arabia

The registration of vital records is considered comprehensive. Saudi Arabia handles adoption under Islamic law. Children are placed within families.

Cost for a certified Birth Certificate	4.00R
Cost for a certified Marriage Certificate	4.00R
Cost for a certified Death Certificate	4.00R

For additional assistance contact:

Director
Department of Statistics
Ministry of Health
Airport Road
Riyadh 11176, Saudi Arabia

National Central Archive
P.O. Box 150486
Riyadh 11745, Saudi Arabia

Royal Embassy of Saudi Arabia   Tel. (202) 337-4076
601 New Hampshire Avenue, NW
Washington, DC 20037

For further information see:

Organization and Status of Civil Registration in the Arab Countries. IIVRS Technical Papers, No. 33. Bethesda, MD: International Institute for Vital Registration and Statistics, 1988. 6p.

SENEGAL

Send your requests to:

Chef de Bureau l'État Civil
Direction de la Statistique
Ministère des Finances et des Affaires Économiques
B.P. 116
Dakar, Senegal

Chef de la Division de l'État Civil
Direction des Collectiveites Locales
Ministère de l'Intérieur
B.P. 4002
Dakar, Senegal

Church registers date from the colonial period and vital registration began in 1916 for most French citizens. Modern vital registration began in 1961 and is not comprehensive.

Cost for a certified Birth Certificate	200Fr
Cost for a certified Marriage Certificate	200Fr
Cost for a Divorce Certificate	200Fr
Cost for a certified Death Certificate	200Fr
Cost for an Adoption Certificate	200Fr

For additional assistance contact:

Regional Advisor in Demographic Surveys and Vital Statistics
Immeuble Fahd, Boulevad
Djily MBAYE
B.P. 154
Dakar, Senegal

Embassy of Senegal   Tel. (202) 234-0540
2112 Wyoming Avenue, NW
Washington, DC 20008

For further information see:

Kannisto, Vaino. *Civil Registration and Vital Statistics in the Africa Region, Lessons Learned from the Evaluation of UNFPA Assisted Projects in Kenya and Sierra Leone.* New York, NY: UN Fund for Population Activities, 1984.

Methods and Problems of Civil Registration Practices and Vital Statistics Collection in Africa. IIVRS Technical Papers, No. 16. Bethesda, MD: International Institute for Vital Registration and Statistics, 1981. 27p.

Organization and Status of Civil Registration in Africa and Recommendations for Improvement. IIVRS Technical Papers, No. 31. Bethesda, MD: International Institute for Vital Registration and Statistics, 1988. 15p.

Rodriguez, Edmond. *Difficulties in the Operation of the Civil Registration System of Senegal.* Paper Presented at the 51st International Statistical Institute, Istanbul, Turkey, 1997.

Some Observations on Civil Registration in French-Speaking Africa. IIVRS Technical Papers, No. 39. Bethesda, MD: International Institute for Vital Registration and Statistics, 1990. 13p.

Send your requests to:

Civil Registration Office
(Town), Serbia

This country has no central office for vital records. To obtain copies of birth, marriage, and death certificates write to the Civil Registration District Office in the town where the event occurred. Vital records are generally on file from 1946. Records before that were kept by the local churches.

Cost for a certified Birth Certificate	Free
Cost for a certified Marriage Certificate	Free
Cost for a certified Death Certificate	Free

For additional assistance contact:

Savezni Zavod za Statistiku
(Federal Statistical Office)
Division of Vital Statistics
Knexa Milo a 20
11000 Belgrade, Serbia

Nardona Biblioteka
(National Library)
ul, Skerli eva 1
11000 Belgrade, Serbia

SEYCHELLES

Send your requests for records after 1902 to:

Division of Immigration and Civil Status
Department of Internal Affairs
P.O. Box 430
Mahe, Seychelles

Send your requests for records 1794–1902 to:

National Archives
P.O. Box 720
Las Bastile
Mahe, Seychelles

Vital registration began in Seychelles for the entire population in 1893. It is one of the few countries in Sub-Saharan Africa where the registration of births and deaths is considered to be comprehensive. Vital registration began in Seychelles for the entire population in 1893.

Cost for a certified Birth Certificate	R25
Cost for a certified Marriage Certificate	R25
Cost for a certified Death Certificate	R25

For additional assistance contact:

Civil Status Officer
Civil Status and Identity Card Section
MISD
P.O. Box 206
Mahe, Seychelles

Embassy of Seychelles   Tel. (212) 687-9766
800 Second Avenue, Suite 400
New York, NY 10017

For further information see:

Kannisto, Vaino.*Civil Registration and Vital Statistics in the Africa Region, Lessons Learned from the Evaluation of UNFPA Assisted Projects in Kenya and Sierra Leone.* New York, NY: UN Fund for Population Activities, 1984.

Methods and Problems of Civil Registration Practices and Vital Statistics Collection in Africa. IIVRS Technical Papers, No. 16. Bethesda, MD: International Institute for Vital Registration and Statistics, 1981. 27p.

Organization and Status of Civil Registration in Africa and Recommendations for Improvement. IIVRS Technical Papers, No. 31. Bethesda, MD: International Institute for Vital Registration and Statistics, 1988. 15p.

APPLICATION FOR BIRTH CERTIFICATE

FULL NAME:...

SURNAME:...

DATE OF BIRTH:.....................................

PLACE OF BIRTH:....................................

NAME OF FATHER:....................................

NAME OF MOTHER:....................................

MOTHER'S MAIDEN SURNAME:...........................

APPLICATION FOR MARRIAGE CERTIFICATE

HUSBAND'S NAME:....................................

HUSBAND'S SURNAME:.................................

WIFE'S NAMES:......................................

WIFE'S SURNAME:....................................

DATE OF MARRIAGE :.................................

PLACE OF MARRIAGE:.................................

APPLICATION FOR DEATH CERTIFICATE

NAME OF DECEASED:..................................

MAIDEN SURNAME: ....

PLACE OF DEATH: ....

DATE OF DEATH: ....

SEYCHELLES NATIONAL IDENTITY CARD
(S.S. Act 10/95)

APPLICATION FORM (NEW/RENEWAL)

PLEASE WRITE IN PRINTED FORMAT.		DATE	SERIAL No.

1 Present Surname: _____

2 Other Names: _____

3 Maiden Surname: _____

4 Date of Birth: ___/___/19___ Sex: _____ District: ____

5 Place of Birth Registration _____ Nationality _____

6 Mother's Maiden Surname: _____

7 Mother's First Name: _____

8 Date Arrived in Seychelles: ___/___/19___ (IF APPLICABLE)

9 a) Residential Address: _____

   b) Employment Address: _____

10 Telephone Number: _____

Signature of Applicant: _____

For Official Use only

N.I.N. ☐☐☐ ☐☐☐☐ ☐☐ ☐☐

Status: _____

Remarks: _____

Collection Date: ___/___/19___   Registration Officer _____

Application Check by: _____   I.D. Card Check by: _____

N.I.N. ☐☐☐ ☐☐☐☐ ☐☐ ☐☐

Delivered to: _____

Mr/Mrs/Miss _____

SIGNATURE _____   DATE: ___/___/19___

RENEWAL APPLICATION FEE PAID: R_____ Cr. No. _____   DATE: ___/___/19___

NOTE: 1 9(a) STATE PERMANENT RESIDENCE.

    2. Application for new NIN must be supported by Birth certificate, passport, GOP, certificate of registration or naturalisation, residence permit as may be requested by the Registration officer.

Send your requests to:

Office of Chief Registrar
Births and Deaths Office
Ministry of Health
3 Wilberforce Street
Freetown, Sierra Leone

Vital registration of births and deaths began in Sierra Leone as early as 1801 in Freetown and Granville. Currently the registration is not comprehensive.

Cost for a certified Birth Certificate	Le .75
Cost for a certified Marriage Certificate	Le .75
Cost for a certified Death Certificate	Le .75

For additional assistance contact:

Director
Demographic and Social Statistics Division
Tower Hill
Freetown, Sierra Leone

Public Archives of Sierra Leone
Fourah Bay College
P.O. Box 87
Freetown, Sierra Leone

Embassy of Sierra Leone   Tel. (202) 939-9261
1701 19th Street, NW
Washington, DC 20009

For further information see:

Kannisto, Vaino. *Civil Registration and Vital Statistics in the Africa Region, Lessons Learned from the Evaluation of UNFPA Assisted Projects in Kenya and Sierra Leone.* New York, NY: UN Fund for Population Activities, 1984.

Methods and Problems of Civil Registration Practices and Vital Statistics Collection in Africa. IIVRS Technical Papers, No. 16. Bethesda, MD: International Institute for Vital Registration and Statistics, 1981. 27p.

Organization and Status of Civil Registration in Africa and Recommendations for Improvement. IIVRS Technical Papers, No. 31. Bethesda, MD: International Institute for Vital Registration and Statistics, 1988. 15p.

SINGAPORE

Send your requests to:

Registrar of Births and Deaths   Tel. (011) (65) 3307-668
National Registration Department   Fax (011) (65) 3388-935
10 Kallang Road
Singapore 208718

Send your requests for Marriage Records to:

Registrar of Marriages
National Registration Department
Ministry of Home Affairs
1 Colombo Court #02-01
Singapore 208718

Send your requests for Divorce Records to:

Registrar
Supreme Court
St. Andrew's Court
Singapore 208718

The Registrar of Births and Deaths has records from 1872 on; the Registrar of Civil Marriages has records from 1875. Muslim marriage records are not not filed with the Registrar, but are kept by the religious authorities. The Supreme Court has divorce records from 1937. Responsibility to hear divorce cases was transferred from the High Court to the Family Courts in 1996.

Cost for a certified Birth Certificate	if the date is known S$8.00, with search S$10.00
Cost for a Marriage Certificate	if the date is known S$8.00, with search S$10.00
Cost for a Divorce Certificate	if the date is known S$8.00, with search S$10.00
Cost for a certified Death Certificate	if the date is known S$8.00, with search S$10.00

For additional assistance contact:

Singapore National Archives
1 Canning Rise
Singapore 179868

Embassy of Singapore   Tel. (202) 537-3100
3501 International Place, NW
Washington, DC 20008

The Family History Library of Salt Lake City, Utah has microfilmed original and published records of Singapore.

APPLICATION FORM FOR A SEARCH AND/OR CERTIFIED EXTRACT FROM REGISTER OF BIRTHS

Part A	Birth Registration No.	Number of Copies Applied For

SUBJECT'S PARTICULARS

Name		
Sex	Date of Birth	Identification Document and No.

Part B	To be completed only if the applicant is unable to furnish the birth registration number or subject is holding a foreign identification document.

BIRTH PARTICULARS

Date of Registration
Place & Address of Birth
Birth Registered At

FATHER'S PARTICULARS

Identification Document & No.
Name
Alias (if any)

MOTHER'S PARTICULARS

Identification Document & No.
Name
Alias (if any)

Part C	Identification Document and No.

APPLICANT'S PARTICULARS

Name in full	Relationship to Child
Address	Telephone No.
Reasons for Application	

....
DATE   *SIGNATURE/THUMB IMPRESSIONS OF APPLICANT*

Part D	SEARCH	EXTRACT

FOR OFFICIAL USE ONLY

SEARCH		EXTRACT
Fee Paid $		Fee Paid $
Receipt No. And Date		Receipt No. And Date
Search Conducted By		Application No.
Result of Search TRACED/UNTRACED	Application No.	Extract No. And Date
Notified Applicant On		Extract Issued On

Entered By : ....   *Date :* ....   *BD 40*

APPLICATION FORM FOR A SEARCH AND/OR CERTIFIED EXTRACT FROM REGISTER OF DEATHS

Part A	Death Registration No.	Number of Copies Applied For

DECEASED'S PARTICULARS	Name		
	Alias (if any)		
	Sex	Date of Death	Identification Document and No.

Part B	To be completed only if the applicant is unable to furnish the dealth registration No.		

SUPPLEMENTARY INFORMATION	Date of Birth/Age	Race/Dialect Group	Nationality
	Address of Death		
	Death Registered At		

Part C	Identificatin Document & No.

APPLICANT'S PARTICULARS	Name in full	Relationship to Deceased
	Address	Telephone No.
	Reasons for Application	

_____   _____
DATE   *SIGNATURE/THUMB IMPRESSIONS OF APPLICANT*

Part D	SEARCH	EXTRACT

FOR OFFICIAL USE ONLY	Fee Paid $		Fee Paid $
	Receipt No. And Date		Receipt No. And Date
	Search Conducted By		Application No.
	Result of Search TRACED/UNTRACED	Application No.	Extract No. And Date
	Notified Applicant On		Extract Issue On

BD 41

Entered By : ....   Date : ....

Send your requests to:

Ministerstvo Vnútra Slovenskej Republiky
Odbor Archívnictva a Spisovej Služby
(Ministry of the Interior, Department of Archives & Records Management)
Križkova 7
81104 Bratislava, Slovakia

Slovakia, formerly part of Czechoslovakia, was created in January 1993. The Archives charges an hourly fee for a search. Church records are available from 1785 but modern civil registration did not begin until 1919. The Ministry of Health is in charge of orphanages for children under three years of age, and the MInistry of Education is responsible for orphanages for children ages three to eighteen.

Cost for a certified Birth Certificate	$15
Cost for a certified Marriage Certificate	$15
Cost for a certified Death Certificate	$15

Send your requests for Adoption Records to:

Ministry of Labor, Social Affairs and Family   Tel. (011) (42) (7) 44-2415
Spitalska 46   Fax (011) (42) (7) 36-2150
81643 Bratislava, Slovakia

If the exact place of the Adoption is known, write to:

District Officer for Local Administration
Section of Social Affairs
Okresny Urad
Odbor Socialnych Veci
(Town), Slovakia

For additional assistance contact:

Department of Social Statistics and Demography
Mileticova 3
82467 Bratislava, Slovakia

Embassy of the Slovak Republic   Tel. (202) 965-5160
2201 Wisconsin Avenue NW, Suite 250
Washington, DC 20007

SLOVENIA

Send your requests to:

Civil Registration Office
(Town), Slovenia

This country has no central office for current vital records. To obtain copies of birth, marriage, and death certificates write to the Civil Registration District Office in the town where the event occurred. Vital records are on file from 1946.

Cost for a certified Birth Certificate	Free
Cost for a certified Marriage Certificate	Free
Cost for a certified Death Certificate	Free

Send your requests for records before 1895 to:

Arhiv Republike Slovenije
(National Archives of Slovenia)
Zvezdarska 1, p.p. 21
1127 Ljubljana, Slovenia

Tel. (011) (386) 61 24 14 200
Fax (011) (386) 61 24 14 269

For additional assistance contact:

Director
Statistical Office of the Republic of Slovenia
Vozarski Pot 12
61000 Ljubljana, Slovenia

Narodna in Univerzitetna Knjiznica
(National and University Library)
Turjaska 1
P.O. Box 259
61000 Ljubljana, Slovenia

Embassy of Slovenia
1525 New Hampshire Avenue, NW
Washington, DC 20036

Tel. (202) 667-5363

Priloha č.

Žiadosť o vyhotovenie jednotlivého výpisu z matriky, resp.
duplikátu matričného dokladu /narodenie, sobáš, úmrtie/
Application for individual vital statistics records or
duplicates of the certificates /birth, marriage, death/
Ansuchen um Herstellung eines genealogischen Auszuges, bzw. um
Ausfertigung einer Geburts-, Heirats-, oder Sterbeurkunde

----

1. Meno a adresa žiadateľa:
   Name and address of applicant:
   Name und Adresse des Gesuchstellers:_____

   ----

2. Typ požadovaného dokladu:
   /narodenie, sobáš, úmrtie/
   Type of certificate requested:
   /birth, marriage, death/
   Art der beanspruchte Urkunde:
   /Geburts-, Heirats-, Sterbeurkunde/:_____

3. Informácie o osobe, ktorá je predmetom výskumu:
   Information on person searched for:
   Angaben über die gesuchte Person:
   a/ Meno:
      Name:
      Name:_____
   b/ Dátum narodenia: +/- 3 roky
      Date of birth: +/- 3 years
      Datum der Geburt:+/- 3 Jahre_____
   c/ Miesto narodenia:
      Place of birth:
      Geburtsort:_____
   d/ Bližšie určenie miesta narodenia /kraj, blizke väčšie
      mesto, farský úrad/
      Further identify the locality /county, larger town,
      parish nearby/
      Hilfsangaben zur Identifizierung des Geburtsortes
      /Kreis, nahe liegende grösere Stadt, Pfarramt/:_____

      ----
   e/ Vierovyznanie:
      Religion:
      Konfession:_____
   f/ Meno otca:
      Name of father:
      Name des Vaters:_____
      Vierovyznanie:
      Religion:
      Konfession:_____

g./ Meno matky:
   Name of mother:
   Name der Mutter:_____

   Vierovyznanie:
   Religion:
   Konfession:_____

h/ Dalšie informácie:
   Other information:
   Weitere Angaben:_____

4. Taktiež žiadam o:
   I also request:
   Ich ersuche auch um:
   Duplikáty dokladov
   Duplicates of records
   Duplikat der Urkunde:_____
   _____

5. Najvyššia čiastka, ktorú uhradim za rešerš:
   My limit on research fee:
   Mein geldliches Limit für die beanspruchte Arbeit:_____

6. Beriem na vedomie, že správa mi bude doručená po prijati
   úhrady.
   I accept the mailing of the report upon the receipt of my
   payment.
   Ich akzeptiere, dass mir der genealogische Bericht erst
   nach dem Empfang meiner Zahlung zugestellt wird.

Dátum:
Date:
Datum: _____
                              Podpis:
                              Signature:
                              Unterschrift:

_____
Žiadateľ hradí cenu za výskum. Duplikáty matričných dokladov
doruči a správny poplatok vyberie príslušný orgán Slovenskej
republiky.
Applicant will pay the research fee. The duplicates of the
birth-marriage-death certificates will be sent through
competent and responsible authority of the Slovak Republic;
applicant will be advised to pay the administrative charges by
this authority as well.

Der Gesuchsteller bezahlt die Forschungsgebühr. Die Duplikaten der Geburts-, Heirats- oder Sterbeurkunden stellt zu und die Verwaltungsgebühr zieht ein die zuständige Stelle.

Vypočítanie cien
Cena sa vypočíta podľa náročnosti a množstva pracovného času. Účtuje sa i cena za kópie a poštovné. Žiadateľ uhradí i negatívnu odpoveď.
- jednoduchá rešerš: 350.00.-Sk/1hod.
- zložitá rešerš: 550.00.-Sk/1hod.
- zložitá kombinovaná rešerš: 600.00.-Sk/1hod.
- kancelárska práca: 80.00.-Sk/1hod.
- manipulačný poplatok: 100.00/200.00.-Sk

Fee calculation
Fee is calculated on the basis of amount of working hours and difficulty of the research; copies, postage and handling are paid as well. Negative answer must be paid as well.
- simple research: 350.00.-Sk/1hour
- demanding research: 550.00.-Sk/1hour
- very demanding research: 600.00.-Sk/1hour
- typing: 80.00.-Sk/1hour
- archives administrative fee: 100.00/200.00.-Sk

Errechnung der Zahlung
Die Zahlung wird gemäss der Schwierigkeit der Forschung und Ausmass der verwendeten Arbeitszeit errechnet. Es werden auch die gelieferten Kopien sowie das Porto zugerechnet. Auch für eine negative Antwort wird die Zahlung errechnet.
- einfache Recherche   350.00.-SK/1Stunde
- komplizierte Recherche   550.00.-Sk/1Stunde
- komplizierte kombinierte Recherche   600.00.-Sk/1Stunde
- Schreibarbeiten   80.00.-Sk/1Stunde
- Manipulationsgebühr   100.00/200.00.-Sk

Žiadosť o vypracovanie genealogického výskumu formou správy
Application for genealogical research in the form of running account
Ansuchen um eine genealogische Forschung

----

1. Meno a adresa žiadateľa:
   Name and address of applicant:
   Name und Adresse:_____

----

2. Informácia o osobe, ktorá je predmetom výskumu:
   Information on person searched for:
   Angaben über die gesuchte Person:
   a/ Meno:
      Name:
      Name:_____
   b/ Dátum narodenia: +/- 3 roky
      Date of birth: +/- 3 years
      Datum der Geburt:+/- 3 Jahre_____
   c/ Miesto narodenia:
      Place of birth:
      Geburtsort:_____
   d/ Bližšie určenie miesta narodenia /kraj, blizke väčšie
      mesto, farský úrad/
      Further identity of the locality /county, larger town,
      parish nearby/
      Zusatz Angaben über Geburtsort /Kreis, naheliegende
      grösere Stadt, Pfarramt/_____
      ----
   e/ Vierovyznanie:
      Religion:
      Konfession:_____
   f/ Meno otca:
      Name of father:
      Name des Vaters:_____
      Vierovyznanie:
      Religion:
      Konfession_____
   g/ Meno matky:
      Name of mother:
      Name der Mutter:_____
      Vierovyznanie:
      Religion:
      Konfession:_____
   h/ Dalšie informácie, resp. kópie dokladov /nie je záväzné/
      Other information or copies of records /optional/
      Weitere Angaben, bzw. Kopien der vorhandenen Dokumenten
      /nicht verpflichtend/:_____

      ----

3. Taktiež žiadam o:
   I also request:
   Ich ersuche auch um:
   Duplikáty matričných dokladov /ak nejde o úradnú
   potrebu, vyhotovujú sa iba výpisy z matrík/
   Duplicates of records /in case of non official use, the
   extracts of records are offered/
   Duplikate der Geburts-, Heirats- oder Sterbeurkunden
   /wenn keine Unterlagen für Amtshandlung erforderlich
   sind, werden nur Matrikauszuge verfertigt/:_____
   _____

4.   Príbuzní osoby, ktorá je predmetom výskumu: /je nezáväzné,
   ale často velmi užitočné/
   Relatives of the person being searched /this is optional
   but often very helpful/
   Verwandte der gesuchten Person /nicht erforderlich, aber
   oft sehr nützlich/
   a/ Manžel/ka: dátum narodenia: miesto:
      Husband/Wife: date of birth: place:
      Eheman/Ehefrau: Datum der Geburt: Ort:

      Vierovyznanie:
      Religion:
      Konfession:_____
   b/ Deti: dátum narodenia: miesto:
      Children: date of birth: place:
      Kinder: Datum der Geburt: Ort:
      Meno:
      Name:
      Name:
      Meno:
      Name:
      Name:
      Vierovyznanie:
      Religion:
      Konfession:_____
   c/ Bratia a sestry: dátum narodenia: miesto:
      Brothers and sisters: date of birth: place:
      Brüder und Schwester: Datum der Geburt: Ort:
      Meno:
      Name:
      Name:
      Meno:
      Name:
      Name:
      Vierovyznanie:
      Religion:
      Konfession:_____

5. Privital by som údaje o narodeni všetkých bratov a sestier
   v priamej linii predkov:
   uveďte   áno - nie
   I would like birth dates of all brothers and sisters of
   direct-line ancestors:
   indicate   yes - no
   Ich habe Interesse auch um die Ermittlung der Geburtsdatum
   aller Brüder und Schwester meiner Vorfahren:
   Ja - Nein: ---------------------------

6. Žiadam iba o výskum predkov v priamej linii:
   uveďte áno - nie
   Please research direct-line ancestors only:
   indicate yes - no
   Ich ersuche nur um Ermittlung der Geburts-/Heirats-, oder
   Sterbedaten/ meiner Vorfahren:
   Ja - Nein   ---------------------------

7. Najvyššia čiastka, ktorú uhradim za rešerš je:
   My limit on research fee is:
   Mein geldliches Limit für die genealogische Forschung:
                                       ----

8. Beriem na vedomie, že správa mi bude doručená po prijati
   úhrady
   I accept the mailing of the report upon the receipt of my
   payment
   Ich akzeptiere, dass mir der genealogische Bericht erst
   nach dem Empfang meiner Zahlung zugestellt wird

Dátum:
Date:
Datum: -------------------------------------
                        Podpis:
                        Signature:
                        Unterschrift:

Vypočitanie cien:
Cena za rešeré sa vypočita podľa náročnosti a množstva
pracovného času. Účtuje sa i cena za kópie a poštovné.
Žiadateľ uhradi i negativnu odpoveď.
- jednoduchá rešerš: 350.00.-Sk/1hod.
- zložitá rešeré: 550.00.-SK/1hod.
- zložitá kombinovaná rešerš: 600.00.-Sk/1hod.
- kancelárska práca: 80.00.-Sk/1hod.
- manipulačný poplatok: 100.00/200.00.-Sk
Fee calculation:
Fee is caculated on the basis of amount of working hours and
difficulty of the research; copies, postage and handling are
paid as well. Negative answer must be paid as well.
- simple research: 350.00.-SK/1hour
- demanding research: 550.00.-Sk/1hour
- very demanding research: 600.00.-Sk/1hour
- typing: 80.00.-Sk/1hour
- administrative fee: 100.00/200.00.-Sk

Errechnung der Zahlung
Die Zahlung wird gemäss der Schwierigkeit der Forschung und
Ausmass der verwendeten Arbeitszeit errechnet. Es werden auch
die gelieferten Kopien sowie das Porto zugerechnet. Auch für
eine negative Antwort wird die Zahlung errechnet.
- einfache Recherche   350.00.-SK/1Stunde
- komplizierte Recherche   550.00.-Sk/1Stunde
- komplizierte kombinierte Recherche   600.00.-Sk/1Stunde
- Schreibarbeiten   80.00.-Sk/1Stunde
- Manipulationsgebühr   100.00/200.00.-Sk

SOLOMON ISLANDS

Send your requests for Birth and Death Records to:

Ministry of Health and Medical Services
P.O. Box G11
Honiara, Solomon Islands

Send your requests for Marriage and Divorce Records to:

Ministry of Police and Justice
Magistrates Division
Honiara, Solomon Islands

Current vital registration in the Solomon Islands is considered to be 75 percent comprehensive.

Cost for a certified Birth Certificate	A$.50
Cost for a certified Marriage Certificate	A$.50
Cost for a certified Death Certificate	A$.50

For additional assistance contact:

Senior Administrator on Registration Matters
Ministry of Home Affairs
P.O. Box 745
Honiara, Solomon Islands

Solomon Islands National Archives
Ministry of Home Affairs
P.O. Box 781
Honiara, Solomon Islands

Tel. (011) (677) 21-339
Fax (011) (677) 21-397

Solomon Islands National Library
P.O. Box 165
Honiara, Solomon Islands

Tel. (011) (677) 21-601

Solomon Islands Mission to the U.N.
800 Second Avenue, 4th Floor
New York, NY 10017

Tel. (212) 599-6192

There is currently no organized vital registration program in Somalia.

For assistance contact:

Library
Jaamacadda Ummadda Soolaaliyeed
(National University of Somalia)
P.O. Box 15
Mogadishu, Somalia

For further information see:

Kannisto, Vaino.*Civil Registration and Vital Statistics in the Africa Region, Lessons Learned from the Evaluation of UNFPA Assisted Projects in Kenya and Sierra Leone.* New York, NY: UN Fund for Population Activities, 1984.

Methods and Problems of Civil Registration Practices and Vital Statistics Collection in Africa. IIVRS Technical Papers, No. 16. Bethesda, MD: International Institute for Vital Registration and Statistics, 1981. 27p.

Organization and Status of Civil Registration in Africa and Recommendations for Improvement. IIVRS Technical Papers, No. 31. Bethesda, MD: International Institute for Vital Registration and Statistics, 1988. 15p.

SOUTH AFRICA

Send your requests to:

Registration Office
Department of Home Affairs
Private Bag X114
Pretoria, 0001, South Africa

Tel. (011) (27) (12) 324-1860
Fax (011) (27) (12) 326-4820

The Registration Office has records from 1924.

Send your requests for Adoption Records to:

Registrar of Adoptions
Private Bag X730
Pretoria 0001, South Africa

Tel. (011) (27) (12) 317-6500

Send your requests for Divorce Records to:

National Archives Repository
24 Hamilton Street
Private Bag X236
Pretoria 0001, South Africa

Cape Archives Repository
72 Roeland Street
Private Bag X9025
Cape Town 8000, South Africa

Free State Archives Repository
37 Elizabeth Street
Private Bag X20504
Bloemfontein 9300, South Africa

National Archives Repository
231 Pietermaritz Street
Private Bag X20504
Pietermaritzburg 3200, South Africa

Cost for a certified Birth Certificate	Short Form R6.00 Long Form R30.00
Cost for a certified Marriage Certificate	Short Form R6.00 Long Form R30.00
Cost for a Divorce Record	Short Form R6.00 Long Form R30.00
Cost for a certified Death Certificate	Short Form R6.00 Long Form R30.00
Cost for Adoption Records	Free

For further information see:

Kannisto, Vaino.*Civil Registration and Vital Statistics in the Africa Region, Lessons Learned from the Evaluation of UNFPA Assisted Projects in Kenya and Sierra Leone*. New York, NY: UN Fund for Population Activities, 1984.

Methods and Problems of Civil Registration Practices and Vital Statistics Collection in Africa. IIVRS Technical Papers, No. 16. Bethesda, MD: International Institute for Vital Registration and Statistics, 1981. 27p.

Organization and Status of Civil Registration in Africa and Recommendations for Improvement. IIVRS Technical Papers, No. 31. Bethesda, MD: International Institute for Vital Registration and Statistics, 1988. 15p.

DEPARTMENT OF HOME AFFAIRS

APPLICATION FOR BIRTH CERTIFICATE

(Complete in block letters please)

N.B.—For use in the **Republic of South Africa** an abridged birth certificate, or where possible, a computer printed certificate of birth particulars is normally issued. Such a certificate usually complies with the requirements for which a birth certificate is required.

An unabridged certificate is available on request and is issued mainly for overseas purposes. If such a certificate is required, indicate with a X in the block hereunder and state fully the purpose for which the certificate is required.

☐ Purpose for which required ....

....

....

I. PARTICULARS OF PERSON CONCERNED

1. Identity Number

2. Surname ....

3. Maiden name if a married woman ....

4. Forenames in full ....

5. Date of birth ....

6. District of birth ....

II. PARTICULARS OF FATHER AND MOTHER

1. Full name of father ....

2. Surname of father ....

3. Full name of mother ....

4. Maiden name ....

III. PARTICULARS OF APPLICANT

1. Name of applicant ....

2. Address of applicant ....

3. Postal code .... 4. Tel. No.: W .... H..

5. ....   6. ....
            Signature   *Date*

APPLICATION FOR MARRIAGE CERTIFICATE

(Complete in block letters please)

Indicate in the appropriate square whether an abridged or a full certificate is required.

N.B.—An abridged certificate generally answers the purpose for which a marriage certificate is required in the Republic of South Africa. A full certificate is issued mainly for *overseas* purposes.

If a full certificate is required, state fully the purpose for which it is required:

....

....

....

☐ **Abridged certificate**   ☐ **Full certificate**

Full names and surname of husband ....

....

Identity number of husband ☐☐☐☐☐☐ ☐☐☐☐ ☐☐ ☐

Date of birth of husband ....

Full names and maiden name of wife ....

....

Identity number of wife ☐☐☐☐☐☐ ☐☐☐☐ ☐☐ ☐

Date of birth of wife ....

Date of marriage ....

Name of church or magistrate's office ....

Place where marriage took place ....

Name of marriage officer (if married in church)..

Name of applicant..

Address of applicant..

....

....

Postal code ....   Tel. No.: Work...

                                                                          Home...

....
                    Signature

Date ....

APPLICATION FOR DEATH CERTIFICATE

(Complete in block letters please)

Identity number: ☐☐☐☐☐☐ ☐☐☐☐ ☐☐ ☐

Surname ....

Maiden name if a married woman ....

Forenames in full ....

Population group ....

Date of birth ....

Date of death ....

District where death occurred ....

N.B.—Two types of certificates are issued, viz. an abridged certificate and a full certificate.

An abridged certificate usually answers the purpose for which it is required in the Republic of South Africa.

A full certificate is issued mainly for overseas purposes.

Make a cross (X) in the appropriate block if a full certificate is required and state the purpose for which it is required.

☐ A full certificate is required for ....

....

....

Name of applicant ....

Address of applicant ....

....

....

Postal code ....   Tel. No.: Work ....

Home ....

....
Signature

Date ....

SPAIN

Send your requests to:

Registro General del Ministerio de Justicia   Tel. (011) (34) (1) 91 390 20 11
San Bernardo   http://www.mju.es/img003.htm
45. 28015 Madrid
Spain
or
Registro Civil
(Town), Spain

Vital records from 1870 are on file. The Registro General (Central Registry) directs the work of the local registrars. Current vital registration is considered to be more than 90 percent complete.

Cost for a certified Birth Certificate	Free
Cost for a certified Marriage Certificate	Free
Cost for a certified Death Certificate	Free

For additional assistance contact:

Jefe de Area del Movimiento Natural de la Población
Instituto Nacional de Estadística
Paseo de la Castellana, 183
28046 Madrid, Spain

Subdirección General de los Archivos Estatales
Dirección General del Libro, Archivos y Bibliotecas
Ministerio de Educación y Cultura
Plaza del Rey 1
Planta 0
28071 Madrid, Spain

Embassy of Spain   Tel. (202) 452-0100
2375 Pennsylvania Avenue, NW
Washington, DC 20037

The Family History Library of Salt Lake City, Utah has microfilmed original and published records of Spain. For further details on their holdilngs please consult your nearest Family History Center.

For further information see:

Atienza Lopez, Jose Ignacio. *Registro Civil.* Madrid, Spain: Centro de Estudios Financieros, 1998. 190p.

Borrajeiros, Manuel Taboada Roca, conde de. *Los Titulos Nobiliarios su Acceso al Registro Civil.* Madrid, Spain: Ediciones Hidalguia, 1961. 29p.

Ley y Reglamento del Registro Civil, Concordancias, Comentarios, Apendices y Formularios, Doctrina de la Dirección General de los Registros Notariado. Madrid, Spain: Editoria COLEX, 1989. 496p.

Registro Civil. 4th ed. Madrid, Spain: Boletin Oficial del Estado, 1983. 498p.

_____. 5th. ed. Madrid, Spain: Boletin Oficial del Estado, 1987. 362p.

Ruiz Gutierrez, Urbano. *Ley y Reglamento del Registro Civil.* Madrid, Spain: Editorial Tecnos.

Send your requests to:

Registrar General of Marriages, Births and Deaths
Ministry of Home Affairs
340, R.A. De Mel Mawatha
Colombo 3, Sri Lanka

Sri Lanka, originally known as Lanka and more recently as Ceylon, has had vital registration since the Dutch period. The British improved coverage with laws passed from 1815 on. By 1867 registration included the entire population and it is now more than 90 percent complete. Marriages are kept by separate Marriage Registrars, by religion. Divorces for marriages other than Muslim or Kandyan are handled by District Courts. Muslim divorces are recorded in their own registers. Kandyan divorces are recorded by the District Registrar. Adoptions are finalized by local District Court. Copies of adoption certificates are obtained from the Registrar General. The nation requires each person to register and obtain a national identity card at age 18.

Cost for a certified Birth Certificate	R 2.00
Cost for a certified Marriage Certificate	R 2.00
Cost for a certified Death Certificate	R 2.00

For more Adoption Record information contact:

Department of Census and Statistics
Ministry of Policy Planning and Implementation
No. 6, Albert Crescent
P.O. Box 563
Colombo 7, Sri Lanka

Department of Probation and Child Care Services
P.O. Box 946
Colombo, Sri Lanka

For more assistance contact:

National Archives of Sri Lanka   Fax (011) (94) 1 694419
P. O. Box 1414
7 Reid Avenue
Colombo 7, Sri Lanka

For further information see:

Jayasuriya, D. C. *Laws Regulating and Influencing the Vital Registration System in Sri Lanka.* Colombo, Sri Lanka: Department of Census and Statistics, Ministry of Plan Implementation, 1980. 87p.

Munasinghe, D. S. *The Development and Organization of Civil Registration in Sri Lanka.* IIVRS Technical Papers, No. 41. Bethesda, MD: International Institute for Vital Registration and Statistics, 1990. 9p.

SUDAN

Send your requests to:

Director of Civil Registration and Vital Statistics
Central Bureau of Statistics
P.O. Box 700
Khartoum, Sudan

Vital registration only began in Sudan in recent times and is not uniform throughout the country. Sudan became independent in 1956.

Cost for a certified Birth Certificate	Free
Cost for a certified Marriage Certificate	Free
Cost for a certified Death Certificate	Free

For additional assistance contact:

Ministry of Health and Social Welfare
Khartoum, Sudan

The National Records Office   Tel. (011) (249) (11) 7-6082
Jumhuria Avenue
P. O. Box 1914
Khartoum, Sudan

Embassy of Sudan   Tel. (202) 338-8565
2210 Massachusetts Avenue, NW
Washington, DC 20008

For further information see:

Kannisto, Vaino.*Civil Registration and Vital Statistics in the Africa Region, Lessons Learned from the Evaluation of UNFPA Assisted Projects in Kenya and Sierra Leone.* New York, NY: UN Fund for Population Activities, 1984.

Methods and Problems of Civil Registration Practices and Vital Statistics Collection in Africa. IIVRS Technical Papers, No. 16. Bethesda, MD: International Institute for Vital Registration and Statistics, 1981. 27p.

Organization and Status of Civil Registration in Africa and Recommendations for Improvement. IIVRS Technical Papers, No. 31. Bethesda, MD: International Institute for Vital Registration and Statistics, 1988. 15p.

Organization and Status of Civil Registration in the Arab Countries. IIVRS Technical Papers, No. 33. Bethesda, MD: International Institute for Vital Registration and Statistics, 1988. 6p.

Send your requests to:

Registrar General
Central Bureau of Civil Registration
Ministry of Interior Affairs
Coppenamelaan 177
Paramaribo, Suriname

The Registrar General is actively computerizing the vital records, concentrating on the Marowijne, Brokopondo, and Sipaliwini districts. Current registration is considered to be at 95 percent.

Cost for a certified Birth Certificate	Gldr 1.00
Cost for a certified Marriage Certificate	Gldr 1.00
Cost for a certified Death Certificate	Gldr 1.00

For additional assistance contact:

Director
Bureau of Public Health
Rode Kruislaan 22
P.O. Box 767
Paramaribo, Suriname

Landsarchiefdienst
(Archives)
Doekhieweg 18A
Paramaribo, Suriname

Bibliotheek
(Library)
Stichting Cultureel Centrum Suriname
Gravenstr 112-114
P.O. Box 1241
Paramaribo, Suriname

Embassy of Suriname   Tel. (202) 244-7488
4301 Connecticut Avenue, NW, Suite 460
Washington, DC 20008

The Family History Library of Salt Lake City, Utah has microfilmed records of Suriname. For further details on their holdings please consult your nearest Family History Center.

SWAZILAND

Send your requests to:

Registrar General
Register General's Office
Ministry of Justice
P.O. Box 460
Moabane, Swaziland

Vital registration began in Swaziland in 1900 for the foreign population. In 1927 it was expanded to the entire nation, although it is not comprehensive.

Cost for a certified Birth Certificate	Free
Cost for a certified Marriage Certificate	Free
Cost for a certified Death Certificate	Free

For additional assistance contact:

Government Statistician
Central Statistical Office
P.O. Box 456
Moabane, Swaziland

Swaziland National Archives
P. O. Box 946
Moabane, Swaziland

Swaziland National Library
P.O. Box 1461
Moabane, Swaziland

Embassy of Swaziland   Tel. (202) 362-6683
3400 International Drive, NW, Suite 3M
Washington, DC 20008

For further information see:

Kannisto, Vaino.*Civil Registration and Vital Statistics in the Africa Region, Lessons Learned from the Evaluation of UNFPA Assisted Projects in Kenya and Sierra Leone.* New York, NY: UN Fund for Population Activities, 1984.

Methods and Problems of Civil Registration Practices and Vital Statistics Collection in Africa. IIVRS Technical Papers, No. 16. Bethesda, MD: International Institute for Vital Registration and Statistics, 1981. 27p.

Organization and Status of Civil Registration in Africa and Recommendations for Improvement. IIVRS Technical Papers, No. 31. Bethesda, MD: International Institute for Vital Registration and Statistics, 1988. 15p.

Send your requests for records from 1895–1991 to:

Lutheran Church Pastor
Pastorsämbete
(Town), Sweden

Send your requests for records after July 1, 1991 to:

Lokala Skattemyndigheten
(Local Tax Office)
(Town), Sweden

Send your requests for pre-1895 records to:

Provincial Archives
(Provincial Seat), Sweden

Microfilm of pre-1895 records may be purchased from:

Swedish National Archives, Microfilm Sales
SVAR
P.O. Box 160, S-880
40 Ramsele, Sweden

The local Lutheran pastors have kept Sweden's records since the 1600s, when the Church Law of 1686 went into effect. Records before 1895 are at the eight Provincial Archives. Addresses for the local *Pastorsämbete* are listed annually in the government publication, *Rikets Indelningar*. Since July 1, 1991 the local tax officers have had the responsibility of keeping vital records. Current vital registration is considered to be comprehensive. While there is no central office for vital records in Sweden, the nation instituted a national personal identification number to every person living in Sweden on January 1, 1947.

Cost for a certified Birth Certificate	Kr 1.00
Cost for a certified Marriage Certificate	Kr 1.00
Cost for a certified Death Certificate	Kr 1.00

For additional assistance contact:

Riksarkivet   Fax: (011) (46) (8) 737 6474
(National Archives)
Box 12541
102 29 Stockholm, Sweden

Embassy of Sweden   Tel. (202) 467-2600
1501 M Street, NW
Washington, DC 20005

The Family History Library of Salt Lake City, Utah has microfilmed many of the original and published vital records and church registers of Sweden. For further details on their holdings please consult your nearest Family History Center.

For further information see:

The Impact of Computerization on Population Registration in Sweden. IIVRS Technical Papers, No. 65. Bethesda, MD: International Institute for Vital Registration and Statistics, 1996. 6p.

Lag om folkbokföringsregister m.m. Stockholm, Sweden: Delbetänkande av organisationskommittén för folkbokföringen, 1990. 214p.

Ny Folkbokforingslag. Stockholm, Sweden: Sweden Folkbokforingskommittee; Allmanna Forlaget, 1990.

SWITZERLAND

Send your requests to:

Zivilstandsamt
(Town), Switzerland

To obtain copies of birth, marriage, and death certificates write to the Civil Registration District Office (*Zivilstandsamt*) in the town where the person was born. These records date from January 1, 1876. Current vital registration is considered to be comprehensive.

Cost for a certified Birth Certificate	Fr 1.00
Cost for a certified Marriage Certificate	Fr 1.00
Cost for a certified Death Certificate	Fr 1.00

For additional assistance contact:

Office Federal de l'État Civil
Department of Justice
Bundesgasse 32
3003 Berne, Switzerland

Department of Population and Employment
Federal Statistical Office
Hallwylstr, 15
3003 Berne, Switzerland

Archives fédérales suisses   Fax: (011) (41) (31) 322-8989
(Swiss National Archives)
Archivstrasse 24
3003 Bern, Switzerland

Embassy of Switzerland   Tel. (202) 745-7900
2900 Cathedral Avenue, NW
Washington, DC 20008

The Family History Library of Salt Lake City, Utah has microfilmed original and published records of Switzerland. For further details on their holdings please consult your nearest Family History Center.

For further information see:

Huber, Ernst. *Das Recht der Urkundspersonen in den Schweizerischen Kantonen.* Affoltern, Switzerland: J. Weiss, 1910. 180p.
Jaques, Pierre B. *La Rectification des Actes de l'état Civil.* Ph.D., Dissertation, Université de Lausanne, 1949. 358p.
Tüzemen, Ekrem. *Les Registres de l'état Civil.* Dissertation, Ph.D., Université de Lausanne, 1940. 269p.

Send your requests to:

General Director
General Directorate of Civil Registration
Ministry of Interior Affairs
Fardos Street
Damascus, Syria

Vital registration began in Syria in 1923 and currently is considered almost comprehensive for births and is 54 percent complete for deaths. Syria handles adoption under Islamic law. Children are placed within families.

Cost for a certified Birth Certificate	Free
Cost for a certified Marriage Certificate	Free
Cost for a certified Death Certificate	Free

For additional assistance contact:

Director General
Central Bureau of Statistics
Office of the Prime Minister
Abu Rumaneh
Damascus, Syria

Embassy of Syria   Tel. (202) 232-6313
2215 Wyoming Avenue, NW
Washington, DC 20008

For further information see:

Organization and Status of Civil Registration in the Arab Countries. IIVRS Technical Papers, No. 33. Bethesda, MD: International Institute for Vital Registration and Statistics, 1988. 6p.

TAJIKISTAN

Send your requests to:

Chief
Registration Directorate
Ministry of Justice
1 Karabayeva Street
734043 Douchanbé, Tajikistan

Cost for a certified Birth Certificate	$25.00
Cost for a certified Marriage Certificate	$25.00
Cost for a certified Death Certificate	$25.00

For additional assistance contact:

Head
Republican Department of the Statement of Civil Condition
Ministry of Justice
3, N Karabeva Street
Douchanbé, Tajikistan

Direction générale des Archives près le Conseil des Ministres de la République du Tadjikistan (Glavarkhiv)
Douchanbé, Tajikistan

The Family History Library of Salt Lake City, Utah has microfilmed records of Tajikistan and the former Soviet Union. For further details on their holdings please consult your nearest Family History Center.

TANZANIA

Send your requests to:

Registrar General
Office of the Administrator General
Ministry of Justice
P.O. Box 9183
Dar es Salam, Tanzania

Tel. (011) (255) (51) 28-811

Vital records began August 28,1917 for Europeans, expanded in 1923 to include Asians and in 1966 to include the major towns. The Registrar General has birth and death records from 1917, and marriage and divorce records from 1921. The registration is not comprehensive.

Cost for a certified Birth Certificate	T.Shs. 600/=
Cost for a certified Marriage Certificate	T.Shs. 700/=
Cost for a certified Divorce Certificate	T.Shs. 600/=
Cost for a certified Death Certificate	T.Shs. 600/=

For additional assistance contact:

Committee on Civil Registration
Demographic and Social Statistics Division
Department of Statistics
Ministry of Planning
P.O. Box 874
Zanzibar, Tanzania

National Archives
P. O. Box 2006
Dar es Salaam, Tanzania

Zanzibar National Archives
Department of Antiquities, Archives and Museum
P. O. Box 116
Zanzibar

Fax (011) (255) (51) 32-337

Embassy of Tanzania
2139 R Street, NW
Washington, DC 20008

Tel. (202) 939-6125

For further information see:

Kannisto, Vaino.*Civil Registration and Vital Statistics in the Africa Region, Lessons Learned from the Evaluation of UNFPA Assisted Projects in Kenya and Sierra Leone.* New York, NY: UN Fund for Population Activities, 1984.

Methods and Problems of Civil Registration Practices and Vital Statistics Collection in Africa. IIVRS Technical Papers, No. 16. Bethesda, MD: International Institute for Vital Registration and Statistics, 1981. 27p.

Organization and Status of Civil Registration in Africa and Recommendations for Improvement. IIVRS Technical Papers, No. 31. Bethesda, MD: International Institute for Vital Registration and Statistics, 1988. 15p.

THAILAND

Send your requests to:

Administrative and Civil Registration Division
Department of Local Administration
Ministry of Interior
Nakhon Sawan Road
Bangkok 10300, Thailand

Thailand began formal vital registration in 1909. In 1956 family registration was also required, and in 1982 the nation instituted a computerized national identification card system to centralize data on all individuals. All recorded birth, marriage, divorce, and death information is available from the Division of Civil Registration.

Cost for a certified Birth Certificate	Free
Cost for a certified Marriage Certificate	Free
Cost for a certified Death Certificate	Free

Send your requests for Adoption Records to:

Child Adoption Center
Department of Public Welfare   Tel. (011) (66) (2) 245-9525
Thanon Mitmaitri
Dindaeng
Huay Kwang
Bangkok 10400, Thailand

For additional assistance contact:

Director
Health Statistics Division
Ministry of Public Health
Devaves Palace
275 Samsen Road
Bangkok 10200, Thailand

National Archives of Thailand   Fax (011) (66) (2) 281-6947
Samsen Road
Bangkok 10300, Thailand

Ho Samut Haeng Chat   Tel. (011) (66) (2) 281-5212
(National Library of Thailand)
Samsen Road
Bangkok 10300, Thailand

Royal Thai Embassy   Tel. (202) 944-3600
1024 Wisconsin Avenue, NW
Washington, DC 20007

Send your requests to:

Division des Affaires Politiques et Administratives
Ministère de l'Intérieur
Lome, Togo

While vital registration in Togo began in 1923 in the larger urban areas, it was not expanded to the entire nation until 1962. Currently the registration is not considered to be comprehensive throughout the country.

Cost for a certified Birth Certificate	50F
Cost for a certified Marriage Certificate	50F
Cost for a certified Death Certificate	50F

For additional assistance contact:

Directeur
Direction de la Statistique
B.P. 118
Lomé, Togo

Archives nationales   Fax (011) (228) 22 19 67
(National Archives)
B.P. 1002
Lome, Togo

Embassy of Togo   Tel. (202) 234-4212
2208 Massachusetts Avenue, NW
Washington, DC 20008

For further information see:

Kannisto, Vaino.*Civil Registration and Vital Statistics in the Africa Region, Lessons Learned from the Evaluation of UNFPA Assisted Projects in Kenya and Sierra Leone.* New York, NY: UN Fund for Population Activities, 1984.

Methods and Problems of Civil Registration Practices and Vital Statistics Collection in Africa. IIVRS Technical Papers, No. 16. Bethesda, MD: International Institute for Vital Registration and Statistics, 1981. 27p.

Organization and Status of Civil Registration in Africa and Recommendations for Improvement. IIVRS Technical Papers, No. 31. Bethesda, MD: International Institute for Vital Registration and Statistics, 1988. 15p.

Some Observations on Civil Registration in French-Speaking Africa. IIVRS Technical Papers, No. 39. Bethesda, MD: International Institute for Vital Registration and Statistics, 1990. 13p.

TONGA

Send your requests to:

Registrar General
Registrar of the Supreme Court
Justice Department
P.O. Box 11
Nuku'alofa, Tonga

Tel. (011) (676) 23 599
Fax (011) (676) 23 098

The Registrar General has birth and death records from 1867, marriage records from 1892, and divorce records from 1905. Current vital registration is considered to be 95 percent complete for births and 90 percent complete for deaths.

Cost for a certified Birth Certificate	T$3.00
Cost for a certified Marriage Certificate	T$3.00
Cost for a certified Divorce Certificate	T$2.00
Cost for a certified Death Certificate	T$3.00

For additional assistance contact:

Government Statistician
Statistics Department
P.O. Box 149
Nuku'alofa, Tonga

The Family History Library of Salt Lake City, Utah has microfilmed original and published vital records and church registers of Tonga. For further details on their holdings please consult your nearest Family History Center.

APPLICATION FOR BIRTH CERTIFICATE

NUMBER OF COPIES REQUIRED: ....

NAME OF CHILD..

DATE AND YEAR OF BIRTH...

PLACE AND PARISH OF BIRTH..

FATHER'S FULL NAME ....

MOTHER'S FULL NAME ....

MOTHER'S MAIDEN SURNAME..

ENTRY NUMBER..

FULL NAME AND ADDRESS OF APPLICANT:

....

....

....

....

APPLICATION FOR MARRIAGE CERTIFICATE

NUMBER OF COPIES REQUIRED...................

HUSBAND'S FULL NAME..

WIFE'S FULL NAME...

WIFE'S MAIDEN SURNAME..

DATE AND YEAR OF MARRIAGE ....

PLACE AND PARISH OF MARRIAGE...

MARRIAGE OFFICER'S NAME ....

ENTRY NUMBER.....................................

FULL NAME AND ADDRESS OF APPLICANT:

....

....

....

....

TRINIDAD and TOBAGO

Send your requests to:

Registrar General's Office
Ministry of Legal Affairs
Red House
St. Vincent Street
Port of Spain, Trinidad and Tobago

Tel. (868) 623-5793

The Registrar General's Office has records for Trinidad from January 1, 1848 and for Tobago from January 30, 1868. Trinidad and Tobago were united in 1889. Current registration is considered to be comprehensive. The local churches also have their own records. The country's Adoption Board approves all adoptions, which are finalized by the local courts and registered with the Registrar General.

Cost for a certified Birth Certificate	TT $25.00
Cost for a certified Marriage Certificate	TT $25.00
Cost for a certified Death Certificate	TT $25.00

For additional assistance contact:

Director of Statistics
Central Statistical Office
35-41 Queen Street
Port of Spain, Trinidad and Tobago

National Archives
105 St. Vincent Street
P.O. Box 763
Port of Spain, Trinidad and Tobago

Tel. (868) 625-2689
Fax (868) 625-2689

Embassy of Trinidad and Tobago
1708 Massachusetts Avenue, NW
Washington, DC 20036

Tel. (202) 467-6490

The Family History Library of Salt Lake City, Utah has microfilmed original and published records of Trinidad and Tobago. For further details on their holdings please consult your nearest Family History Center.

For further information see:

Registration of Vital Events in the English-Speaking Caribbean. IIVRS Technical Papers, No. 32. Bethesda, MD: International Institute for Vital Registration and Statistics, 1988. 10p.

REQUEST FOR A BIRTH CERTIFICATE

(Particulars of person for whom Certificate is required)

Particulars:

Birth of ....

Date of Birth ....

Father's Name ....

Mother's Maiden Name ....

Place of Birth ....

....
Applicant

For Official use

Year .... Volume ....

Folio .... Entry No. ....

....
Search Clerk

Fee of $ /2.5.0 ....in stamps received and affixed on
Certificate No.

....
Cashier

G.P., Tr./To.—I 1528—100,000.— /92

REQUEST FOR A MARRIAGE CERTIFICATE

Particulars:

   (a) Civl   (b) Hindu
   (c) Muslim   (d) In Extremis

Names of Parties
   (i) ....
   (ii) ....

Date of Marriage ....

....
Applicant

For Official Use

Year .... Volume ....

Folio .... Entry No. ....

....
Search Clerk

Fee of $ 12.50 ....In stamps received and affixed
on Certificate No.

....
Cashier

G.P., Tr./To.—F3300—30,000 /89

REQUEST FOR A DEATH CERTIFICATE

Particulars:—

Death of ....

Date of Death ....

Place of Death ....

....
Applicant

For Official use

Year .... Volume ....

Folio .... Entry No. ....

....
Search Clerk

Fee of $ 12.50 ....In stamps received and affixed
on Certificate No.

....
Cashier

G.P., Tr./To.—F1495—20,000.— /89

TUNISIA

Send your requests to:

Registrar
Centres d'État Civil
(Town), Tunisia

Vital registration of births and deaths began in Tunisia in 1958, with marriages and divorces being added in 1958. Registration of births is considered to be more than 90 percent comprehensive.

Cost for a certified Birth Certificate	Free
Cost for a certified Marriage Certificate	Free
Cost for a certified Death Certificate	Free

For additional assistance contact:

Ingénieur Principal de la Statistique
Charge des Statistiques de l'État Civil
Institute National de la Statistiques
70 rue Echam
1002 Tunis, Tunisia

El Archive al Watani　　　　　　　　　　Tel. (011) (216) (1) 26-0556
(National Archives)　　　　　　　　　　Fax (011) (216) (1) 56-9175
Premier Ministère, La Kasha
1020 Tunis, Tunisia

Bibliothéque Nationale　　　　　　　　　Tel. (011) (216) (1) 25-6921
(National Library)　　　　　　　　　　　Fax (011) (216) (1) 34-2700
20 Souk el Attarine
1008 Tunis, Tunisia

Embassy of Tunisia　　　　　　　　　　　Tel. (202) 862-1850
1515 Massachusetts Avenue, NW
Washington, DC 20005

For further information see:

Kannisto, Vaino. *Civil Registration and Vital Statistics in the Africa Region, Lessons Learned from the Evaluation of UNFPA Assisted Projects in Kenya and Sierra Leone.* New York, NY: UN Fund for Population Activities, 1984.

Methods and Problems of Civil Registration Practices and Vital Statistics Collection in Africa. IIVRS Technical Papers, No. 16. Bethesda, MD: International Institute for Vital Registration and Statistics, 1981. 27p.

Organization and Status of Civil Registration in Africa and Recommendations for Improvement. IIVRS Technical Papers, No. 31. Bethesda, MD: International Institute for Vital Registration and Statistics, 1988. 15p.

Organization and Status of Civil Registration in the Arab Countries. IIVRS Technical Papers, No. 33. Bethesda, MD: International Institute for Vital Registration and Statistics, 1988. 6p.

Send your requests to:

General Directorate of Population and Citizenship Affairs
Ministry of Internal Affairs
T.C. Icisleri Bakanligi
Nufus ve Vatandaslik Isleri Gn. Md.
Bakanliklar, Ankara, Turkey

The modern government of Turkey was founded in 1923. Efforts have been made to make vital registration compulsory, but it is currently not considered to be comprehensive.

Cost for a certified Birth Certificate	45.00L
Cost for a certified Marriage Certificate	45.00L
Cost for a certified Death Certificate	45.00L

For additional assistance contact:

Devlet Arşivleri Genel Müdürlügü   Tel. (011) (90) (312) 344-2500
(General Dictorate of the State Archives)   Fax (011) (90) (312) 315-1000
Ivedik Caddesi 59, Yenimahalle
06180 Ankara, Turkey

Embassy of Turkey   Tel. (202) 612-6740
2525 Massachusetts Avenue, NW
Washington, DC 20008

For further information see:

Chanlett, Eliska. *Organization and Methods of The Dual Report System in Turkey.* Chapel Hill, NC: International Program of Laboratories for Population Statistics, 1971. 24p.

TURKMENISTAN

For information contact:

Natsional'naia Beblioteka
(National Library)
pl. Karl Marksa
744000 Ashgabat, Turkmenistan

Archives Administration within the Cabinet of Ministers of Turkmenistan
Makhtumkuly Avenue 88
744000 Ashgabat, Turkmenistan

Embassy of Turkmenistan   Tel. (202) 588-1500
2207 Massachusetts Avenue, NW
Washington, DC 20008

The Family History Library of Salt Lake City, Utah has microfilmed records of Turkmenistan and the former Soviet Union. For further details on their holdings please consult your nearest Family History Center.

TURKS and CAICOS ISLANDS

Send your requests to:

Registrar General's Office   Tel. (649) 946-2791
Post Office Building   Fax (649) 946-2821
Front Street
Grand Turk, Turks and Caicos
British West Indies

The Registrar General's Office has records from January 2, 1863. Current registration is considered to be more than 90 percent complete.

Cost for a certified Birth Certificate	US $1.68
Cost for a certified Marriage Certificate	US $1.00
Cost for a certified Death Certificate	US $1.68

For further information see:

Registration of Vital Events in the English-Speaking Caribbean. IIVRS Technical Papers, No. 32. Bethesda, MD: International Institute for Vital Registration and Statistics, 1988. 10p.

APPLICATION FOR BIRTH CERTIFICATE

TO: Registrar of Births
        Registrar General's Office
        Grand Turk

        I desire to have a search made for and .... certified copy/ies
supplied of the Registrar of Birth of

....
                        (Enter all names)

Born at ....

in the Parish of ....

in or about the year ....

Father's full name ....

Mother's full name ....

                        Name of applicant

                        Mr/Mrs/Miss

                        Date   ....

Entry No ....

Stamp Duty Required   80¢
Office fees   88¢
                        $1.68

APPLICATION FOR MARRIAGE CERTIFICATE

TO: Registrar of Marriages
       Registrar General's Office
       Grand Turk

       I desire to have a search made for and .... certified copy/ies
supplied of the Registrar of Marriages of

....
                    (enter all names)

Place of marriage ....

in the Parish of ....

in or about the year ....

                         Name of Applicant

                         Mr/Mrs/Miss

                         Date ....

Entry No............

Office fees $1.00
                     $1.00

APPLICATION FOR DEATH CERTIFICATE

TO: Registrar of Death
         Registrar General's Office
         Grand Turk

        I desire to have a search made for and .... certified copy/ies
supplied of the Registrar of Death of

....
                    (Enter all names)

Died at...
in the Parish of ....
in or about the year....................................

                    Name of Applicant

                    Mr/Mrs/Miss

                    Date   ....

Entry No ....

Stamp Duty Required   80¢
Office fees   88¢
                       $1.68

Send your requests to:

Registrar General
Medical Division
Office of the Prime Minister
Fanafuti, Tuvalu

Tuvalu, consisting of nine islands in the Pacific, became independent in 1978. Current vital registration in Tuvalu is considered to be comprehensive.

Cost for a certified Birth Certificate	$.50
Cost for a certified Marriage Certificate	$.50
Cost for a certified Death Certificate	$.50

For additional assistance contact:

Senior Medical Officer
Medical Division
Ministry of Health, Education and Community Affairs
Funafuti, Tuvalu

National Library and Archives   Tel. (011) (688) 711
P.O. Box 36   Fax (011) (688) 819
Fanafuti, Tuvalu

The Family History Library of Salt Lake City, Utah has microfilmed records of Tuvalu. For further details on their holdings please consult your nearest Family History Center.

UGANDA

Send your requests to:

Registrar General of Births and Deaths
Ministry of Justice and Constitutional Affairs
P.O. Box 7183
Kampala, Uganda

Vital registration of births and deaths began in Uganda as early as 1905 for Europeans, and was expanded in 1915 to include Asians. Registration for the entire population did not begin until 1973. Currently the registration is not considered to be comprehensive.

Cost for a certified Birth Certificate	3Sh
Cost for a certified Marriage Certificate	3Sh
Cost for a certified Death Certificate	3Sh

For additional assistance contact:

Chief Government Statistician
Ministry of Finance and Economic Planning
P.O. Box 13
Entebbe, Uganda

Embassy of Uganda   Tel. (202) 726-7100
5911 16th Street, NW
Washington, DC 20011

For further information see:

Kannisto, Vaino.*Civil Registration and Vital Statistics in the Africa Region, Lessons Learned from the Evaluation of UNFPA Assisted Projects in Kenya and Sierra Leone.* New York, NY: UN Fund for Population Activities, 1984.

Methods and Problems of Civil Registration Practices and Vital Statistics Collection in Africa. IIVRS Technical Papers, No. 16. Bethesda, MD: International Institute for Vital Registration and Statistics, 1981. 27p.

Organization and Status of Civil Registration in Africa and Recommendations for Improvement. IIVRS Technical Papers, No. 31. Bethesda, MD: International Institute for Vital Registration and Statistics, 1988. 15p.

ZAGS (Ukrainian Office of Vital Records)
Kiev, Ukraine

Russian American Genealogical Archival Service (RAGAS)
1929 18th Street, NW
Washington, DC 20009

E-mail: ragas@cityline.ru
ragas@dgs.dgsys.com

By an agreement between the United States National Archives and the Archives of Russia Society RAGAS will receive and process requests for vital records in Ukraine. For information to establish whether records exist for your subject it is $50.00. If indications are good and you wish to pursue a fuller request there is a non-refundable deposit of $100.00 to initiate the search.

Send your requests for Adoption Records to:

The Adoption Center
Ministry of Education
27 Taras Shevchenko Boulevard
252032 Kiev, Ukraine

Tel. (011) (380) (44) 246-5431
Fax (011) (380) (44) 246-5452

For additional assistance contact:

Direction des Archives d'Ukraine
Main Archival Administration of Ukraine

Tel. (011) (380) (44) 277-2777
Fax (011) (380) (44) 277-3655

Solomyanskja St. 24
252601 Kiev 100, Ukraine

Embassy of Ukraine
3350 M Street, NW
Washington, DC 20007

Tel. (202) 333-7507

The Family History Library of Salt Lake City, Utah has microfilmed records of Ukraine and the former Soviet Union. For further details on their holdings please consult your nearest Family History Center.

RAGAS INFORMATIONAL REQUEST FORM:

RAGAS
1929 18th St., NW
Washington, DC 20009

(© copyright 1997 Russian-American Genealogical Archival Service)

A $50.00 non-refundable fee is required to complete this preliminary report. You will have a reply from RAGAS/Moscow office within one-two months to inform you whether a search is feasible and which sources are available. The reply will include a detailed description of archival records, the current address of each archive which will be useful to you for your research, and an estimate of actual costs to complete a full search. You may also be advised that it is not possible to accept a request for this area. With this information you will then be able to determine whether you wish to submit a request for a fuller search. In the case of some archives it may require additional travel and research expense for a special investigation.

Please type or print:

1. PLACE:

It is essential for any search to be successful to have as a starting point the exact geographic location. Many regions have several towns with the same name. Include the name of the region, district, town, village or rural area.

2. TIME FRAME:

Please give dates a report should cover and, if specific dates for individual events are known, include them within the time frame.

3. Please enclose a stamped self-addressed envelope.

SPECIFIC INFORMATION FORM
PLEASE PRINT OR TYPE (пожалуйста, пишите печатными буквами)

RAGAS
1929 18th St., NW
Washington, DC 20009

It is realized that you may not have answers to some questions. Fill in to the best of your knowledge.
(Возможно, Вы не сможете ответить на все вопросы. Постарайтесь ответить как можно более подробно)

Search for information about a specific event or a specific document.

Record to be searched:	☐ Birth Рождение	☐ Baptism Крещение	☐ Marriage Брак	☐ Death Смерть

☐ Military Service Records
О Военной Службе

☐ Civil Service Records
О Гражданской Службе

☐ Property Records
Об Имущественной Собственности

Approximate date (within 5 years) & place of event (guberniya/region, district, town, village, parish; in large cities – ward, quarter, parish, street, house)
Дата (приблизительно – в пределах 5 лет) и место события (губерния/область, уезд /район, волость, стан, округаж город, село, деревня, церковный приход, синагога; в крупных городах – район, участок=. церковный приход, улица, дом)

First name Имя	Patronymic Отчество	Last name Фамилия	Sex Пол

All other names used at any time (including maiden name if married) Другие имена (включая девичью фамилию)

Variant spelling Возможные разночтения фамилии, имени, отчества

Citizenship Гражданство	Ethnic group Национальность	Religion Вероисповедание	Class: Сословие
			☐ Nobility Дворянство ☐ Clergy Духовенство ☐ Middle Class Мещанство
			☐ Merchant class Купечество ☐ Peasantry Крестьянство ☐ Working class Рабочий класс
			☐ Foreign national working in Russia Иностранцы на русской службе

PARENTS (РОДИТЕЛИ)

Father ОТЕЦ	Full name Фамилия, имя, отчество	Date of birth Дата рождения	Place of birth Место рождения	Other information Дополнительная информация
Mother МАТЬ	Full name Фамилия, имя, отчество	Date of birth Дата рождения	Place of birth Место рождения	Other information Дополнительная информация

FULLER GENEALOGICAL SEARCH FORM
PLEASE PRINT OR TYPE (пожалуйста, пишите печатными буквами)

RAGAS
1929 18th St., NW
Washington, DC 20009

It is realized that you may not have answers to some questions. Fill in to the best of your knowledge. (Возможно, Вы не сможете ответить на все вопросы. Постарайтесь ответить как можно более подробно)

FOCUS OF SEARCH: ☐   To link several generations (Установить связи между несколькими поколениями)

ЦЕЛЬ ПОИСКА   ☐   To link family members within a generation (Установить связи между членами семьи одного поколения)

  ☐   To confirm several events in the life of a single individual (Подтвердить определенные события из жизни одного человека)

First name Имя Patronymic Отчество Last name Фамилия	Sex Пол	Date of birth Дата рождения
All other names used at any time (including maiden name if married) Другие имена	Place of birth Место рождения	
Variant spelling Возможные разночтения фамилии, имени, отчества		

Citizenship Гражданство	Ethnic group Национальность	Religion Вероисповедание	Class: Сословие ☐ Nobility Дворянство ☐ Clergy Духовенство ☐ Middle Class Мещанство ☐ Merchant class Купечество ☐ Peasantry Крестьянство ☐ Working class Рабочий класс ☐ Foreign national working in Russia Иностранцы на русской службе Transfer from one class to another Переход из одного класса в другой

PARENTS (РОДИТЕЛИ)

Father ОТЕЦ Full name Фамилия, имя, отчество	Date of birth Дата рождения	Place of birth Место рождения	Other information Дополнительная информация
Mother МАТЬ Full name Фамилия, имя, отчество	Date of birth Дата рождения	Place of birth Место рождения	Other information Дополнительная информация

BROTHERS AND SISTERS (БРАТЬЯ И СЕСТРЫ)

Name including maiden name Фамилия, имя, отчество (включая девичью фамилию)	Sex Пол	Date of Birth Дата рождения	Place of Birth Место рождения	Other information Дополнительная информация

SPOUSE(S) OF PERSON TO BE SEARCHED (МУЖЬЯ, ЖЕНЫ)

Name including maiden name Фамилия, имя, отчество (включая девичью фамилию)	Date of birth Дата рождения	Place of birth Место рождения	Other information Дополнительная информация

B R O T H E R S   A N D   S I S T E R S (БРАТЬЯ И СЕСТРЫ)

Name including maiden name Фамилия, имя, отчество (включая девичью фамилию)	Sex Пол	Date of Birth Дата рождения	Place of Birth Место рождения	Other information Дополнительная информация

SPOUSE(S) OF PERSON TO BE SEARCHED (МУЖЬЯ, ЖЕНЫ)

Name including maiden name Фамилия, имя, отчество (включая девичью фамилию)	Date of birth Дата рождения	Place of birth Место рождения	Other information Дополнительная информация

C H I L D R E N (ДЕТИ)

Name Имя	Date of birth Дата рождения	Place of birth Место рождения	Other information Дополнительная информация

P L A C E S   O F   R E S I D E N C E (МЕСТО ЖИТЕЛЬСТВА)

	Place of residence Место жительства	~~Time~~ Время проживания
1.		
2.		

NAME AND ADDRESS OF THE REQUESTER

ФАМИЛИЯ И АДРЕС ЗАЯВИТЕЛЯ

RAGAS
1929 18th St., NW
Washington, DC 20009

CHILDREN (ДЕТИ)

Name Имя	Date of birth Дата рождения	Place of birth Место рождения	Other information Дополнительная информация

PLACES OF RESIDENCE (МЕСТО ЖИТЕЛЬСТВА)

	Place of residence Место жительства	Date Время проживания
1.		
2.		

OTHER INFORMATION (ДОПОЛНИТЕЛЬНАЯ ИНФОРМАЦИЯ)

Education (Name and address of institution)
Образование (Название и адрес учебного заведения)

Place of service or work
Место службы или работы

Titles, Ranks, Awards
Звания, чины, награды

Real estate ownership
Земельные владения

Adoption, guardianship
Усыновление, опекунство

Legal actions
Нахождение под судом

Place and date of emigration
Место и дата эмиграции

Membership in organizations (cultural, fraternal)
Членство в организациях (культурных, общественных)

Military service (rank, organization, dates)
Военная служба (звание, название части, время службы)

Other information that might help in identification
Дополнительная информация, которая могла бы облегчить поиски

NAME AND ADDRESS OF THE REQUESTER
ФАМИЛИЯ И АДРЕС ЗАЯВИТЕЛЯ

RAGAS
1929 18th St., NW
Washington. DC 20009

UNITED ARAB EMIRATES

Send your requests to:

Registration
Central Preventive Medicine Directorate
Ministry of Health
Abu Dhabi, United Arab Emirates

Registration is not considered to be comprehensive. Adoptions are handled under Islamic law. Children are placed within families.

Cost for a certified Birth Certificate	Dh 4.00
Cost for a certified Marriage Certificate	Dh 4.00
Cost for a certified Death Certificate	Dh 4.00

For additional assistance contact:

National Archives
Airport Road
P.O. Box 2380
Abu Dhabi, United Arab Emirates

Tel. (011) (971) (2) 44-7797
Fax (011) (971) (2) 44-5639

National Library
P.O. Box 2380
Abu Dhabi, United Arab Emirates

Tel. (011) (971) (2) 21-5300
Fax (011) (971) (2) 21-7472

Embassy of the United Arab Emirates
1255 22nd Street, NW
Washington, DC 20037

Tel. (202) 955-7999

For further information see:

Organization and Status of Civil Registration in the Arab Countries. IIVRS Technical Papers, No. 33. Bethesda, MD: International Institute for Vital Registration and Statistics, 1988. 6p.

UNITED KINGDOM — ENGLAND and WALES

Records are available for all births, deaths, and marriages registered in England and Wales since July 1837; adoptions since 1927; and some births, deaths, and marriages of British citizens overseas since 1761, including those of the armed forces. Payment for applications from abroad should be made by credit card or by check, draft (payable in London), or International Money Order made out to "ONS" and expressed in pounds sterling. Expedited service is available, with payment by credit card, for a fee of £27.00 (£24.00 with accurate FRC index citation, or for short form birth certificate, with accurate FRC index citation). For priority service you can order by phone, fax, or e-mail (priority.certificates@ons.gov.uk).

If Applying in Person

Cost for a certified Birth, Marriage, or Death Certificate	£6.50
Coast for a full Adoption Certificate	£6.50
Cost for a short form Adoption Certificate	£5.00
Cost for priority service	£22.50

If Applying by Mail

Cost for a certified Birth, Marriage or Death Certificate	£11.00
If the index citation is given	£8.00
Cost for a short form Birth Certificate	£13.00
Cost for a full Adoption Certificate	£11.00
Cost for a short form Adoption Certificate	£9.50
Cost for a duplicate short form Adoption Certificate, ordered at the same time	£5.00
Cost for duplicate Birth, Marriage, Death, or full Adoption certificates, when ordered at the same time	£6.50

The Family History Library of Salt Lake City, Utah has microfilmed many of the United Kingdom's original and published vital records and church registers. For further details on their holdings please consult your nearest Family History Center.

For further information see:

Baxter, Angus. *In Search of Your British & Irish Roots.* 4th ed. Baltimore: Genealogical Publishing Co., 1999. 320 p.

Bigland, Ralph. *Observations on Marriages, Baptisms and Burials as Preserved in Parochial Registers. With Sundry Specimens of the Entries of Marriages, Baptisms, etc. in Foreign Countries Interspersed with Divers Remarks Concerning Proper Methods Necessary to Preserve a Remembrance of the Several Branches of Families.* London, England: W. Richardson & S. Clark, 1764. 96p.

Christensen, Penelope Janet. *Using Register Offices for English and Welsh Certificates.* Rev. ed. Toronto, Ontario: Heritage Productions, 1997. 78p.

Eagle, William. *The Acts for Marriages and Registration, 6 & 7 Will. IV. C. 85 & 86, with Explanatory Notes and Index.* London, England: Shaw & Sons, 1837. 180p.

Headrick, T. E. *The Town Clerk in English Local Government.* Toronto, Ontario: Royal Institute of Public Administration, by the University of Toronto Press, 1962. 223p.

Herber, Mark D. *Ancestral Trails.* Baltimore: Genealogical Publishing Co., 1998. 688 p.

Registrar General. *The Act for Suspending the Operation of Two Acts Passed in the Last Session for Registering Births, Deaths, and Marriages in England, and the Act for Explaining and Amending the Said Two Acts.* London, England: G. Eyre and A. Spottiswoode, printers to the Queen's Most Excellent Majesty, 1837. 31p.

Reid, Judith Prowse, and Simon Fowler. *Genealogical Research in England's Public Record Office: A Guide for North Americans.* 2nd ed. Baltimore: Genealogical Publishing Co., 2000. 164 p.

COPIES
....

APPLICATION FOR BIRTH CERTIFICATE
General Register Office, PO Box 2, Southport, Merseyside PR8 2JD

Applicant

Mr/Mrs/Miss ....

Full
postal
address ....

....

Telephone number ....

Number of certificates required
.... Full Certificate .... Short Certificate

Please tick appropriate box
.... Birth register .... Adoption Register

Particulars of the person whose certificate is required.
Remember, we need full details to ensure a positive search.
PLEASE COMPLETE IN BLOCK CAPITALS

Surname at Birth ....

Forenames ....

Date of birth ....

Place of birth ....

Father's surname ....

Father's forenames ....

Mother's maiden surname ....

Mother's forenames ....

Reference information from GRO Index

Qtr/Year	Vol. No.	Page No.	District
....	....	....	....

NOTES

THIS OFFICE HOLDS RECORDS OF BIRTHS REGISTERED IN
ENGLAND AND WALES SINCE 1ST JULY 1837.

You can also obtain certificates on application in person or by post
to the Superintendent Registrar for the district where the birth
occurred.

Short Certificate - shows only the name, sex, date of birth and
place of birth.

Please allow 28 days for despatch of certificates

FOR OFFICE PAS ....
USE ONLY
Amount Received ....
Fees ....Certificates FULL...........................
                                              SHORT
Total charge ....
Refund ....
Despatched ....
Sub-District ....

LB	MB	CB	MD	City of	County of

Entry

Year M J S D
Year M J S D
D/S Year M J S D
Yes
No Restricted to

METHODS OF PAYMENT
Cheques, postal orders, etc, should be made payable to "**ONS**".
Payment from abroad may be made by cheque, international money
order, draft in favour of "**ONS**". Credit card orders, cheques and
drafts should always be expressed in STERLING. Cheques and
drafts must bear the name and address of a London clearing bank.
PLEASE DO NOT SEND CASH.

APPLICANT TO COMPLETE
*I enclose a cheque/postal order made payable to ONS to the value
of £....................

*or debit my Access/Visa/Master/Switch card. Amount £................

Card no. ....

Expiry date ....

Signature .... Date ....

* *Delete as appropriate*

Adoption Certificate - the full certificate is a copy of the entry
with the date of birth, particulars of the adoption and the adoptive
parent or parents; a short certificate bears no reference to adoption.

Searching by ONS Staff
If the search is likely to be too time consuming because of lack of
identifying details, or if the search to be made is a general one (eg to
trace a family tree), we cannot undertake the task. The applicant
should conduct the search personally or arrange for someone else to
search on their behalf, at The Family Records Centre, 1 Myddelton
Street, London.

COPIES

....

APPLICATION FOR MARRIAGE CERTIFICATE
General Register Office, PO Box 2, Southport, Merseyside PR8 2JD

Applicant

Mr/Mrs/Miss ....

Full
postal ....
address ....

....

Telephone number ....

Number of certificates required
.... Certificate

**Particulars of the person whose certificate is required.
Remember, we need full details to ensure a positive search.**

PLEASE COMPLETE IN BLOCK CAPITALS

Man's	Surname	....
	Forenames	....
Woman's	Surname	....
	Forenames	....

Date of marriage ....

Place of marriage ....

Name of man's father ....

Name of woman's father ....

Reference information from GRO Index

Qtr/Year	Vol. No.	Page No.	District
....	....	....	....

NOTES
THIS OFFICE HOLDS RECORDS OF MARRIAGE
REGISTERED IN ENGLAND AND WALES SINCE
1ST JULY 1837.

You can also obtain certificates on application in person or by
post to the Superintendent Registrar for the district where the
marriage occurred.

FOR OFFICE   PAS ....
USE ONLY
Amount Received ....
Fees .... Certificates ....
Total charge ....
Refund ....
Despatched
Sub-District ....

LB	MB	CB	MD	City of	County of
Entry		Year	M	J	S	D
D/S		Year	M	J	S	D
Yes		Year	M	J	S	D
No		Restricted to			

METHODS OF PAYMENT
Cheques, postal orders, etc, should be made payable to
"ONS". Payment from abroad may be made by cheque,
international money order, draft in favour of "ONS". Credit
card orders, cheques and drafts should always be expressed in
STERLING. Cheques and drafts must bear the name and
address of a London clearing bank.
PLEASE DO NOT SEND CASH.

APPLICANT TO COMPLETE
*I enclose a cheque/postal order made payable to ONS to the
value of £..................
*or debit my Access/Visa/Master/Switch card. Amount £.......

Card no. ....

Expiry date ....

Switch Card Issue no. ....

Signature .... Date ....

* *Delete as appropriate*

Searching by ONS Staff
If the search is likely to be too time consuming because of lack
of identifying details, or if the search to be made is a general
one (eg to trace a family tree), we cannot undertake the task.
The applicant should conduct the search personally or arrange
for someone else to search on their behalf, at The Family
Records Centre, 1 Myddelton Street, London.

If we cannot find the entry, after a one year search either side
of the date given, a search fee will be retained and the balance
refunded.

PAS 8M

Please allow 28 days for despatch of certificates

COPIES .... PAS ....

APPLICATION FOR DEATH CERTIFICATE
General Register Office, PO Box 2, Southport, Merseyside PR8 2JD

Applicant
Mr/Mrs/Miss ....

Full   ....
postal   ....
address   ....

Telephone number   ....

Number of certificates required
         Certificate
Particulars of the person whose certificate is required.
Remember, we need full details to ensure a positive search.
PLEASE COMPLETE IN BLOCK CAPITALS

Surname   ....
Forenames   ....
Date of death ....
Place of death ....
            ....
            ....
Age at death ....
Occupation   ....
Marital status
(if female) ....

Reference information from GRO Index

Qtr/Year   Vol.No.   Page No.   District

....

NOTES

THIS OFFICE HOLDS RECORDS OF DEATHS REGISTERED IN
ENGLAND AND WALES SINCE 1ST JULY 1837.

You can also obtain certificates on application in person or by
Post to the Superintendent Registrar for the district where the .
death occurred.

Searching by ONS Staff

If the search is likely to be too time consuming because of lack of
identifying details, or if the search to be made is a general one (eg
to trace a family tree), we cannot undertake the task. The
applicant should conduct the search personally or arrange for
someone else to search on their behalf at The Family Records
Centre, 1 Myddelton Street, London.

If we cannot find the entry, after a one year search either side of the
date given, a search fee will be retained and the balance refunded.

FOR OFFICE   PAS
      USE ONLY
      Amount Received ....
Fees .... Certificates ....
Total charge ....
Refund ....
      Despatched ....
Sub-District ....

LB	MB	CB	MD	City of		County of
Entry						
		Year		M	J	S	D
		Year		M	J	S	D
D/S		Year		M	J	S	D

Yes

No   Restricted to

APPLICANT TO COMPLETE
* I enclose a cheque/postal order made payable to ONS
  to the value of £ ....
*or debit my Access/Visa/Master/Switch card. Amount £ ....
Card no. ....
Expiry date ....
Switch Card Issue no. ....
Signature .... Date ....

* Delete as appropriate

METHOD OF PAYMENT
Cheques, postal orders, etc should be made payable to "ONS"
Payment from abroad may be made by cheque, international
money order, draft in favour of "ONS". Credit card orders,
cheques and drafts should always be expressed in STERLING.
Cheques and drafts must bear the name and address of a
London clearing bank.
PLEASE DO NOT SEND CASH

Please allow 28 days for despatch of certificates

PAS 8D

UNITED KINGDOM — NORTHERN IRELAND

Send your requests to:

General Register Office
Oxford House
49–55 Chichester Street
Belfast BT1 4HL, Northern Ireland

Tel. (011) (44) 28 9025 2021
Fax (011) (44) 28 9025 2120
E-mail: gro.nisra@dfpni.gov.uk
http://www.nisra.gov.uk/grohome.htm

The General Register Office maintains birth and death records from January 1, 1864. Marriage records are on file from April 1, 1845, with Roman Catholic marriage records beginning on January 1, 1864. The County Heritage Centres provide direct access to many of Ireland's earliest vital records. The Adoption Children Register has records from July 1, 1930. Payment for applications from outside the United Kingdom should be by credit card, or by check or money order payable to the "Registrar General" in pounds sterling, and should include return postage. Expedited service is available for an extra £10.00.

Cost for a certified Birth Certificate	£7.00
Cost for a short form Birth Certificate	£7.00
Cost for a certified Marriage Certificate	£7.00
Cost for a certified Death Certificate	£7.00
Cost for a duplicate copy, when ordered at the same time	£4.00

For additional assistance contact:

County Armagh Genealogy—Armagh Ancestry
42 English Street
510033-Armagh
Co Armagh BT61 7BA No. Ireland

Tel. (011) (44) 1861 521802
Fax (011) (44) 1861

http://www.mayo-ireland.ie/Geneal/Armagh.htm

County Derry or Londonderry Genealogy Centre
10–16 Pump Street
Londonderry BT48 6JG Northern Ireland

Tel. (011) (44) 1504 260329
Fax (011) (44) 1504 374818
http://www.mayo-ireland.ie/Geneal/Derry.htm

The Irish Family History Foundation

http://www.irishroots.net/

The Irish Family History Foundation is the co-ordinating body for a network of government-approved genealogical research centers in the Republic of Ireland and in Northern Ireland which have computerized tens of millions of Irish ancestral records of different types.

The Family History Library of Salt Lake City, Utah has microfilmed many of the original and published vital records and church registers of Northern Ireland. For further details on their holdings please consult your nearest Family History Center.

Birth Certificate Application

❖ Please complete Sections 1, 2, 4 and 5 in CAPITAL letters.
❖ For the certificate of an **adopted** child, please complete
   Sections 1, 3, 4 and 5.

Section 1 Applicant (Person Applying)

1	Full name	*(Mr / Mrs / Miss / Ms)*
	Full postal address	
		Postcode
	Daytime telephone no.	

For purposes of detection and prevention of crime, information relating to this application may be passed on to other Government or Law Enforcement Agencies.

2 Are you applying for your own certificate?   Yes ☐   No ☐

3 If No, please state your relationship to the person to whom the certificate relates.

4 Please give reasons for wanting a certificate :

Section 2 Details of the person whose certificate is required

	Surname at birth	Forename(s)	Date of birth	Place of birth *(Hospital or address)*
5 Details of person				

	Surname	Forename(s)	Maiden surname	Mother's residence *(at time of child's birth)*
6 Father				
Mother				

Section 3 Certificate / Search from Adopted Children Register (from 1 January 1931 only)

	Surname	Forename(s)	Date of birth
7 Adopted person			
8 Name of Adopters			

	Name of Court which made the order	Date of order
9 Adoption Order		

Section 4 Number and type of certificate(s) required

10   number ☐ FULL   number ☐ SHORT

Section 5 Payment

11 I enclose cash (if applying in person) cheque / postal order for £ ☐ made payable to **REGISTRAR GENERAL.** (For postal applications please enclose the correct fee as refunds cannot be made.)

12 or debit my Visa ☐ or Mastercard ☐ by £ ☐ card no. ☐☐☐☐☐☐☐☐☐☐☐☐☐☐☐☐ expiry date ☐

(Please tick appropriate box)

Cardholders name (CAPITAL letters)

13 Your signature ....   Date ....

Please return to :   The Registrar General, Oxford House, 49/55 Chichester Street, Belfast BT1 4HL
Telephone (028) 90252022/24/23/21 Opening hours 9.30am - 4.00pm

Marriage Certificate Application

❖ Please complete all sections in CAPITAL letters

Section 1 Applicant (Person Applying)

1 Applicant's full name

Full postal address

Postcode

Daytime telephone no.

For purposes of detection and prevention of crime, information relating to this application may be passed on to other Government or Law Enforcement Agencies.

Section 2 Details of Certificate Required

MAN

2 Forename(s)

Surname

WOMAN

3 Forename(s)

Maiden surname

4 Any other surname before this marriage

5 Place of marriage

Full postal address

Postcode

6 Date of marriage

Day   Month   Year

Please note that marriages before 1922 cannot be traced unless the CHURCH and DISTRICT are known.

Section 3 Number of Certificates Required

7 Number of certificates required

Section 4 Payment

8 I enclose cash (if applying in person) cheque / postal order for £ .... made payable to **REGISTRAR GENERAL.** (For postal applications please enclose the correct fee as refunds cannot be made.)

9 or debit my Visa ☐ or Mastercard ☐ by £ .... card no. ☐☐☐☐☐☐☐☐☐☐☐☐☐☐☐☐ expiry date ....

(Please tick appropriate box) Cardholders name (CAPITAL letters)

10 Your signature .... Date ....

Please return to : **The Registrar General, Oxford House, 49/55 Chichester Street, Belfast BT1 4HL Telephone (028) 90252022/24/23/21 Opening hours 9.30am - 4.00pm**

Death Certificate Application

❖ Please complete all sections in CAPITAL letters

Section 1 Applicant (Person Applying)

1 **Full name**

Full postal address

Postcode

Daytime telephone no.

For purposes of detection and prevention of crime, information relating to this application may be passed on to other Government or Law Enforcement Agencies.

2 Please give reasons for wanting a certificate.

3 Please state your relationship to the deceased.

Section 2 Details of Certificate Required

4 **Forename(s)**

Surname

5 **Date of death**   6 **Place of death**

Please note that deaths before 1922 are difficult to trace if the place of death is not known.

7 **Usual address**

Postcode

8 **Date of birth or age at death**   years

9 If person was married or widowed at death, please give the name of spouse.

10 If death occurred within the last 3 years was the Coroner notified?   Yes ☐   No ☐

Section 3 Number of Certificates Required

11 **Number of certificates required**

Section 4 Payment

12 I enclose cash (if applying in person) cheque / postal order for   £   made payable to **REGISTRAR GENERAL.**   (For postal applications please enclose the correct fee as refunds cannot be made.)

13 or debit my Visa ☐ or Mastercard ☐ by £   card no. ⬚⬚⬚⬚⬚⬚⬚⬚⬚⬚⬚⬚⬚⬚⬚⬚   expiry date

(Please tick appropriate box)   Cardholders name (CAPITAL letters)

14 **Your signature**   Date

Please return to : **The Registrar General, Oxford House, 49/55 Chichester Street, Belfast BT1 4HL**
Telephone (028) 90252022/24/23/21 Opening hours 9.30am - 4.00pm

UNITED KINGDOM — SCOTLAND

Send your requests to:

General Register Office for Scotland
New Register House
3 West Register Street
Edinburgh, EH1 3YT, Scotland

Tel. (011) (44) 131 314 4440
Tel. (credit card orders) (011) (44) 131 314 4411
Fax (011) (44) 131 314 4400
E-mail: records@gro-scotland.gov.uk
http://www.gro-scotland.gov.uk/

The General Register Office has records of governmental registers from January 1, 1855. In addition they hold many old parish registers dating back to 1553; adoptions from October 1909; births and deaths of Scots at sea, on military service, 1881–; and some returns for persons of Scottish descent in Bangladesh, Ghana, India, Pakistan, and Sri Lanka. The Office has divorce records from May 1, 1984. Divorces before that date are noted on the Registrar's copy of the marriage certificate. Checks need to be in British pounds sterling, payable to the "Registrar General"; payment can also be made by credit card. Expedited service is available for an additional fee of £10.00.

A fully searchable index of Scottish birth and marriage records from 1553 to 1899, death records from 1855 to 1924; and the 1891 census is now available on the Internet **(http//www.origins.net/GRO/)**. There is a fee to view and get a copy of these records.

Cost for a certified Birth Certificate	£13.00 (ordered by mail);
	£11.00 (ordered in person);
	£16.00 (ordered over the Internet)
Cost for a certified Marriage Certificate	£13.00 (ordered by mail);
	£11.00 (ordered in person);
	£16.00 (ordered over the Internet)
Cost for a certified Divorce Certificate	£13.00 (ordered by mail);
	£11.00 (ordered in person);
	£16.00 (ordered over the Internet)
Cost for a certified Death Certificate	£13.00 (ordered by mail);
	£11.00 (ordered in person);
	£16.00 (ordered over the Internet)

The Family History Library of Salt Lake City, Utah has microfilmed many of the original and published vital records and church registers of Scotland. For further details on their holdings please consult your nearest Family History Center.

For further information see:

Baxter, Angus. *In Search of Your British & Irish Roots.* 4th ed. Baltimore: Genealogical Publishing Co., 1999. 320 p.

Brownlee, David. *Computerisation of the Indexes to the Statutory Registers of Births, Deaths and Marriages in Scotland.* IIVRS Technical Papers, No. 42. Bethesda, MD: International Institute for Vital Registration and Statistics, 1990. 8p.

Cory, Kathleen B. *Tracing Your Scottish Ancestry.* 2nd ed. Baltimore: Genealogical Publishing Co., 1999. 228 p.

Herber, Mark D. *Ancestral Trails.* Baltimore: Genealogical Publishing Co., 1998. 688 p.

Telephone: Direct line   0131-314 4440, 4441, 4451
            Switchboard   0131-314 0380
            Facsimile   0131-314 4400

APPLICATION FOR CERTIFICATE(S)
Searching undertaken by GRO(S) staff for a particular event ('Particular Search'). For details see Leaflet S2.

Please complete this application overleaf and return it to the address above along with the appropriate fee. Details of charges are given below, including the PRIORITY SERVICE for urgent orders.

Please indicate in the appropriate box(es) below how many of each certificate you want.

1.	☐	Extract of entry in register of births. ('Full Certificate')	Price	£ 13	per extract
2.	☐	Abbreviated certificate of birth. This shows the person's name, surname, sex, date and place of birth, but not parentage. Not applicable to records before 1855	Price	£ 13	per extract
3.	☐	Extract of entry in register of adopted children. This shows the person's adopted name, not the name in the register of births which may be different. It is however a legal "birth certificate" which may be used for all purposes	Price	£ 13	per extract
4.	☐	Extract of entry in register of marriages (see note)	Price	£ 13	per extract
5.	☐	Extract of entry in register of divorces (see note)	Price	£ 13	per extract
6.	☐	Extract of entry in register of deaths	Price	£ 13	per extract
7.	☐	Additional priority fee (applicable to birth, death, marriage extracts from 1855 to date; divorce extracts from 1 May 1984 to date; adoption extracts from 1930 to date. For further details, see leaflet S2	Price	£ 10 extra	per extract

---

Note: recording of marriages ending in divorce

When a **decree of divorce** was granted by the Court of Session, it was formerly the practice to enter a note on the marriage entry to show that the marriage had ended in divorce. This practice was discontinued on 1 May 1984. Where a divorce was notified to the Registrar General on or after that date, there will be no note regarding divorce on the corresponding marriage entry or on any extract of the entry. A separate Register of Divorces was set up from 1 May 1984, from where extracts are available.

Prior to 1 May 1984 an extract of divorce granted in Scotland is obtainable from the Court issuing the decree.

If you order an extract(s) by post, you may pay by a personal cheque in British pounds Sterling, crossed and **made** payable to 'The Registrar General'. **PLEASE DO NOT SEND CASH.** You can also if you wish, quote your **Switch, Visa** or **Mastercard** number (plus the cardholder's name, the expiry date and your signature, as they appear on the card) since this enables us to charge you exactly the right amount. For **Switch** please also **quote** the start date/issue number on card. If you order by fax, you must pay by **Switch, Visa** or **Mastercard.**

Cardholder's Name: ....   Cardholder's Signature: ....

Card Number: ☐☐☐☐   ☐☐☐☐   ☐☐☐☐   ☐☐☐☐

Start Date   .... / ......   Expiry Date   ..../.......   Cardholder's Address: ....

....

Issue number on card   ☐   for Switch transactions only.

APPLICANT	
Mr/Mrs/Miss/Ms	
Full	
postal	
address	
Telephone number	
Date of application	

FOR OFFICE USE ONLY

APPLICATION FOR A BIRTH, ADOPTION, MARRIAGE, DIVORCE, DEATH or OLD PARISH REGISTER CERTIFICATE

Searching undertaken by GRO(S) staff for a particular event ('Particular Search'). For details see Leaflet S2. Tick as appropriate (see notes overleaf on birth or divorce certificates)

BIRTH / ADOPTION

Surname at Birth/Adoption *

Forename(s)

Male/Female *

Place (town or parish) in which Birth occurred (adopted persons please state date of adoption, if known)

PARENTS/ADOPTIVE PARENTS *

Father's surname

Father's forename(s)

Mother's maiden surname

Mother's forename(s)

Date of Birth

Day	Month	Year

RD No	Year	Entry No
RCE		

MARRIAGE / DIVORCE

Groom's surname

Forename(s)

Bride's surname

Forename(s)

Place (town or parish) in which Marriage occurred

Widow or Divorcee please state former married name

Date of Marriage

Day	Month	Year

Date of Divorce *(if applicable)*

Day	Month	Year

RD No	Year	Entry No
RCE		

DEATH

Surname

Forename(s)

Age at Death

Place (town or parish in which Death occurred)

PARENTS *

Father's surname

Father's forename(s)

Mother's maiden surname

Mother's forename(s)

Date of Death

Day	Month	Year

RD No	Year	Entry No
RCE		

FOR OFFICE USE

* Delete as applicable

URUGUAY

Send your requests to:

Registro Civil Central
Av. Uruguay 753
11.100 Montevideo, Uruguay

Tel. (011) (598) (2) 4373-8441
http://www.nubilis.com/Planif/RegCiv.html

Church registers date from the 1500s, and vital registration began July 1, 1879. The Registro Civil Central has 14 regional offices and 40 local offices. Adoptions are approved by the Instituto Nacional del Menor, finalized by the Juzgado de la Familia (Family Court), and registered with the Registro Civil Central.

Cost for a certified Birth Certificate	N$ 5.00
Cost for a certified Marriage Certificate	N$ 5.00
Cost for a certified Death Certificate	N$ 5.00

For more Adoption Record information contact:

Instituto Nacional del Menor (INAME)
Instituto de Adopción
Rio Branco 1394
Montevideo, Uruguay

For additional assistance contact:

Director General de Estadística y Censos
Cuareim 2052
11.100 Montevideo, Uruguay

Embassy of Uruguay
2715 M Street, NW, 3rd Floor
Washington, DC 20007

Tel. (202) 331-1313

The Family History Library of Salt Lake City, Utah has microfilmed original and published records of Uruguay. For further details on their holdings please consult your nearest Family History Center.

For further information see:

Diagnostico del Registro Civil Latinoamericano, enero de 1980. Montevideo, Uruguay: UN Fund for Population Activities, 1982. 142p.

Report on the First Latin American Training Centre on Statistics and Censuses Held at Mexico City from 2 September to 10 December 1948 by the Food and Agriculture Organization of the UN and the Government of the United States of Mexico with the Cooperation of the Statistical Office of the UN and the InterAmerican Statistical Institute. Lake Success, NY: Statistical Office of the UN, 1948. 33p.

Rivero de Arhancet, Mabel. *Estado Civil, Registro de Estado Civil.* Montevideo, Uruguay: Acali Editorial, 1984. 56p.

Revista de la Asociacion de Escribanos del Uruguay. Montevideo, Uruguay: Association, 1904– .

UZBEKISTAN

Send your requests to:

Civil Registration Office
ZAGS
(Town), Uzbekistan

Adoptions are approved by the local town mayor (Hokimiate) and registered with the local civil registrar (ZAGS). The Tayanch, a sub-organization of the Uzbekistan Red Crescent, maintains ongoing records and reports on adoptees who leave Uzbekistan.

For additional assistance contact:

Gosudarstvennaia Respublikanskaia Biblioteka
National Librarian   Tel. (011) (7) (3712) 33-0547
Alleja Naradov 5
700000 Tashkent, Uzbekistan

Embassy of the Republic of Uzbekistan   Tel. (202) 887-5300
1746 Massachusetts Avenue, NW
Washington, DC 20036

The Family History Library of Salt Lake City, Utah has microfilmed records of Uzbekistan and the former Soviet Union. For further details on their holdings please consult your nearest Family History Center.

VANUATU

Send your requests to:

> Registrar General
> Civil Registration Office
> Ministry of Home Affairs
> Private Bag 050
> Port Vila, Vanuatu

Vital registration was not formally introduced to Vanuatu until 1975, and so the Registrar General's Office has initiated a program to retroactively register each birth and marriage of the current residents. They also maintain the records of all divorces and deaths. Current vital registration in Vanuatu is considered to be 40 percent complete for births and 30 percent complete for deaths.

Cost for a certified Birth Certificate	50.00V
Cost for a certified Marriage Certificate	50.00V
Cost for a certified Death Certificate	50.00V

For additional assistance contact:

> Principal Statistician
> Statistics Office
> Private Mail Bag 019
> Port Vila, Vanuatu

> National Archives of Vanuatu   Tel. (011) (678) 22-498
> P.O. Box 184   Fax (011) (678) 23-142
> Port Vila, Vanuatu

> Vanuatu Mission to the U.N.   Tel. (212) 593-0144
> 865 United Nations Plaza, Suite 441
> New York, NY 10017

VENEZUELA

Send your requests to:

Dirección de Registro y Notaria
Ministerio de Justicia
Torre Norte, Centro Simon Bolivar, Piso 20
Caracas, Venezuela

While church registers date from the 1500s, vital registration began in 1873.

Cost for a certified Birth Certificate	50c
Cost for a certified Marriage Certificate	50c
Cost for a certified Death Certificate	50c

For more Adoption Record information contact:

Instituto Nacional del Menor (INAM)
Caracas, Venezuela

For additional assistance contact:

Embassy of the Republic of Venezuela   Tel. (202) 342-2214
1099 30th Street, NW
Washington, DC 20007

The Family History Library of Salt Lake City, Utah has microfilmed original and published records of Venezuela. For further details on their holdings please consult your nearest Family History Center.

For further information see:

Almenar de Ochoa, Elena. *Funcionamiento del Registro Civil en Venezuela.* Caracas, Venezuela: Venezuela, División de Estadística Vital, 1964. 34p.

Ascanio Rodriguez, Juan Bautista. *Apuntes y Documentos para la Historia del Registro Civil en Venezuela.* Caracas, Venezuela: Tip. Americana, 1925. 137p.

Diagnostico del Registro Civil Latinoamericano, enero de 1980. Montevideo, Uruguay: UN Fund for Population Activities, 1982. 142p.

Report on the First Latin American Training Centre on Statistics and Censuses Held at Mexico City from 2 September to 10 December 1948 by the Food and Agriculture Organization of the UN and the Government of the United States of Mexico with the Cooperation of the Statistical Office of the UN and the InterAmerican Statistical Institute. Lake Success, NY: Statistical Office of the UN, 1948. 33p.

Sanavia, Victor. *Interpretación Judicial de la Ley de Registro Publico; Decisiones Publicadas hasta el 31 de Diciembre de1960.* Caracas, Venezuela: Corte Federal y de Casación, Mene Grande Oil, Departamento Legal, 1961. 191p.

Send your requests to:

Registrar
Police Station
(Town), Vietnam

Vietnam has a personal identity card, family registration, and a vital registration system. These systems have varied widely during the violent changes of government in Vietnam. Currently all three systems are administered by the local police. Each household in Vietnam is required to keep a family registration record, which gives the vital information on each person in the household. These booklets are copied and registered at the local police station. All changes in the household, address changes, etc., must be recorded with the police.

Cost for a certified Birth Certificate	10,000 D
Cost for a certified Marriage Certificate	10,000 D
Cost for a certified Death Certificate	10,000 D

For additional assistance contact:

Embassy of the Socialist Republic of Vietnam   Tel. (202) 861-0737
1233 20th Street, NW, Suite 400
Washington, DC 20036

For further information see:

Hiôên tròang vâê õææang ký hòô tòich và thâông kê dân sâô Viòêt Nam 1992. (Status of Civil Registration and Population Statistics, Vietnam, 1992). Hanoi, Vietnam: Statistical Pub. House, 1992. 65p.

WESTERN SAMOA

Send your requests to:

Registrar General
Justice Department
P.O. Box 49
Apia, Western Samoa

Vital registration began in the mid-1800s and is now centrally administered by the Registrar General. The Registrar of the Supreme Court is required to send copies of all divorces to the Registrar General.

Cost for a certified Birth Certificate	50 sene
Cost for a certified Marriage Certificate	50 sene
Cost for a Divorce Certificate	50 sene
Cost for a certified Death Certificate	50 sene

For additional assistance contact:

Mission of Samoa   Tel. (212) 599-6196
800 Second Avenue, Suite 400J
New York, NY 10017

The Family History Library of Salt Lake City, Utah has microfilmed many of the original and published records of Samoa. For further details on their holdings please consult your nearest Family History Center.

YEMEN

Send your requests to:

Registrar General
Ministry of Justice & AWQAF
P.O. Box 5030
Maalla, Aden, Yemen

The registration is not considered to be comprehensive.

Cost for a certified Birth Certificate	2.00R
Cost for a certified Marriage Certificate	2.00R
Cost for a certified Death Certificate	2.00R

For additional assistance contact:

Chairman
Central Statistical Organization
P.O. Box 1272
Tawahi, Aden, Yemen

National Archives
P. O. Box 846
Al Zubeiri Street
Sanaa, Yemen

Fax (011) (967) (1) 288 161

Embassy of Yemen
2600 Virginia Avenue, NW
Washington, DC 20037

Tel. (202) 965-4760

For further information see:

Organization and Status of Civil Registration in the Arab Countries. IIVRS Technical Papers, No. 33. Bethesda, MD: International Institute for Vital Registration and Statistics, 1988. 6p.

ZAMBIA

Send your requests to:

Registrar General
Department of National Registration, Passport and Citizenship
Kundalila House
P.O. Box 32311
10101 Lusaka, Zambia

Vital registration is not considered to be comprehensive.

Cost for a certified Birth Certificate	Free
Cost for a certified Marriage Certificate	Free
Cost for a certified Death Certificate	Free

For additional assistance contact:

Director of Census and Statistics
Central Statistical Office
P.O. Box 31908
Lusaka, Zambia

National Archives of Zambia   Fax (011) (260) (1) 254 080
P. O. Box 500 10
Lusaka, Zambia

Embassy of Zambia   Tel. (202) 265-9717
2419 Massachusetts Avenue, NW
Washington, DC 20008

For further information see:

Kannisto, Vaino.*Civil Registration and Vital Statistics in the Africa Region, Lessons Learned from the Evaluation of UNFPA Assisted Projects in Kenya and Sierra Leone*. New York, NY: UN Fund for Population Activities, 1984.

Methods and Problems of Civil Registration Practices and Vital Statistics Collection in Africa. IIVRS Technical Papers, No. 16. Bethesda, MD: International Institute for Vital Registration and Statistics, 1981. 27p.

Organization and Status of Civil Registration in Africa and Recommendations for Improvement. IIVRS Technical Papers, No. 31. Bethesda, MD: International Institute for Vital Registration and Statistics, 1988. 15p.

ZIMBABWE

Send your requests to:

Registrar General of Zimbabwe
Central Registry
Ministry of Home Affairs
Bag 7734
Causeway, Harare, Zimbabwe

The registration is not considered to be comprehensive.

Cost for a Certified Birth Certificate	Z$.25
Cost for a Certified Marriage Certificate	Z$.25
Cost for a Certified Death Certificate	Z$.25

For additional assistance contact:

Director of Census and Statistics
Central Statistical Office
P.O. Box 8063
Causeway
Harare, Zimbabwe

National Archives   Fax (011) (263) (4) 792 398
Private Bag 7729
Causeway
Harare, Zimbabwe

Embassy of Zimbabwe   Tel. (202) 332-7100
1608 New Hampshire Avenue, NW
Washington, DC 20009

For further information see:

Kannisto, Vaino. *Civil Registration and Vital Statistics in the Africa Region, Lessons Learned from the Evaluation of UNFPA Assisted Projects in Kenya and Sierra Leone.* New York, NY: UN Fund for Population Activities, 1984.

Methods and Problems of Civil Registration Practices and Vital Statistics Collection in Africa. IIVRS Technical Papers, No. 16. Bethesda, MD: International Institute for Vital Registration and Statistics, 1981. 27p.

Organization and Status of Civil Registration in Africa and Recommendations for Improvement. IIVRS Technical Papers, No. 31. Bethesda, MD: International Institute for Vital Registration and Statistics, 1988. 15p.